COMBAT: *The Civil War*

COMBAT

The

EDITED AND WITH COMMENTARY BY
DON CONGDON

Civil War

SMITHMARK

This edition published in 1994 by SMITHMARK Publishers Inc.,
16 East 32nd Street, New York, NY 10016

SMITHMARK books are available for bulk purchase for sales
promotion and premium use. For details write or call the
manager of special sales, SMITHMARK Publishers Inc.,
16 East 32nd Street, New York, NY 10016; (212) 532-6600.

This edition published by special arrangement
with W.S. Konecky Associates, Inc.

ISBN: 0-8317-1335-6

Printed in the United States of America

10 9 8 7 6 5 4 3 2 1

ACKNOWLEDGMENTS

"Stuart's Ride Around McClellan" from Volume I of *Lee's Lieutenants*, by Douglas Southall
Freeman. Copyright 1942 by Charles Scribner's Sons. Reprinted with the permission of the
publisher.

"Shiloh, Bloody Shiloh" from *Sherman: Fighting Prophet*, by Lloyd Lewis. Copyright 1932 by
Harcourt, Brace & World, Inc.; renewed 1960 by Kathryn Lewis. Reprinted with the permission
of the publishers.

"The Seizure of New Orleans" from *Mr. Lincoln's Navy*, by Richard S. West, Jr. Copyright © 1957
by Richard S. West, Jr. Reprinted with the permission of David McKay Co., Inc.

"Gettysburg: Second Day" from *The Twentieth Maine*, by John J. Pullen. Copyright © 1957 by
John J. Pullen. Reprinted with the permission of J.B. Lippincott Company.

SELECTIONS WERE ALSO TAKEN FROM THE FOLLOWING BOOKS:

Decisive Battles of the Civil War by Colonel Joseph B. Mitchell. Copyright 1955 by
Joseph B. Mitchell. Reprinted by permission of G. P. Putnam's Sons.

The Growth of the American Republic, Fifth Edition, by Samuel Eliot Morison and Henry Steele
Commager. Copyright © 1962 by Oxford University Press, Inc. Reprinted by permission of the
publisher.

The Coming Fury by Bruce Catton. Copyright © 1961 by Bruce Catton. Reprinted by permission
of Doubleday & Company, Inc., and, for the Brutish Commonwealth, Victor Gallancz, Ltd.

Terrible Swift Sword by Bruce Catton. Copyright © 1963 by Bruce Catton. Reprinted by
permission of Doubleday & Company, Inc., and, for the Brutish Commonwealth, Victor
Gollancz, Ltd.

Never Call Retreat by Bruce Catton. Copyright 1965 by Bruce Catton. Reprinted by permission
of Doubleday & Company, Inc., and, for the British Commonwealth, Victor Gallancz, Ltd.

The Blue and the Gray by Henry Steele Commager. Copyright 1950 by the Bobbs-Merrill
Company, Inc. Reprinted by permission of the Bobbs-Merrill Company, Inc.

This Hallowed Ground by Bruce Catton. Copyright © 1955, 1956 by Bruce Catton. Reprinted by
permission of Doubleday & Company, Inc., and, for the British Commonwealth, Victor
Gollancz, Ltd.

CONTENTS

CONTENTS

CONTENTS

CONTENTS

MAPS

ILLUSTRATIONS

COMBAT: *The Civil War*

EDITOR'S NOTE

This anthology is the sixth in a series. As in his previous combat collections, the editor has wherever possible selected narratives which project the intense personal experience of men actually fighting in the front lines. He believes that this method, though arbitrary, is the one most likely to give the reader an intimate understanding of "what the war was like."

The editor has not attempted to present an overall history of the Civil War. Battles fought west of the Mississippi are not included because they lacked the scope of major engagements in the East and had no comparable effect upon the progress of the war.

Each combat selection is preceded by introductory material which should help clarify the grand strategy of the war, campaign by campaign, and thus show individual battles in true perspective. The rest is up to the reader. He will find Billy Yank and Johnny Reb out yonder, warming up their muzzle-loaders on the picket line.

THE NATION IS DISSOLVED

THE ELECTION OF Abraham Lincoln to the Presidency of the United States was considered by many southerners as the final affront in a long series of provocations that had pushed their states to the brink of secession. Ironically, it was the southern political leaders themselves who had split the Democratic ticket in 1860, thus insuring Lincoln's election as a Republican. But the new President was anathema to the South; "he appeared to the South not as we (now) know him but as a malignant baboon, with abolitionist serpents as attendants. His election inspired the same fear and loathing that would arise today among conservatives if a Communist were elected President."*

Southerners for years had been reacting with increasing violence to all pressures relating to slavery. John Brown's Raid on Harper's Ferry in 1859 and his subsequent election to martyrdom by the northern abolitionists were, they felt, a widespread conspiracy to murder southern women and children.† When northerners attacked slavery, southerners defended the institution by pointing to the miserable conditions of northern factory workers. Southerners were incensed when northerners did not cooperate in the return of runaway slaves; the law of the land clearly guaranteed the return of such "legal property." And howls of frustration were heard when the South was prevented from insuring that a new state in the Union might introduce or encourage slavery. All these stemmed from the two great exacerbating issues that divided the nation: the primacy of states' rights over national interests and the right not only to maintain slavery but to extend it to new states and territories. Both issues had been debated since the formation of the federal government, and the debate had intensified as the first half of the nineteenth century drew to a close.

The case for secession, according to Morison and Commager, was based on "the axiom that the Federal Constitution created a confederacy, not a government, and did not impair state sovereignty. . . . In 1800 the vast majority of American citizens felt more loyal to their respective states than to the Union. In 1830 none but Virginians, Georgians, and the South

* Samuel Eliot Morison and Henry Steele Commager, *The Growth of the American Republic*, p. 668.

† Brown attacked the Federal arsenal at Harper's Ferry to secure arms to begin an insurrection of the slaves. Unsuccessful, he was tried for treason and hanged.

I

Carolinians would have followed their states out of the Union, on any possible issue. After 1844, with the growth of southern self-consciousness, the phrase and the idea of state rights gave place in that section to 'Southern rights.' "*

In December, 1860, a month after Lincoln's election, South Carolina took the bull by the horns and seceded, proclaiming that the Union of South Carolina with the other states under the name of the United States of America was dissolved. By February, Texas, Florida, Mississippi, Georgia, Alabama, and Louisiana had followed South Carolina out of the Union. These states dealt forthrightly with the issue of slavery: the people in the North were interfering with the South's practice of that "peculiar institution." South Carolina's proclamation said, in part: "They [the North] have denounced as sinful the institution of slavery; they have permitted the open establishment among them of abolition societies, and have united in the election of a man to the high office of President of the U.S. whose opinions and purposes are hostile to slavery."

Why was the issue of slavery so inflamed for southerners? An important reason was the South's dependency on a single-crop economy. The invention of the cotton gin and the consequent demand for cotton in the world market had turned southern planters away from such staples as tobacco and rice. By planting cotton, they were guaranteed a good profit, but this profit depended on cheap labor. So long as the slaves worked the field, and a steady demand for cotton continued in the world market (part of this demand came from the mills in the North), slavery and cotton were a highly successful combination. By mid-century more than three-quarters of the slave work force (some two and a half million slaves) picked cotton.

The North had given up slavery long before, largely because it was uneconomical. The invention of the reaper had provided farmers in the North and Midwest with a means to expand their production of wheat and corn, neither of which depended upon slave labor. The North also had access to a cheap labor force, provided by European immigrants streaming into the northern cities; they were not slaves but poorly paid laborers. They would, however, be an essential part of the increasing industrialization of the North.

The differences between the two sections of the country were not easily understood by southerners. So long as their one-crop agricultural economy worked, their society appeared rich and stable. But could it survive a serious disruption, such as war? The South, by 1860, was in no mood for sober judgments—passions ruled the day. In seceding, the South was throwing down the gauntlet, confident the North would not go to war over slavery; but if the challenge was accepted, the South would fight. In fact, many a southerner was "rarin' for a fight."

Through the crucial months, President Buchanan did nothing; he sympathized with the South's position but hated to see the Union dissolved. The North was unable to act in concert. Northerners had heard the South talk of secession for years, but when it came there was no public outcry. A few feeble efforts by Congress to achieve a new compromise failed miserably.

* Morison and Commager, *op. cit.,* p. 670.

On March 4, 1861, Lincoln took the oath of office. His inaugural address made his position on secession crystal clear to any southerner who cared to listen:

"In your hands and not in mine, is the momentous issue of the civil war. The Government will not assail you. I hold that, in contemplation of universal law and the Constitution, the Union of these states is perpetual. . . . No state, upon its own mere action can lawfully get out of the Union. . . . I shall take care, as the Constitution itself expressly enjoins upon me, that the laws of the Union be faithfully executed in all the States. . . . The power confided to me will be used to hold, occupy, and possess the property and places belonging to the Government, and to collect the duties and imposts."

On February 8, 1861, delegates from the seven seceded states met at Montgomery, Alabama, and founded the Confederate States of America. On the ninth, the Congress of delegates elected Jefferson Davis as their President.

Among the moves taken to protect the security of their new nation was the seizure of the coastal forts and navy yards in the southern harbors. By the time Lincoln was inaugurated only two forts remained under the Federal flag—Fort Sumter at Charleston and Fort Pickens at Pensacola.

"From the extreme southern point of view, the jurisdiction of such places passed with secession to the states, and their retention by the Federal government was equivalent to an act of war. Confederate commissioners came to Washington to treat for their surrender, a few days after Lincoln's inauguration. Although Seward refused to receive the gentlemen, he assured them indirectly that no supplies or provisions would be sent to the forts without due notice, and led them to expect a speedy evacuation. . . .

"Major Anderson, commanding Fort Sumter, notified the war department that his supplies were giving out, and that new Confederate batteries commanded his position. Fort Sumter had no strategic value in case of civil war. Why, then, risk war by holding it? The Confederacy made it clear that any attempt to reinforce or even to supply Sumter would be regarded as a hostile act, which would probably pull Virginia into the Confederacy. If, however, the forts were tamely yielded, would not the principle of union be fatally compromised? Could a recognition of the Confederacy thereafter be avoided?

"Lincoln delayed decision, not from fear, but because he was watching Virginia. Jefferson Davis, too, was watching Virginia. The Old Dominion was a stake worth playing for. Although long since fallen from her primacy in wealth and statesmanship, her sons were the ablest officers in the United States Army, and her soil was almost certain to be the theater of any war between the sections. The 'panhandle' of western Virginia thrust a salient between Pennsylvania and Ohio, to within 100 miles of Lake Erie. If Virginia seceded, she must carry North Carolina with her; and Maryland, Kentucky, Tennessee, and Missouri would probably follow."*

Meanwhile, in Charleston Harbor, which Fort Sumter guarded, tension

* *Ibid.,* pp. 676–77.

grew between the militant citizens of Charleston and the small force stationed in the fort to guard the Union's interests. Work had been going on to strengthen Sumter, ostensibly from invasion from without—perhaps England, Secretary Stanton might have said, if cornered—but actually against a possible takeover by southern sympathizers. There were two forts in the harbor, the other being Fort Moultrie, much less defensible than Sumter. The commander at Moultrie had been transferred with his men to Sumter on December 26, 1860.

The Fall of Fort Sumter*

BY CAPTAIN JAMES CHESTER

THE TRANSFER OF MAJOR ANDERSON'S COMMAND from Moultrie to Sumter was neatly executed early in the evening of December 26th, 1860. It was a few minutes after sunset when the troops left Moultrie; the short twilight was about over when they reached the boats; fifteen or twenty minutes more carried them to Sumter. The workmen had just settled down to an evening's enjoyment when armed men at the door startled them. There was no parleying, no explaining; nothing but stern commands, silent astonishment, and prompt obedience. The workmen were on the wharf, outside the fort, before they were certain whether their captors were secessionists or Yankees.

Fort Sumter was unfinished, and the interior was filled with building materials, guns, carriages, shot, shell, derricks, timbers, blocks and tackle, and coils of rope in great confusion. Few guns were mounted, and these few were chiefly on the lowest tier. The work was intended for three tiers of guns, but the embrasures of the second tier were incomplete, and guns could be mounted on the first and third tiers only.

The complete armament of the work had not yet arrived, but there were more guns on hand than we could mount or man. The first thing to be considered was immediate defense. The possibility of a sudden dash by the enemy, under cover of darkness and guided by the discharged workmen then in Charleston, demanded instant attention. It was impossible to spread 65 men over ground intended for 650, so some of the embrasures had to be bricked up. Selecting those, therefore, essential to artillery defense, and mounting guns in them, Anderson closed the rest. This was the work of many days; but we were in no immediate danger of an artillery attack. The armament of Moultrie was destroyed; its guns were spiked, and their carriages burned; and it would take a longer time to put them in condition than it would to mount the guns of Sumter.

* Condensed from "Inside Sumter in '61," *Battles and Leaders*, Vol. I.

On the parade were quantities of flag-stones standing on end in masses and columns everywhere. We dared not leave them where they were, even if they had not been in the way, because mortar shells bursting among them would have made the very bomb-proofs untenable. A happy idea occurred to some one in authority, and the flag-stones were arranged two tiers high in front of the casemates, and just under the arches, thus partly closing the casemates and making excellent splinter-proofs.

Moving such immense quantities of material, mounting guns, distributing shot, and bricking up embrasures kept us busy for many weeks. But order was coming out of chaos every day, and the soldiers began to feel that they were a match for their adversaries. Still, they could not shut their eyes to the fact that formidable works were growing up around them. The secessionists were busy too, and they had the advantage of unlimited labor and material. Fort Moultrie had its armament again in position, and was receiving the framework of logs which formed the foundation for its sandbag bomb-proofs. The Stevens's Point floating battery was being made impregnable by an overcoat of railroad iron; and batteries on Morris, James, and Sullivan's islands were approaching completion. But our preparations were more advanced than theirs; and if we had been permitted to open on them at this time, the bombardment of Sumter would have had a very different termination. But our hands were tied by policy and instructions.

The heaviest guns in Sumter were three ten-inch columbiads—considered very big guns in those days. They weighed fifteen thousand pounds each, and were intended for the gorge and salient angles of the work. We found them skidded on the parade ground. Besides these there was a large number of eight-inch columbiads—more than we could mount or man—and a full supply of 42, 32, and 24-pounders, and some eight-inch sea-coast howitzers. There was an ample supply of shot and shell, and plenty of powder in the magazines, but friction primers were not abundant and cartridge-bags were scarce. The scarcity of cartridge-bags drove us to some strange makeshifts. During the bombardment several tailors were kept busy making cartridge-bags out of soldiers' flannel shirts, and we fired away several dozen pairs of woolen socks belonging to Major Anderson. In the matter of friction primers strict economy had to be observed, as we had no means of improvising a substitute.

Our first efforts in preparation were directed toward mounting the necessary guns on the lowest tier. These consisted of 42 and 32-pounders, and as the necessary trucks, gins, and tackle were on hand, the work went on rapidly. The men were in fine condition and as yet well fed; besides, they had the assistance of the engineer workmen, who soon became experts at this kind of work. Meantime a party of mechanics were making the main gate secure. This was situated at the middle of the gorge or base of the pentagon (the trace of the work was pentagonal), which was also the south-west side. It was closed by two heavy iron-studded gates, the outer a folding pair, and the inner arranged on pulleys, so that it could be raised or lowered at will. It was clear that the enemy, if he meant to bombard us, would erect batteries on Morris Island, and thus would be able to deliver an oblique fire on the gate sufficient to demolish it in a very few minutes. The gate once demolished, a night assault would become practicable.

To meet this possible emergency the main entrance was closed by a substantial brick wall, with a man-hole in the middle two feet wide and opposite to the man-hole in the gate. This wall was about six feet high, and to increase the security and sweep the wharf, an eight-inch sea-coast howitzer was mounted on its upper carriage without any chassis, so as to fire through the man-hole. The howitzer was kept loaded with double canister. To induce the belief that the folding gates were our sole dependence at this point, their outer surface was covered with iron.

The lower tier of guns being mounted, the more difficult operation of sending guns up to the third tier began. The terreplein of the work was about fifty feet above parade level—a considerable hoist—but a pair of shears being already in position, and our tackle equal to the weight of eight-inch columbiads, the work went on amidst much good humor until all the guns of that caliber were in position.

We had now reached a problem more difficult to solve, namely, sending up our ten-inch columbiads. We were extremely desirous to have them— or at least two of them—on the upper tier. They were more powerful guns than any the enemy had at that time, and the only ones in our possession capable of smashing the iron-clad defenses which might be constructed against us. We had rumors that an iron-clad floating battery was being built in Charleston, which the enemy proposed to anchor in some convenient position so as to breach Sumter at his leisure. We had no faith in the penetrating power of the eight-inch guns, and if we wished to demolish this floating adversary, it was necessary that the ten-inch guns should be mounted. Besides, an iron-clad battery was well on the road to completion at Cumming's Point (twelve hundred yards from the weakest side of Sumter), which, from what we could see of it, would be impervious to any less powerful gun.

There was in the fort a large coil of very heavy rope, new, and strong enough to sustain fifteen thousand pounds, but some of the doubtful workmen had cut several strands of it at various points on the outside of the coil; at least we could account in no other way for the damage. Besides, we had no blocks large enough to receive the rope even if it had been uninjured. The rope was uncoiled and examined. The portion on the inner side of the coil was found uninjured, and a few splices gave rope enough for a triple tackle sixty feet long. The improvisation of blocks of sufficient size and strength now became the sole remaining difficulty, and it was overcome in this way: the gun-carriages of those days were made of well-seasoned oak, and one of them was cut up and the material used for the construction of blocks. When the blocks were finished the iron-clad battery was shorn of half its terrors.

The tackle thus improvised was rigged on the shears, the first gun was rolled into position for hoisting, the sling was attached, and the windlass was manned. After carefully inspecting every knot and lashing, the officer in charge gave the word, "Heave away," and the men bent to their work steadily and earnestly, feeling, no doubt, that the battle with the iron-clad had really begun. Every eye watched the ropes as they began to take the strain, and when the gun had fairly left the skids, and there was no accident, the song which anxiety had suspended was resumed, all hands joining in the chorus, "On the Plains of Mexico," with a sonorous heartiness that might well have been heard at Fort Moultrie. The gun made the vertical passage of fifty feet successfully, and was safely landed on the terreplein. The chassis and carriage were then sent up, transported to the proper emplacement, and put in position, and the gun was mounted.

The ten-inch columbiad threw a shot weighing one hundred and twenty-eight pounds, and it was now necessary that a supply of such shot should be raised. Of course, they could have been sent up at the derrick, but that would have been a slow process, and, moreover, it would have required the derrick and the men, when they were needed for other work. So after retreat roll-call, when the day's work was over, the men were bantered by some designing sergeant as to their ability to carry a ten-inch shot up the stairway. Some of the soldiers, full of confidence and energy, shouldered a shot each and started. They accomplished the feat, and the less confident, unwilling to be outdone by comrades no bigger than themselves, shouldered a shot each and made the passage. In a few minutes sixty shot were deposited near the gun; and it became the custom to carry up a ten-inch shot after retreat—just for fun—as long as there were any to carry.

The second ten-inch columbiad was less fortunate than its fellow. It reached the level of the terreplein without accident, but almost at the first haul on the watch tackle to swing it in, it broke away and fell with a dull thud. There was no mirth in the faces of the men at the watch tackle as they looked over the edge of the parade wall to see how many of the men at the windlass were left. The gun had descended, breech first, like a bolt from a catapult, and had buried itself in the sand up to the trunnions; but beyond breaking the transoms of the derrick, no damage was done. The cause of the accident was easily discovered. The amateur block-maker, unwilling to weaken the blocks by too much trimming, had left their upper edges too sharp, and the strap of the upper block had been cut in consequence. In four days the derrick was repaired, and the gun safely landed on the terreplein.

The third ten-inch columbiad was not sent up. It was mounted as a mortar on the parade, for the purpose of shelling Charleston should that become advisable. A mortar platform already existed there. A ten-inch top carriage was placed on it and the gun mounted pointing toward the city.

A breach was not dreaded by the garrison, for, weak as it was, it could have given a good account of itself defending a breach. The greatest danger was a simultaneous attack on all sides. Sixty-four men could not be made very effective at a dozen different points. The possibility of the enemy, under cover of darkness, getting a foothold in force on the narrow bit of riprapping between tide-water and the foundation of the scarp was ever present in our minds.

The most likely place to land was the wharf, a stone structure in front of the main entrance. There an assaulting column might be formed and the main gate stormed, while the bulk of the garrison was defending the embrasures. To checkmate any such attempt, means of blowing the wharf out of existence were devised. Two five-gallon demijohns filled with powder were planted as mines, well under the wharf pavement, in such a way as to insure the total demolition of the structure by their explosion. These mines were arranged so that both should explode at the same instant. The means of firing were twofold: first, a powder-hose leading from the mines through a wooden trough buried under the pavement, and terminating in a dry well just inside the gate; second, a long lanyard connected with friction primers inserted in the corks of the powder demijohns, and extending through the trough into the well, whence it branched like a bell wire to convenient points inside the fort.

Another place offering special advantages to a storming party was the esplanade. This was a broad promenade extending the whole length of the gorge wall on the outside, and paved with immense blocks of dressed granite. As Fort Sumter was not designed to resist attack by storm, the esplanade was unswept by any fire. To remedy this defect the stone fougasse was resorted to. To the uninitiated the fougasse looked like a harmless pile of stones resting against the scarp wall. The only thing that would be likely to attract his attention was the bin-like inclosure of solid masonry open at the outer side, which looked like an immense dust-pan, and which he might think was a rather elaborate arrangement to hold merely a pile of stones together. There was nothing to indicate that beneath the stones, in the angle close to the scarp wall, a magazine of gunpowder lay concealed, and that behind were arrangements for firing it from the inside of the works. These harmless-looking piles of stones were mines of the deadliest kind. In addition, two eight-inch sea-coast howitzers were mounted on their upper carriages only, and placed in front of the main entrance, pointing to the right and left so as to sweep the esplanade.

Another contrivance, the "flying fougasse," or bursting barrel, a device of Captain Truman Seymour, consisted of an ordinary cask or barrel filled with broken stones, and having in its center a canister of powder, sufficient to burst the barrel and scatter its contents with considerable force.

With the exception of the mounting of the guns, the preparations described were chiefly intended to ward off assault. The actions of the enemy now indicated that he proposed to bombard the work at an early day. If we would meet Moultrie, and the numerous batteries which were being constructed against us, on anything like even terms, we must be prepared to shoot accurately.

Aiming cannon consists of two distinct operations: namely, alignment and elevation. In the former, according to instructions and practice, the gunner depends upon his eye and the cannon-sights. But for night firing or when the enemy is enveloped in smoke—as he is sure to be in any artillery duel—the eye cannot be depended on. Visual aiming in a bombardment is a delusion and a snare. To overcome this difficulty, on clear days, when all the conditions were favorable to accuracy, and we could work at our leisure, every gun in the armament was carefully aimed at all the prominent objects within its field of fire, and its position marked on the traverse circle, the index being a pointer securely fastened to the traverse fork. After this had been done, alignment became as easy as setting a watch, and could be done by night or day, by the least intelligent soldier in the garrison.

The elevation was more difficult to deal with. The ordinary method by the use of a breech-sight could not be depended on, even if there had been a sufficient supply of such instruments, because darkness or smoke would render it inapplicable or inaccurate; and the two quadrants in the outfit could not be distributed all over the fort.

Before the correct elevation to carry a shot to a given object can be determined, it is necessary to know the exact distance of the object. This was obtained from the coast-survey chart of the harbor. The necessary elevation was then calculated, or taken from the tables, and the gun elevated accordingly by means of the quadrant. The question then became, How can the gunner bring the gun to this elevation in the heat of action, and without the use of a quadrant? There was an abundance of brass rods, perhaps a quarter-inch in diameter, in the fort. Pieces of such rods, eighteen inches long, were prepared by shaping one end to fit into a socket on the cheek of the carriage, and the other into a chisel edge. They were called by the men pointing rods. A vertical line was then drawn on the right breech of the gun, and painted white. The non-commissioned officer who attended to this preparation, having carefully elevated the gun with the quadrant for a particular object, set the pointing rod in the socket, and brought its chisel end down on the vertical line. The point thus cut was marked and the initials of the object to be struck with that elevation written opposite. These arrangements, which originated with Captain Doubleday, were of great value during the bombardment.

The opening of he bombardment was a somewhat dramatic event. A relieving fleet was approaching, all unknown to the Sumter garrison, and General Beauregard, perhaps with the hope of tying Major Anderson's hands in the expected fight with that fleet, had opened negotiations with him on the 11th of April looking toward the evacuation of the fort. But Major Anderson declined to evacuate his post till compelled by hunger. The last ounce of breadstuffs had been consumed, and matters were manifestly approaching a crisis. It was evident from the activity of the enemy that something important was in the wind. That night we retired as usual. Toward half-past three on the morning of the 12th we were startled by a gun fired in the immediate vicinity of the fort, and many rose to see what was the matter. It was soon learned that a steamer from the enemy desired to communicate with Major Anderson, and a small boat under a flag of truce was received and delivered the message. Although no formal announcement of the fact was made, it became generally known among the men that in one hour General Beauregard would open his batteries on Sumter.

The men waited about for some time in expectation of orders, but received none, except an informal order to go to bed, and the information that reveille would be sounded at the usual hour. This was daylight, fully two hours off, so some of the men did retire. The majority perhaps remained up, anxious to see the opening, for which purpose they had all gone on the ramparts. Except that the flag was hoisted, and a glimmer of light was visible at the guard-house, the fort looked so dark and silent as to seem deserted. The morning was dark and raw. Some of the watchers surmised that Beauregard was "bluffing," and that there would be no bombardment. But promptly at 4:30 A.M. a flash as of distant lightning in the direction of Mount Pleasant, followed by the dull roar of a mortar, told us that the bombardment had begun. The eyes of the

Confederate floating battery bombards Fort Sumter

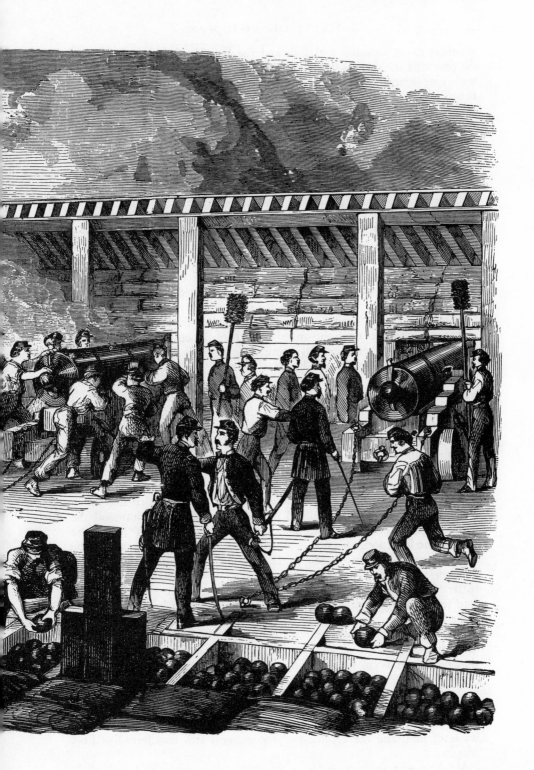

watchers easily detected and followed the burning fuse which marked the course of the shell as it mounted among the stars, and then descended with ever-increasing velocity, until it landed inside the fort and burst. It was a capital shot. Then the batteries opened on all sides, and shot and shell went screaming over Sumter as if an army of devils were swooping around it. As a rule the guns were aimed too high, but all the mortar practice was good. In a few minutes the novelty disappeared in a realizing sense of danger, and the watchers retired to the bomb-proofs, where they discussed probabilities until reveille.

Habits of discipline are strong among old soldiers. If it had not been for orders to the contrary, the men would have formed for roll-call on the open parade, as it was their custom to do, although mortar-shells were bursting there at the lively rate of about one a minute. But they were formed under the bomb-proofs, and the roll was called as if nothing unusual was going on. They were then directed to get breakfast, and be ready to fall in when "assembly" was beaten. The breakfast part of the order was considered a grim joke, as the fare was reduced to the solitary item of fat pork, very rusty indeed. But most of the men worried down a little of it, and were "ready" when the drum called them to their work.

By this time it was daylight, and the effects of the bombardment became visible. No serious damage was being done to the fort. The enemy had concentrated their fire on the barbette batteries, but, like most inexperienced gunners, they were firing too high. After daylight their shooting improved, until at 7:30 A.M., when "assembly" was beaten in Sumter, it had become fairly good. At "assembly" the men were again paraded, and the orders of the day announced. The garrison was divided into two reliefs, and the tour of duty at the guns was to be four hours. Captain Doubleday being the senior captain, his battery took the first tour.

There were three points to be fired upon—the Morris Island batteries, the James Island batteries, and the Sullivan's Island batteries. With these last was included the famous iron-clad floating battery, which had taken up a position off the western end of Sullivan's Island to command the left flank of Sumter. Captain Doubleday divided his men into three parties: the first, under his own immediate command, was marched to the casemate guns bearing on Morris Island; the second, under Lieutenant Jefferson C. Davis, manned the casemate guns bearing on the James Island batteries; and the third—without a commissioned officer until Dr. Crawford joined it—was marched by a sergeant to the guns bearing on Sullivan's Island. The guns in the lower tier, which were the only ones used during the bombardment—except surreptitiously without orders—were 32 and 42-pounders, and some curiosity was felt as to the effect of such shot on the iron-clad battery. The gunners made excellent practice, but the shot were seen to bounce off its sides like peas. After battering it for about an hour and a half, no visible effect had been produced, although it had perceptibly slackened its fire, perhaps to save ammunition. But it was evident that throwing 32-pounder shot at it, at a mile range, was a waste of iron, and the attention of the gunners was transferred to Fort Moultrie.

Moultrie was, perhaps, a less satisfactory target than the iron-clad. It was literally buried under sand-bags, the very throats of the embrasures being closed with cotton-bales. The use of cotton-bales was very effective as against shot, but would have been less so again shell. The fact that the embrasures were thus closed was not known in Sumter till after the bombardment. It explained what was otherwise inexplicable. Shot would be seen to strike an embrasure, and the gunner would feel that he had settled one gun for certain, but even while he was receiving the congratulations of his comrades the supposed disabled gun would reply. That the cotton-bales could not be seen from Sumter is not surprising. The sand-bag casemates which covered the guns were at least eighteen feet thick, and the cotton-bale shutter was no doubt arranged to slide up and down like a portcullis inside the pile of sand-bags. The gunners of Sumter, not knowing of the existence of these shutters, directed their shot either on the embrasures for the purpose of disabling the enemy's guns, or so as to graze the sand-bag parapet for the purpose of reaching the interior of the work. The practice was very good, but the effect, for reasons already stated, was inconsiderable.

At the end of the first four hours, Doubleday's men were relieved from the guns and had an opportunity to look about them. Not a man was visible near any of the batteries, but a large party, apparently of noncombatants, had collected on the beach of Sullivan's Island, well out of the line of fire, to witness the duel between Sumter and Moultrie. Doubleday's men were not in the best of temper. They were irritated at the thought that they had been unable to inflict any serious damage on their adversary, and although they had suffered no damage in return they were dissatisfied. The crowd of unsympathetic spectators was more than they could bear, and two veteran sergeants determined to stir them up a little. For this purpose they directed two 42-pounders on the crowd, and, when no officer was near, fired. The first shot struck about fifty yards short, and, bounding over the heads of the astonished spectators, went crashing through the Moultrie House. The second followed an almost identical course, doing no damage except to the Moultrie House, and the spectators scampered off in a rather undignified manner.

The smoke which enveloped the Confederate batteries during the first day, while not so thick as entirely to obscure them, was sufficiently so to make visual aiming extremely unreliable; and during the second day, when Sumter was on fire, nothing could be seen beyond the muzzles of our guns. But the aiming arrangements, due to the foresight and ingenuity of Captain Doubleday, enabled us to fire with as much accuracy when we could not see the object as when we could.

Major Anderson had given orders that only the casemate batteries should be manned. While this was undoubtedly prompted by a desire to save his men, it operated also, in some degree, to save the Confederates. Our most powerful batteries and all our shell guns were on the barbette tier, and, being forbidden their use, we were compelled to oppose a destructive shell fire with solid shot alone. This, especially as we had no mortars, was a great disadvantage. Had we been permitted to use our shell guns we could have set fire to the barracks and quarters in Moultrie; for, as it was, we wrecked them badly with solid shot, although we could not see them. Then the cotton-bale shutters would have been destroyed, and we could have made it much livelier generally for our adversaries. This was so apparent to the men, that one of them—a man named Carmody —stole up on the ramparts and deliberately fired every barbette gun in position on the Moultrie side of the work. The guns were already loaded and roughly aimed, and Carmody simply discharged them in succession; hence, the effect was less than it would have been if the aim had been carefully rectified. But Carmody's effort aroused the enemy to a sense of his danger. He supposed, no doubt, that Major Anderson had determined to open his barbette batteries, so he directed every gun to bear on the barbette tier of Fort Sumter, and probably believed that the vigor of his fire induced Major Anderson to change his mind. But the contest was merely Carmody against the Confederate States; and Carmody had to back down, not because he was beaten, but because he was unable, single-handed, to reload his guns.

The first night of the bombardment was one of great anxiety. The fleet might send reënforcements; the enemy might attempt an assault. Both would come in boats; both would answer in English. It would be horrible to fire upon friends; it would be fatal not to fire upon enemies. The night was dark and chilly. Shells were dropping into the fort at regular intervals, and the men were tired, hungry, and out of temper. Any party that approached that night would have been rated as enemies upon general principles. Fortunately nobody appeared; reveille sounded, and the men oiled their appetites with the fat pork at the usual hour by way of breakfast.

The second day's bombardment began at the same hour as did the first; that is, on the Sumter side. The enemy's mortars had kept up a very slow fire all night, which gradually warmed up after daylight as their batteries seemed to awaken, until its vigor was about equal to their fire of the day before. The fleet was still off the bar—perhaps waiting to see the end. Fire broke out once or twice in the officers' quarters, and was extinguished. It broke out again in several places at once, and we realized the truth and let the quarters burn. They were firing red-hot shot. This was about 9 o'clock. As soon as Sumter was noticed to be on fire the secessionists increased the fire of their batteries to a maximum. In the perfect storm of shot and shell that beat upon us from all sides, the flag-staff was shot down, but the old flag was rescued and nailed to a new staff. This, with much difficulty, was carried to the ramparts and lashed to some chassis piled up there for a traverse.

We were not sorry to see the quarters burn. They were a nuisance. Built for fire-proof buildings, they were not fire-proof. Neither would they burn up in a cheerful way. The principal cisterns were large iron tanks immediately under the roof. These had been riddled, and the quarters below had been deluged with water. Everything was wet and burned badly, yielding an amount of pungent piney smoke which almost suffocated the garrison.

The scene inside the fort as the fire gained headway and threatened the magazine was an exciting one. It had already reached some of our stores of loaded shells and shell-grenades. These must be saved at all hazard. Soldiers brought their blankets and covered the precious projectiles, and thus the most of them were saved. But the magazine itself was in danger. Already it was full of smoke, and the flames were rapidly closing in upon it. It was evident that it must be closed, and it would be many hours before it could be opened again. During these hours the fire must be maintained with such powder as we could secure outside the magazine. A number of barrels were rolled out for this purpose, and the magazine door—already almost too hot to handle—was closed.

It was the intention to store the powder taken from the magazine in several safe corners, covering it with damp soldiers' blankets. But safe corners were hard to find, and most of the blankets were already in use covering loaded shells. The fire was raging more fiercely than ever, and safety demanded that the uncovered powder be thrown overboard. This was instantly done, and if the tide had been high we should have been well rid of it. But the tide was low, and the pile of powder-barrels rested on the riprapping in front of the embrasure. This was observed by the enemy, and some shell guns were turned upon the pile, producing an explosion which blew the gun at that embrasure clear out of battery, but did no further damage.

The fire had now enveloped the magazine, and the danger of an explosion was imminent. Powder had been carried out all the previous day, and it was more than likely that enough had sifted through the cartridge-bags to carry the fire into the powder-chamber. Major Anderson, his head erect as if on parade, called the men around him; directed that a shot be fired every five minutes; and mentioned that there was some danger of the magazine exploding. Some of the men, as soon as they learned what the real danger was, rushed to the door of the magazine and hurriedly dug a trench in front of it, which they kept filled with water until the danger was considered over.

It was during this excitement that ex-Senator Wigfall of Texas visited the fort. It came the turn of one of the guns on the left face of the work to fire—we were now firing once in five minutes—and as the cannoneer approached for the purpose of loading, he discovered a man looking in at the embrasure. The man must have raised himself to the level of the embrasure by grasping the sill with his hands. A short but lively altercation ensued between the man and the cannoneer, the man pleading to be taken in lest he should be killed with his own shot and shell. He was hauled in, Thompson, the cannoneer, first receiving his sword, to the point of which a white handkerchief was attached, not by way of surrender, but for convenience. Once inside, the bearer asked to see Major Anderson. The major was soon on the spot and opened the conversation by asking, "To what am I indebted for this visit?" The visitor replied, "I am Colonel Wigfall, of General Beauregard's staff. For God's sake, Major, let this thing stop. There has been enough bloodshed already." To which the major replied, "There has been none on my side, and besides, your batteries are still firing on me." At which Wigfall exclaimed, "I'll soon stop that," and turning to Thompson, who still held the sword under his arm, he said, pointing to the handkerchief, "Wave that out there." Thompson then handed the sword to Wigfall, saying, in substance, "Wave it yourself." Wigfall received back his sword and took a few steps toward the embrasure, when the major called him back, saying, "If you desire that to be seen you had better send it to the parapet." There was a good deal more said on the subject of the white flag both by Wigfall and the major which the writer cannot recall, but the end of it all was that a white flag was ordered to be displayed from the parapet at the request of Colonel Wigfall, and pending negotiations with him, which was instantly done, a hospital sheet being used for the purpose. Then the firing gradually ceased, and the major and his officers and Colonel Wigfall retired into the hospital bomb-proof, the only habitable room left. This was about 3 o'clock in the afternoon.

Wigfall's conference was not of long duration. He left the fort in the small boat which brought him from Morris Island, and which was manned by negroes. Shortly after his departure another small boat from Sullivan's Island, containing officers in full uniform (Wigfall wore citizen's dress with the sword), approached the fort. The officers in this boat were very much astonished and annoyed at being warned off by the sentinel, and compelled to show a white flag before they were permitted to approach. They were received by the officer of the day, who apologized for not meeting them afloat, saying that all our boats had been destroyed by shot or burned up. They were indignant at their reception, and demanded to know whether or not the fort had surrendered. What was said in reply was not distinctly heard by the writer, but it was believed to be a negative. The officer then asked what the white flag meant, and Wigfall's name was mentioned in reply. About this time Major Anderson made his appearance, and the visitors, still talking in an indignant tone, addressed themselves to him. What was said seemed to be a repetition of what had just been said to the officer of the day. The major's replies were inaudible where the writer of this stood, except when he raised his hand in a sweeping sort of gesture in the direction of Fort Moultrie, and said, "Very well, gentlemen, you can return to your batteries." They did not return, however, immediately, but were conducted into the hospital where Wigfall had been, and remained there some time. When they left we learned that there would be no more firing until General Beauregard had time to hear from his Government at Montgomery.

About seven o'clock in the evening another white flag brought the announcement that the terms agreed upon between General Beauregard and Major Anderson had been confirmed, and that we would leave Fort Sumter the following day; which we did, after saluting our flag with fifty guns.

THE Nation GIRDS ITSELF

THE FALL OF FORT SUMTER ended President Lincoln's hopes of avoiding war. On April 15, he called for 75,000 volunteers. In May he asked for 40,000 more, and on April 19 he ordered a blockade of all southern ports. The call to arms met an enthusiastic response in the North, but it had an opposite effect in the border states. Two days after the President's call, Virginia fell into the Confederate camp. North Carolina, Tennessee, and Arkansas followed, and the other border states continued to teeter.

With Virginia in the Confederacy, Washington was vulnerable to attack from across the Potomac River. To strengthen the capital guard and to further increase his armed forces, President Lincoln called Congress into emergency session on July 4. In his message he asked for 400,000 men and four hundred million dollars. Congress gave the President everything he asked for—and more the day after the Battle of Bull Run!—endorsing and legalizing necessary emergency measures to deal with a nation at war.

Regiments of Union militia began to arrive in Washington in late April. By early July a Union army of 35,000 existed, although their experience was limited to parade-ground marching. General McDowell, in charge of the District of Columbia defenses, was handed the troops and directed to invade Virginia and head for Richmond, the Confederate capital, and, it was hoped, end the war before it had time really to begin.

As Bruce Catton says: "McDowell was not concerned with broad strategy. He commanded what was called the Department of Northeastern Virginia, with headquarters at Arlington, in the pillared house occupied until recently by Robert E. Lee, and he knew that he was expected to take action against the enemy in his immediate front. This enemy was General Beauregard, who had an army drawn up in front of Manassas Junction, thirty-odd miles from Washington, behind a sluggish stream known as Bull Run. McDowell had nothing resembling an adequate staff, but his intelligence service was good, and he had an only mildly exaggerated count of Beauregard's numbers: about 25,000 of all arms, he believed, with perhaps 10,000 more up in the Shenandoah Valley led by Joe Johnston. Since there was a railroad line from Manassas to the Valley, Johnston could quickly come to Beauregard's aid when the Yankees moved. Let the Federals along the upper Potomac, then, keep Johnston so busy that he could send no help; McDowell himself, with 30,000 men in column and another 10,000 in reserve, could march down to give Beauregard a battle. . . .

"The direct route from Centreville to Manassas ran off mainly south by west, crossing Bull Run by a number of fords—Mitchell's, Blackburn's, McLean's, Union Mills. Nearly all of Beauregard's army was waiting in this area, snugly posted behind the river in good defensive positions, and McDowell had no intention of making a head-on attack. He wanted to get beyond the Confederate left, which appeared to be anchored along the Warrenton Pike at the stone bridge, and so he had his men moving out at two in the morning in the flat white light of the moon, marching toward the positions from which they could take the Rebels by surprise. Some would be retained in the vicinity of Centreville, in reserve. A few would go down to the lower fords just to put in an appearance and make Beauregard think something was apt to happen there. A much larger contingent would move straight off for the stone bridge, under instructions to fire cannon and make other warlike noises, so that the Confederates on the left would looked fixedly at the bridge and would pay no attention to anything that might be going on farther upstream.

"Farther upstream was where things really would happen. McDowell would take 14,000 men off on a wide circle to the right, coming to Bull Run at a ford by a place known as Sudley Springs, several miles north and west of the stone bridge. Crossing here, this force could march south and come in well behind the Confederate flank, and if the job were done right, it ought to roll up the whole Confederate army like a rug.

"The Confederate army that was waiting for him was in no better shape than his own as far as training and discipline went, except that it did not contain any ninety-day regiments whose time was about up. McDowell had many of these; a few, learning on the literal eve of battle that their ninety days had been spent, insisted on marching off to the rear despite McDowell's earnest entreaties. Beauregard had nearly 25,000 men, drawn up in a line eight miles long on the far side of Bull Run. He had most of his strength on his right, and he was planning to make a grand left wheel, hitting the invader in the flank; he reported that his men were 'badly armed and suffering from the irregularity and inefficiency of the Quartermaster's and Commissary's Departments,' but he believed they would do well enough. They did have one advantage: they had not had to tire themselves out and disrupt their organization with a long and wearing march. Like McDowell, Beauregard was worried for fear his men could not tell friend from foe once the fight began—in each army some men wore blue and others wore gray, there were all manner of fancy-dress uniforms in use, and some Confederates had no uniforms at all. McDowell had ordered that the United States flag be displayed constantly in all units, and Beauregard hoped that the ladies of Richmond might contribute colored scarves which his men could loop over their shoulders. The ladies did their best, but the supply was short, and what resulted was a sort of rosette which men were asked to pin to their coats. Beauregard noted that a good many of his regiments had no flags at all.

"It was going to be, in short, a battle of amateurs, and both commanders knew it. Looking back long afterward, Beauregard believed that a special weight rested on both sides: 'There was much in this decisive conflict about to open not involved in any after battle, which pervaded the two armies and the people behind them and colored the responsibility of the respective commanders. The political hostilities of a generation were now face to face with weapons instead of words.' "*

Bull Run: A Union Soldier†

BY CAPTAIN HENRY N. BLAKE

O N JULY 16, 1861, the Eleventh Regiment Massachusetts Volunteers formed a part of a brigade commanded by Col. Franklin, and a division commanded by Gen. Heintzelman. In compliance with orders, the regiment marched from Alexandria at 2 P.M., and left all the diseased and feeble in the camp, under the charge of a sick captain, to guard the tents and knapsacks of the men during their absence. The soldiers composing the expedition displayed the highest emotion of joy; and those who were compelled by their physical weakness to remain in the rear were affected with grief, and some shed tears. Each person carried his musket and equipments, containing forty rounds of ammunition; and bore upon his shoulder a woollen blanket enclosed in one made of gum or rubber, and a canteen and haversack. The latter was filled with rations for three days, which consisted of three or four pounds of salt pork or beef ("junk"), thirty crackers ("hard-tack"), and a small quantity of sugar and coffee. No one seemed to be informed concerning the object of the movement; but it was generally surmised that a battle was one of the events of the uncertain future. The column marched over a narrow and miserable road (one of the chief features of the barbarism of Virginia) south of the Orange and Alexandria Railroad, and formed the left wing of the invading army, which was commanded by Gen. McDowell. Sixteen horses could not draw a thirty-two-pound Parrott gun over the rugged course; and two companies were detached from the regiment to assist the jaded animals in performing this labor. The men sustained the fatigues of their first march during the afternoon and evening in an excellent manner; and there were few cases of utter exhaustion or straggling, although the halts were infrequent. The houses, or, to speak truly, hovels, upon the road, were small in number and dimension, and the country was thickly wooded. The population that was visible comprised aged men, women with their children, and the negroes.

Our progress was extremely slow after sunset; and the column for seven hours advanced, at irregular intervals of time, five, twenty, or one

* *The Coming Fury,* pp. 440, 447, 448, 449.
† From *Three Years in the Army of the Potomac.*

hundred feet. No orders to halt were received during the night from the brigade commander: the delays of a few seconds or minutes were uncertain in their duration; and the men did not know when they could enjoy them. As soon as they had broken ranks, and prepared to rest after a sudden stop, they would be commanded to "fall in"; and another pause frequently occurred before the moving mass had travelled the length of a company. The troops, expecting to start at once, sometimes stood in their places half of an hour before the march was resumed; and were fatigued during this time, as if they had been in motion. The soldiers were completely exhausted by this severe mode of manoeuvring them, for which there was no excuse; and many fell asleep upon the roadside. The regiment reached its halting-place near Pohick Church at 3:45 A.M., on the 17th, and welcomed repose without seeking any shelter. A single tree formed the bridge over Pohick Creek, a run which was about twenty-five feet in width, and too deep to be forded; and the troops, assisted by a feeble light, crossed upon it in one rank. The column had been delayed several hours by this obstacle, which could have been easily removed by the pioneers, who carried fifty axes, with which they might have felled the trees that were standing upon the banks of the streamlet, and built a bridge. The most tedious portion of the march could have been prevented by the use of the most ordinary judgment by the brigade commander, who displayed a profound ignorance of the first lesson in the school of a general—the art of marching men: instead of conducting troops a great distance with a small expenditure of strength, he reversed the rule, and caused more fatigue in marching the brigade fourteen miles than they would have suffered in moving twice this distance under an intelligent officer.

The troops rested only an hour, and were awakened at four o'clock, and ordered to resume the march; during which they nibbled their rations, for there were no chances to eat a regular meal. From this early moment until 3 P.M., the brigade was marched in the heedless style that characterized the previous night; and no stated halts took place, although there was an intense heat. Hundreds were obliged to leave the ranks, because they had been deprived of bodily vigor by the hardships of the two days; while the brigadier and his staff, riding upon their horses and suffering no inconvenience, unjustly reprimanded them for straggling. These unfortunate soldiers did not wish to avoid the dangers of a battle: on the contrary, the only apprehension which they expressed was, that the rebels, following the precedent established at Harper's Ferry and Alexandria, might evacuate Manassas. No public road was followed during a portion of the route, which passed through fields and forests in a thinly settled country. The forms of one half of the brigade arrived at Sangster's Station at three o'clock, about two hours after the South-Carolina troops retreated upon the railroad from Fairfax Court House; and the bridges which they had set on fire were burning when the column halted. Squads of the missing fragment of the command constantly joined it during the next six hours, until there were no absentees. Three or four men were killed on both days by the carelessness of soldiers who bore loaded muskets upon their shoulders for the first time.

A drove of pigs, and flock of sheep numbering about one hundred and fifty, were captured by these men within an hour after their arrival; and it was ascertained that they had been collected for the purpose of feeding a detachment of the rebel army which had been stationed at this point. Some were killed, and roasted upon the camp-fires by means of a rammer, or forked twig, while the flesh quivered. The brigade commander issued an order authorizing the officers to shoot every man who was detected in the act of killing these hogs or sheep, and the soldiers stealthily cooked in the night what they had slaughtered and concealed; but the largest portion of the number was abandoned to nourish the poorly supplied enemy. A circular was transmitted by Gen. McDowell, reproaching the volunteers as plunderers, and denouncing their conduct in such strong terms of undeserved censure, that a feeling of indignation pervaded the ranks. My facilities for seeing any depredations that might have been committed were excellent, because the regiment had a position in the rear of the division; and the behavior of the troops towards the people upon the road was unexceptionable. A house which had been deserted by its owner, who had joined the forces of Beauregard, was burned during the night by some men who were exasperated on account of the wearisome manner in which they were delayed. They rushed to the wells near some of the dwellings to procure fresh water, because the officers in charge of the command did not halt and allow them to fill their canteens, the contents of which had become too warm for use. Certain mounted officers were very conspicuous in using oaths, and driving the troops from these places which belonged to traitors who were toiling upon the intrenchments of Manassas. The painful experiences and stringent orders of the 16th and 17th excited in the minds of many privates a strong prejudice against some of their superiors in rank, and opinions were freely expressed regarding their wisdom and loyalty. The soldiers listened for the first time to the reports of rebel cannon upon the afternoon of the 18th; and gladly advanced in the direction of the firing at 5 P.M., and bivouacked near Centreville at midnight.

Stacks of arms, and batteries, surrounded us in the field near the old road over which Gen. Braddock led his ill-fated expedition to Fort du Quesne. The army rested two days at this point, and listened to the whistle of the locomotives that were bringing to the junction re-enforcements for the rebel hordes. The soldiers eagerly walked long distances to see prisoners; and a defiant sergeant told the crowd of spectators that they would "double-quick back to Washington" within a week; a prophecy which was fulfilled upon the 21st. Citizens searching for runaway negroes, or presenting claims for damages to their property, were protected by Gen. McDowell, who allowed them to examine every encampment, and ascertain the number and position of the troops and batteries; after which they rode to Manassas, and communicated the valuable information which they had acquired. A private of the regiment, who was wounded and captured in the battle, saw a person, that applied for compensation on account of the injury to his crops, dressed in the nondescript uniform of the Southern soldiers. He spoke to him when he was posted upon guard, and asked, "How much money did you get for your wheat?" The rebel laughed at the question, but admitted that he was a spy, and entertained his companions by narrating the facts. Rations of pork and beef for two days were boiled on the 20th, and issued to the command at midnight. The regiment was formed in line at 1 A.M., upon the 21st: the division commenced to move into the road at half-past two, and marched a mile towards the commanding heights of Centreville, when it was halted to allow the commands of Tyler and Hunter to file by it. Infantry and artillery, during the following three hours, occupied the solitary avenue over which the entire army passed to the front. The appearance of this large force inspired all with confidence; and the order to advance was awaited with impatience.

The head of the column started at the end of this unforeseen delay, advanced upon the Warrenton Turnpike through the little village of Centreville, and crossed the bridge that spans Cub Run, near which I noticed about twenty barouches and carriages that contained members of Congress and their friends, who had left Washington for the purpose of witnessing the approaching conflict. The divisions of Hunter and Heintzelman debouched from the main road, at a point two and a half miles from Centreville, and, accompanied by a guide, followed a narrow pathway which was not often used, and led in its tortuous course through a dry territory that was well shaded by the forest. An open space of fifteen acres sometimes intervened; but it was always enclosed by dense woods. The day was one of the hottest of the year: there was no friendly cloud to obstruct the rays of the sun; and it was impossible for the army to march a long distance with unusual speed. Nevertheless, for twelve miles, the men were pushed forward at an unnatural gait, generally walking as rapidly as possible, and double-quicking one-fourth of the time, to keep the different regiments of the column within supporting distance of each other. Nearly every man impatiently asked, "How far is it to the Junction?" whenever the loyal citizen residing in the vicinity, who acted as a guide, rode along the line. He always answered the question in a good-natured manner by saying, "Six miles." The brigade commander never attempted to secure a rest for the soldiers; and some of them sank upon the ground, wholly overcome by faintness, which was produced by the intolerable heat and the furious rate at which they were marched. There was a very small number, if any, in the Union host, that wished to evade the unknown perils of the combat; and many, throwing away their blankets and rations to facilitate their progress, merely retained their muskets and ammunition. The thirty-two-pound Parrott gun opened its mouth of iron near the "stone bridge" over Bull Run at 6 A.M.; and the artillery upon the left continued to fire at regular intervals in the vicinity of the fords, while the right wing was hastening to turn the left of the rebel line, which was posted in the rear of the Bull Run. The scarcity of water to allay the thirst produced by the causes that have been described was another impediment; but the cannonading inspired the men with patriotism, and gave them a physical strength which they could not have possessed under similar circumstances in the avocations of a peaceful life.

They occasionally emerged from the woods, and beheld the long clouds of dust in the south, which showed that the rebels were moving in the same direction; and it required no deep knowledge of mathematics to demonstrate that the two lines of march, if extended, would soon intersect. The column arrived at eleven o'clock at a point that was a short

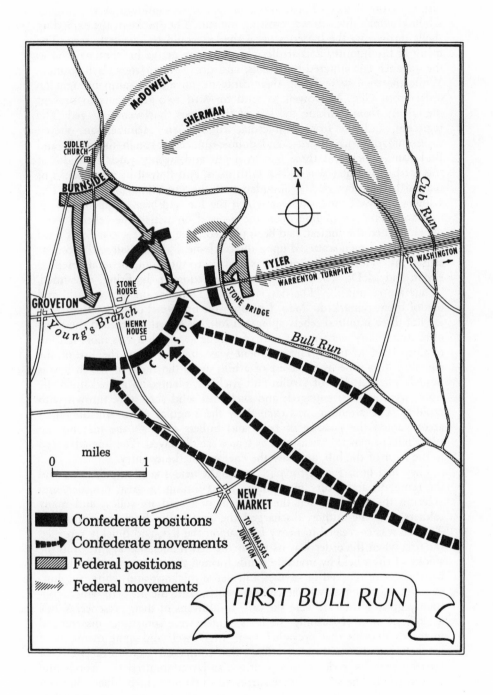

MCDOWELL

SHERMAN

SUDLEY
CHURCH

BURNSIDE

N

Cub Run

TYLER

WARRENTON TURNPIKE

TO WASHINGTON

STONE
HOUSE

GROVETON

Young's Branch

HENRY
HOUSE

STONE BRIDGE

JACKSON

Bull Run

miles

0   1

NEW
MARKET

TO MANASSAS JUNCTION

■■■ Confederate positions
▪▪▪▶ Confederate movements
▨▨▨ Federal positions
▨▨▨ Federal movements

FIRST BULL RUN

distance from Sedley's Ford; and a slight rest was enjoyed by the brigade while Hunter's division was crossing the run. The smoke of the exploding shells thrown by the batteries upon the left could be distinctly seen. The firing of the infantry and artillery became very active in front, as soon as the advance encountered the rebels, and drove them from their position. While the men were filling their canteens, an aide-de-camp brought an order from Gen. McDowell to send forward two regiments to prevent the enemy from flanking the left of the troops that were engaged. The regiment, and one from Minnesota, led by Gen. Heintzelman, obeyed the command with alacrity, and double-quicked through the fields, and Bull Run, which was three feet in depth and twenty yards in width at this ford. The water was yellow with mud, and flowed between banks of red earth that showed the abundance of the sandstone in the soil. The soldiers followed the road over which the foe had been compelled to retire, and deployed in line upon the ground on which the rebel battery, which opened the contest, had been planted. The strange spectacle of dead and wounded men scattered upon the battle-field affected all with peculiar sensations. While the regiment was moving to the front, Generals Heintzelman and McDowell, pointing in the direction of the firing, exclaimed, "They are running!" "The day is ours!" "They are on the retreat!" and one of them remarked, "Men, I pledge you my word of honor that there are not three hundred rebels upon that hill." When they reached the scene of contest, many were in that state of fatigue in which it was more natural to sleep than to fight. The regiment was shielded from the fire of the enemy at this time by the crest of a hill, upon the slope of which it was posted. The batteries of Griffin and Ricketts, planted in a field upon the right, were actively engaged; and shell and solid shot were thrown with rapidity. The attention was excited by the singular shrill whistling that accompanied the passage of balls and bullets through the air; but no symptoms of general uneasiness or fear were displayed. The line advanced to the crest of the hill, and saw the enemies of the country.

They had been forced to quit the height near the Henry House; and the remnant, about fifty in number, was running in great disorder, and entering the woods, when the regiment delivered its volley, and many soldiers, like the author, discharged the first bullet from their muskets. The foe was concealed in heavy force upon the left, and quickly returned the fire, when the order was issued to "lie down and load again;" and the smoke of rifles held by invisible hands formed the next target. The hostile batteries were masked in ravines and dense thickets; and white, sulphurous clouds, rising slowly at certain points, and the reports which constantly greeted the ear, were the only indications of their presence. While the officers were re-forming the lines, which were sometimes disarranged in the excitement that prevailed, Gen. McDowell and some members of his staff, together with other officers that composed a group of twelve or thirteen persons, rode to this position, and reconnoitred the woods and hills in front. The soldiers were surprised to witness the boldness that was thus displayed; and expected to see them fall; but were amazed when they retired without receiving a bullet. When the regiment, inferring that the rebels had been forced from their last line of defence, advanced to the same point, a shower of lead welcomed it, and traced little channels in the ground upon which it stood. The enemy was again pushed back: the brigade filed to the right, and held a portion of the Leesburg Road, which ran through the stream at Sedley's Ford; and victory seemed to be no longer a matter of doubt. The national troops had pursued a retreating army a mile and a half: the Warrenton Pike was in their possession; and the left wing of Beauregard's force had been completely turned, so that his line of battle was formed at right angles with the Bull Run, which they had vainly attempted to defend. A lull in the infantry firing took place a few minutes after one o'clock, and continued half of an hour; during which the men that were unoccupied should have attacked the rebels, who were enabled by this blundering delay to re-organize their shattered ranks, and offer a firm resistance when the offensive was assumed. These were the precious moments when a small fraction of the large reserve should have been ordered to complete the triumph that had been already won. The commanding general never submitted an excuse for this omission of duty that satisfied those who took an active part in the engagement. I had a good opportunity to notice the topography of this portion of the field, which became the centre of the most stubborn fighting, while the soldiers were waiting for orders in the narrow Leesburg Road, that had been excavated seven or ten feet below the surface of the adjoining ground, and made a fair protection against an assault. There was a small wooden house, occupied by an infirm old lady, Mrs. Henry, who languished upon the bed of sickness during the contest, and was killed by the troops who fired at the dwelling when it was filled with rebel sharpshooters. The open space of ground was very irregular, and located between successive chains of abrupt hills about a quarter of a mile apart, which varied from one to two hundred feet in height. Thickets of pine and oak flourished upon the parts of the field in which the lines of the enemy were established; and the country was adapted by nature for defensive purposes, so that the rebels, when dislodged from one stronghold, always found another a short distance in the rear of it. They were concealed in forests which no telescope could penetrate; but the formation of the Union divisions took place in the open ground, and could be easily perceived by the hostile generals from the summit of a commanding height that overlooked the scene. The principal portion of the cleared soil was uncultivated, and covered with dry grass, and the black weeds which thrive upon land that has been poisoned by the culture of tobacco. The rain had formed brooks that cut numerous deep gullies in the slopes of the hills and every section of the field, and afforded an excellent refuge for the wounded who could not be carried to the hospitals.

The brigade was near the centre of the line at this time, and missiles of lead and iron were continually flying over it. Although the batteries had been placed in the extreme advance, contrary to the well-known precepts of military authors, the success which had hitherto followed our arms tempted Gen. McDowell to make greater risks. The regular artillery, which had rendered splendid service, was removed from a secure position, and pushed to the open field in front, which was destitute of any natural barrier or protection.

"Put the battery upon that hill, and the day is ours!" shouted an officer of high rank. The order was promptly obeyed, and the nation lost the victory. Members of the regiment destroyed a portion of the Virginia rail-fence upon the sides of the road, to allow the cannons to be drawn to the new point that had been designated. The gunners were proud of the success which had been achieved; and one of them said with truth, as he rode by the company, "We made the secesh battery change position three times in half an hour." The regiment was not actively engaged at that moment; and most of the men were watching the section of Griffin's Battery, which was planted near them. A heavy volley from many rifles ended the silence that had existed in the infantry-firing, before it had discharged two rounds: horses, officers, and men were killed or disabled in the space of a second; and, during my subsequent experience in a score of engagements, I never saw the work of destruction more sudden or complete. The battery of Rickett, which was in line of that of Griffin, had been annihilated in the same decisive manner before the support could be placed in position. I did not satisfactorily ascertain by whose stupidity this body of rebels was permitted to approach within two hundred feet of the lines without molestation, until I read the testimony of Gen. Griffin before the Committee on the Conduct of the War. I quote his language, because this disaster was the first check that had occurred in the action, and the chief cause of the defeat. "Major Barry said, 'I know it is the battery support: it is the regiment taken there by Col. ———.' I said. 'They are confederates; as certain as the world, they are confederates.' He replied, 'I know they are your battery support.'"

The few cannoneers that survived this fatal volley immediately rushed to the rear: wounded horses, in their agony, galloped through the ranks of the infantry, and trampled upon the dead and helpless who were lying upon the field. Three animals, which were harnessed, and attached to a caisson, dashed through the regiment at a furious rate of speed, and dragged one that was severely injured: a soldier, whose legs had been shattered by a solid shot, sat upon the carriage, clinging to it with his hands; and a stream of blood sprinkled the earth, and made a trail by which the course of the caisson could be traced. The troops now lost the confidence of victory which they had hitherto possessed; while the defeated and disheartened rebels who saw eleven pieces of artillery in an instant placed *hors de combat,* at once renewed their efforts, and their yells of exultation were heard above the din of the conflict. A squadron of their cavalry attempted to make a charge; but many of their saddles were emptied, and they were easily repulsed by a body of men who belonged to different regiments. In the mean time, the rebel leaders had rallied their stragglers and fugitives, and advanced their lines to capture the guns which were now powerless to do them any injury. They were triumphantly driven three times to the woods, and victory was once more within the grasp of the Union general. The soldiers seized some of the pieces, and pulled them a few yards to the rear; but were compelled to leave them, because the defeat of the enemy required the presence of every man in the line of battle. The regiment at one time stood upon the ground which was held by the foe when the first volley was discharged, and the dead and wounded were seen upon every side. The Mississippi troops had sustained a heavy loss at this point; and one of them, who was dying, remarked to the men, "You have fought for your country, and I have fought for mine." The mangled artillerists rested beneath the guns, in serving which they had so bravely fallen.

It was three o'clock, and the soldiers had been engaged upon the march, or in action, during the long period of thirteen hours. A large number, from various causes, had left their commands and escaped to the rear, or fought without regard to the rules of discipline; but the colors of the regiments, and the organizations, with many of the officers and companies, still remained. The exhausting march, the terrible heat, the lack of water, the horrors of the battle, and, above all, the loss of the artillery, had affected those who remained, to such an extent that they became every minute more unfitted to resist the onset of the enemy, who maintained an irregular fire from the forest. Some officers behaved in the most cowardly manner; and certain companies were commanded by sergeants, because the captains and lieutenants absented themselves during the engagement. An uninjured colonel, who pretended to be severely wounded, and declared that he was unable to walk, was borne from the field by four members of his regiment. There was no general demoralization in the army, although many of the troops acted like all novices in the dreadful art of war, and executed some movements with great confusion. Two men placed their hands upon their ears to exclude the noise of the musketry and artillery, and rushed to the woods in the rear of the regiment. A timid Catholic took his service-book from his pocket, and read some of the prayers when the brigade was posted in the road. The shells struck rifles with such force, that some were twisted into the form of circles. A cannon-ball severed the arm of a sergeant, and threw it into the face of a soldier, who supposed, from the blow and the amount of blood upon his person, that he was dangerously wounded. One man stumbled over some briers while the column was ascending a hill; and a solid shot passed over him and killed his file-leader, when he fell upon the ground. The ghastly faces of the dead, and the sufferings of the wounded, who were begging for water, or imploring aid to be carried to the hospital, moved the hearts of men who had not by long experience become callous to the sight of human agony.

The firing in front was very feeble at four o'clock; but a succession of severe volleys was poured from the woods upon the right flank and rear. The troops were unable to offer any resistance, and began to retire from the field upon which they had maintained, unaided, the long struggle. The fresh soldiers that arrived at this opportune moment belonged to Kirby Smith's brigade, and formed a part of the rebel army of Johnson in the Shenandoah Valley. Generals and mounted officers, among whom were Burnside, Wadsworth, and Gov. Sprague, attempted in every way to form a new line, and prevent the retreating regiments from leaving the field; but the position that was selected had no natural strength, and could be discerned by the enemy, who followed with the energy of conquerors. The colors of some commands were planted firmly; and every man was ordered to rally around them, and make one more effort to win the battle; and officers shouted, "Rally round the old flag!" or, "Zouaves, remember Ellsworth!"

When the foe advanced with loud yells, and it was certain that the thousands who had remained in the reserve at Centreville, and rendered no service during the protracted contest, would not assist the diminished numbers that were formed upon the field, despair was visible on every face; and the regiments fell back about half-past four o'clock. The rebel artillery opened as I passed the Stone Church, which had been used as a hospital; and their cavalry followed at a safe distance in the rear of the mass of the army, after they had received a few rounds of canister. The men were overcome by their thirst; when they forded the run, and drank copious quantities of the water, which was constantly disturbed and filled with particles of mud by the tramp of horses and soldiers through it. The disorder that existed was increased at this point; and the sorrowful troops, who had been forced to show their backs to the enemy, discussed the causes of the repulse while the shells were bursting in their midst. All seemed to wish to reach some rallying-point like Centreville, so that they would not be taken prisoners; and some officers removed their shoulder-straps to conceal their rank, and rushed to Washington. The infantry did not attempt to pursue the retreating columns; and the cavalry halted for the night upon the south bank of Cub Run, which flows into Bull Run. The disorganized brigades marched upon the road over which they had passed in the morning; squads were scattered in all directions, stopping occasionally to eat the refreshing blackberries under their feet; and few bodies of men were moving with regularity.

The gunners of the Washington Artillery obtained an excellent range upon the bridge over Cub Run, and demolished an army wagon, which was not removed by the teamsters who blocked up the way in their eagerness to escape. The stream was not fordable: trains and batteries that had not yet crossed were abandoned, and one-third of the loss that was sustained in the munitions of war occurred at this place. The general that allowed the wagons to go to the front committed an inexcusable error: if they had been parked at Centreville with the reserve, not one of them would have been captured. The so-called panic, about which so much has been said by persons that have given a description of the battle, occurred at this time. The drivers, finding it impossible to cross the run with the wagons and artillery, took their horses, and sometimes cut the traces to expedite their movements; because the shells were continually bursting near them, and there were no troops upon that side of the stream to resist the cavalry if they made a charge. Some government teamsters, who belonged to no army organization, and were upon the safe bank, beyond the range of the rebel guns, cowardly deserted their wagons, and rode, without halting, until they saw the dome of the Capitol. The foot-soldiers, alarmed by this strange conduct and the absence of general officers, double-quicked and ran; and hundreds cast aside muskets, axes, and equipments, so that their flight could not be retarded. The appearance of so many full regiments at Centreville, that had been unemployed during the day, caused much excitement; and the troops that had undergone the perils of the fight were very severe in their comments upon the ability and loyalty of the commanding general. "We have been sold," was a common remark in their conversation. The last shot was fired a few minutes before sunset; and the armies no longer heard, "in tones of thunder, the diapason of the cannonade." The shells and bullets ceased to sing their songs of death in the forests of Manassas, but rushed in silence, until they struck the homes of their victims, in the peaceful villages of the north.

I was obliged to leave the ranks during the latter part of the march, on account of exhaustion produced, in the battle, by a fragment of shell which had inflicted a mere scratch. I walked in the direction of Centreville, at daybreak, on the 22d, after a sound sleep in a clump of bushes, and expected to find the army established upon the heights. In travelling on the road which led through this town and Fairfax Court House, the amount of government property that was needlessly destroyed, during the retreat, was easily ascertained. There were ten or twelve commissary and ammunition wagons in the streets of Centreville; and three had been abandoned within a mile of the last-named place, when the rebels were at least ten miles from them. Blankets, rifles, and equipments of many descriptions, were scattered in the road, and the woods that bordered upon it; and some had been thrown away by men who were near Alexandria. Crowds of women and negroes, like wreckers in a stranded ship, were taking flour and provisions from the deserted wagons; and the commissary department of the enemy obtained a small number of rations at the expense of the national treasury.

The houses upon the public way, and especially those of Centreville, were filled with the wounded who could not walk: there were no surgeons or nurses to dress and bandage their injuries; and they implored all the able-bodied persons to tell the general to send doctors and ambulances. Squads of stragglers, and slightly wounded men, with bandaged heads, arms in slings, and limping upon sticks, were walking to overtake the army, which had marched during the night. A steady rain fell during the day; and with my musket, and equipments for companions, I arrived at night at Alexandria, completely saturated. Upon the line of retreat, the natives, comprising old men and the female portion of the community, openly expressed their joy at the result of the conflict, and misled the soldiers by wilfully deceiving them about the direction of the roads; while others, and the Irish settlers near the railroad, in every way assisted the stragglers. When I passed through Centreville at half-past seven o'clock in the morning, a loyal man, without any hat upon his head, which was adorned with the white hair of age, stood at the intersection of the streets, pointed out to all that which led to Fairfax Court House, and earnestly advised them to hurry as much as possible, because the rebel cavalry could cut them off as soon as they knew that the troops had marched to Alexandria. Most of the wagons which had been purposely or shamefully abandoned were marked "U.S."; and I did not see a regimental team upon the route. There was an important distinction between the drivers: those of the first were hireling civilians, while the last were soldiers detailed for this duty from the volunteers.

Near Fairfax there was a squad of fifty men, two of whom had fastened white handkerchiefs to their bayonets to prevent the rebels from firing upon them. Other groups marched together under a commander of their choice, kept in good order, and avowed an intention to resist the cavalry, which was momentarily expected. Three men tied their muskets to the saddle of a horse which they had found, and each one rode a portion of the way. A soldier knocked down an officer who was mounting his steed,

The first shock of battle at Bull Run (THE BETTMANN ARCHIVE)

jumped upon the animal, and, in a few minutes, there was an impassable gulf between the owner and the thief. Many of the ambulances and wagons, from which the stores had been removed, instead of conveying the wounded, were crowded with officers and men who wished to secure a ride.

The reports of the fighting at Bull Run were distorted accounts of a single feature of the retreat; and the journals and people spoke of nothing except the "panic-struck troops" or a "routed army." Certain general and staff officers shrewdly and dishonorably availed themselves of this fact, and threw the cause of the defeat upon the "disorganized volunteers," to shield themselves from the share of public censure which they justly deserved. Major Barry, with remarkable assurance, testified concerning "uninstructed," "raw," and "green" troops, "panics," "indolent officers," and "infantry support broken in confusion, and scattered in all directions." The wisdom of Gen. Scott, in opposing the appointment of Gen. McDowell, was fully confirmed; and the soldiers that formed his command considered that his incompetency was the primary reason of the unfortunate defeat. The effective strength of the army was diminished by the mode in which it was manœuvred and separated. Gen. Runyon was stationed near Fairfax Court House, which was a day's march from the battle-field, with seven or ten thousand men, and performed no more service for the country than the Queen's Guard in London. Another body of eleven thousand troops, under Col. Miles, who was intoxicated, and unrelieved when the fact was reported at headquarters, was posted in the morning at Centreville, upon the left, and remained there during the day, without rendering any aid to their comrades upon the right. A few skirmishers rarely exchanged shots; and the artillery quickly dispersed a small rebel force that reconnoitred the position by firing nine or ten rounds of canister. Nearly two brigades of the division commanded by Col. Tyler were halted upon the north bank of Bull Run, and most unwillingly acted the part of spectators. It will be observed that less than three-eighths of Gen. McDowell's force (about fifteen thousand men) actively participated in the combat; and the remainder (about twenty-five thousand) did not fire a cartridge at the enemy. Of forty-nine pieces of artillery which was attached to the army, only twenty-two were planted upon the field of strife. This small number of gallant soldiers, at times basely deserted by certain brigadiers, overcame serious obstacles, gained a brilliant success, which was not followed up, and was finally repulsed by fresh troops. If the list of casualties is apportioned among those that actually fought, and it is remembered that the contending troops were unused to the disturbing events of battle, and could not aim with the deadly accuracy of veterans, their bravery is vindicated. It is an interesting fact, that, while the so-called generals of the rebel army suffered a severe loss, not one was killed upon the Union side.

Bull Run: A Confederate Soldier*

BY McHENRY HOWARD

At 2 a.m., sunday, july 21, we were aroused by the shrill whistle of the locomotive and marched down from our somewhat elevated position to take the train, but delays ensued as usual and it was daybreak before we started. The cars were filled to their utmost capacity and I rode part of the way on the platform and part on top of a car. The engine made slow time and there were frequent stops. Having had scanty fare since leaving Winchester, indeed dating from before that in our company, the blackberries on the side of the embankment were an irresistible temptation during these stops. But while the side of the road was crowded with eager pickers on one of these occasions, I heard a voice exclaiming furiously, "If I had a sword I would cut you down where you stand," and raising my eyes I beheld the crowd scattering for the cars before an officer striding up from the rear. I stood still but felt very uncomfortable as he came up close and glared at me, thinking he was going to strike me and wondering what I would do, and when he turned off I was glad to regain my position on the car top. This was Brigadier-General E. Kirby Smith, but we did not know him, seeing him thus for the first time. So we straggled from the cars no more.

As we neared Manassas Junction we distinctly heard the booming of cannon at intervals and could even see the smoke from some of the discharges a few miles to the left, but we had no idea that a general engagement was then actually going on. We arrived at the railroad junction, a few hundred yards west of the station, about 1 p.m. and immediately disembarking, threw off our knapsacks into a pile and formed in line. Colonel Elzey galloped down the front, his eyes sparkling, followed by General Kirby Smith who with the back of his hand raised to the front of his cap, exclaimed, "This is the signal, men, the watchword is 'Sumpter'"; this was to distinguish friend from foe. Enthusiastic cheers were given in response, and I now suddenly realized that we were going straight into our first battle.

We were marched north, partly across the country, towards the firing, which, cannon and musketry, became more and more distinct and as of a real battle. We took a quick step at first, but presently in our excitement broke into a double quick, with a cheer, and kept up that gait for a considerable time, the whole distance passed over being about five miles. The dust was most distressing, so thick at times that it was impossible to see more than a few feet ahead of one, and floating high above the tree tops,

* From *Recollections of a Maryland Confederate Soldier.*

so that, as is well known, the enemy were able to trace the march of our column and mark its progress—as we did theirs. Once we halted for a few minutes and, being parched with thirst, some of the men eagerly lapped the muddy water which stood in the fresh deep prints of horses' feet in the road—a little miry at that point—while others picked a few huckleberries on the right and left. As we neared the front the signs were very discouraging—would have been so to older troops and were particularly calculated to try the nerves of raw soldiers. We passed a great many wounded, and still more unwounded, going to the rear, many of whom assured us that "we were getting cut to pieces this time," "we were catching hell," "we were sure to be whipped, but to go in," etc. Sometimes a man with no greater injury than a finger hurt would be supported by a comrade or two on either side. Wagons and ambulances with wounded and dead also drove by. Twice we passed directly over regiments lying as flat as they could get to the ground, some of the men raising their heads and feebly exhorting us to "go in," to which our fellows responded with an invitation, in strong language, to come in with us themselves. Marching steadily, we presently came out into an open field, the ground rising to a low crest in front, behind (this side of) which was drawn up a small body of horse, which I understood to be the Black Horse Troop. This was a little way to our right. Here a shell exploded seventy or eighty yards to the right, our first shot from an enemy. After halting for a few minutes we again moved forward and some shots began to fall closer; I saw one shell strike in a ravine fifteen yards to the right which burst with what I thought was a tremendous explosion. Soon after the head of the column (we had been all the time marching in the usual formation of fours) passed a low thicket which had screened us in front, when there was a succession of sharp reports like a pack of fire crackers and many bullets whistled around. A shell also exploded quite close to the side of the column. I saw General Kirby Smith, who was riding a little on my right, fall from his horse and two men (John Berryman and ———) of Dorsey's company, C, which was leading, also fell to the ground not more than fifteen or twenty feet in front of me; for although, as second sergeant, the left or rear file closer of my company H, which came next, I had insensibly gotten ahead and was then with the file closers of Company C. Only these two companies had got well out into the open ground. Looking around I saw that the file closers had crossed over to the other (left) side of the column under the impression that the firing came from our own men in rear, and that the last half of our company had squatted down to the ground looking about for the hidden enemy. The first half went on, however, and I with it, feeling as if in a dream, the whole thing was so sudden, unexpected and novel. I passed directly by the two men who had been shot, Berryman raising himself on his elbow with an expression of agony, having received a terrible wound in the groin, I did not soon forget. The firing soon ceased and although the regiment was quickly ordered to form line forward on first company and the movement was executed with tolerable promptness under the circumstances, we encountered no further opposition, the enemy, a skirmish line of New York Zouaves, having hastily retreated. We therefore lay down just in rear of a slight eminence, some shells passing overhead, while Colonel

Elzey, who succeeded General Smith in command of the brigade, rode off to reconnoitre. It must have been now about three o'clock.

Colonel Elzey soon returned and moved us first to the left oblique in column across open ground and then forward in line of battle through a wood, the Maryland regiment now in the centre, and when about twenty or thirty yards from its further edge we received an unexpected volley and saw a line drawn up on high ground in the middle of the field beyond. Colonel Elzey, who happened to be immediately behind the left of our company, called out to his aide de camp, "My glass, Contee, quick, quick." His staff gathered around him and all peered anxiously through and under the foliage which partly obstructed the view. After looking through his glass for a few moments, Elzey dropped his hand, his eye lighted up—I was a few feet directly in front of him—and he hastily cried, "Stars and Stripes! Stars and Stripes! Give it to them, boys!" The words were scarcely out of his mouth, the men seeming to take the command from his eye, when a rolling volley was poured into the enemy. Once or twice we loaded and fired, or many did, and we had the satisfaction of seeing the line disappear behind the crest in confusion. I think it doubtful if we did much execution, and on our side we had only one man killed—Private Swisher of Company—although the bullets cut off twigs and leaves overhead.* The order was now given to charge bayonets (only our two right companies, Dorsey's and Murray's, had bayonets), and we pressed forward with a cheer, not in a very regular line but each one striving to be foremost. But in passing over the stubble or pasture field we discovered it bore an abundant crop of blackberries, and being famished with hunger and our throats parched with thirst, the temptation was too strong to be resisted, the men stopped with one accord and the charging line of battle resolved itself into a crowd of blackberry pickers. Officers swore or exhorted, according to their different principles, and presently succeeded in getting the line to move on. Still, whenever an unusually attractive bush was passed over, we reached down without stopping and stripped off berries, leaves and briers, which we crammed into our mouths; for days afterwards I was occupied extracting the thorns from the palms of my hands. Just before reaching the top of the ridge we were halted and Colonel Elzey ordered Lieutenant T. O. Chestney of his staff to ride forward and see if there was any enemy on the other side, a duty which he performed in a very gallant manner and to our great admiration. No enemy was to be seen and he waved us forward and we advanced some distance over the open ground until near a pine wood in front, or a little to the left oblique. At this moment an irregular fire was poured into this wood by a part of our line, it being supposed that the enemy had halted there and some asserting that from it a fire had been first opened on us. Our fire was presently stopped by the exertions of the officers, but the entire line, consisting of the 1st Maryland, 10th Virginia and 3d Tennessee, was halted while the Newtown Battery, Captain Beckham, attached to our brigade, from the extreme left shelled

* The left of our company had got crowded up, several deep, and Nick Watkins in firing shot through the cap of George Lemmon who was in his front. Taking off his damaged cap and looking at it, George turned slowly around and in his drawling tone said, reproachfully, "Nick Watkins, what did you do that for?"

the woods for some time. When this ceased we again advanced and had scarcely entered the woods when we saw abundant evidence of the place having been occupied by the enemy and of our execution, both from artillery and small arms, for I do not think it had been the scene of a conflict earlier in the day. At one spot I noticed five dead bodies (Federal) lying close together and their faces seemed to me to be already turning dark in the intense heat of the weather. Their guns, Minie muskets, were lying near, but I hesitated to appropriate one in exchange for my smooth bore. We passed other dead but came to the edge of the open ground without encountering a living enemy. The line having been a good deal disarranged in passing through the thick old field pines, we now halted to reform it. A little stream ran along the front, but, in our inexperience, many of the men would not drink it, being told there were or might be dead or wounded in it. Here a stranger was observed to take a place in our ranks who attempted to pass himself off as a stray South Carolinian, but on cross-examination he proved to be a Federal straggler and was taken into custody.

Repenting that I had not taken one of the Minie guns seen while passing through the woods, I now asked permission of Captain Murray to take advantage of the halt to run back for it. This being granted, a few steps carried me within the dense foliage which seemed to have the effect of shutting out all sound of conflict, and every other. It was literally as still as death, and a disagreeable feeling succeeded to excitement, tempting me to give up my enterprise and get back among my comrades. Besides, it struck me as not unlikely that I might fall in with some stray party of the enemy, especially as we did not know how the battle was going on our right and left. Cocking my piece, I walked cautiously on, looking about and listening. I presently stumbled against something which gave a metallic ring and looking down, perceived what I took to be a bright piece of lead pipe, bent in the shape of a siphon, and wondered how it got there. But a closer examination showed it was a gun barrel, which had probably been struck on the end by one of Beckham's shells. I had scarcely taken ten steps more when I was startled by hearing a voice calling me and discovered a man lying with his head and shoulders propped against a tree. Walking over to him, I saw that he evidently had but a short time to live, an hour or two at most, being horribly torn about the waist by a shell. He belonged to a Maine regiment, was a fine looking man of middle age, having a heavy dark beard, and belonging to a respectable class in society. I told him I was sorry to see him in such a condition—was there anything I could do? "Yes," he replied in a perfectly composed manner, "you can do one thing for me, and I wish you to do it—for God's sake, take your bayonet and run me through, kill me at once and put an end to this." I replied that I could not do that, and remembering what I had read of the sufferings of wounded men on battlefields, asked if he did not want some water. He answered, yes, but that made no matter, and reiterated his request to be put out of misery. I told him he had but a few more hours to live, and recommended him to make his preparation for death. He said he was ready to die and earnestly, but without excitement, begged me to run my bayonet through his heart. Having no canteen, I ran back to the company where I found

Thomas H. Levering with one full of water and got him to go back with me. He drank eagerly but still begged us to kill him and as we moved away his voice followed us until we were out of hearing.

Without much difficulty I found the place where I had before observed the five Minie guns and hastily selected one and a set of accoutrements which had evidently belonged to one of the dead men lying near by. While doing so I heard Levering's voice, who had gone in a slightly different direction, calling out that he had found a wounded man trying to cut his own throat. I told him to take away the knife, which, stooping down, he apparently did. We rejoined the company just as the line was about to move forward.

We continued advancing (not all the time in line of battle, I think), until we came to the Warrenton and Centreville Turnpike Road but did not overtake the enemy, now in full retreat along his whole front. We found here a lot of haversacks and other stuff and I made a good meal out of one, in spite of a comrade's earnest warning that the rations might be poisoned. It contained crackers, beef, and mixed ground coffee and sugar; from this mixture I sucked out the sugar and chewed the coffee.

About this time President Davis and Generals Johnston and Beauregard came on this part of the field and were greeted by us with enthusiastic cheers. We were presently moved back, or to the right, to the Henry house where we halted for half an hour. Here there were some captured pieces of artillery and one of them was directed on the flying column of the enemy seen pressing confusedly along the Turnpike near the stone bridge over Bull Run. This plateau witnessed the hardest share of the fighting during the day and numbers of dead and wounded men and horses gave evidence of the stubbornness of the contest for it. Under one tree, in particular, had been collected many wounded, belonging to Rickett's (?) Battery (Federal) and other organizations, with whom we talked freely, our ranks having been broken (dismissed) for awhile. (Visiting the battlefield later in the summer, a long trench marked the spot where these men had been lying and, no doubt, containing many of their bodies.)

Our ranks were presently re-formed and I think we now marched forward and across the stone bridge, or perhaps only the bridge over Young's Branch of Bull Run; it may have been that we made this movement before going to the Henry house, but I am almost sure it was at this time. After going some hundred yards beyond it, however, we turned about and struck off towards the railroad—not, however, by the route we had come. I think it was near sunset when we had made the halt at the Henry house and now night had come and found us trudging wearily on, although the men were terribly exhausted from fatigue and want of sleep. At length, when the night was half over, we went into bivouac in an open field, somewhere between Manassas and Bull Run and we sank down exhausted around blazing piles of fence rails.

THE NAVY AT WAR

NEITHER SIDE WAS PREPARED for naval war. In 1861, the U.S. fleet consisted of 90 vessels, more than half of which were wooden sailing ships.

Lincoln's decision to blockade the southern coast caught the Navy totally unprepared. The President and Secretary Welles foresaw "a cordon of fast and efficient steamers . . . stretched from end to end, without so much as a gap in the whole four thousand miles of coast. The reduction or even the passage of fortifications required powerful and well-equipped fleets engaged solely in these enterprises. The vast network of interior waterways in which the Army's base and communications must be protected, could only be occupied successfully by another and equally numerous fleet. Finally, the protection of commerce demanded from the very nature of things, far more vessels than its destruction."*

Secretary Welles was slow to begin a building program to obtain the new vessels. As for contracting for the new ironclads, the Navy and the Congress argued the issue back and forth until late in the summer of 1861, when a board of officers was appointed to study the situation. Three designs were agreed upon from which to begin; of the three by far the most successful was that for the *Monitor*.

"The main features of the *Monitor* were the revolving turret, the low freeboard, and the projecting overhang. By means of these devices the ship was made to present a very small target, and her engines, battery, screw, rudder, and anchor, as well as her crew, were thoroughly protected, and neither rams nor guns could make much impression on her. On the other hand, the low freeboard had also one distinctive disadvantage, in that it reduced the vessel's reserve of flotation, thus making it possible for a small influx of water to sink her. The idea of mounting guns in a revolving circular turret had been suggested before at various times, but had never been carried to the point of useful application. . . .

"The contract for the *Monitor* was finally signed on the 4th of October. The extraordinary energy of the contractors when they had once undertaken the work pushed it to completion with unexampled speed. But the time which had been of the greatest value, namely, the six months from

* From J. R. Soley, "The Union and Confederate Navies," *Battles and Leaders*, I, 615.

March to September, had been lost, and thus it happened that the new ironclad was not finished in season to prevent the raid of the *Merrimac* in Hampton Roads, and the obliteration of the *Congress* and the *Cumberland*.

"It must be remembered that the Navy Department had possessed from the beginning five frigates, sister ships of the *Merrimac*, any one of which could have been armored more efficiently than she was, in half the time and with half the money, and without waiting for Congressional action. Evidently the department little imagined, while it was dallying for six months with the question of ironclads, that the first twenty-four hours of the *Monitor*'s career would be so big with fate.*

"The South entered upon the war without any naval preparation, and with very limited resources by which its deficiencies could be promptly supplied. Indeed, it would hardly be possible to imagine a great maritime country more destitute of the means for carrying on a naval war than the Confederate States in 1861. No naval vessels, properly speaking, came into their possession, except the *Fulton*, an old side-wheeler built in 1837, and at this time laid up at Pensacola, and the sunken and half-destroyed hulks at Norfolk, of which only one, the *Merrimac*, could be made available for service."†

Aboard the Merrimac‡

BY COLONEL J. T. WOOD

IN THE SPRING OF 1861 Norfolk and its large naval establishment had been hurriedly abandoned by the Federals, why no one could tell. It is about twelve miles from Fort Monroe, which was then held by a large force of regulars. A few companies of these, with a single frigate, could have occupied and commanded the town and navy yard and kept the channel open. However, a year later, it was as quickly evacuated by the Confederates, and almost with as little reason.

The yard was abandoned to a few volunteers, after it was partly destroyed, and a large number of ships were burnt. Among the spoils were upward of twelve hundred heavy guns, which were scattered among Confederate fortifications from the Potomac to the Mississippi. Among the ships burnt and sunk was the frigate *Merrimac* of 3500 tons and 40 guns, afterward rechristened the *Virginia*, and so I will call her. During the

---

* Nearly sixty ironclads, all of which were of the *Monitor* type except three, were built during the war.

† Soley, *op. cit., pp.* 618, 619, 624.

‡ From "The First Fight of Iron-Clads," *Battles and Leaders*, Vol. I.

summer of 1861 Lieutenant John M. Brooke, an accomplished officer of the old navy, who with many others had resigned, proposed to raise and rebuild this ship as an iron-clad. His plans were approved, and orders were given to carry them out. She was raised and cut down to the old berth-deck. Both ends for seventy feet were covered over, and when the ship was in fighting trim were just awash.

The South was almost without a maritime population. In the old service the majority of officers were from the South, and all the seamen from the North.

Every one had flocked to the army, and to it we had to look for a crew. I visited every camp (at Yorktown) and the commanding officers were ordered to parade their men, and I explained to them what I wanted. About 200 volunteered, and of this number I selected 80 who had had some experience as seamen or gunners. Other commands at Richmond and Petersburg were visited, and so our crew of three hundred was made up. They proved themselves to be as gallant and trusty a body of men as any one would wish to command, not only in battle, but in reverse and retreat.

Notwithstanding every exertion to hasten the fitting out of the ship, the work during the winter progressed but slowly, owing to delay in sending the iron sheathing from Richmond. At this time the only establishment in the South capable of rolling iron plates was the Tredegar foundry. Its resources were limited, and the demand for all kinds of war material most pressing. And when we reflect upon the scarcity and inexperience of the workmen, and the great changes necessary in transforming an ordinary iron workshop into an arsenal in which all the machinery and tools had to be improvised, it is astonishing that so much was accomplished. The unfinished state of the vessel interfered so with the drills and exercises that we had but little opportunity of getting things into shape. It should be remembered that the ship was an experiment in naval architecture, differing in every respect from any then afloat. The officers and the crew were strangers to the ship and to each other. Up to the hour of sailing she was crowded with workmen. Not a gun had been fired, hardly a revolution of the engines had been made, when we cast off from the dock and started on what many thought was an ordinary trial trip, but which proved to be a trial such as no vessel that ever floated had undergone up to that time. From the start we saw that she was slow, not over five knots; she steered so badly that, with her great length, it took from thirty to forty minutes to turn. She drew twenty-two feet, which confined us to a comparatively narrow channel in the Roads; and, as I have before said, the engines were our weak point. She was as unmanageable as a water-logged vessel.

It was at noon on the 8th of March that we steamed down the Elizabeth River. Passing by our batteries, lined with troops, who cheered us as we passed, and through the obstructions as Craney Island, we took the south channel and headed for Newport News. At anchor at this time off Fort Monroe were the frigates *Minnesota, Roanoke,* and *St. Lawrence,* and several gun-boats. The first two were sister ships of the *Virginia* before the war; the last was a sailing frigate of fifty guns. Off Newport News, seven miles above, which was strongly fortified and held by a large Federal garrison, were anchored the frigate *Congress,* 50 guns, and the sloop *Cumberland,* 30. The day was calm, and the last two ships were swinging lazily by their anchors. [The tide was at its height about 1:40 P.M.] Boats were hanging to the lower booms, washed clothes in the rigging. Nothing indicated that we were expected; but when we came within three-quarters of a mile, the boats were dropped astern, booms got alongside, and the *Cumberland* opened with her heavy pivots, followed by the *Congress,* the gun-boats, and the shore batteries.

We reserved our fire until within easy range, when the forward pivot was pointed and fired by Lieutenant Charles Simms, killing and wounding most of the crew of the after pivot-gun of the *Cumberland.* Passing close to the *Congress,* which received our starboard broadside, and returned it with spirit, we steered direct for the *Cumberland,* striking her almost at right angles, under the fore-rigging on the starboard side. The blow was hardly perceptible on board the *Virginia.* Backing clear of her, we went ahead again, heading up the river, helm hard-a-starboard, and turned slowly. As we did so, for the first time I had an opportunity of using the after-pivot, of which I had charge. As we swung, the *Congress* came in range, nearly stern on, and we got in three raking shells. She had slipped her anchor, loosed her foretop-sail, run up the jib, and tried to escape, but grounded. Turning, we headed for her and took a position within two hundred yards, where every shot told. In the meantime the *Cumberland* continued the fight, though our ram had opened her side wide enough to drive in a horse and cart. Soon she listed to port and filled rapidly. The crew were driven by the advancing water to the spardeck, and there worked her pivot-guns until she went down with a roar, the colors still flying. No ship was ever fought more gallantly. The *Congress* continued the unequal contest for more than an hour after the sinking of the *Cumberland.* Her losses were terrible, and finally she ran up the white flag.

As soon as we had hove in sight, coming down the harbor, the *Roanoke, St. Lawrence,* and *Minnesota,* assisted by tugs, had got under way, and started up from Old Point Comfort to join their consorts. They were under fire from the batteries at Sewell's Point, but the distance was too great to effect much. The first two, however, ran aground not far above Fort Monroe, and took but little part in the fight. The *Minnesota,* taking the middle or swash channel, steamed up half-way between Old Point Comfort and Newport News, when she grounded, but in a position to be actively engaged.

Previous to this we had been joined by the James River squadron, which had been at anchor a few miles above, and came into action most gallantly, passing the shore batteries at Newport News under a heavy fire, and with some loss. It consisted of the *Yorktown* (or *Patrick Henry*), 12 guns, Captain John R. Tucker; *Jamestown,* 2 guns, Lieut.-Commander J. N. Barney; and *Teaser,* 1 gun, Lieut-Commander W. A. Webb.

As soon as the *Congress* surrendered, Commander Buchanan ordered the gun-boats *Beaufort,* Lieut-Commander W. H. Parker, and *Raleigh,* Lieut.-Commander J. W. Alexander, to steam alongside, take off her crew, and set fire to the ship. Lieutenant Pendergrast, who had succeeded Lieutenant Smith, who had been killed, surrendered to Lieutenant Parker, of the *Beaufort*. Delivering his sword and colors, he was directed by Lieutenant Parker to return to his ship and have the wounded transferred as rapidly as possible. All this time the shore batteries and small-arm men were keeping up an incessant fire on our vessels. Two of the officers of the *Raleigh*, Lieutenant Tayloe and Midshipman Hutter, were killed while assisting the Union wounded out of the *Congress*. A number of the enemy's men were killed by the same fire. Finally it became so hot that the gun-boats were obliged to haul off with only thirty prisoners, leaving Lieutenant Pendergrast and most of his crew on board, and they all afterward escaped to the shore by swimming or in small boats. While this was going on, the white flag was flying at her mainmasthead. Not being able to take possession of his prize, the commodore ordered hot shot to be used, and in a short time she was in flames fore and aft. While directing this, both himself and his flag-lieutenant, Minor, were severely wounded. The command then devolved upon Lieutenant Catesby Jones.

It was now five o'clock. The *Minnesota* was aground and at our mercy. But the pilots would not attempt the middle channel with the ebb tide and approaching night. So we returned by the south channel to Sewell's Point and anchored, the *Minnesota* escaping, as we thought, only until morning.

Our loss in killed and wounded was twenty-one. The armor was hardly damaged, though at one time our ship was the focus on which were directed at least one hundred heavy guns, afloat and ashore. But nothing outside escaped. Two guns were disabled by having their muzzles shot off. The ram was left in the side of the *Cumberland*. One anchor, the smoke-stack, and the steam-pipes were shot away. Railings, stanchions, boat-davits, everything was swept clean. The flag-staff was repeatedly knocked over, and finally a boarding-pike was used. Commodore Buchanan and the other wounded were sent to the Naval Hospital, and after making preparations for the next day's fight, we slept at our guns, dreaming of other victories in the morning.

But at daybreak we discovered, lying between us and the *Minnesota*, a strange-looking craft, which we knew at once to be Ericsson's *Monitor*, which had long been expected in Hampton Roads, and of which, from different sources, we had a good idea. She could not possibly have made her appearance at a more inopportune time for us, changing our plans, which were to destroy the *Minnesota*, and then the remainder of the fleet below Fort Monroe. She appeared but a pigmy compared with the lofty frigate which she guarded. But in her size was one great element of her success.

After an early breakfast, we got under way and steamed out toward the enemy, opening fire from our bow pivot, and closing in to deliver our starboard broadside at short range, which was returned promptly from her 11-inch guns. Both vessels then turned and passed again still closer. The *Monitor* was firing every seven or eight minutes, and nearly every shot struck. Our ship was working worse and worse, and after the loss of the smoke-stack, Mr. Ramsey, chief engineer, reported that the draught was so poor that it was with great difficulty he could keep up steam. Once or twice the ship was on the bottom. Drawing 22 feet of water, we were confined to a narrow channel, while the *Monitor*, with only 12 feet immersion, could take any position, and always have us in range of her guns. Orders were given to concentrate our fire on the pilot-house, and with good result, as we afterward learned. More than two hours had passed, and we had made no impression on the enemy so far as we could discover, while our wounds were slight. Several times the *Monitor* ceased firing, and we were in hopes she was disabled, but the revolution again of her turret and the heavy blows of her 11-inch shot on our sides soon undeceived us.

Coming down from the spar-deck, and observing a division standing "at ease," Lieutenant Jones inquired:

"Why are you not firing, Mr. Eggleston?"

"Why, our powder is very precious," replied the lieutenant; "and after two hours' incessant firing I find that I can do her about as much damage by snapping my thumb at her every two minutes and a half."

Lieutenant Jones now determined to run her down or board her. For nearly an hour we manoeuvred for a position. Now "Go ahead!" now "Stop!" now "Astern!" The ship was as unwieldy as Noah's ark. At last an opportunity offered. "Go ahead, full speed!" But before the ship gathered headway, the *Monitor* turned, and our disabled ram only gave a glancing blow, effecting nothing. Again she came up on our quarter, her bow against our side, and at this distance fired twice. Both shots struck about half-way up the shield, abreast of the after pivot, and the impact forced the side in bodily two or three inches. All the crews of the after guns were knocked over by the concussion, and bled from the nose or ears. Another shot at the same place would have penetrated. While alongside, boarders were called away; but she dropped astern before they could get on board. And so, for six or more hours, the struggle was kept up. At length, the *Monitor* withdrew over the middle ground where we could not follow, but always maintaining a position to protect the *Minnesota*. To have run our ship ashore on a falling tide would have been ruin. We awaited her return for an hour; and at two o'clock P.M. steamed to Sewell's Point, and thence to the dockyard at Norfolk, our crew thoroughly worn out from the two days' fight. Although there is no doubt that the *Monitor* first retired—for Captain Van Brunt, commanding the *Minnesota,* so states in his official report—the battle was a drawn one, so far as the two vessels engaged were concerned. But in its general results the advantage was with the *Monitor*. Our casualties in the second day's fight were only a few wounded.

In the Monitor *Turret**

BY COMMANDER S. DANA GREENE

So hurried was the preparation of the *Monitor* that the mechanics worked upon her day and night up to the hour of her departure, and little opportunity was offered to drill the crew at the guns, to work the turret, and to become familiar with the other unusual features of the vessel. The crew was, in fact, composed of volunteers. Lieutenant Worden, having been authorized by the Navy Department to select his men from any ship-of-war in New York harbor, addressed the crews of the *North Carolina* and *Sabine,* stating fully to them the probable dangers of the passage to Hampton Roads and the certainty of having important service to perform after arriving. The sailors responded enthusiastically, many more volunteering than were required. Of the crew Captain Worden said, in his official report of the battle, "A better one no naval commander ever had the honor to command."

We left New York in tow of the tug-boat *Seth Low* at 11 A.M. of Thursday, the 6th of March. On the following day a moderate breeze was encountered, and it was at once evident that the *Monitor* was unfit as a sea-going craft. Nothing but the subsidence of the wind prevented her from being shipwrecked before she reached Hampton Roads. The berth-deck hatch leaked in spite of all we could do, and the water came down under the turret like a waterfall. It would strike the pilot-house and go over the turret in beautiful curves, and it came through the narrow eye-holes in the pilot-house with such force as to knock the helmsman completely round from the wheel. The waves also broke over the blower-pipes, and the water came down through them in such quantities that the belts of the blower-engines slipped, and the engines consequently stopped for lack of artificial draught, without which, in such a confined place, the fires could not get air for combustion. Newton and Stimers, followed by the engineer's force, gallantly rushed into the engine-room and fire-room to remedy the evil, but they were unable to check the inflowing water, and were nearly suffocated with escaping gas. They were dragged out more dead than alive, and carried to the top of the turret, where the fresh air gradually revived them. The water continued to pour through the hawse-hole, and over and down the smoke-stacks and blower-pipes, in such quantities that there was imminent danger that the ship would founder. The steam-pumps could not be operated because the fires had been nearly extinguished, and the engine-room was uninhabitable on account of the suffocating gas with which it was filled. The hand-pumps were then

* From *Battles and Leaders,* Vol. I.

rigged and worked, but they had not enough force to throw the water out through the top of the turret—the only opening—and it was useless to bail, as we had to pass the buckets up through the turret, which made it a very long operation. Fortunately, toward evening the wind and the sea subsided, and, being again in smooth water, the engine was put in operation. But at midnight, in passing over a shoal, rough water was again encountered, and our troubles were renewed, complicated this time with the jamming of the wheel-ropes, so that the safety of the ship depended entirely on the strength of the hawser which connected her with the tug-boat. The hawser, being new, held fast; but during the greater part of the night we were constantly engaged in fighting the leaks, until we reached smooth water again, just before daylight.

It was at the close of this dispiriting trial trip, in which all hands had been exhausted in their efforts to keep the novel craft afloat, that the *Monitor* passed Cape Henry at 4 P.M. on Saturday, March 8th. At this point was heard the distant booming of heavy guns, which our captain rightly judged to be an engagement with the *Merrimac,* twenty miles away. He at once ordered the vessel stripped of her sea-rig, the turret keyed up, and every preparation made for battle. As we approached Hampton Roads we could see the fine old *Congress* burning brightly, and soon a pilot came on board and told of the arrival of the *Merrimac,* the disaster to the *Cumberland* and the *Congress,* and the dismay of the Union forces. The *Monitor* was pushed with all haste, and reached the *Roanoke* (Captain Marston), anchored in the Roads, at 9 P.M. Worden immediately reported his arrival to Captain Marston, who suggested that he should go to the assistance of the *Minnesota,* then aground off Newport News. As no pilot was available, Captain Worden accepted the volunteer services of Acting Master Samuel Howard, who earnestly sought the duty. An atmosphere of gloom pervaded the fleet, and the pygmy aspect of the new-comer did not inspire confidence among those who had witnessed the destruction of the day before. Skillfully piloted by Howard, we proceeded on our way, our path illumined by the blaze of the *Congress.* Reaching the *Minnesota,* hard and fast aground, near midnight, we anchored, and Worden reported to Captain Van Brunt. Between 1 and 2 A.M. the *Congress* blew up—not instantaneously, but successively. Her powder-tanks seemed to explode, each shower of sparks rivaling the other in its height, until they appeared to reach the zenith—a grand but mournful sight. Near us, too, at the bottom of the river, lay the *Cumberland,* with her silent crew of brave men, who died while fighting their guns to the water's edge, and whose colors were still flying at the peak.

The dreary night dragged slowly on; the officers and crew were up and alert, to be ready for any emergency. At daylight on Sunday the *Merrimac* and her consorts were discovered at anchor near Sewell's Point. At about half-past seven o'clock the enemy's vessels got under way and steered in the direction of the *Minnesota.* At the same time the *Monitor* got under way, and her officers and crew took their stations for battle. Captain Van Brunt, of the *Minnesota,* officially reports, "I made signal to the *Monitor* to attack the enemy," but the signal was not seen by us; other work was in hand, and Commander Worden required no signal.

The pilot-house of the *Monitor* was situated well forward, near the

Monitor *and* Merrimac *clash at close range* (THE BETTMANN ARCHIVE)

bow; it was a wrought-iron structure, built of logs of iron nine inches thick, bolted through the corners, and covered with an iron plate two inches thick, which was not fastened down, but was kept in place merely by its weight. The sight-holes or slits were made by inserting quarter-inch plates at the corners between the upper set of logs and the next below. The structure projected four feet above the deck, and was barely large enough inside to hold three men standing. It presented a flat surface on all sides and on top. The steering-wheel was secured to one of the logs on the front side. The position and shape of this structure should be carefully borne in mind.

Worden took his station in the pilot-house, and by his side were Howard, the pilot, and Peter Williams, quartermaster, who steered the vessel throughout the engagement. My place was in the turret, to work and fight the guns; with me were Stodder and Stimers and sixteen brawny men, eight to each gun.

The physical condition of the officers and men of the two ships at this time was in striking contrast. The *Merrimac* had passed the night quietly near Sewell's Point, her people enjoying rest and sleep, elated by thoughts of the victory they had achieved that day, and cheered by the prospects of another easy victory on the morrow. The *Monitor* had barely escaped shipwreck twice within the last thirty-six hours, and since Friday morning, forty-eight hours before, few if any of those on board had closed their eyes in sleep or had anything to eat but hard bread, as cooking was impossible. She was surrounded by wrecks and disaster, and her efficiency in action had yet to be proved.

Worden lost no time in bringing it to test. Getting his ship under way, he steered direct for the enemy's vessels, in order to meet and engage them as far as possible from the *Minnesota*. As he approached, the wooden vessels quickly turned and left. Our captain, to the "astonishment" of Captain Van Brunt (as he states in his official report), made straight for the *Merrimac,* which had already commenced firing; and when he came within short range, he changed his course so as to come alongside of her, stopped the engine, and gave the order, "Commence firing!" I triced up the port, ran out the gun, and, taking deliberate aim, pulled the lock-string. The *Merrimac* was quick to reply, returning a rattling broadside (for she had ten guns to our two), and the battle fairly began. The turrets and other parts of the ship were heavily struck, but the shots did not penetrate; the tower was intact, and it continued to revolve. A look of confidence passed over the men's faces, and we believed the *Merrimac* would not repeat the work she had accomplished the day before.

The fight continued with the exchange of broadsides as fast as the guns could be served and at very short range, the distance between the vessels frequently being not more than a few yards. Worden skillfully ma-noeuvred his quick-turning vessel, trying to find some vulnerable point in his adversary. Once he made a dash at her stern, hoping to disable her screw, which he thinks he missed by not more than two feet. Our shots ripped the iron of the *Merrimac,* while the reverberation of her shots against the tower caused anything but a pleasant sensation. While Stodder, who was stationed at the machine which controlled the revolving motion of the turret, was incautiously leaning against the side of the tower, a

large shot struck in the vicinity and disabled him. He left the turret and
went below, and Stimers, who had assisted him, continued to do the
work.

The drawbacks to the position of the pilot-house were soon realized. We
could not fire ahead nor within several points of the bow, since the blast
from our own guns would have injured the people in the pilot-house, only
a few yards off. Keeler and Toffey passed the captain's orders and messages to me, and my inquiries and answers to him, the speaking-tube
from the pilot-house to the turret having been broken early in the action.
They performed their work with zeal and alacrity, but, both being lands-
men, our technical communications sometimes miscarried. The situation
was novel: a vessel of war was engaged in desperate combat with a powerful foe; the captain, commanding and guiding, was inclosed in one place,
and the executive officer, working and fighting the guns, was shut up in
another, and communication between them was difficult and uncertain.
It was this experience which caused Isaac Newton, immediately after the
engagement, to suggest the clever plan of putting the pilot-house on top
of the turret and making it cylindrical instead of square; and his suggestions were subsequently adopted in this type of vessel.

As the engagement continued, the working of the turret was not altogether satisfactory. It was difficult to start it revolving, or, when once
started, to stop it, on account of the imperfections of the novel machinery,
which was now undergoing is first trial. Stimers was an active muscular
man, and did his utmost to control the motion of the turret; but, in spite
of his efforts, it was difficult, if not impossible, to secure accurate firing.
The conditions were very different from those of an ordinary broadside
gun, under which we had been trained on wooden ships. My only view
of the world outside of the tower was over the muzzles of the guns, which
cleared the ports by only a few inches. When the guns were run in, the
portholes were covered by heavy iron pendulums, pierced with small
holes to allow the iron rammer and sponge handles to protrude while they
were in use. To hoist these pendulums required the entire gun's crew
and vastly increased the work inside the turret.

The effect upon one shut up in a revolving drum is perplexing, and it
is not a simple matter to keep the bearings. White marks had been placed
upon the stationary deck immediately below the turret to indicate the
direction of the starboard and port sides, and the bow and stern; but these
marks were obliterated early in the action. I would continually ask the
captain, "How does the *Merrimac* bear?" He replied, "On the starboard-
beam," or "On the port-quarter," as the case might be. Then the difficulty
was to determine the direction of the starboard-beam, or port-quarter, or
any other bearing. It finally resulted, that when a gun was ready for
firing. the turret would be started on its revolving journey in search of the
target, and when found it was taken "on the fly," because the turret could
not be accurately controlled. Once the *Merrimac* tried to ram us; but
Worden avoided the direct impact by the skillful use of the helm, and
she struck a glancing blow, which did no damage. At the instant of collision I planted a solid 180-pound shot fair and square upon the forward
part of her casemate. Had the gun been loaded with thirty pounds of
powder, which was the charge subsequently used with similar guns, it is

probable that this shot would have penetrated her armor; but the charge being limited to fifteen pounds, in accordance with peremptory orders to that effect from the Navy Department, the shot rebounded without doing any more damage than possibly to start some of the beams of her armor-backing.

The battle continued at close quarters without apparent damage to either side. After a time, the supply of shot in the turret being exhausted, Worden hauled off for about fifteen minutes to replenish. The serving of the cartridges, weighing but fifteen pounds, was a matter of no difficulty; but the hoisting of the heavy shot was a slow and tedious operation, it being necessary that the turret should remain stationary, in order that the two scuttles, one in the deck and the other in the floor of the turret, should be in line. Worden took advantage of the lull, and passed through the port-hole upon the deck outside to get a better view of the situation. He soon renewed the attack, and the contest continued as before.

Two important points were constantly kept in mind: first, to prevent the enemy's projectiles from entering the turret through the port-holes—for the explosion of a shell inside, by disabling the men at the guns, would have ended the fight, as there was no relief gun's crew on board; second, not to fire into our own pilot-house. A careless or impatient hand, during the confusion arising from the whirligig motion of the tower, might let slip one of our big shot against the pilot-house. For this and other reasons I fired every gun while I remained in the turret.

Soon after noon a shell from the enemy's gun, the muzzle not ten yards distant, struck the forward side of the pilot-house directly in the sight-hole, or slit, and exploded, cracking the second iron log and partly lifting the top, leaving an opening. Worden was standing immediately behind this spot, and received in his face the force of the blow, which partly stunned him, and, filling his eyes with powder, utterly blinded him. The injury was known only to those in the pilot-house and its immediate vicinity. The flood of light rushing through the top of the pilot-house, now partly open, caused Worden, blind as he was, to believe that the pilot-house was seriously injured, if not destroyed; he therefore gave orders to put the helm to starboard and "sheer off." Thus the *Monitor* retired temporarily from the action, in order to ascertain the extent of the injuries she had received. At the same time Worden sent for me, and leaving Stimers the only officer in the turret, I went forward at once, and found him standing at the foot of the ladder leading to the pilot-house.

He was a ghastly sight, with his eyes closed and the blood apparently rushing from every pore in the upper part of his face. He told me that he was seriously wounded, and directed me to take command. I assisted in leading him to a sofa in his cabin, where he was tenderly cared for by Doctor Logue, and then I assumed command. Blind and suffering as he was, Worden's fortitude never forsook him; he frequently asked from his bed of pain of the progress of affairs, and when told that the *Minnesota* was saved, he said, "Then I can die happy."

When I reached my station in the pilot-house, I found that the iron log was fractured and the top partly open; but the steering gear was still intact, and the pilot-house was not totally destroyed, as had been feared. In the confusion of the moment resulting from so serious an injury to the commanding officer, the *Monitor* had been moving without direction. Exactly how much time elapsed from the moment that Worden was wounded until I had reached the pilot-house and completed the examination of the injury at that point, and determined what course to pursue in the damaged condition of the vessel, it is impossible to state; but it could hardly have exceeded twenty minutes at the utmost. During this time the *Merrimac,* which was leaking badly, had started in the direction of the Elizabeth River; and, on taking my station in the pilot-house and turning the vessel's head in the direction of the *Merrimac,* I saw that she was already in retreat. A few shots were fired at the retiring vessel, and she continued on to Norfolk. I returned with the *Monitor* to the side of the *Minnesota,* where preparations were being made to abandon the ship, which was still aground.

LINCOLN AND McCLELLAN

AFTER THE BATTLE OF BULL RUN, both North and South forsook the illusion of quick, decisive victory. Preparations for a major war were set in motion.

President Lincoln brought Major General George McClellan from West Virginia to command the Federal troops shielding Washington. McClellan was an excellent organizer. He welded the Union soldiers into proud, finely disciplined units, fired their commanders with ambition, and strengthened the capital's defenses as well. Much pleased, Lincoln asked McClellan to begin a campaign against the Confederates who were entrenched at Manassas Junction. Lincoln wanted action before winter weather made troop movements difficult, but week after week went by and McClellan did not move. In late December the general contracted typhoid fever. He did not take up his duties again until January 13.

Exasperated by the delay, Lincoln issued a general order that all armies would move forward on February 22, in honor of Washington's birthday. Now McClellan offered a new plan of attack. He would send the newly named Army of the Potomac to the mouth of the Rappahannock River (which empties into the Chesapeake Bay about fifty miles east of Richmond), and strike up the peninsula at Richmond. If frontal attacks on the city's defenses failed, cross the James River to the south and attack Richmond from the rear. After thorough discussion, President Lincoln approved the expedition. He ordered McClellan to have his troops embarked by March 18.

The Confederate general, Joseph E. Johnston, had anticipated McClellan's move. In early March he withdrew from Manassas and took up positions around Culpeper Courthouse south of the Rappahannock River. There he waited for the Yankees.

Up the Peninsula with McClellan*

BY PRIVATE WARREN L. GOSS

IN THE EARLY SPRING OF 1862, when the Army of the Potomac was getting ready to move from Washington, the constant drill and discipline, the brightening of arms and polishing of buttons, and the exasperating fussiness on the part of company and regimental officers during inspections, conveyed to us a hint, as one of our comrades expressed it, that "some one higher in command was punching them to punch us." There was unusual activity upon the Potomac in front of our camp. Numerous steamtugs were pulling huge sailing vessels here and there, and large transports, loaded with soldiers, horses, bales of hay, and munitions for an army, swept majestically down the broad river. Every description of water conveyance, from a canal-boat to a huge three-decked steamboat, seemed to have been pressed into the service of the army.

We formed in two ranks and marched on board a little steamer lying at the wharf near our quarters. "Anything for a change," said Wad Rider, really delighted to move. All heavy baggage was left behind. I had clung to the contents of my knapsack with dogged tenacity; but, notwithstanding my most earnest protest, I was required to disgorge about one-half of them, including a pair of heavy boots and my choice brick from the Harper's Ferry engine-house. To my mind I was now entirely destitute of comforts.

The general opinion among us was that at last we were on our way to make an end of the Confederacy. We gathered in little knots on the deck, here and there a party playing "penny ante"; others slept or dozed, but the majority smoked and discussed the probabilities of our destination, about which we really knew as little as the babes in the wood. That we were sailing down the Potomac was apparent.

The next day we arrived at Old Point Comfort, and looked with open-eyed wonder at Fortress Monroe, huge and frowning. Negroes were plentier than blackberries, and went about their work with an air of importance born of their new-found freedom. These were the "contrabands" for whom General Butler had recently invented that sobriquet. We pitched our tents amid the charred and blackened ruins of what had been the beautiful and aristocratic village of Hampton. The first thing I noticed about the ruins, unaccustomed as I was to Southern architecture, was the absence of cellars. The only building left standing of all the village was the massive old Episcopal church. Here Washington had worshipped, and its broad aisles had echoed to the footsteps of armed

---

* Condensed from Warren L. Goss, *Recollections of a Private.*

men during the Revolution. In the church-yard the tombs had been
broken open. Many tombstones were broken and overthrown, and at the
corner of the church a big hole showed that some one with a greater
desire for possessing curiosities than reverence for ancient landmarks
had been digging for the corner-stone and its buried mementos.

Along the shore which looks towards Fortress Monroe were landed
artillery, baggage-wagons, pontoon trains and boats, and the level land
back of this was crowded with the tents of the soldiers. Here and there
were groups frying hard-tack and bacon. Near at hand was the irre-
pressible army mule, hitched to and eating out of pontoon boats; those
who had eaten their ration of grain and hay were trying their teeth, with
promise of success, in eating the boats. An army mule was hungrier than
a soldier, and would eat anything, especially a pontoon boat or rubber
blanket. The scene was a busy one. The red cap, white leggings, and baggy
trousers of the Zouaves mingled with the blue uniforms and dark
trimmings of the regular infantrymen, the short jackets and yellow
trimmings of the cavalry, the red stripes of the artillery, and the dark blue
with orange trimmings of the engineers; together with the ragged, many-
colored costumes of the black laborers and teamsters, all busy at something.

One morning we broke camp and went marching up the Peninsula.

During our second day's march it rained, and the muddy roads, cut up
and kneaded, as it were, by the teams preceding us, left them in a state of
semi-liquid filth hardly possible to describe or imagine. When we arrived
at Big Bethel the rain was coming down in sheets.

After leaving Big Bethel we began to feel the weight of our knapsacks.
Castaway overcoats, blankets, parade-coats, and shoes were scattered along
the route in reckless profusion, being dropped by the overloaded soldiers,
as if after ploughing the roads with heavy teams they were sowing them
for a harvest.

To each baggage-wagon were attached four or six mules, driven usually
by a colored man, with only one rein, or line, and that line attached to
the bit of the near leading mule, while the driver rode in a saddle upon the
near wheel mule. Each train was accompanied by a guard, and while the
guard urged the drivers the drivers urged the mules. The drivers were
usually expert and understood well the wayward, sportive natures of the
creatures over whose destinies they presided. On our way to Yorktown
our pontoon and baggage-trains were sometimes blocked for miles, and
the heaviest trains were often unloaded by the guard to facilitate their
removal from the mud. Those wagons which were loaded with whiskey
were most lovingly guarded, and when unloaded the barrels were often
lightened before they were returned to the wagons.

When procuring luxuries of eggs or milk we paid the people at first
in silver, and they gave us local scrip in change; but we found on attempting to pay it out again that they were rather reluctant to receive it,
even at that early stage in Confederate finance, and much preferred
Yankee silver or notes.

On the afternoon of April 5, 1862, the advance of our column was
brought to a standstill, with the right in front of Yorktown and the left
by the enemy's works at Lee's mills. We pitched our camp on Wormly
Creek, near the Moore house on the York River, in sight of the enemy's

water battery and their defensive works at Gloucester Point. The day after our arrival I was detailed to go to Shipping Point, some eight miles distant, on the York River, and we made the march, with pack mules, over the very worst mud roads I had ever seen in all my experience. A depot of supplies had been established here, and speedily the roads leading to this place were corduroyed and thus rendered decently passable. We found the place had been strongly fortified by the Confederates, and contained about two hundred log huts built for their accommodation. They were, however, rendered useless to them by being flanked or cut off by our advance. In one of the huts, evidently belonging to one of their officers, I picked up a paper, which proved to contain a detail of negro servants from different plantations to work upon the fortifications, which showed that the Confederates were even then using their slaves for military purposes, thus leaving their soldiers fresh for other military duties. The camp and fortifications were almost on a level with the water of the river, very muddy and dirty, and we were not sorry to be recalled to our camp at Yorktown.

One of the impediments to an immediate attack on Yorktown was the difficulty of using light artillery in the muddy fields in our front, and at that time the topography of the country ahead was but little understood, and had to be learned by reconnaissance in force. We had settled down to the siege of Yorktown; began bridging the streams between us and the enemy, constructing and improving the roads for the rapid transit of supplies, and for the advance.

A comrade in Hooker's division gave me an account of his experiences about as follows: "Marching over the muddy road late in the afternoon, we found our farther advance prevented by a force which had preceded us, and we halted in the mud by the roadside just as it began to rain. About five o'clock we resumed our march by crossing over to the Hampton road, and did not halt till eleven in the evening, when we lay down in our blankets, bedraggled, wet, and tired, chewing hard-tack and the cud of reflection, the tenor of which was, 'Why did we come for a soldier?' Before daylight we were on the march, plodding in the rain through the mire. By daybreak we came out on the edge of the dense woods in front of Fort Magruder and its cordon of redoubts stretching across the Peninsula, which is here narrowed by the head-waters of two streams which empty into the York on the one hand and the James River on the other. Here we had an opportunity of viewing the situation while waiting for orders to attack. The main fort, called Magruder, was a strong earthwork with a bastioned front and a wide ditch. In front of this muddy-looking heap of dirt was a level plain, sprinkled plentifully with smaller earthworks; while between us and the level plain the dense forest, for a distance of a quarter of a mile, had been felled, thus forming a labyrinth of tangled abatis difficult to penetrate. A mile away lay the village of Williamsburg.

"We were soon sent out as skirmishers, with orders to advance as near the enemy's rifle-pits as possible. They immediately opened fire upon us with heavy guns from the fort, while from their rifle pits came a hum of bullets and crackle of musketry. Their heavy shot came crushing among the tangled abatis of falling timber, and ploughed up the dirt in our front, rebounding and tearing through the branches of the woods in our rear. The constant hissing of the bullets, with their sharp *ping* or *bizz* whispering around and sometimes into us, gave me a sickening feeling and a cold perspiration. I felt weak around my knees—a sort of faintness and lack of strength in the joints of my legs, as if they would sink from under me. These symptoms did not decrease when several of my comrades were hit. The little rifle-pits in our front fairly blazed with musketry, and the continuous *snap, snap, crack, crack* was murderous. Seeing I was not killed at once, in spite of all the noise, my knees recovered from their unpleasant limpness, and my mind gradually regained its balance and composure. I never afterwards felt these disturbing influences to the same degree.

"We slowly retired from stump to stump and from log to log, finally regaining the edge of the wood, and took our position near Webber's and Bramhall's batteries, which had just got into position on the right of the road, not over seven hundred yards from the hostile fort. While getting into position, several of the battery men were killed, as they immediately drew the artillery fire of the enemy, which opened with a noise and violence that astonished me.

"Our two batteries were admirably handled, throwing a number of shot and shell into the enemy's works, speedily silencing them, and by nine o'clock the field in our front, including the rifle-pits, was completely 'cleaned out' of artillery and infantry. Shortly afterwards we advanced along the edge of the wood to the left of Fort Magruder, and about eleven o'clock we saw emerging from the little ravine to the left of the fort a swarm of Confederates, who opened on us with a terrible and deadly fire. Then they charged upon us with their peculiar yell. We took all the advantage possible of the stumps and trees as we were pushed back, until we reached the edge of the wood again, where we halted and fired upon the enemy from behind all the cover the situation afforded. We were none of us too proud, not even those who had the dignity of shoulder-straps to support, to dodge behind a tree or stump. I called out to a comrade, 'Why don't you get behind a tree?' 'Confound it,' said he, 'there ain't enough for the officers.'

"I don't mean to accuse officers of cowardice, but we had suddenly found out that they showed the same general inclination not to get shot as privates did, and were anxious to avail themselves of the privilege of their rank by getting in our rear. I have always thought that pride was a good substitute for courage, if well backed by a conscientious sense of duty; and most of our men, officers as well as privates, were too proud to show the fear which I have no doubt they felt in common with myself. Occasionally a soldier would show symptoms which pride could not overcome. One of our men, Spinney, ran into the woods and was not seen until after the engagement. Some time afterwards, when he had proved a good soldier, I asked him why he ran, and he replied that every bullet which went by his head said 'Spinney,' and he thought they were calling for him. In all the pictures of battle I had seen before I ever saw a battle, the officers were at the front on prancing steeds, or with uplifted swords were leading their followers to the charge. Of course, I was surprised to find that in a real battle the officer gets in the rear of his men, as is his right and duty—that is, if his ideas of duty do not carry him so far to the rear as to make his sword useless.

"The 'Rebs' forced us back by their charge, and our central lines were almost broken. The forces withdrawn from our right had taken the infantry support from our batteries, one of which, consisting of four guns, was captured. We were tired, wet, and exhausted when supports came up, and we were allowed to fall back from under the enemy's fire, but still in easy reach of the battle. I asked one of my comrades how he felt, and his reply was characteristic of the prevailing sentiment: 'I should feel like a hero if I wasn't so blank wet.' The bullets had cut queer antics among our men. A private who had a canteen of whiskey when he went into the engagement, on endeavoring to take a drink found the canteen quite empty, as a bullet had tapped it for him. Another had a part of his thumb-nail taken off. Another had a bullet pass into the toe of his boot, down between two toes, and out along the sole of his foot, without much injury. Another had a scalp wound from a bullet, which took off a strip of hair about three inches in length from the top of his head. Two of my regiment were killed outright and fourteen badly wounded, besides quite a number slightly injured. Thus I have chronicled my first day's fight, and I don't believe any of my regiment were ambitious to 'chase the enemy any farther' just at present. Refreshed with hot coffee and hard-tack, we rested from the fight, well satisfied that we had done our duty. When morning dawned, with it came the intelligence that the enemy had abandoned their works in our front, and were again in full retreat, leaving their wounded in our hands."

A theory generally entertained is that Hancock's brilliant action on our right caused the retreat of the rebels. The facts, I imagine, are that the rebels only intended to fight till night, and under cover of the darkness, continue their retreat, and thus save their trains and rear-guard from capture.

On the morning following the fight Couch's men took possession of Fort Magruder and the abandoned redoubts, and a force was sent out to bury the dead.

In this first battle of the Peninsula, whose only redeeming feature was the bravery of those who fought it, our loss was shown by official report to have been: in killed, wounded, and prisoners, 2228; of these 1700 were of Hooker's force. The loss of the enemy was 1560; the protection their position afforded accounting for their small loss as compared with ours.

The 6th of May was a beautiful morning, with birds singing among the thickets in which lay the dead. The next morning we marched through quaint, old fashioned Williamsburg. The most substantial buildings of the town were those of William and Mary College, which were of brick. In most of the houses there were no signs of life; blinds and shutters were closed, but a white hand was occasionally seen through the blinds, showing that a woman was gazing stealthily at us. Occasionally a family of black people stood in the doorway, the women and children greeting us with senseless giggles, and in one instance waving their red handkerchiefs. I asked one of the black women where the white people were, and she replied, "Dey's done gone and run away."

On our tramp to White House Landing, on the Pamunkey River, we began to realize some of the more substantial discomforts of a march; the dust, rising in clouds, filled our nostrils and throats, and thoroughly impregnated our clothing, hair, and skin, producing intolerable choking and smothering sensations; our usual thirst was intensified, and made us ready to break ranks at sight of a brook, and swarm like bees around every well on the route. No one can imagine the intolerable thirst of a dusty march who has not had a live experience of it; canteens often replenished were speedily emptied, and, unless water was readily attainable, there was great suffering. During the frequent showers, which came down with the liberality common to the climate, it was not unusual to see men drinking from a puddle in the road; and at one place where water was scarce I saw men crowding round a mud-puddle drinking heartily, while in one edge of it lay a dead mule. There was little to choose between the mud and the dust, and we usually had one or the other in profusion.

Near New Kent Court-House, a little settlement of two or three houses, we came upon several Confederate sick. One of them was full of fighting talk. I asked him what he was fighting for. He said he didn't know, except it be "not to get licked!"

The roads were narrow and very muddy between the White House and the Chickahominy, and it was with great trouble that our trains were moved over them. A few miles west of the Pamunkey we found the country beautiful and undulating, with graceful round-topped hills, here and there crowned with trees and clothed in the varied tints of early summer. The picture is present with me as I write; the beautiful, undulating country, dotted with tents, and the picturesque groups of men around their camp-fires at the hush of evening.

On our entire march up the Peninsula, we did not see a dozen white men left upon the soil. At last, on the twenty-third of May, we arrived upon the banks of the sluggish Chickahominy—a small mill-stream, forty or fifty feet wide, with swampy lowland bordering on either side; the tops of the trees growing in the swamp being about on a level with the crests of the bluffs just beyond, on the Richmond side. Our first camp was pitched on the hills in the vicinity of Gaines's Farm.

The engineers soon began the construction of bridges for the passage of the troops, as it was very important to gain a foothold on the west bank, preparatory to our advance. While Duane's bridge was being constructed, we were ordered on duty along the banks: and upon approaching the river we found, in the thickets near it, one of our dead cavalrymen lying in the water, evidently having been killed while watering his horse. The bridges were thrown out with marvellous quickness, and the corduroy approaches were soon constructed. A small force was ordered to cross, to reconnoitre and to observe the condition of the roads with respect to the passage of artillery. I happened to be one of that squad. With orders not to return the fire if assailed, we advanced across the bridge and through the woods, a quarter of a mile; and, seeing the sloughy condition of the roads, were returning, when the crack of a rifle told us the enemy were upon us. At the first fire one of our men fell. He entreated us to leave him and save ourselves; while we were carrying him, the enemy wounded two more of our men, but not seriously. On each side of the narrow defile were woods with but little screening underbrush, and it was through this we were advancing when attacked. We could not see the enemy, who were secreted in the tree tops around us, but the *zip, zip* of their bullets pursued us as we retreated.

The comrade who had been shot, apparently through the lungs, was examined by our surgeon, who at first thought the case fatal, as the bullet came out of the chest on the side opposite to which it entered; but it was found that the bullet had been deflected by a rib, and glanced round, beneath the skin, only causing a painful flesh-wound. In three weeks our comrade was on light duty about camp. Before seeing very much service we discovered that a man may be hit with bullets in a great many places without killing him. Later I saw a man who had both his eyes destroyed by a bullet without injuring the bridge of his nose, or otherwise marking his face.

In the barn at Gaines's Farm there were a number of Confederate sick and wounded—men captured in some skirmish during our advance; and while taking a peep at them through a crack, I saw a North Carolina lieutenant whom I recognized as a former school acquaintance. I obtained permission to speak to him, but they told me he was violent and bitter in his language. On approaching him, and inquiring if he knew me, something like a smile of recognition lighted up his face; hesitating a moment, he finally extended his hand. We talked for fifteen or twenty minutes about our school-fellows and early days, but not one word about the war.

Considerable foraging was done, on the sly, about the neighboring plantations, but as a rule foraging was severely condemned by our commanders. There was much tobacco raised in this section of country, and we found the barns filled with the best quality of tobacco in leaf; this we appropriated without objection on the part of our officers. As all trades were represented in our ranks, that of cigar-maker was included, and the army rioted in cigars without enriching the sutlers.

By the lower bridges two of the army corps were sent across to take position near Seven Pines. Some of the bridges were of boats, with corduroy approaches. While they were in process of finishing, on the night of May 30, a terrible storm occurred; the rain-fall was immense, and the thunder the most terrific I ever heard, its sharp, crackling rattle at times sounding like the cannonading of an engagement. When morning dawned, our boat bridges were found dangling midway in a stream which covered the whole swampy and bottom land on both sides the original channel, and the water was waist-deep throughout the greater part of the swamp.

THE BATTLE OF SEVEN PINES (FAIR OAKS)

We were ordered on duty with Sumner's corps, which was stationed at Tyler's house, and held the centre of the general line of the army. Not long after noon of the 31st, we heard the dull reverberation of cannonading in the direction of Seven Pines, and the companies and regiments fell into line, ready to march at a moment's notice. About two in the afternoon the march was begun to the approaches of Sumner's upper bridge, also called the "Grapevine" bridge, which had been built of logs over the swampy bottom, and which was sustained in place by ropes tied to stumps on the upstream side. At first it seemed impossible to cross, so swollen was the stream by the overflow; but when the troops were well on the bridge, it was held in place by the moving weight and rendered passable, although covered with water and swaying in the rushing torrent, which every moment threatened to float it away piecemeal. The men grumbled some, after the manner of soldiers. "If this bridge goes down I can't swim a stroke," said one. "Well," said "Little" Day, always making the best of everything, "there will be, in that case, plenty of logs for you to float on." If we had gone down with all our marching equipment, there would have been but little chance even for a good swimmer. Kirby's battery of Napoleon guns preceded us; we found them mired on the west shore. They were unlimbered, and the men of different regiments tugged and lifted at them, knee-deep in the mire, until they were extricated, and finally almost carried them to dry land, or rather firm land, as by no stretch of courtesy could anything in the vicinity be called dry.

Sedgwick's division, being nearer the Grapevine bridge, took the lead at that crossing, while Richardson's division moved toward Sumner's lower bridge. There French's brigade crossed by wading to the waist, the other brigades being ordered to turn back and follow Sedgwick. It was this delay which kept Richardson out of the first day's fight.

A private of the Fifteenth Massachusetts (Gorman's brigade) afterward gave me his recollections of that forced march through water and mud. "Most of our artillery," he said, "became so badly mired that we were obliged to proceed without it, but the little battery of twelve-pound Napoleon guns, commanded by an energetic regular officer (Lieutenant Kirby), notwithstanding it was continually mired to its axles, was pluckily dragged along by horses and men. Despite the mire, we cracked jokes at each other, shouted and sang in high spirits, and toiled through the morass in the direction of the heavy firing."

About 3:30 P.M. we began to meet stragglers from the front. They all told in substance the same story: "Our companies and regiments are all cut to pieces!" One straggler had a strapping Confederate prisoner in charge. He inquired for a Pennsylvania regiment, saying that during the fight in the woods he lost his company, and while trying to find his way out came across the "reb," and was trying to "take him in." "Stranger," said the prisoner, "yer wouldn't have taken me in if I'd known yer war lost."

Meanwhile the thunder of the conflict grew louder and louder, and about five o'clock we came upon fragments of regiments of that part of Couch's command which had become isolated at Fair Oaks Station; they had fallen back half a mile or so, and when we joined them beyond the Courtney house they were hotly engaged with the enemy, who were in overwhelming numbers.

As we came up through a stumpy field we were greeted with the quick *crack, crack* of the infantry in our front. The smoke of battle hung in clouds over the field, and through it could be seen the flashes of the artillery. The *ping, zip, zip* of bullets, and the wounded men limping from the front or carried by comrades, were a prelude to the storm to come. We formed on the left of Abercrombie's shattered brigade, near the Adams house, and were welcomed with hearty cheers. Presently there was a terrible explosion of musketry, and the bullets pattered around us, causing many to drop; a line of smoke ahead showed where the destructive fire came from. Kirby's five Napoleon guns came up, and in the angle of the woods opened with splendid precision upon the Confederate columns. The recoil of the pieces was often so great as to bury the wheels nearly to the hub in mud. Soon the "rebel yell" was heard as they charged on the right of Kirby's battery, which changed front to the right, and delivered a destructive fire of canister. This caused the enemy to break in confusion, and retreat to the cover of the woods. Shortly afterward the enemy developed in greater force in our front, and the hum of shot and shell was almost incessant; but in a few minutes the fire slackened, and the Confederate lines came dashing upon us with their shrill yells. We received them with a volley from our rifles, and the battery gave them its compliments. The gray masses of the enemy were seen dimly through the smoke, scattering to cover. Presently the order ran down the line, "Fix bayonets!" While waiting the moment for the final order, John Milan said: "It's light infantry we are, boys, and they expect us to fly over them criss-cross fences." Then the final order came: "Guide right—Double-quick—Charge!" Our whole line went off at double-quick, shouting as we ran. Some scattering shots were fired by the enemy as we struggled over the fences, and then their line broke and dissolved from view.

That night we lay under the stars, thinking of the events of the day and the expected conflict of the morrow. Until dawn of Sunday (June 1) our officers were busy gathering together the scattered and separated forces. About five o'clock next morning we heard firing on our left flank, which was covered by Richardson's division of Sumner's corps. It was a line of Confederate pickets deploying in an open field on the south side of Fair Oaks Station. Shortly after six o'clock there was a furious fire of musketry on our left, which continued for an hour.

During the day I went over a portion of the battle-field in the road through the woods, where the Confederates had made the unsuccessful charge upon Kirby's battery. Here the dead lay very thick, and a number of their wounded were hidden in the thickets. They had fallen in many instances on their faces in the headlong charge; some with their legs torn off, some with shattered arms, and others with ghastly wounds in the head.

On the 2d of June the whole line moved forward, and from Fair Oaks to the Williamsburg road occupied the positions which had been held previous to the battle. About that time I went over the battleground in front of Casey's position where the battle began. Many of the dead remained unburied. Some of the men who first took possession of the works informed me that they found large quantities of Confederate arms; also a number of the enemy who had become intoxicated on Yankee whiskey. The camp had been well plundered, and the enemy had adopted a system of exchange in dress, throwing aside their ragged uniforms, and clothing themselves in the more comfortable and cleanly garments of the

White Oak Swamp: *Union batteries check Confederate pursuit*

Federal soldiers. I saw a Sibley tent in which I counted over two hundred bullet-holes.

A comrade who visited the scene of the charge made by Sedgwick's men said that in the woods beyond, where the Confederate lines had been formed, a number had been killed while in the act of getting over the fence, and were suspended in the positions in which they had been shot. In the woods just beyond this fence were some swampy pools, to which a number of the enemy's wounded had crept for water and died during the night. There were two or three of these pools of stagnant water, around which were clusters of wounded and dead men.

When my company reached the vicinity of Fair Oaks, about a week after the battle, I was surprised to find how many limbs of trees had been cut away by bullets and shot. At one place a cannon-ball had apparently passed entirely through the stem of a large tree, splitting it for some distance; but the springy wood had closed together again so closely that the point of a bayonet could not be inserted in its track. The forests in the rear were marked in such a manner by bullets as to indicate that the enemy must have shot at times a long way over their intended mark.

In the advance, where Naglee's brigade made its struggle until overwhelmed by the enemy, graves were plenty in every direction, and some of the enemy's dead were found standing, in the swamp near by, in the position in which they were shot. They had decomposed so rapidly that the flesh had partly dropped from the bones.

Many of Casey's men had lost their knapsacks, blankets, and clothing, as well as their tents, and were in a sad plight for soldiering.

Thereafter our lines were constantly engaged in skirmishing, and we were kept in position for battle day after day, expecting an attack. Often the bugler at brigade headquarters sounded the alarm to "fall in," on one day sounding it ten times. During one of the frequent thunder-storms the Confederates made reconnoissance, and fired volleys so timed that they might be mistaken for thunder; but our men were not deceived and stood to their arms, expecting an attack. At one time the men in our rear were practising the drill with blank cartridges, and were mistaken for the enemy. Thus the alarms of war kept our attention occupied.

WHERE IS JACKSON?

IT HAD TAKEN TWO MONTHS for McClellan to move up the peninsula and get in position before Richmond. His troops outnumbered the Confederates about two to one, but McClellan chose to believe rumors that the Rebel forces were much larger. As late as May 14, he wrote to Lincoln that he fully expected to have to fight twice his number before Richmond. In fact, as Bruce Catton says, "the general Confederate situation in Virginia was desperate. On the peninsula, Johnston with 55,000 men faced an army approximately twice that large. At Norfolk, which was about to be abandoned, the Confederate Major General Benjamin Huger had 10,000 soldiers, who presumably would join Johnston; they were balanced by 12,400 Federals under old General Wool at Fort Monroe, who would eventually be put under McClellan's command. In northern Virginia, from the Shenandoah Valley to the tidewater city of Fredericksburg, there were some 75,000 Federal troops in the separated commands of McDowell and Banks and in the Washington lines. In addition, Pathfinder Frémont had upwards of 17,000 scattered up and down the mountain valleys of western Virginia; he was beginning to pull them together and was contemplating a move south to break the railroad line that connected Virginia and Tennessee. To meet this immense array—which, for all anyone in Richmond knew, might at any moment be welded into one army—the Confederacy had 13,000 men under Brigadier General Joseph R. Anderson, below the Rappahannock watching McDowell; 6000 or more under Stonewall Jackson in the upper Shenandoah; 2800 under Brigadier General Edward Johnson west of Staunton, to keep an eye on Frémont; and 8500 under Major General Richard Ewell, poised at one of the gaps in the Blue Ridge, ready at need to join Jackson against Banks or to move east and join Anderson against McDowell. Since the Confederate authorities had a fairly accurate count on Federal strength, a simple exercise in addition was all anyone needed in order to understand the inadequacy of Confederate manpower in Virginia."*

McClellan continued to ask for more men. Secretary of War Stanton considered sending McDowell's 40,000 troops, now deployed along the

* _Terrible Swift Sword,_ p. 293.

Rappahannock River, but Lincoln wanted to keep McDowell within quick marching distance of the capital, ready to defend against a sudden strike by "Stonewall" Jackson.

Thomas Jonathan Jackson had earned his nickname at Bull Run by standing fast under heavy Union attack. Now he was marching and countermarching up and down the Shenandoah Valley with frightening speed, making his Federal opponents seem hopelessly ponderous by comparison. Late in May, 1962, Stonewall Jackson turned up at Harper's Ferry, and Lincoln's fears seemed about to become reality.

The Valley Campaign*

BY GENERAL RICHARD TAYLOR

Ewell's DIVISION REACHED THE WESTERN BASE of Swift Run Gap on a lovely spring evening, April 30, 1862, and in crossing the Blue Ridge seemed to have left winter and its rigors behind. Jackson, whom we moved to join, had suddenly that morning marched toward McDowell, some eighty miles west, where after uniting with a force under General Edward Johnson, he defeated the Federal general Milroy. Some days later he has suddenly returned. Meanwhile we were ordered to remain in camp on the Shenandoah near Conrad's store, at which place a bridge spanned the stream.

The great Valley of Virginia was before us in all its beauty. Fields of wheat spread far and wide, interspersed with woodlands, bright in their robes of tender green. Wherever appropriate sites existed, quaint old mills, with turning wheels, were busily grinding the previous year's harvest; and grove and eminence showed comfortable homesteads. The soft vernal influence shed a languid grace over the scene. The theatre of war in this region was from Staunton to the Potomac, one hundred and twenty miles, with an average width of some twenty-five miles; and the Blue Ridge and Alleghenies bounded it east and west. Drained by the Shenandoah with its numerous affluents, the surface was nowhere flat, but a succession of graceful swells, occasionally rising into abrupt hills. Resting on limestone, the soil was productive, especially of wheat, and the underlying rock furnished abundant metal for the construction of roads. Railway communication was limited to the Virginia Central, which entered the Valley by a tunnel east of Staunton and passed westward through that town; to the Manassas Gap, which traversed the Blue Ridge at the pass of that name and ended at Strasburg; and to the Winchester and Harper's Ferry, thirty miles long. The first extended to Richmond by

* From *Destruction and Reconstruction*.

Charlottesville and Gordonsville, crossing at the former place the line from Washington and Alexandria to Lynchburg; the second connected Strasburg and Front Royal, in the Valley, with the same line at Manassas Junction; and the last united with the Baltimore and Ohio at Harper's Ferry. Frequent passes or gaps in the mountains, through which wagon roads had been constructed, afforded easy access from east and west; and pikes were excellent, though unmetaled roads became heavy after rains.

But the glory of the Valley is Massanutten. Rising abruptly from the plain near Harrisonburg, twenty-five miles north of Staunton, this lovely mountain extends fifty miles, and as suddenly ends near Strasburg. Parallel with the Blue Ridge, and of equal height, its sharp peaks have a bolder and more picturesque aspect, while the abruptness of its slopes gives the appearance of greater altitude. Midway of Massanutten, a gap with good road affords communication between Newmarket and Luray. The eastern or Luray valley, much narrower than the one west of Massanutten, is drained by the east branch of the Shenandoah, which is joined at Front Royal, near the northern end of the mountain, by its western affluent, whence the united waters flow north, at the base of the Blue Ridge, to meet the Potomac at Harper's Ferry.

While in camp near Conrad's store, the 7th Louisiana, Colonel Hays, a crack regiment, on picket down stream, had a spirited affair, in which the enemy was driven with the loss of a score of prisoners. Shortly after, for convenience of supplies, I was directed to cross the river and camp some miles to the southwest. The command was in superb condition, and a four-gun battery from Bedford county, Virginia, Captain Bowyer, had recently been added to it. The four regiments, 6th, 7th, 8th, and 9th Louisiana, would average above eight hundred bayonets. The 6th, Colonel Seymour, recruited in New Orleans, was composed of Irishmen, stout, hardy fellows, turbulent in camp and requiring a strong hand, but responding to kindness and justice, and ready to follow their officers to the death. The 9th, Colonel Stafford, was from North Louisiana. Planters or sons of planters, many of them men of fortune, soldiering was a hard task to which they only became reconciled by reflecting that it was "niddering" in gentlemen to assume voluntarily the discharge of duties and then shirk. The 8th, Colonel Kelly, was from the Attakapas—"Acadians," the race of which Longfellow sings in "Evangeline." A home-loving, simple people, few spoke English, fewer still had ever before moved ten miles from their natal cabanas; and the war to them was "a liberal education," as was the society of the lady of quality to honest Dick Steele. They had all the light gayety of the Gaul, and, after the manner of their ancestors, were born cooks. A capital regimental band accompanied them, and whenever weather and ground permitted, even after long marches, they would waltz and "polk" in couples with as much zest as if their arms encircled the supple waists of the Celestines and Melazies of their native Teche. The Valley soldiers were largely of the Presbyterian faith, and of a solemn, pious demeanor, and looked askant at the caperings of my Creoles, holding them to be "devices and snares."

At nightfall of the second day in this camp, an order came from General Jackson to join him at Newmarket, twenty odd miles north; and it was stated that my division commander, Ewell, had been apprised of the

order. Our position was near a pike leading south of west to Harrisonburg, whence, to gain Newmarket, the great Valley pike ran due north.
All roads near our camp had been examined and sketched, and among
them was a road running north-west over the southern foot-hills of
Massanutten, and joining the Valley pike some distance to the north of
Harrisonburg. It was called the Keazletown road, from a little German
village on the flank of Massanutten; and as it was the hypothenuse of the
triangle, and reported good except at two points, I decided to take it.
That night a pioneer party was sent forward to light fires and repair the
road for artillery and trains. Early dawn saw us in motion, with lovely
weather, a fairish road, and men in high health and spirits.

Later in the day a mounted officer was dispatched to report our approach and select a camp, which proved to be beyond Jackson's forces,
then lying in the fields on both sides of the pike. Over three thousand
strong, neat in fresh clothing of gray with white gaiters, bands playing
at the head of their regiments, not a straggler, but every man in his place,
stepping jauntily as on parade, though it had marched twenty miles and
more, in open column with arms at "right shoulder shift," and rays of
the declining sun flaming on polished bayonets, the brigade moved down
the broad, smooth pike, and wheeled on to its camping ground.

After attending to necessary camp details, I sought Jackson, whom I
had never met.

The mounted officer who had been sent on in advance pointed out a
figure perched on the topmost rail of a fence overlooking the road and
field, and said it was Jackson. Approaching, I saluted and declared my
name and rank, then waited for a response. Before this came I had time
to see a pair of cavalry boots covering feet of gigantic size, a mangy cap
with visor drawn low, a heavy, dark beard, and weary eyes—eyes I afterward saw filled with intense but never brilliant light. A low, gentle voice
inquired the road and distance marched that day. "Keazletown road, six
and twenty miles." "You seem to have no stragglers." "Never allow straggling." "You must teach my people; they straggle badly." A bow in reply.
Just then my Creoles started their band and a waltz. After a contempla-
tive suck at a lemon, "Thoughtless fellows for serious work" came forth.
I expressed a hope that the work would not be less well done because
of the gayety. A return to the lemon gave me the opportunity to retire.
Where Jackson got his lemons "no fellow could find out," but he was
rarely without one.

Quite late that night General Jackson came to my camp fire, where
he stayed some hours. He said we would move at dawn, asked a few
questions about the marching of my men, which seemed to have impressed him, and then remained silent. If silence be golden, he was a
"bonanza." He sucked lemons, ate hard-tack, and drank water, and praying and fighting appeared to be his idea of the "whole duty of man."

In the gray of the morning, as I was forming my column on the pike,
Jackson appeared and gave the route—north—which, from the situation
of its camp, put my brigade in advance of the army. After moving a short
distance in this direction, the head of the column was turned to the east
and took the road over Massanutten gap to Luray. Scarce a word was
spoken on the march, as Jackson rode with me. From time to time a

courier would gallop up, report, and return toward Luray. An ungraceful horseman, mounted on a sorry chestnut with a shambling gait, his huge feet with outturned toes thrust into his stirrups, and such parts of his countenance as the low visor of his shocking cap failing to conceal wearing a wooden look, our new commander was not prepossessing. That night we crossed the east branch of the Shenandoah by a bridge, and camped on the stream, near Luray.

Off the next morning, my command still in advance, and Jackson riding with me. The road led north between the east bank of the river and the western base of the Blue Ridge. Rain had fallen and softened it, so as to delay the wagon trains in rear. Past midday we reached a wood extending from the mountain to the river, when a mounted officer from the rear called Jackson's attention, who rode back with him. A moment later, there rushed out of the wood to meet us a young, rather well-looking woman, afterward widely known as Belle Boyd. Breathless with speed and agitation, some time elapsed before she found her voice. Then, with much volubility, she said we were near Front Royal, beyond the wood; that the town was filled with Federals, whose camp was on the west side of the river, where they had guns in position to cover the wagon bridge, but none bearing on the railway bridge below the former; that they believed Jackson to be west of Massanutten, near Harrisonburg; that General Banks, the Federal commander, was at Winchester, twenty miles northwest of Front Royal, where he was slowly concentrating his widely scattered forces to meet Jackson's advance, which was expected some days later. All this she told with the precision of a staff officer making a report, and it was true to the letter.

Convinced of the correctness of the woman's statements, I hurried forward at "a double," hoping to surprise the enemy's idlers in the town, or swarm over the wagon bridge with them and secure it. Doubtless this was rash, but I felt immensely "cocky" about my brigade, and believed that it would prove equal to any demand. Before we had cleared the wood Jackson came galloping from the rear, followed by a company of horse. He ordered me to deploy my leading regiment as skirmishers on both sides of the road and continue the advance, then passed on. We speedily came in sight of Front Royal, but the enemy had taken the alarm, and his men were scurrying over the bridge to their camp, where troops could be seen forming. The situation of the village is surpassingly beautiful. It lies near the east bank of the Shenandoah which just below unites all its waters, and looks directly on the northern peaks of Massanutten. The Blue Ridge with Manassas Gap, through which passes the railway, overhangs it on the east; distant Allegheny bounds the horizon to the west; and down the Shenandoah, the eye ranges over a fertile, well-farmed country. Two bridges spanned the river—a wagon bridge above, a railway bridge some yards lower. A good pike led to Winchester, twenty miles, and another followed the river north, whence many cross-roads united with the Valley pike near Winchester. The river, swollen by rain, was deep and turbulent, with a strong current. The Federals were posted on the west bank, here somewhat higher than the opposite, and a short distance above the junction of waters, with batteries bearing more especially on the upper bridge.

Under instructions, my brigade was drawn up in line, a little retired from the river, but overlooking it—the Federals and their guns in full view. So far, not a shot had been fired. I rode down to the river's brink to get a better look at the enemy through a field-glass, when my horse, heated by the march, stepped into the water to drink. Instantly a brisk fire was opened on me, bullets striking all around and raising a little shower-bath. Like many a foolish fellow, I found it easier to get into than out of a difficulty. I had not yet led my command into action, and, remembering that one must "strut" one's little part to the best advantage, sat my horse with all the composure I could master. A provident camel, on the eve of a desert journey, would not have laid in a greater supply of water than did my thoughtless beast. At last he raised his head, looked placidly around, turned, and walked up the bank.

This little incident was not without value, for my men welcomed me with a cheer; upon which, as if in response, the enemy's guns opened, and, having the range, inflicted some loss on my line. We had no guns up to reply, and in advance as has been mentioned, had outmarched the troops behind us. Motionless as a statue, Jackson sat his horse some few yards away, and seemed lost in thought. Perhaps the circumstances mentioned some pages back had obscured his star; but if so, a few short hours swept away the cloud, and it blazed, Sirius-like, over the land. I approached him with the suggestion that the railway bridge might be passed by stepping on the cross-ties, as the enemy's guns bore less directly on it than on the upper bridge. He nodded approval. The 8th regiment was on the right of my line, near at hand; and dismounting, Colonel Kelly led it across under a sharp musketry fire. Several men fell to disappear in the dark water beneath; but the movement continued with great rapidity, considering the difficulty of walking on ties, and Kelly with his leading files gained the opposite shore. Thereupon the enemy fired combustibles previously placed near the center of the wagon bridge. The loss of this structure would have seriously delayed us, as the railway bridge was not floored, and I looked at Jackson, near by, who was watching Kelly's progress. Again he nodded, and my command rushed at the bridge. Concealed by the cloud of smoke, the suddenness of the movement saved us from much loss; but it was rather a near thing. My horse and clothing were scorched, and many men burned their hands severely while throwing brands into the river. We were soon over, and the enemy in full flight to Winchester, with loss of camp, guns, and prisoners. Just as I emerged from flames and smoke, Jackson was by my side. How he got there was a mystery, as the bridge was thronged with my men going at full speed; but smoke and fire had decidedly freshened up his costume.

In the angle formed by the two branches of the river was another camp held by a Federal regiment from Maryland. This was captured by a gallant little regiment of Marylanders, Colonel Bradley Johnson, on our side. I had no connection with this spirited affair, saving that these Marylanders had acted with my command during the day, though not attached to it. We followed the enemy on the Winchester road, but to little purpose, as we had few horsemen over the river. Carried away by his ardor, my commissary, Major Davis, gathered a score of mounted orderlies and couriers, and pursued until a volley from the enemy's rear guard laid him low on the road, shot through the head.

Late in the night Jackson came out of the darkness and seated himself by my camp fire. He mentioned that I would move with him in the morning, then relapsed into silence. I fancied he looked at me kindly, and interpreted it into an approval of the conduct of the brigade. The events of the day, anticipations of the morrow, the death of Davis, drove away sleep, and I watched Jackson. For hours he sat silent and motionless, with eyes fixed on the fire. I took up the idea that he was inwardly praying, and he remained throughout the night.

Off in the morning, Jackson leading the way, my brigade, a small body of horse, and a section of the Rockbridge (Virginia) artillery forming the column. Major Wheat, with his battalion of "Tigers," was directed to keep close to the guns. Sturdy marchers, they trotted along with the horse and artillery at Jackson's heels, and after several hours were some distance in advance of the brigade, with which I remained.

A volley in front, followed by wild cheers, stirred us up to a "double," and we speedily came upon a moving spectacle. Jackson had struck the Valley pike at Middletown, twelve miles south of Winchester, along which a large body of Federal horse, with many wagons, was hastening north. He had attacked at once with his handful of men, overwhelmed resistance, and captured prisoners and wagons. The gentle Tigers were looting right merrily, diving in and out of wagons with the activity of rabbits in a warren; but this occupation was abandoned on my approach, and in a moment they were in line, looking as solemn and virtuous as deacons at a funeral. Prisoners and spoil were promptly secured. The horse was from New England, a section in which horsemanship was an unknown art, and some of the riders were strapped to their steeds. Ordered to dismount, they explained their condition, and were given time to unbuckle. Many breastplates and other protective devices were seen here, and later at Winchester. We did not know whether the Federals had organized cuirassiers, or were recurring to the customs of Gustavus Adolphus. I saw a poor fellow lying dead on the pike, pierced through breastplate and body by a rifle ball. Iron-clad men are of small account before modern weapons.

A part of the Federal column had passed north before Jackson reached the pike, and this, with his mounted men, he pursued. Something more than a mile to the south a road left the pike and led directly west, where the Federal General Fremont, of whom we shall hear more, commanded "the Mountain Department." Attacked in front, as described, a body of Federals, horse, artillery, and infantry, with some wagons, took this road, and, after moving a short distance, drew up on a crest, with unlimbered guns. Their number was unknown, and for a moment they looked threatening. The brigade was rapidly formed and marched straight upon them, when their guns opened. A shell knocked over several men of the 7th regiment, and a second, as I rode forward to an eminence to get a view, struck the ground under my horse and exploded. The saddle cloth on both sides was torn away, and I and Adjutant Surget, who was just behind me, were nearly smothered with earth; but neither man nor horse received a scratch. The enemy soon limbered up and fled west. By some well-directed shots, as they crossed a hill, our guns sent wagons flying in the air, after which we left them and marched north.

At dusk we overtook Jackson, pushing the enemy with his little mounted force, himself in advance of all. I rode with him, and we kept on through the darkness. There was not resistance enough to deploy infantry. A flash, a report, and a whistling bullet from some covert met us, but there were few casualties. I quite remember thinking at the time that Jackson was invulnerable, and that persons near him shared that quality. An officer, riding hard, overtook us, who proved to be the chief quartermaster of the army. He reported the wagon trains far behind, impeded by a bad road in Luray Valley. "The ammunition wagons?" sternly. "All right, sir. They were in advance, and I doubled teams on them and brought them through." "Ah!" in a tone of relief.

To give countenance to this quartermaster, if such can be given of a dark night, I remarked jocosely: "Never mind the wagons. There are quantities of stores in Winchester, and the General has invited me to breakfast there to-morrow."

Jackson, who had no more capacity for jests than a Scotchman, took this seriously, and reached out to touch me on the arm. Without physical wants himself, he forgot that others were differently constituted, and paid little heed to commissariat; but woe to the man who failed to bring up ammunition! In advance, his trains were left far behind. In retreat, he would fight for a wheelbarrow.

Moving with the first light of morning, we came to Kernstown, three miles from Winchester, and the place of Jackson's fight with Shields. Here heavy and sustained firing, artillery and small arms, was heard. A staff officer approached at full speed to summon me to Jackson's presence and move up my command. A gallop of a mile or more brought me to him. Winchester was in sight, a mile to the north. To the east Ewell with a large part of the army was fighting briskly and driving the enemy on to the town. On the west a high ridge, overlooking the country to the south and southeast, was occupied by a heavy mass of Federals with guns in position. Jackson was on the pike, and near him were several regiments lying down for shelter, as the fire from the ridge was heavy and searching. A Virginian battery, Rockbridge artillery, was fighting at a great disadvantage, and already much cut up. Poetic authority asserts that "Old Virginny never tires," and the conduct of this battery justified the assertion of the muses. With scarce a leg or wheel for man and horse, gun or caisson, to stand on, it continued to hammer away at the crushing fire above.

Jackson, impassive as ever, pointed to the ridge and said, "You must carry it." I replied that my command would be up by the time I could inspect the ground, and rode to the left for that purpose. A small stream, Abraham's creek, flowed from the west through the little vale at the southern base of the ridge, the ascent of which was steep, though nowhere abrupt. At one point a broad, shallow, trough-like depression broke the surface, which was further interrupted by some low copse, out-cropping stone, and two fences. On the summit the Federal lines were posted behind a stone wall, along a road coming west from the pike. Worn somewhat into the soil, this road served as a countersink and strengthened the position. Further west, there was a break in the ridge, which was occupied by a body of horse, the extreme right of the enemy's line.

There was scarce time to mark these features before the head of my column appeared, when it was filed to the left, close to the base of the ridge, for protection from the plunging fire. Meanwhile, the Rockbridge battery held on manfully and engaged the enemy's attention. Riding on the flank of my column, between it and the hostile line, I saw Jackson beside me. This was not the place for the commander of the army, and I ventured to tell him so; but he paid no attention to the remark. We reached the shallow depression spoken of, where the enemy could depress his guns, and his fire became close and fatal. Many men fell, and the whistling of shot and shell occasioned much ducking of heads in the column. This annoyed me no little, as it was but child's play to the work immediately in hand. Always an admirer of delightful "Uncle Toby," I had contracted the most villainous habit of his beloved army in Flanders, and, forgetting Jackson's presence, ripped out, "What the h—— are you dodging for? If there is any more of it, you will be halted under this fire for an hour." The sharp tones of a familiar voice produced the desired effect, and the men looked as if they had swallowed ramrods; but I shall never forget the reproachful surprise expressed in Jackson's face. He placed his hand on my shoulder, said in a gentle voice, "I am afraid you are a wicked fellow," turned, and rode back to the pike.

The proper ground gained, the column faced to the front and began the ascent. At the moment the sun rose over the Blue Ridge, without cloud or mist to obscure his rays. It was a lovely Sabbath morning, the 25th of May, 1862. The clear, pure atmosphere brought the Blue Ridge and Allegheny and Massanutten almost overhead. Even the cloud of murderous smoke from the guns above made beautiful spirals in the air, and the broad fields of luxuriant wheat glistened with dew.

As we mounted we came in full view of both armies, whose efforts in other quarters had been slackened to await the result of our movement. I felt an anxiety amounting to pain for the brigade to acquit itself handsomely; and this feeling was shared by every man in it. About half way up, the enemy's horse from his right charged; and to meet it, I directed Lieutenant-Colonel Nicholls, whose regiment, the 8th, was on the left, to withhold slightly his two flank companies. By one volley, which emptied some saddles, Nicholls drove off the horse, but was soon after severely wounded. Progress was not stayed by this incident. Closing the many gaps made by the fierce fire, steadied the rather by it, and preserving an alignment that would have been creditable on parade, the brigade, with cadenced step and eyes on the foe, swept grandly over copse and ledge and fence, to crown the heights from which the enemy had melted away.

Breaking into column, we pursued closely. Jackson came up and grasped my hand, worth a thousand words from another, and we were soon in the streets of Winchester, a quaint old town of some five thousand inhabitants. There was a little fighting in the streets, but the people were all abroad—certainly all the women and babies. They were frantic with delight, only regretting that so many "Yankees" had escaped, and seriously impeded our movements.

Past the town, we could see the Federals flying north on the Harper's

Ferry and Martinsburg roads. Cavalry, of which there was a considerable force with the army, might have reaped a rich harvest, but none came forward. Raised in the adjoining region, our troopers were gossiping with their friends, or worse. Perhaps they thought that the war was over. Jackson joined me, and, in response to my question, "Where is the cavalry?" glowered and was silent. After several miles, finding that we were doing no good—as indeed infantry, preserving its organization, cannot hope to overtake a flying enemy—I turned into the fields and camped.

The following day my command was moved ten miles north on the pike leading by Charleston to Harper's Ferry, and after a day some miles east toward the Shenandoah. This was in consequence of the operations of the Federal General Shields, who, in command of a considerable force to the east of the Blue Ridge, passed Manassas Gap and drove from Front Royal a regiment of Georgians, left there by Jackson. Meanwhile, a part of the army was pushed forward to Martinsburg and beyond, while another part threatened and shelled Harper's Ferry. Jackson himself was engaged in forwarding captured stores to Staunton.

On Saturday, May 31, I received orders to move through Winchester, clear the town of stragglers, and continue to Strasburg. Few or no stragglers were found in Winchester, whence the sick and wounded, except extreme cases, had been taken. I stopped for a moment, at a house near the field of the 25th, to see Colonel Nicholls. He had suffered amputation of the arm that morning, and the surgeons forbade his removal; so that, much to my regret and more to his own, he was left. We reached camp at Strasburg after dark, a march of thirty odd miles, weather very warm. Winder, with his brigade, came in later, after a longer march from the direction of Harper's Ferry. Jackson sat some time at my camp fire that night, and was more communicative than I remember him before or after. He said Fremont, with a large force, was three miles west of our present camp, and must be defeated in the morning. Shields was moving up Luray Valley, and might cross Massanutten to Newmarket, or continue south until he turned the mountain to fall on our trains near Harrisonburg. The importance of preserving the immense trains, filled with captured stores, was great, and would engage much of his personal attention; while he relied on the army, under Ewell's direction, to deal promptly with Fremont. This he told in a low, gentle voice, and with many interruptions to afford time, as I thought and believe, for inward prayer. The men said that his anxiety about the wagons was because of the lemons among the stores.

Dawn of the following day (Sunday) was ushered in by the sound of Fremont's guns. Our lines had been early drawn out to meet him, and skirmishers pushed up to the front to attack.

We found the right of our line held by a Mississippi regiment, the colonel of which told me that he had advanced just before and driven the enemy. Several of his men were wounded, and he was bleeding profusely from a hit in his leg, which he was engaged in binding with a handkerchief, remarking that "it did not pester him much." The brigade moved forward until the enemy was reached, when, wheeling to the left, it walked down his line. The expression is used advisedly, for it was nothing but a "walk-over." Sheep would have made as much resistance as we met.

Men decamped without firing, or threw down their arms and surrendered, and it was so easy that I began to think of traps. At length we got under fire from our own skirmishers, and suffered some casualties, the only ones received in the movement.

Our whole skirmish line was advancing briskly as the Federals retired. I sought Ewell, and reported. We had a fine game before us, and the temptation to play it was great; but Jackson's orders were imperative and wise. He had his stores to save, Shields to guard against, Lee's grand strategy to promote; and all this he accomplished, alarming Washington, fastening McDowell's strong corps at Fredericksburg and preventing its junction with McClellan, on whose right flank he subsequently threw himself at Cold Harbor. He could not waste time chasing Fremont, but we, who looked from a lower standpoint, grumbled and shared the men's opinion about the lemon wagons.

Fremont made no further sign, and as the day declined the army was recalled to the pike and marched south. Jackson, in person, gave me instructions to draw up my brigade facing west, on some hills above the pike, and distant from it several hundred yards, where I was to remain. He said that the road was crowded, and he wanted time to clear it, that Fremont was safe for the night, and our cavalry toward Winchester reported Banks returned to that place from the Potomac, but not likely to move south before the following day; then rode off, and so rapidly as to give me no time to inquire how long I was to remain, or if the cavalry would advise me in the event that Banks changed his purpose. This was near sunset, and by the time the command was in position darkness fell upon us. No fires were allowed, and, stacking arms, the men rested, munching cold rations from their haversacks. It was their first opportunity for a bite since early morning.

I threw myself on the ground, and tried in vain to sleep. No sound could be heard save the clattering of hoofs on the pike, which as the night wore on became constant. Hour after hour passed, when, thinking I heard firing to the north, I mounted and looked for the pike. The darkness was so intense that it could not have been found but for the white limestone. Some mounted men were passing, whom I halted to question. They said their command had gone on to rejoin the army, and, they supposed, had missed me in the dark; but there was a squadron behind, near the enemy's advance, which, a large cavalry force, had moved from Winchester at an early period of the day and driven our people south. This was pleasant; for Winder's brigade had marched several hours since, and a wide interval existed between us.

More firing, near and distinct, was heard, and the command was ordered down to the pike, which it reached after much stumbling and swearing, and some confusion. Fortunately, the battery, Captain Bowyer, had been sent forward at dusk to get forage, and an orderly was dispatched to put it on the march. The 6th (Irish) regiment was in rear, and I took two companies for a rear guard. The column had scarce got into motion before a party of horse rushed through the guard, knocking down several men, one of whom was severely bruised. There was a little pistol-shooting and sabre-hacking, and for some minutes things were rather mixed. The enemy's cavalry had charged ours, and driven it on the infantry. One

Federal was captured and his horse given to the bruised man, who congratulated the rider on his promotion to a respectable service. I dismounted, gave my horse to Tom to lead, and marched with the guard. From time to time the enemy would charge, but we could hear him coming and be ready. The guard would halt, about face, front rank with fixed bayonets kneel, rear rank fire, when, by the light of the flash, we could see emptied saddles. Our pursuers' fire was wild, passing over head; so we had few casualties, and these slight; but they were bold and enterprising, and well led, often charging close up to the bayonets. I remarked this, whereupon the Irishmen answered, "Devil thank 'em for that same." There was no danger on the flanks. The white of the pike alone guided us. Owls could not have found their way across the fields. The face of the country has been described as a succession of rolling swells, and later the enemy got up guns, but always fired from the summits, so that his shells passed far above us, exploding in the fields. Had the guns been trained low, with canister, it might have proved uncomfortable, for the pike ran straight to the south. "It was a fine night intirely for divarsion," said the Irishmen, with which sentiment I did not agree; but they were as steady as clocks and chirpy as crickets, indulging in many a jest whenever the attentions of our friends in the rear were slackened. They had heard of Shields's proximity, and knew him to be an Irishman by birth, and that he had Irish regiments with him. Expressing a belief that my "boys" could match Shields's any day, I received loud assurance from half a hundred Tipperary throats: "You may bet your life on that, sor." During the night I desired to relieve the guard, but was diverted from my purpose by scornful howls of "We are the boys to see it out."

Daylight came, and I tried to brace myself for hotter work, when a body of troops was reported in position to the south of my column. This proved to be Charles Winder with his (formerly Jackson's own) brigade. An accomplished soldier and true brother-in-arms, he had heard the enemy's guns during the night, and, knowing me to be in rear, halted and formed line to await me. His men were fed and rested, and he insisted on taking my place in rear. Passing through Winder's line, we moved slowly, with frequent halts, so as to remain near, the enemy pressing hard during the morning. The day was uncommonly hot, the sun like fire, and water scarce along the road; and our men suffered greatly.

Just after midday my brisk young aide, Hamilton, whom I had left with Winder to bring early intelligence, came to report that officer in trouble and want of assistance. My men were so jaded as to make me unwilling to retrace ground if it could be avoided; so they were ordered to form line on the crest of the slope at hand, and I went to Winder, a mile to the rear. His brigade, renowned as the "Stonewall," was deployed on both sides of the pike, on which he had four guns. Large masses of cavalry, with guns and some sharp-shooters, were pressing him closely, while far to the north clouds of dust marked the approach of troops. His line was on one of the many swells crossing the pike at right angles, and a gentle slope led to the next crest south, beyond which my brigade was forming. The problem was to retire without giving the enemy, eager and persistent, an opportunity to charge. The situation looked so blue that I offered to move back my command; but Winder thought he could pull through, and splendidly did he accomplish it. Regiment by regiment, gun by gun, the brigade was withdrawn, always checking the enemy, though boldly led. Winder, cool as a professor playing the new German game, directed every movement in person, and the men were worthy of him and of their first commander, Jackson. It was very close work in the vale before he reached the next crest, and heavy volleys were necessary to stay our plucky foes; but, once there, my command showed so strong as to impress the enemy, who halted to reconnoiter, and the two brigades were united without further trouble.

The position was good, my battery was at hand, and our men were so fatigued that we debated whether it was not more comfortable to fight than retreat. We could hold the ground for hours against cavalry, and night would probably come before infantry got up, while retreat was certain to bring the cavalry on us. At this juncture up came General Turner Ashby, followed by a considerable force of horse, with guns. This officer had been engaged in destroying bridges in Luray Valley, to prevent Shields from crossing that branch of the Shenandoah, and now came, much to our satisfaction, to take charge of the rear. He proceeded to pay his respects to our friends, and soon took them off our hands. We remained an hour to rest the men and give Ashby time to make his dispositions, then moved on.

Before sunset heavy clouds gathered, and the intense heat was broken by a regular downpour, in the midst of which we crossed the bridge over the west branch of the Shenandoah—a large stream—at Mount Jackson, and camped. There was not a dry thread about my person, and my boots would have furnished a respectable bath. Not withstanding the flood, Tom soon had a fire, and was off to hunt forage for man and beast. Here we were less than ten miles from Newmarket, between which and this point the army was camped. Jackson was easy about Massanutten Gap. Shields must march south of the mountain to reach him, while the river, just crossed, was now impassable except by bridge.

We remained thirty-six hours in this camp, from the evening of the 2d until the morning of the 4th of June—a welcome rest to all. Two days of light marching carried us thence to Harrisonburg, thirty miles. Here Jackson quitted the pike leading to Staunton, and took the road to Port Republic. This village, twelve miles southeast of Harrisonburg, lies at the base of the Blue Ridge, on the east bank of the Shenandoah. Several streams unite here to form the east (locally called south) branch of that river; and here too was the only bridge from Front Royal south, all others having been destroyed by Ashby to prevent Shields from crossing. This commander was pushing a part of his force south, from Front Royal and Luray, on the east bank.

The army passed the night of June 5 in camp three miles from Harrisonburg toward Port Republic. Ewell's division, which I had rejoined for the first time since we met Jackson, was in rear; and the rear brigade was General George Stewart's (Steuart's) composed of one Maryland and two Virginia regiments. My command was immediately in advance of Stewart's (Steuart's). Ashby had burnt the bridge at Mount Jackson to delay Fremont, and was camped with his horse in advance of Harrisonburg. The road to Port Republic was heavy from recent rains, causing much delay to trains, so that we did not move on the morning of the 6th. Early in the day Fremont, reenforced from Banks, got up; and his cavalry, vigorously led, pushed Ashby through Harrisonburg, where a sharp action occurred, resulting in the capture of many Federals—among others, Colonel Percy Wyndham, commanding brigade, whose meeting with Major Wheat has been described. Later, while Ewell was conversing with me, a message from Ashby took him to the rear. Federal cavalry, supported by infantry, was advancing on Ashby. Stewart's (Steuart's) brigade was lying in a wood, under cover of which Ewell placed it in position. A severe struggle ensued; the enemy was driven, and many prisoners were taken.

On the 7th of June we marched to a place within four miles of Port Republic, called Cross Keys, where several roads met. Near at hand was the meeting-house of a sect of German Quakers, Tunkers or Dunkards, as they are indifferently named. Here Jackson determined to await and fight Fremont, who followed him hard; but as a part of Shields's force was now unpleasantly near, he pushed on to Port Republic with Winder's and other infantry, and a battery, which camped on the hither bank of the river. Jackson himself, with his staff and a mounted escort, crossed the bridge and passed the night in the village.

Ewell, in immediate charge at Cross Keys, was ready early in the morning of the 8th, when Fremont attacked. The ground was undulating, with much wood, and no extended view could be had. In my front the attack, if such it could be called, was feeble in the extreme—an affair of skirmishers, in which the enemy yielded to the slightest pressure. A staff officer of Jackson's, in hot haste, came with orders from his chief to march my brigade double-quick to Port Republic. Elzey's brigade, in second line to the rear, was asked to take my place and relieve my skirmishers; then, advising the staff officer to notify Ewell whom he had not seen, we started on the run, for such a message from Jackson meant business. Two of the intervening miles were quickly passed, when another officer appeared with orders to halt. In half an hour, during which the sound of battle at Cross Keys thickened, Jackson came. As before stated, he had passed the night in the village, with his staff and escort. Up as usual at dawn, he started alone to recross the bridge, leaving his people to follow. The bridge was a few yards below the last house in the village, and some mist overhung the river. Under cover of this a small body of horse, with one gun, from Shields's forces, had reached the east end of the bridge and trained the gun on it. Jackson was within an ace of capture. As he spurred across, the gun was fired on him, but without effect, and the sound brought up staff and escort, when the horse retired north. This incident occasioned the order to me. After relating it (all save his own danger), Jackson passed on to Ewell. Thither I followed, to remain in reserve until the general forward movement in the afternoon, by which Fremont was driven back with loss of prisoners. We did not persist far, as Shields's force was near upon us. From Ewell I learned that there had been some pretty fighting in the morning, though less than might have been expected from Fremont's numbers. I know not if the presence of this commander had a benumbing influence on his troops, but certainly his advanced cavalry and infantry had proved bold and enterprising.

In the evening we moved to the river and camped. Winder's and other brigades crossed the bridge, and during the night Ewell, with most of the army, drew near, leaving Trimble's brigade and the horse at Cross Keys. No one apprehended another advance by Fremont. The following morning, Sunday, June 9, my command passed the bridge, moved several hundred yards down the road, and halted. Our trains had gone east over the Blue Ridge. The sun appeared above the mountain while the men were quietly breakfasting. Suddenly, from below, was heard the din of battle, loud and sustained, artillery and small arms. The men sprang into ranks, formed column, and marched, and I galloped forward a short mile to see the following scene:

From the mountain, clothed to its base with undergrowth and timber, a level—clear, open, and smooth—extended to the river. This plain was some thousand yards in width. Half a mile north, a gorge, through which flowed a small stream, cut the mountain at a right angle. The northern shoulder of this gorge projected farther into the plain than the southern, and on an elevated plateau of the shoulder were placed six guns, sweeping every inch of the plain to the south. Federal lines, their right touching the river, were advancing steadily, with banners flying and arms gleaming in the sun. A gallant show, they came on. Winder's and another brigade, with a battery, opposed them. This small force was suffering cruelly, and its skirmishers were driven in on their thin supporting line. As my Irishmen predicted, "Shields's boys were after fighting." Below, Ewell was hurrying his men over the bridge, but it looked as if we should be doubled up on him ere he could cross and develop much strength. Jackson was on the road, a little in advance of his line, where the fire was hottest, with reins on his horse's neck, seemingly in prayer. Attracted by my approach, he said, in his usual voice, "Delightful excitement." I replied that it was pleasant to learn he was enjoying himself, but thought he might have an indigestion of such fun if the six-gun battery was not silenced. He summoned a young officer from his staff, and pointed up the mountain. The head of my approaching column was turned short up the slope, and speedily came to a path running parallel with the river. We took this path, the guide leading the way. From him I learned that the plateau occupied by the battery had been used for a charcoal kiln, and the path we were following, made by the burners in hauling wood, came upon the gorge opposite the battery. Moving briskly, we reached the hither side a few yards from the guns. Infantry was posted near, and riflemen were in the undergrowth on the slope above. Our approach, masked by timber, was unexpected. The battery was firing rapidly, enabled from elevation to fire over the advancing lines. The head of my column began to deploy under cover for attack, when the sounds of battle to our rear appeared to recede, and a loud Federal cheer was heard, proving Jackson to be hard pressed. It was rather an anxious moment, demanding instant action. Leaving a staff officer to direct my rear regiment—the 7th Colonel Hays —to form in the wood as a reserve, I ordered the attack, though the deployment was not completed, and our rapid march by a narrow path had occasioned some disorder. With a rush and shout the gorge was passed and we were in the battery. Surprise had aided us, but the enemy's infantry rallied in a moment and drove us out. We returned, to be driven a second time. The riflemen on the slope worried us no little, and two companies of the 9th regiment were sent up the gorge to gain ground above and dislodge them, which was accomplished. The fighting in and around the battery was hand to hand, and many fell from bayonet wounds. Even the artillerymen used their rammers in a way not laid down in the Manual, and died at their guns. As Conan said to the devil, " 'Twas claw for claw." I called for Hays, but he, the promptest of men, and his splendid regiment, could not be found. Something unexpected had occurred, but there was no time for speculation. With a desperate rally, in which I believe the drummer-boys shared, we carried the battery for the third time, and held it. Infantry and riflemen had been driven off, and we began to feel a little comfortable, when the enemy, arrested in his advance by our attack, appeared. He had countermarched, and, with left near the river, came into full view of our situation. Wheeling to the right, with colors advanced, like a solid wall he marched straight upon us. There seemed nothing left but to set our backs to the mountain and die hard. At the instant, crashing through the underwood, came Ewell, outriding staff and escort. He produced the effect of a reenforcement, and was welcomed with cheers. The line before us halted and threw forward skirmishers. A moment later, a shell came shrieking along it, loud Confederate cheers reached our delighted ears, and Jackson, freed from his toils, rushed up like a whirlwind, the enemy in rapid retreat. We turned the captured guns on them as they passed, Ewell serving as a gunner. Though rapid, the retreat never became a rout. Fortune had refused her smiles, but Shields's brave "boys" preserved their organization and were formidable to the last; and had Shields himself with his whole command, been on the field, we should have had tough work indeed.

Jackson came up, with intense light in his eyes, grasped my hand, and said the brigade should have the captured battery. I thought the men would go mad with cheering, especially the Irishmen. A huge fellow, with one eye closed and half his whiskers burned by powder, was riding cock-horse on a gun, and, catching my attention, yelled out, "We told you to bet on your boys." Their success against brother Patlanders seemed doubly welcome. Strange people, these Irish!

While Jackson pursued the enemy without much effect, as his cavalry, left in front of Fremont, could not get over till late, we attended to the wounded and performed the last offices to the dead, our own and the Federal. I have never seen so many dead and wounded in the same limited space. A large farmhouse on the plain, opposite the mouth of the gorge, was converted into a hospital. Ere long my lost 7th regiment, sadly cut up, rejoined. This regiment was in rear of the column when we left Jackson to gain the path in the woods, and before it filed out of the road his thin line was so pressed that Jackson ordered Hays to stop the enemy's rush. This was done, for the 7th would have stopped a herd of elephants, but at a fearful cost. Colonel Hays was severely wounded, among many others, and the number of killed was large.

Many hours passed in discharge of sad duties to the wounded and dead, during which Fremont appeared on the opposite bank of the river and opened his guns; but, observing doubtless our occupation, he ceased his fire, and after a short time withdrew. It may be added here that Jackson had caused such alarm at Washington as to start Milroy, Banks, Fremont, and Shields toward that capital, and the great valley was cleared of the enemy.

We passed the night high up the mountain, where we moved to reach our supply wagons. A cold rain was falling, and before we found them every one was tired and famished. I rather took it out on the train-master for pushing so far up, although I had lunched comfortably from the haversack of a dead Federal. It is not pleasant to think of now, but war is a little hardening.

On the 12th of June the army moved down to the river, above Port Republic, where the valley was wide, with many trees, and no enemy to worry or make us afraid.

LITTLE MAC'S RIGHT
FLANK IS IN THE AIR

STONEWALL JACKSON HAD TORMENTED the Federal troops in the Shenandoah and forestalled the early moves to reinforce McClellan. But once Jackson's forces had retreated down the Valley and successfully fought off his pursuers at Harrisonburg and Port Republic, his strategy became clear. Having won a valuable respite for the main southern army, he would reinforce Johnston at Richmond. Lincoln was now free to send McDowell south to strengthen McClellan's right flank.

Near the end of May, a heavy rainstorm brought the Chickahominy River to flood crest, catching two Union corps south of the swollen stream, while the other three corps of McClellan's army were still on the northern bank. Any use of the bridges across the river was questionable, and in effect, McClellan's army was temporarily cut in two. Confederate General Johnston saw his opportunity. He launched an attack against the two Union corps south of the river.

Catton says: "Johnston's battle plan was excellent, but its execution was sadly bungled. Orders were misunderstood, James Longstreet got his division on a road someone else was supposed to use, Huger's division ran into this roadblock and was crowded completely out of action, a number of Longstreet's brigades were unable to reach the firing line, and the pulverizing attack which was to have been delivered by overwhelming numbers turned into a straight slugging match in which much of the Confederate advantage was unused. McClellan ordered Sumner to take his corps across the river and get into the fight, and Sumner—a tough, literal-minded old-timer, who had been an Army officer before McClellan was born and who joined a complete lack of imagination to an unshakable belief in the overriding importance of obeying orders—got his men across on a bridge that was beginning to float away, and gave the shaken Federal lines the stiffening they had to have. Much of the fighting took place in a wooded swamp, where fighting men stood in water to their knees, and where details went along the firing lines to prop wounded men against trees or stumps to keep them from drowning. The Confederates gained a good deal of ground on May 31, lost most of it the next morning, and finally accepted a drawn battle which left things just about as they had been before the fighting started."[*]

[*] Bruce Catton, *Terrible Swift Sword*, pp. 312–13.

The battle's most important casualty was the Confederate General Joseph E. Johnston. His place was taken by General Robert E. Lee. The appointment of this brilliant strategist to the command of the Army of Northern Virginia was the best move the Confederacy ever made.

General Lee immediately set the Confederate troops to digging trenches and improving fortifications around Richmond. By strengthening his field works so they could be held by fewer troops, Lee was able to marshal a stronger striking force on the Federal flanks. He was already probing McClellans' right flank which ended somewhere north of Richmond. To determine its strength and extent, he sent for his chief cavalry officer, Brigadier General J. E. B. Stuart. He explained the need for information and instructed Stuart to select troops for the expedition. The following day, June 11, he supplemented his orders with written instructions: "You will return as soon as the object of your expedition is accomplished, and you must bear constantly in mind, while endeavoring to execute the general purpose of your mission, not to hazard unnecessarily your command or to attempt what your judgment may not approve; but be content to accomplish all the good you can without feeling it necessary to obtain all that might be desired. I recommend that you take only such men as can stand the expedition, and that you take every means in your power to save and cherish those you take. You must leave sufficient cavalry here for the service of this army, and remember that one of the chief objects of your expedition is to gain intelligence for the guidance of future operations. . . . Should you find upon investigation that the enemy is moving to his right, or is so strongly posted as to render your expedition inopportune—as its success, in my opinion, depends upon its secrecy—you will, after gaining all the information you can, resume your former position."

Stuart's Ride Around McClellan[*]

BY DOUGLAS S. FREEMAN

THESE, THEN, WERE AMONG THE MEN Stuart selected—Fitz Lee, his cousin "Rooney," Will Martin, Jim Breathed, von Borcke, John S. Mosby, Redmond Burke, William Farley—these and the best 1200 troopers that the cavalry had. Stuart chose them quietly on the 11th but apparently did not notify them. The secrecy which the commanding General enjoined on him was to be respected to the letter. All the cavalry heard was a vague rumor that something was afoot.

At 2 A.M. on the 12th, Stuart himself, in the cheeriest of moods, awak-

[*] From *Lee's Lieutenants*, Vol. I.

ened his staff. "Gentlemen, in ten minutes," he announced, "every man must be in the saddle." Soon the troopers were astir in the camps near Mordecai's and around Kilby's Station on the R. F. & P. Railroad. Quietly and with no sounding of the bugle, the long column presently was in motion. Its route was toward Louisa Court House, as if it were bound for the Valley of Virginia, whence reports had come of a dazzling victory by Jackson. Reinforcement of "Stonewall" presumably was the mission of the cavalry, though nothing was confided by Stuart.

Along empty roads, past farms where the women waved handkerchiefs or aprons and the old men stared admiringly at the display of so much horse flesh, the troopers rode all day. Twenty-two miles they covered and then they went into camp on the Winston Farm near Taylorsville, close to the South Anna River. Scouts were sent out; troopers were left to their sleep. When everything was in order, Stuart mounted with "Rooney" Lee and rode to near-by Hickory Hill, the home of Mrs. Lee's family and of Col. William C. Wickham of the Fourth Cavalry. With him and with the other members of the household, "Rooney" Lee had high converse. Stuart, for his part, went to sleep in his chair.

Back at camp before day, Stuart had a few rockets sent up as signal for the start, but again he permitted no reveille. He had, by that time, reports from his scouts that residents said the enemy was not in any of the country to the southeastward, as far as Old Church, twenty miles distant by the shortest road. Confidently, then, when men and beasts were fed, the column got under way again. The moment it turned toward the East, a stir went down the files: despite the ostentatious suggestion of a march to Louisa, the men had suspected that McClellan's flank was their objective, and now they knew it. The day for which they had waited long had come at last. They were to measure swords with the enemy. Greatly must the leading squadron have been envied; deep must have been the resentment of Will Martin's Legion that it was designated as rearguard.

Stuart ere long left the road and called the field officers in council. Every eye was fixed expectantly on him as he sat with careless rein on his horse. Not more than five feet ten in height, wide of shoulder and manifestly of great physical strength, he had a broad and lofty forehead, a large, prominent nose with conspicuous nostrils. His face was florid; his thick, curled mustache and his huge wide-spreading beard were a reddish brown. Brilliant and penetrating blue eyes, now calm, now burning, made one forget the homeliness of his other features and his "loud" apparel. The Army boasted nothing to excel that conspicuous uniform—a short gray jacket covered with buttons and braid, a gray cavalry cape over his shoulder, a broad hat looped with a gold star and adorned with a plume, high jack boots and gold spurs, an ornate and tasselled yellow sash, gauntlets that climbed almost to his elbows. His weapons were a light French saber and a pistol, which he carried in a black holster. On the pommel of his regulation saddle an oilcloth overall was strapped; behind the saddle was a red blanket wrapped in oilcloth. When he gave commands, it was in a clear voice that could reach the farthest squadron of a regiment in line. On this particular morning of the 13th of June—a Friday at that—the information he had to confide to his field officers was not to be shouted on the battlefield: it was to be explained in an undertone. He gave his instructions for the next stage of the reconnaissance and aroused among his young companions no less enthusiasm than he exhibited.

The officers galloped off to take their places with their regiments. On moved the column, through the woods and past fields where the young corn was showing itself. When the force came in sight of Hanover Court House, which straggled on either side of the road, horses and men were observed. Scouts reported that the enemy was there, but in what strength, nobody in the neighborhood knew. Quickly it was decided that Fitz Lee should take his regiment and swing around on a detour to the right, which would bring him back into the Courthouse road, South of the village. When sufficient time had elapsed for Lee to reach that intersection, Stuart was to advance with the remainder of the column. The Federals would be cut off and would be forced either to surrender or else to scatter where they might be caught.

Fitz Lee and the 1st regiment slipped off; the Ninth Virginia and the Jeff Davis Legion waited impatiently. At length, fingering his watch, Stuart gave the word. Scouts near the Courthouse came out from their hiding places. The Southerners prepared to charge. Almost immediately a few shots rang out from the village. The game was flushed! Stuart shouted a command. The column dashed down the road. It was too late. The "blue birds," the Confederates dubbed their enemy, had taken alarm and had fled under cover of the dust they raised. Stuart found nothing in the village except its few residents, the old Courthouse where Patrick Henry had won his first reputation as a lawyer, and the tavern where the great Revolutionary had worked for his father-in-law. Ill luck it was to lose the first covey! Fitz Lee made it worse by getting his regiment into a marsh, the passage of which was so slow that the enemy passed the crossroads before he arrived.

"Rooney" Lee's 9th Virginia was now in front. Its advance squadron, scouting ahead of the regiment, was under the eye of the regimental Adjutant, Lt. W. T. Robins, a daring man. As the Federals had escaped down the Courthouse road, that approach to the village of Old Church was certain to be guarded. Stuart accordingly left the highway about a mile below Hanover Courthouse and, turning South, followed the route via Taliaferro's Mill and Enon Church. The march was hard and rapid. As the sun climbed toward noon, heat radiated from every field, but nobody heeded it. Only one thing mattered—to find and to drive the enemy.

Seven miles were covered from the turnout. Enon Church was passed. Then, near Haw's Shop, anxious eyes caught a glimpse of bluecoats. Some were ahead, some in a field on one flank. Before Stuart's leading squadron knew what was astir, the Federals came forward with a roar. They dashed almost to the head of the column, fired a shot or two and veered off.

"Form fours! Draw saber! Charge!" Stuart commanded. Almost as uttered, his orders were obeyed. The Confederates swept forward—and again to no purpose. A few videttes were surprised and captured. Some dismounted men were bagged. The others escaped. All the satisfaction the Southerners had was in the behavior of their captives. Some of the prisoners stared at Col. Fitz Lee, then broke into grins of recognition and greeted him as "Lieutenant." They were of the 5th United States Cavalry, formerly the 2nd, with which Lee had served as a junior officer. He was as glad to see his former troopers as they were to hail him. Inquiries were made concerning old friends; familiar jests were revived. It was difficult to believe that the disarmed, laughing troopers and the smiling young Colonel represented opposing armies mustered to slaughter each other.

Rumors, coming presumably from the prisoners, were that the 5th was in front and would make a stand, but Stuart's column moved on at a trot and encountered no opposition. When the van approached Totopotomoy Creek, a difficult little stream, with its banks a maze of underbrush, there was every reason to assume that the Federals would contest the crossing. Perhaps the very fact that the bridge had not been destroyed was a reason for suspecting an ambush. Cautiously Stuart held back the main column, dismounted half a squadron, and sent these men forward as skirmishers. Once again there was disappointment. The Federals had left the barrier unguarded.

It was now about 3 P.M. Old Church was distant only two and a half miles. There, if anywhere, the enemy would offer resistance, because wagon trains from Piping Tree Ferry and from New Castle Ferry would have to pass that point in order to supply the right wing of the Federals North of the Chickahominy. Inasmuch as the Federal cavalry were known to be under Stuart's own father-in-law, Brig. Gen. Philip St. George Cooke, a Virginian and a renowned trooper of the "old army," it could not be that he had neglected that important and exposed crossroad.

For the first time that day, military logic was vindicated. Word came back that the enemy was at a stand and apparently was awaiting attack. Stuart did not hesitate. Straight up the road, the only avenue of approach, he ordered the column to charge. With a shout and a roar, the leading squadron, that of Capt. William Latané, dashed forward and threw itself squarely against the Federals. For a few minutes there was a mad melee, sword against pistol; then the Federals made off. A brief second stand, a short distance to the rear, ended in the same manner. When the clash was over, Captain Latané was dead, pierced by five bullets. The Federal Captain who had met him in combat was said to have been wounded badly by a blow from Latané's saber. A few Federals had been shot or slashed. Several bluecoats were killed; others were taken prisoner. Five guidons were among the trophies—the first that had fallen into the hands of the expedition.

Fitz Lee was all entreaty to push on and to rout his old regiment. Stuart gave ready permission but admonished the Colonel to return quickly. In a few moments the 1st Virginia rushed on and soon reached the camp of the troops who had disputed the advance. The tents were deserted, though supplies were there in abundance. As there was no time to collect even what the men most coveted, the place was fired; but an ambulance that contained a keg of whiskey, a regal seizure in the eyes of some, was rescued and made ready to move with the column. Of men, only a few near-by stragglers could be found. The Federals, strong or weak, had disappeared. Nothing was to be gained, of course, by pursuing them toward their main force, which could not be far distant.

Stuart was now fourteen miles from Hanover Court House. He had established the main fact he had been directed to ascertain: there was no Federal force of any consequence on the watershed down which he had ridden. Of that he could be sure in the report he made General Lee when he returned . . . but should he return the way he had come? The enemy would expect him to do so. If alert, the Federals would burn the bridge across the Totopotomoy. In event they neglected that, they would of course watch the route by which the column had advanced, and they could waylay the Confederates at or near Hanover Court House, to which the most direct road led. Stuart could not skirt the village and strike for the South Anna, in an effort to cross that stream and swing back to Richmond on a wide arc. The bridge across the river had been burned; the fords were impassably high. So Stuart reasoned. If he turned back, danger and perhaps disaster, he concluded speedily, would be his.

Perhaps, at the moment, or when he came to write his report, Stuart magnified the difficulties of a march to the rear, because he yearned for the more exciting adventure that lay ahead. Nine miles to the Southeast was Tunstall's Station on the York River Railroad, McClellan's main line of supply. A great achievement it would be to tear up that railway and, if only for a day, or even for a few hours, to have the Federal Army cut off from the base at the White House. How the public would praise that feat!

Escape from Tunstall's would not be impossible. By turning South there, and riding eleven miles, Stuart could reach Forge Bridge on the Chickahominy. That crossing, his troopers from the neighborhood told him, had been burned but not beyond quick repair. At Forge Bridge, moreover, there was every reason to believe the column would be well beyond the left flank of the enemy. Once he was across the Chickahominy, Stuart told himself, General Lee could make a diversion that would keep the enemy from dispatching a sufficient force to trap the returning column.

Was the whole plan feasible? Did it hang together? When the expedition had been planned, Stuart had suggested that the cavalry might ride entirely around the enemy: why not prove himself correct? Would the Federals have along the railroad sufficient infantry to destroy him? Could Union troops be sent down the railroad in time to intercept him? Cavalry he could beat off, but a heavy column of infantry . . . well, it was certain that the enemy would not expect him to do what he was contemplating. That was an excellent reason for doing it. Besides, whatever the risk, there was a chance of striking terror into the heart of "a boastful and insolent foe." He would do it!

There was not a shadow of misgiving on his face. Nor, when he found that his Colonels doubted the wisdom of his choice of routes, was there any hesitation. Their misgiving hardened his resolution. He thanked them for their ready promise to go on, if he saw fit to do so, and he prepared to start forthwith. Ostentatiously he inquired of the farmers around Old Church which road he should take to Hanover Court House, and how far it was. Quietly he picked his guides from soldiers who resided in the country he was to enter. Over them he placed R. E. Frayser, who knew every bypath to Tunstall's. Then, turning to John Esten Cooke, he said: "Tell Fitz Lee to come along. I'm going to move on with my column."

"I think," Cooke replied laughingly, "the quicker we move now the better."

"Right! Tell the column to move on with a trot."

Stuart touched the flank of his horse and was off. He was relishing every moment of the drama he was shaping. "There was something of the sublime," he later wrote, "in the implicit confidence and unquestioning trust of the rank and file in a leader guiding them straight, apparently, into the very jaws of the enemy, every step appearing to them to diminish the faintest hope of extrication."

The road of this adventure skirted to Pamunkey River. Southward, the country was populous. To the North and Northeast were great plantations that ran down to the meadows and swamps by the streamside. As the column passed, the women, the girls and the old men at every house came out to greet the first gray-clad soldiers they had seen in weeks. Now and again there would be a delighted scream of recognition, whereupon some dust-covered boy would break ranks, would leap from his horse and embrace mother or sister.

None of these jubilant residents knew much concerning the enemy's strength or position. Vessels were known to be at Garlick's Landing; wagon trains passed frequently; a guard was on the railroad at Tunstall's. That was all the information Stuart could get. Once, at a great distance to the Southwest, tents could be seen. It was surmised that they were McClellan's headquarters. A strange and thrilling experience it was, surely, to look on the opposing commander's lodging place from his own rear!

At Tignor's house, two miles and a little more from Old Church, Frayser turned out of the road that led East to Piping Tree Ferry, and took the right fork toward Tunstall's Station. Weary though the men were, they straightened up expectantly: the New Kent boys explained that the column was getting closer to the point where the enemy must be waiting. Stuart turned ere long to Cooke: "Tell Colonel Martin," said he, "to have his artillery ready, and look out for an attack at any moment." The staff officer hurried back, delivered his message to the commander of the rearguard, and was returning to the front, when a cry was raised: "Yankees in the rear!" Swords instantly were gripped tightly. In a moment there was relieved laughter. Some one had attempted a joke. The men slumped back in their saddles, but not too comfortably. Next time the alarm might not be false.

At length, the weary horses brought their tired riders to Wynne's Shop and Hopewell Church, whence a road led two miles East to Garlick's Landing. Satisfied that stores were there under scant guard, Stuart detached two squadrons to swoop down on the place, to bring off any horses they might find, and to apply the torch to what could not be moved off. The main column continued on its way. Its road now showed evidence of heavy travel and of vast alarm. Overturned wagons and booty of all sorts lay temptingly at hand, where it had been left or thrown away by Federals who had been warned that "the rebels" were descending upon them. Perhaps, at Tunstall's, which now was distant only two miles, the enemy might be squarely across the front of advance.

Stuart accordingly sought to close the column and to bring the artillery to the front. Breathed was most willing, but, at the moment, he was engaged with a foe distinctly his own. Both the rifle and the howitzer were in mud from which all the lashing of the teams and all the tugging and swearing of the gunners could not extricate them. Ankle-deep in the hole, the fieldpieces seemed in fixed position. Further pulling at them settled them more deeply.

"Gott, Lieutenant," said a sergeant of German stock, "it can't be done!"

Then he eyed the ambulance which, with its treasured keg of liquor, had been captured in the camp at Old Church. "But," the sergeant added, "yust put dat keg on der gun, Lieutenant, und tell the men they can have it if only they vill pull through!"

Lt. William McGregor thought the experiment worth trying, so, with a laugh, he had the keg placed on the gun. In a moment, the gunners sprang into the knee-deep mud and, with one mighty effort, lifted the piece to dry ground. The other gun the artillerists handled in the same way.

They had their reward, but they missed the excitement. While they were wrestling with the pieces, before the sergeant made his proposal, Frayser dashed up to Stuart from the direction of Tunstall's Station, which the head of the column was approaching. The scout reported that one or two companies of Federal infantry were guarding the station and that the commander of these troops had seen and greeted him, in broad Germanic accent, with the odd challenge, "Koom yay!" as if he hoped Frayser would ride into the lines and surrender. Stuart did not take time to laugh at this. Swiftly he advanced the head of the column within striking distance and then ordered: "Form platoons! Draw saber! Charge!"

Down swept the cavalry at a thunderous gallop. The Federals, too few to resist, scattered almost instantly. Some were captured. Others fled to the woods. Immediately, designated Confederates began to tear up the railroad in the delighted knowledge that, if they succeeded, they would separate the Federal Army from its base. Redmond Burke hurried off to set fire to the bridge across Black Creek. His fellow scouts proceeded to chop down the two telegraph poles nearest the station. The excited troopers who were ordered to remain in their saddles watched and yearned to search the countryside for prisoners and abandoned wagons for booty. It was a high moment—perhaps the most triumphant the cavalry had known since the time when the earliest volunteers had galloped across the fields that bordered Bull Run.

Now, above the chatter of the troopers and the sound of the axes on the telegraph poles, there came a shrill whistle from the westward. A train was approaching—did it bring infantry to oppose the raiders? From the boldness of the whistle blast, the engineer could not know that Tunstall's was in the hands of the Confederates. Derail the train, then; shoot or capture the troops on it. Quickly the orders were given. Lieutenant Robins ran to a near-by switch and tried to throw it, so that the train would run into the siding, but he had no success in hammering at the heavy lock. Such obstructions as near-by men could find at the moment they hurled on the track. The troopers in ranks were hurried into ambush alongside the railway to open fire if the train stopped or left the track when it hit the obstructions.

All this was swift work, not well done. Before the slowest of the cavalry-men could get to cover, the train came in sight—a locomotive and a string of flatcars loaded with soldiers. Almost immediately, the brakes began to squeak. Was the engineer going to make a regular stop at the station or had he seen the obstructions? Slower still the train. A few of its passengers stepped off as if they knew it would remain at Turnstall long enough for them to stretch their legs or to find water. Then, nervously, one excited trooper in ambush fired his pistol. The engineer heard it, perhaps sensed danger and immediately put on full steam. All along the right of way, Southerners' pistols rang out. Startled Federals on the train dropped from wounds or threw themselves face down on the flatcars to escape the fire. Will Farley seized Heros von Borcke's rifle, spurred his horse till it caught up with the locomotive and, at a gallop, shot the engineer. The train continued on its way, fast and faster. A moment more, and it was out of range. Very different the story might have been if only the artillery had been near the head of the column. Now that the train had escaped them, there was nothing for the disappointed troopers to do except to round up the men who had fled from the station or had jumped from the train.

Stuart, for his part, had to make another decision: should he continue on his way, cross the Chickahominy and make for his own lines, or should he rush down the railroad and attempt to capture the Federal base at the White House? A vast prize that was, distant a bare four miles. If it could be destroyed, McClellan would be compelled to retreat. The world would resound with praise for the leader of 1200 men who had forced 100,000 to break off an attempted siege of Richmond. Such a prospect was alluring, but was it not an enticement? A start could not be made until the arrival of the two squadrons that had been sent to Gar-lick's Landing. Billowing, high-mounting smoke from that direction showed that those troopers had reached their objective. They probably had escaped, but some time might elapse before they rejoined. Every mo-ment that passed after the arrival of the train at White House would be devoted to preparation for defense by a garrison that might be consider-able. If it put up a good fight, reinforcements from McClellan's front might come down the railroad and close the Confederates' line of retreat. Regretfully, then, but decisively, Stuart shut his mind to this highest adventure of all.

It was now close to nightfall, but not too dark to observe that many army wagons with deserted teams were standing around the station. Some of the vehicles had been in plain sight from the moment the column had arrived. A larger, tangled park was at a little distance. As rapidly as might be, the mules were unhitched. Then the wagons, which were loaded with grain and coffee, were set afire. While this was being done, something more than an hour after the train had passed, the squadrons from Garlick's Landing arrived. Their commander, Capt. O. M. Knight, reported that he had destroyed two schooners and many wagons loaded with fodder. Not to be outdone by this feat, the rearguard, when it closed, presented the General with twenty-five prisoners who had surrendered in the belief that they were surrounded.

As the bogged guns also had come up, without any evidence on the part of the gunners that the liquor in the keg had been too abundant, the column started at once for the Chickahominy. Stuart had no additional report of pursuit but he knew, of course, that the reflection of the fires and the report of the escaped trainmen and passengers would bring quickly toward Tunstall's Station a powerful force. He had reasoned at Old Church that the worst of his danger would be behind him after he passed Tunstall's. Now it did not seem so probable that retreat and return would be unmolested.

As the column wound southeastward to the vicinity of old St. Peter's Church, and then turned southward to Talleysville, the road grew worse. When Talleysville was reached by the vanguard at eight thirty, a Federal hospital of 150 patients was found. Stuart did not molest it or disturb the surgeons and attendants. Close by, a well-stocked sutler's store naturally did not fare so well—fared so ill, in fact, that its entire contents were taken and devoured, to the distress of some who ate too much as surely as to the grief of the sutler, who lost all.

A bright moon now had risen, one day past the full, and lighted the bad road, but the column was strung out almost back to Tunstall's. It had to be closed again. Midnight came before the exhausted artillery horses dragged the pieces to Talleysville. From that point, the distance to Forge Bridge on the Chickahominy was less than seven miles. With good fortune, it could be negotiated before daylight. To expedite the march, which must be rapid if the column was to escape, the 165 prisoners were mounted on such of the captured animals as were not required for the troopers whose horses had broken down. By putting two prisoners on each of the fresh Federal mules, Stuart saved the time that would have been lost had any of the captives been afoot.

Long as each minute seemed, the night was almost ended. If all went well, the winding, marshy river soon would lie between the Confederates and their pursuers. Lt. Jonas Christian, who lived at Sycamore Springs on the bank of the Chickahominy, told his commander that he knew a blind ford on the plantation that was nearer than Forge Bridge. The columns could slip across at that ford and would not waste precious hours putting timbers in place on the site of the destroyed bridge. Should the Federals be near, they scarcely would learn of this plantation crossing and would press on to Forge Bridge.

Hopeful as was the outlook, the ride from Talleysville to the river was the hardest part of the long, long march. The 9th Virginia, in advance, became separated from the 1st and made Stuart acutely anxious for a few minutes. When he relaxed after finding that the 9th was ahead, he became so sleepy that he, the tireless man who never knew exhaustion, put one knee over the pommel of the saddle and nodded often. Sometimes he lurched so far that John Esten Cooke had to ride closely by his side to keep him from falling off. Like Stuart, the whole column dragged. Troopers snatched sleep, horses staggered. There was no alarm. If Federals were in pursuit, the rearguard caught no glimpse of them.

The moon was just being dimmed by a faint light in the East when

Jonas Christian turned from the main road into the lane of Sycamore Springs, and led the head of the 9th Regiment past the house and down toward the blind ford. An hour more and, with the stream behind the rearguard, a halt could be called and some rest could be given men and mounts. In a double sense, day was dawning. Presently young Christian halted in startled surprise. He was at the ford, but it had a different appearance from the easy crossing he had known all his life. In front of him was a wide, swift and evil-looking stream that extended far beyond its banks. The placid Chickahominy was an angry torrent, the ford might be a death trap. Col. "Rooney" Lee, the first officer of rank to arrive at Sycamore Springs, stripped quickly and swam into the stream to test it. Strong and powerful though he was, he had to battle to escape being drowned or swept downstream.

"What do you think of the situation, Colonel?" John Esten Cooke asked when the Colonel pulled himself ashore.

"Well, Captain," replied the half-exhausted swimmer, with all the courtesy of his stock, "I think we are caught."

That was the feeling of the soldiers. The jig was up! Some of the boys, reconciled to the worst, merely stretched out on the ground. They were too weary to stand, but almost intuitively, they held their bridle reins over their arms, in order to be ready were an alarm sounded. Other exhausted cavalrymen sat glumly on the ground and ate the remnants of what they had grabbed at Talleysville from the sutler's store. Gloom was written darkly on the face of all of them.

At that moment Stuart rode down to the ford. He had little to say. Carefully he surveyed the stream from the vantage point of his horse's back. Then he stroked his beard with a peculiar twist that his staff officers noticed he never employed except when he was anxious. He looked dangerous—just that. Silently he observed while young George Beale, son of the Lieutenant Colonel of the 9th, went into the water, and swam across with his father's steed, which he tied on the opposite bank. Then young Beale did the same thing with his own mount, an animal he had caught the previous day after his horse had run off. The boy was an excellent swimmer and he got over, as did the captured animal, but when Beale started back to the shore where the troopers were waiting, the horse insisted on coming back with him.

Encouraged by this success, the most experienced swimmers began in the same way to cross the river with their horses, but only a few of the men had enough skill in the water to breast so wrathful a stream. Stuart continued silently to watch. Presently the General summoned Turner Doswell and asked that daring courier if he thought he could reach the other side. When Doswell said he could, Stuart gave him a dispatch for General Lee. Doswell must ride hard, because the dispatch was a request to the commanding General to make a diversion that would keep the Federals from attempting to intercept the column on its return. It would return. Of that Stuart was certain; of the means, he was not.

Axes were sent for. Trees were felled in the hope that the men might clamber over them. The trees crashed in the desired direction, but they were too short to bridge the swollen stream. Thereupon, mustering their ingenuity, some of the men tried to make a crude ferry. They strung bridle reins and halters together to serve in place of a rope and, from fence rails, they made a raft. This floated so promisingly that some of the men put their belongings on it and ventured with it into the water. It tipped promptly and dropped its cargo.

Time was passing. The summer sun was up. A rumor was afloat that Federal infantry in large force were close at hand. Stuart decided that his one hope of escaping was to patch together a crude bridge. He directed the men who already had swum to the right bank—some thirty-five they were—to make their way downstream under Lt. Col. R. L. Beale. The main body, with a brief command, he ordered to the site of Forge Bridge. This familiar crossing of the Chickahominy, one mile below Sycamore Springs, was on the road from Providence Forge to Charles City Court House. From the north bank, a narrow stream of considerable depth led to an island. Beyond this island was the south channel, spanned in normal times by a second bridge. At the western end of the island, above this bridge, was a swampy ford which could be used in emergency.

All Stuart's information had been that the main bridge across the north channel was destroyed but that enough remained to make possible a reconstruction of the span. He found conditions precisely as described. The stream was swift but the channel was narrower than at the Sycamore Springs ford. Stone abutments on either side were intact. Stuart at once threw out videttes, posted his artillery and entrusted to Redmond Burke, as resourceful as dauntless, the task of building a bridge. Burke went instantly to work in the knowledge that delay might mean disaster, perhaps the destruction of the whole force. A skiff was found on the bank and was moored unsteadily in midstream by a rope tied to a tree. From a large abandoned warehouse near at hand, boards were stripped. Troopers and prisoners hustled several of these to the bank, placed the ends aboard the skiff, as if it were a pontoon, and in that way made a narrow if treacherously unstable bridge. Across this, one by one, troopers made their way. With their right arms they carried their saddles and with the left they held the rein of horses that swam on the downstream side of the bridge.

This soon proved too slow a procedure, and, besides, it would not permit of the passage of the guns. Burke accordingly decided to try the one expedient left him—to secure the main timbers of the warehouse and to see if they were long enough to span the river from the abutments. Battering-rams knocked down the frame of the structure. Tired men shouldered the old uprights and brought them to the streamside. From the skiff, with much effort, they were pushed across and then were lifted up toward the abutments. Stuart watched all the while and counselled with calm cheer. Ere long, the dangerous look faded from his face. He began to hum a tune. His eye told him the timbers were long enough, but even he must have held his breath when, with a final "pull together" the long beam was set. It rested safely on both banks, but with few inches to spare.

A shout went up from the men. They could save the guns! Quickly the bridge was floored. Over it, in renewed strength, the men made their way. Undamaged, the rifle and the howitzer lumbered across. The rearguard was drawn in. Fitz Lee, listening and watching the road, left five men to fire the bridge and then he, too, crossed to the island. By the time the rear of the column had passed out of sight, the flames were crackling. Then—as if to add the perfect dramatic touch to the climax—a little knot of Federal lancers appeared on the north bank and opened fire. The margin of escape from a clash with this contingent was ten minutes. Time consumed in building the bridge was three hours.

Now on the island, the Confederate cavalry found that the ford from the western end to the south bank of the Chickahominy was difficult but not impracticable. Horses might flounder through the successive swamps but, with luck, they and even the guns could pass. The prisoners went across first, and a most unhappy time they had. Again and again a mule, with two bluecoats astride him, would lose his footing and, in scrambling to recover it, would jettison his riders. The Confederate guard would laugh; the prisoners would swear. One of them, entangled in a third swamp, exploded violently: "How many damned Chicken-hominies are there, I wonder, in this infernal country!"

Downstream, meantime, Lieutenant Colonel Beale, early on the ground, had rebuilt a bridge, but the column did not know of this easy crossing until one of the limbers had been caught hopelessly in the swampy ford above. Had the artillery been sent down the island to Beale's bridge, Stuart might have been able to report that, except for the death of Captain Latané, and the runaway of a few horses which he had replaced five for one, he had sustained no casualties and had lost nothing entrusted to him.

When on the right bank of the Chickahominy at last, Stuart was thirty-five miles from Richmond. Twenty miles of this distance was East of the left flank of the enemy. The return meant tedious riding for the troopers and more suffering for their worn horses, but it was nothing compared with what had endured on the other side of the river. Stuart himself turned over the command to Fitz Lee, and hurried on to report. He rested for two hours at Thomas Christian's, then rode on to Judge Isaac Christian's plantation near Charles City Court House, stopped again for a cup of coffee at Rowland's Mill and, on the morning of June 15, forty-eight hours from the time he had left the Winston Farm at the beginning of the ride, reported to General Lee. The column moved more slowly from the river to Buckland, the seat of Col. J. M. Wilcox, and arrived in Richmond on the 16th, to receive a conqueror's welcome.

Stuart's satisfaction was as boyish as his feat had been extraordinary. Whether the raid was well conceived by Lee—whether it did or did not put McClellan on guard for the security of his right flank—is a question much disputed. That the whole was flawlessly executed, none would dispute. Stuart became the hero of his troopers and one of the idols of the public. Lee's confidence in him and his confidence in himself were confirmed. What was not less important, the cavalry was shown to be as truthworthy as the infantry.

"That was a tight place at the river, General," John Esten Cooke said to Stuart when it was all over. "If the enemy had come down on us, you would have been compelled to have surrendered."

"No," answered Stuart, "one other course was left."

"What was that?"

"To die game."

GENERAL LEE ATTACKS

STUART'S RIDE PROVED to Robert E. Lee that, just as he suspected, George McClellan's right flank was vulnerable. The main body of Little Mac's army was south of the Chickahominy in the swamp facing Richmond, while a single Union corps, under Fitz John Porter, extended less than ten miles north of the river. A Confederate flanking movement, if successful, would leave the main Federal supply route, the Richmond and York railroad, naked to attack.

General Lee, showing his willingness to gamble, ordered Jackson to come in from the Shenandoah Valley and upon his arrival reinforced him with one division. Jackson was to hit the Federal right flank, turn it, and roll up the Federal troops from the rear. Meanwhile Lee would mass 60,000 troops in an attack on Porter's flank to the south of Jackson's strike.

Lee's risk was considerable. He left only 25,000 troops in the trenches before Richmond. If McClellan detected Lee's withdrawal, the Federals would have a troop superiority of three to one and McClellan could march over the trenches right into the Confederate capital. But Lee's stake was more than just the frustration of McClellan's capture of Richmond; he was bent on the complete roll-up and encirclement of the Federal armies, bringing the war in the east to an end.

McClellan got wind of part of the Confederate strategy—a Confederate deserter confided the details of Jackson's plan of attack. But the cautious McClellan thought this to be only another sign of Confederate strength so great that they could mount attacks on two fronts at once. McClellan was only too willing to accept anything the Confederates wanted him to believe. And now he became an unsuspecting audience to Confederate theatricals. Catton says: "Magruder would be responsible for the defense of Richmond while Lee was making his attack north of the river, and although he would soon reveal grave shortcomings as a field commander he had undeniable talents in the dramatic arts; in the Old Army he had been an enthusiastic dabbler in amateur theatricals, and he at least knew how to create an illusion. Magruder now was told to move his men about, making a big noise and a great to-do, causing his outnumbered battalions to look both aggressive and numerous, acting as if he were about to unleash a terrible offensive all along the line—and, if none of this worked, to hold the line with the bayonet, dying hard and slowly until either

Lee or the end of everything came to him. Magruder had done this earlier with vast success. During the first few days at Yorktown he had sprinkled 5000 men along a 13-mile front, making McClellan believe that the position was much too strong for anything but the famous siege train; the whole operation leading Joe Johnston, when he reached the scene, to report that "no one but McClellan could have hesitated to attack. What Magruder had done once he could doubtless do again. Lee was betting the Confederacy's life on it.

"In the end Magruder played his role to perfection. The actor who put on such a poor performance that the entire production almost failed was, of all people, Stonewall Jackson himself.

"Famous for the speed of his marches, Jackson here came in late. He was supposed to arrive opposite A. P. Hill on the morning of June 26; at 3 P.M. on that day neither Jackson nor any tidings of him had arrived, and the hot-blooded Hill went ahead without him: crossed the river, marched east through Mechanicsville, drew up his men in a broad battle line facing the Federal position behind Beaver Dam Creek, and without further ado opened his attack.

"When Hill did this the entire operation was put in motion, irreversibly. Longstreet and D. H. Hill dutifully crossed the river in his wake, and Lee went with them, supposing that he would at once come in touch with Jackson, whose moving column ought to be just beyond A. P. Hill's left flank. Lee quickly discovered that no one had seen anything of Jackson; he was presumably on the way, but when he would show up was anyone's guess. Hill had made his move strictly on his own hook, and now Lee had two thirds of his army north of the Chickahominy and there was nothing in the world to do but go on with the assault even though it was exactly the sort of operation Lee had planned to avoid—a straight frontal attack on a position which was altogether too strong to be carried that way. Regardless of what had happened to Jackson, the offensive must be pressed hard; the thing that could not be forgotten for a moment was that McClellan right now was closer to Richmond than Lee was. If the Federal General were allowed to look up, even for a moment, he might see it.

"The Federal position was immensely strong, and Hill's men never had a chance. The attack was rebuffed with heavy loss—Hill's division sustained between 1300 and 1500 casualties, inflicting fewer than 400 on the enemy—and McClellan was elated. During the morning, when scouts confirmed the rumors that Jackson was approaching, he had sent Stanton an anxious wire: 'There is no doubt in my mind now that Jackson is coming upon us, and with such great odds against us we shall have our hands full. No time should be lost if I am to have any more reinforcements.' During the evening, while the fight was still going on, he telegraphed that 'my men are behaving superbly, but you must not expect them to contest too long against great odds,' but by nine o'clock at night he was full of confidence, reporting: 'Victory of today complete and against great odds. I almost begin to think we are invincible.' "*

* *Terrible Swift Sword*, pp. 327–28.

The Seven Days *

BY GENERAL THOMAS L. LIVERMORE

O<small>N THE 21ST, OR A DAY OR TWO SOONER</small>, we found ourselves camped close to the Chickahominy River, though not where we could see it. The atmosphere seemed to teem with miasma from the swamp through which the river ran, and these with the heat prostrated a large number of our men. The malaria worked in a singular manner. Men would be on duty up to the day they must lie down, and then all at once give up, and go to hospital or tent and to bed, some never to rise again. I had not yet recovered fully from my miserable weakness of the spring and seemed to be a fit subject for the disease, and it was not more than a week before the most debilitating diarrhœa seized me. Whiskey was issued to us at this time, but after the first few issues it was rather new and raw, and did not help me any. We used to get a gill a day, and when rations were issued nearly every man in the company, and the little drummer fifteen years old, marched up with a tin cup to take his grog.

On the 28th Colonel Cross was ordered to construct a bridge over the Chickahominy capable of bearing up artillery and wagons. We marched to the river where the 1st Minnesota Regiment, I think, had commenced the construction of a bridge, and went to work. Large details were sent into the water, and there up the stream they cut logs and floated them down to the bridge, where parties built great log piers and laid stringers from one to another, and across these laid logs corduroy fashion. The work was mainly done in the water, sometimes waist-deep, and amid mud and tangled underbrush. The men worked away with spirit, and did not let anything dismay them, and as we were composed largely of men who could wield the axe we got along finely. Details from the 64th and 69th New York were sent to aid us, and the colonel had a barrel of whiskey broached, at which the soaked soldiers could slake their thirst and fan up their fires *ad libitum,* and such was the effect of this generosity that the Irishmen of the 69th cheered Colonel Cross as the best of men. By the evening of the 30th, whether three or five days, the bridge was completed seventy rods in length, and it has been considered a remarkably difficult task to perform. General Sumner, I believe, christened it the "Grapevine Bridge," whether from the surrounding vines or its sinuosity, if it had such, I do not know. General McClellan says that it was the only bridge available above Bottom's Bridge to cross on, when Sumner's corps crossed the next day, as the rains had swelled the current so high that the rest were rendered useless.

* From *Days and Events.*

On the second day of our bridge-building or thereabouts the surgeon informed me that unless I lay down and kept still I should be attacked with the fever, and as death was not far from that, I complied with his directions and lay down in my shelter tent, a sick man. I could eat nothing which would do me any good, and it seemed as though my viscera were dissolving and passing away; I believe that such was partly the case. The surgeon tried three medicines on three days, with no effect, and he, I think, knew that my condition was critical. Sergeant George F. Goodwin, ordinarily a strong and lusty man, lay near me sick also. Time flew slowly with me unused to such pains and inactivity, and if our camp had remained stationary a week longer I might have been rolled up in my blanket and covered with earth.

All this time I, as one of the line, was in ignorance of what was transpiring, but the fact was that two corps had been pushed over the river and lay in imminent danger of an attack by the rebels in full force, and on the 31st it came. The enemy attacked the Fourth Corps, and, driving in Casey's division, bade fair to drive the whole back into the river. Orders were sent to General Sumner to move across. He hurried away with the 2d Division, and as soon as they had crossed we were ordered to follow. Of all this I was ignorant, but on the afternoon of the 31st I heard the firing across the river, and presently the regiment was ordered to move. The men began to pack up, and I was under the surgeon's directions to lie still, but I thought that it might be my only battle; that my promotion might depend on this chance; and I already had declined the place of sergeant major when Cummings was promoted in May that I might take a second lieutenancy when I was promoted and in my own company if I could; in short, I could not bear the idea of marching so far and enduring so much only to lose the first battle. So I got up, and packed my knapsack, buckled on my equipments, and rifle in hand took my place.

We marched along up the river until we came to the bridge, and then crossed its length in safety, though the swollen current already hid some of the timbers and threatened to lift them from their places. On the flat on the other side a battery struggled in a morass, but we halted not, and soon the muddy waters, horses, and guns were out of sight. The sounds of musketry were very distinct, sometimes rolling in prolonged volleys; but as we neared and the shades of evening fell, they seemed to be of platoons and companies and fitful. We hurried along anxious to reach the field before it was done, and to our unpracticed ears the volleys seemed to denote the close of the battle. It was a weary march to me, so weak that body and soul did not seem to care for each other's companionship. I sometimes fell down or lagged a little behind in difficult places, but I would not have feared death in my struggle to reach the front, and I kept with my company.

Night closed around us still marching, and the sounds of battle ceased. Our men feared it was over, and some grumbled; one, Watson, said, "This regiment never *will* get into a fight"; another, Howard, hoped we should; and I cared for nothing but battle, I think. We drew near the field and silence fell on the ranks, and as we marched naught was heard but an occasional low-spoken word, the fall of many feet, and the tinkling of canteens. Once we heard General Meagher bawling for the

Irish Brigade, and then we passed him and moved into what seemed a large field with woods around it. Some lights flashed in the distance, and the unaccustomed groans of a wounded man reached our ears, and as the column moved on a movement of the men in front and a word warned us to avoid a human form right in our track. One wounded man, dimly perceived in the darkness, moaned that he was cold. I think I smelled here the damp, mouldy odor which I have attributed to blood on other battle-fields; it might have been only the smell of the torn soil. We filed down silently across the field, and near the railroad went into line of battle, and then lay down on our arms. Some dark forms lay around which might have been the dead, but I chose to lie down and not search. Gove and I lay together, I think, and every little while a whisper would steal along, "Rise up!" "The rebels are coming!" but every time we lay down again.

We were within three hundred yards of the enemy's lines and we heard them shout, and a speech from one afterwards said to be Longstreet. On our right were woods, in our front the railroad parallel with our line, running along the edge of a deep wood, and on our left were woods and bush. The darkness was almost impenetrable around us, and the eye saw only a black wall where the trees commenced. Colonel Cross in the night, maybe toward morning, walked to the right of our line and entered a tent there standing a little way removed from us. He asked what regiment was there, and was informed by the inmates that the tent was the headquarters of a Texan regiment, or some other rebel regiment, and then he quietly walked back.

As it grew light, we stood to arms, and a party was dispatched into the woods on our right, where they stirred up and drove away a whole nest of rebels, though the regiment the colonel had stumbled on had discovered its proximity and stolen away before light. At some time early we had changed our position, I think, to the rear and stood in line of battle, and there we waited to give or receive.

A rebel courier rode up in front of us and inquired, through the twilight, if any one could direct him to General Pryor (a rebel). "Yes," said Colonel Cross, "this way, sir"; and stepping briskly out to him caught his rein and with drawn revolver made him his prisoner. The man had dispatches said to be important and rode a valuable horse; the former the colonel forwarded to headquarters and the latter to New Hampshire, confiscated to his own use, which last, though conflicting with the rule that captured property belongs to the Government, was doubtless a tempting thing ot do under the circumstances. (Perhaps, though, the colonel paid for the animal.)

The light of the day of June 1, Sunday, had hardly crept around the shadows of the woods, when over the railroad, a little to the left of our front in the woods, a thundering roll of musketry broke forth, and increased in noise until it was almost deafening; and if there were shouts and loud commands they were drowned in that awful noise. Bullets commenced to whiz over our heads in piping tones; sometimes they sounded like a very small circular saw cutting through thin strips of wood, and sometimes like great blue flies; some flew high, and some low, but none hit any one that I observed. Presently old General Sumner rode up to our colonel, and said in his deep voice, plain enough for us in the ranks to hear, "If they come out here, give 'em the bayonet; give 'em the bayonet, they can't stand that"; and rode away. The feelings of that first half-hour, while listening to our comrades in front, are indescribable. I can remember, though, that I waited with the most harrowing (if I may use the word) curiosity. The time was now come to shoot for country and liberty; we stood on our first field with the bullets whizzing around us. When *would* the time come? We did not see, that I recollect, any wounded men, and no horror abated the enthusiasm which the thunders of the fusillade excited; and yet we were all grave, and I for one was patient to rest or go, only the suspense was dreadful.

At length we moved forward in line of battle over the railroad. On the way some of the men in my company, poor fellows, marched into a pit full of water up to their chins, but they kept on. We lay down in the bushes at the edge of the woods and waited again. Up the railroad to our right the rebels we had driven out commenced to fire scattering shots at us, and I think our skirmishers replied. I do not know how near our troops connected on our right, but I believe that if the rebels could have known our exposed flank to be so near they could have made hot work for us. Some frightened, fleeing rebels came from the front right into our ranks, and were captured and told or shown how their lines must have been broken. In half an hour the musketry commenced subsiding, and suddenly our time came and we were commanded to rise up and march to the left on the railroad. The colonel was near our company on foot when he met General French on the railroad, his usual red face all afire and his eyes winking harder than ever; he was without a staff. The colonel asked him something about the fight, and he stammered out in the most excited way that his brigade (the 3d of our division) had met the enemy in the woods and were all cut to pieces. But the colonel, marching gallantly at our head, marched on, and when he had got just in rear of where the fight had been hottest, halted us. I think it was then that we saw two regiments of the Irish Brigade a little farther down the railroad, huddled into masses with their colors flying, trying to charge across the railroad, but as long as we saw them they only lost men and were unable to advance; they yelled, cheered, and swore, but somebody had got them into such an inextricable confusion they could do nothing.

Colonel Cross hurriedly strove to get orders from some one as to where to go in. General Howard had been wounded, and no one in command was near by, but time was not to be lost, so the gallant man ordered his line right forward. Firing had ceased in our front, and we knew not where we should meet our friends or our foes, but we plunged down the embankment into the dense woods and marched boldly ahead. My company struck an old road which lay right in our course, but those on the right penetrated through a jungle thick and swampy. We soon came to some of our dead men, and saw their blood in our path, and then I saw a man sitting up against a tree with his face toward us; he bore a ghastly wound upon his head, if my memory serves me right, and the poor fellow could not speak, for he motioned with his hand over his shoulder constantly, evidently, gallant fellow, telling us that our enemy were there. It was said that we drove in a rebel skirmish line, but this man was the only living creature I saw, and we had gone but a few rods farther, when we were quickly ordered to lie down and to fire by file.

We had eight hundred rifles, and I never shall forget how we made those woods ring with our firing. The rebels opened at once, and the bullets flew in myriads around us, humming deadly songs, hitting our men, and splintering the trees around us so that I thought the fine pieces of wood flew in my face. I, acting as a file closer, had to help keep the men at work, so I kept my eyes on them, and I do not recollect seeing many hit. Whether it was apathy from my sickness or ignorance of battle, or both, that kept my apprehension down, I do not know, but I lay there careless of bullets and death, noting my men and the splintering of the trees. The bushes were thick, and I did not see the rebels, and though perhaps the smell of the burning powder inspirited me a little, yet I was far more indifferent to everything than I could have supposed before. Orders had been issued for file closers to reserve their fire until they could aim at officers, and as I saw none I fired not at all, but presently Lieutenant Ballou turned to me and asked if I had fired. I said, "No," and he said I'd better, so I aimed in front low and where I supposed the rebels to be in the smoke, and loaded again. I fired perhaps once, maybe twice more, when we were ordered to cease firing and rise up. No bullets came then from the rebels, and we moved back a few feet and halted to re-form our line.

The rebels had gone, and we marched back over the railroad. Our dead lay in some places within three rods of the enemy's. Just as the fight was closing as I have related, Colonel Cross received a shot in the thigh and fell. He said afterwards that he was just about to order a charge when he was shot, but that then he told Lieutenant-Colonel Langley to do as he pleased, and he was carried off by some men (whom he sent back as soon as he reached another regiment, risking himself with strangers that they might help fight). Colonel Langley alleged that so many men had fallen he thought it best to fall back a little way to re-form, but whether he formed this determination before the rebel fire slacked or not I am ignorant. But it was lucky for him that the rebels left upon our rising or before as they did, for otherwise he would have had hard work to reconcile a necessity to re-form with our straight line and undaunted courage. It was said, and probably truly, that the 69th New York, or some other Irish regiment behind our backs, fired wildly into us and killed some of the men in the right companies, and they were reported in the newspapers as having charged and pinned the rebels to the trees with their bayonets. We moved into the open field whence we had moved at light and then counted our killed and wounded. The regiment had lost 186 all told, and among them were Colonel Cross and Major Cook, both wounded in their legs. As we stood there, old "Fighting Dick" came out of the scene of action with his coat off, looking very much exhausted. There were but few more shots on the field, if any, after our fusillade, and we moved into the adjoining bushes and lay down to rest and watch for the reappearance of the enemy.

First Lieutenant Somes, of "I" Company, resigned after "Fair Oaks" (the action just described), and then Frank Butler was promoted to his place and I to be second lieutenant of my own company in place of Butler.

We lay in the bushes all day June 1, and the night following, when all the bivouac was still, somewhere in the middle of the night, we were startled from our slumbers by a most hideous yell, which rang through the bush and roused us to arms in a twinkling, where we stood with beating hearts, to receive the enemy, until word was passed along that a private in a nightmare had encountered a rebel who gained hold of his throat, when he vented the yell which woke us. A grumbling chuckle stole along the ranks, which then sank down to slumber again.

When the retreat of the rebels was certain in a day or so, we moved up the railroad track two or three hundred yards toward Richmond, and then to the right two hundred more. How we got there, and how many times we moved, I do not remember, but we got there and pitched our tents and threw up a long line of works breast high, and near our position there was a fort or redoubt into which a battery went. I went down to the house where our wounded were treated, and saw our fellows. The surgeons were at work cutting off legs and arms with the most business-like air, and near by the rebel dead, to the number of hundreds, perhaps, were being buried in a long trench, where they were laid without mark or distinction, side by side, and covered with four or five feet of earth decently and without injury. The surgeons gave chloroform to a wounded rebel and amputated a limb, and while under the effects of the vapors, the poor fellow burst out with "I wish I had a cabbage," which was comic, notwithstanding the circumstances; but reflection might invest this homely wish with the garden, the cottage, and the loved ones who haunted his wandering imagination then, and one might wonder if he ever saw them again, but wonder in vain.

Colonel Cross did not forget his duty in caring for his wound, but directed a lot of arms to be collected from the field and turned in to his credit, which I think I assisted in doing. I could find no shoulder straps for sale, but I discarded my gun and knapsack, and put as good a blouse on as I could find, and with a sword and belt felt, if I did not look, the officer at last.

The pickets raised alarms quite often, and we would rouse to arms at once night or day, and sometimes lie upon them, and once in this month of June, while we lay in the night on our arms, I saw an annular eclipse of the moon.

I must not omit to mention that some new regiments joined our division after Fair Oaks; one was the 2d Delaware and the other the 7th New York Volunteers. The 7th New York was a regiment of Dutchmen and Germans, commanded by a handsome man with light complexion, blue eyes, light side whiskers and hair, named Von Schaack, said to be a captain in the Household Guards of Prussia, who, traveling in this country when the war broke out, got leave of absence and came out as major of the regiment and by the casualties of the service had risen to colonel. The regiment had been stationed in barracks at Newport News, and was a very trim battalion with clean clothes and changes in their knapsacks. Their drill was exact, but they had been taught a few changes on the Prussian plan in the manual, such as coming from the "right shoulder shift" to "order," and *vice versa;* at least it was supposed to be

Prussian, and that movement was so commended to us we adopted it afterwards. This regiment came into our brigade. The men of the 7th were heard to complain that they had had no soft bread for *three days,* at which our men laughed greatly. Finally we went into camp along the line of breastworks within a few feet of them and devoted ourselves to what we were pleased to call the siege of Richmond.

The woods in front of us were cleared away to the depth of a hundred or more yards, and this space our batteries and ourselves overlooked; beyond this in the woods we maintained a continuous picket line which was opposed by the rebels' picket line at a distance from it of two hundred yards, more or less. While the lines were in the woods the men were posted where practicable behind the trees, but when it ran into the open ground they hid behind the bushes and stumps. Each regiment took its turn at doing picket duty, and did it well or indifferently as the regiment differed from the rest. We soon found out which were reliable on this duty from the number of alarms, for the poor picket line would become alarmed at a single shot sometimes, and imagining that the rebels were advancing would rattle away along the whole front until the whole camp was in arms and somebody would stop them. This did not trouble us much except in standing .to arms at first, and we took a deal of grim comfort in doing our own duty without such alarms. But at length our reliability proved our bane, for when one of these regiments would run in we would have to march out and take their places and thus do double duty.

When we went out, each man took his tree and there watched intently in his front until relieved. It was the duty of the officers to go to their posts occasionally and see that all of them were awake and alive; this was dangerous in a greater or less degree, as the rebels chose to fire more or less, and at two hundred yards they sometimes made it quite lively work to get from one tree to the other. On occasions this duty was tremendous, as, for instance, once my company was on duty, each man behind his tree, for thirty-six hours, and for some reason unknown to us we had no reliefs. It was excessively hard to keep awake, and I think it was at this time that we found ———— asleep lying under a bush as he had been stationed. It was a hard case to punish a man for sleeping who was obliged to lie so long on the ground, but his fault might imperil the army, and the captain ordered him to take post behind the roots of an upturned stump which barely sheltered him, while the rebels could fire right down a road at him if he showed a hand's-breadth. He moved once and a bullet struck just above him; again, and another came, when he got mad, and then with great care got his rifle up over the stump, aimed and fired at the fellow who abused him; but at the instant he fired, Johnny fired, too, and the bullet struck close by him, and then he kept quiet. The captain sent him there with the remark that he thought he wouldn't sleep much there, and he didn't, I think, for his life depended on vigilance.

Once on a rainy day we were cold and cross, and for fear of alarm or with a view to cease hostilities between pickets, we were ordered not to fire unless the enemy advanced; but there was a rebel behind a tree who would fire at our men, and I went to Russell, who stood opposite him, to see if he couldn't still him. Russell raised his piece, but his hand trembled so that he couldn't aim. I got him a drink of whiskey and quinine which warmed him, when he fired, but Johnny reported himself surviving with a rifle ball. Russell tried again, but Johnny lived, and at length Captain Cross came up and took the rifle and fired. We could see the bark fly from the tree, and Johnny kept still thereafter, but whether from lead or caution I knew not.

At another time Charles Bailey reported that he had seen a rebel in the bushes very carefully pull down a tall stem, tie a handkerchief filed with leaves to it, let it spring back, and then, crouched low, begin to agitate it gently, with the evident purpose of inducing some one to expose himself in firing at it, that he might kill him; that he did fire, but, instead of at the handkerchief, at a point where he supposed his body to be; and that afterwards the handkerchief hung still upon the bush.

On one occasion a part of our regiment was on picket just in front of the redoubt before mentioned, when after dark the rebels made an advance, or our men believed they did, and a fusillade of a violent character broke out along the line, whereupon a battery in the redoubt opened upon the rebels, with canister, perhaps, and shortly after one of our men was brought in, his back torn its whole length by one of the missiles from the battery. He had lain down, but the guns were depressed so much that the shot raked the ground almost. The month wore along, and we in our ignorance supposed and hoped that ere long we should march to Richmond, and some climbed the trees and looked wistfully at the spires of the city which were in sight.

On the 25th a reconnoissance in force went out from Heintzelman's corps, which lay on our left, and after a spirited engagement drove the rebel picket line out of sight amid great cheering from ourselves, who had mounted the works and witnessed the encounter. But even this success did not tempt our commander to move forward, and we still waited and watched. On the 26th we heard the gruff notes of artillery far to our right, and our surmises of a battle were confirmed by the news that Mechanicsville had been fought and won, but under what circumstances we knew not. On the 27th we heard again the sounds of battle on the right, and sometimes the fusillade would be heard muttering far to the right, and then would come nearer and nearer until it would roll down to our own front, when the pickets, nervously expecting the battle, would join in the rattling chorus; but each time the fire subsided and we who had rushed to arms again relinquished them. Our men climbed into the trees and saw the quick flashes of the guns at nightfall, and from them and the rapidly succeeding discharges we knew how hot the fight was. During the day Sergeant Cook, of the 8th Illinois, rode by us, and I engaged in a little conversation with him. The light of another morning found us still waiting for the battle, and again we passed a day of alarms, but now we hoped for a relief from suspense, for we struck tents; but we moved only a little to the left, and took post at the works, waiting as we supposed for an attack, but at night we pitched tents again, and then struck them and lay down to sleep.

The rumors which came to us were various: at first the battle was said to have been won, and then a "change of base" was expected and soon, until we closed our eyes with the sage conclusion that McClellan, having decoyed the main force of the enemy away to our right, was about to

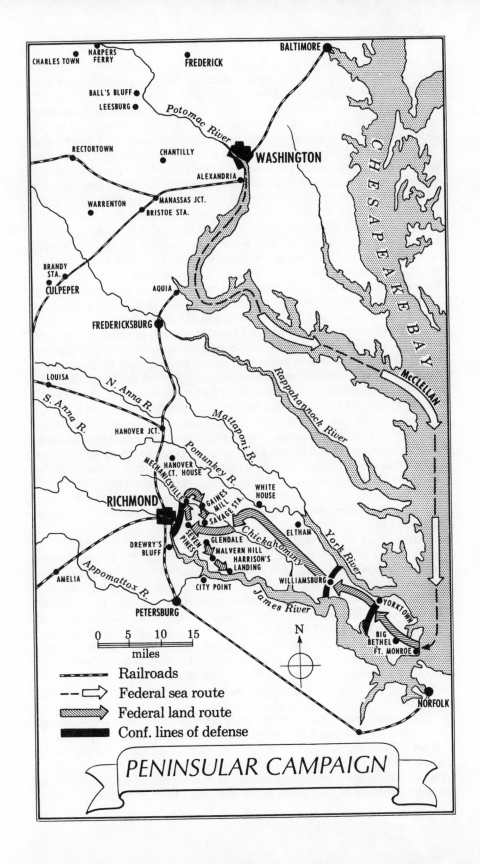

CHARLES TOWN •   HARPERS FERRY •   FREDERICK   BALTIMORE •

BALL'S BLUFF •
LEESBURG •

Potomac River

RECTORTOWN •   CHANTILLY •

WASHINGTON

ALEXANDRIA

WARRENTON •   MANASSAS JCT. •
BRISTOE STA. •

CHESAPEAKE BAY

BRANDY STA. •
CULPEPER

AQUIA •

FREDERICKSBURG •

McCLELLAN

LOUISA •
N. Anna R.

S. Anna R.

HANOVER JCT. •

Rappahannock River

Mattaponi R.

Pomunkey R.

HANOVER CT. HOUSE •
MECHANICSVILLE •

RICHMOND

GAINES MILL
SAVAGE STA.

WHITE HOUSE

Chickahominy

ELTHAM •

York River

DREWRY'S BLUFF •

SEVEN PINES
GLENDALE
MALVERN HILL
HARRISON'S LANDING

WILLIAMSBURG

AMELIA •

Appomattox R.

CITY POINT •

James River

YORKTOWN

BIG BETHEL
FT. MONROE

PETERSBURG

N

NORFOLK •

0   5   10   15
miles

—·—·— Railroads
- - -▷ Federal sea route
▨▨▷ Federal land route
▬▬ Conf. lines of defense

PENINSULAR CAMPAIGN

advance on our left and carry Richmond by storm. To think of this and then of the real state of affairs is sickening. We whipped the rebels at Fair Oaks, but McClellan did not follow up his victory for the reason that he did not dare to send over the rest of the army at New Mechanicsville bridges in front of the rebel batteries, although in four days after he did send over a division in front of the same batteries. Then he lingered and lingered, waiting for good weather and to make his bridges better, but promising the President that as soon as the river fell he would attack the rebels in their works; yet he did nothing until the 25th, although the weather was good enough and he did cross *some* troops over the bridges. All this time, after having nearly lost one corps by separating his army by the river, he had, after defeating the attack upon it, left his army in precisely the same predicament, and wrote that an attack on his part would open the way to defeat in detail, perhaps never reflecting that defeat in detail could come from an attack by the enemy as well. He went over to the right and did the very thing necessary for defeat in either case, by ordering his troops to stay there and receive the attack, and letting his troops on the left remain idle. The rebels *did* come down on his right, and defeat it after one repulse, and then McClellan ordered it to retreat to our side of the river, and the whole army to move in retreat to Turkey Bend, choosing to do this rather than to stand and fight or assault and capture Richmond while the rebels were getting across the Chickahominy.

I have been informed that General Hooker wanted to move forward on the 25th, but McClellan wouldn't let him, and General Hincks has informed me since that he condemned McClellan at the same time or before we left Fair Oaks. And, by the way, his regiment, the 19th Massachusetts, with another part of the Second Corp, were engaged in the reconnoissance of the 25th. But we were ignorant of all these matters, and on the morning of the 29th we only knew that a defeat had been experienced, which information came to us perhaps with the Irish Brigade, which had been up to help Porter's men on the right who had been defeated by the rebels at Gaines's Mill.

Camps were all dismantled, wagons were loaded and sent away, the whole line of works, with bare tent poles behind it, amid bunks and nests, assumed a lonesome look, and finally the head of our column countermarched away to the left. We passed by the old field in which we had lain on the morning of June 1 and entered the copse beyond, and here Lieutenant Ballou, with ten men of our company, was detached and sent out toward the railroad and we marched on a little farther, then the rest of us were sent out as skirmishers and the regiment moved on. Captain Cross took half of the men and deployed on the other side of the railroad among the buildings around which the Irish Brigade fought June 1, while I deployed mine in the edge of the bushes in which we had slept on that night.

The ground had been a commissary's depot where I stood. Around me were tents standing, and the various bunks and arbors of a camp; behind, on the edge of the railroad, a pile of boxes of hard bread, as tall and large a few yards, a little ravine ran with whiskey and molasses which had been spilled out; other commissary stores were scattered about, rendered as nearly worthless as they could be by dirt, and just at the left of my line, as an ordinary dwelling-house, perhaps, said to have contained 8000 boxes, the rations of bread for our army sufficient for three days, was on fire. The flames roared and snapped, and its vicinity was exceedingly hot, and we had a sort of savage joy in seeing the destruction which would keep our rations from the enemy.

Presently there were some shots in front of us from Ballou's party, and then a man, Corporal Law, I think, came running through my line. I stopped him, and he said that five hundred rebels had come on them and they were obliged to run, but I saw no occasion to go yet, so I put Tom in the line, and waited. Presently, to my astonishment, I saw the tall forms of the men of the right section striding back over the railroad in a great hurry for the rear, which struck me with astonishment, as they composed the captain's line. I looked back in vain for the regiment, which had moved clear out of sight into the woods, and the last I heard from it was the voice of Captain Rice, who, standing in the plain behind us, cried out, "When you retreat come this way!" I had been under the captain's orders, and I knew not where he was, so I held on still. I heard a shout on my right, and looking saw in among the trees some men in blue gesticulating and indicating that the enemy were coming in on my right, but as the enemy had not struck me yet, and my left was well protected by the infernally hot pile of bread, I walked along and cautioned my men (numbering with the one or more from Ballou's force a dozen or so) to hold their ground and to fire when they saw a head. So, crouched behind bushes, boxes, and tents, we waited, and it was not long, for presently the rebels came, and standing in or beyond the bushes opened a lively fusillade upon us. I stood this a little while, and then, thinking they were coming too close, I ordered a retreat. My men came back coolly and with precision, and we halted among the trees a few rods away, where we felt at home. Here I found those who had warned me on my right, they proving to be Ballou and his men. He and I held a council of war, and as the rest seemed to have left us to our fate, we resolved to post our men behind the trees and stay here until we were driven away. So we did, and when the rebels showed themselves in front we banged away at them, and kept them back. We did this a few minutes when a new feature appeared. The roar of a battery behind us was followed by the shriek of a shell which burst in our rear and hurtled in fragments around us, and as there seemed to be no knowledge behind us of the advanced position in which we were fighting, we concluded to retreat far enough to get out of our own fire.

We took up a new line a hundred yards back and waited events. The rebels did not get very near to us this time. Some one in our rear, frightened evidently, cried out for us to come in, but we sent a man back to inquire of the colonel if those were the orders, and received word to stay where we were until ordered in. However, a relief was soon sent to us, and we moved back and took post in the regiment, which lay along the edge of the woods in which we were. Behind was a large plain on which troops were moving, and we then perceived that the regiment lay in line with a large number of other troops. A few crackling shots and the skirmish line came in on the run, reporting that the rebels were coming, and we laughed at the sticking-out of Keller's and Cross's eyes. Then we lying down opened fire, and the rattle of musketry continued for a mile on our right. For my own part I could not see the rebels, but the flying bullets proved that they were in front, and we urged the men in their firing, and I never had a jollier time in a fight. Ballou and I saw a stump close to us and took shelter behind it. It was a poor one, though, for a bullet came through it right between us and hit Corporal Gay in the thumb.

We cracked away a few minutes, and then the rebels left our front and we threw out skirmishers. I was on the line, and for half an hour or more we watched carefully, suspecting every yellow log or bush, but saw no rebels. Just behind or near me a man lay in a red shirt. I went to him and saw that he was dead drunk; he probably had partaken too freely of the stream of whiskey and molasses.

While we lay here our artillery and the enemy's fired at each other. Old Conell went up to a house to get some water and found such a crowd around the pump or well as to prevent his approach, but presently a shell dropped among them or in the house, at which they all ran away but Conell, who then deliberately filled his canteens.

Presently, at about noon, the order to move was given, and the regiment moved out into the plain on the retreat. As we neared a piece of woods our once gallant and trim band filed out of their cover and joined the column, forlorn and dirty, and with instruments battered into ugliness. They evidently had been demoralized a little. (I should say that our loss was not great, perhaps half a score, and that this fight has gone by the names of "Peach Orchard" and "Orchard Station.") Long columns marched away in front of us and on the side of the railroad, the bed of which we pursued. The sun's heat was intense, and our men suffered a great deal. Our march was but two miles or so, however. We halted near Savage's Station and lay down on the ground. By the middle of the afternoon some of our men were sunstruck, and Captain Cross sent one or two to a hospital, not far away, for ice. They succeeded in getting there just before the enemy, who were advancing on our position, and then brought the ice to us, with which we revived our sufferers.

At about 4 P.M. the enemy attacked the lines in front, which were concealed from us by a gentle eminence, and soon the roar of battle was quite heavy; added to this the columns of fire and smoke from burning stores, and clouds of dust from moving bodies, made the heat more terrific. Once a great pillar of white smoke shot up hundreds of feet in the air and in sight of all. This was said to be the railroad bridge being blown up, but I have read somewhere since then that a train of cars laden with ammunition, headed by a locomotive, was set to going and then exploded while under headway. Be that as it may, I do not recollect more than one explosion. Some shells flew over our heads and some struck near by, but I do not recall any casualty from them in my regiment. When the musketry grew hot over the hill, we were ordered up to support the line engaged, and lay down pretty near the crest. Standing on this about dusk I saw the Irish Brigade, or a portion of it, charge down the slope on the double-quick and cheering lustily, and I presume they repulsed the enemy, as we were not called on. There were troops from other corps, however, engaged, and I could not see the whole engagement, but the firing gradually grew less heavy, and at perhaps nine o'clock ceased.

We had no idea that we were to run away immediately, and some of us had taken satisfaction in visiting the spot where the 7th New York had lain and taking from the plethoric knapsacks, which they had abandoned, bedding for the night. But we soon were put on the move and left the hospitals and field in the hands of the enemy. The Adjutant General's Report of New Hampshire troops gives Hiram W. Carlton as killed on this day, but I do not think he was killed then, though whether on June 1 or afterwards I cannot remember. It grew pitch dark and walking became insecure. Sometimes we were stopped, and we waited for the brigade in front of us to move along, and when we came up to where they had delayed, would find that some declivity or difficult passage had impeded their march, and I have a dim recollection of hearing General Meagher's voice in our front at one of these places. Sometimes we hurried along almost at a trot, and passed quickly woods, fields, white with dry grass or weeds, bushes, and stragglers, and finally, at perhaps two in the morning, we caught up with a lot of troops and trains halted, and after marching among them for some time came to a dead stop. Then we heard through the darkness General Richardson swearing like a trooper, and after considerable of that we moved on. Our weary feet carried us over a narrow bridge on each side of which was blackness.

We climbed a hill, deviated a little to the right, and lay down, tired and sleepy, and our rest on the ground was too sweet to relinquish without a sigh; but hardly had we made ourselves quiet and comfortable, when the quick command to rise up came to us, and we hurried down the hill again with orders to tear up the bridge, but when we got there a stream of fugitives hurrying across forbade our touching it, and we waited watching them. Here came a regiment of stragglers in disorderly haste, some hobbling with sore feet, some too lazy to move very fast in other circumstances, and some loaded with too many traps. Among the last was a gray-haired old sergeant of the Irish Brigade, with many years of service indicated by the chevrons on his arm, and the cause of his straggling made evident by a woman and child—his wife and child, probably—whom he guarded. It seemed a cruel time for them. Sutlers and bummers, drummers and cooks, came filing along in a stream which grew thinner and thinner, and then the astonishing spectacle of a noble battery greeted our eyes, unattended by infantry, and the drivers urging their horses toward the bridge; they had been left by mistake.

The crowd had dwindled to a few flying men when we commenced taking up the planks and timbers. Our men plunged into the water, and we quickly took up everything on which a living thing could cross and carried all to our side. The dawn came stealing on us and revealed the plain on the other side lonesome and bare, with perhaps a few rebel cavalry who came in sight on the farther edge searching for stragglers and reconnoitering, and the swamp in front of us, black and tangled, seemed to put a barrier between them and us. A few yards above and a few yards below the clearing which had bordered the bridge ceased, and the white-oak trees and tangled brush hid the passes if there were any. This was called the "White-Oak Swamp." We crawled up the hill again and rested by a little house awhile, and then moved a little farther on and halted in column.

The sun rose and darted his fiery rays upon us, and as most of us had eaten, we stuck our rifles up by the bayonets, fastened our blankets in the locks, and lay down in their shade to shun the scorching rays, and sleep. The dust of the barren plain was a sweet couch, and the stifling heat which enveloped us could not prevent profound sleep. A few, perhaps, bestirred themselves to complete the breakfasts which had been begun at our first halt when we had crossed the bridge, but there seemed to be a soothing quiet around us, and we could praise the economy of Nature which made the pleasure of sleep so intense as to requite us almost for our labors and deprivations before. What I thought or dreamed of I do not know, but suddenly, whatever visions of peace hovered around me were dispelled by the thunders of artillery, the shriek of shells, and the horrid humming of their fragments. Hell seemed to have opened upon us. In a twinkling every man was on his feet, the blankets were slung over our shoulders, and the men were in their places, shrinking under the storm, perhaps, but steady and prepared for action. The rebels had planted a large number of cannon on the other side of the swamp, and having pointed them at the host which lay on the plain had fired them all at once. And what a scene it was! As far as the eye could see the tired troops were springing to arms; batteries were whirling into position or hurrying out of reach with horses on the gallop; wagons drawn by teams of frightened mules, driven by frantic drivers, rattled away to the woods; the teams of six mules which belonged to a pontoon train which were surprised watering at the swamp, fled up the hill and away, leaving their boats; stragglers and non-combatants of all kinds fled in all directions from the fire; while the air was filled with clouds of dust and wreaths of smoke which spread out from the fierce clouds, breathing fire of bursting shells, and the ear was dimmed with explosions, shouts, and a storm of other noises. The ——— New York Volunteers was said to have run away when the first shell burst in front of it, and ——— battery, also of New York, I think, disgraced itself in like manner. But the rest of the troops quickly formed lines of battle, and when we in a very few minutes had reached our position and lain down in line with our faces to the enemy, order had come out of chaos. Near us, in front and rear and right, the troops of our own division lay in parallel lines; on other parts of the plain Smith's division and Naglee's brigade were in similar order, and a few rods in front the welcome sight of Hazzard's battery of our corps, firing with rapidity at the enemy, greeted our eyes. The enemy's fire was unremitting, and from noon until nearly dark we endured the slow torture of seeing our comrades killed, mangled, and torn around us, while we could not fire a shot, as our business was to lie and wait to repel attacks and protect our batteries. With every discharge of the enemy's guns, the shells would scream over our heads and bury themselves in the woods beyond, burst over us and deal death in the ranks, or ricochet over the plain, killing whenever they struck a line.

The ——— New York Volunteers in changing position either attempted to escape to the rear or mistook its colonel's orders and retreated right down toward us. General Caldwell, who was near, galloped to our rear and cried out, "5th New Hampshire, rise up!" and we rose, leveled our bayonets, and received the ——— at their points. This was a decisive barrier to further retreating, and after a little confusion they went back and behaved themselves. We were pleased to have rebuked this cowardice, but were sorry for Colonel ———, who was a brave man.

The shot hit some of our men and scattered their vitals and brains upon the ground, and we hugged the earth to escape this horrible fate, but nothing could save a few who fell victims there. I saw a shot strike in the 2d Delaware, a new regiment with us, which threw a man's head perhaps twenty feet into the air, and the bleeding trunk fell over toward us. The men seemed paralyzed for a moment, but presently gathered up the poor fellow's body in a blanket and carried it away. I do not know that I have ever feared artillery as I did then, and I can recollect very well how close I lay to the ground while the messengers of death, each one seemingly coming right into us, whistled over us.

In the midst of the storm I heard my name called. I could not believe that any one could call me to come at such a time, and waited; another call told me that Colonel Langley wanted me. I got up and walked to him with as much composure as I could assume, and he, pointing to a wood perhaps a quarter of a mile away, and the approach to which was under fire all the way, said, "Go over to General Caldwell in that wood and tell him that my men are getting killed where we are lying, and that I wish permission to move back three rods to get behind a knoll which will shelter me." The prospect was frightful, but it did not occur to me to do anything but obey, and I started. Ricker has told me that he lay and bet with a sergeant as to how far I would go before I got killed. I walked, sometimes, perhaps, ran, between the lines, and when I heard the thunder of a salvo stooped low to avoid the shells which whistled over. Men were killed very likely near me as I went, and a shot struck the wood into which I was about to go, but nothing hit me, and I reached the general and delivered my message. He asked how many had been killed, and I replied, I think, seven or eight, and he said, "Certainly! Tell the colonel to move where he pleases if he don't go off the field."

I retraced my steps through the same dangers, and proudly, maybe, delivered the message. I had just reached my place, when the order was given to rise up and face about. A cannon shot came quicker than the wind through my company, and close by me. Tibbetts fell and Nichols fell. We reached the line designated with a few hasty steps, and resumed our line with faces to the front. Nichols got up, and came back to the captain and said, "Captain, I am wounded and want to go to the rear." The poor fellow held up one arm with the other hand, for it dangled only by a strip of flesh. Some men went forward and hastily gathered up Tibbetts in a blanket and bore him away; the shot had gone through his body. We felt a little safer now. Hazzard's battery withdrew, cut to pieces, and with Captain Hazzard mortally wounded; and for a short time it seemed as if the rebels would fire unmolested, but Pettit galloped up with his battery of 10-pounder Parrotts and went into action, and then iron *did* fly, and the rebels had their hands full. Captain Keller sat up on a knapsack in front of us and gave warning when the shells were coming, and perhaps saved lives by it; anyhow it was a brave thing to do.

It was not a long time before we perceived that Captain Pettit's fire was getting too hot for the rebels, and they only fired at intervals; and at last

Pettit would hold up until they fired, when he would fire his whole battery at them, and as his shells went screaming over the tops of the trees to where the smoke was seen, our hearts bounded, for we perceived that their range was almost perfect; the rebels grew timid, and finally toward night they ceased firing, and we felt grateful to Pettit for it.

Once during the afternoon we saw a battery heavily engaged on our side close to the swamp on the right, and I think that we heard in that direction the rattle of musketry, perhaps where the rebels were attempting a crossing. The portion of the pontoon train which was left on the plain was set fire to in the afternoon, and the smoke and flames added to the infernal aspect of affairs. If ever stillness and rest were appreciated, I think it was on the verge of that evening, and even the dusty plain must have assumed a lovely hue when it was no longer disturbed by ricocheting shot. We found out the handiness of the outfit of the ——— New York again, for we got from the scattered knapsacks brushes to clean our clothes with. The discipline of our regiment was well illustrated this day, aside from its coolness in taking position and driving back the ——— New York, by Colonel Langley's asking permission to move so short a distance at such a time, and by poor Nichols's requesting permission to go to the rear when his arm was nearly severed from his body. He was safely carried away, but poor Tibbetts found his grave on that field. He was company clerk, had been a clerk, I think, at home, wrote a fine hand, and was a gentlemanly little fellow. The captain wanted him to go with the train on this march, but he was determined to see a fight, and had bravely carried his musket on the retreat until this time. We were told by those who came from the field hospital that he did not know that he was mortally hurt and lived three or four hours, and that he was buried there.

The sun had set and twilight approached when an order came for us to move. I should not omit to mention that during the afternoon on our left troops of ours, mostly out of sight in the woods and bushes, fired briskly for a long time, and that later the rattle of musketry extended farther to the left and finally to the rear of our position.

When McClellan retreated from his intrenchments, Lee, after he comprehended the almost inconceivable blunder of our commander, sent Magruder and Huger (whatever their positions as commanders were) chasing after us on the right flank, Hill and Longstreet in the center and Jackson on the left flank. It was Magruder who touched us at Peach Orchard and Savage's Station. He then deflected to the right as well as Hill and Longstreet, and it was Jackson who came upon and opened so fiercely on us at the White-Oak Swamp, and it was Hill and Longstreet whose musketry we heard on the left farther up the creek; the history cited says that Lee and Jefferson Davis accompanied the latter division of the rebels in their attack, and that after encountering our troops at the crossing they waited until 3 P.M. for Magruder and Huger to come and assist them. It probably was the encounter of the divisions of Longstreet and Hill or the right of Jackson which we heard on our left early in the afternoon. But they all moved off to the field in our rear, where the fight raged hottest at evening, or else they gave up the contest on our part of the field and kept still. At any rate, as I have said, firing ceased in our front, and it did in our vicinity on the left, but the rattle of musketry and fierce discharges of artillery were incessant in our rear, and at length, as I have said, the order came to move.

We marched hurriedly out of the plain and into the woods, following a road. We passed some of Rush's lancers, who carried lances with red pennants, apparently stationed or skulking along the road, and probably assuming the latter we laughed at them and called their flags hospital flags (being of the same color). But I have since been told that they fought bravely. A mile or two brought us close to the field, and here we met a stream of men, cannon, and horses coming to the rear, wounded, disabled, and stragglers. They hurried along, seeming jolly, and spreading reports of the hotness of the battle. We took the double-quick step and set up a cheer and rushed for the melee. A turn to the left took us into a road in the woods. On the right we caught glimpses and heard the soul-stirring cheers of a line of battle charging the rebels, which I have reason to believe was a part of the Second Corps, a part of the 2d Division, I think, in which General Hincks, then colonel of the 19th Massachusetts of the Irish Brigade, was wounded, though I may well be mistaken in this, for the fight raged far out of sight on either hand. As we filed in among the trees we recognized the battle-field by the bullets which spattered into the trees about us. We formed line of battle along the edge of the road, lay down, and listened to the roaring around us while we waited our turn. On each side and in front the musketry rolled and cannon flashed and roared, and to this day I can recollect one loud-sounding battery, the roar of which would burst out and echo in the forests with an almost gloomy sound, followed by the long, horrid shriek of its shell; but such was the confusion of positions to us that we could not tell whether it was a battery of friend or foe, nor where its shell sped to with its horrid shriek. Some thought it was a gunboat.

Darkness fell upon us, and still we waited, though once our men fired, I think in the left companies, upon the rebels who were close to us in the bushes, and we took some prisoners who strayed near us. Some of the Pennsylvania Reserves who had been engaged came straggling along from the left, and we thought they were retreating. After a while we were ordered across the road and lay down to rest a little, but a horseman came along and in the darkness held an altercation with Colonel ——, in which he accused him of leaving a battery which had been captured in our front, and threatened to report him. Colonel —— asked leave to explain before he did it, but he swore that he would grant no such leave, and then rode up to Captain Sturtevant, commanding our regiment, and said, "What regiment is this?" "The 5th New Hampshire," said the captain. "You have a fine regiment, Captain," said he; "and now I want you to go in there and capture that battery at the point of the bayonet without firing a shot." Word was passed around that this was General Phil Kearny, and we rose and marched silently across the road. By this time the sounds of battle had ceased in our front, but far down to the right the rattle of musketry still vexed the night. We marched into a grassy road over dead bodies, through shadows, and then halted behind a thick hedge or fence, and lay down in line of battle, and here we found not a rebel; but just across the fence, in what seemed to be a field, their torches flashed in their hands as they searched for their wounded, and cries for this regiment and that regiment arose in various quarters as they searched for the wounded of their corps, or some man wounded called his friends. They came very close to us sometimes, and I have the impression that our men reached out and took some of them prisoners as they ventured too near.

Colonel —————— was never censured that I know of, and it was said to be the fact that he had stood face to face with a rebel regiment and fired until all his ammunition was gone, and that then the rebel commander commanded him to surrender, at which Colonel —————— charged him with the bayonet and took his colors. The battery, I imagine, was nothing but the fence, and that the rebels did not care to move on when it was abandoned, or did not know it was abandoned, was evident. That it was the position of our lines is pretty certain to me, as our dead lay there and the rebels searched beyond it for their wounded.

At last musket and cannon, cheer and curse, had ceased. The whippoorwill with inexpressible melancholy wailed in the woods, the searchers for the wounded now and then spoke, and when one moved on the road, some poor wounded man in the woods would cry mournfully for water or moan for help. The darkness was intense and the time the most mournful of my experience on the field of battle at that time. Colonel —————— had left the regiment, and I was sent to find him for some purpose, but after wandering down the road awhile I gave it up and came back. In one place there lay asleep a crowd of soldiers on the side of the road. I waked one, and found they were the —————— New York deployed as stragglers. There was something said about General —————— being out of the way, too; where he was is more than I ever knew. At midnight or thereabouts the order came to move silently away, and we shook the men to wake them. The dead men lay so near them that in the darkness they could not be distinguished from the living except by touch, and some, I think, perhaps I, strove to wake a dead man. As we marched away a few of the wounded moaned and cried for aid, but cruel war did not permit us to stop, and we marched on; and I hope that in the immutable course of Nature it was their fortune to be succored on the next day, but no one has ever told me.

Captain ——————, it was afterwards ascertained, left the regiment and went away a short distance and lay down to sleep, and when we marched away he was left, and taken prisoner by the rebels. We marched silently away on the road through the woods, and at length came beside another column and we both moved together on the road. I recollect passing a church or house on the right of us, and that I was awakened from sleep by Lieutenant Ballou in the midst of another regiment, for I was so tired and sleepy I went to sleep marching and had walked into the other regiment's ranks. Ballou saw and followed me. I was cross at being waked even so kindly. What the road was, and how we passed it, I cannot recall. I know simply that it was darkness and toil, until we began climbing a hill and were greeted with advancing dawn.

At length, the welcome halt was called on an eminence and we lay down. Rations were very scarce, but I had a cracker or two to nibble and enjoyed them for my breakfast while the surgeon amputated the finger of a man beside me, who bore it without murmur or chloroform. The column was again formed and we marched almost to the farther verge of the hills we were on, and finally past a large house (Randolph's), and, if my memory serves me correctly, over the verge, and formed line of battle on the side of the hill, facing outward on the right flank of what I suppose was our semi-circular line of battle on that day. Again we moved, and coming up in front of the house mentioned before, formed column and moved in splendid array (for so shabby a division in looks) down through a field of green grass, and again formed line of battle, facing the right, on the crest of the hill, where we looked off for miles over the undulating surface of a beautiful country, with woods, fields of grain, and houses, as yet untouched by war. The peaceful prospect was not marred by a visible enemy, and we rested.

This was the morning of July 1, and we were on Malvern Hill. The army had retreated during the day before and that night, and on this morning were placed in position to meet the advancing enemy again, and I have an indistinct recollection of seeing General McClellan on the field that morning, but he went on board a gunboat soon after and stayed until late in the day. The sun rose as hot as ever and again prostrated some of the men.

Presently a battery appeared in our front and opened fire on us at the distance of perhaps three quarters of a mile. As we lay directly on the crest of the hill, we presented a fair mark and our quarters were decidedly uncomfortable.

Ammunition was sent to us, and I was ordered to distribute it. As I was performing the work, or about that time, a cannon shot took off the foot of a man lying near by, and I was glad when I could lie down again.

The slow hours dragged along until the middle of the afternoon, when the battle opened in earnest on our left far down in front. Cannon and muskets roared and rattled, the blue smoke made the air heavy, and cheers and yells made the heavens ring. We did not remain long in suspense; an order came to move, and setting our faces to the fighting ground, we shook from our feet the dust of that ground where we were fired at without the privilege of a return fire. We moved down the hill, in front of the woods, and into a road, and marched toward the left flank. On our right was a wheatfield and beyond it another field. Through this last one, as we passed it, the shot came whirling over and through our ranks, spending their force in the woods, where they cracked and crashed through limbs, trunks, and foliage. Our men in the line of battle cheered and cheered again, and our hearts bounded to think that we had met with a success. A color sergeant, with his colors all torn, came by us and reported victory. We filed into the field on our right and moved forward. But I must not omit to mention that while we marched by the flank a shot crashed through the ranks of the 61st New York which led us. Captain —— fell and cried out in mortal agony, "One man! two men! three men! carry me off the field!" The pitying men sprang forward and raised him up gently to find that the shot had only taken off his coat-tail.

As I have said, we formed line on our right and moved forward. At this time Colonel Barlow, of the 61st New York, was with General Caldwell, and seemed to be maneuvering the brigade for him and in a very cool manner. We moved forward, and as we neared the fight could see our men crouching behind the fences and hedges, firing with a will. The rest of the brigade moved away from us, where I knew not, and we halted behind what was, I think, West's house by the Quaker road. Here we lay down for a few minutes in peace, but very soon a rebel battery close in front opened on us with fury. Some of our officers had got into an out-building just in front of us for shelter, but a shell came right in among them and they left. General Howe, a fine-looking man, whose command was near by, rode up and ordered Captain Sturtevant to move over to the right and support one of our batteries. In order to do this the quickest way, we had to move directly in front of the rebel battery within not more than four hundred yards, over an open plain with no obstacle between us. The general rode away, and Captain Sturtevant, who was honest and brave, but a little wanting in decision, got up and, beginning to scratch his leg, said, "There! I am ordered to go and support that battery. If I go clear out of range I shall be too long, and if I go across we shall go right into the fire of the rebels; I don't know what to do!" Perhaps my boldness arose from having been placed in command of "I" Company that day, its officers being absent; but whatever might be the cause, I said to him, "Well, Captain, we might just as well go across under fire as to lie here, for we shall get killed here; so let us go!" "That's so," said he; "rise up, men! Forward, march!"—and away we went on the double-quick; and then how the rebel battery did pepper us! Shells flew all around us, and the wonder was that more were not hurt. I turned my head to the left and saw the battery and the gunners, springing to their work amid the smoke. I saw one pull the string, saw the flash of the piece, heard the roar, and the whiz of the shell, heard it burst, heard the humming of the fragments, and wondered if I was to be hit, and quicker than a flash something stung my leg on the calf, and I limped out of the ranks, a wounded man. My first impulse was to go to the rear, but the plain for a quarter of a mile was dotted with dust raised by the flying pieces and ricocheting shot, and I concluded that if I could, 'twere better to stay at the front than to be killed going to the rear. So I stooped down, opened the ragged hole in my trousers leg, and saw no blood, but the form of a piece of shell two or three inches long, printed in a cruel bruise on my leg; then I limped to the regiment, which had halted and lain down. I took my place, and was so vexed with pain that I swore at a Frenchman in my company roundly for being out of his place, and then commenced behaving myself. The same shell wounded two or three others, I believe.

We lay just behind the crest of a gentle slope and in front of some trees. In front of us first came the open field and then some woods. The rebel battery had been silenced somehow, but sharpshooters in the farther woods shot at us with uncomfortable precision. The battery on our left threw shell into the woods and I imagine made hot quarters for the sharp-shooters. In the course of an hour my leg had swelled badly, and my lameness was such that I could hardly step otherwise than on my toes. It was a matter of honor and pride with me to stay with the regiment as long as I could, but Captain Sturtevant and Captain Cross both urged me to go to the hospital, for (they said) we were liable to move on the enemy at any moment, and as I seemed to grow lamer, I might be in such a plight that I should give out in a bad place and lose my life or be taken prisoner. The force of these arguments was evident, and at length I hobbled away. I passed some of the Third Corps in a field where the wheat was stacked in many piles, and reached the road on which we had marched down, and then climbed the hill and searched for the hospital.

Long before light in the morning I was awakened by some one and told that the army was moving, and divining that it was retreating I looked about for the means of transportation, but the hospital wagon was full, and supposing that I must move or be captured, I commenced a painful march, following the road on which the army marched. For a long time I walked in darkness, and the rain began falling to make the road more difficult. By the hospital, down a precipitous hill, along a muddy road, and creeping along the edge of a bluff, I now picture my toil. The labor was painful, and sometimes I very gladly accepted the arms of my good comrades who were with me, and of my new servant. Daylight came and revealed only a disheartening prospect. The army was straggling without order or discipline, and no one seemed to think of aught but reaching the river, which was said to be near and our halting-place. The artillery struggled along the muddy road with weary horses urged by eager drivers, and the siege pieces were pulled along by the teams and men of the 1st Connecticut Artillery, who had hold of long ropes and worked gallantly. The rain poured down ceaselessly, and the mud grew deeper. I had gone through much hardship for a week, and was tired before I was wounded, but now, limping along on my toes, and the rain and mud wetting my wounded leg, I was more miserable than ever, perhaps, and would gladly have lain down in one of the wheat stacks to sleep for a day; but the fact was irresistible and relentless that I must march or be taken prisoner. The river was reported to be within a mile or two several times, and I strained my eyes to see masts or pipes across the flat country on the right, but to no purpose; and while it was true that the river was close by, yet our course was *down* the river, and it was seven or eight miles from Malvern Hill to where I halted that day at Harrison's Landing. As we trudged along where the crowd was thickest, my surprised eyes rested on a sleek, black mule, saddled and bridled, wandering without an owner within a few rods. One of my men quickly made him prize and brought him to me, and I mounted. No man probably ever felt better to mount a mule. My pain fled, weariness was not to be thought of, and the river and camp were but a short distance away to such a team, and I rode along joyfully. My equestrian career continued for a few hundred yards, and then I dismounted, for a brook lay across my course, of unknown depth. One bridge alone spanned it, and over that the artillery was galloping in a continual stream, which rendered it folly for me to attempt to cross it. In haste to be over, I crossed on a log, giving the rein to my servant that he might lead my steed across. Once over I looked around, and my gallant steed manifested his existence only by his head, which was just out of water, and he could not stir, for he had stuck in the mud. To extricate him seemed impossible, and to kill him with a pistol dangerous when so many were near. It was a pity to leave him, but it seemed useless for me to stay, and indeed dangerous, and I trudged along. Poor mule!

At last the stream of stragglers with whom I was marching came to an open plain, at the entrance of which men were posted who cried out the names of their corps and divisions and directed the men to the places designated for their assembling; and then I fully realized how utterly broken up the army was by this last retreat, for there was no semblance of order or organization in the masses who tramped in the mire of the plain, at least as they entered it. In a little while I found a few of the men of the 5th, and, entirely exhausted, I lay down under a bush in the rain and slept for twenty-four hours.

THE WAR IN THE WEST

GENERAL MC CLELLAN CHOSE to blame the rout of the Army of the Potomac on Lincoln and Stanton. He wrote Stanton at the end of June, "As it is, the Government must not and cannot hold me responsible for the result. ... If I save this army now, I tell you plainly that I owe no thanks to you or to any other persons in Washington. You have done your best to sacrifice this army." Such a mutinous dispatch should have brought on Mc-Clellan's relief, but Stanton's aides cut the last bitter sentences before showing it to the Secretary. McClellan's failures merely caused President Lincoln to turn to the West for help. Major General Halleck was brought to Washington and appointed General-in-Chief of the Armies of the United States.

Soon after his arrival, Halleck visited McClellan at Harrison's Landing. There he was apprised of McClellan's usual "estimate" that Lee's troops outnumbered his own men three to one. (At this time McClellan had 101,000 troops to Lee's 70,000.) Halleck wasn't as familiar with McClellan's pleas as were Lincoln and Stanton, but in August he decided that if McClellan wouldn't mount another attack on Richmond, then his army should evacuate the peninsula and withdraw to Acquia Creek, which was situated well up the Potomac River, northeast of Fredericksburg.

General Halleck was regarded as a successful commander in the West, but his reputation stemmed largely from competent administration. As Lincoln learned to his dismay, there was a good deal of all too familiar caution in Halleck. Yet almost any western general looked good in comparison to George McClellan. No western general had yet won a major battle, but both Halleck and General U. S. Grant had seemed anxious to engage the enemy. At least, they moved their men. Perhaps the differences in geography between East and West had something to do with it. As Commager says in his *The Blue and the Gray:*

"While the war in the East surged back and forth between Washington and Richmond, the Chesapeake Bay and the Valley, the war in the West raged and burned over an enormous territory, from Missouri to the Gulf, from the Alleghenies to the Mississippi, with outcroppings in Missouri, Arkansas, Louisiana, and even in Texas and New Mexico.

"Not only were the geographical circumstances of the war in the West profoundly different from those in the East, the strategic objectives, too,

were different. The objectives of fighting in Virginia and Maryland were
the capture of the rival capitals and the destruction of the rival armies. The
war in the West was of necessity directed to different ends. There was,
first, the control of the belt of border states—Kentucky and Missouri—and
of eastern Tennessee, heavily Unionist in sentiment and commanding the
approaches to the East and the South. There was, second, control of the
great arteries of commerce: the Mississippi, the Cumberland, Tennessee,
and Red rivers, and the railroads which connected the deep South with
the Atlantic coast, the border states with the Gulf. The greatest strategical
objective was, of course, control of the Mississippi River, and the separation
of the Trans-Mississippi West from the rest of the Confederacy. Almost
all the major battles of the Western theater involved some strategic point
on some river or railroad: Fort Donelson, Island No. 10, Shiloh, Murfreesboro, Vicksburg, Port Hudson, Chattanooga, and others. The otherwise
confusing cavalry raids, too, fall into a logical pattern when we see them
against the background of lines of communication; and the cavalry leaders
of the Western armies—men like Forrest and Morgan and Grierson—
played a very different role from Eastern cavalry leaders like Stuart and
Buford.

"Most of the campaigns of the West involved control of rivers or railroads."*

By the end of summer, 1861, the war was at full tide but it appeared
to have, as Bruce Catton says, "two ends and no middle" because the
border state, Kentucky, was still neutral. Both sides vied for Kentuckians
to join their cause. "The stakes were high. In Confederate hands, Kentucky
would effectively blockade the Ohio River and deprive the Federals of any
feasible base for a large-scale offensive in the Mississippi Valley, fundamental in the Union's grand strategy. . . . Conversely, if the state were
held by the Union, the Confederacy had no good way to save Tennessee,
hold the Mississippi, and stave off a drive into the deepest South."†

The South moved first to force a decision. On September 3, Confederate
General Polk ordered troops into the state to fortify the bluffs overlooking the Mississippi River at Columbus. As Catton says, the war in the
West "was going to be fought along the rivers amphibious as no war had
ever been before, and the generals were going to have to learn the rules
as they went along. One of the rules was the unanticipated fact that in
such warfare the defensive can be much more difficult than the offensive.
It seemed obvious that guns on top of a high bluff could keep gunboats,
transports, and supply steamers from getting past; Columbus had very
high bluffs, and that was why General Polk had had the place occupied.
But an invader blocked at Columbus could still invade if he could float
south on some other stream that would put him close enough to the
stronghold's rear to enable him to snip its lifelines."‡

General Grant, from his headquarters at Cairo, countered the Confederate move by sending an expedition up the Ohio River to occupy
Paducah, Kentucky. The Confederates had triggered the "invasion"; now

* Henry Steele Commager, *The Blue and the Gray,* p. 338.
† Bruce Catton, *Terrible Swift Sword,* p. 37.
‡ *Ibid.,* p. 42.

the Kentucky legislature, which had favored the Union all along, requested Federal help to drive out the Confederates. General Robert Anderson, of Fort Sumter fame, was asked to gather and train an army. Anderson appointed Generals Sherman and Thomas to help.

In the early stages of the campaign for Kentucky, the Confederates had the best of it, even though Confederate General Albert S. Johnston had less than 30,000 men to hold a line three hundred miles long from the eastern perimeter of the Cumberland Gap to the Mississippi River. Johnston was outnumbered two to one, but by conducting numerous raids and feints he kept the Federals off balance. Anderson had retired because of ill health, and the command had been given to General William Tecumseh Sherman. Sherman, who confessed to have little faith in the fighting capacity of his green troops, failed to carry the attack to the Confederates stationed at the Cumberland Gap. (Commanding raw troops at the First Battle of Bull Run had left its mark on Sherman, though he later recovered from the shock.) Sherman was relieved of his command, and General Don Carlos Buell took over.

The Union strategy had two objectives: to get into eastern Tennessee, where there were many sympathetic and loyal Unionists, and there encourage rebellion against the South; and to cut the main southern rail artery connecting Richmond to the western states. Unfortunately for the Union, Buell was no more aggressive than Sherman.

The Federals made some progress in late January when General George Thomas destroyed a force of Confederates at Logan's Cross Roads in Kentucky, but the strike through the Cumberland Gap still seemed insurmountable to Buell because of the lack of good roads and forage for his men.

While the Federal forces sputtered and stalled in eastern Kentucky, General Grant asked for and was given permission to attack two Forts in western Kentucky—Fort Henry on the banks of the east side of the Tennessee River and Fort Donelson on the west side of the Cumberland River. Only a dozen miles separated the two fortifications, and Grant could count on help from Navy Commodore Foote's gunboats.

When the ships opened fire on Fort Henry it soon became obvious that the works could not be defended. The Confederate garrison withdrew and marched overland to Fort Donelson. The batteries at Fort Henry exchanged fire with the gunboats for a short time, and then surrendered. Grant's troops had scarcely been engaged. He decided to march on Fort Donelson.

The Capture of Fort Donelson*

BY GENERAL LEW WALLACE

W HEN GENERAL JOHNSTON ASSUMED COMMAND of the Western Department, the war had ceased to be a new idea. Battles had been fought. Preparations for battles to come were far advanced. Already it had been accepted that the North was to attack and the South to defend. The Mississippi River was a central object; if opened from Cairo to Fort Jackson (New Orleans), the Confederacy would be broken into halves, and good strategy required it to be broken. The question was whether the effort would be made directly or by turning its defended positions. Of the national gun-boats afloat above Cairo, some were formidably iron-clad. Altogether the flotilla was strong enough to warrant the theory that a direct descent would be attempted; and to meet the movement the Confederates threw up powerful batteries, notably at Columbus, Island Number Ten, Memphis, and Vicksburg. So fully were they possessed of that theory that they measurably neglected the possibilities of invasion by way of the Cumberland and Tennessee rivers. Not until General Johnston established his headquarters at Nashville was serious attention given to the defense of those streams. A report to his chief of engineers of November 21st, 1861, establishes that at that date a second battery on the Cumberland at Dover had been completed; that a work on the ridge had been laid out, and two guns mounted; and that the encampment was then surrounded by an abatis of felled timber. Later, Brigadier-General Lloyd Tilghman was sent to Fort Donelson as commandant, and on January 25th he reports the batteries prepared, the entire field-works built with a trace of 2,900 feet, and rifle-pits to guard the approaches were begun. The same officer speaks further of reënforcements housed in four hundred log-cabins, and adds that while this was being done at Fort Donelson, Forts Henry and Heiman, over on the Tennessee, were being thoroughly strengthened.

Pacing the parapets of the work on the hill above the inlet formed by the junction of Hickman's Creek and the Cumberland River, a sentinel, in the serviceable butternut jeans uniform of the Confederate army of the West, might that day have surveyed Fort Donelson almost ready for battle. In fact, very little was afterward done to it. There· were the two water-batteries sunk in the northern face of the bluff, about thirty feet above the river; in the lower battery nine 32-pounder guns and one 10-inch Columbiad, and in the upper another Columbiad, bored and rifled as a 32-pounder, and two 32-pounder carronades. These guns lay between

* Condensed from "The Capture of Fort Donelson" in *Battles and Leaders*, Vol. I.

the embrasures, in snug revetment of sand in coffee-sacks, flanked right and left with stout traverses. The satisfaction of the sentry could have been nowise diminished at seeing the backwater lying deep in the creek; a more perfect ditch against assault could not have been constructed. The fort itself was of good profile, and admirably adapted to the ridge it crowned. Around it, on the landward side, ran the rifle-pits, a continuous but irregular line of logs, covered with yellow clay. From Hickman's Creek they extended far around to the little run just outside the town on the south. If the sentry thought the pits looked shallow, he was solaced to see that they followed the coping of the ascents, seventy or eighty feet in height, up which a foe must charge, and that, where they were weakest, they were strengthened by trees felled outwardly in front of them, so that the interlocking limbs and branches seemed impassable by men under fire. At points inside the outworks, on the inner slopes of the hills, defended thus from view of an enemy as well as from his shot, lay the huts and log-houses of the garrison.

The morning of the 13th—calm, spring-like—found in Fort Donelson a garrison of 28 regiments of infantry: 13 from Tennessee, 2 from Kentucky, 6 from Mississippi, 1 from Texas, 2 from Alabama, 4 from Virginia. There were also present 2 independent battalions, 1 regiment of cavalry, and artillerymen for 6 light batteries, and 17 heavy guns, making a total of quite 18,000 effectives.

It may be doubted if General Grant called a council of war. The nearest approach to it was a convocation held on the *New Uncle Sam,* a steamboat that was afterward transformed into the gun-boat *Blackhawk.* The morning of the 11th of February, a staff-officer visited each commandant of division and brigade with the simple verbal message: "General Grant sends his compliments, and requests to see you this afternoon on his boat."

There were in attendance on the occasion some officers of great subsequent notability. Of these Ulysses S. Grant was first. The world knows him now; then his fame was all before him. A singularity of the volunteer service in that day was that nobody took account of even a first-rate record of the Mexican War. The battle of Belmont, though indecisive, was a much better reference. A story was abroad that Grant had been the last man to take boat at the end of that affair, and the addendum that he had lingered in face of the enemy until he was hauled aboard with the last gang-plank, did him great good. From the first his silence was remarkable. He knew how to keep his temper. In battle, as in camp, he went about quietly, speaking in a conversational tone; yet he appeared to see everything that went on, and was always intent on business. He had a faithful assistant adjutant-general, and appreciated him; he preferred, however, his own eyes, word, and hand. His aides were little more than messengers. In dress he was plain, even negligent; in partial amendment of that his horse was always a good one and well kept. At the council he smoked, but never said a word. In all probability he was framing the orders of march which were issued that night.

Fort Henry, it will be remembered, was taken by Flag-Officer Foote on the 6th of February. The time up to the 12th was given to reconnoitering the country in the direction of Fort Donelson. Two roads were discovered: one of twelve miles direct, the other almost parallel with the first, but, on account of a slight divergence, two miles longer.

By eight o'clock in the morning, the First Division, General McClernand commanding, and the Second, under General Smith, were in full march. The infantry of this command consisted of twenty-five regiments in all, or three less than those of the Confederates. Against their six field-batteries General Grant had seven. In cavalry alone he was materially stronger. The rule in attacking fortifications is five to one; to save the Union commander from a charge of rashness, however, he had also at control a fighting quality ordinarily at home on the sea rather than the land. After receiving the surrender of Fort Henry, Flag-Officer Foote had hastened to Cairo to make preparation for the reduction of Fort Donelson. With six of his boats, he passed into the Cumberland River; and on the 12th, while the two divisions of the army were marching across the Donelson, he was hurrying, as fast as steam could drive him and his following, to a second trial of iron batteries afloat against earth batteries ashore. The *Carondelet,* Commander Walke, having preceded him, had been in position below the fort since the 12th. By sundown of the 12th, McClernand and Smith reached the point designated for them in orders.

On the morning of the 13th of February General Grant, with about twenty thousand men, was before Fort Donelson. We have had a view of the army in the works ready for battle; a like view of that outside and about to go into position of attack and assault is not so easily to be given. At dawn the latter host rose up from the bare ground, and, snatching bread and coffee as best they could, fell into lines that stretched away over hills, down hollows, and through thickets, making it impossible for even colonels to see their regiments from flank to flank.

We have now before us a spectacle seldom witnessed in the annals of scientific war—an army behind field-works erected in a chosen position waiting quietly while another army very little superior in numbers proceeds at leisure to place it in a state of siege. Such was the operation General Grant had before him at daybreak of the 13th of February. Let us see how it was accomplished and how it was resisted.

In a clearing about two miles from Dover there was a log-house, at the time occupied by a Mrs. Crisp. As the road to Dover ran close by, it was made the headquarters of the commanding general. All through the night of the 12th, the coming and going was incessant. Smith was ordered to find a position in front of the enemy's right wing, which would place him face to face with Buckner. McClernand's order was to establish himself on the enemy's left, where he would be opposed to Pillow.

A little before dawn Birge's sharp-shooters were astir. Theirs was a peculiar service. Each was a preferred marksman, and carried a long-range Henry rifle, with sights delicately arranged as for target practice. In action each was perfectly independent. They never manœuvred as a corps. When the time came they were asked, "Canteens full?" "Biscuits for all day?" Then their only order, "All right; hunt your holes, boys." Thereupon they dispersed, and, like Indians, sought cover to please themselves behind rocks and stumps, or in hollows. Sometimes they dug holes; sometimes they climbed into trees. Once in a good location, they remained there the day. At night they would crawl out and report in camp. This morning, as I have said, the sharp-shooters dispersed early to find places within easy range of the breastworks.

The movement by Smith and McClernand was begun about the same time. A thick wood fairly screened the former. The latter had to cross an open valley under fire of two batteries, one on Buckner's left, the other on a high point jutting from the line of outworks held by Colonel Heiman of Pillow's command. Graves commanded the first (Kentucky), Maney the second (Tennessee); both were of Tennessee. As always in situations where the advancing party is ignorant of the ground and of the designs of the enemy, resort was had to skirmishers, who are to the main body what antennae are to insects. Theirs it is to unmask the foe. Unlike sharp-shooters, they act in bodies. Behind the skirmishers, the batteries started out to find positions, and through the brush and woods, down the hollows, up the hills the guns and caissons were hauled. At Donelson the proceeding was generally slow and toilsome. The officer had to find a vantage-ground first; then with axes a road to it was hewn out; after which, in many instances, the men, with the prolonges over their shoulders, helped the horses along. In the gray of the dawn the sharp-shooters were deep in their deadly game; as the sun came up, one battery after another opened fire, and was instantly and gallantly answered; and all the time behind the hidden sharp-shooters, and behind the skirmishers, who occasionally stopped to take a hand in the fray, the regiments marched, route-step, colors flying, after their colonels.

About eleven o'clock Commander Walke, of the *Carondelet,* engaged the water-batteries. The air was then full of the stunning music of battle, though as yet not a volley of musketry had been heard. Smith, nearest the enemy at starting, was first in place; and there, leaving the fight to his sharp-shooters and skirmishers and to his batteries, he reported to the chief in the log-house, and, like an old soldier, calmly waited orders. McClernand, following a good road, pushed on rapidly to the high grounds on the right. The appearance of his column in the valley covered by the two Confederate batteries provoked a furious shelling from them. On the double-quick his men passed through it; and when, in the wood beyond, they resumed the route-step and saw that nobody was hurt, they fell to laughing at themselves. The real baptism of fire was yet in store for them.

On the 14th of February the Confederates were completely invested, except that the river above Dover remained to them. The infantry on both sides were in cover behind the crests of the hills or in thick woods, listening to the ragged fusillade which the sharp-shooters and skirmishers maintained against each other almost without intermission. There was little pause in the exchange of shells and round shot.

These circumstances, the sharp-shooting and cannonading, ugly as they may seem to one who thinks of them under comfortable surroundings, did in fact serve a good purpose the day in question in helping the men to forget their sufferings of the night before. The weather had changed during the preceding afternoon: from suggestions of spring it turned to intensified winter. From lending a gentle hand in bringing Foote and his iron-clads up the river, the wind whisked suddenly around to the north and struck both armies with a storm of mixed rain, snow, and sleet. All night the tempest blew mercilessly upon the unsheltered, fireless soldier, making sleep impossible. Inside the works, nobody had overcoats; while thousands of those outside had marched from Fort Henry as to a summer fete, leaving coats, blankets, and knapsacks behind them in the camp. More than one stout fellow has since admitted, with a laugh, that nothing was so helpful to him that horrible night as the thought that the wind, which seemed about to turn his blood into icicles, was serving the enemy the same way; they, too, had to stand out and take the blast.

Up to this time, it will be observed, there had not been any fighting involving infantry in line. This was now to be changed. Old soldiers, rich with experience, would have regarded the work proposed with gravity; they would have shrewdly cast up an account of the chances of success, not to speak of the chances of coming out alive; they would have measured the distance to be passed, every foot of it, under the guns of three batteries. Nor would they have omitted the reception awaiting them from the rifle-pits. They were to descend a hill entangled for two hundred yards with underbrush, climb an opposite ascent partly shorn of timber; make way through an abatis of tree-tops; then, supposing all that successfully accomplished, they would be at last in face of an enemy whom it was possible to reënforce with all the reserves of the garrison—with the whole garrison, if need be. A veteran would have surveyed the three regiments selected for the honorable duty with many misgivings. Not so the men themselves. They were not old soldiers. Recruited but recently from farms and shops, they accepted the assignment heartily and with youthful confidence in their prowess. It may be doubted if a man in the ranks gave a thought to the questions, whether the attack was to be supported while making, or followed up if successful, or whether it was part of a general advance. Probably the most they knew was that the immediate objective before them was the capture of the battery on the hill.

The line when formed stood thus from the right: the 49th Illinois, then the 17th, and then the 48th, Colonel Haynie. At the last moment, a question of seniority arose between Colonels Morrison and Haynie. The latter was of opinion that he was the ranking office. Morrison replied that he would conduct the brigade to the point from which the attack was to be made, after which Haynie might take the command, if he so desired.

Down the hill the three regiments went, crashing and tearing through the undergrowth. Heiman, on the lookout, saw them advancing. Before they cleared the woods, Maney opened with shells. At the foot of the descent, in the valley, Graves joined his fire to Maney's. There Morrison reported to Haynie, who neither accepted nor refused the command. Pointing to the hill, he merely said, "Let us take it together." Morrison turned away, and rejoined his own regiment. Here was confusion in the beginning, or worse, an assault begun without a head. Nevertheless, the whole line went forward. On a part of the hillside the trees were yet standing. The open space fell to Morrison and his 49th, and paying the penalty of the exposure, he outstripped his associates. The men fell rapidly; yet the living rushed on and up, firing as they went. The battery was the common target. Maney's gunners, in relief against the sky, were shot down in quick succession. His first lieutenant (Burns) was one of the first to suffer. His second lieutenant (Massie) was mortally wounded. Maney himself was hit; still he staid, and his guns continued their punishment; and still the farmer lads and shop boys of Illinois clung to their purpose. With marvelous audacity they pushed through the abatis and reached a point within forty yards of the rifle-pits. It actually looked as if the prize were theirs. The yell of victory was rising in their throats. Suddenly the long line of yellow breastworks before them, covering Heiman's five regiments, crackled and turned into flame. The forlorn-hope stopped—staggered—braced up again—shot blindly through the smoke at the smoke of the new enemy, secure in his shelter. Thus for fifteen minutes the Illinoisans stood fighting. The time is given on the testimony of the opposing leader himself. Morrison was knocked out of his saddle by a musket-ball, and disabled; then the men went down the hill. At its foot they rallied round their flags and renewed the assault. Pushed down again, again they rallied, and a third time climbed to the enemy. This time the battery set fire to the dry leaves on the ground, and the heat and smoke became stifling. It was not possible for brave men to endure more. Slowly, sullenly, frequently pausing to return a shot, they went back for the last time; and in going their ears and souls were riven with the shrieks of their wounded comrades, whom the flames crept down upon and smothered and charred where they lay.

Considered as a mere exhibition of courage, this assault, long maintained against odds—twice repulsed, twice renewed—has been seldom excelled. One hundred and forty-nine men of the 17th and 49th were killed and wounded. Haynie reported 1 killed and 8 wounded.

There are few things connected with the operations against Fort Donelson so relieved of uncertainty as this: that when General Grant at Fort Henry became fixed in the resolution to undertake the movement, his primary object was the capture of the force to which the post was intrusted. To effect their complete environment, he relied upon Flag-Officer Foote and his gun-boats, whose astonishing success at Fort Henry justified the extreme of confidence.

Foote arrived on the 14th, and made haste to enter upon his work. The *Carondelet* (Commander Walke) had been in position since the 12th. Behind a low output of the shore, for two days, she maintained a fire from her rifled guns, happily of greater range than the best of those of the enemy.

At nine o'clock on the 14th, Captain Culbertson, looking from the parapet of the upper battery, beheld the river below the first bend full of transports, landing troops under cover of a fresh arrival of gun-boats. The disembarkation concluded, Foote was free. He waited until noon. The captains in the batteries mistook his deliberation for timidity. The impinging of their shot on his iron armor was heard distinctly in the fort a mile and a half away. The captains began to doubt if he would come at all. But at three o'clock the boats took position under fire: the *Louisville* on the right, the *St. Louis* next, then the *Pittsburgh,* then the *Carondelet,* all iron-clad.

Five hundred yards from the batteries, and yet Foote was not content! Foote forged ahead within 400 yards of his enemy, and was still going on.

His boat had been hit between wind and water; so with the *Pittsburgh* and *Carondelet*. About the guns the floors were slippery with blood, and both surgeons and carpenters were never so busy. Still the four boats kept on, and there was great cheering; for not only did the fire from the shore slacken; the lookouts reported the enemy running. It seemed that fortune would smile once more upon the fleet, and cover the honors of Fort Henry afresh at Fort Donelson. Unhappily, when about 350 yards off the hill a solid shot plunged through the pilot-house of the flag-ship, and carried away the wheel. Near the same time the tiller-ropes of the *Louisville* were disabled. Both vessels became unmanageable and began floating down the current. The eddies turned them round like logs. The *Pittsburgh* and *Carondelet* closed in and covered them with their hulls.

Seeing this turn in the fight, the captains of the batteries rallied their men, who cheered in their turn, and renewed the contest with increased will and energy. A ball got lodged in their best rifle. A corporal and some of his men took a log fitting the bore, leaped out on the parapet, and rammed the missile home. "Now, boys," said a gunner in Bidwell's battery, "see me take a chimney!" The flag of the boat and the chimney fell with the shot.

When the vessels were out of range, the victors looked about them. The fine form of their embrasures was gone; heaps of earth had been cast over their platforms. In a space of twenty-four feet they had picked up as many shot and shells. The air had been full of flying missiles. For an hour and a half the brave fellows had been rained upon; yet their losses had been trifling in numbers. Each gunner had selected a ship and followed her faithfully throughout the action, now and then uniting fire on the *Carondelet*. The Confederates had behaved with astonishing valor. Their victory sent a thrill of joy through the army. The assault on the outworks, the day before, had been a failure. With the repulse of the gun-boats the Confederates scored success number two, and the communication by the river remained open to Nashville. The winds that blew sleet and snow over Donelson that night were not so unendurable as they might have been.

The night of the 14th of February fell cold and dark, and under the pitiless sky the armies remained in position so near to each other that neither dared light fires. Overpowered with watching, fatigue, and the lassitude of spirits which always follows a strain upon the faculties of men like that which is the concomitant of battle, thousands on both sides lay down in the ditches and behind logs and whatever else would in the least shelter them from the cutting wind, and tried to sleep. Very few closed their eyes. Even the horses, after their manner, betrayed the suffering they were enduring.

That morning General Floyd* had called a council of his chiefs of brigades and divisions. He expressed the opinion that the post was untenable, except with fifty thousand troops. He called attention to the heavy reënforcements of the Federals, and suggested an immediate attack upon their right wing to reopen land communication with Nashville, by way of Charlotte. The proposal was agreed to unanimously. General Buckner

* The Confederate commander.

proceeded to make dispositions to cover the retreat, in the event the sortie should be successful. Shortly after noon, when the movement should have begun, the order was countermanded at the instance of Pillow. Then came the battle with the gun-boats.

In the night the council was recalled, with general and regimental officers in attendance. The situation was again debated, and the same conclusion reached. According to the plan resolved upon, Pillow was to move at dawn with his whole division, and attack the right of the besiegers. General Buckner was to be relieved by troops in the forts, and with his command to support Pillow by assailing the right of the enemy's center. If he succeeded, he was to take post outside the intrenchments on the Wynn's Ferry road to cover the retreat. He was then to act as rearguard. Thus early, leaders in Donelson were aware of the mistake into which they were plunged. Their resolution was wise and heroic. Let us see how they executed it.

Preparations for the attack occupied the night. The troops for the most part were taken out of the rifle-pits and massed over on the left to the number of ten thousand or more. The ground was covered with ice and snow; yet the greatest silence was observed. It seems incomprehensible that columns mixed of all arms, infantry, cavalry, and artillery, could have engaged in simultaneous movement, and not have been heard by some listener outside. One would think the jolting and rumble of the heavy gun-carriages would have told the story. But the character of the night must be remembered. The pickets of the Federals were struggling for life against the blast, and probably did not keep good watch.

Oglesby's brigade held McClernand's extreme right. Here and there the musicians were beginning to make the woods ring with reveille, and the numbed soldiers of the line were rising from their icy beds and shaking the snow from their frozen garments. As yet, however, not a company had "fallen in." Suddenly the pickets fired, and with the alarm on their lips rushed back upon their comrades. The woods on the instant became alive.

The regiments formed, officers mounted and took their places; words of command rose loud and eager. By the time Pillow's advance opened fire on Oglesby's right, the point first struck, the latter was fairly formed to receive it. A rapid exchange of volleys ensued. The distance intervening between the works on one side and the bivouac on the other was so short that the action began before Pillow could effect a deployment. His brigades came up in a kind of echelon, left in front, and passed "by regiments left into line," one by one, however; the regiments quickly took their places, and advanced without halting. Oglesby's Illinoisans were now fully awake. They held their ground, returning in full measure the fire that they received. The Confederate Forrest rode around as if to get in their rear, and it was then give and take, infantry against infantry. The semi-echelon movement of the Confederates enabled them, after an interval, to strike W. H. L. Wallace's brigade, on Oglesby's left. Soon Wallace was engaged along his whole front, now prolonged by the addition to his command of Morrison's regiments. The first charge against him was repulsed; whereupon he advanced to the top of the rising ground behind which he had sheltered his troops in the night. A fresh assault followed, but, aided by a battery across the valley to his left, he repulsed the enemy a second time. His men were steadfast, and clung to the brow of the hill as if it were theirs by holy right. An hour passed, and yet another hour, without cessation of the fire. Meantime the woods rang with a monstrous clangor of musketry, as if a million men were beating empty barrels with iron hammers.

Buckner flung a portion of his division on McClernand's left, and supported the attack with his artillery. The enfilading fell chiefly on W. H. L. Wallace. McClernand, watchful and full of resources, sent batteries to meet Buckner's batteries. To that duty Taylor rushed with his Company B; and McAllister pushed his three 24-pounders into position and exhausted his ammunition in the duel. The roar never slackened. Men fell by the score, reddening the snow with their blood. The smoke, in pallid white clouds, clung to the underbrush and tree-tops as if to screen the combatants from each other. Close to the ground the flame of musketry and cannon tinted everything a lurid red. Limbs dropped from the trees on the heads below, and the thickets were shorn as by an army of cradlers. The division was under peremptory orders to hold its position to the last extremity, and Colonel Wallace was equal to the emergency.

It was now ten o'clock, and over on the right Oglesby was beginning to fare badly. The pressure on his front grew stronger. The "rebel yell," afterward a familiar battle-cry on many fields, told of ground being gained against him. To add to his doubts, officers were riding to him with a sickening story that their commands were getting out of ammunition, and asking where they could go for a supply. All he could say was to take what was in the boxes of the dead and wounded. At last he realized that the end was come. His right companies began to give way, and as they retreated, holding up their empty cartridge-boxes, the enemy were emboldened, and swept more fiercely around his flank, until finally they appeared in his rear. He then gave the order to retire the division.

W. H. L. Wallace from his position looked off to his right and saw but one regiment of Oglesby's in place, maintaining the fight, and that was John A. Logan's 31st Illinois. Through the smoke he could see Logan riding in a gallop behind his line; through the roar in his front and the rising yell in his rear, he could hear Logan's voice in fierce entreaty to his "boys." Near the 31st stood W. H. L. Wallace's regiment, the 11th Illinois, under Lieutenant-Colonel Ransom. The gaps in the ranks of the two were closed up always toward the colors. The ground at their feet was strewn with their dead and wounded; at length the common misfortune overtook Logan. To keep men without cartridges under fire sweeping them front and flank would be cruel, if not impossible; and seeing it, he too gave the order to retire, and followed his decimated companies to the rear. The 11th then became the right of the brigade, and had to go in turn. Nevertheless, Ransom changed front to rear coolly, as if on parade, and joined in the general retirement. Forrest charged them and threw them into a brief confusion. The greater portion clung to their colors, and made good their retreat. By eleven o'clock Pillow held the road to Charlotte and the whole of the position occupied at dawn by the First Division, and with it the dead and all the wounded who could not get away.

Pillow's part of the programme, arranged in the council of the night before, was accomplished. The country was once more open to Floyd. Why did he not avail himself of the dearly bought opportunity, and march his army out?

Without pausing to consider whether the Confederate general could now have escaped with his troops, it must be evident that he should have made the effort. Pillow had discharged his duty well. With the disappearance of W. H. L. Wallace's brigade, it only remained for the victor to deploy his regiments into column and march into the country. The road was his. Buckner was in position to protect Colonel Head's withdrawal from the trenches opposite General Smith on the right; that done, he was also in position to cover the retreat. Buckner had also faithfully performed his task.

On the Union side the situation at this critical time was favorable to the proposed retirement. My division in the center was weakened by the dispatch of one of my brigades to the assistance of General McClernand; in addition to which my orders were to hold my position. As a point of still greater importance, General Grant had gone on board the *St. Louis* at the request of Flag-Officer Foote, and he was there in consultation with that officer, presumably uninformed of the disaster which had befallen his right. It would take a certain time for him to return to the field and dispose his forces for pursuit. It may be said with strong assurance, consequently, that Floyd could have put his men fairly *en route* for Charlotte before the Federal commander could have interposed an obstruction to the movement. The real difficulty was in the hero of the morning, who now made haste to blight his laurels. General Pillow's vanity whistled itself into ludicrous exaltation. Imagining General Grant's whole army defeated and fleeing in rout for Fort Henry and the transports on the river, he deported himself accordingly. He began by ignoring Floyd. He rode to Buckner and accused him of shameful conduct. He sent an aide to the nearest telegraph station with a dispatch to Albert Sidney Johnston, then in command of the Department, asseverating, "on the honor of a soldier," that the day was theirs. Nor did he stop at that. The victory, to be available, required that the enemy should be followed with energy. Such was a habit of Napoleon. Without deigning even to consult his chief, he ordered Buckner to move out and attack the Federals. There was a gorge, up which a road ran toward our central position, or rather what had been our central position. Pointing to the gorge and the road, he told Buckner that was his way and bade him attack in force. There was nothing to do but obey; and when Buckner had begun the movement, the wise programme decided upon the evening before was wiped from the slate.

When Buckner reluctantly took the gorge road marked out for him by Pillow, the whole Confederate army, save the detachments on the works, was virtually in pursuit of McClernand, retiring by the Wynn's Ferry road—falling back, in fact, upon my position. My division was now to feel the weight of Pillow's hand; if they should fail, the fortunes of the day would depend upon the veteran Smith.

When General McClernand perceived the peril threatening him in the morning, he sent an officer to me with a request for assistance. This request I referred to General Grant, who was at the time in consultation with Foote. Upon the turning of Oglesby's flank, McClernand repeated his request, with such a representation of the situation that, assuming the responsibility, I ordered Colonel Cruft to report with his brigade to Mc-Clernand. Cruft set out promptly. Unfortunately a guide misdirected him, so that he became involved in the retreat, and was prevented from accomplishing his object.

I was in the rear of my single remaining brigade, in conversation with Captain Rawlins, of Grant's staff, when a great shouting was heard behind me on the Wynn's Ferry road, whereupon I sent an orderly to ascertain the cause. The man reported the road and woods full of soldiers apparently in rout. An officer then rode by at full speed, shouting, "All's lost! Save yourselves!" A hurried consultation was had with Rawlins, at the end of which the brigade was put in motion toward the enemy's works, on the very road by which Buckner was pursuing under Pillow's mischievous order. It happened also that Colonel W. H. L. Wallace had dropped into the same road with such of his command as staid by their colors. He came up riding and at a walk, his leg over the horn of his saddle. He was perfectly cool, and looked like a farmer from a hard day's plowing. "Good-morning," I said. "Good-morning," was the reply. "Are they pursuing you?" "Yes." "How far are they behind?" That instant the head of my command appeared on the road. The colonel calculated, then answered: "You will have about time to form line of battle right here." "Thank you. Good-day." "Good-day."

At that point the road began to dip into the gorge; on the right and left there were woods, and in front a dense thicket. An order was dispatched to bring Battery A forward at full speed. Colonel John M. Thayer, commanding the brigade, formed it on the double-quick into line; the 1st Nebraska and the 58th Illinois on the right, and the 58th Ohio, with a detached company, on the left. The battery came up on the run and swung across the road, which had been left open for it. Hardly had it unlimbered, before the enemy appeared, and firing began. For ten minutes or thereabouts the scenes of the morning were reënacted. The Confederates struggled hard to perfect their deployments. The woods rang with musketry and artillery. The brush on the slope of the hill was moved away with bullets. A great cloud arose and shut out the woods and the narrow valley below. Colonel Thayer and his regiments behaved with great gallantry, and the assailants fell back in confusion and returned to the intrenchments. W. H. L. Wallace and Oglesby re-formed their commands behind Thayer, supplied them with ammunition, and stood at rest waiting for orders. There was then a lull in the battle. Even the cannonading ceased, and everybody was asking, What next?

Just then General Grant rode up to where General McClernand and I were in conversation. He was almost unattended. In his hand there were some papers, which looked like telegrams. Wholly unexcited, he saluted and received the salutations of his subordinates. Proceeding at once to business, he directed them to retire their commands to the heights out of cannon range, and throw up works. Reënforcements were *en route,* he said, and it was advisable to await their coming. He was then informed of the mishap to the First Division, and that the road to Charlotte was open to the enemy.

In every great man's career there is a crisis exactly similar to that which now overtook General Grant, and it cannot be better described than as a crucial test of his nature. A mediocre person would have accepted the news as an argument for persistence in his resolution to enter upon a siege. Had General Grant done so, it is very probable his history would have been then and there concluded. His admirers and detractors are alike invited to study him at this precise juncture. It cannot be doubted that he saw with painful distinctness the effect of the disaster to his right wing. His face flushed slightly. With a sudden grip he crushed the papers in his hand. But in an instant these signs of disappointment or hesitation—as the reader pleases—cleared away. In his ordinary quiet voice he said, addressing himself to both officers, "Gentlemen, the position on the right must be retaken." With that he turned and galloped off.

Seeing in the road a provisional brigade, under Colonel Morgan L. Smith, consisting of the 11th Indiana and the 8th Missouri Infantry, going, by order of General C. F. Smith, to the aid of the First Division, I suggested that if General McClernand would order Colonel Smith to report to me, I would attempt to recover the lost ground; and the order having been given, I reconnoitered the hill, determined upon a place of assault, and arranged my order of attack. I chose Colonel Smith's regiments to lead, and for that purpose conducted them to the crest of a hill opposite a steep bluff covered by the enemy. The two regiments had been formerly of my brigade. I knew they had been admirably drilled in the Zouave tactics, and my confidence in Smtih and in George F. McGinnis, colonel of the 11th, was implicit. I was sure they would take their men to the top of the bluff. Colonel Cruft was put in line to support them on the right. Colonel Ross, with his regiments, the 17th and 49th, and the 46th, 57th, and 58th Illinois, were put as support on the left. Thayer's brigade was held in reserve. These dispositions filled the time till about 2 o'clock in the afternoon, when heavy cannonading, mixed with a long roll of musketry, broke out over on the left, whither it will be necessary to transfer the reader.

The veteran in command on the Union left had contented himself with allowing Buckner no rest, keeping up a continual sharp-shooting. Early in the morning of the 14th he made a demonstration of assault with three of his regiments, and though he purposely withdrew them, he kept the menace standing, to the great discomfort of his *vis-à-vis*. With the patience of an old soldier, he waited the pleasure of the general commanding, knowing that when the time came he would be called upon. During the battle of the gun-boats he rode through his command and grimly joked with them. He who never permitted the slightest familiarity from a subordinate, could yet indulge in fatherly pleasantries with the ranks when he thought circumstances justified them. He never for a moment doubted the courage of volunteers; they were not regulars—that was all. If properly led, he believed they would storm the gates of his Satanic Majesty. Their hour of trial was now come.

From his brief and characteristic conference with McClernand and myself, General Grant rode to General C. F. Smith. What took place between them is not known, further than that he ordered an assault upon the outworks as a diversion in aid of the assault about to be delivered on the right. General Smith personally directed his chiefs of brigade to get their regiments ready. Colonel John Cook by his order increased the number of his skirmishers already engaged with the enemy.

Taking Lauman's brigade, General Smith began the advance. They were under fire instantly. The guns in the fort joined in with the infantry who were at the time in the rifle-pits, the great body of the Confederate right wing being with General Buckner. The defense was greatly favored by the ground, which subjected the assailants to a double fire from the beginning of the abatis. The men have said that "it looked too thick for a rabbit to get through." General Smith, on his horse, took position in the front and center of the line. Occasionally he turned in the saddle to see how the alignment was kept. For the most part, however, he held his face steadily toward the enemy. He was, of course, a conspicuous object for the sharp-shooters in the rifle-pits. The air around him twittered with minie-bullets. Erect as if on review, he rode on, timing the gait of his horse with the movement of his colors. A soldier said: "I was nearly scared to death, but I saw the old man's white mustache over his shoulder, and went on."

On to the abatis the regiments moved without hesitation, leaving a trail of dead and wounded behind. There the fire seemed to get trebly hot, and there some of the men halted, whereupon, seeing the hesitation, General Smith put his cap on the point of his sword, held it aloft, and called out, "No flinching now, my lads? — Here—this is the way! Come on!" He picked a path through the jagged limbs of the trees, holding his cap all the time in sight; and the effect was magical. The men swarmed in after him, and got through in the best order they could—not all of them, alas! On the other side of the obstruction they took the semblance of re-formation and charged in after their chief, who found himself then between the two fires. Up the ascent he rode; up they followed. At the last moment the keepers of the rifle-pits clambered out and fled. The four regiments engaged in the feat—the 25th Indiana, and the 2d, 7th, and 14th Iowa— planted their colors on the breastwork. Later in the day, Buckner came back with his division; but all his efforts to dislodge Smith were vain.

We left my division about to attempt the recapture of the hill, which had been the scene of the combat between Pillow and McClernand. If only on account of the results which followed that assault, in connection with the heroic performance of General C. F. Smith, it is necessary to return to it.

Riding to my old regiments—the 8th Missouri and the 11th Indiana—I asked them if they were ready. They demanded the word of me. Waiting a moment for Morgan L. Smith to light a cigar, I called out, "Forward it is, then!" They were directly in front of the ascent to be climbed. Without stopping for his supports, Colonel Smith led them down into a broad hollow, and catching sight of the advance, Cruft and Ross also moved forward. As the two regiments began the climb, the 8th Missouri slightly in the lead, a line of fire ran along the brow of the height. The flank companies cheered while deploying as skirmishers. Their Zouave practice proved of excellent service to them. Now on the ground, creeping when the fire was hottest, running when it slackened, they gained ground with astonishing rapidity, and at the same time maintained a fire that was like a sparkling of the earth. For the most part the bullets aimed at them passed over their heads and took effect in the ranks behind them. Colonel Smith's cigar was shot off close to his lips. He took another and called for a match. A soldier ran and gave him one. "Thank you. Take your place now. We are almost up," he said, and, smoking, spurred his horse forward. A few yards from the crest of the height the regiments began loading and firing as they advanced. The defenders gave way. On the top there was a brief struggle, which was ended by Cruft and Ross with their supports.

The whole line then moved forward simultaneously, and never stopped until the Confederates were within the works. There had been no occasion to call on the reserves. The road to Charlotte was again effectually shut, and the battle-field of the morning, with the dead and wounded lying where they had fallen, was in possession of the Third Division, which stood halted within easy musket-range of the rifle-pits. It was then about half-past 3 o'clock in the afternoon. I was reconnoitering the works of the enemy preliminary to charging them, when Colonel Webster, of General Grant's staff, came to me and repeated the order to fall back out of cannon range and throw up breastworks. "The general does not know that we have the hill," I said. Webster replied: "I give you the order as he gave it to me." "Very well," said I, "give him my compliments, and say that I have received the order." Webster smiled and rode away. The ground was not vacated, though the assault was deferred. In assuming the responsibility, I had no doubt of my ability to satisfy General Grant of the correctness of my course; and it was subsequently approved.

When night fell, the command bivouacked without fire or supper. Fatigue parties were told off to look after the wounded; and in the relief given there was no distinction made between friend and foe. The labor extended through the whole night, and the surgeons never rested. By sunset the conditions of the morning were all restored. The Union commander was free to order a general assault next day or resort to a formal siege.

A great discouragement fell upon the brave men inside the works that night. Besides suffering from wounds and bruises and the dreadful weather, they were aware that though they had done their best they were held in a close grip by a superior enemy. A council of general and field officers was held at headquarters, which resulted in a unanimous resolution that if the position in front of General Pillow had not been reoccupied by the Federals in strength, the army should effect its retreat. A reconnoissance was ordered to make the test. Colonel Forrest conducted it. He reported that the ground was not only reoccupied, but that the enemy were extended yet farther around the Confederate left. The council then held a final session.

General Simon B. Buckner, as the junior officer present, gave his opinion first; he thought he could not successfully resist the assault which would be made by daylight by a vastly superior force. But he further remarked, that as he understood the principal object of the defense of Donelson was to cover the movement of General Albert Sidney Johnston's army from Bowling Green to Nashville, if that movement was not completed he was of opinion that the defense should be continued at the risk of the destruction of the entire force. General Floyd replied that General Johnston's army had already reached Nashville, whereupon General Buckner said that "it would be wrong to subject the army to a virtual massacre, when no good could result from the sacrifice, and that the general officers owed it to their men, when further resistance was unavailing, to obtain the best terms of capitulation possible for them."

Both Generals Floyd and Pillow acquiesced in the opinion. Ordinarily the council would have ended at this point, and the commanding general would have addressed himself to the duty of obtaining terms. He would have called for pen, ink, and paper, and prepared a note for dispatch to the commanding general of the opposite force. But there were circumstances outside the mere military situation which at this juncture pressed themselves into consideration. As this was the first surrender of armed men banded together for war upon the general government, what would the Federal authorities do with the prisoners? This question was of application to all the gentlemen in the council. It was lost to view, however, when General Floyd announced his purpose to leave with two steamers which were to be down at daylight, and to take with him as many of his division as the steamers could carry away.

General Pillow then remarked that there were no two persons in the Confederacy whom the Yankees would rather capture than himself and General Floyd (who had been Buchanan's Secretary of War, and was under indictment at Washington). As to the propriety of his accompanying General Floyd, the latter said, coolly, that the question was one for every man to decide for himself. Buckner was of the same view, and added that as for himself he regarded it as his duty to stay with his men and share their fate, whatever it might be. Pillow persisted in leaving. Floyd then directed General Buckner to consider himself in command. Immediately after the council was concluded, General Floyd prepared for his departure. His first move was to have his brigade drawn up. The peculiarity of the step was that, with the exception of one, the 20th Mississippi regiment, his regiments were all Virginians. A short time before daylight the two steamboats arrived. Without loss of time the general hastened to the river, embarked with his Virginians, and at an early hour cast loose from the shore, and in good time, and safely, he reached Nashville. He never satisfactorily explained upon what principle he appropriated all the transportation on hand to the use of his particular command.

Colonel Forrest was present at the council, and when the final resolution was taken, he promptly announced that he neither could nor would surrender his command. The bold trooper had no qualms upon the subject. He assembled his men, all as hardy as himself, and after reporting once more at headquarters, he moved out and plunged into a slough formed by backwater from the river. An icy crust covered its surface, the wind blew fiercely, and the darkness was unrelieved by a star. There was fearful floundering as the command followed him. At length he struck dry land, and was safe. He was next heard of at Nashville.

General Buckner, who throughout the affair bore himself with dignity, ordered the troops back to their positions and opened communications with General Grant, whose laconic demand of "unconditional surrender," in his reply to General Buckner's overtures, became at once a watchword of the war.

The Third Division was astir very early on the 16th of February. The regiments began to form and close up the intervals between them, the intention being to charge the breastworks south of Dover about breakfast-time. In the midst of the preparation a bugle was heard and a white flag was seen coming from the town toward the pickets. I sent my adjutant-general to meet the flag half-way and inquire its purpose. Answer was returned that General Buckner had capitulated during the night, and was now sending information of the fact to the commander of the troops in this quarter, that there might be no further bloodshed. The division was ordered to advance and take possession of the works and of all public property and prisoners. Leaving that agreeable duty to the brigade commanders, I joined the officer bearing the flag, and with my staff rode across the trench and into the town, till we came to the door of an old tavern, where I dismounted. The tavern was the headquarters of General Buckner, to whom I sent my name; and being an acquaintance, I was at once admitted.

I found General Buckner with his staff at breakfast. He met me with politeness and dignity. Turning to the officers at the table, he remarked: "General Wallace, it is not necessary to introduce you to these gentlemen; you are acquainted with them all." They arose, came forward one by one, and gave their hands in salutation. I was then invited to breakfast, which consisted of corn bread and coffee, the best the gallant host had in his kitchen. We sat at the table about an hour and a half, when General Grant arrived and took temporary possession of the tavern as his headquarters. Later in the morning the army marched in and completed the possession.

TO PITTSBURG LANDING

AFTER THE CAPTURE OF FORT DONELSON, Ulysses Simpson Grant was a hero to the North. His initials now stood for "Unconditional Surrender" Grant. Unfortunately, his superior, General Halleck, was bucking for command of the whole western theater from the Rockies to the Alleghenies and the promotion hadn't come through yet. Because Grant was his closest competitor, Halleck began to criticize him to Washington, and for a time Grant's star sank as fast it had risen. Then President Lincoln interceded, asking Congress to give Grant the rank of Major General. Halleck was then given command in the West—whereupon he withdrew his objections to Grant, ordering him to join the troops at Pittsburg Landing, just north of the Mississippi border where General Sherman had assembled them. Lloyd Lewis says: "Old Brains had won, and it was his new favorite, Sherman, who led the advance guard. With orders to precede the army far up the Tennessee, land, march inland, and break the Memphis and Charleston Railroad, Sherman steamed rapidly. At one point he saw a wharf beside some aged warehouses at the foot of yellow cliffs—Pittsburg Landing, where travelers went ashore for the twenty-mile trip overland to Corinth. Quickly Sherman sent a courier back to Smith, commanding the main flotilla, with the news that here concentration would be easiest. By the time he had returned from his railroad raid—a failure due to unfordable streams—he was met by orders to disembark at the spot he had chosen.

"Up sticky saffron bluffs he led his regiments. On the heights peach orchards spread over rough country, their blossoms beginning to show like a faint pink rain. On the right was Snake Creek, fed by Owl Creek, on the left was Lick Creek—all of them swollen by spring storms and making the high ground a natural citadel. If an enemy attacked, he must come marching down between the streams as a Lilliputian would stride down the ribs of an open fan toward the Landing in the handle. Pushing forward two miles from the river, Sherman pitched his camp on a knoll hard by a log church—Shiloh Meeting-house. . . .

"No superior officer ordered Sherman to intrench. Brigadier General James Birdseye McPherson, chief engineer of the army, thought when he arrived that breastworks were unnecessary. General Smith, whose illness, due to an infected leg, kept him on board a transport, told Grant when the latter was given the active command, 'By God, I want nothing better than to have the Rebels come out and attack us! We can whip them to hell. Our men suppose we have come here to fight, and if we begin to spade, it will make them think we fear the enemy.' Grant and Sherman agreed that digging was bad psychology.

"Newspaper correspondents, at some time around April 1, asking Sherman what prospects there might be of Confederate attacks, were told, 'We are in great danger.' And when they asked him why he didn't urge his views on Grant, he said with a shrug of his shoulders, 'Oh, they'd call me crazy again.' Most of the time, however, he expected no attack. 'Beauregard is not such a fool as to leave his base of operation and attack us in ours,' he told his officers. Perhaps this was only his gesture of showing army men that he did not overestimate the enemy—his recent failing.

"Grant, arriving for inspection on March 17, learned from Sherman that the enemy in Corinth numbered no more than 20,000. In reality 40,000 were there. Grant, confident that no attack would come from them, returned to his headquarters at Savannah, some nine miles down the river.

"It seemed safe by the sleepy church among the peach blossoms. Soon there were 33,000 men on or near the yellow bluffs. The Army of the Tennessee—henceforth to be Grant's or Sherman's—was forming. Seven miles north down the river camped Lew Wallace's division, 7,000 strong, while a little farther back Buell rested with 20,000 more—the Army of the Ohio. Thus in the region there were 60,000 Federals, young, strong assurance of victory running through them. From the hills by the Shiloh Meeting-house, the boys could see Southern cavalrymen now and then. Sherman knew of one private who wrote a letter—'I gazed from a lofty eminence, my darling sweetheart, and looked upon the Rebels with vigor and contempt.'

"Through the Southern ranks at Corinth ran the same naïve confidence —'One Southerner can whip three Yankees.' Sometimes it was 'ten Yankees.' Their generals were planning the very thing that Grant, McPherson, and, perhaps, Sherman were sure they would not dare—a surprise attack upon Grant before Buell could arrive. In after years there would be interminable quarrels as to whether the plan was made by Albert Sidney Johnston or by Beauregard. The former was known to be eager to redeem his loss of Kentucky and Tennessee. Beauregard, sick with throat trouble, was anxious for a victory that would show the Richmond authorities how wrong they had been to remove him from the Eastern command so soon after his 'victory' at Bull Run.

"At noon on Thursday, April 3, Johnston set 40,000 men walking toward Pittsburg Landing. 'You can march to a decided victory over your mercenary enemies,' he told them. 'The eyes and hopes of eight millions of people rest upon you.' With Johnston, Beauregard, and Bragg at their head, the Confederates overshadowed their opponents in prestige. Except for the confidence that the Federals had in Grant, the conqueror of Donelson, the situation was almost identical with that at Bull Run. Of the twenty-six officers, from Johnston down, who commanded units of brigade size or larger, ten were West Point graduates and eleven had seen fighting in the Mexican War. Of a similar number that ranged from Grant to the lowest brigade officer in the Federal army, only four were West Point graduates and only one, McPherson, had come directly from the regular military force. No more than seven were veterans of Mexican War battles. Sherman was the only one of six division commanders to have had regular army experience.

"But the scarcity of battle-trained officers was not to prove as serious a handicap in the West as in the East. Western farmers were in no event as dependent upon leadership as were the clerks and factory hands of the seaboard States. The industrial and social regimentation that had been working for generations in the Northeast had been largely absent from the Northwest, where a farmer's only master was Nature, and where individuals boasted that they were 'as good as the next man.' The Western excess of independence might make discipline more difficult than in the East, but it meant superior initiative and self-reliance in fights.

"Fresh from log schoolhouses, Western boys in their teens treated officers as though they were teachers, stealing clothing, books, and liquor from them with prankish delight. When the uniformed schoolmaster grew too strict with discipline, it was common for the martial pupils to threaten him with defeat at the next election of officers three years hence. Many officers, having been politicians and office-holders before the war, feared to punish insubordinates lest they offend constituents back home.

"Weapons were of comic assortment. Hundreds, perhaps thousands, of Confederates carried shotguns because muskets were lacking. Others sneered at the guns that had been issued and fondly patted the bowie knives in their belts. Most of the Federals still carried flintlocks remodeled into percussion-cap weapons. A few shouldered the cumbersome foreign muskets that they had not yet found opportunity to lose.

"On Thursday night rain fell in torrents, turning the yellow roads to mire and making the Southern privates fearful that their powder was damp. To see if their guns would work, they discharged them into the air, blazing away in spite of the pleadings of their officers that quiet was necessary to a surprise attack. The rain dribbled down the necks of officers as they squabbled about the right of way. Orders were misunderstood and repeated in comic jumbles. Bishop Polk's men stalled and held up the whole advance, the bishop growing irate when accused of inefficiency. So ridiculous were the delays that by Saturday night the Confederates had progressed only eighteen miles—one of the slowest military marches on record. In that time the Southern boys had whooped, cheered, and shot at deer that broke cover at their approach; they had eaten up their five days' provisions in two days' time and thrown their haversacks away.

"Disgusted with the conduct of the men, on Saturday night Beauregard wanted to give up the whole enterprise, arguing that by no amount of negligence could the Federals have missed discovering the approach of 40,000 men of whom so many were yelling and shooting. 'We will find the enemy intrenched to the eyes,' he said, all the leaders but Johnston agreeing.

"Johnston had sent his underlings through the regiments to learn their temper, and when the report came back to him that if the army retreated now it would melt away, the disappointed boys leaving for their homes, he made up his mind to attack Grant at all costs. Neither he nor the South could afford another retreat such as he had made from Bowling Green. 'I would fight them if they were a million,' he announced, and ordered the attack for dawn.

"The night was starry, with 33,000 Northern boys snoring in their tents and 40,000 Southern boys drowsing fitfully on their muskets a mile or two away—two virgin armies ready for their maiden embrace."*

Shiloh, Bloody Shiloh! †

BY LLOYD LEWIS

THE DAWN CAME UP ON SUNDAY, APRIL 6, to shine red on the peach blossoms that were flowering in Tennessee. Among the fluttering petals, buglers in blue uniforms stood up and their horns wailed "The-devil-is-loose, the-devil-is-loose." The routine reveille snarled through the tents and the Army of the Tennessee awakened to remember that they were soldiers face to face with another day of camp life. There had been a little scare on Friday evening when some gray cavalry had galloped up with a few cannon to annoy the outposts, but that meant nothing more than bluff. Sherman had pursued the enemy for five miles with his brigade, only to find no respectable force menacing him. On Saturday afternoon Colonel Jesse J. Appler of the Fifty-third Ohio, holding the most advanced position, had sent Sherman word that a large force of the foe was approaching, and the red-haired commander, bulging with confidence, had answered, "Take your damned regiment back to Ohio. There is no enemy nearer than Corinth." That afternoon he had wired Grant, "I do not apprehend anything like an attack upon our position."

Ever since his arrival at Pittsburg Landing, Sherman had been listening to wild-eyed pickets rushing in with tales of massed armies "out there," and always he had found on investigation merely a few squads of Southern cavalrymen scampering away. He had had enough of these camp rumors in Kentucky and would not make the same mistake again. In Sherman's tent, his new aide-de-camp, Lieutenant John T. Taylor, asked why he didn't march out to fight the "Rebs" over in Corinth. Sherman replied, "Never mind, young man, you'll have all the fighting you want before this war is over."

Now the Confederates, looking at the red dawn, exclaimed, "The sun of Austerlitz!"—so filled were they with Napoleonic mottoes. No bugles blew; the whole Southern army stepped quietly into battle array. "Tonight we will water our horses in the Tennessee," said Johnston, his large

* Lloyd Lewis, *Sherman: Fighting Prophet*, pp. 213, 214, 215.
† From *Sherman: Fighting Prophet*.

mustachios flaring. At half-past five the brigades, spread wide, came marching through the dew, straight down the ribs of the giant fan, aiming at the Landing in the handle. Men in the ranks carried their muskets at right-shoulder shift; the skirmishers ahead bore their guns like quail-hunters.

Johnston's battle scheme was to strike the Union right, then let the whole Southern line, as it came up, roll down the length of the Union front—a method that would begin with Sherman, proceed to Prentiss, then engage Hurlbut and W. H. L. Wallace on the left.

"What a beautiful morning this is!" said boys of the Eighty-first Ohio as they washed their faces in front of their tents, stuffed their shirt tails inside their trousers, and stretched themselves. The birds and insects sang with that especial loudness which they seemed to possess on Sundays. Breakfast was cooking. Shots popped among the trees, far away. "Those pickets again," everybody said. The Eighty-first, well to the rear—they were in W. H. L. Wallace's division—did not know that the shooting came from skirmishers whom Prentiss had sent out to reconnoiter. Prentiss, the volunteer officer, was warier than his neighbor Sherman, the trained soldier.

In Sherman's lines, so much nearer the sound of this first clash between the opposing skirmishers, there was deadly calm. One man, the timorous leader, Colonel Appler of the Fifty-third Ohio, took alarm and had his drums sound the long roll. He had cried "Wolf" so often that his men, grumbling, took their own time about falling into formation. Suddenly a private of the Twenty-fifth Missouri, one of Prentiss's outposts, stumbled out of the thicket, holding a wound and calling, "Get into-line, the Rebels are coming!" Appler sent a courier to Sherman, who sent back word, "You must be badly scared over there." Neighboring regiments, accustomed to Appler's chronic uneasiness, went on with their breakfasts.

An officer of the Fifty-third who had gone into the bushes half dressed came scrambling back howling, "Colonel, the Rebels are crossing the field!" Appler hurried two companies out to see and one of their captains rushed back with the news, "The Rebels are out there thicker than fleas on a dog's back!" At that moment the quail-hunting skirmishers of the Confederate advance stalked into view within musket shot of Appler's right flank. "Look, Colonel!" an officer shouted. A Union skirmisher dashed in yelling, "Get ready, the Johnnies are here thicker than Spanish needles in a fence corner!"

"This is no place for us," wailed Appler, and ordering battalions right to meet the Southern threat, shook in his shoes. His men, who had never held a battalion drill, were confused and milled about pathetically. Cooks left their camp kettles and ran. The sick, one third of the regiment, were carried to the rear. Sherman, one orderly behind him, rode up and trained his glasses on a part of the field that was as yet clear. The quail-hunters raised their rifles. "Sherman will be shot!" cried the Fifty-third. "General, look to your right!"

The general looked, threw up his hand, snapping, "My God, we're attacked!" As he said it the Confederates fired and his orderly fell dead, the first mortality at Shiloh. "Colonel Appler, hold your position! I'll support you!" shouted Sherman, and he spurred away for reënforcements.

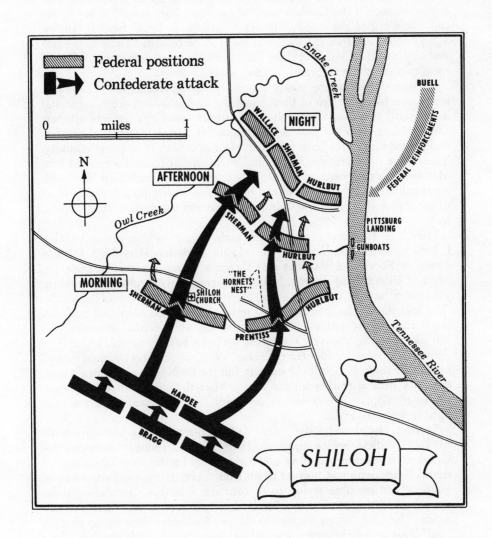

Appler received the encouraging news, walked over to a tree, and lay down behind it, his face like ashes. His men, forming in a wavering line, began to shoot at the Confederates, whose main line, guns flashing in the sun, came out of the woods. "Retreat! Save yourselves!" bawled Appler, and jumping up from the shelter of the tree, he bounded away to the rear and so out of the Civil War. The Fifty-third wavered. Some boys followed their colonel; the rest began to shoot at the enemy.

An incessant humming was going on among the tree tops. The boys said it sounded like a swarm of bees. Then the leaden swarm drew lower and lower until men began to fall down under its stings. It was all new and puzzling. When a man fell wounded his friends dropped their guns and helped him to the rear, staring at the blood with horror and curiosity. There were no stretchers, no hospital attendants at hand, no first-aid kits. Men bled to death because no comrade knew how to stanch the flow with a twisted handkerchief. One boy of the Fifty-third was hit a glancing blow in the shin and sat down, rubbing the place and squalling loudly. It hurt, bad!

Private A. C. Voris of the Seventeenth Illinois, which stood close by, left his regiment and came over to help the leaderless Fifty-third. He had served at Fort Donelson and was therefore a veteran among these apprentice killers. Walking calmly among them, Voris taught the trembling youngsters how to use their guns. He would aim, fire, reload, and talk. "I've met the elephant before and the way to do is to keep cool and aim low." His rifle would go "Crack!" then his voice would resume: "It's just like shooting squirrels, only these squirrels have guns, that's all." The Fifty-third began to do better. Soon Voris, seeing his own regiment moving off, called "Goodby!" and left, but the Ohio boys never forgot him, even if a little later they all ran away. After their flight they re-formed, promoted Captain Jones to the colonelcy, and marched back into the fight in scattered units.

Recruits like those of the Fifty-third were scampering away from all parts of the field before nine o'clock, and soon a number, estimated by Grant to be 8,000 were hiding under the bluffs by the river screeching in terror. Grant, who had hurried down from Savannah at the first sound of guns, wasted no time trying to re-form the fugitives. "Excluding these troops who fled, panic-stricken before they had fired a shot, there was not a time," he said, "when during the day we had more than 25,000 men in line." This 25,000, however, learned the business of battle quickly. Considering their lack of training it would not have been surprising if they had all run; so said British military critics when they studied the battle years later. The average Federal stood his ground, shooting at enemies sometimes not more than thirty feet away. When the Confederates derisively shouted "Bull Run!" the Union boys gave them back "Donelson!" in a jeering bellow.

To join them came a thin trickle of soldiers who, after fleeing, regained self-command on the river bank. Surgeon Horace Wardner, Twelfth Illinois, was working among the wounded on the wharf when he heard a large splash and looked up to see a demoralized horseman trying to swim the river on horseback. Some fifty yards from shore the animal wheeled, unseating its rider, and headed back. Frantically the cavalryman caught the passing tail and was towed to land. The ducking had cooled his blood and, gathering up weapons, he mounted and rode toward the battle.

So stoutly did Sherman hold the Union right that Johnston failed in his scheme for rolling up the Federal line like a sheet of paper. With his face and red beard black with powder, Sherman dashed up and down the field, re-forming regiments as fast as they crumbled, plugging leaks in the human dike, drawing back his force, step by step, and succeeding, somehow, in keeping the stormy tide of Southerners from breaking through. Confederate batteries were shelling his force heavily and volleys of musket balls and buckshot swept the ground. One buckshot penetrated his palm, but without taking his eyes off the enemy he wrapped a handkerchief about it and thrust his hand into his breast. Another ball tore his shoulder strap, scratching the skin. Captain William Reuben Rowley, aide-de-camp to Grant, arriving to ask how the battle was going, found Sherman standing with his uninjured hand resting on a tree, his eyes watching his skirmishers.

"Tell Grant," he said, "if he has any men to spare I can use them; if not, I will do the best I can. We are holding them pretty well just now—pretty well—but it's hot as hell."

Four horses had died between Sherman's knees. At the death of the first, Lieutenant Taylor dismounted and handed his reins to the general. Swinging into the saddle, Sherman said, "Well, my boy, didn't I promise you all the fighting you could do?" Albert D. Richardson, collecting descriptions of Sherman from his men after the battle, said that at this point in the encounter:

> All around him were excited orderlies and officers, but though his face was besmeared with powder and blood, battle seemed to have cooled his usually hot nerves.

Other soldiers said that during the battle Sherman hadn't waved his arms when he talked, nor talked so much, as in the past. His lips were shut tight, his eyelids narrowed to a slit. He let his cigars go out more often than in peace times. He didn't puff smoke as furiously as in camp. John Day of Battery A in the Chicago Light Artillery saw Sherman halt his spurring progress over the field by the guns, again and again. Brass missionaries, the cannoneers called their pieces, having vowed to "convert the Rebels or send 'em to Kingdom Come." Day remembered that during the fight "Sherman had trouble keeping his cigar lit and he used up all his matches and most of the men's."

Thomas Kilby Smith, officer of the Fifty-fourth Ohio, and a family friend of the Ewings, watched Sherman with worshipful eyes and wrote home, "Sherman's cheek never blanched." For the second time in his life, Sherman had found something to make him forget himself, completely, utterly. He had caught that sharp rapture of absorption as a youth painting pictures on canvas in South Carolina. Now he had found it again—the strange joy of profound selflessness. Here in the storm and thunder of Shiloh, the artist found his art. His nerves, so close to the thin skin, congealed into ice. Sometimes when he held his horse motionless for a period, studying the enemy, the dead and wounded piled high before him.

He did not notice them, yet they were the same boys for whose safety he had worried himself in Louisville to the brink of lunacy.

Soldiers around him thought he saw and foresaw everything. When his right wing fell back, he grinned, saying, "I was looking for that," and loosed a battery that halted the charging Confederates in stricken postures. When his chief of staff, Major Dan Sanger, pointed out Southern cavalry charging the battery, Sherman produced two companies of infantry that had been held for this emergency. They shot riders from saddles while Sherman went on with his cannonade.

For all its absorption, his mind—perhaps his subconscious mind—was photographing hideous pictures, sharp negatives, and storing them away. Later on they would become vivid positives:

> . . . our wounded mingled with rebels, charred and blackened by the burning tents and grass, crawling about begging for some one to end their misery . . . the bones of living men crushed beneath the cannon wheels coming left about . . . 10,000 men lying in a field not more than a mile by half a mile.

The field of which he spoke was a cocklebur meadow in the front. Across it Beauregard had sent his Irish-born dare-devil General Patrick R. Cleburne, to lose one third of the brigade in the fury of Sherman's fire. Probably all that saved the life of Cleburne was an accident; his horse stumbled at the start of the charge, sinking the general in the mud and separating him from his command. When the day was done, many observers said that a man could have walked all over the cocklebur meadow using bodies for stepping-stones.

Novitiates though the Northern boys might be at the profession of war, most of them were trained squirrel-shooters who, once they had mastered the complexities of the newfangled muskets, did lavish execution at point-blank range. After the first flurry, nothing could terrify them, not even the Rebel yell that had first been heard at Fort Donelson. This incoherent battle cry was distinguished by a peculiar shrillness from the deeper shouts of the Federals.

By ten o'clock the Northerners had steadied enough to begin counter-charges, the Twentieth Illinois, for instance, fighting back and forth through its camps a half-dozen times. At this hour Grant, making the rounds, had ridden quietly up to Sherman, upon whom the full fury of Southern determination continued to fall. Grant said that he had antici-pated Sherman's need of cartridges, and that he was satisfied the enemy could be held. He said that he was needed more elsewhere and galloped away. It was their first meeting under fire, and in the smoke they gauged each other. Later Grant said, "In thus moving along the line, I never deemed it important to stay long with Sherman."

It was at this hour of 10 A.M. that the battle settled into what most of those participants who survived the war would describe as the fiercest they ever saw. Regiments mixed, blue and gray, in the hit-trip-smother. Men carried away confused memories—awful sheets of flame . . . the endless *zip-zip* of musket balls, canister . . . the shudder of grapeshot . . . dirt, gravel, twigs, pieces of bark, flying in their faces . . . splinters like knives ripping open bodies . . . men tearing paper cartridges, ramming them down musket barrels, capping the guns, firing, and as likely as not forgetting to remove the ramrods, not missing them, in fact, until they saw them quivering like arrows in the throats of enemies fifty feet away. Sense and hearing were stunned by the crash of exploding powder and the death shrieks of boys. Fountains of warm wet blood sprayed on the faces and hands of the living, brains spattered on coat sleeves. Men moved convulsively, wondering whether this moment—now—would be their last. When the Fifty-fifth Illinois retreated into a blind ravine, Confederates slaughtered them from the gully edge. "It was like shooting into a flock of sheep," said Major Whitfield of the Ninth Mississippi, and years later he was still saying, "I never saw such cruel work during the war."

Prentiss, who had been forced slowly backward, finally anchored his regiments in a sunken road and by a concentrated fire was achieving a carnage hitherto unimagined by any one of the youths involved. The Hornet's Nest, the Southerners called this sector as they worked in it for six hours, trampling their own dead and wounded. Federals noted how the charging lines would wave like standing grain when a volley cut through them. Others said the lines when hit wobbled like a loose rope shaken at one end. At times the graycoats simply bent their heads as to a sleet storm. For beginners the Southerners were as brave as the Federals, and vice versa—farm boys all, learning a new trade.

A young private of the Fourteenth Illinois came up to Lieutenant Colonel Cam, fumbling at his entrails, which were trying to escape through a great slit in his abdomen, made by a passing shell. The slippery intestines kept working through his fingers. "Oh, Colonel, what shall I do?" he pleaded. Cam laid him gently behind a tree, whipped tears off his own cheeks, then walked back into the killing. Johnson, an officer of the same regiment, spurred his horse after an elderly Confederate officer, shot him through the body, reached out and seized his victim by the hair. To his horror the whole scalp came off as the Southerner slipped dead from the saddle. A roar of laughter arose above the battle clash, and Johnson saw that he held a wig.

Private Robert Oliver of the Fifty-fifth Illinois saw Private James Goodwin walk off the field resembling Mephistopheles in a play: "He looked like he had been dipped in a barrel of blood." Goodwin carried seven bullet holes in his skin. The Union Sergeant Lacey saw George F. Farwell, a company bugler, sitting against a tree reading a letter. Lacey shook him and found that he was dead, his sightless eyes still fast upon his wife's handwriting. Colonel (afterwards General) Joseph Wheeler of the Southern force said, "The Yankee bullets were so thick I imagined if I held up a bushel basket it would fill in a minute." A boy of the Fifty-third Ohio, joining another outfit, was wounded and sent to the rear, but was soon back saying, "Captain, give me a gun, this damned fight ain't got any rear." Units were surrounded at times without knowing it and were rescued only by the equality of their enemy's ignorance.

Lieutenant James H. Wilson of Grant's staff caught a youth starting for the rear, shook him, and called him a coward. The soldier protested indignantly. "I've only lost confidence in my colonel," he said. Private Sam Durkee of Waterhouse's Battery, close to Sherman often during the day, felt a blow on the seat of his trousers as he bent over his cannon, and looking around, he saw the heels of his lieutenant's horse flirting past. Durkee yelled above the cannonade, "Why did you let your horse kick me?" "I didn't," screamed the officer. Sam felt his posterior with his hand and found blood. "Oh, I'm wounded!" he screeched. Ed Russell, thumbing the vent of a cannon near by, went down with a solid shot through his abdomen, lived twenty minutes, and shook hands with every man in the battery before he died. Men with lung wounds lay heaving, every breath hissing through holes in their chests.

The most ghastly killing of all took place when Albert Sidney Johnston assailed the Peach Orchard, a knob left of the Union center. Hurlbut, defending it, placed his men on their stomachs in a double row to shoot Johnston's men like rabbits "a-settin'." Before such a blast the Confederate boys at length withered and refused to try again. Johnston rode along the front. In one hand he carried a small tin cup that he had picked up in the sack of a Union camp and forgotten to drop. He touched bayonets with it, crying, "Men, they are stubborn; we must use the bayonet!" The Southern boys admitted that Johnston was magnificent and that his horse Fire-eater was beautiful, but they did not want to go into that sheet-flame death again. Suddenly Johnston swung his horse toward the foe and shouted, "Come, I will lead you!" Boys felt hot blood in their veins once more and, rushing past him, took the Peach Orchard, although they left comrades in rows behind them.

Fire-eater was hit four times. Johnston's clothes were pierced, one ball ripping the sole of his boot. He flapped the sole, laughing—"They didn't trip me that time!" Then he reeled. Searching hands could at first find no wound, but at length came upon a boot full of blood. Johnston was dead at two-thirty in the afternoon. A tourniquet might have saved him from the thigh wound that drained his life.

The capture of the Peach Orchard was not decisive. Hurlbut fell back to another strong position, and his men fired so rapidly as to shave down saplings and thickets as if with gardeners' shears. Between the lines thirsty men from both forces drank side by side. Wounded soldiers died while drinking, staining the water red. The Bloody Pool, it was called long afterwards.

In the retirement from the orchard, two wounded gunners tried to move their cannon with one horse. Mud stalled them. They decided to give up. Just then a stray bullet obligingly struck the horse at the base of the tail and with an astonished snort and lurch the animal took the gun off to safety.

Battered slowly, steadily backward, Grant did not lose confidence. At 3 p.m. he calmly began to assemble cannon on high ground near the Landing, parking the guns wheel to wheel and collecting enough ammunition for a final burst of flame, which at close quarters was expected to destroy any possible number of assailants.

At 4 p.m. the crisis of the battle came. In nine hours of fighting the Confederates had captured 23 cannon, and pushed the Union line back a mile or more. At the beginning Sherman had prevented them from turning the Union flank, yet they had seized three out of five Northern division camps, shooting some Federals in night clothes among the tent ropes. Some of the attackers who reached the camps so suddenly owed their success to their blue uniforms, Union batteries having let them advance unmolested. These rows of tents had helped save the Northern battle line from complete breakage, for the Confederates halted to loot the camps. It had been almost twelve hours since many of them had eaten, and they forgot the battle in their hunger for the half-cooked breakfasts standing on Union fires. They rifled haversacks, drank whisky, and read the letters of Federal privates that fluttered on tent floors.

The Confederates had been at fault, too, in attacking in long lines on so rough and broken a front. The battle had promptly split up into many individual struggles, with coöperation between generals impossible. Bragg, smashing fiercely at Prentiss, finally surrounded him, but could find no brother Confederate to push in through the open spaces on right and left to divide the Union line into three sections. By the time Prentiss had surrendered to save the lives of his remaining 2,000 men, Grant had patched up a solid front line again, Sherman and McClernand had fallen back into a more solid array, and the Federals waited for the next assault.

It never came. Beauregard, succeeding to the Confederate command on Johnston's death, saw that his men had had enough. Many had left their posts to go over and stare at the Union prisoners. Organization was broken, officers were separated from men, losses had been frightful. Furthermore, a dull, heavy, and monotonous *pum-pum* had begun to sound from the river. Two Union gunboats, escorting Buell's army in its advance up the stream, had begun to throw shells into the Confederate lines.

Shortly after six o'clock that morning, Grant had sent word for Buell's advance guard, under General "Bull" Nelson of Kentucky, to make haste. A steamer with rush orders had gone on to tell Buell at Savannah to bring up his whole force. To his men Buell seemed negligent as he listened to the distant guns. Boys of the Fifty-first Indiana Volunteers said he was "seemingly unconcerned—a condition of mind and heart almost universally attributed to him by the men of his command." Their regimental historian described the scene:

> Colonel Streight stormed around at a great rate and Captain Will Searce became so impatient that he cried like a child and railed out against Buell, characterizing him as a rebel. Looking up he saw Buell not forty feet away. He had certainly heard the remark but took no notice. We paced up and down the bank like caged animals.

Although there was no convincing proof of the not uncommon charge that Buell's loyalty was doubtful, the man had too much of his friend McClellan's jealousies and prima donna's outlook ever to fit into the Western way of war. Twenty-two years after Shiloh, Sherman wrote James B. Fry, one of Buell's officers:

> General Grant believes, and we all do, that you [Buell's army] were derelict in coming by the short line . . . so deliberately and slowly as to show a purpose, while Sidney Johnston moved around by the longer line and made his concentration and attack on us before you arrived, and long after you should have been there to help us on the *first day*.

Shiloh: *Confederates overrun McClernand's headquarters*

Buell arrived at the Landing in mid-afternoon, in advance of his men, and concluded from the sight of 8,000 fugitives at the wharf that the Army of the Tennessee had been defeated. He later insisted that Grant, whom he soon met, gave him a similar impression. But Sherman, who conversed with Grant at almost the same time, declared that the latter had talked quite differently, saying that at Donelson he had noticed that there came a time "when either side was ready to give way if the other showed a bold front." He had decided to be the bold one, and had won. Now, he said, the enemy had shot its bolt and with Buell's force available by morning, victory was sure.

Near dusk, Sherman, meeting Buell and Fry, told them that the Army of the Tennessee had 18,000 men in line, that Lew Wallace's 6,000 "had just come in and that I had orders from General Grant in person to attack at daylight the next morning." He was glad Buell had come, but thought victory certain even without him. Buell regarded this as a poor way to welcome him, "the savior of the day."

The battle dwindled as twilight spread. Grant and Sherman had narrow escapes at almost the same moment. A shell, missing Grant, tore the whole head, except for a strip of chin, from a captain beside him, ripped a cantle from a saddle behind him, and bowled on to clip both legs from one of Nelson's men as he came up from the river bank.

Sherman was swinging into his saddle when his horse pranced sufficiently to tangle around his neck the reins held by Major Hammond. As he bowed while Hammond raised the reins, a cannon ball cut the straps two inches below the major's hand and tore the crown and back rim of Sherman's hat.

Up from the Landing poured Nelson's men, stepping over piles of wounded on the wharf. The 8,000 fugitives had already trampled these bloody victims, sailors had dragged heavy cables across them, and they were now so caked with mud and dried blood that they were as black as Negroes.

The fresh legions cursed the cowards at the Landing. They thought them as terrorized as sheep who have been visited by killer dogs. In answer to these taunts, the deserters answered, *"You'll* catch it; *you'll* see. They'll cut you to pieces!" Nelson wanted to fire upon them. Colonel Jacob Ammen, the Virginia-born leader of a Union brigade, found his way blocked by a clergyman who exhorted the refugees, "Rally for God and country! Oh, rally round the flag! Oh, rally!" Always a pious Episcopalian, Ammen forgot himself this once and burst out, "Shut-up, you God-damned old fool! Get out of the way!"

The first of Nelson's men to reach the top were Rousseau's brigade—the Kentuckians who had originally disliked Sherman at Muldraugh's Hill. Now when they saw him with his hat in tatters, black powder on his red beard, his hand bandaged, they put their hats on their bayonets and cheered for Old Sherman. He pretended not to notice, but he remembered it always. It was the first really good word he had had since the beginning of the war.

While the Union officers rearranged their battered forces, Bragg had been moaning, "My God! My God!" because Beauregard would not order the one final charge that, Bragg was sure, would bring complete victory.

But several days later he admitted to his wife that "our force was disorganized, demoralized and exhausted and hungry." Some of his men he described as

> too lazy to hunt the enemy's camps for provisions. They were mostly out of ammunition and though millions of cartridges were around them, not one officer in ten supplied his men. . . . Our failure is entirely due to a want of discipline and a want of officers. Universal suffrage, furloughs and whisky have ruined us.

It was just such a letter as Sherman would have written had he been in Bragg's shoes.

That night Bragg and Beauregard slept in Sherman's vacated tent. Near by, the captive Prentiss slept among Confederates he had known before the war. He twitted his hosts about the defeat awaiting them on the morrow. "Do you hear that?" he would say, awakening them in the night, when the boom of the United States Navy cannon came from the river, Colonel Nathan Bedford Forrest, lately a slave-trader, now an unmilitary but surpassingly warlike cavalry leader in the Southern army, walked through the bivouacs of his men confiding to brother officers, "If the enemy attack us in the morning they will whip us like hell."

Grant was riding through the Union camps with substantially the same message, hunting out his commanders in the chaos to tell them that he was going to attack at daylight. To General Rusling, he said quietly, "Whichever side takes the initiative in the morning will make the other retire, and Beauregard will be mighty smart if he attacks before I do."

Across the torn field, men slept with the roar of the gunboats and the screams of the wounded ripping the air. Hospitals had broken down. Surgeons, swamped with work, did what they could, slicing and sawing in desperate haste. Flies had been blackening wounds all day. A mixture of whisky and chloroform was the only antiseptic, and when it was poured on mangled flesh it brought out maggots "on a canter," as the sufferers grimly said. Rain fell, bringing misery to the tentless warriors and relief to the burning lips of the sufferers.

When the lightning flashed the wet and weary Confederates saw sickening sights all around them—naked, bloating flesh, ghastly white faces—and they heard the moaning refrains, "Water! Water!" in the storm. A. H. Mecklin, a Bible student who had joined a Mississippi regiment, thought he heard wild hogs in the bushes. "Through the dark I heard the sound of hogs quarreling over their carnival feasts." He admitted, however, that the sound was not unmistakable.

As the night grew gray with morning, Lieutenant William George Stevenson, of Beauregard's staff, rode the field searching for his chief. Stevenson had seen a cannon ball take off the head of an earlier mount and was sick of everything. His new horse balked at a little ravine. He said afterward:

> He hesitated and I glanced down to detect the cause. The rain had washed leaves out of the narrow channel down the gully some six inches wide, leaving the hard clay exposed. Down this pathway ran

a band of blood nearly an inch thick, filling the channel. Striking my rowels into the horse to escape the horrible sight, he plunged his foot into the stream of blood and threw the already thickening mass in ropy folds up on the dead leaves on the bank.

Through both battered and bleeding armies ran the folk saying, "Nobody ever wins who starts a battle on Sunday."

Monday saw sharp, bitter fighting, but victory for the North was certain. General Lew Wallace with 5,000 men arrived and took their places in the line. Wallace had started early on Sunday morning to march the five miles to Shiloh Meeting-house, but had wandered around the country all day within sound of the battle without being able to find it. Whether the mistake was his or that of Grant's aides was a matter of dispute for years to come. Beauregard, calling the roll at dawn, found only half of his original 40,000 men at hand—and these were disorganized. Nevertheless the Confederates fought stoutly for eight hours more.

At 3 P.M. on Monday Grant, gathering up fragments of regiments led them in one last charge that broke Confederate resistance, and Shiloh was won. That evening the cold, drizzling rain resumed, gradually turning to sleet and hail that bruised the butchered Southern boys who lay in the young spring grass or who had been piled like bags of grain into open wagons for the jolting trip to Corinth. Against orders, Confederate privates crowded into the tent of General Breckinridge and stood there packed and wretched while the water ran in under the tent flap. In defeat they had lost their awe of great men.

The hail pelted Union wounded too, as they lay shrieking on the field of victory; it knocked from the trees the last few peach blossoms that the bullets had spared.

OPENING THE LOWER MISSISSIPPI

To ABRAHAM LINCOLN, the Mississippi River was the backbone of the Confederacy; if it could be broken, the defeat of the South was a certainty. Admiral David Porter claimed after the war that if strikes had been made at both ends of the river simultaneously—and before the Confederates had time to fortify its banks and turn the guns in the government's forts against the Union forces—the war could have been brought to an early close. Porter said: "Their harbors were all more or less closed against our ships-of-war, either by the heavy forts built originally by the General Government for their protection, or by torpedoes and sunken vessels. Through four of these seceding States ran the great river Mississippi, and both of its banks, from Memphis to its mouth, were lined with powerful batteries. On the west side of the river were three important States, Louisiana, Arkansas, and Texas, with their great tributaries to the Mississippi—the White, the Arkansas, and the Red—which were in a great measure secure from the attacks of the Union forces. These States could not only raise half a million soldiers, but could furnish the Confederacy with provisions of all kinds, and cotton enough to supply the Rebel Government with the sinews of war. New Orleans was the largest Southern city, and contained all the resources of modern warfare, having great workshops where machinery of the most powerful kind could be built, and having artisans capable of building ships in wood or iron, casting heavy guns, or making small arms."

Porter was in command of a vessel taking part in the blockade of the entrance to the Mississippi below New Orleans. He observed the vulnerability of the South in the early months and was tempted to sail up the river to New Orleans on his own and demand the surrender of the city. He says: "Any three vessels could have passed Forts Jackson and St. Philip a month after the commencement of the war, and could have gone on to Cairo, if necessary, without any trouble. But the Federal Government neglected to approach the mouth of the Mississippi until a year after hostilities had commenced, except to blockade. The Confederates made good use of this interval, putting forth all their resources and fortifying not only the approaches to New Orleans, but both banks of the river as far north as Memphis.

"While in command of the *Powhatan*, engaged in the blockade of the southwest Pass of the Mississippi—a period of seventy-six days—I took pains to obtain all possible information concerning the defenses of the river. I learned from the fishermen who supplied the city with oysters and fish that very little progress had been made in strengthening the forts, and that no vessel of any importance was being built except the ram *Manassas,* which had not much strength and but a single gun. The only Confederate vessel then in commission was a small river-boat, the *Ivy,* mounting one 4-pounder rifled gun. Had I been able to cross the bar with my ship, I would have felt justified in going up to the city and calling on the authorities to surrender. I could easily have passed the forts under cover of the night without the aid of a pilot, as I had been up and down the river some thirty times in a large mail steamer. But the *Pow-hatan* drew three feet too much water, and there was no use thinking about such an adventure."

Instead, Porter went to Washington to persuade Lincoln and the Navy Department to outfit a mortar ship expedition to reduce the forts as soon as possible. "By the latter part of January, the mortar-flotilla got off. In addition to the schooners, it included seven steamers and a store ship. Seven hundred picked men were enlisted, and twenty-one officers were selected from the merchant marine to command the mortar-schooners."

In the meantime the South took advantage of the delay. "They had been working night and day ever since the expedition was planned by the Federal Government. Forts Jackson and St. Philip were strong defenses, the former on the west and the latter on the east bank of the Mississippi. As they are to hold an important place in the following narration of events, it will be well to give a description of them.

"Fort Jackson was built in the shape of a star, of stone and mortar, with heavy bomb-proofs. It was back about one hundred yards from the levee, with its casemates just rising above it. Its armament consisted of 42 heavy guns in barbette, and 24 in casemates; also 2 pieces of light artillery and 6 guns in water-battery—in all, 74 guns. The last was a very formidable part of the defenses, its heavy guns having a commanding range down the river. The main work had been strengthened by covering its bomb-proofs and vulnerable parts with bags of sand piled five or six feet deep, making it proof against the projectiles of ordinary guns carried by ships-of-war in those days. The fort was also well supplied with provisions and munitions of war, which were stowed away in a heavily built citadel of masonry situated in the center of the works. Altogether, it was in a very good condition to withstand either attack or siege.

"Fort St. Philip was situated on the other side of the river, about half a mile above Fort Jackson, and, in my opinion, was the more formidable of the two works. It covered a large extent of ground, and although it was open, without casemates, its walls were strongly built of brick and stone, covered with sod. The guns were mounted in barbette, and could be brought to bear on any vessel going up or down the river. There were in all 52 pieces of ordnance. One heavy rifled gun bore on the position of the mortar-fleet, and caused us considerable disturbance until the second or third day after the bombardment commenced, when it burst.

"The best passage up the river was near the west bank close under the guns of Fort Jackson, where the current was not very rapid and few eddies existed. Across this channel the Confederates had placed a raft of logs, extending from the shore to the commencement of a line of hulks which reached to the other side of the river. These hulks were anchored and connected to each other by chains. The raft was so arranged that it could be hauled out of the way of passing vessels, and closed when danger threatened. Although this plan of blocking the river was better than the first one tried by the Confederates, viz., to float a heavy chain across on rafts, it was not very formidable or ingenious.

"In addition to the defenses at the forts, the Confederates worked with great diligence to improvise a fleet of men-of-war, using for this purpose a number of heavy tugs that had been employed in towing vessels up and down the river, and some merchant steamers. These, with the ram *Manassas* and the iron-clad *Louisiana,* made in all twelve vessels.

"The iron-clad *Louisiana,* mounting 16 heavy guns, with a crew of 200 men, was a powerful vessel, almost impervious to shot, and was fitted with a shot-proof gallery from which her sharp-shooters could fire at an enemy with great effect. Her machinery was not completed, however, and during the passage of the Union fleet she was secured to the river-bank and could only use one broadside and three of her bow guns."*

The naval commander of the expedition was Admiral David G. Farragut, a sixty-year-old southerner who had impressed Secretary Welles by his decision to remain loyal to the Union. Richard West says, "Farragut's squadron was a heterogeneous group of vessels that included sailing sloops, converted merchant steamers of assorted sizes, old steam frigates, and a class of brand-new gunboats whose shakedown cruise was their voyage to Ship Island. The U.S.S. *Mississippi* was a lumbering side-wheel battleship, veteran of Perry's opening of Japan. The *Varuna* was a light merchantman purchased only a month before Farragut left for the Gulf. The Mortar Flotilla was made up of whaling schooners and a miscellany of side-wheel ferryboats and new navy-built 'double-enders' like the *Miami.*"

Farragut reached Ship Island, which was about 95 miles north of the lower opening of the Mississippi, on February 20. It took him a few weeks to get coal for his ships, and then to work them over the shallow bar in the mouth of the river. Finally, they were all assembled at Pilot Town, "a muddy village on South West Pass whose houses were perched precariously on posts to keep them above floodwater. Farragut placed all the inhabitants on parole and requisitioned several buildings as storage sheds for masts, spars, and other gear not wanted up the river, and he prepared other dwellings for possible use as hospitals.

"To his captains he now issued detailed instructions for preparing the ships for action. 'I wish you to understand,' he concluded, 'that the day is at hand when you will be called upon to meet the enemy in the worst form for our profession. . . . I expect every vessel's crew to be well exercised at their guns. . . . Hot and cold shot will no doubt be freely dealt to us, and there must be stout hearts, and quick hands. . . . I shall expect the most prompt attention to signals and verbal orders. . . .' "†

* From David Porter, "The Opening of the Lower Mississippi," *Battles and Leaders,* II, 22, 23, 30, 31.

† From Richard S. West, Jr., *Mr. Lincoln's Navy,* pp. 140, 143.

The Seizure of New Orleans*

BY RICHARD S. WEST, JR.

WHILE THE MORTAR SCHOONERS stripped for action at Pilot Town, sending ashore their spars, sails, and inessential furniture, a Coast Survey vessel under gunboat escort triangulated the river below the forts to mark positions and ranges for the mortar schooners. There was bitter fighting between boats' crews protecting the surveyors and Confederate sharp-shooters in the flooded forest who sniped at the Federals by day and re-moved their surveyors' markers by night.

A *New York Times* reporter, impressed by the energy displayed in mosquito-infested Pilot Town, wrote: "The mortar captains, a jolly set of fellows, may become ill . . . if something is not done soon. They begin to fret at the lack of opportunity for ridding themselves of the large amount of superfluous energy with which they are imbued." Regular sea dogs in Farragut's squadron shook their heads and predicted that the bottoms of the mortar schooners would drop out at the tenth fire. But these oldsters approved of the smart dress parade which Porter staged when he towed his schooners up the river to battle positions. "They looked very pretty," confessed a seaman on the *Hartford,* "as they ranged along the shore in line of battle, with their flagship, the *Harriet Lane,* at their head."

The three divisions of the flotilla were anchored in marked positions. The First and Third Divisions under Lieutenants Watson Smith and K. R. Breese were placed along the western bank below the lower limit of Fort Jackson's casemate fire and were sheltered behind cottonwood trees laden with vines. The Second Division under Lieutenant W. W. Queen was moored on the east bank in a position exposed but favorably located for attacking Fort St. Philip. The crippling of two vessels in this group shortly after the bombardment began caused Porter to place it below the other divisions against the western bank.

The bombardment, continuing past the anticipated forty-eight hours, lasted for six days and nights. The schooners dressed their tops with bushes, both to hide masts and to shield spotters who perched aloft to check accuracy of firing. Trees on shore shortly became black with powder dust, as did the gunners themselves. "The enemy's fire was excellent," wrote General J. K. Duncan, commander of the forts, "a large proportion of his shells falling within Fort Jackson. The . . . parapets and platforms were very much cut up, as well as much damage done to the casemates. The magazines were considerably threatened, and one shell passed into the casemate containing fixed ammunition."

* From *Mr. Lincoln's Navy.*

After rowing up the river the first night to check on damages, Porter was convinced that the mortars alone might compel a surrender. Farragut permitted him to prolong his firing, especially since the high wind now blowing from the north would retard vessels in passing the forts. Shot from Fort Jackson tore through the point of forest which shielded the "bombards," splintering and uprooting trees. As rapidly as the brush was stripped from the schooners' masts, it was replaced by the powder-streaked gunners. Here and there a vessel's crew would take time out to sleep on a quivering deck not twenty feet from their next neighbor's thundering mortar.

Porter found that too many shells exploded in midflight. After fruitlessly struggling to adjust the length of the unreliable fuses, he finally put in full-length fuses to burst the shells after they had entered the ground. The swamp had encroached upon the fort as a result of bomb damage and recent rains, and the bombshells, after embedding themselves twenty feet in the ground, blew geysers of mud into the air, "not doing a great deal of harm, but demoralizing the men."

To obtain relief from the concentrated rain of thirteen-inch mortar shells, General Duncan sent fire barges down the river and made repeated calls upon Commander J. K. Mitchell of the Confederate ironclad battery *Louisiana* to bring down from New Orleans his uncompleted vessel to draw some of the fire away from the forts. Commander Mitchell shifted his ironclad with workmen and tenders to a mooring half a mile above Fort St. Philip, where work on her was continued. Although 150 men were now detailed from the forts to man the ironclad's guns, the vessel's engines were not functioning, so that she could not be employed against Farragut. Fire rafts at first caused confusion among Farragut's closely packed vessels. Several ships collided or lost anchors in working clear of these menaces. But the Federals developed a system for grappling and dowsing or towing the barge torches clear of the fleet. One night the crews of fifty small boats quenched an inferno by pouring on buckets of water and salvaged a barge load of fat pine logs. Another night a fire raft that had been guided through the fleet ignited the trees for half a mile along the bank where it was brought to rest.

On the night of April 20 Farragut sent Captain Bell, his fleet captain, up the river to break the chain barrier. In the swift current and under fire of the forts, Bell's vessels fouled the obstructions, ran aground, and broke electric wires leading to petards placed on the hulks, but one of his gunboats, after slipping the chain over the bow of a hulk, rammed into the chain and broke it, opening a gap in the barrier wide enough for the fleet to enter in single file.

In preparation for running past Forts Jackson and St. Philip, all of Farragut's ships hung sheet cables up and down on the sides as a sort of loosely woven chain mail to protect their engines. And, since they would be exposed to raking fire from the forts before they could bring their own broadsides into action, each commander tried to stop fore and aft shot from penetrating boilers or machinery by packing in exposed areas clothes bags and hammocks, sacks of ashes, sand, and coal. Some lined their bulwarks with hammocks, others with splinter nettings of woven rope. Some rubbed their vessels with mud to make them less visible, and whitewashed their gundecks to make tackle, marline spikes, and ammunition visible without use of lanterns.

Farragut organized his attack squadron into three divisions: Bailey's flying the red pennant, Farragut's the blue, and Bell's the red and blue.

Bailey's division, with the stout *Pensacola* and the *Mississippi,* was expected to pass close by and devote its chief attention to Fort St. Philip. Farragut, with the three heaviest broadsides of the fleet, planned to concentrate upon Fort Jackson; while Bell with the light gunboats, primarily useful for maneuvering in the upper river, would simply sprint upstream while covered by the first two divisions.

During Farragut's attempt to run the gantlet, the mortars behind Point of Woods were to increase their rate of fire; and Porter, with six of the light steamers of the Mortar Flotilla, was to move up into an exposed position close to the barrier and enfilade Fort Jackson's water battery.

At 2:00 A.M. on April 24, two dull red lanterns hung from the mizzen peak of the flagship *Hartford* signaled to the fleet to get under way, but, because of difficulty in purchasing their anchors, the line did not begin moving until after three. Captain Bailey, in his little "pilot fish" *Cayuga,* led the procession through the gap in the barrier at 3:30. A quarter of an hour later the forts opened fire. The *Cayuga* sped through the area of danger between the forts in fifteen minutes and was struck forty-two times. Her masts were mangled, smokestack riddled, but, with her crews prone on deck when not serving her two guns, she came through with only six wounded.

In the blackness the slower *Pensacola* lost sight of the leading gunboat, and, after cruising close alongside of her appointed target, Fort St. Philip, lost her bearings and sheered to the opposite side of the river where she came under the cross fire of both forts. Lieutenant Roe, who conned the ship, saw gun crews decimated with horrible groans, shrieks, and wails. "My signal quartermaster and my boy aid (Flood) were both swept away from my side. The quartermaster lost his leg by a cannon ball . . . shell burst all about me. At daylight I found the right leg of my pantaloons and drawers cut away by the knee, and the skirt of my coat cut in a strip; yet my body was untouched." The muzzles of the *Pensacola*'s guns almost scraped the plated sides of the dreaded Confederate *Manassas,* but this turtle-backed ironclad ran on downstream squaring off for a bout with the side-wheeler *Mississippi.*

The Confederate ram attempted to butt the port paddle wheel of the *Mississippi* and was balked in her effort by Lieutenant George Dewey who maneuvered the big ship so skillfully that she received only a glancing blow on her quarter. The future hero of Manila Bay, leaning far out over the rail, saw in the lurid light from shellburst and fire raft, where planks had been ripped off his vessel, about fifty gleaming ends of copper bolts "cut as clean as if they were hair under a razor's edge." A few minutes after the *Manassas* had made a feint toward the flagship, Farragut hailed the *Mississippi* to run down the ram. The *Mississippi,* quickly backing one wheel and driving forward the other, turned on her axis and dashed after the *Manassas* only to see her plough into the river bank. The *Mississippi* poured two broadsides into the stalled Confederate and left her breathing out smoke through a row of fresh punctures that resembled portholes.

The Confederate tug *Mosher* pushed a fire barge toward the flagship, in attempting to avoid which Farragut's ship ran aground. The inferno continued to be shoved against the grounded ship. Flames blowing through the ports and running up the rigging endangered the *Hartford* as much as the gunfire of the forts which was now concentrated against her. But she extinguished her flames, backed herself free of the bank, and proceeded upstream, her gunners the while never slacking in the broadsides they delivered to the forts.

In the darkness and blinding smoke the captain of the *Brooklyn,* next in line after the *Hartford,* lost sight of the latter, missed the gap in the barricade, and crashed over one of the anchored hulks. "For a few moments I was entangled and fell athwart the stream, our bow grazing the shore on the left bank of the river," wrote Captain T. T. Craven. "Whilst in this situation I received a pretty severe fire from Fort St. Philip. Immediately after extricating my ship from the rafts her head was turned upstream and a few minutes thereafter she was feebly butted by the celebrated ram *Manassas.* She came butting into our starboard gangway, first firing from her trapdoor when within about 10 feet of the ship, directly toward our smokestack, her shot entering about 5 feet above the water line and lodging in the sandbags which protected our steam drum. I had discovered this queer-looking gentleman while forcing my way over the barricade, lying close in to the bank, and when he made his appearance the second time I was so close to him that he had not an opportunity to get up his full speed, and his efforts to damage me were completely frustrated, our chain armor proving a perfect protection to our sides. He soon slid off and disappeared in the darkness."

Above the forts there was a brief melee between Farragut's van ships and the Confederate River Defense Fleet. These latter river craft and steam tugs, some of them fitted with rams and light metal plating across the bow, made a heroic struggle. The *Governor Moore,* under Confederate Lieutenant Beverly Kennon, twice rammed the Federal *Varuna,* and, being unable otherwise to aim his pivot gun at his target, fired downward through his own vessel's bow. The *Varuna,* the only converted merchantman to attempt to run past the forts, was the only vessel sunk by the Confederates. Her skipper Commander C. S. Boggs, ran her into the bank, let go her anchors, tied her to the trees, and, while she was slowly sinking, continued to operate her guns until the muddy water swirled around her gun trucks. Then he abandoned ship. Only three small gunboats at the rear of Farragut's line failed to get through. One was crippled by a boiler injury, and the others, daylight having arrived, found the wrath of the forts concentrated against them. By simply dropping their crews on deck, the *Kennebec,* the *Itasca,* and the *Winona* drifted downstream out of action.

At the quarantine station four miles above the forts, Farragut stopped long enough to bury his dead and temporarily plug the leaks in his vessels. His losses had been 36 killed and 135 wounded. To Porter he sent a cheerful note—"You supported us most nobly." Leaving two gunboats to protect General Butler's landing of troops, Farragut pushed on toward the city of New Orleans. All the morning of the twenty-fifth his ships dodged the evidences of panic in New Orleans. "Cotton-loaded ships on fire came floating down, and working implements of every kind, such as are used in shipyards." At the English Turn, the site of Andrew Jackson's victory over the British in 1815, Farragut discovered new earthwork forts on both shores. About 10:30 A.M., with his fleet in two lines, Farragut passed between these defenses. The river here was too narrow actually for two vessels to operate in tandem; his crews were so excited that the flag officer's greatest fear was that they would fire into each other. "Captain Wainwright and myself were hallooing ourselves hoarse at the men not to fire into our ships," Farragut wrote to Fox. But this engagement, "one of the little elegancies of the profession; a dash and a victory," was quickly decided and Farragut moved on up to the city and dropped anchor.

Meanwhile, when Confederate General Mansfield Lovell at New Orleans learned of Farragut's passing the forts, he evacuated his troops from New Orleans, taking with them as much food and military stores as the retreating trains could carry. Then he ran a torch along the length of the levee. Patriotic citizens participated in the frenzy of destruction by emptying warehouses, tossing cotton on the fires, or staving in barrels of molasses and sugar and pouring them in the gutters. When Farragut arrived he found the levee "one scene of destruction; ships, steamers, cotton, coal, etc., were all in one common blaze, and our ingenuity much taxed to avoid the floating conflagration."

"The river was filled with ships on fire," wrote the New York *Herald* reporter billeted on board the *Hartford,* "and all along the levee were burning vessels, no less than eighteen vessels being on fire at one time and the enemy firing others as fast as they could apply the torch. . . . The atmosphere was thick with smoke and the air hot with flames. It was a grand but sad sight. . . . At the levee just by the Custom House lay a burning ram (the *Anglo-Norman*). The unfinished frames of two or three more were on the stocks at Algiers [across the river]. . . . While men were hastening up the levee firing ships and river craft as fast as possible, the people were rushing to and fro. Some of them cheered for the Union, when they were fired upon by the crowd. Men, women and children were armed with pistols, knives and all manner of weapons. Some cheered for Jeff. Davis, Beauregard, etc., and used the most vile and obscene language toward us and the good old flag. Pandemonium was here a living picture."

Farragut seized all steamboats that had not been destroyed and sent them down to quarantine to bring General Butler's troops to New Orleans. He ordered Lee of the *Oneida* to seek out the unfinished Confederate ironclad *Mississippi,* but that vessel, having already been set afire and cut from her moorings, presently drifted through the fleet in flames.

Captain Theodorus Bailey was sent ashore to demand surrender of the city. He could find no civil official willing to undertake that responsibility. Mayor John T. Monroe claimed that the city was ruled by General Lovell under martial law. Lovell, when summoned, returned the city to the mayor, as his troops had now departed. Monroe replied that he would not haul down the Louisiana State flag. Any citizen who did so, he avowed, would be mobbed. Lowering the Confederate flag "would have to be performed by the invading forces themselves."

The Stars and Stripes emblem which Captain Morris of the *Pensacola* raised over the United States Mint building was torn down by a group of hot Secessionists and desecrated. Farragut sent a battalion of marines to lower Secession flags and raise the Stars and Stripes over public buildings. To Mayor Monroe, Farragut wrote on the twenty-sixth: "I shall speedily and severely punish any person or persons who shall commit such outrages as were witnessed yesterday by armed men firing upon helpless women and children for giving expression to their pleasure at witnessing the 'old flag.'" To this Monroe answered that the people of New Orleans "do not allow themselves to be insulted" by deserters in their midst who "might remind them too forcibly that they are the conquered and you the conquerors.... Your occupying of the city does not transfer allegiance from the government of their choice to one which they have deliberately repudiated, and they yield the obedience which the conqueror is entitled to extort from the conquered."

Meanwhile, for three days the situation below the forts was one of uncertainty. Farragut's fleet had gone to New Orleans leaving the forts unreduced and, in the absence of accurate information, the ram *Louisiana* was believed to be "as lively as ever." Under flag of truce Porter demanded surrender of the forts, and, the demand refused, he expended the remainder of his available ammunition in renewed bombardment. Then he sent the defenseless mortar schooners to Pilot Town twenty-five miles away and with his light steamers mounted guard behind the Point of Woods.

General Butler, with naval assistance, transferred the Twenty-sixth Massachusetts from inside the river below the forts, out through Pass a L'Outre, and around to a landing from the Gulf side behind Fort St. Philip. The troops made their way up a bayou known as Maunels Canal which empties into the Gulf and, after their galleys touched bottom, they waded the last mile and a half in water and mud that was sometimes hip deep. After they reached quarantine, some were ferried by Farragut's gunboats, the *Wissahickon* and the *Kineo,* across to the Fort Jackson side of the river. Both forts were thus cut off from their escape routes to New Orleans, since the flooded condition of the countryside left only these narrow trails of dry land along the levees which were now occupied by Federal troops.

At midnight on the twenty-seventh the troops in Fort Jackson seized the guards and posterns and turned their guns on the officers who sought to check their mutiny, and the next day General Duncan came off to the *Harriet Lane* and surrendered the forts. Because of disunity between the Confederate forces ashore and afloat, the Confederate ships were not included in the capitulation. While the surrender negotiations were in process between General Duncan and Commander Porter of the Mortar Flotilla, word was brought to the *Harriet Lane* that the ironclad *Louisiana* had been set on fire and cast adrift. "This is sharp practice," Porter remarked to the Confederate officers, "but if you can stand the explosion when it comes we can. We will go on and finish the capitulation." Several minutes after the signing was completed the boom of the explosion was heard. Everything in the cabin was jolted from side to side, but not an officer left his seat.

"New Orleans falling seems to have made a stampede in 'Secessia,'" Porter jubilantly wrote to Fox. "You may put the rebellion down as 'spavined,' 'broken-backed,' and 'wind-galled.' . . . You good people at home can go to work now, cut down the Navy's pay, and disrate us to your heart's content. You will soon have no use for us in this contest."

Butler's transports arrived in New Orleans on May 1, and Farragut turned over to the political general the arduous chore of governing New Orleans. Fortunately, Butler proved to be unusually gifted in what to the United States Army was then the novel science of military administration. Quasi-rebellious citizens were held in check. The destitute were fed. Law and order were made to prevail. The sanitary situation was corrected as it had never been before. And these matters were of no small import in view of the use to be made of New Orleans as a naval base for future operations both within the river and on the Gulf coast.

If Lincoln's Navy in seizing New Orleans had not yet succeeded in opening the Mississippi River and splitting the Confederacy in two, it had made a long stride in that direction.

LET US GET VICKSBURG

THE PROGRESS OF THE UNION ARMIES south through Kentucky and Tennessee was slow but inexorable. Federal troops pressed the Confederates back into Mississippi and Alabama. Before Grant could turn east in a flanking movement, the Mississippi Valley had to be won. The Union Navy could dominate the Mississippi River but traffic would be almost impossible until the land fortifications at Port Hudson and Vicksburg were reduced.

Vicksburg was the key. Supplies from the west bound for southern states in the east had to go through Vicksburg by rail. Admiral Porter said, "It means hog and hominy without limit, fresh troops from all the states of the far south, and a cotton country where they can raise the staple (cotton) without interference. Let us get Vicksburg and all that country is ours."

While the Navy worked to clear the river, U. S. Grant moved his armies into position above Vicksburg. Taking the city would be a formidable task. Colonel Joseph Mitchell in his *Decisive Battles of the Civil War* describes the forbidding barriers facing Grant: "It is extremely difficult for an army to approach it [Vicksburg] from the North. The line of hills, of which Vicksburg forms a part, turns abruptly to the northeast following the Yazoo River. Between these hills and the Mississippi is a vast bottom land known as the Yazoo delta, stretching northward for 175 miles. It is sixty miles wide in places, and covers an area of several thousand square miles. Most of this land is very soft and very low. If it were not for the levees along the Mississippi it would be under water a great part of the year. Crisscrossed with small streams, large bayous, and rivers, it presented an almost impassable obstacle to a large army with heavy guns and wagons.

"On the other side of the Mississippi opposite Vicksburg the bottom land, though not as wide as the Yazoo delta, extends both north and south of the city. The problem confronting an army trying to capture Vicksburg was to reach the high ground east of the Yazoo River or south of the city, and assault Vicksburg from the rear. Either solution presented immense difficulties. The first involved crossing the Yazoo delta. The alternative meant finding a way through the bottom land on the opposite bank, then crossing the Mississippi to the eastern shore. Supply would be difficult in either case, perhaps impossible by the second method because the supply ships would have to run down past the Vicksburg batteries to reach the troops operating below the city. . . .

"General Grant's first effort to capture Vicksburg by a combined land and water movement had failed. This had been in November and December of 1862. From then on the Union forces were based on the west side of the river opposite, but somewhat north of the city. For the next four months they tried various ways to cross the Yazoo delta or to by-pass the city. A total of four more unsuccessful attempts were to be made before the fifth finally succeeded and General Grant's Army of the Tennessee could engage the Confederate forces in open warfare."*

While Grant schemed to get his troops into position before Vicksburg, he set in motion five separate operations to divert the Confederates' attention from his main effort. The foremost of these was a raid into Mississippi by a brigade of cavalry under Colonel Benjamin Grierson. The brigade's mission was to cut the railroad east of Vicksburg and generally cause as much trouble as they could.

On April 17, 1863, Grierson's 1,700 troopers left La Grange, Tennessee, heading south. The first four days of marching carried the column some 130 miles into Rebel territory. Let us pick up the story on the fifth day.

Grierson's Raid †

BY SERGEANT RICHARD W. SURBY

FIFTH DAY

LEFT CAMP ON THE MORNING OF THE TWENTY-FIRST at daylight, the seventh Illinois in advance; Colonel Hatch with the second Iowa and one piece of artillery turned eastward from Clear Springs with orders to proceed toward Columbus, Mississippi, and destroy as much as possible of the Mobile and Ohio railroad, and make his way to Le Grange again. Some fears were felt for his success, as forces were concentrating in our rear, expecting to intercept us on our return. It was of the utmost importance that a feint should be made in the direction of Columbus in order to draw the enemies' forces that way and conceal the real movement which was then making all speed south.

Belonging to the non-commissioned staff I was a privileged character, and undoubtedly took many liberties not allowed me, consequently I had a good opportunity of observing many things, and learning some the designs of our commanders. Possessed of a venturesome disposition I naturally wanted to be in the front, and it occurred to me I could do so; I immediately suggested my ideas to Lieut. Col. Blackburn (formerly my

---

* *Decisive Battles of the Civil War*, pp. 133–34.
† Condensed from *Grierson Raids*.

captain), that of having some scouts in the advance dressed in citizens' clothes, where they could by proper management gain much valuable information, although not without running some danger. Colonel Blackburn immediately had an interview with Colonel Grierson stating the object of the organization; Colonel Grierson approved the plan provided the right men could be found, Colonel Blackburn said he knew just the men, and without further consideration, he had full permission to organize and control the scouts; it was not long before I was ordered to report to him, and was somewhat surprised when he requested me to act as scout, and take command of a squad of men. This suited me, and without any hesitation I accepted the position with thanks, fully resolved not to abuse the confidence reposed in me. I received orders to take six or eight men, proceed at once on the advance and procure citizens' dress, saddles, shot guns, and everything necessary for our disguise. It did not take long to do this, and by noon reported myself and men ready for duty; we excited some little curiosity and sold the sixth Illinois boys completely, they thought we were prisoners and bored us with a thousand questions; after this we went by the name of "The Butternut Guerillas."

My instructions from Colonel Blackburn were to keep in the advance, from a quarter of a mile to two as the case required, to obtain all information respecting different roads, their destination, distance, and condition, also that of the streams, bridges, and the whereabouts of the enemy, their force, and was to exercise my own judgment in all cases where it required immediate action, to report to him or Colonel Prince from time to time. Another advantage was, that we would more easily find forage, and save trouble and delay by sending out squads for that purpose.

The advance guard each day being advised and cautioned about us, did not find or take us prisoners, and our signs were soon understood by both parties. We passed through Starkville, Ochtibleher County, and camped eight miles south of that place. Between Starkville and camp the scouts captured a Lieutenant belonging to Vicksburg, who was seated in a fine buggy with a beautiful span of iron gray horses attached; the horses Colonel Grierson assigned to the battery. Also a mounted rebel was secured and taken along.

SIXTH DAY

Morning of the twenty-second left camp at an early hour—weather favorable. Before leaving camp Captain Graham of the seventh, commanding a battalion, was sent to burn a Confederate shoe and saddle manufactory near Starkville; he succeeded in destroying several thousand pairs of boots and shoes besides a large quantity of leather and hats, capturing a quarter-master from Port Hudson, who was getting supplies for his regiment (the twelfth Tennessee). Previous to leaving camp, the field officers had a consultation and were convinced that it was of the utmost importance to intercept and destroy the railroad and telegraph between Okalona and Macon, as near Macon as possible. This work Colonel Prince offered Captain Forbes, Company B, seventh Illinois, whose company numbered thirty-five men and officers; Captain Forbes accepted at once, though he knew he would be obliged to repulse all attacks and travel at least fifty miles more than the command, would run great risk in being captured, as it was not known what force was at Macon, nor what force was following us; he was instructed, that if a force should be at Macon, to endeavor to cross the Ranox Bar and move toward Decatur, in Newton County, by the shortest route.

The Captain proceeded on his perilous journey, and many feared that they would never see him again. The country through which we were passing was not of a prepossessing appearance—it was low and swampy. The scouts were quite successful during the day in finding several droves of horses and mules, with Negroes concealed in the woods, to avoid being captured by our forces. The manner in which we obtained our information was quite easy in our assumed characters, when conversing with the hunters we passed ourselves off as confederates, belonging to commands in Tennessee; that we were ordered to keep in advance of the Yankees, watch their movements and when opportunity presented, to report to the nearest post; this story invariably was credited among them, and in a little while by ingratiating ourselves into their favor, we obtained their confidence, and was told where they had concealed their fine animals; I would then leave a man to inform the Colonel when the column came up, and a squad of men would often bring in twenty-five horses and mules, with as many Negroes, who would of their own accord accompany us.

I was very much amused one day; had taken three of my men with me and proceeded two miles from the main road expecting to find a Confederate captain at home, but he had left quite suddenly; found some good mules, upon which I mounted some Negroes who were standing round with mouths wide open showing teeth like circular saws, at the sight of a Yankee, having never seen one before. On my return I passed a very fine residence—my attention was suddenly attracted by a motion made at one of the windows, I gave the order to halt; no sooner done than the front door flew open and three lovely looking females dressed in white appeared at the opening, their faces beaming with smiles, and in a voice soft and sweet invited us to dismount and come in. It was raining, we were all wet to the skin, and spattered with mud, contrasting strongly with the elegant appearance of everything around; I therefore begged to be excused as my time was limited, and we were watching the advanced movements of the Yankees; no sooner said than out they bounded, regardless of the rain, and coming to the gate (were joined by an elderly lady whom they addressed as mother), insisted upon our remaining over night. Various were the questions asked about the "Yanks" all of which we could answer satisfactorily; they informed us their father and brothers were in the Confederate Army.

One of the boys complained of being hungry; no sooner said than one of the ladies ran into the house, and soon returned with two black servants following, loaded down with eatables; we had to accept half a ham, that would make a hungry man laugh; biscuits, sweet cakes, fried sausage, and peach pie, all in abundance were pressed upon us, while one of the young ladies plucked some roses and presenting one to each bade us adieu, with many blessings and much success in our "holy cause"; on my way back I met a company of the sixth Illinois, and cautioned them to still deceive the "ladies," and I presume it was some time ere they learned how bad they had been sold.

Another instance occurred where I visited a plantation, accompanied by two of my scouts. We found two young men at home, both belonging to the Confederate army. They were somewhat surprised to hear the Yankees were coming that way; all was excitement, the Negroes were called up, and received orders to get all the horses and mules, and saddle two of them. We were invited into the house. Having told them that we would accompany them some distance, the demijohn was brought out, glasses placed upon the table, and a cordial invitation given to help ourselves to some "old rye," which invitation a soldier never refuses. The blacks soon announced all ready, and we started out, the young men armed with shot guns, eight Negroes following with fourteen mules and six fine horses. It was about one and a half miles to the road, upon which the column was advancing, and in the direction that we were going; when about half way I had a curiosity to examine their guns, which they seemed proud to exhibit; making a motion to one of my men he followed suit, thus we had them disarmed, and in a good humored way informed them they were our prisoners; they laughed, thinking it a good joke, saying they were old soldiers, and not easily scared. We soon came in sight of the column, when our Confederate friends "smelt a rat," and with downcast countenances became uncommunicative. Shortly after this we passed through Whitefield, a small place of little importance.

After leaving this place the country began to look decidedly swampy, we were crossing the Big Black or Okaxuler River, which was much swollen by the recent rains. In many places we had to swim our horses and mules. Many troopers lost their animals and equipments, barely escaping with their lives. It was a tedious task piloting our way through this bottom, which extended in breadth nearly six miles, and was covered with water to the depth of three feet. You will ask how did we get our artillery over; this was accomplished by taking the ammunition out of the caissons, and packing it over our own horses, thereby keeping it dry. Unfortunately one of the gun carriages broke down, causing some delay, but through the ingenuity of Capt. Smith, commanding the guns, it was mounted next day on buggy wheels.

The sixth Illinois cavalry succeeded in crossing and reached camp about two o'clock; the seventh did not arrive until three the next morning. After leaving this dismal swamp, the country became more rolling, the roads were in better condition, vegetation more forward, and the citizens were impressed with the idea that we belonged to the rebel General Van Dorn's command, and complimented us on our fine appearance, and said we were right good looking men. No couriers had preceded us on this road, and we enjoyed ourselves very much at the expense of the deluded citizens.

While passing a schoolhouse the teacher gave her pupils recess; the way they flocked to the roadside was not slow, hurrahing for Beauregard, Van Dorn, and the Southern Confederacy. One little urchin imagined she recognized in one of the men an old acquaintance, and very impatiently inquired how John was, and if her uncle was along.

Before reaching Louisville the scouts captured a mailcoach containing the Port Hudson mail, together with some Confederate money, which was handed to Colonel Grierson. The letters were mostly in French, which was translated into English by Sergeant-Major Le Sure of the seventh; they contained some valuable information. Louisville is a neat little town of pretty location, in Winston County. After leaving it ten miles in our rear, we camped for the night, having traveled this day fifty miles. On this evening Captain Lynch of Company E, of the sixth Illinois, and one of his men, Corporal W. H. H. Bullard, disguised themselves in citizens' dress, and started on a reconnoitering expedition towards Macon, with what success will appear hereafter.

SEVENTH DAY

We left camp at an early hour and were now drawing near Pearl River Valley. A glance at the map will show the importance of this river on the Talla Hoga, and knowing it to be quite high from recent rains, and a possibility of news of our approach reaching them from other routes, it became necessary to secure the bridge. I was instructed to proceed rapidly and cautiously forward, and if possible, to secure it with my squad. When within two miles of the bridge, I met an old citizen mounted upon a mule. We passed the time of day and entered into conversation; he informed me that a picket was stationed at the bridge, composed of citizens, numbering five in all, his son being one of the party; all were armed with shot-guns. They had torn up several planks from the centre of the bridge, and had placed combustibles on it ready to ignite on our approach.

I then wrote down the old man's name, and the whereabouts of his residence, which was on the opposite side of the river. He began to mistrust that all was not right, and says, "Gentlemen you are not what you seem to be, you certainly are Yankees, for we got news in Philadelphia last night that 'you'ens' all were coming this way." I had now fully resolved upon scaring the old man into an unconditional surrender of the bridge. So, looking him in the face, I told him it now lay in his power to save his buildings from the torch, his own life, and probably that of his son, by saving the bridge. We started, and when within one half mile of our object we descended into a low bottom land, considerably flooded with water, making progress slowly. Unless the enemy had a picket, or vidette, thrown out we could approach to within three hundred yards without being discovered. I now told the old man, who was trembling with fear, that he was to visit his friends, and tell them, that if they would surrender, they should not be harmed, but would be paroled as soon as we reached town, but if they did any damage to the bridge, his property would suffer for it.

The old man said he was confident of saving the bridge, but would not promise the surrender of his friends; that we cared nothing about—the bridge was the important point. I impatiently followed the figure of the old man with my eye; when within a dozen yards of the bridge, he halted, and commenced telling his errand; but ere he had got hardly half through, I could perceive some signs of uneasiness on the side of his listeners, they all at once jumped upon their horses and away they went. We then advanced to the bridge, replaced the planks, found two shot guns, that they had left in their flight, and leaving one man to wait for the column and turn the old man over to the Colonel, I proceeded with the rest to Philadelphia.

This incident is mentioned as one of the many in which the *Power above* seemed shielding us from harm, as the destruction of the bridge would have been fatal to the expedition. In my case others might have acted differently; my object was to save life if possible, the bridge at all hazards. We now proceeded toward Philadelphia, occasionally firing a shot at some mounted citizens who were armed but took care to keep at a respectful distance. The nearer we approached the larger the force became in our advance, yet, they showed no disposition to come within range, until within about three hundred yards of town, when they were discovered drawn up in line across the road, upon which we were approaching. I immediately sent a man back, requesting the commanding officer of the advance guard to send me ten men. I waited long enough to see they were coming, and turning to my men ordered them to charge, and as we neared them amid a cloud of dust, we commenced to discharge our revolvers at them, which had the desired effect of stampeding them; they fired but a few shots, and in a few minutes we had full possession of the town; resulting in the capture of six prisoners, nine horses with equipments. One of the prisoners being the county judge—a very worthy man. At first they evinced much uneasiness and thought their time was near to depart from this world. Colonel Grierson soon quieted their fears by telling them that he did not come among them to insult them, or destroy private property, that he was in quest of Confederate soldiers and government property. We left the Philadelphians in better humor and with a more favorable opinion of our intentions, and the conduct of our army.

The last I saw of them they were standing in line with arms extended perpendicular, and Colonel Prince was swearing them not to give any information for a certain length of time. Just as we were leaving Philadelphia, up came Captain Lynch and his corporal in disguise, having just arrived from their expedition to Macon, the particulars of which I obtained from Captain Lynch.

On his departure from Louisville he pushed through to Macon, traveling all night, arriving within half a mile of the place at eight o'clock next morning; traveling seventy-five miles, meeting with no trouble until halted by the picket in sight of the town; they demanded his business. The Captain told them that he had been sent out from Enterprise to ascertain the whereabouts of the Yankees. "Why," says the guard, "you need not go any further, they are now within two miles of here. General Loring sent out a squad of cavalry to reconnoitre; they have all returned but one who is either killed or taken prisoner." The Captain then inquired what force they had to defend the place, and was told that re-enforcements had arrived from Mobile—two regiments of cavalry, one of infantry, and two pieces of artillery. The Captain made an excuse to withdraw by stating that he had left two men at a plantation about a mile from there; he would return for them and be back in a few hours. The guards thought it all right and allowed him to depart.

The Captain made good time, forfeiting his word to return. After traveling all night and next day until about one hour of sunset, they reached the command, just as they were leaving Philadelphia. After proceeding seven miles south of the latter place the command halted to feed and rest for a few hours on the plantation of Esquire Payn. While so doing, at a council of the officers Lieut. Col. Blackburn offered a proposition, which was to take two hundred men and proceed to Newton Station, on the Southern railroad, to intercept the trains and destroy the track; his plan was favored by Colonel Grierson, and at ten o'clock Colonel Blackburn started with the first battalion of seventh Illinois. I was ordered by him to take two of my men and accompany him. The night was a beautiful starlight one, the roads in good condition, and meeting with no enemy, nothing occurred to interrupt the stillness that reigned until midnight, when the column was startled by the report of firearms, in the advance, which occurred in the following manner: In coming to a point where the road forked, I was at a loss which one to take, and to decide the question, sent George Stedman back to a house to inquire, in the meantime I had advanced on the road leading to the right a short distance, and halted, with my horse standing crosswise the road, leaving a narrow neck of timber between me and the other road. Scout number two had preceded me a short distance, and was waiting by the shade of the timber. In a few minutes Stedman came trotting back, and as he neared me I asked him if this was the right road; he did not seem to comprehend what I said but came up within a few feet of me and peering into my face a moment, without saying a word, wheeled his horse and galloped off. His actions puzzled me a little at first, and was giving no further thought to it, supposing he had gone back to the column with his information, when the first thing I heard was the report of firearms; though somewhat startled at first I did not move my position until the third shot had been fired, which impressed me with the idea that some one was firing at me, by hearing and seeing the fire-sparks fly from a stone the ball hit just beneath my horse's head, the next whizzed a few feet over me. I began to think it was time for me to get out of that, so I turned left about and retreated a few yards into the timber. Soon, *whiz, whiz,* came another shot, tearing through the timber; I immediately decided on a retreat, and went pell-mell through the scrub-oaks and briars for about two hundred yards, then coming to a halt, I heard another shot, then all was quiet again.

I now took time to think, and was of the opinion that we were ambushed from the point of timber between the two roads, and that the enemy had let us pass, and were firing into the advance of our column; still I could not account for the shots fired at me. I concluded to flank around and get to the column if possible. At that moment up came scout number two. We struck out and circled about a mile, striking the middle of the column, and soon learned that I was the sole object of all the firing. It appears that Stedman, when he rode up, did not recognize me, but hastily retreated to the fork of the road, and commenced firing at me with his revolver, causing the advance to hurry forward, who in turn began to fire with their carbines. Loss sustained, one hat. George was cautioned against firing upon his comrades again. It reminds me of the saying, "Better born lucky than rich."

When within four miles of Decatur I was ordered by Colonel Blackburn to take one of my men and proceed to the town and try and ascertain if there was any force stationed at Newton Station, their position; if any artillery, and any information I could obtain. We started, feeling secure of our disguise, and no couriers ahead to tell of our coming. About three o'clock in the morning we entered the quiet town of Decatur, in Newton County. No one seemed astir, the sleeping occupants little dreaming that two "Yanks" were treading on their sacred soil. After going up and down, surveying all the streets, and satisfying ourselves that no one was astir, we halted in front of an old fashioned country inn, with its pigeon-hole windows standing half way up the slanting roof. Dismounting and leaving my horse in care of my comrade, I stepped boldly up on the verandah, approached the door, knocked loudly; no answer. Repeated the summons; still no answer. Tried another door, with the same result. Began to think the hotel was evacuated. Made a forward movement, which proved the right one. After knocking at the door, a gruff voice on the inside inquired "Who's there?" I answered in a loud voice, "A Confederate soldier, on important business, in quest of information." In a moment the door opened, and an invitation to come in was extended, which I at once accepted, stepping into what appeared to be a sitting room and bed chamber in one.

I begged to be excused for disturbing them at so unseasonable an hour. No excuses were necessary. The old gentleman, who proved to be the proprietor of the establishment, scraped out a few coals in the fire place, which threw a lurid light across the room, drew forth a chair, and told me to be seated. At the same time he sprang into bed again, from beneath whose covering I could see a pair of sparkling, roguish black eyes, tresses black as the raven's wing, a mischievous mouth, belonging to a young and charming woman. Can it be possible, thinks I, that she is married to this old man. It must be so, for it is quite fashionable in the South, old husbands and young wives. My hospitable friend, in a mild tone, at once demanded my business. I told him in a few words. Before answering me he was careful to ask me to whose command I belonged, where I came from, and why I was sent through there. I answered him by stating that I belonged to Van Dorn's command, a portion of which was stationed at Columbus, Miss., and I was sent with a portion of them across the country to obtain all the information I could respecting a Yankee raid, which was then being made somewhere in the interior of the State, and supposed to be meditating an attack on the Southern railroad. I wished to know how far it was to any of our forces, at what points stationed, their strength, &c., as it was of the utmost importance that I should communicate to them.

This story seemed to satisfy the old gentleman. He then told me that the nearest force was at Newton Station, that our hospital was there, and about one hundred sick and wounded soldiers occupied it, and he was under the impression that two corps of infantry were stationed there. He also said that a considerable force of cavalry had passed a few days previous within five miles of Decatur, going east. He had heard the day before many conflicting reports about the Yankees, but had no idea that they would ever reach this far. Had he known that the "blue coats" were then within rifle shot, that dreaded disease, the "cholera," would not have caused more consternation in town. My partner called me. A sweet voice invited me to call if I came that way again. I promised, and, bidding good-bye, left them to slumber.

I met the column just entering the town, reported to Colonel Blackburn, and again assumed my place in front. It was not long after leaving this town that streaks of daylight began to appear in the east, and a glorious sun arose to crown the day.

EIGHTH DAY

The eighth day found us passing through a timbered country somewhat rolling, and displaying but little cultivation. Decatur is a small place in Newton County. It being night, I could see but little of the town. When within five miles of Newton Station Colonel Blackburn ordered me to proceed lively with my two men to the station, reconnoitre, and report what force was stationed there, what time the train would arrive, and so forth.

This suited us. On we went, meeting with no obstacles, approached to within half a mile of town, found an elevated position, from whence I could obtain a pretty good view of the place; could not see any camp; saw several persons walking and standing around a large building, which I took to be the hospital. I felt pretty well satisfied that there was no force stationed there, or we would have seen their pickets ere we approached so close to town.

I told the men we would proceed and see a little more before reporting. We started leisurely along and stopped at a house just at the edge of town; found a white man, called for a drink of water, and asked him how long before the train would be in. He said it was due in about three quarters of an hour. I ascertained that no force was stationed here. Was obtaining other information, when my ears were startled by the whistle of a locomotive. It seemed a long way off. I then inquired what train that was. The man said it was the freight train coming from the east, due at nine o'clock, A.M.

I now allowed there was no time to lose in order to capture the train. The column must be here. I at once sent back one man to tell the Colonel to hasten with all speed or lose the train. I then, with my scout, made for the depot to secure the telegraph, but found, upon reaching there, no office. By this time the convalescents began to pour out of the hospital, (which building stood within one hundred yards of the depot) to see who and what we were. I knew the column would be here in a few minutes, and, with revolver in hand, approached it and told them to remain inside, not to come out on peril of their lives.

In a moment the column came charging down the street, which was immediately picketed to prevent any one leaving town. The horses were led back behind the buildings, and one man sent to each switch, to lay concealed until the train passed, then to spring forward and alter it. Every "blue coat" was ordered to lay behind the buildings until the train was secured. On she came, puffing and blowing with the weight of twenty-five cars, loaded with railroad ties, bridge timber and plank. In a few minutes this train was in our possession and switched on a side track. Another train would be due in a few minutes from the west. Men were placed near the switches. The command was ordered to hide themselves from view, and everything was perfected just as the whistle sounded. On she came rounding the curve, her passengers unconscious of the surprise that awaited them. The engineer decreased her speed. She was now nearly opposite the depot. Springing upon the steps of the locomotive, and presenting my revolver at the engineer, told him if he reversed that engine I would put a ball through him. He was at my mercy, and obeyed orders. It would have done any one good to have seen the men rush from their hiding places amid the shouts and cheers which rent the air of "the train is ours." It contained twelve freight cars and one passenger car, four loaded with ammunition and arms, six with commissary and quartermasters' stores, and two with dry goods and household property belonging to families moving from Vicksburg.

This train being switched off on the side track with the other, the private property thrown out, fires were kindled in each car. The whole soon became one continuous flame. By eleven o'clock the heat had reached the shells, which began to explode, and must have sounded at a distance like a sharp artillery duel. Such was the impression it had on Colonel Grierson and the rest of the command, who were eight miles in our rear, following us up. As soon as they heard the reports of the bursting shells, they allowed that Colonel Blackburn was attacked, and the order was given, "trot, gallop, march," and on they came, expecting battle, but instead, found the men had charged on a barrel of whisky, which they were confiscating. I did not see a man that had more or less than a canteen full.

As soon as Colonel Grierson came up, two battalions, under command of Major Starr, of the sixth Illinois, were sent to destroy the bridges and tressel-work for six miles on the east side of the station, while one battalion of the seventh, under command of Captain Hening, destroyed them the same distance on the west, also effectually destroying the telegraph lines for some distance.

TENTH DAY

Left camp at five o'clock—the sixth Illinois in advance. Three soldiers had to be left behind this morning, they being too feeble to travel further. About eight o'clock we passed through Raleigh, Smith County, a small place having rather a deserted appearance. On entering the place I discovered a man hastily mounting his horse and riding away at full speed, which looked rather suspicious; he was requested to halt, but paying no attention, kept increasing his speed. I told two of my men to give him chase; they being well mounted soon came up within pistol shot of him, when a few shots fired convinced him that there was danger in his rear, he concluded to halt, and very reluctantly returned to town, where he was delivered over to Colonel Grierson, together with five thousand Confederate "greenbacks," and a bundle of papers; he proved to be the county sheriff, and possessed some valuable information.

During the day we traveled through considerable pine timber plantations, few and far between. We experienced some scarcity of forage. It
was just about dusk when I stopped at a plantation to dry my clothes,
it having rained all the afternoon; had a very lively conversation with the
proprietor who proved to be another sheriff (but minus the five thousand), one that had no little conceit of his own abilities; he imagined we
were hunting up deserters, and did not trouble himself to ask our business particularly, not half so much as we did to try the quality of his
home-made whisky, which he very generously supplied.

Imagine his astonishment when I ordered his Negro servant to bring
his master's horse to the door without delay, at the same time allowing
the sheriff permission to procure a change of clothing, which he crammed
into his saddle bags with an oath, exclaiming that it was d——d strange
that he should be ordered round in his own house in this style, that he
was not subject to conscription, and he be d——d if somebody should not
have to pay for this trouble. He did not seem well posted in military
matters. By this time up came the column, and Mr. Sheriff was introduced
to Colonel Grierson, under the impression that he was in the presence of
some noted general in the Confederate army. He was ready to tell all he
knew, and more too. We were now nearing Stony River and near West-
ville, in Simpson County, when the column was overtaken by two messengers from Captain Forbes, who was then about thirty miles in our
rear, requesting us not to burn any more bridges, as he was endeavoring
to overtake us. This was joyful news to us. One of the messengers, whose
name is Wood, was one of the scouts, and had rendered much valuable
assistance on the expedition that was now trying to reach us, of which I
will speak hereafter. About nine o'clock the Sixth Illinois camped on the
plantation of Major ———; the Seventh, going a mile further, crossed
Stony River bridge and camped at Mr. Smith's plantation. The rebel
Major was quietly seated in his house, when Colonel Grierson halted before it. Coming out he wished to know whose command this was. No
one seemed to pay any attention to him, but riding in through his gate
into his garden, dismounting and hitching their horses to the beautiful
shade trees. This was more than he bargained for, and he foamed and
tore around, swearing that it was an insult upon his dignity, and he'd
be d——d if he would not report the commanding officer to General
Pemberton; he would not stand such abuse and insult on his own
premises; his garden was ruined, and they were feeding up all of his corn
and fodder. The Major learned his mistake before morning, respecting
our character, and had nothing more to say about his garden. Distance
marched this day forty-two miles. Though tired and sleepy, there were
those who did not rest or sleep longer than to feed their horses and prepare supper. As the citizens were arming themselves, and the news was
flying in every direction, it was a matter of life or death that Pearl River
should be crossed and the New Orleans and Southern railroad reached,
without any delay. So thought Colonel Prince; and acting on the impulse
he had an interview with Colonel Grierson, and obtained permission to
move directly forward, and with two hundred picked men of his regiment
to secure the ferry across Pearl River before the enemy should destroy it.
The following companies were detached: I, C, E and L. The distance to

the river was thirteen miles, and from thence to Hazelhurst Station twelve miles. The remainder of the two regiments were to come forward as soon as they were sufficiently rested. The Colonel left with the four companies at two o'clock on the morning of the twenty-seventh. Some of the scouts accompanied him, they being permitted to sup.

ELEVENTH DAY

At daylight the remainder of the command moved out, and it was discovered that Mr. Sheriff number two had effected his escape during the night, and availed himself of a fine horse belonging to one of Colonel Grierson's orderlies. Taking the advance I reached Pearl River, and found that Col. Prince had succeeded in crossing about one hundred of his men. He had reached the bank of the river before daylight, and, contrary to the information he had received, the flat-boat was upon the opposite side. Not daring to arouse any of the citizens, the Colonel called for a volunteer, who, with a powerful horse, undertook to swim the river; but the rapidity of the swollen stream carried him far below the landing, where there was quicksand, and he barely escaped to the shore with his life; his name was Henry Dower, company I, Seventh Illinois. A few minutes later a man from the house came down toward the river, and, with North Carolina accent, wanted to know if we wished to cross, to which the Colonel replied, in a very fair imitation of the same tongue, that a few of us would like to get across, and it was harder to wake his Negro ferry-men than to catch the d——d conscripts. The proprietor apologized, and woke up his ferrymen, who brought the boat across, from which time it remained in federal possession. For all the proprietor knew it was in the possession of the first regiment Alabama cavalry, from Mobile. The Colonel says the breakfast he gave the first Alabama will long be highly appreciated. The importance of this dispatch in this instance was proved half an hour later, by the capture of a courier, who was flying to the ferry with the news that the "Yanks" were coming, and that the ferry must be destroyed immediately. By the time that Colonel Prince had crossed his two hundred men the rest of the command came up, having left a guard at Stony River bridge to await the arrival of Captain Forbes. It was known that a rebel transport was some seven miles up the river, that carried two pieces, six-pounders. Colonel Grierson sent a detachment of men two or three miles above the ferry, where they could lay behind the river bank, secure from artillery, and engage the transport if she attempted to come down; but she did not make her appearance, probably apprehending capture. Leaving the rest of the command crossing—a slow, tedious task, as only twenty-four horses could go at a time—Colonel Prince with his two hundred men proceeded toward Hazelhurst. The scouts were ordered ahead, and had not advanced more than four miles before we began to pick up citizens, who were collecting together and arming themselves to repel the invader. One small man, with sandy whiskers and foxy eyes, trying to look as savage as a meat-axe, had secured in an old belt around his waist two large old flint-lock dragoon pistols, and slung over his shoulder a large leather pouch and powder-horn, and on his left shoulder, with his hand resting on the stock, an old United States musket, flint-lock. As I came up to him he brought his gun to a carry arms, and between a grin and a laugh exclaimed: "They is coming, Capting, and I am ready; I've jist bid the old woman good-bye, and told her that she need not expect me back until I had killed four Yankees, and they were exterminated from out our Southern *sile;* I'm good for three of them, anyhow; I've been through the Mexican war, and know how to use them ere weapons." I gave the men the wink, which they understood, and approaching the "exterminator" began to compliment him on the appearance of his arms, and requested to look at them. Without any hesitation he passed over his musket to me; the other men in the meantime had his pistols. I informed him he was a prisoner, and would soon have a chance to see the General.

When within four miles of Hazelhurst, Colonel Prince handed me a written dispatch and ordered me to send two of my men with it to the station, to be handed to the telegraph operator. I at once hastened forward and sent Stedman and Kelly. The dispatch was addressed to General Pemberton, at Jackson, Miss., stating that the Yankees had advanced to Pearl River, but finding that the ferry was destroyed, and that they could not cross, had left, taking a northeast course. The scouts had no difficulty in reaching the station, found the telegraph office, the operator and six or eight Confederate officers and soldiers standing and seated around, not having the least idea that any Yankees were on the south side of Pearl River. The dispatch was examined and various questions asked by the parties, all of which were satisfactorily answered. The dispatch being sent the men complained of being hungry, and said they would cross over to the hotel, and mounting their horses they were half way over when up rode, in great haste, Mr. Sheriff number two, who had escaped the night before. He at once recognized the scouts as two of the party who had helped to drink his whisky; the men knew him, too, and began to feel for their revolvers, while the sheriff, with naked sword in one hand and horse-pistol in the other—which proved to be empty—began to assume rather a dangerous character; at the same time shouting for help, and ordering everybody to stop them d——d Yankees. The men thought it would not pay to resist, so they prudently commenced a retreat. Several persons tried to stop their horses, but the sharp crack of a revolver impressed them with the idea that it would not be a safe business, and gave them a wide berth. They met me within one mile of town. After stating their adventures I immediately sent one man back to report to the Colonel, also to tell the advance guard to come on double quick, while with the remainder of my men we charged back into town, the rain at the time pouring down in torrents. The first place to visit was the depot. Not a soul was there except two old men; the rest had all absconded, the operator tearing up his instrument and taking it with him. He had not countermanded the dispatch, as was ascertained. When the two scouts retreated the Confederates thought that the Yankees were then in sight, and without waiting to secure their private property skedaddled, the honest sheriff with them. Upon inquiry we learned that a train was soon due from the north. The usual precaution was taken to secure it; but after waiting half an hour beyond the time for its arrival the command became careless, and no further attention was given it, supposing that news had reached the next station of our approach. This was a sad mistake, for when every one was scattered around town, thinking of anything else, the train came around the corner, from which point the engineer had a good view of a score of "blue coats." He "smelt a rat," and reversing his engine retreated safely with seventeen commissioned officers and eight millions in Confederate money, which was *en route* to pay off troops in Louisiana and Texas. A large lot of empty and loaded freight cars was burned, considerable commissary stores, four car-loads of ammunition, the telegraph cut in several places, the track torn up and some tressel-work destroyed.

The depot was spared on account of its being so near private buildings; they would undoubtedly have caught fire. This was a humane act, and was highly appreciated by the citizens. Though every precaution was taken by the officers to prevent the destruction of private property, the flames were soon seen to burst forth from a drug-store on the east side of the depot, resulting in the burning of three other buildings, two of which were empty stores and the third a private residence; none of the buildings was of very large dimensions. Every exertion was made to extinguish the fire and prevent its spreading.

Hazelhurst is in Copiah County, and is not a very large place; the buildings are somewhat scattered. But little taste or neatness is displayed, though we found some very clever people there, and some who still entertained a strong feeling for the old Union, and were bitterly opposed to secessionism. Two or three barrels of eggs and a quantity of sugar, flour and hams was found in the depot, which was taken to the hotel and cooked for all hands as long as it lasted.

The explosion of boxes of ammunition and bursting of some shells not only alarmed the citizens to some extent, but had a startling effect on Colonel Grierson and the column with him, which was about half way between the station and ferry. The order was given at once to "trot," then "gallop, march!" and they came charging into town, expecting to find Colonel Prince hotly engaged with the enemy. It was only the explosion of the ammunition and shells, that we had purposely fired, and they were sold again, as at Newton Station.

Captain Forbes, who was sent to Macon, rejoined the command just as the rear guard was crossing Pearl River. After the whole command reached Hazelhurst they rested four or five hours, giving me a good opportunity to listen to Captain Forbes relating his adventures.

When within three miles of Macon he had decided to camp. Before reaching this place the scouts had captured twelve Confederate soldiers, picking them up one, two and three at a time. The Captain being informed that there were about four hundred troops, mostly conscripts, stationed in Macon, plus nine hundred troops who had arrived that day from Mobile, he concluded not to visit Macon, and early next morning started back. After marching eight miles the scouts picked up a soldier belonging to the Second Mississippi Artillery. He happened to be one of those individuals that had been opposed to the war, but rather than be conscripted had volunteered. This man proved of considerable service to the Captain, he having a good knowledge of the country; just the man the Captain wanted, and he used him to good advantage. Striking towards the railroad, with the intention of cutting the telegraph and burning a bridge between Macon and Enterprise, to prevent a force being sent from the former to the latter place; but on nearing the railroad he learned that the bridge was strongly guarded; he concluded to avoid it, and destroying the telegraph proceeded towards Newton Station, at which place he was informed that Colonel Grierson had gone to Enterprise. The Captain had a tedious time reaching this point, having to go through swamps, swim streams, travel through timber without any roads, for hours at a time, in order to avoid forces that were patroling the country in quest of us. From Newton Station he went the nearest route to Enterprise, and when within one mile of the town learned that a force of three thousand rebel troops were just getting off the cars. He promptly raised a white flag and rode forward, demanding the surrender of the town in the name of Colonel Grierson! To this demand the rebel commander, Colonel Goodwin, asked an hour to consider upon it, and inquired of the Captain where he would be found at the end of that time. Captain Forbes replied that he would fall back to the reserve. It is not known whether Enterprise surrendered or not, although an article was read in the Jackson-Granada-Memphis-Appeal, of April 26th, that fifteen hundred "Yanks" had demanded the surrender of the place. The Captain made good use of the hour in getting to the reserve. He followed our trail for four days, making forced marches of sixty miles a day, swimming streams, over which we had burned the bridges, to prevent the enemy following us.

When near Raleigh, Robinson learned that a company of guerrillas were in that place. The Captain ordered a charge, and so complete was the surprise (they thinking that all the "Yanks" had passed) that not one of them escaped. They were taking dinner, and ere they knew it, they were surrounded; they numbered twenty-nine men. Their arms were destroyed, men turned loose, the horses and captain of the company taken along. After leaving this place, Lieut. McCausland suggested to Captain Forbes that if he would let him he would send three men, well mounted, to overtake Colonel Grierson. His request was granted, and I have previously mentioned how successful they were. Captain Forbes was highly complimented by Colonel Grierson for his success.

At seven o'clock the command left Hazelhurst, the Sixth Illinois in advance. Taking a northwest course it proceeded towards Galiton. It now became necessary to use every precaution. We had passed within twenty-five miles of the capital of the State—cut the railroad and telegraph communications on the New Orleans and Great Northern Railroad. The enemy's scouts had been sent out, and were watching our movements; couriers were flying in every direction, spreading the news, forces were concentrating and sent to intercept us, hem us in and annihilate us, as they boasted, and felt confident of accomplishing. They certainly had every advantage on their side—a perfect knowledge of the country— every road, public or private—every stream of water, small or large—the fordable places and bridges—forces above and below us on the railroad, in our front at Port Gibson, Grand Gulf and Port Hudson—following in our rear—retreat was impossible, even if such an idea had occurred to us, we having destroyed our only hope in that quarter—bridges and ferries. Colonel Grierson was not one of the retreating kind; his motto was "onward." With one of Colton's maps—a small pocket companion—with the states and counties on it, he made his way through the enemy's country. The road selected, it was then the duty of the scouts to keep its communication open, thereby causing no delay to the column.

Colonel Grierson was, just at this time, executing one of his flank movements, which had so many times thrown the enemy off our track, leaving them far in our rear. It was about nine o'clock when we entered the small town of Galiton, driving out a few guerrillas. We had not proceeded many miles further when a train of wagons was discovered ahead, drawn by oxen. The scouts were withdrawn; the Sixth Illinois dashed ahead, and after a few shots fired, captured a thirty-two pound Parrott gun, fourteen hundred pounds of powder, two wagons, and some provisions, *en route* for Grand Gulf. The gun was spiked, wagon and powder destroyed. After proceeding a few miles further, we went into camp at Hargrove's.

FIFTEENTH DAY

On the morning of the first of May, just as daylight began to appear, the command left camp, taking a southwest course—Seventh Illinois in advance—and as we wended our way through the woodlands, we little dreamed what a change would be produced in a few hours. The sun arose in all his glory—not one cloud visible in the sky to obscure its dazzling brightness.

About ten o'clock we emerged into the Clinton and Osyko road. I at once discovered, by the newly made tracks, that a column had passed, and could not have been long before. Sending a man back to Colonel Grierson, he soon came up and examined closely. It was the opinion of all the officers that a considerable force had passed, and was going in the same direction as ourselves. I was then ordered by Colonel Grierson to advance cautiously, to let nothing escape my observation on either side of the road, and if I saw any object that I could not satisfy myself about, to report at once to him, and not to get more than half a mile from the advance. After receiving these instructions I started, followed by my scouts; had proceeded about two and a half miles when I discovered horses hitched in the edge of the timber, near the road-side on our left; I could see that they were saddled, but could not discover any person around. We were then about three hundred yards from them. I immediately sent one man back to report to Colonel Grierson, and taking two of them with me started on, using the necessary precaution of having our revolvers ready at hand. As we approached nearer I could see that there were but three horses and three men, two of them sitting upon a log talking, the third lying down. They were well armed, each man carrying a carbine and revolver. They did not seem to think strange of our approach. We rode up to them and I said, "Hello, boys, on picket?" "Yes; been on about an hour and feel devilish tired; been traveling night and day after the d——d 'Yanks,' and I'll bet my horse they will get away yet." "That is just our case," I replied, "but where is your command?" "Over in the rush bottom, resting"—pointing with his hand. "Whose command is it, and how many have you?" Just then two shots were heard in our rear, and sounded as though fired on the right of the road. At this they began to open their eyes and prick up their ears. There was no time for further questioning, so giving the men the sign, each one of us covered his man with his revolver, demanding their surrender, and to hand over their arms at once or we would blow them through, and ordering them to mount, double-quicked them back to the column, which was halted some four hundred yards in our rear. In order that the reader may more fully understand the situation of affairs, I will try and describe the surrounding country. On our left as we advanced was timber; on our right a large plantation, a two-story frame-house, painted white, standing back from the road some three hundred yards; between the house and main road the ground was covered with a dense growth of live-oaks and silver-poplars, completely hiding from the house the view of any passing column. Two roads wended their way through this little forest from the main road to the house, one above and the other below it, taking an oblique direction. It appears that when the column was stopped, the advance was just opposite the house, and while waiting for further developments from the scouts, several men under command of Lieutenant Gaston, company G, Seventh Illinois, proceeded to the house. As they rode up to the gate they were surprised at seeing four armed rebels standing around in the yard, their horses being tied outside the gate. The "rebs" were surprised as well, and both parties showed a disposition to fight. Our men demanded their surrender, which they had no notion of complying with. Both parties commenced firing upon each other, which resulted in our men taking two, putting the other two to flight, and an easy capture of the four horses. One of our men was struck in the breast by a buck-shot, striking one of his ribs and glancing off without inflicting a serious wound. This explained the firing while at the picket-post, and these four "rebs" belonged to that post, but had gone to the house to procure something to eat, not expecing the "Yanks" to come that way. They paid little or no attention to their duty.

I was again ordered to proceed cautiously, and upon reaching the place where we had taken in the picket I thought I could see two mounted men off to my right, in an oblique direction, and about one quarter of a mile off; an open field was between us, having a gradual descent towards them. On surveying the road with my eye I could see that after following it for a quarter of a mile it turned a right angle, and then at the distance of another quarter it entered the timber, at which point those two men appeared sitting on their horses, and not moving but looking very earnestly at us. That a force was down in the bottom, and that not very far off, was pretty well understood; but what that force was, and their number, we did not know, but, as the game says, we had to "go it blind." Leaving a man at this point with instructions to stop the column, which could advance this far without being seen by those who appeared to be watching us from below, and at the same time see all that was going on in the bottom, outside of the timber, I proceeded with Stedman. Fowler and Wood had taken the right-hand road, and advanced on it about one hundred yards, when one of the horsemen cried out in a loud voice, "What in h——l does all that firing mean?" I answered that reinforcements were coming up, and that his picket had fired on our advance, thinking that they were "Yanks," but no one was hurt, and it was all right. At this one of them broke out in a roar of laughter, and said "Is that all?" and putting spurs to his horse started towards us at a gallop, leaving his comrade behind. I told Fowler to let him ride up between us, and I would manage him. Each one of us carried our revolvers in our hands ready for instant use. Up he came, looking much pleased, and said, "How are you, boys; how much force have you got?" We had now halted, and as he rode in between us I turned my horse in an oblique direction, changing my revolver into my left hand, cocked it, and pointing it at his breast, attracted his attention to it, and in a quiet way told him not to speak or make a motion, but hand over his arms to Fowler or I would blow him through; he at once complied, though not without some astonishment at our proceedings. I then directed my attention to "reb" number two, and discovered that he was coming slowly towards us. Stedman, who had dismounted for some reason, was leading his horse and advancing to meet him. He had returned his revolver to its holster, feeling confident that he had an easy prey. They met about one hundred yards from where I was then standing. Stedman was so anxious to secure his man that he forgot for a moment the character he was to play, which came near proving fatal to him. As they met Stedman let go his bridle-rein and grasped that of his opponent, at the same time laying his hand firmly on his revolver holster and ordered him to surrender. This proceeding somewhat confused the "reb's" ideas, and for a moment he did not know what to think, at the same time he looked up the hill and must have seen the column advancing. He was a large, athletic man, while Stedman was very small. With a quick movement he tried to release the hold Stedman had on his holster, at the same time saying. "Who and what in h——l are you?" It only took a moment to see something was wrong, and calling to Wood to come on I put spurs to my horse, and in a few moments was presenting a revolver at his head, threatening to blow his brains out if he did not surrender; he at once complied. I could not but admire his manly proportions, and face beaming with courage and bravery. I noticed the gold bars on his collar, which in the Southern army denotes captain. I ordered him to follow me, and told him not to be alarmed, that we were Illinois boys and he would be treated well. Smilingly he said, in a clear, firm voice, "I am not afraid, sir; I would not have been your prisoner had it not been that I was deceived in your dress." He proved to be a Captain Scott, and commanded the force then within rifle-shot. Just at this time Colonel Blackburn came galloping up, alone, and said to me, "Sergeant, bring along your scouts and follow me, and I'll see where those rebels are." I called one of my men and told him to take the Captain back to the column, which by this time had descended the hill, and were advancing within four hundred yards of us. I then started, followed by Kelly, Wilson and Wood. The Colonel being some distance ahead we had to increase our speed to a gallop to overtake him. It seemed to me that this was a rash movement on the part of Colonel Blackburn, but he had ordered me to follow him, and it was my duty to obey. As soon as we reached the spot where the two horsemen were first seen, we were at the end of a lane, and a few yards further all was timber. A considerable stream of water could be seen wending its way through the marshy and heavily timbered bottom. A little to the left, about seventy-five yards, is the crossing, a narrow plank bridge, some fifty feet in length, better known as Wall's Bridge, across the Trickafaw River, in Hunt County, and within one mile of Wall's post-office. Just before we reached the bridge we were saluted by a few shots fired from the opposite side of the stream, which did not check our speed, but rather increased it. Closely following Colonel Blackburn all dashed upon the bridge, but ere the last one of us had reached the opposite side we were greeted by a loud volley of carbines and musketry, coming from some eighty of Colonel Wirt Adams' cavalry, who lay in ambush not more than fifty yards distant. It seemed as though a flame of fire burst forth from every tree. The Colonel fell, along with his horse, both pierced by the fatal bullet. One of my comrades had his horse shot under him. A Minié ball struck me on my right thigh, passing through it into my saddle, just grazing my horse's back. Three shots were all I could get. I began to feel a faintness creeping over me, but still clinging to my revolver I turned my horse about and tried to retrace my steps amid the flying bullets. When the first few shots were fired it was heard by Colonel Grierson, who then occupied the advance, and was the advance guard of the column. On they came, most gallantly, led by Lieutenant Styles, who charged across the bridge, followed by only twelve men. No sooner over the bridge than they were checked by a well directed volley. They rally and charge, but it is useless—they were too few and exposed, while the enemy were protected by the surrounding timber. The little band have to retreat back across the bridge, leaving one man killed and two wounded, and seven dead horses. They had no support; the column was too far behind to lend assistance in time, but just as they re-crossed the bridge the column came up on the double-quick. Colonel Prince, by order of Colonel Grierson, ordered companies A and D of his regiment to dismount. They were sent to the right and left as skirmishers. One section of Captain Smith's battery was brought up, the woods were shelled, the enemy put to flight, and our men were pursuing them; and as they pass Colonel Blackburn, who laid mortally wounded, with one leg under his horse, cries out to them, "Onward! follow them, boys!" and cheers. The Sixth now take the advance—no halt is made—the Seventh look after the killed and wounded; they are all borne by friendly hands, and with tender care placed in the ambulances and carried forward one mile and left at the plantation of Mr. Newman. Their horses, equip-ments and arms are turned over to comrades and friends to take through with them. Many a kind farewell was given, and friends parted, some never to meet again on this side of the grave.

The command was now in Louisiana, Amit County being the last county passed through in Mississippi. We found the roads in good condi-tion, and were making not less than six miles per hour. It was about two o'clock, P.M., the column was about six miles from Wall's Bridge, and the scouts, who were in the advance, discovered off to the right about forty rebels advancing on a side road leading into the main one. The scouts made a halt at this corner and fired several shots, which was replied to by the "rebs," who still kept advancing, seeming determined to gain the main road, but ere they could accomplish this the Sixth came in sight, and at the distance of six hundred yards brought one of their guns into position and threw a few shells among them, which had the desired effect, causing them to beat a hasty retreat. This was most opportune, for had they gained the main road nothing could have prevented them from reaching the Amit River and effectually destroying the extensive bridge over that stream, which would have resulted most seriously with us. About 4 P.M. the command passed through Greensborough, a small town in St. Helena County. It was here that Lieutenant Newall, company G, Sixth Illinois, overtook the command, having been sent early that morning with a few men to procure horses and provisions.

As the scouts entered this place Samuel Nelson discovered a mounted "reb," who was armed with a shot-gun, and apparently standing picket on a cross-road. Samuel approached him, and saluting him inquired who he was and what he was doing there. He replied that he was the County Clerk, and was waiting for a courier to come up that he might learn the news. Samuel then asked him if he knew who he was talking too. The fellow replied that he did not remember seeing him before, but thought he was a soldier and belonged to Port Hudson. Samuel says, "No, sir; you are mistaken—you are talking to a live Yankee, and here is some Yankee whisky." "Reb" looked somewhat surprised at first, but displayed good taste and judgment—took the proffered canteen, and raising it to his lips took a good drink. As soon as the column came up Samuel turned him over, but before they parted company he very politely asked Samuel for "another nip of that Yankee whisky."

On leaving town the column took a southwest course. The night was a clear, starlight one, and moderately warm, the moon not making its appearance until about eleven o'clock, which added to the beauty of the surrounding country. Yet there was little interest displayed in the scenery, the men being too much exhausted for want of rest, and nearly every man was nodding as he rode along. For the last hour previous to reaching the Amit River considerable delay was occasioned by waiting for the scouts, who were ordered to visit different plantations and obtain all the information they could respecting the situation of the bridge and whether any force was stationed there. Before reaching the bridge the scouts learned that a post of couriers was stationed during the day, and at night withdrawn, one half mile from the bridge, on the south side of the river. If this should prove to be the case, what a considerable advantage would be gained? Once across this bridge and all was comparatively safe. So thought Colonel Grierson, who was fully awake to the interests of his command. When within one mile of the bridge the roads became very muddy and rough. The column was halted, and the scouts were ordered to proceed to the bridge and ascertain if any picket was stationed there. Samuel taking the advance arrived at the bridge, dismounted and proceeded across on foot. The bridge was about two hundred yards in length, over a deep and rapid stream. He found it all right, and was not long in reporting this good news to Colonel Grierson, who gave the order "Forward!" and in a few minutes the horse's hoofs could be heard rattling upon the planks. It was a striking scene to witness the column crossing this long bridge at the hour of midnight. After crossing the column passed through a delightful country. The distance from the Amit to the Comit River is seventeen miles, and better roads are seldom traveled in the interior of any state. No alarm had been given in crossing the bridge. The couriers, who numbered ten men, were asleep at a house about half a mile from the bridge, little dreaming that the Yankee raiders were then within rifle-shot. They were not disturbed, and not until daylight did they learn what a rich prize had escaped their vigilance.

SIXTEENTH DAY

On crossing the bridge over Big Sandy Creek the scouts discovered a camp not more than two hundred yards from the bridge, but could not discover any sentinels, and upon approaching nearer saw two Negroes, who were busy building a fire. Without being seen the scouts withdrew and reported to Colonel Grierson, who immediately ordered Lieut.-Col. Loomis to send forward two companies of the Sixth to open fire, while the rest of the regiment brought up the rear. Captain Marshall, company H, dismounted his men, crossed the bridge silently—being supported by Captain Lynch, with company E, mounted—and when within one hundred yards raised a tremendous yell, shooting and charging down through the long rows of tents, which must have somewhat startled the unconscious sleepers, who felt so perfectly secure as not to have out any pickets. Instead of finding a considerable force here, as was expected, there were only about forty men, principally convalescents, nearly all of whom were captured. The force stationed at this place numbered six hundred (Williams' cavalry). They had the day previous to this been ordered to push forward to Brookhaven and intercept the Yankees. Colonel Grierson at once ordered Colonel Prince to move forward on the advance, while the Sixth stopped long enough to destroy the camp and garrison equipage, and secure the prisoners, one of whom escaped and was afterwards captured, and related his experience that night by stating that he rushed from his tent, reached his horse, sprang upon his back, and away he went, barebacked, with nothing on but his shirt and drawers and socks; he never stopped until he reached home, some sixty miles distant. The only casualty that happened while capturing this place was the wounding of one rebel.

We will now follow the Seventh, who are in the advance, going at a lively pace, over a good road, which began to show some signs of dust. The morning was beautiful, with a clear sky and a bright sun. The country had the appearance of being very level—on our right somewhat low and swampy, for several miles on our left fine and extensive plantations. After proceeding about a mile and a half a single horseman was seen, by two members of company A, to emerge into the road about two hundred yards in their advance, and between them and the scouts. The road was so straight and level that most any moving object could be seen for the distance of two miles. As soon as he came into the road he was ordered to halt, but did not feel inclined to obey orders, and using his spurs away he dashed, hotly pursued, exchanging a few shots. In a few minutes he overtakes our scouts, whom he takes for some of his own men, and brandishing his revolver over and around his head excitedly says, "Get out of here, boys; the road is full of 'Yanks' in our rear!" "Yes," says one of the scouts, as they closed in around him, "and you are right among them now." Imagine his surprise. His name was Hinson, and a Lieut.-Col. of cavalry. He had heard the firing in the direction of the camp that morning, and was on his way to give notice to a picket-post between them and Baton Rouge. After proceeding about three miles Samuel Nelson, who was somewhat in advance of his companions, met a man walking, a citizen, and asked him if there were any soldiers around. He replied that there was one at the next house, about a quarter of a mile further, on the right-hand side of the road. Samuel pushed ahead and stopped in front of the house. Dismounting and stepping up to the door, which was wide open, he confronted a female, who very politely invited him to enter. On stepping into the room he saw a soldier and three females seated around a table, enjoying a meal. The lady invited him to partake of their hospitality, which invitation he very readily accepted, and while eating had a very lively conversation with the "reb," from whom he learned that there was a company stationed on the road about four miles from there.

After Samuel had got all the information he wanted from the "reb," he asked him where he belonged. He answered that he was a lieutenant, and his command was at Natchez. Samuel then said, "You may consider yourself my prisoner."

Just at this time a squad of company A appeared in front of the house. Samuel again took his place in the advance, reporting to Colonel Grierson the information he had obtained respecting the force ahead. Nothing occurred until the column had arrived within half a mile of the Comit River, at which place the force spoken of was expected to be found. The scouts were ordered to advance cautiously and reconnoitre the ground, and find out the position of the camp. Owing to the situation of the ground the scouts could approach to within three hundred yards of the camp without being seen, the enemy not having out any vidette on that side, and as yet no report had reached them of the Yankees coming that way. The scouts then halted, and Wood volunteered to go and reconnoitre and see what he could discover. Just then a soldier was seen coming up from the creek, and approaching the scouts said, "How are you, gentlemen; have you come to relieve us?" "Yes; the company will be up in a few minutes." "It's about time you come to relieve us; we've been here now four days, and are just about out of rations." The scouts told him they would soon be relieved. In the meantime Wood returned, having obtained all desired information. The camp was situated along the east bank of the stream, shaded by timber, just at the end of the lane, and could not be approached only by charging down the road, which was fenced on either side. After the scouts had reported to Colonel Grierson the command moved forward slowly until within three hundred yards of the camp, when the following companies were ordered to proceed: company A to flank through the field on the left, while companies D, E and I kept the road, the former commanded by Lieutenant Bradshaw, the latter by Captain Ashmead. They charged most gallantly upon the unsuspecting foe. So complete was the surprise that the rebels, forgetting everything, tried to seek safety in flight; but a very few of them escaped, and not more than a dozen shots were fired. The confusion was indescribable—shot guns, saddles, camp-kettles, rifles, old blankets, coats and hats scattered in all directions, while men and loose horses were stampeding from all quarters. It did not take long for our men to flank the woods and pick up the stragglers. One man, a member of company I, found sixteen rebels hid in a hole that the water had washed out by the bank of the stream. They all surrendered to him. While the Seventh was thus engaged gathering up their booty the Sixth was ordered in the advance, so as to save time. It was now about nine o'clock A.M., and in half an hour's time the Seventh followed the Sixth, having captured forty-two prisoners belonging to Stewart's cavalry, together with all their horses and equipments, without sustaining any loss or damage. In order to cross this stream the command had to move up its bank about a half mile and ford it. All those owning large horses had the advantage—they could ford it without swimming, while the small ones had to resort to the latter extremity. After proceeding three miles the whole command stopped to rest and feed, the first for man or horse for the last thirty hours, having traveled eighty miles night and day, with scarcely a halt, and it is to be remembered that nearly the whole command was asleep on their horses while marching the greater portion of the last night.

The command was now within six miles of Baton Rouge, and all felt quite safe. The raid had been one grand success. A kind Providence had smiled upon our efforts all through our perilous journey, and finally crowned it with victory. Nearly eight hundred miles had been traveled in sixteen days, passing through fourteen counties, and through the interior of the State of Mississippi, destroying a great amount of government property, besides the destruction of railroad property, and effectually cutting off communication in various directions, preventing supplies from reaching Vicksburg and Port Hudson, drawing out a force from Jackson, at a time when General Grant was making a rapid flank movement on that place, and on the last morning surprising two camps, capturing and bringing in four hundred prisoners, not including the six hundred that were paroled and left on the route at different points, besides eight hundred horses and mules, and some five hundred Negroes that followed us, a large number of cattle, and a considerable train of vehicles of various descriptions. But what must be considered the crowning glory of the expedition is the fact that during the entire march, and more especially the last forty hours, men and horses hungry and jaded though they were, not a murmur was heard from the lips of either officers or men. Our loss did not exceed twenty men.

While feeding and resting a company of the First Louisiana Cavalry, Union forces, came out from Baton Rouge, the report having reached there that a large force was crossing Comit River and advancing towards that place. This company was sent out to reconnoitre. Picture their astonishment when they learned whose command it was, and where it came from. It was some time before they could be convinced of the fact.

Our prisoners felt quite jubilant. They allowed that a force had to come all the way from Tennessee purposely to capture them; they considered it an honor to be taken by Illinois troops. Altogether they were a jolly set of fellows—the most of them living in Louisiana and Mississippi, and men of wealth. Their captain, at the time their camp was taken, escaped by climbing a tree, where he remained concealed by the Spanish moss, which abounds in that section of the country, and presents a beautiful sight, hanging in long clusters from every limb.

After being formed, and when within four miles of Baton Rouge, the column was met by Captain Godfry, First Louisiana Cavalry, who escorted us into the city. For one half mile before entering the city we were met by citizens and soldiers, both white and black; male and female, old and young, rich and poor, paper collars and ragged urchins; everybody's curiosity was at its highest pitch. The streets were densely crowded, and amid the shouts and cheers of thousands, the waving of banners and flags, interspersed with music, the tired soldiers, all covered with dust, marched through the principal streets, around the public square, down to the river, watered their horses, and then proceeded to Magnolia Grove, two miles south of the city, a most delightful spot, shaded by the magnolia, whose long green leaves encircle a beautiful white flower, which fills the air with its rich perfume.

It was just at sunset that the command entered this grove, and that night, for the first time in sixteen days, they slept soundly under federal protection.

THAT DEVIL FORREST

GRIERSON'S RAID COVERED SIXTEEN DAYS and, in the words of General Grant, "was one of the most brilliant cavalry exploits of the war. . . . It was Grierson who first set the example of what might be done in the interior of the enemy's country without any base from which to draw supplies."

The raid mounted by Colonel Abel Streight into Alabama did not share so fortunate a fate. Starting with about 2,000 officers and men, he was to drive into Alabama and reach Georgia if possible, destroying the railroads connecting Chattanooga to Atlanta and Knoxville.

"A body of men, of well-attested pluck and endurance, were to be selected, armed, and equipped with a special view to the success of this undertaking. They were to be transported by steamers from Nashville down the Cumberland and Ohio and up the Tennessee to Eastport, Mississippi, near the Alabama interstate line. This would bring the troops, at the beginning of their overland journey, safe from all unnecessary exertion or fatigue until the crucial moment should come.

"From twenty to forty miles south of the Tennessee River, and running nearly east and west across the northern portion of the State of Alabama, is a mountainous belt of country sparsely inhabited, and at that time without railroad or telegraphic communications. A good proportion of the inhabitants of this barren tract were Union sympathizers, and many of them had relatives in the Federal army. For the reason that these sympathizers lived along this line, and on account of its remoteness from the telegraph, Colonel Streight had wisely selected this as his route for the movement into Georgia. As there were many rugged hills and mountains to cross, and as the roads were generally in a wretched condition, it was deemed a wise precaution to mount the troops for this expedition on mules, since these hardy animals are surer of foot in difficult going and can stand greater hardships on less forage than horses."[*]

---

[*] John A. Wyeth, *That Devil Forrest*, p. 166.

The Pursuit and Capture of
Streight's Raiders*

BY JOHN A. WYETH

ON THE AFTERNOON OF THE 10TH OF APRIL the leader of this expedition received orders from General Garfield to embark at once on steamers and proceed to Palmyra, on the Cumberland River. At this point he was to land his troops and march across the country to Fort Henry, on the Tennessee. Streight reached Palmyra on the 11th, disembarked, and sent the fleet around to the Ohio and up the Tennessee to Fort Henry, where he arrived on the 15th, one day ahead of the boats. He brought with him every mule in all that country upon which he could lay his hands, for he had orders to strip the land of these useful animals as he went. On the 17th the expedition was again afloat convoyed by two gunboats and General Ellet, with a brigade of marines, and reached Eastport, Mississippi, on the 19th of April, where his command was finally disembarked.

Due notice of his coming had been given by General Rosecrans: "Colonel Streight, with near two thousand picked men, will probably reach Eastport by Thursday. Dodge, with the marine brigade and the gunboats, can occupy or whip the Tuscumbia forces, and let my force go directly to its main object—the destruction of the railroads. This great enterprise, fraught with great consequences, is commended to Dodge's care, enjoining on him to despatch Streight by every means to his destination. Nothing should for a moment arrest his progress."

Colonel Streight had no sooner set foot on land than he hastened to a conference with General Grenville M. Dodge, who with 5,500 infantry and cavalry had already arrived at Bear Creek, twelve miles from Eastport. This officer had encountered a small force of Confederate cavalry west of Bear Creek, at Glendale, but these had retired before his advance to the creek; and on April 17th, without much difficulty, he succeeded in crossing this stream, and marched thirteen miles toward Tuscumbia. Colonel P. D. Roddey, with a small brigade of cavalry, attacked one of his columns here with such vigor that he threw it into confusion, captured two pieces of artillery, twenty-two artillerists, and one company of mounted infantry; and although Dodge retook one of the guns, he was so troubled over the results of the day and the nonarrival of Streight's column that he fell back to Bear Creek to await his arrival and to send for more help. He telegraphed to Corinth for Fuller's brigade, 2,000 strong, and another battery, all of which reached

* from *That Devil Forrest*.

him in good time, increasing his force, exclusive of Streight's raiders, to 7,500 men. At that time he was confronted only by a single brigade of cavalry under Roddey.

At Eastport the woes which an unkind fate had in store for the gallant Hoosier raider and his band began to be in evidence. While he was absent, in conference with General Dodge until midnight, the great cargo of mules had been put ashore, and with clarion tones these noisy animals were celebrating their deliverance from their natural dread of a watery grave. Some irresponsible Westerner, who had nothing to do but to wear a blue uniform, carry a musket, and fight, suggested that since this species of animal did not appear upon the roster of the original ark, they had determined on this occasion to celebrate loud enough to make up for all past slights. The braying of mules was not an unusual sound to Roddey's cavalry, who were hovering about the Federal encampment, with the true instinct of Confederate cavalrymen seeking what they might devour. Many of them in this busy time of war were glad enough to get even a mule to ride, and it is said of the men who took General Dodge's cannon only a few days before that they were experts in selecting those which were fast.

During the night, after the fashion of Comanches, they crept into Colonel Streight's corral and, with hoots and yells and the firing of guns and pistols, stampeded this army of mules. This officer says: "Daylight next morning revealed to me the fact that nearly four hundred of our best animals were gone. All of that day and part of the next were spent in scouring the country to recover them, but only about two hundred of the lost number were recovered. The remainder fell into the hands of the enemy. The loss of these animals was a heavy blow to my command, for besides detaining us nearly two days at Eastport, and running down our stock in searching the country to recover them, it caused still further delay at Tuscumbia to supply their places."

Colonel Roddey and his troopers were doing very effective work. They never did better service than this, and when the gallant fight they made under brave Colonel W. A. Johnson at Brice's Crossroads is recalled, no greater compliment could be paid them. The delay thus caused in the execution of this bold conception of the Federal commander and his trusted subordinate was fatal to its success. It gave General Bragg time to hear of it and to select for its defeat the man of all men capable of its accomplishment.

Colonel Streight with his caravan filed out of Eastport on the afternoon of April 21, 1863, and brought up the rear of Dodge's troops, which were continually skirmishing with the enemy as they advanced as far as Tuscumbia. So thoroughly was Roddey doing his work that it took the Union forces (four times his number) until 5 P.M. on the 24th of April to reach Tuscumbia. At this place General Dodge, according to Streight, supplied him with two hundred mules and six wagons to haul his ammunition and rations; but General Dodge officially reports: "I took horses and mules from my teams and mounted infantry and furnished him some six hundred head. I also turned over ten thousand rations hard bread." The troops were now carefully inspected by the surgeon of the command, and all men not fit for the arduous duties to be undertaken were sent to the rear. The colonel says: "This reduced my command to fifteen hundred men."

On the 25th, Colonel Streight received a piece of news which gave him great concern: "General Dodge informed me there was no doubt but Forrest had crossed the Tennessee River and was in the vicinity of Town Creek!" Dodge's information was not altogether correct. Forrest was coming like a whirlwind, by night-and-day marches, and was not far away; but as yet the lion was not in Streight's path, and the way was open. If ever delay was dangerous, the leader of this expedition was now incurring it. Properly employed, the 25th and 26th of April were worth a world to Colonel Abel D. Streight.

At Spring Hill, on April 23rd, a message had arrived from General Braxton Bragg, directing Forrest to make a forced march with his old brigade to Decatur, Alabama, and, uniting there with the brigade of Colonel Roddey, to take charge of all the Confederate troops and check the Federal advance. On receipt of this order, Colonel Edmondson's Eleventh Tennessee was hurried off with directions to reach Bainbridge on the Tennessee River as soon as possible, cross there, and effect a junction with Roddey. Following with the Fourth, Ninth, and Tenth Tennessee regiments and Morton's battery, Forrest crossed the Tennessee River at Brown's Ferry, near Courtland, Alabama, on the 26th, and was soon in position to dispute the farther advance of General Dodge. Just before crossing this formidable stream he had directed Colonel Dibrell to take his Eighth Tennessee regiment and one gun, march along the northern bank of the river in the direction of Florence, and to use his artillery at every opportunity in order to create as much of a diversion in the Union rear as was possible.

Help had come none too soon for Roddey's brigade, which had struggled manfully with the overwhelming force under the Union leader. General Dodge had pushed out with his legions, and on Monday, April 27th, had driven the Confederates across Town Creek, when he ascertained "that the enemy were in force under Forrest on the opposite bank."

On the 28th, although "the resistance of the enemy was very strong, and their sharp-shooters very annoying," the Union commander succeeded in crossing the creek, the Confederates retiring toward Courtland. Notwithstanding his advantage, Dodge again withdrew to Town Creek that night and there encamped.

It was here, about dark on the evening of the 28th of April, when the fighting had ceased and the Union forces were going into camp on Town Creek, that a well-known citizen of Tuscumbia, Mr. James Moon, after a hurried ride around and through various Federal detachments, reached General Forrest with the startling intelligence that a very considerable body of mounted Union troops, estimated at about two thousand, had passed through Mount Hope in the direction of Moulton, and were probably now at the latter place. In his original plan, General Rosecrans had intended that Dodge should advance no farther than Tuscumbia in aid of Streight; but when at this point he informed the leader of the raiders that Forrest was at Town Creek, Streight insisted that Dodge should attack the latter and drive him at least as far as

Courtland, or even to Decatur, and thus hold Forrest off. Streight says, moreover: "It was understood that in the event Forrest took after me in the direction of Moulton, Dodge and his cavalry were to follow Forrest." Swinging loose from all support, and taking advantage of the darkness of night to conceal his departure, Streight's "lightning brigade" marched out of Tuscumbia in the direction of Mount Hope on the 26th of April. Although Mount Hope was the first point aimed for, it must have been that evil forebodings filled the heart of the raider chief as he stumbled and groped his way along the almost impassable roads of northern Alabama. He says: "It was raining very hard, and the mud and darkness of the night made our progress very slow."

Sergeant H. Briedenthal, of Company A, Third Ohio Infantry, in his journal says: "We were aroused from our refreshing slumbers in camp at Tuscumbia at eleven o'clock at night, and prepared our meals and mules. We were in the saddle at 1 A.M., and started on the Russellville road, but made only five miles by daylight, on account of the badness of the roads, and the depth of the streams swollen by the recent rains. We reached Russellville at 10 A.M., a distance of eighteen miles northwest of Tuscumbia. Halted long enough to feed, and at 11 A.M. were in our saddles, and took a westerly direction. At sunset reached Mount Hope, a small village thirty-six miles from Tuscumbia, where we went into camp somewhat fatigued and hungry."

On the night of the 27th, at Mount Hope, Colonel Streight received the cheering news from Dodge that he had Forrest on the run; that he had crossed east to Town Creek, had driven the Confederates away, and that he must now push on. Colonel Streight did push on through mud and slush and rain, and late on the afternoon of the 28th of April woke up the sleepy village of Moulton with the largest procession of Union troopers that secluded spot had yet entertained. Here he fed and rested his weary cavalcade until 1 A.M. (29th), when, saddling up, he moved eastward, with Blountsville as his next objective.

Sergeant Briedenthal says: "After a ride of twelve miles over the most miserable roads, we arrived at dark in Moulton, the capital of Lawrence County, and bivouacked about 9 P.M. At one o'clock on the morning of the 29th we were mounted and off in a westerly (easterly) direction."

As Streight was filing out of Mouton at one o'clock on the morning of the 29th of April, sixteen miles away to the north another body of mounted men was leaving the suburbs of Courtland and heading after them. The plucky raider, relying upon the understanding with Dodge, little dreamed at this midnight hour that the man of all men he most dreaded, at the head of a determined lot of fighters, made veterans under his iron hand and absolutely devoted to his service, had boldly cut loose from in front of Dodge and with rapid stride was bearing down upon him.

When Forrest, at dark on the 28th of April, had received information of the presence of so large a body of mounted troops so far detached from their main column, his quick perception took in the situation at a glance. Calling his staff at once, he gave explicit directions as to the disposition of the troops whose duty it would be to confront Dodge and hold him where he was or retard any pursuit. He sent a courier to Dibrell to attack at once Dodge's outposts near Florence; to use his artillery freely, and create the impression that a considerable force was threatening the rear of the Union commander. This he did with the hope that it would draw him back to Tuscumbia. In order to prevent any possibility of a return of the raiders to unite with General Dodge's column, or prevent any reinforcements to them from this source, he directed Colonel Roddey to take his Alabama regiment, the Eleventh Tennessee regiment (Edmondson's), and Julian's battalion, to interpose these troops between Dodge and Streight, and then follow on directly after the raiders. Starnes's and Biffle's regiments, two pieces of John W. Morton's battery, and Ferrell's six pieces (heretofore with Roddy) were speedily prepared for the pursuit. Forrest did not leave the details of preparation to any subordinate, however faithful and reliable. He selected the best horses and harness, and double-teamed his artillery and caissons. He even stood by to see the ammunition carefully distributed, with directions to the captains of companies to say to each man that "no matter what else gets wet he must keep his carridge box dry." He saw to it that the farriers were busy shoeing the horses and tightening the shoes which were loose.

Three days' rations were cooked, and shelled corn issued for two days' forage. To the successful commander, close personal attention to these details was essential, and he knew it. At the bottom of his remarkable and almost unbroken series of brilliant achievements, may not this patient attention to the smallest detail explain in part the wonderful measure of his success?

By one o'clock on the morning of the 29th of April all was ready, and as the cavalcade rode out of the town of Courtland, in the cold drizzling rain which was falling and making the muddy roads still more difficult, there began a race and running fight between two bodies of cavalry which, in the brilliant tactics of the retreat and stubbornness in defense on one side, and the desperate bravery of the attack and relentlessness in pursuit upon the other, has no analogue in military history.

Steadily throughout that night, and well into the daylight of the 29th, the Confederate leader rode without a halt. The mud was deep and the night so dark that even the animals could scarcely find their way. At eight o'clock, an hour for feeding and resting the horses, and then through to Moulton on the forenoon of this day.

In the meantime, Colonel Streight had not been idle. From Moulton he had struck a steady gait and kept it up, and had placed seventeen miles to his credit on the 29th, reaching at dark a defile or gorge which leads to the summit of Sand Mountain and is known as Day's Gap. In addition to this good march over rough and muddy roads on a direct line, his men had swept the country for several miles on each side of the highway, taking all the horses and mules, not only to replace any which might break down, but to prevent them from being used by the enemy, should pursuit be made. He says: "We destroyed during the day a large number of wagons laden with provisions. We were now in the midst of devoted Union people. I could learn nothing of the enemy." And here, at the foot of Sand Mountain, he rested for the night, still unconscious of the fact that the "Wizard of the Saddle" was on his trail.

While the Union troops were sleeping, Forrest's hardy riders were reel-

ing off mile after mile of their heavy task. At Moulton they had stolen
another hour of rest, with the saddles off to cool the horses' backs while
feeding the hungry animals. Just as the bugle sounded to "saddle up," the
sunlight broke though a rift in the western sky, and as their chieftain
mounted his horse and gave that ever-famous command, "Move up, men,"
twelve hundred hats were lifted, and the rebel yell that split the air might
well have shaken the sparkling pendants of rain from the tender green
leaves of that April afternoon. The moment was auspicious. The wild
enthusiasm of his men was to him the harbinger of success. Never was
mortal man more in his element than Nathan Bedford Forrest at this hour.
Of him and these men Lord Wolseley says:

They were reckless men, who looked to him as their master, their
leader, and over whom he had obtained the most complete control. He
possessed that rare tact—unlearnable from books—which enabled him
not only effectively to control these fiery, turbulent spirits, but to attach
them to him personally "with hooks of steel." In him they recognized
not only the daring, able, and successful leader, but also the commanding officer who would not hesitate to punish with severity when he
deemed punishment necessary. He thoroughly understood the nature
and disposition of those with whom he had to deal, their strong and
their weak points, what they could and could not accomplish. He never
ventured to hamper their freedom of action by any sort of stiff, barrack-
yard drill, or to embarrass it by any preconceived notions of what a
soldier should look like. They were essentially irregulars by nature, and
he never attempted to rob them of that character. They possessed as an
inheritance all the best and most valuable fighting qualities of the
irregulars, accustomed as they were from boyhood to horses and the use
of arms, and brought up with all the devil-may-care, lawless notions of
the frontiersman. But the most volcanic spirit among them felt he must
bow before the superior iron will of the determined man who led them.
There was a something about the dark-gray eye of Forrest which
warned his subordinates he was not to be trifled with and would stand
no nonsense from either friend or foe. He was essentially a practical
man of action, with a dauntless, fiery soul, and a heart that knew no
fear.

A little after midnight, Forrest, at the head of the column, had arrived
within four miles of Day's Gap. Here he learned that the Union troops
were encamped at the foot of the mountain, in the mouth of this defile.
Now assured that he had his adversary in striking distance, he halted
the men and told them to feed and rest until near daylight. The roadside
was soon lined with the weary troopers so soundly sleeping that dreams
of neither war nor peace disturbed them. It took several hours for the
column to close up. The trying pace had told on many of the horses,
and it was near daylight when the last of the stragglers caught up. They
in turn were allowed a short respite.

Not all the Confederates, however, were allowed to rest. The general
thought his brother, Captain William Forrest, and his famous "Forty
Scouts" did not need sleep. He ordered him to "keep right on down the

road and get up close to the enemy and see what they are doing." Captain Bill moved on, and in the moonlight succeeded in getting between an unsuspecting rear vedette of the Federals and their main column, and capturing them. He then advanced to within sight of the campfires of Streight's command, and without disturbing their slumbers concluded to give his own men a rest. It is said that man proposes, but that the disposition is elsewhere. In any event, the famous scouts were not to sleep for the short part of the night now at their disposal. One of this company relates that when they were here, close to the Union camp, just before daylight, there broke out the most awful noise to which mortal man had ever been called upon to listen. In one mighty effort nearly two thousand mules, braying in far-reaching and penetrating chorus, set the echoes in vibration among the Alabama mountains. So loud and continuous was this unusual noise that Forrest's scouts discarded all idea of sleep and laughed at the drollery of their serenade.

Over in Streight's camp, the salute to the morning which had so disturbed the Confederate scouts was the breakfast call of the hungry drove. Colonel Streight had determined to be up and away before daylight, and in good time his men were bestirring themselves to feed the animals. At the head of his column, with wagons near the front, and before the day was yet breaking, on April 30th, the Federal commander moved slowly up the narrow, winding, and rocky road by which Sand Mountain is here ascended. In and out as the way runs, it is more than a mile to the summit. From boulders and knobs and trees the gap should be easily held from direct assault, by one against four. It took an hour to make the ascent, and was sunrise when the great undulating plateau was reached.

The caravan almost filled the snakelike highway from top to bottom, and when the advance was on the crest the rear guard of the Union troopers and some loiterers were still lounging about the campfires when suddenly, and from a distance of not over five hundred yards, a cannon boomed on the morning air, and a whizzing shell exploded among the startled stragglers. These and the rear guard did not stand upon the order of their going, but went. In wild disorder the campfires and kettles were abandoned as they chased after the column of raiders climbing up the mountain, with Captain William Forrest and his company in swift pursuit.

Colonel Streight says: "We moved before daylight. I had not proceeded more than two miles at the head of the column before I was informed that the rear-guard had been attacked, and at that moment I heard the boom of artillery."

General Forrest had also moved by daylight, and was in the immediate vicinity of the Union rear before his presence was suspected. Seeing the difficulty of driving Streight from so formidable a position by direct assault, he ordered Biffle's and Starnes's regiments, under McLemore, to hasten by a neighboring pass and take the enemy in flank and rear. The wily Hoosier, however, did not wait for this. His two Alabama companies from this immediate section knew the passes and the country, and in this the Confederates had no advantage. They had told him of the other routes. "I soon learned that the enemy had moved through the gap, and were endeavoring to form a junction in my advance." He therefore hurried on across the mountain, his rear guard followed steadily by Captain Bill Forrest's men and the advance of Edmondson's and Roddey's regiments and Julian's battalion. About two miles from the top or western crest of Sand Mountain, Colonel Streight saw he had to make a stand, and standing or running, by night or by day, and without regard to odds, Forrest was determined to fight him whenever he saw him. His order was: "Shoot at everything blue, and keep up the scare."

The country through which Streight was now passing "was of open sand-ridges, very thinly wooded, and afforded fine defensive positions." It was well named Sand Mountain, the topsoil or covering being fine sand or sandstone, in various grades of pulverization. It is the lower or southwestern termination of the great Appalachian range. The elevation is about five hundred feet above the valleys which bound it, and the plateau varies in width from twelve to twenty miles. On top, the land is slightly undulating, with numerous small streams or creeks worn deeply into the surface of the earth, like small canyons or deep ravines, with steep banks, heavily fringed with a thick growth of small trees and dense mountain laurel. Away from these streams there is a fairly rich growth of various species of oak, pine, and hickory trees.

For defensive warfare, as Colonel Streight reports, it is admirably adapted, and here, about two miles from the crest of the mountain, he laid the first ambuscade. His line of battle was formed "along the crest of a ridge circling to the rear. Our right rested on a precipitous ravine, and the left was protected by a marshy run that was easily held against the enemy." Skirmishers extended well beyond either flank to guard against surprise. The mules were to the rear and out of range. In the center of his line and concealed by brush were two twelve-pounder howitzers. He had scarcely got everything in shape, guns loaded, and men all lying down, when his rear guard of the Alabama companies came scurrying down the road, with Bill Forrest leading his men right on their heels.

As soon as Streight's men passed through the gap in the line left open for them, the Federals from either side of the road poured a furious and effective volley into the Confederate scouts. A Minié ball crushed the brave captain's thigh bone, and several of his men were killed or wounded by this deadly fusillade before they could check their horses and run out of range.

General Forrest now rode to the front to inspect the Federal position. He had at hand only a portion of Edmondson's and Roddey's regiments, Julian's battalion, his escort company, and the remnants of Captain Forrest's company. In the hard ride since leaving Courtland a number of the horses had not been able to keep up with the advance. Those that came in late to the bivouac, four miles west of Day's Gap, had been left to rest and care for their animals, and were not yet on the ground. There were not one thousand Confederates all told on the top of Sand Mountain at this hour. Dismounting Edmondson's men, Forrest threw them into line, while Roddey and Julian, mounted, were deployed to the right, and to the left his escort and the scouts were placed. The two guns of Morton's battery, having just arrived, were brought up and opened upon the Union line. Edmondson's trained veterans advanced steadily, and when they had reached a point within about a hundred yards of the Federal troops, the two mounted companies on the left rode into the skirmishers on this flank.

At this moment Roddey's and Julian's men recklessly urged their horses well in front of the alignment of Edmondson's men, and by their advanced and exposed position brought on themselves a murderous volley from the greater portion of the Federal line. A number of men and horses were killed or wounded, and, seeing they had been thrown into confusion, the able Federal commander seized the moment to order a charge which, gallantly made, swept the mounted Confederates from the field. As Edmondson was now overlapped and enfiladed, and in danger of having the right files of his regiment captured, he and the escort and Captain Forrest's scouts also fell back, yet steadily without confusion. Reaching the two guns, they made an effort to take these away, but as several of the horses, having been shot, had become entangled in the gearing, the pieces with their caissons could not be extricated in time and fell into the hands of the advancing Federals.

Whether justly or unjustly, General Forrest never forgave the lieutenant in charge of the artillery for the loss of these guns in this encounter at Day's Gap. In the reorganization of his troops a few weeks later he requested that the artillerist be transferred to another command, and although he preferred no charges against the young officer, the latter, resenting what he interpreted as a reflection upon his courage, in an unfortunate moment attempted to kill his commander.

To those who have been with General Forrest when his troops suffered even a temporary repulse, and know how furious he became, it is not difficult to depict the state of mind he was now in at the loss of his two pet guns. He was praying for Starnes and Biffle to come up; but, alas, they were off on the flank movement and could not be had. He rode in among the men with his saber drawn and accompanied his deft employment of this weapon with a series of remarks well calculated to increase the temperature of the mountain atmosphere. He told every man to get down and hitch his horse to a sapling. There would be no horse-holders in this fight; men were too scarce. Those guns had to be retaken if every man died in the attempt, and if they did not succeed they would never need their horses again. One of Forrest's staff (Captain Henry Pointer), when at last the men were lined up for the charge and the general was riding along to tell every trooper just what he expected of him, rode up to a fellow member of the military family (Major Anderson), drew a modest little bundle of sliced ham and bread from an inside pocket, and, offering half of it to him, remarked: "Major, we had better eat this now, I reckon, for from the way the old man is preparing to get his guns back it might spoil before we get another chance at it."

The order to move up was soon given, and the line of dismounted troopers in desperate mood moved steadily forward. As they neared the strong position from which they had been repulsed, the enemy again opened fire upon them, but without artillery and in feeble, scattering shots. The charge was now ordered, and the men went forward only to see the rear guard of the Union column mount their mules and scamper away in the direction of Blountsville. This was about 11 A.M., on the 30th of April. Streight was satisfied with the first repulse and the capture of the guns, and as soon as the Confederates gave way he had hastily departed, taking the captured pieces with him. He admits in this skirmish a loss of about thirty killed and wounded. Among the mortally wounded was Lieutenant Colonel Sheets, of the Fifty-first Indiana. Forrest claimed about fifty or seventy-five of their killed and wounded were found on the field. The Confederates should naturally have suffered more severely, as they were the assailants and received the fire of the Federals, who were better protected. Of the Confederate officers, Captain William Forrest, brother of the general, was desperately wounded. Fortunately his injury did not prove fatal or permanently unfit him for service.

By the time the Confederate troopers could get back to their horses and resume the pursuit, their vigilant and energetic adversary had a start of nearly an hour. The running fight had opened. The tactics of both leaders were now in evidence. With Colonel Streight it was to move with celerity, until his rear was too hard pressed, and then, whenever a suitable position offered, to ambuscade his adversary, and thus discourage direct assault. Forrest would thus be compelled to attempt to ride around him and head him off.

The raiders were now on the run, and Forrest had no idea of letting them rest until he had worried them into a surrender. His chief anxiety was that Streight might sheer off on some byroad toward the Tennessee River, take the back track, and break for safety by reuniting with Dodge. He did not think Dodge's cavalry was near him, and yet he wanted to make his work sure. With great rapidity he now pressed on after the flying column. Six miles eastward from the battleground of the morning a byroad came in, and along this he saw the Fourth and Ninth Tennessee regiments riding swiftly after their detour around Day's Gap. The distance had, however, been too great to enable them to accomplish the object of this movement. The Federals had passed before they could strike the road. The arrival of these veteran regiments gave great satisfaction to the Confederate leader. He now ordered Colonel Roddey with his regiment and Julian's battalion to retrace their steps and place themselves in observation in front of General Dodge. To preclude the possibility of Streight's escape toward Guntersville, on the Tennessee, Edmondson's regiment, accompanied by Major Charles W. Anderson of the staff, was dispatched toward Somerville and Brooksville in a general direction parallel with the route upon which Streight was moving, and between him and the river.

Under his immediate leadership, in the direct pursuit of Streight, he retained his escort, Captain Forrest's scouts, and the regiments of Biffle and Starnes, and with these moved rapidly on. It was not long before they began to overhaul the swift-marching raiders. The mule tracks in the road grew fresher and fresher at every stride of the pursuers, and soon the moist and dark-colored sand in the deepest hollow of the hoofprints told that they had just been made.

Nine miles from Day's Gap the blue coats of the Federal rear guard came in sight, and the vedettes of the Fourth Tennessee were soon crowding them up on the moving column. For a mile the skirmishing went on, increasing in briskness and gradually demanding more and more attention from the Federal colonel. He says: "Finally the enemy pressed upon our rear so closely that I was compelled to prepare for battle. I selected a strong position on a ridge called Hog Mountain. The whole force soon became engaged about one hour before dark. The enemy strove first to carry our right, then charged the left, but with the help of the two pieces captured in the morning and the two mountain howitzers we were able to repulse them."

This obstinate and plucky encounter did not cease until ten o'clock at night, when Streight retreated. Forrest in person led his men again and again in the assault, with seeming desperation. The Federals stood their ground, and much of the fighting was at close range and at times hand to hand, with no light by which to distinguish friend from foe, except the flash of pistol and carbine and the artillery, which the Federals alone had in the action. Ever in the thickest of the fray, the Confederate commander had one horse killed and two others wounded under him in this bloody encounter; nor did Streight's picked veterans yield until Biffle, with a strong detachment and the daring escort company, had under cover of darkness made a flank movement and borne down upon the mule-holders in the Union rear. Streight then quickly mounted and retreated, leaving his dead and wounded to the Confederates. In the hurry of his retreat he was unable to carry off the two guns he had captured that day, and left them again in the hands of the Southerners. The Union leader says: "The ammunition we had captured with the guns was exhausted, and being very short of horses, I ordered the guns spiked and the carriages destroyed."

The Hoosier colonel had scarcely started again before he had to turn and fight the persistent Tennesseeans who, with the ferocity of blood-hounds, were at his heels. The extreme peril of his situation now began to dawn upon him. He realized that the only safety lay in the integrity of this end of the column. Colonel Hathaway's Seventy-third Indiana regiment was given this important duty, and, as Colonel Streight says: "I remained in the rear in person. We had scarcely got under way when I received information of the enemy's advance." This information came from the cracking carbines of Biffle's picked hundred, who were now Forrest's advance guard. They came on so boldly and became so noisy and insistent that Colonel Streight concluded to give them another check. It was now late in the night; the clouds had disappeared and the moon was shining brightly. The position for the ambuscade was well selected. On each side of the road along this barren region was a dense thicket of young pines which had sprung up in the track of a hurricane which years ago had mowed a wide swath through the primitive forest of oaks. Here he quickly dismounted Hathaway's men, hurried the mules some distance up the road, and concealed his troops within short gunshot range of the highway by having them lie down in the dark shadows of the saplings.

As the Confederate advance vedette came on at a stiff pace and approached the ambuscade, he was made to suspect the nearness of the enemy by the conduct of his horse, which, with a keener sense of sight and smell than his rider, stopped suddenly in the roadway. Retracing his steps until other troopers of the advance guard came up, he informed the lieutenant in command of the suspected proximity of the Federals. General Forrest was soon notified of the situation, and called for volunteers to draw the enemy's fire. From these, three were selected and told to ride forward, observe closely, and retreat as soon as they recognized the presence of the enemy or received their fire. Moving at a cautious gait, these daring riders became aware of the proximity of Hathaway's men as they were rising from the prone position to deliver their fire. Wheeling quickly about and throwing their bodies well down upon the horses' sides farthest from the enemy, the trained scouts saved themselves from the death trap so skilfully laid. One of these, Private Granville Pillow, of Grove's company, Biffle's regiment, quickly made his way to the rear and guided General Forrest near the position of the ambuscaders.

Forrest ordered one gun of Ferrell's battery, under Lieutenant Jones, to be double-shotted with canister; this was noiselessly shoved by hand along the soft, sandy road until, as indicated by the scout, it was within two hundred yards of the thicket from which the Union troopers had fired. It was a novel experience to the artillerist, but, carefully aiming his piece by the moonlight, he pulled the lanyard, and the charge went crashing through the pines. The Indianians responded with a return salute of small arms. The Confederates brought up a second piece near enough, and several shells were then fired along the road. The raiders, not expecting this turn in affairs, sought their mules and resumed their flight.

Colonel Streight says: "We were not again disturbed until we had marched several miles, when they attacked our rear-guard vigorously. I again succeeded in ambuscading them, and we continued our march, and reached Blountsville by ten o'clock in the morning." This last ambuscade was between 2 and 3 A.M. on May 1st, and was practically a repetition of the other. From Day's Gap to Blountsville Colonel Streight had not had a minute's rest or peace, and in making this distance of forty-three miles he had consumed twenty-eight hours.

Forrest now had his antagonist so far from his base at Tuscumbia that he was assured he could not escape in that direction. Should he at Blountsville turn north toward Guntersville, Edmondson and Anderson would head him off until he could close in upon him from behind and destroy him. The only other alternative opened to the raider was to plunge farther into the hopeless distance which lay between him and the arsenals at Rome and the Western and Atlantic Railroad at Dalton. Forrest knew he could wear Streight down before he should reach his goal, and with this in mind, at three o'clock in the morning of May 1st, all hands were ordered to dismount, unsaddle, feed what corn they had brought to their animals, and lie down for a two hours' sleep. This was a short nap, considering the fact that out of the last forty-eight hours they had ridden steadily for forty-four, and for eighteen hours they had fought almost without cessation.

While the Confederates slept, Streight's tired and weary yet determined band was winding down the eastern slope of the Sand Mountain plateau into the valley of corn and plenty. They reached Blountsville at 10 A.M. on May Day, and instead of the usual festivities the citizens of this quiet country town amused themselves in entertaining their first *visitors in blue.*

They furnished corn for two thousand hungry animals, and had the pleasure of seeing every horse and mule in all that region gathered up and carried away in speeding the parting guests. Moreover, they witnessed a lively cavalry fight, which was followed by a second entertainment of a second tired and hungry army of horses and men, and all within the short space of three hours. It was the liveliest day in the history of Blountsville, and the pretty Queen of the May was for once neglected.

Colonel Streight did not tarry longer than was necessary to impress all the horses and mules, and corn enough for feed, and to give men and stock a much-needed though very brief respite. The persistent hammering Forrest had given him had taught him the urgent need of a faster pace, and he now determined to rid himself of every possible encumbrance to more rapid flight. A fresh supply of ammunition was distributed to the men, rations issued, and the contents of the wagons transferred to pack mules. The wagons were then bunched and set on fire, but just as the smoke was rising in the air General Forrest, at the head of his escort and a portion of the Fourth Tennessee, charged into the village, driving Captain Smith's rear guard in a whirlwind of dust through and out of the town, to seek shelter in the main column of the flying raiders. Taking possession of the deserted camp, the Confederates soon extinguished the fire in the burning wagons, and secured a rich and much-needed booty.

Colonel Streight says: "After resting about two hours, we resumed our march in the direction of Gadsden. The column had not got fairly under motion before our pickets were driven in, and a short skirmish ensued between Forrest's advance and our rear-guard, under Captain Smith, in the town of Blountsville. The enemy followed closely for several miles, continually skirmishing with the rear-guard, but were badly handled by small parties of our men stopping in the bushes by the side of the road, and firing at them at short range." Despite the great advantages of the Federal leader's position, the Confederates never for a moment relaxed their relentless pursuit, and their general was at the front of it by night and day.

The methods employed by General Forrest to insure discipline and to impress upon the mind of his troopers the importance of obtaining information which was absolutely reliable, and not hearsay, were original and at times extremely severe.

Not far from Blountsville a scout belonging to Captain Bill Forrest's company, who had wandered off a mile or two from the main road to a country blacksmith's shop for the purpose of getting his horse shod, came back to the column at full speed and in great perturbation, anxiously inquiring for General Forrest. Riding up to the commander, he told him in an excited tone that a heavy force of Union cavalry was moving on the road which ran parallel with the one upon which his command was marching, and that they were then not more than four miles off. Forrest said: "Did you see the Yankees?" The man replied: "No; I did not see them myself, but while I was at the blacksmith's shop a citizen came galloping up on horseback and told me he had seen them."

He had scarcely delivered himself of this piece of information when General Forrest, with both hands, seized the astonished soldier by the throat, dragged him from his horse, and, shoving him against a tree near the roadside, proceeded to bump his head vigorously against the rough bark of the trunk. Having sufficiently punished the unreliable scout, this overbearing leader of men, who, when he found it necessary for the good of his command, constituted himself judge, jury, and executioner, said: "Now, damn you, if you ever come to me again with a pack of lies, you won't get off so easily!" Macbeth, springing upon the messenger with unpleasant and uncertain news, with that fierce denunciation, "The devil damn the black, thou pale-fac'd loon," was not more ungovernable nor unreasonable than was Forrest in his furious rage.

From Blountsville to the Black Warrior River, a run of about ten miles, the peril of Streight's rear increased to such an extent that he was compelled to turn on his pursuers once more to secure a crossing of this swift and dangerous stream. Under cover of a heavy line of skirmishers he hurried the main portion of the command through the rocky ford, with the loss of only two pack mules (each carrying two boxes of hard bread), which, stumbling over the large, loose stones in the bed of this mountain torrent, went under and were carried away with the current and drowned. On the east bank the two howitzers covered the pell-mell withdrawal of the skirmish line, from which, as the Tennesseeans vigorously charged, several prisoners were taken.

With the exception of two companies, which were ordered to push onward after the Federals and "worry them," Forrest gave his command another respite here for three hours. Some of the Confederates were not so weary of body but that they found time from sleep to strip off and wade in the Warrior, to relieve the dead pack mules of what was *"hard tack"* before it got wet. It did not matter to the hungry troopers if it was wet, for as one freckle-faced, brawny youth remarked, while struggling up the steep bank with the heavy, soaking box on his shoulder: "Boys, it's wet and full of mule hair, but it is a damned sight better than anything the old man's a-givin' us now."

Streight reports that it was about 5 P.M. on the 1st of May when the last of his command crossed the east branch of the Black Warrior. "With the exception of small parties who were continually harassing the rear of the column, we proceeded without further interruption until about nine o'clock the next morning, May 2d, when the rear-guard was fiercely attacked at the crossing of Black Creek near Gadsden."

After the short halt at the Warrior, General Forrest had once more roused his men for their fourth consecutive night march, and, pushing on, overtook his faithful advance guard, which was then skirmishing with the raiders at Big Will's Creek. Sending Biffle's men to the rear for a well-earned rest, and taking their place with his escort, he in person now took charge of the attack, and, gaining rapidly on the Union column, closed in upon the raiders about four miles eastward from where he first struck them, at the ever-famous Black Creek bridge.

Black Creek is a crooked, deep, and sluggish stream with precipitous clay banks and mud bottom. It has its source on the plateau of Lookout Mountain, the southern limit of which range is less than one mile to the north. Only a little farther away, in a series of precipitous falls and whirling cascades, pure and crystal while a mountain stream, leaping from rock to rock it falls from its high estate to mingle with the stained and muddy waters of the lowlands.

Spanning the creek on the main road leading from Blountsville to Gadsden there stood in 1863 a rude, uncovered wooden bridge. There was no other means of crossing the stream (deemed impassable except by bridge or boat) nearer than two miles, where there was a second structure, so rickety and unsafe, however, that it had been abandoned. Colonel Streight, sorely pressed by his pursuers, had built his hopes of escape more upon this obstacle in Forrest's path than any other possible to him before he reached the Chattooga River near Rome, and he bent every energy to cross his command over and destroy this bridge before the Confederates could close in upon him.

This accomplished, and believing the creek could not be forded, he could take it easy for at least half a day and allow his worn-out cavalcade to sleep and to recuperate. By nine o'clock on the morning of May 2nd, despite Forrest's persistent rush at the rear guard for the last four miles, all of his men were over except the rear vedette. His howitzers were in position on the eastern bank, fence rails were piled upon the structure, and it was well in flames. At this moment a cloud of dust came sweeping down the road; in front of it, at full speed, a man on horseback wearing a blue uniform, and in the whirlwind, though not yet distinguishable, a squadron of Confederates. The man in blue, seeing the bridge ablaze and escape now impossible, checked his horse, threw up his hands, and surrendered. The foremost man in the pursuing squadron was General Forrest.

Close by the roadside and some two hundred yards from the westerly approach to the bridge was a plain farmhouse, having only a single story, with two or three rooms on either side of a wide-open passageway, after the fashion of the primitive dwellings of this section of the South. Owning this home, and the small tract of land on which it had been built, there lived a widow and two young unmarried daughters. Their chief means of support had been an only son and brother, and they had sent him to the war in 1861, in one of the first companies that left Gadsden to join the Southern army. He was then away in the Nineteenth Alabama Infantry, and they, with all they had of help given to the cause which they believed was right, were struggling to make the little farm yield enough for their support.

They owned no slaves, nor did at least one-half of the families in the South who gave life and whatever property they possessed to the Southern cause. They fought no war for slavery, but for what they believed to be their right to live like freemen, as they were born, and under whatever form of government the majority decreed. This was the faith of these honest women. The outside world can scarcely appreciate the influence of the women of the Southern states in carrying on the fight when it was once started. Such were their devotion and intensity of purpose that from sixteen to sixty-five years of age no able-bodied male was free from the pressure they exercised in various ways to attach him to the active service. It was this spirit that actuated the widow Sansom and her daughters, and on the 2nd of May, 1863, one of these daughters, Emma Sansom, wrote her name in history.

As Forrest came dashing down the road, close on the fleeing Federals, this girl of sixteen years, recognizing him as a Confederate officer and knowing, as she says, "we were now in the midst of our own men," told him that the bridge was destroyed, and in reply to his questions informed him that there was no other bridge nearer than two miles, but that there was near by, on her mother's farm, an old ford where at times, in very low water, she had noticed the cows wading across the creek, and she believed that he and his men might be able to cross there. No one but her folks knew anything about this "lost ford," and she would guide him to it. So many exaggerated versions of this simple affair have found their way in print that I determined to get from the one best able to give it— viz., Emma Sansom, now Mrs. C. B. Johnson, of Calloway, Texas—a true statement of the incident.

Emma Sansom was born at Social Circle, Walton County, Georgia, in 1847. In 1952 her father moved from Georgia to the home on Black Creek, Alabama, and there died in 1859. She writes:

When the war came on, there were three children—a brother and sister older than I. In August, 1861, my brother enlisted in the second company that left Gadsden, and joined the Nineteenth Alabama Infantry. My sister and I lived with our mother on the farm. We were at home on the morning of May 2, 1863, when about eight or nine o'clock a company of men wearing blue uniforms and riding mules and horses galloped past the house and went on towards the bridge. Pretty soon a great crowd of them came along, and some of them stopped at the gate and asked us to bring them some water. Sister and I each took a bucket of water, and gave it to them at the gate. One of them asked me where my father was. I told him he was dead. He asked me if I had any brothers. I told him I had "six." He asked where they were, and I said they were in the Confederate Army. "Do they think the South will whip?" "They do." "What do you think about it?" "I think God is on our side and we will win." "You do? Well, if you had seen us whip Colonel Roddey the other day and run him across the Tennessee River, you would have thought God was on the side of the best artillery."

By this time some of them began to dismount, and we went into the house. They came in and began to search for fire-arms and men's saddles. They did not find anything but a side-saddle, and one of them cut the skirts off that. Just then some one from the road said, in a loud tone: "You men bring a chunk of fire with you, and get out of that house." The men got the fire in the kitchen and started out, and an officer put a guard around the house, saying: "This guard is for your protection." They all soon hurried down to the bridge, and in a few minutes we saw the smoke rising and knew they were burning the bridge. As our fence extended up to the railing of the bridge, mother said: "Come with me and we will pull our rails away, so they will not be destroyed." As we got to the top of the hill we saw the rails were already piled on the bridge and were on fire, and the Yankees were in line on the other side guarding it.

We turned back towards the house, and had not gone but a few steps before we saw a Yankee coming at full speed, and behind were some more men on horses. I heard them shout, "Halt! and surrender!" The man stopped, threw up his hand, and handed over his gun. The officer to whom the soldier surrendered said: "Ladies, do not be alarmed, I am General Forrest; I and my men will protect you from harm." He inquired: "Where are the Yankees?" Mother said: "They have set the bridge on fire and are standing in line on the other side, and if you go down that hill they will kill the last one of you." By this time our men had come up, and some went out in the field, and both sides commenced shooting. We ran to the house, and I got there ahead of all.

General Forrest dashed up to the gate and said to me: "Can you tell me where I can get across that creek?" I told him there was an unsafe bridge two miles farther down the stream, but that I knew of a trail about two hundred yards above the bridge on our farm, where our cows used to cross in low water, and I believed he could get his men over there, and that if he would have my saddle put on a horse I would show him the way. He said: "There is no time to saddle a horse; get up here behind me." As he said this he rode close to the bank on the side of the road, and I jumped up behind him. Just as we started off mother came up about out of breath and gasped out: "Emma, what do you mean?" General Forrest said: "She is going to show me a ford where I can get my men over in time to catch those Yankees before they get to Rome. Don't be uneasy; I will bring her back safe." We rode out into a field through which ran a branch or small ravine and along which there was a thick undergrowth that protected us for a while from being seen by the Yankees at the bridge or on the other side of the creek. This branch emptied into the creek just above the ford. When we got close to the creek, I said: "General Forrest, I think we had better get off the horse, as we are now where we may be seen." We both got down and crept through the bushes, and when we were right at the ford I happened to be in front. He stepped quickly between me and the Yankees, saying: "I am glad to have you for a pilot, but I am not going to make breastworks of you." The cannon and the other guns were firing fast by this time, as I pointed out to him where to go into the water and out on the other bank, and then we went back towards the house.

He asked me my name, and asked me to give him a lock of my hair. The cannon-balls were screaming over us so loud that we were told to leave and hide in some place out of danger, which we did. Soon all the firing stopped, and I started back home. On the way I met General Forrest again, and he told me that he had written a note for me and left it on the bureau. He asked me again for a lock of my hair, and as we went into the house he said: "One of my bravest men has been killed, and he is laid out in the house. His name is Robert Turner. I want you to see that he is buried in some graveyard near here." He then told me good-bye and got on his horse, and he and his men rode away and left us all alone. My sister and I sat up all night watching over the dead soldier, who had lost his life fighting for our rights, in which we were overpowered but never conquered. General Forrest and his men endeared themselves to us forever.

Emma Sansom's presence of mind and coolness under circumstances which would have paralyzed the faculties of most women enabled Forrest to overcome a very formidable obstacle in his pursuit of Streight, and gained for him at least three hours in time, inestimable in value, since it enabled him to overtake and compel Streight's surrender almost within sight of Rome.

In less than thirty minutes from the time of Forrest's arrival at Black Creek, the artillery was up, and the Federals were driven away from the opposite bank. The "lost ford" was soon cleared and made passable. The cavalry went over, carrying by hand the ammunition from the caissons. The guns and empty caissons, with long ropes tied to the poles, were then rolled by hand to the water's edge, one end of the rope taken to the top of the opposite bank and hitched to double teams of horses. In this original manner the artillery soon made a subaqueous passage to the east bank. The advance guard had already hurried on after the raiders, who, to their great surprise, were hustled out of Gadsden, less than four miles distant from Black Creek bridge, before they could do much damage to the small commissary supplies there.

Another all-night march now became necessary for Colonel Streight, although he says: "The command was in no condition to do so. I only halted at Gadsden sufficiently long to destroy a quantity of arms and stores found there, and proceeded. Many of our animals and men were entirely worn out and unable to keep up, and were captured. It now became evident to me that our only hope was in crossing the river at Rome and destroying the bridge, which would delay Forrest a day or two and allow the command a little time to sleep, without which it would be impossible to proceed."

But alas for all such hope! The relentless hand which had smote him for three successive days and nights, and banished sleep from his worn-out cavalcade, was striking at him yet and had no thought of giving him a respite. Streight, in fact, was not allowed to stop in Gadsden. As he approached the town, he surrounded it, in order to corral all the horses and mules belonging to the citizens. Impressing these, he set fire to several houses containing small quantities of commissaries, and then moved onward with all the speed possible to his mules and men, all now physically exhausted, and the latter mentally dispirited yet ready to fight.

If the state of his men and horses was so deplorable from fatigue and loss of sleep, what must have been the condition of those which were pursuing him? Forrest's men had had no opportunities for obtaining fresh horses or mules when theirs succumbed to the terrible strain to which they were being subjected. The Federals had swept the country clear of livestock as they marched, and in this, as in the tremendous tactical advantage of the ambuscade, they had the Confederate leader at great disadvantage. Many of his men had not tasted food in twenty-four hours, and a number fell from their horses from sheer exhaustion and slept by the roadside as their commands rode almost over their seemingly lifeless bodies. Despite the inspiring example of their leader—who did more work and fighting than any subordinate—and notwithstanding the details, whose duty it was to keep the men awake, rouse up the sleepers, and put them on their horses, Forrest's command had now crumbled away to a mere remnant. From 1 A.M. on April 29th to noon of May 2nd they had marched 119 miles and fought almost without cessation, and still the strongest of them pushed on in desperate emulation of their indomitable leader. Edmondson and Anderson were not up yet—and did not get up until after the surrender. Their duty was to keep Streight from escaping northward, and they were doing this.

Forrest's ever-faithful and efficient escort, now reduced to about forty effectives, some twenty of the remnant of his brother's scouts, and not over five hundred of Starnes's and Biffle's regiments (his entire command) made up the full quota of the troops with which he marched east of Gadsden. In front of him, and fleeing in despair, were more than twice as many brave and picked men of the enemy. From Gadsden on, Streight says, "the enemy followed closely, and kept up a continuous skirmish with the rear of the column, until 4 P.M., at which time we reached Blount's plantation, fifteen miles from Gadsden, where we procured forage for our animals. Here I decided to halt. The command was dismounted, a detail made to feed the horses and mules, while the balance of the command formed in line of battle. Meanwhile the rear-guard became severely engaged, and was driven in."

Forrest, continuing his tactics of worrying his antagonist, and knowing the perilous weakness of his own command, advanced his sharpshooters and made all possible show of strength and of assault. This he kept up vigorously until dark. Colonel Streight had set a skillful and dangerous ambuscade, in which he hoped to entrap his enemy and destroy him, but such cunning was as native to the Confederate leader as to his adversary, and he did not take the bait.

In this affair Streight's right-hand man, brave Colonel Gilbert Hathaway, fell wounded and expired in a few minutes from a carbine bullet fired by a sharpshooter, Private Joseph Martin. The death of Hathaway sealed the doom of the raiders. The Federal commander says: "His loss to me was irreparable. His men almost worshipped him, and when he fell it cast a deep gloom of despondency over his regiment which was hard to overcome. We remained in ambush but a short time when the enemy, who by some means had learned of our whereabouts, commenced a flank movement. I then decided to withdraw as silently as possible."

On through the night struggled this plucky remnant of Rosecrans's picked band of raiders. Bragg's important communications between Chattanooga and Atlanta looked very safe now, but these men were dying gamely. Forrest was at last sure of his quarry, provided he could keep his remnant from destruction by ambush. From Gadsden, by a parallel route, he had dispatched a horseback, to go right through to Rome, a courier who would arrive there in good time to warn the citizens to guard or burn the bridge, and thus stop the raiders short of their spoil. It was too great a danger, with his handful of men, to risk a night fight, with all the advantage on the other side. Therefore, picking out a squadron of his best-mounted troopers to follow on and "devil them all night," he gave his men their first night's rest since leaving Courtland. Forrest's foresight in hurrying a courier to Rome was not the least important of his brilliant moves in this campaign, and was well timed. Colonel John H. Wisdom outdid Paul Revere in this famous ride.

Near Turkeytown, eight miles east of Gadsden, at nightfall of May 2nd, Streight picked out 200 of the best-mounted men of his command, and, placing them under Captain Milton Russell, ordered him to hurry on to Rome and seize and hold the bridge until he could get there with the main column. Captain Russell pushed on, crossed the Chattooga River in a small ferryboat, and on the 3rd approached the city to find the bridge barricaded and defended by a strong company of home guards. He concluded not to attack, and sent word back to his chief of the condition of affairs.

Meanwhile things were going desperately with Streight, without regard to Russell's failure, of which as yet he was in ignorance. With heroic persistence he urged his weary, sleepy, and worn-out cavalcade by starlight, and by the moon when it came out, as far as the Chattooga River, where Captain Russell had crossed. Alas! his subordinate had not left a guard to hold the ferryboat, and some citizens, by this time apprised of the warlike character of the soldiers who had used it, had spirited the boat away to parts undiscoverable.

Many a man would have given up in despair at this moment, but Abel D. Streight was not that sort of man. Several miles distant up this stream there was a bridge, and, Moseslike, he led his people thitherward and verily through a wilderness. He says: "We had to pass over an old coal-chopping for several miles, where the timber had been cut and hauled off for charcoal, leaving innumerable wagon-roads running in every direction. The command was so worn out and exhausted that many were asleep, and in spite of every exertion I, with the aid of such of my officers as were able for duty, could make, the command became scattered and separated in several squads, travelling in different directions, and it was not until near daylight that the last of the command had crossed the river." This bridge was also burned, and still onward Streight plodded with his troopers past Cedar Bluff, twenty-eight miles from Gadsden, at sunup, and then wearily on in the direction of Rome, until at 9 A.M., May 3rd, he stopped at Lawrence to rest and feed. So exhausted were his men that, as soon as they were ordered to halt, they sank down upon the ground and many of them fell asleep at once.

It was with great difficulty that a sufficient number could be kept on their feet long enough to give the mules and horses the measure of provender due them. It was not so, however, with their commander. He had just received a message from Captain Russell that the bridge at Rome was too heavily guarded, and he could not take it. He also had heard that a second column of Confederates was moving parallel with him, and were now nearer to Rome than himself. This was all very depressing news, but at this same moment his quick ear caught a sound he knew too well, and which, more than all else, banished hope as well as sleep. As Sherman called him, "that devil Forrest" was at his heels again, and once more the cracking rifles of his rear guard and their relentless pursuers came ringing through the wood. The Confederate commander had not been long delayed at the Chatooga, where Streight had burned the last bridge. He had discovered that the walking on the bottom of this stream was no worse than at Black Creek, even if still more inconvenient than crossing dry on a bridge.

Ten hours of refreshing sleep and rest had wrought wonders in Forrest's fragment of a command, and by dawn of day, on May 3rd, his less than six hundred were once more in full cry after the raiders. When they reached the burned bridge near Gaylesville, the ammunition was carried over in small boats. The horses swam or forded with the men on their backs, and the cannon and empty caissons were pulled over on the river bottom. So little time was lost by these adepts at war that by 9 A.M. they were up with the Union column, although the latter had trudged along all through the night.

Forrest advanced at once, making the greatest possible display of his small force, yet careful not to make an assault which would demonstrate his numerical weakness. In crescentic line, and at good distance apart, he advanced his skirmishers until he had more than halfway surrounded the Federal position. From the noise these men made, and the orders given as to the disposition and formation of the troops and artillery, one might well have thought a brigade or two was being moved in battle array rather than a corporal's guard of a little over half a thousand men.

In this dire extremity, Colonal Streight gathered his officers about him, and with them tried to arouse his sleeping men. Some of these, when vigorously shaken, raised themselves to a sitting posture, stared drowsily about as if dazed and uncertain as to where they were, then, nodding, closed their eyes, fell over on the earth, and were again asleep. Others made no response whatever to the energetic effort made to awaken them. After strenuous exertion about one-half of the Federal command struggled to their feet, and once more pluckily rallied to their colors. Their commander lined them up for one more desperate effort, and then ordered them to lie down for better protection. They did lie down, their heads to the foe, their loaded guns pointed along the ground in the direction in which Forrest and his men were coming.

Then, instead of shutting one eye in deadly aim along the gleaming barrels of their rifles, both eyes were closed. Gunstock and hammer, barrel and sight and hated foeman faded from their vision in the darkness which overcame them. The brave fellows were asleep in line of battle. The exultant rebel yell, the crack and crackle of pistol and carbine, and the tattoo of horses' feet upon the ground as the rear guard and pickets came rushing into camp no longer aroused them. The man of iron had worn them out. Colonel Streight, in his official report, says: "Nature was exhausted. A large portion of my best troops actually went to sleep while lying in line of battle under a severe skirmish fire."

It was at this propitious moment that General Forrest sent Captain Henry Pointer, of his staff, with a flag of truce to the Union commander, demanding the surrender of himself and command. The wily Confederate, knowing his man, and his own questionable position as well, expressed an earnest desire to avoid "the further effusion of blood," but took especial pains to leave off that terrifying threat of "no quarter, if he had to sacrifice his men in the assault," with which he was wont to bluff his antagonists ever since he used it so successfully in his first attack on Murfreesboro.

Colonel Streight replied that he would meet General Forrest to discuss the question, and in the conference asked what his proposition was. Forrest replied: "Immediate surrender—your men to be treated as prisoners of war; the officers to retain their side-arms and personal property." Colonel Streight requested a few minutes in which to consult his officers. Forrest said: "All right, but you will not require much time. I have a column of fresh troops at hand, now nearer Rome than you are. You cannot cross the river in your front. I have men enough right here to run over you." In all of this there was not one word of truth; but this was war, and in war everything is fair.

Just then one piece of a section of Ferrell's battery, under Lieutenant R. G. Jones, came in sight. This officer says: "I was riding a little in advance of the gun when, suddenly looking up, I saw General Forrest, Captain Pointer, one or two other officers, and several Federal officers sitting down on the north side of the road. A little distance up the road I saw a crowd of Yankees. Captain Pointer motioned for me to halt. He then approached me and said: 'Colonel Streight objects to your coming up so close; drop back a little.' I moved back with the gun, and came to 'action front,' with one wheel in the road and the other at the edge of the wood. Soon Sergeant Jackson came up with the other piece and took position in the other half of the roadway."

Streight returned to his command, called his officers together, and talked over the situation. They voted unanimously to surrender, and their commander, though personally opposed to it, and still ready to fight to the death, yielded to the decision of his subordinates. The men stacked their guns, and were marched away to an open field or clearing, but it was not until the Confederate general got his small command between the Federal troopers and their arms that he felt himself secure.

For seventy-two hours, with no troops in reach excepting the regiments of Biffle and Starnes, his brother's company of scouts, about thirty in number, and his personal escort company, and two pieces of artillery, Forrest had pursued and fought Streight with four regiments and two companies of picked troops and two twelve-pounder howitzers. Moving in front, the Federal commander had cleared up the country of all horses and mules, and in this way kept his men supplied with fresh mounts. He says: "I do not think that at the time of surrender we had a score of the mules drawn at Nashville left." On the other hand, Forrest had had no opportunity of supplying his men with animals. When, from casting a shoe or other injury, or from exhaustion, one of his horses gave out, that was the end of both man and horse as far as this expedition was concerned.

Starting from Courtland, Alabama, at one o'clock on the morning of the 29th of April, he and his command marched sixteen miles to Moulton, thence seventeen miles to Day's Gap. They rode and fought nearly all day of April 30th and through the greater portion of that night, reaching Blountsville, seventy-six miles from the starting point, at ten o'clock on the morning of May 1st, the time consumed being fifty-seven hours, for fifty-two of which his troops were in the saddle. From Blountsville to Gadsden forty-three miles additional were covered, and from Gadsden to Lawrence, where Streight surrendered, thirty-one miles more, making a total distance of one hundred and fifty miles. As the greater part of this march was through a mountainous region and over bad roads, it is not surprising that the thousand troops with which he had started had dwindled down to considerably less than six hundred at the finish. To this small force Colonel Abel D. Streight surrendered all that was left of the two thousand picked troops of the Union army which had left Nashville on April 10th.

CROSSING THE RIVER

WHILE GRIERSON AND STREIGHT kept the enemy in an uproar, U. S. Grant was moving his army down the west side of the Mississippi trying to find a proper crossing. General Grant says: "The winter of 1862–63 was unprecedented for continuous high water in the Mississippi, and months were spent in ineffectual efforts to reach high land above Vicksburg from which we could operate against that stronghold, and in making artificial waterways through which a fleet might pass, avoiding the batteries to the south of the town, in case the other efforts should fail.

"In early April, 1863, the waters of the Mississippi having receded sufficiently to make it possible to march an army across the peninsula opposite Vicksburg, I determined to adopt this course and moved my advance to a point below the town. It was necessary, however, to have transports below both for the purpose of ferrying troops over the river and to carry supplies. These had necessarily to run the batteries. Under the direction of Admiral Porter this was successfully done. On the 29th, Grand Gulf, the first bluff south of Vicksburg on the east side of the river and about fifty miles below, was unsuccessfully attacked by the navy.

"The night of the same day the batteries of that place were run by the navy and transports, again under the direction of Admiral Porter, and on the following day the river was crossed by the troops, and a landing effected at Bruinsburg, some nine miles below.

"I was now in the enemy's country, with a vast river and the stronghold of Vicksburg between me and my base of supplies. My total force was then about thirty-three thousand men. The enemy occupied Grand Gulf, Vicksburg, Haynes's Bluff, and Jackson, with a force of nearly sixty thousand men. My first problem was to capture Grand Gulf to use as a base, and then if possible beat the enemy in detail outside the fortifications of Vicksburg."*

Grant was taking a huge risk. As Catton says: "A great many things could go wrong with such a plan. All told the Confederates had more soldiers in Mississippi than Grant had, and it was perfectly possible for them to swarm in on him and beat him—and to be beaten so far down in enemy territory, without any open road for retreat, would be to meet

* "The Vicksburg Campaign," *Battles and Leaders*, III, 494, 495.

complete and final disaster. There was also the prospect that once he crossed the river Grant would have no secure line of supply. His army might simply be starved into surrender if the Confederates played their cards right and had a little good luck. It was certain that the whole proposition would scare cautious Halleck right to the tips of his wispy hair. Therefore, Halleck would not be let in on the secret until it was too late for him to countermand it."*

General Grant continues his story of the Vicksburg operation: "The crossing of troops at Bruinsburg commenced April 30th. On the 18th of May the army was in rear of Vicksburg. On the 19th, just twenty days after the crossing, the city was completely invested and an assault had been made: five distinct battles—besides continuous skirmishing—had been fought and won by the Union forces; the capital of the State had fallen, and its arsenals, military manufactories, and everything useful for military purposes had been destroyed; an average of about 180 miles had been marched by the troops engaged; but 5 days' rations had been issued, and no forage; over 6,000 prisoners had been captured, and as many more of the enemy had been killed or wounded; 27 heavy cannon and 61 field-pieces had fallen into our hands; 250 miles of the river, from Vicksburg to Port Hudson, had become ours. The Union force that had crossed the Mississippi River up to this time was less than 43,000 men. One division of these—Blair's—only arrived in time to take part in the battle of Champion's Hill, but was not engaged there; and one brigade—Ransom's—of McPherson's corps reached the field after the battle. The enemy had at Vicksburg, Grand Gulf, Jackson, and on the roads between these places, over sixty thousand men. They were in their own country, where no rear-guards were necessary. The country is admirable for defense, but difficult to conduct an offensive campaign in. All their troops had to be met. We were fortunate, to say the least, in meeting them in detail: at Port Gibson, 7,000 or 8,000; at Raymond, 5,000; at Jackson, from 8,000 to 11,000; at Champion's Hill, 25,000; at the Big Black, 4,000. A part of those met at Jackson were all that were left of those encountered at Raymond. They were beaten in detail by a force smaller than their own, upon their own ground. Our loss up to this time was: 4,379 casualties.

"My line was more than fifteen miles long, extending from Haynes's Bluff to Vicksburg, thence south to Warrenton. The line of the enemy was about seven. In addition to this, having an enemy at Canton and Jackson, in our rear, who was being constantly reënforced, we required a second line of defense facing the other way. I had not troops enough under my command to man these. But General Halleck appreciated the situation, and, without being asked, forwarded reënforcements with all possible dispatch.

"The ground about Vicksburg is admirable for defense. On the north it is about two hundred feet above the Mississippi River at the highest point, and very much cut up by the washing rains; the ravines were grown up with cane and underbrush, while the sides and tops were covered with a dense forest. Farther south the ground flattens out somewhat, and was in cultivation. But here, too, it was cut by ravines and small streams. The

* Bruce Catton, *This Hallowed Ground*, p. 229.

enemy's line of defense followed the crest of a ridge, from the river north of the city, eastward, then southerly around to the Jackson road, full three miles back of the city; thence in a south-westerly direction to the river. Deep ravines of the description given lay in front of these defenses.

"As there is a succession of gullies, cut out by rains, along the side of the ridge, the line was necessarily very irregular. To follow each of these spurs with intrenchments, so as to command the slopes on either side, would have lengthened their line very much. Generally, therefore, or in many places, their line would run from near the head of one gully nearly straight to the head of another, and an outer work, triangular in shape, generally open in the rear, was thrown up on the point; with a few men in this outer work they commanded the approaches to the main line completely.

"We had no siege-guns except six 32-pounders, and there were none in the west to draw from. Admiral Porter, however, supplied us with a battery of navy-guns, of large caliber, and with these, and the field artillery used in the campaign, the siege began. The first thing to do was to get the artillery in batteries, where they would occupy commanding positions; then establish the camps, under cover from the fire of the enemy, but as near up as possible; and then construct rifle-pits and covered ways, to connect the entire command by the shortest route. The enemy did not harass us much while we were constructing our batteries. Probably their artillery ammunition was short; and their infantry was kept down by our sharp-shooters, who were always on the alert and ready to fire at a head whenever it showed itself above the rebel works.

"In no place were our lines more than six hundred yards from the enemy. It was necessary, therefore, to cover our men by something more than the ordinary parapet. To give additional protection sand-bags, bullet-proof, were placed along the tops of the parapets, far enough apart to make loop-holes for musketry. On top of these, logs were put. By these means the men were enabled to walk about erect when off duty, without fear of annoyance from sharp-shooters. The enemy used in their defense explosive musket-balls, thinking, no doubt, that, bursting over the men in the trenches, they would do some execution; but I do not remember a single case where a man was injured by a piece of one of the shells. When they were hit, and the ball exploded, the wound was terrible. In these cases a solid ball would have hit as well. Their use is barbarous, because they produce increased suffering without any corresponding advantage to those using them.

"The enemy could not resort to the method we did to protect their men, because we had an inexhaustible supply of ammunition to draw upon, and used it freely. Splinters from the timber would have made havoc among the men behind.

"There were no mortars with the besiegers, except what the navy had in front of the city; but wooden ones were made by taking logs of the toughest wood that could be found, boring them out for six or twelve pounder shells, and binding them with strong iron bands. These answered as coehorns, and shells were successfully thrown from them into the trenches of the enemy.

"The labor of building the batteries and intrenching was largely done by the pioneers, assisted by Negroes who came within our lines and who were paid for their work, but details from the troops had often to be made. The work was pushed forward as rapidly as possible, and when an advanced position was secured and covered from the fire of the enemy, the batteries were advanced. By the 30th of June there were 220 guns in position, mostly light field-pieces, besides a battery of heavy guns belonging to, manned, and commanded by the navy. We were now as strong for defense against the garrison of Vicksburg as they were against us. But I knew that Johnston was in our rear, and was receiving constant reën-forcements from the east. He had at this time a larger force than I had prior to the battle of Champion's Hill."*

Up to Vicksburg†

BY CAPTAIN S. H. M. BYERS

IN A LITTLE TIME, FEBRUARY, 1863, Grant's army was again off to try for Vicksburg. This time it was to go on that campaign, so laughable now, but romantic always, called the "Yazoo Pass expedition." We were to go down the Mississippi River in big steamers to Helena, and there transfer ourselves on to a fleet of little steamers, cut the levee into the overflooded country, and try floating a whole army a hundred miles across the planta-tions and swamps of Mississippi.

On the 22d of March, near Helena, my regiment went aboard the pretty little schooner called the *Armada*. Shortly, dozen of these small boats, crowded with regiments, accompanied by gunboats, were floating about, awaiting the order to sail through a big cut that our engineers had made in the river levee and get down the pass into Moon Lake. The Mississippi was high and raging. All the low-lying country for half a hundred miles was flooded till it looked like a vast sea, with forests of trees standing in its midst. Here and there, too, a plantation, higher than the surrounding country, was noticeable. The first pass into Moon Lake was but a mile long. But through that pass swirled and roared the waters of the Missis-sippi, so suddenly let loose by the break in the levee.

At just four in the evening our little steamer got the order to turn out of the river and into the rushing waters of the pass. We would not have been more excited at being told to start over Niagara Falls. Our engines are working backward and we enter the crevasse slowly, but in five minutes the fearful, eddying current seized us, and our boat was whirled round and round like a toy skiff in a washtub. We all held our breath

* "The Vicksburg Campaign," pp. 519, 520, 521, 522.
† Condensed from S. H. M. Byers, *With Fire and Sword*.

as the steamer was hurled among floating logs and against overhanging trees. In ten minutes the rushing torrent had carried us, backward, down into the little lake. Not a soul of the five hundred on board the boat in this crazy ride was lost. Once in the lake we stopped, and with amazement watched other boats, crowded with soldiers, also drift into the whirl and be swept down the pass. It was luck, not management, that half the little army was not drowned.

Now for days and days our little fleet coursed its way toward Vicksburg among the plantations, swamps, woods, bayous, cane-brakes, creeks, and rivers of that inland sea. Wherever the water seemed deepest that was our course, but almost every hour projecting stumps and trees had to be sawn off under the water to allow our craft to get through. Sometimes we advanced only four or five miles a day. At night the boat would be tied to some tall sycamore. Here and there we landed at some plantation that seemed like an island in the flood. The Negroes on the plantation, amazed at our coming, wondered if it was the day of Jubilee or if it was another Noah's flood and that these iron gunboats were arks of safety.

We soldiers, if not on duty pushing the boat away from trees, had nothing to do but sleep and eat and read. Most of the soldiers slept on the decks, on the guards, and on the cabin floors. Four of us had a little stateroom. I had with me a copy of Shakespeare, cribbed by one of the boys somewhere, and the Bard of Avon was never studied under stranger circumstances.

The Yazoo Pass, though not so crazy as the crevasse we had come through, was nevertheless bad and dangerous. Two of our craft sank to the bottom, but the soldiers were saved by getting into trees. All the boats were torn half to pieces. One day as we pushed our way along the crooked streams amid the vine-covered forests we ran onto a Rebel fort built on a bit of dry land. In front of it were great rafts that completely obstructed our way. An ocean steamer was also sunk in the channel in front of us. To our amazement we learned that it was the *Star of the West,* the ship that received the first shot fired in the war of the Rebellion. That was when it was trying to take supplies to Fort Sumter. Our gunboats shelled this "Fort Greenwood" in vain, and now Rebels were gathering around and behind us and guerrillas were beginning to fire on the boats. The waters, too, might soon subside, and our fleet and army be unable to get back into the Mississippi. We could not go ahead. Suddenly the orders came to turn about and steam as fast as possible to a place of safety.

By April 8 we had made the journey through the woods and cane-brake back to the pass. The picturesque farce was ended. We could now hunt some other road to Vicksburg. We know nothing of what the generals thought of this fiasco, but we private soldiers had great fun, and the long stay on the boats had been a rest from hard campaigning. We had not lost a man. A whole campaign and not a soldier lost!

The attempt on Vicksburg was not to be given up. In the spring of 1863 the whole army moved down the Mississippi to begin one of the most noted campaigns of history.

The notion was, if possible, to get across the Mississippi *below* the town (Sherman had failed trying it above) and throw the whole army on to the fortifications at the rear. If the town's defenders should be bold and come out and fight us, so much the better. We wanted that.

Soon General Grant built long stretches of wagon roads and corduroy bridges that ran snakelike for forty miles among the black swamps, canebrakes, and lagoons on the west bank of the Mississippi River. He then marched half his army down these roads to a point below Vicksburg, below Grand Gulf, and bivouacked them on the shore of the river. The other half, of which my regiment was a part, remained near the river above the city. Possibly we were twenty-five thousand men there.

The moon was down by ten o'clock of the night of April 16. Under the starlight one hardly saw the dark river or the cane-brakes, swamps, and lagoons along its border. The whole Northern fleet lay anchored in silence. Grant's army too, down below, was silent and waiting. A few miles below us lay Vicksburg, dark, sullen, and sleeping. Not a gun was being fired. A few lonesome Confederate river guards floated above the town in rowboats watching to give the alarm at the approach of any foe on the water.

Three mysterious looking Northern steamboats, with crews of volunteer soldiers on board, lay out in the middle of the Mississippi River in front of Milliken's Bend, a dozen miles above Vicksburg. Down in the dark hold of each vessel stand a dozen determined men. They have boards, and pressed cotton, and piles of gunny sacks beside them there, to stop up holes that shall be made pretty soon by the cannon of the enemy. They have none of war's noise and excitement to keep them up—only its suspense. They are helpless. If anything happens they will go to the bottom of the river without a word. Above the decks the pilot-houses are taken off and the pilot wheels are down by the bows, and the pilot will stand there wholly exposed. Lashed to the sides of each of the three little steamers are barges piled up with bales of hay and cotton. They look like floating breastworks. Anchored still a little further down the stream seven gunboats also wait in silence. They will lead these steamboats and try the batteries first. The boats must all move two hundred yards apart. That is the order.

All is suspense. For a little while the night grows darker and more silent; the moon now is down. The thousands of soldiers standing on the levee waiting, and watching to see them start, almost hold their breath. At the boats there is no noise save the gurgling of the water as it grinds past the hulls of the anchored vessels. That is all the noise the men waiting down in the dimly lighted hulls can hear. On a little tug, near by, General Grant, the commander of the Western armies, waits and listens. The Assistant Secretary of War is at his side. In a yawl, farther down the stream, General Sherman ventures far out on the dark river to watch events. All is ready, all is suspense. Just then a lantern on the levee is moved slowly up and down. It is the signal to start. Down in Vicksburg the unexpectant enemy sleeps. Their guards out on the river, too, almost sleep; all is so safe. Quietly we lift anchors and float off with the current. Our wheels are not moving. There is a great bend in the river, and as we round it the river guard wakened, sends up a rocket, other rockets too go up all along the eastern or Vicksburg shore. That instant, too, a gun is fired from a neighboring bluff. We are discovered. "Put on all steam," calls the captain, and our boats move swiftly into the maelstrom of sulphur

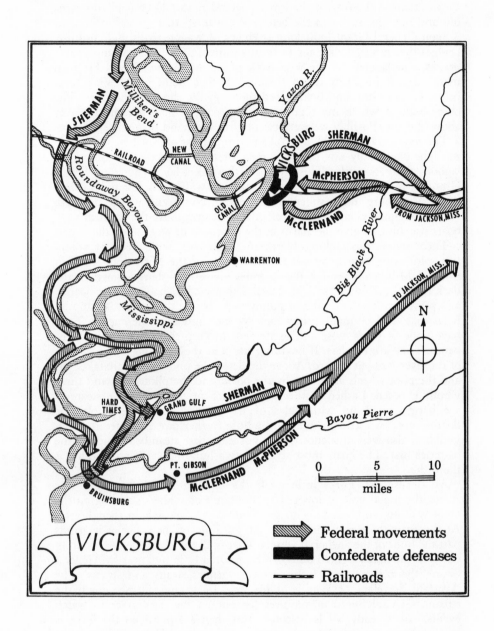

VICKSBURG

Federal movements
Confederate defenses
Railroads

and iron, for the enemy opens fire vigorously. The enemy sets houses on fire all along the levee to illuminate the river, bonfires are lighted everywhere, and suddenly the whole night seems but one terrific roar of cannon. The burning houses make the river almost as light as day. We see the people in the streets of the town running and gesticulating as if all were mad; their men at the batteries load and fire and yell as if every shot sunk a steamboat. On the west side of the river the lagoons and canebrakes look weird and dangerous. The sky above is black, lighted only by sparks from the burning houses. Down on the river it is a sheet of flame. One of the steamers and a few of the barges have caught fire and are burning up, the men escaping in life-boats and by swimming to the western shore. The excitement of the moment is maddening, the heavy fire appalling, while the musketry on the shore barks and bites at the unprotected pilots on the boats. Ten-inch cannon and great columbiads hurl their shot and shell into the cotton breastworks of the barges or through the rigging of the steamers.

Amid all this roar and thunder and lightning and crash of cannonballs above, the men down in the holds of the boats—they are the real heroes—stand in the dim candle-light waiting, helpless, ignorant of events, and in terrible suspense, while sounds like the crash of worlds go on above their heads. Once some of them climb up to the hatchways and look out into the night. One look is enough! What a sight! The whole Mississippi River seems on fire, the roar of the gunboats answering the howling cannon on the shore, the terrific lightnings from the batteries, the screeching shells above the decks. It was as if hell itself were loose that night on the Mississippi River.

Daylight saw the little fleet safe below Vicksburg, where thousands of soldiers welcomed it with cheers. Only one boat and some barges were lost, and only a few of the soldiers were hurt. The cotton bales had proved a miracle of defense. In a week still other steamers, though with greater loss, passed the batteries.

Now that the boats were below the city, we were to begin the Vicksburg campaign in earnest. All the troops that had been left camped on the river levee above at Milliken's Bend hurried by roundabout roads through canebrakes and swamps to the point where our little boats had anchored after running past the batteries that night. Here we joined the rest of the army, and the ferrying of thousands of soldiers across the great river day and night at once commenced.

My own regiment was put on to one of the iron gunboats and ferried over the Mississippi at a point close to Grand Gulf. Here our river navy had silenced the Rebel forts. It was the first gunboat I had ever seen. Its sides bore great scars, indentations made by the enemy's batteries on the preceding day. We hurried on and became a part of the reserve at the hot battle of Port Gibson, as we ourselves did no fighting. In a plantation yard, close by my regiment lay our wounded as they were carried back from the front. It was a terrible sight. Many had been torn by shrapnel and lay there on the grass in great agony. Some seemed with their own hands to be trying to tear their mangled limbs from their bodies. The possession of all Vicksburg did not seem worth the pain and the agony I saw there that afternoon.

The next day, when the battle was over, I was at a Negro cabin getting a loaf of corn bread. I suddenly heard a little cheering down by the river, where some men were putting down pontoons in place of the bridge burned by the enemy. I went down at once, and as I stood by the river bank I noticed an officer on horseback in full general's uniform. Suddenly he dismounted and came over to the very spot where I was standing. I did not know his face, but something told me it was Grant— Ulysses Grant—at that moment the hero of the Western army.

Now he spoke, "Men, push right along; close up fast, and hurry over." Two or three men on mules attempted to wedge past the soldiers on the bridge. Grant noticed it, and quietly said, "Lieutenant, arrest those men and send them to the rear."

My own command crossed the bridge that night by torchlight. It was a strange weird scene. Many of the Rebel dead—killed beyond the stream by our cannon before our approach—still lay at the roadside or in fields unburied. At one turn in the road my regiment marched close by a Rebel battery that had been completely destroyed. Men, horses, and all lay there dead in indiscriminate heaps.

My regiment now entered on all those rapid marches and battles in the rear of Vicksburg—Raymond, Jackson, Champion Hills, and the assaults on the breastworks about the city. For days we scarcely slept at all; it was hurry here and quickstep there, day or night. None of us soldiers or subordinates could tell the direction we were marching. We had few rations, little water, and almost no rest. We had left our base at the river, and in a large sense we were cut off and surrounded all the time. The capture of a Rebel scout at once changed everything. Through him Grant learned how hurrying divisions of the enemy were about to unite. A quick move could checkmate everything. My regiment, like all the others, hurried along the country roads through dust that came to the shoe top. The atmosphere was yellow with it. The moving of a column far away could be traced by it. We followed it in the way that Joshua's army followed the mighty cloud. As we passed farms where there was something to eat the captains would call out to a dozen men of the line to hurry in, carry off all they could, and pass it over to the companies still marching. It was a singular looking army. So whole regiments tramped along with sides of bacon or sheaves of oats on the points of their bayonets. We dared not halt. When we bivouacked, long after dark, often it was the dust of the roadside. We always lay upon our arms. Sometimes there was a little fire, oftener there was none. The fat bacon was eaten raw.

My regiment was in advance at the engagement at Raymond; also at Jackson. At Jackson it rained and thundered fearfully during the battle. A Rebel battery was on a green slope right in front of us, pouring a terrible shelling into us as we approached it from the Raymond road. The shocks of thunder so intermingled with the shocks from the guns that we could not tell the one from the other, and many times a sudden crash of thunder caused us all to drop to the ground, fearing a cannonball would cut its swath through the regiment. We were marching in colunms of fours. Shortly, we formed line of battle, and in rushing to the left through a great cane-brake, while we were advancing in battle line under a fire of musketry, the order was given to lie down.

We obeyed quickly. How closely, too, we hugged the ground and the depression made by a little brook! While I lay there it happened that my major (Marshall) was close behind me on horseback. He had no orders to dismount. I could glance back and see his face as the bullets zipped over our heads or past him. He sat on his horse as quiet as a statue, save that with his right hand he constantly twisted his mustache. He looked straight into the cane-brake. He was a brave man. Could the enemy behind the forests of cane have seen where they were firing he would not have lived a minute. Shortly there was roaring of cannon and quick charges at the other side of the town. Jackson was won.

At daylight the next morning we hurried in the direction of Champion Hills. At our left, as we went down the road, the battlefield of the day before was strewn with corpses of our own men. In a few minutes the brave Seventeenth Regiment of Iowa had lost 80 men at this spot, out of 350 engaged in an assault. My friend Captain Walden received honorable mention, among others, for gallantry in this Jackson charge. A few hundred yards off I noticed a man in a field quite alone, digging in the ground. Out of curiosity I went to him and asked what he was doing alone when the regiments were all hurrying away. A brown blanket covered something near by. He pointed to it and said that two of his brothers lay dead under that blanket. He was digging a grave for them. He went on with his work and I hurried to overtake my command. This was the 15th of May, 1863.

My situation as to the Fifth Regiment was a peculiar one; being the quartermaster sergeant, I belonged to no company in particular. The good colonel, however, knowing my love for adventure, and that I was never lacking in duty, allowed me to attach myself to any company I liked, provided only, that there was a reliable substitute performing my duties with the train at the rear. I had no trouble in securing such a substitute, usually found among the slightly wounded soldiers.

None of us private soldiers now really knew in what direction we were marching. We heard only that the enemy was concentrating at Edwards Ferry Station, between us and Big Black River. General Crocker of my State was now leading our division, and the magnificent General McPherson commanded the army corps. The night of May 15 the division bivouacked in the woods by the side of a road that leads from Bolton toward Vicksburg. We marched hard and late that day. The morning of the 16th my regiment was up and getting breakfast long before daylight. The breakfast consisted of some wet dough cooked on the ends of ramrods; nothing more.

Troops were hurrying past our bivouac by daylight. Once I went out to the roadside to look about a bit. It was scarcely more than early daylight, yet cannon could occasionally be heard in the far distance, something like low thunder. As I stood there watching some batteries hurrying along I noticed a general and his staff gallop through the woods, parallel with the road. They were leaping logs, brush, or whatever came in their way. It was General Grant, hurrying to the front. Shortly came the orders, "Fall in!" and we too were hurrying along that road toward Champion

Hills. By ten o'clock the sound of the cannon fell thundering on our ears, and we hurried all we could, as riders came back saying the battle had already begun. As we approached the field the sound of great salvos of musketry told us the hour had surely come. The sound was indeed terrible.

At the left of the road we passed a pond of dirty water. All who could broke ranks and filled canteens, knowing that in the heat of the fight we would need the water terribly. I not only filled my canteen, I filled my stomach with the yellow fluid, in order to save that in the canteen for a critical moment. Just then there was in front of us a terrific crashing, not like musketry, but more like the falling down of a thousand trees at once. Our brigade, a small one, was hurried into line of battle at the edge of an open field that sloped down a little in front of us and then up to a wood-covered ridge. That wood was full of the Rebel army. Fighting was going on to the right and left of us, and bullets flew into our own line, wounding some of us as we stood there waiting. There was an old well and curb at the immediate right of my regiment, and many of our boys were climbing over each other to get a drop of water. Soon the bullets came faster, *zip*ping, *zip*ping among us, thicker and thicker. We must have been in full view of the enemy as we stood there, not firing a shot. Our line stood still in terrible suspense, not knowing why we were put under fire without directions to shoot. *Zip! zip! zip!* came the Rebel bullets, and now and then a boy in blue would groan, strike his hand to a wounded limb or arm, drop his gun and fall to the rear; or perhaps he fell in his tracks dead, without uttering a word. We too, who saw it, uttered no word, but watched steadily, anxiously at the front.

Then General Grant himself rode up behind us, and so close to the spot where I stood, that I could have heard his voice. He leaned against his little bay horse, had the inevitable cigar in his mouth, and was calm as a statue. Possibly smoking so much tranquillized his nerves a little and aided in producing calmness. Once a badly wounded man was carried by the litter-bearers—the drummers of my regiment—close to the spot where the General stood. He gave a pitying glance at the man, I thought— I was not twenty feet away—but he neither spoke nor stirred. Then I heard an officer say, "We are going to charge." It seems that our troops in front of us in the woods had been sadly repulsed, and now our division was to rush in and fight in their stead, and the commander-in-chief was there to witness our assault. Two or three of us, near each other, expressed dissatisfaction that the commander of an army in battle should expose himself, as General Grant was doing at that moment. When staff officers came up to him, he gave orders in low tones, and they would ride away. One of them, listening to him, glanced over our heads toward the Rebels awhile, looked very grave, and gave some mysterious nods. The colonel who was about to lead us also came to the General's side a moment. He, too, listened, looked, and gave some mysterious nods. Something was about to happen.

"My time has probably come now," I said to myself, and with a little bit of disgust I thought of the utter uselessness of being killed there without even firing a shot in self-defense. The suspense, the anxiety, was indeed becoming fearfully intense. Soon General Grant quietly climbed upon his horse, looked at us once, and as quietly rode away. Then the colonel came along the line with a word to each officer. As he came near me he called me from the ranks and said: "I want you to act as sergeant-major of the regiment in this battle." I was surprised, but indeed very proud of this mark of confidence in me. "Hurry to the left," he continued. "Order the men to fix bayonets—quick!" I ran as told, shouting at the top of my voice, "Fix bayonets! fix bayonets!" I was not quite to the left, when I heard other voices yelling, "Forward! quick! double quick! forward!" and the line was already on the run toward the Rebels. I kept up my shouting, "Fix bayonets!" for by some blunder the order had not been given in time, and now the men were trying to get their bayonets in place while running. We were met in a minute by a storm of bullets from the wood, but the lines in blue kept steadily on, as would a storm of wind and cloud moving among the tree tops. Now we met almost whole companies of wounded, defeated men from the other division, hurrying by us, and they held up their bleeding and mangled hands to show us they had not been cowards. They had lost twelve hundred men on the spot we were about to occupy. Some of them were laughing even, and yelling at us: "Wade in and give them hell."

On the edge of a low ridge we saw a solid wall of men in gray, their muskets at their shoulders blazing into our faces and their batteries of artillery roaring as if it were the end of the world. Bravely they stood there. They seemed little over a hundred yards away. There was no charging further by our line. We halted, the two lines stood still, and for over an hour we loaded our guns and killed each other as fast as we could. The firing and the noise were simply appalling. Now, I was not scared. The first shot I fired seemed to take all my fear away and gave me courage enough to calmly load my musket at the muzzle and fire it forty times. Others, with more cartridges, fired possibly oftener still. Some of the regiments in that bloody line were resupplied with cartridges from the boxes of the dead. In a moment I saw Captain Lindsey throw up his arms, spring upward and fall dead in his tracks. Corporal McCully was struck in the face by a shell. The blood covered him all over, but he kept on firing. Lieutenant Darling dropped dead, and other officers near me fell wounded.

I could not see far to left or right, the smoke of battle was covering everything. I saw bodies of our men lying near me without knowing who they were, though some of them were my messmates in the morning. The Rebels in front we could not see at all. We simply fired at their lines by guess, and occasionally the blaze of their guns showed exactly where they stood. They kept their line like a wall of fire. When I fired my first shot I had resolved to aim at somebody or something as long as I could see, and a dozen times I tried to bring down an officer I dimly saw on a gray horse before me. Pretty soon a musket ball struck me fair in the breast. "I am dead, now," I said, almost aloud. It felt as if someone had struck me with a club. I stepped back a few paces and sat down on a log to finish up with the world. Other wounded men were there, covered with blood, and some were lying by me dead. I spoke to no one. It would have been useless; thunder could scarcely have been heard at that moment. My emotions I have almost forgotten. I remember only that something said to me, "It is honorable to die so." I had not a thought of friends, or of home, or of religion. The stupendous things going on around me filled my mind. On getting my breath a little I found I was not hurt at all—simply stunned; the obliquely-fired bullet had struck the heavy leather of my cartridge belt and glanced away. I picked up my gun, stepped back into the line of battle, and in a moment was shot through the hand. The wound did not hurt; I was too excited for that.

The awful roar of battle now grew more terrific, if possible. I wonder that a man on either side was left alive. Biting the ends off my cartridges, my mouth was filled with gunpowder; the thirst was intolerable. Every soldier's face was black and, with some, blood from wounds trickled down over the blackness, giving them a horrible look. Once a boy from another part of the line to our left ran up to me crying out: "My regiment is gone! What shall I do?"

There was now a little moment's lull in the howling noise; something was going on. "Blaze away right here," I said to the boy, and he commenced firing like a veteran. Then I heard one of our own line cry, "My God, they're flanking us!" I looked to where the boy had come from. His regiment had indeed given way. The Rebels had poured through the gap and were already firing into our rear and yelling to us to surrender. In a moment we would be surrounded. It was surrender or try to get back past them. I ran like a race-horse—so did the left of the regiment, amid a storm of bullets and yells and curses. I saved my musket, anyway. I think all did that—but that half-mile race through a hot Mississippi sun, with bullets and cannonballs plowing the fields behind us, will never be forgotten. My lungs seemed to be burning up. Once I saw our regimental flag lying by a log, the color-bearer wounded or dead. I cried to a comrade flying near me, "Duncan Teter, it is a shame—the Fifth Iowa running."

Only the day before Teter had been reduced to the ranks for some offense or another. He picked up the flag and with a great oath dared me to stop and defend it. For a moment we two tried to rally to the flag the men who were running by. We might as well have yelled to a Kansas cyclone. Then Captain John Tait, rushing by, saw us, stopped, and, recognizing the brave deed of Corporal Teter, promoted him on the spot. But the oncoming storm was irresistible, and, carrying the flag, we all again hurried rearward. We had scarcely passed the spot where I had seen Grant mount his horse before the charge when a whole line of Union cannon, loaded to the muzzle with grape-shot and canister, opened on the howling mob that was pursuing us. The Rebels instantly halted, and now again it seemed our turn. A few minutes rest for breath and our re-formed lines once more dashed into the woods. In half an hour the battle of Champion Hills was won, and the victorious Union army was shortly in a position to compel the surrender of the key to the Mississippi River.

Six thousand blue- and gray-coated men were lying there in the woods, dead or wounded, when the last gun of Champion Hills was fired. Some of the trees on the battlefield were tall magnolias, and many of their limbs were shot away. The trees were in full bloom, their beautiful blossoms contrasting with the horrible scene of battle. Besides killing and wounding three thousand of the enemy, we had also captured thirty cannon and three thousand prisoners.

When the troops went off into the road to start in pursuit of the flying enemy, I searched over the battlefield for my best friend, poor Captain Poag, with whom I had talked of our Northern homes only the night before. He lay dead among the leaves, a bullet hole in his forehead. Somebody buried him, but I never saw his grave. Another friend I found dying. He begged me only to place him against a tree, and with leaves to shut the burning sun away from his face. While I was doing this I heard the groaning of a Rebel officer, who lay helpless in a little ditch. He called to me to lift him out, as he was shot through both thighs, and suffering terribly. "Yes." I said, "as soon as I get my friend here arranged a little comfortably." His reply was pathetic. "Yes, that's right; help your own first." I had not meant it so. I instantly got to him and, with the aid of a comrade, pulled him out of the ditch. He thanked me and told me he was a lieutenant colonel, and had been shot while riding in front of the spot where he lay. I eased his position as best I could, but all that night, with many another wounded soldier, blue and gray, he was left on the desolate battlefield.

Some weeks after this battle, and after Vicksburg had been won, my regiment was marched in pursuit of Joe Johnston, and we recrossed this same battlefield. We reached it in the night and bivouacked on the very spot where we had fought. It was a strange happening. Our sensations were very unusual, for we realized that all about us there in the woods were the graves of our buried comrades and the still unburied bones of many of our foes. Save an occasional hooting owl the woods were sad and silent. All the night a terrible odor filled the bivouac. When daylight came one of the boys came to our company and said, "Go over to that hollow, and you will see hell." Some of us went. We looked but once. Dante himself never conjured anything so horrible as the reality before us. After the battle the Rebels in their haste had tossed hundreds of their dead into this little ravine and slightly covered them over with earth, but the rains had come, and the earth was washed away, and there stood or lay hundreds of half-decayed corpses. Some were grinning skeletons, some were headless, some armless, some had their clothes torn away, and some were mangled by dogs and wolves. The horror of that spectacle followed us for weeks.

I have written this random but true sketch of personal recollections of a severe battle because it may help young men who are anxious for adventure and war, as I was, to first realize what war really is. My experiences probably were the same as hundreds of others in that same battle. I only tell of what was nearest me. A third of my comrades who entered this fight were lost. Other Iowa and other Western regiments suffered equally or more. General Hovey's division had a third of its number slain. I have been in what history pronounces greater battles than Champion Hills, but only once did I ever see two lines of blue and gray stand close together and fire into each other's faces for an hour and a half. I think the courage of the private soldiers, standing in that line of fire for that awful hour and a half, gave us Vicksburg, made Grant immortal as a soldier, and helped to save this country.

But I must return to that afternoon of the battle. All that could be assembled of our men gathered in line in a road near the field. It was nearly dark. Sergeant Campbell walked about, making a list of the dead and wounded of Company B. As I was not now on the company rolls, being quartermaster sergeant, my name was not put down as one of the wounded. Nor, seeing how many were sadly torn to pieces, did I think my wound worth reporting. Shortly General Grant passed us in the road. Knowing well how the regiment had fought in the battle, he rode to where our colors hung over a stack of muskets and saluted them. We all jumped to our feet and cheered. He spoke a few words to the colonel and rode on into the darkness. That night we marched ahead, and in the morning bivouacked in the woods as a reserve for troops fighting at the Black River bridge. *There it was that Grant reached the crisis of his career.* While sitting on his horse waiting to witness a charge by Lawler's brigade, a staff officer overtook him, bringing a peremptory order from Washington to *abandon the campaign* and take his army to Port Hudson to help General Banks. That moment Grant glanced to the right of his lines and saw a dashing officer in his shirt sleeves suddenly come out of a cluster of woods, leading his brigade to the assault. It was General Lawler, and in five minutes the Rebel breastworks were carried, the enemy in flight or drowning in the rapid river. Then Grant turned to the staff officer and simply said, *"See that charge! I think it is too late to abandon this campaign."*

The next morning (the 18th) my regiment crossed the pontoon bridge over the Big Black and marched eight miles further toward Vicksburg. Now we knew we were getting close to the Richmond of the West. As we crossed the Black River we gazed with curiosity at the half-burned bridge from which so many unfortunates had been hurled into the water by our artillery the day before. After Lawler's charge thousands had tried to get over the stream by the trestle-work and bridge, or by swimming. General Osterhaus, seeing the fugitives from a high point where he stood, cried out to his batteries: "Now, men, is the time to give them hell." Twenty cannon instantly hurled their iron missiles at the bridge, and the flying soldiers fell to the ground or into the foaming river, almost by hundreds. "Lost at Black River," was the only message that ever reached the home of many a Southern soldier of that day.

On the 19th, at two o'clock, a terrible assault was made by the army on the walls of Vicksburg. My own regiment, still in McPherson's corps, lay close to the Jackson wagon road and under a tremendous thundering of the enemy's artillery. We suffered little, however. Once I was ordered to help some men build sheds of brush for the wounded. This was in a ravine behind us. In an hour the work was done, and as I crept up the slope to get forward to my regiment again I heard the loud voice of some officer on horseback. It was General John A. Logan. The enemy's artillery was sweeping the field at this point, but I could still hear Logan's voice above the battle, cheering a number of soldiers that were near. "We have taken this fort and we have taken that," he cried in tones that were simply stentorian. "We are giving them hell everywhere." He was in full uniform, his long black hair swept his shoulders, his eyes flashed fire, he seemed the incarnation of the reckless, fearless soldier. He must have thought cannonballs would not hurt him. For five minutes, perhaps, I stood in a little dip in the ground, comparatively protected, while he rode up and down under a storm of cannonballs, calling at the top of his warrior's voice. I expected every moment to see him drop from his horse, but nothing happened, and I went on to the line where all our men were closely hugging the ground. Soon I, too, was stretched on the ground, making myself as thin as I could.

On the 20th we advanced still closer to the frowning works. It was only a thousand yards to the forts of Vicksburg. We moved up in the darkness that night. I think no one knew how close we were being taken to the enemy. We lay down in line of battle and in the night our line was moved a little. When daylight came my regiment was no little astonished to find that we were on an open place in full view of the enemy. A comrade and I rose from the ground and commenced our toilet, by pouring water into each other's hands from our canteens. Almost at that moment the Rebels had caught sight of our men lying there in long lines so close to them, and instantly commenced throwing shells at us. My friend and I left our morning toilet uncompleted and, seizing our rifles, we all stood in line waiting. We could see the flags of the enemy above the forts distinctly. With a glass the gunners could be seen at their guns, hurling shot and shell at us. We were in a perilous and helpless position. We were also very tired and hungry, for we had had nothing whatever to eat. But here we stayed, and by the next morning our skirmishers had advanced so close to the Vicksburg forts that the Rebel gunners could reach us but little. Our gunboats too, down in the river now commenced hurling shells into the city.

On the morning of the 22d of May all the batteries of the army and the big guns of the river fleet bombarded the city for an hour, and under the fog and the smoke of the battle the infantry advanced to assault the works. It was a perilous undertaking. The day was fearfully hot; the forts, ten feet high, were many and powerful; the ditches in front of them were seven feet deep. That made seventeen feet to climb in the face of musketry. In battle line, my regiment ran down into the ravines in front and then up the opposite slope to the smoking breastwork.

The colonel had ordered me to fasten two ammunition boxes across a mule and follow the regiment into the assault. I was to lead my mule. A soldier with a bush was to beat him from behind, so as to hurry him over an exposed bit of ground at our front. The moment my mule appeared in full sight of the enemy the bullets commenced whizzing past us. The mule, true to his ancestral instinct, commenced pulling backward. Yelling and pounding and pulling helped none at all. Two or three bullets struck the boxes on his back, and before we had pulled him half across he braced himself, held his ears back, and stood stock still. My assistant dodged back to our rifle pit and I hurried down to the ravine in front. The mule, too, as luck would have it, also ran now—ran down into the ravine beside me, right where he was wanted.

My regiment was all lying against the hill close up to the fort. In front of them was the ditch seven feet deep, beyond them an armed fort ten feet high, emitting a constant blaze of cannon and musketry. The sun was

Closing the ring at Vicksburg

broiling hot. I crept along the line of the regiment and gave ammunition to every company; then I crept back a little to where my mule was still alive and his ears still at their antics. Lying there in the line beside the boys, roasting in the sun and suffering from the musketry in front, was our brave Colonel Boomer, leading the brigade. He asked me once what I was doing, and, when I told him, he gave me some compliments in a kind, but sad, low tone. Now I saw a company of men creep by me, dragging little ladders in their hands. They were to make a rush and throw these ladders across the ditch of the forts for the assaulters to cross on. They were all volunteeers for a work that seemed sure death. I looked in each hero's face as he passed me, knowing that he would be dead in a few minutes. Scarcely a dozen of them returned alive. My regiment, with the rest of the assaulters, was simply being shot to pieces without a hope of getting into the forts. We fell back under the smoke of the battle as best we could, only to be led into an assault at another point. McClernand had sent Grant word that he had taken a fort on our left. He wanted help to hold it.

Our division, was double-quicked to the next place of assault. I saved my mule. Again I strapped two ammunition boxes over his back and followed the regiment. This time I did not risk my mule so close in the battle, but took all the cartridges I could carry in my arms and went to the left of the regiment. Once I saw a body lying on the grass by me, with a handkerchief over the face. I went up and looked. It was our own Colonel Boomer, who had spoken so kindly to me in the morning. A useless charge had already been made by the brigade and he, with many brave men, was dead. Some of my own company lay dead there too. One of them had come from Iowa and joined his brother in the company that very morning. All the assaulting of the 22d of May and all the sacrifice of life had been for nothing. Vicksburg was not taken.

Now commenced the regular siege of the city. We hid ourselves behind ridges, in hollows, and in holes in the ground, as best we could. Communication with our gunboats on the Yazoo was opened, and we had plenty to eat and ammunition enough to bombard a dozen cities. Then the bombardment commenced indeed, and lasted to the end, forty-four days. We often threw three hundred cannonballs and shells a day into the city. The whole Rebel army was hidden in holes and hollows. All the people of Vicksburg lived in caves at the sides of the hills or along the bluffs of the river. Their homes now were like swallows' nests, with small entrances in the face of hills and bluffs and big, dug-out chambers inside. It was a strange life. With the eternal hail of cannon over them day and night, and starvation a familiar figure to them, it must have been a horrible one.

Now we advanced our rifle pits and trenches and mines close up to the Rebel forts, though our main lines lay in the ravines and on the ridge a few hundred feet farther back. As for me, when not looking after the ammunition, a trifling duty now, I was in the trenches with the others.

One morning when out there at the front among our riflemen, who were forever blazing day and night at every Rebel fort and rifle pit, I noticed our Colonel Matthies creeping along the trench to where I was. He had a package of brown paper in his hand. Imagine my surprise and pride to have him come to me and say: "Sergeant, this officer's sash is yours." Then he announced my appointment as adjutant of the regiment. He had been made a general now, and would soon leave for his new command. This sash was one that he had worn and honored on many a battlefield. Is it any wonder that now, after the long and perilous years, it is preserved by me as a souvenir of honor? Soon after, I went to a sutler's store on the Yazoo River to buy a sword and uniform. In those days swords were not given to officers by committees in dress coats, until they had been earned. This little trip to get my sword almost cost me my life. My path to the river, six miles away, lay partly along a ridge and partly close to an empty Rebel fort. This fort showed scarcely any signs of having ever been used. I stayed all night with the sutler, whom I knew very well, and at noon on a hot day started, on my big yellow government horse, to go back to my regiment. My sword was buckled on me and my new uniform was tied in a bundle on my saddle-bow. It was too hot to ride fast, and my horse almost slept as he slowly carried me close by the seemingly abandoned fort. Suddenly there was a crash and a whole volley of musketry rattled about my ears. My poor horse fell dead. It was a quick awakening, but I managed to pull my bundle from the saddle-bow and to escape into a ravine where our own troops lay. There I learned that the fort had been occupied by the Rebels in the night, while I was with the sutler. It was a close call for me. One of the boys declared he could save my saddle and bridle. "Take them as a present," I said, "if you can get them." He crept up to where my dead horse lay, and as he rose to his feet to undo the saddle another volley from the fort hastened him to the ravine. I laughed. "If your saddle and bridle were made of gold and silver," he shouted at me as he ran back, "I wouldn't try it again."

Slowly and without perceptible advance the siege went on. The little battery that my regiment had saved at Iuka was still with us and behind some breastworks at our immediate right. It was no uncommon thing to see even Grant himself come along and stop and watch Captain Sears' guns knock the dirt up from some fort in front of us. One day this battery wounded a man who was running between two Rebel breastworks. The enemy tried to secure his body, but every soul that showed himself for an instant was shot by our riflemen. For half an hour this shooting over one poor man's body was kept up, until it seemed that a battle was taking place.

Now our lines were so close together that our pickets often had a cup of coffee or a chew of tobacco with the Rebel pickets at night. Drummer Bain, of my company, had a brother among the soldiers inside Vicksburg. One night he met him at the picket line, and together they walked all through the beleagured town. But such things were dangerous business and had to be kept very quiet. The weather was now very warm and fine, some of the nights clear moonlight, and when the guns had stopped their roaring many a time in the quiet night we heard the bell clock on the Vicksburg Court House measuring out the hours. It is said that this clock never stopped for an instant in all the siege, nor under the hundred cannon that rained iron hail into the town. At night, too, the big mortars from our fleet some miles from us tossed mighty bombs into the air, that sailed like blazing comets and fell at last among the people hidden in their caves.

One day Governor Kirkwood of Iowa visited our regiment and made a speech to us in a hollow back of our line. We cheered, and the Rebels, hearing us and knowing we must be assembled in masses, hurled a hundred cannonballs and shells over our heads, yet I think few were hurt. This was the 3d of June. Every night that we lay there on the line we went to sleep fearing to be waked by an attack from the army of Rebels under Johnston, now assembled at our rear. This was the force we most feared, not the army we had penned up in Vicksburg. Nevertheless, the batteries in front of us gave us enough to do to prevent any ennui on our part. On the 15th of June the enemy got one big gun in a position to rake from our left the ravine in which my regiment was lying. We all stuck close to our little caves on the ridge side, and few got hurt. In the meantime we were working day and night putting more breastworks in front of us, though we were now but four hundred yards away from the Rebel lines. Here, as many times elsewhere, I copy from my diary. "Last night, the 16th, the major of our regiment, Marshall, took two hundred men and worked all night digging new ditches and building breastworks. It was rainy and muddy. The Rebels heard us at the work and in the darkness slipped up and captured a few men. Some of the enemy, however, also got taken in. This is the kind of work that is going on every night until daybreak, and then we fire bullets all the day into the enemy's lines, to prevent their repairing their forts. The cannonading and the rifle shooting never cease. The roar is simply incessant, and yet when off duty we sleep like newborn babes.

"All the region we are in is hills and ravines, brush and cane-brake, with here and there a little cotton field. Nature defends Vicksburg more than a dozen armies could."

The rumors kept coming of a purposed attack on our rear. On the 20th of June, at four o'clock in the morning, all the cannon on Grant's lines and all the cannon on the gunboats opened fire on the town and thundered at it for six mortal hours. They must have been awful hours for the people inside. We private soldiers did not know the exact object of this fearful bombardment. The Rebels probably lay in battle line, expecting an assault, and must have suffered greatly.

In the night of the 22d of June, at midnight, rumors again came of a great Rebel army marching on our rear. It was a beautiful moonlight night, and my regiment, together with whole divisions of the army, received orders to hurry back toward Black River, where cavalry skirmishing had taken place. No battle came on, but for two days we lay in line of battle, or else built breastworks for defense.

On the 3d of July, as we were bivouacked in a little wood, news came that the whole Rebel army in Vicksburg had prepared to surrender the next day, the Nation's jubilee day. Instantly the regiment was ordered to fall in. I had no little pride in reading to the men the dispatch from General Grant announcing the great news. It was the first order I had ever read to the regiment as its adjutant, and its great importance gratified me much. The whole command acted as if they were drunken or had suddenly lost their minds. Privates and officers shook hands and laughed and wept, while majors and colonels turned somersaults on the grass. It was indeed a great moment to us all. Twenty-seven thousand men, with twenty-four generals and one hundred and eighty cannon, was a great capture. We all knew we had made history on that day.

Now the whole Rebel army passed out along the roads where we lay. I sat on a rail fence near our bivouac and watched the host go by. The officers all looked depressed, but the soldiers seemed glad the suspense and danger were over and that now they could have enough to eat. Our regiment freely divided with them all we had.

BRAGG INVADES KENTUCKY

AFTER THE BATTLES OF SHILOH AND CORINTH, Halleck ordered Buell's Army of the Cumberland to drive the Confederates out of East Tennessee and occupy Chattanooga. Buell's progress was so slow that he got no farther than Nashville in the summer of 1862. Meanwhile, Confederate General Bragg had already arrived in Chattanooga; he had been pursuaded to invade Kentucky. In June, while still based in Tupelo, Mississippi, "General Bragg had been visited by many prominent citizens of Kentucky, who had abandoned their homes, and who assured him that Kentuckians were thoroughly loyal to the South, and that as soon as they were given an opportunity it would be proven. Fired with this idea, [Bragg] planned his offensive campaign. . . . Headquarters were established at Chattanooga on July 29th."*

Bragg marched into Kentucky in September, heading for Louisville and the Ohio River. On September 17, he called a council with his officers at Munfordville. "With the map and the cavalry dispatches outspread before him, General Bragg placed General Buell and his army in our rear, with Munfordville on the direct line of his march to Louisville, the assumed objective point of his movement. General Bragg then explained his plan, which was [to continue] our advance, leaving General Buell to pursue his march unmolested. . . . At one o'clock on the morning of the 18th, Bragg was on the point of rescinding the order . . . and of directing instead an immediate offensive movement against Buell. . . . But upon further consideration, he reverted to his previous plans, saying to me with emphasis, 'This campaign must be won by marching, not by fighting.' . . . At the moment he evinced no regret at having allowed Buell to pass on our left flank."†

There was ample opportunity for the armies to obtain battle with each other. Buell had been forced to turn north to try to reach Louisville before Bragg, and on September 25 he marched into the city, a step ahead of the Confederates, who were in the outskirts. Bragg did not offer battle but withdrew to the South.

* Col. David Urquhart, "Bragg's Advance and Retreat," *Battles and Leaders,* III, 600.
  † *Ibid.*, p. 601.

It was now clear to General Bragg "that the reported desire of Kentucky to cast her lot with the South had passed away, if indeed such a disposition had ever existed; for not only was Kentucky unprepared to enter the Confederacy, but her people looked with dread at the prospect of their state being made a battlefield. Under these circumstances he remarked to me . . . 'The people here have too many fat cattle and are too well off to fight.' He was now aware that he had embarked on a campaign that was to produce no favorable result, and that he had erred in departing from his original plan of taking the offensive in the outset against Buell by an operation on that general's communications."*

So Bragg retreated into Tennessee, taking up headquarters at Murfreesboro on November 26. Less than thirty miles away in Nashville, the Army of the Cumberland was resting after having marched all over the state. They had a new commander—General Rosecrans had replaced Buell—and after three weeks of foraging and preparation, Rosecrans made his move.

The Battle of Murfreesboro†

BY CAPTAIN W. F. HINMAN

THE FIRST ORDER FOR THE ADVANCE came to us at four o'clock on the morning of December 24th. We struck tents, loaded wagons—which we were told would be left behind—and waited, momentarily expecting the tap of the drum, till late in the afternoon. Then we were directed to pitch tents again, and prepare for an early march on Christmas morning. We were ready at daylight, but were soon ordered again to unpack. Instead of waiting in camp, however, we went out with a forage train. After our return from this expedition we received an order that the army would positively move on the following day—and that night was the last of our stay at Nashville.

Early on the morning of the 26th, drums and bugles sounded through all the camps of Rosecrans's army. In accordance with previous orders the company wagons were loaded and sent to Nashville, where they were parked to await the issue of the impending campaign. But three wagons were permitted to accompany each regiment. The troops began to march at six o'clock. Crittenden's command, the left wing of the army, moved out by the direct road to Murfreesboro. We got off at nine, in a pelting rain. The entire day was sloppy and disagreeable. There was frequent skirmishing in the advance, with now and then a few artillery shots, that

* *Ibid.*, p. 602.
† From *The Story of the Sherman Brigade.*

quickened the steps of the soldiers and kept us all in a state of excitement. The probabilities of a battle were freely discussed. It was generally believed that at last there was a fair prospect that we would get into a fight. It was noticeable that those who, when they thought the war was about over, had most loudly expressed their disappointment, because they were not going to see a battle, were now the most quiet.

After frequent halts, on account of the delay of the troops in front, just before dark we filed off the pike into a muddy field near Lavergne. A spirited skirmish had taken place here a few hours before. Several dead horses lay around, and here and there the ground had been torn up by shells. Things began to have a practical look. This appearance was more impressed upon our minds when we were informed that we must be ready to move very early the following day, as Wood's division would have the advance. The mud everywhere was shoe deep, churned by the ceaseless tread of thousands of men and horses. Night, dark and dripping, settled down upon the great bivouac. Forty-five thousand men were there and at Triune, a few miles to the right, gathered around the sputtering fires. In the midst of such a multitude there was little chance to get anything to promote comfort. What little there had been was taken by those first to arrive. We could do nothing except spread our blankets upon the wet ground, choosing the spots where there was the least depth of mud.

Rain drizzled down upon us during the whole night. We slept, however, but arose well soaked, and in a most forlorn condition. The Fifty-first Indiana did the picket duty for the brigade. Coffee and hardtack were soon disposed of and we were ready for orders soon after daylight. An early movement was prevented by a dense fog, so thick at times that objects could not be seen at ten yards distance. The rebels were reported to be in force a mile to the front. There was a prospect of a fight as soon as we should attempt to advance. It looked even more that way when, about nine o'clock, the fog having lifted a little, a rebel battery opened fire, throwing several shells in our midst, with the most reckless disregard of consequences. Captain Samuel Neeper, of the Sixty-fourth, was severely wounded in the knee, and two or three men were more or less injured. Captain Bradley placed a section of the Sixth battery in position and gave the enemy his compliments. A desultory fire was kept up for an hour, with frequent rattling of musketry on the picket line. Wood's division stood at arms, ready to receive the enemy should he take the aggressive.

At noon an advance was ordered. We moved in line of battle by brigades, Hascall's leading, with the Twenty-sixth Ohio and Fifteenth Indiana deployed in a heavy skirmish line. There was constant irregular firing, the rebels stubbornly contesting the ground. They slowly yielded, however, and we at no time receded from our forward movement. The Sixty-fifth Ohio and Seventy-third Indiana were in line to the left of the Murfreesboro pike, and the Sixty-fourth Ohio, Thirteenth Michigan and Fifty-first Indiana on its right. As we approached the little straggling village of Lavergne we were much annoyed by the enemy's riflemen, who were concealed in and around the buildings. A few shells from the Sixth battery gave them to understand that we were on the war-path in earnest. A quick advance by the infantry drove them in confusion. The rebel artillery took advantage of every favorable position to retard our progress.

But we did not sit down for half a day whenever a shot was fired, as we did under General Buell. We just kept right on, steadily pressing the enemy. One solid shot, or a shell which fortunately did not explode, struck the ground a few yards in front of the Sixty-fifth, splashing the mud and water in every direction, which made the boys feel solemn. We advanced during the day about six miles, through miry fields, over hills, across swollen streams, and through dense cedar thickets which showered us with water as we forced our toilsome way through them. Long before we stopped for the night we were wet to the skin and thoroughly fatigued.

Toward evening a change of direction brought Harker's brigade in front. One company from each regiment was thrown out upon the skirmish line. As we emerged suddenly from a thick wood we came upon a squad of some thirty rebel cavalry. They were dismounted, and evidently not expecting us so soon. At sight of our advancing line they sprang into their saddles and were off like the wind. Their movements were hastened by a brisk fire from our skirmishers. In their flight the fugitives bore to our right, and dashed into a piece of woods, almost upon the muskets of Union troops which had but a moment before reached that point. They were all captured, except two or three who escaped through a shower of bullets. Having driven the enemy across Stewart's creek, we bivouacked on the north bank of that stream. A bridge which the retreating rebels had fired was saved by a dash of the Third Kentucky. We had another dismal night, with mud everywhere. The Sixty-fifth was detailed for picket, the right wing relieving the left at midnight. Two deserters came in through our line, and were escorted to brigade headquarters.

The 28th was Sunday. We kept it "holy" to the extent of not advancing to disturb the devotions of the enemy—if they had any. We did nothing except to stand picket and wade around in the mud.

Monday, December 29th, was an exciting day. It was in the evening of that day that we had our famous "cornfield skirmish," which was the tightest place we had yet been in, by long odds, and tested the mettle of the boys in standing fire. The army was up betimes. We formed on the colors at four o'clock—long before daylight—and waited patiently, and courageously, for whatever might turn up. But nothing happened to disturb us, and we stood around, half way to our knees in mud, till nearly noon. A spasmodic fire was kept up on the outposts, but neither party appeared to know just what he wanted to do.

We finally moved out, crossing Stewart's creek without opposition. Trouble had been expected here, and before the passage was attempted, two of our batteries threw over a few shells as "feelers," but elicited no reply. We immediately formed line of battle on either side of the pike, as on our advance from Lavergne. Within half an hour we stirred up the enemy's cavalry. Firing began at once, and continued through the day. The companies on the skirmish line were kept busy, but as scarcely anybody got hurt they thought it great sport. The rebel horsemen took care to keep at a good distance, galloping off whenever we began to get within gunshot. The shooting made a great deal of noise, although it was about as harmless as a Fourth of July fusillade. But our skirmishers blazed away incessantly. We marched over the body of one rebel who had been killed. Shots enough were fired that day to destroy half of Bragg's army. Several times Captain Bradley took a hand in the game. His battery was behind us. When opportunity offered he would unlimber two or three pieces; at the command "Lie down!" we would flatten ourselves upon the ground, and the shells would go screaming over us. The rebels had what we used to call a "jackass battery," which replied feebly from time to time. A large house just off the road was set on fire by one of our shells. It was in flames as we passed it, and was soon burned to the ground. We experienced all the fatigue of line-of-battle marching, tearing through woods and thickets, and fording several streams.

About four o'clock we reached the bank of Stone river, soon to be made historic by one of the great battles of the war. The Confederates were in force on the opposite bank. Their appearance seemed to say that if we advanced farther it would be at our peril. Not long after we halted, General Rosecrans and General Crittenden rode up and took a view of the situation. The enemy occupied a ridge half a mile from the river. A mile beyond lay Murfreesboro. Rosecrans, just at nightfall, acting upon a mistaken rumor that the rebels were evacuating, ordered Crittenden to occupy the town immediately, with one of his divisions. Wood's division was designated for this duty. The movement began at once, ours being the leading brigade.

"Skirmishers—forward, promptly!" said Colonel Harker and ordered the brigade to follow.

Descending the steep bank to the brink of the stream, we plunged in and waded to the other side, the water being in places thigh deep. By this time darkness was fast enveloping us. Such a movement by night, over unknown ground, against an enemy in position, was one of extreme hazard, and General Wood protested to General Crittenden against its execution. Crittenden, however, refused to suspend a peremptory order which he had received from Rosecrans. An hour later the latter revoked the order and directed the recall of the troops that had crossed.

But in the meantime there had been no hesitation on the part of Colonel Harker and his brigade. Without pausing for an instant to question the expediency of the movement, he had ordered the line to push forward rapidly. Emerging from the river, we plunged into a thicket so dense that it seemed scarcely possible for even an unincumbered man to penetrate it. But we got through, with torn clothes and scratched faces, and entered a large cornfield, in which the dry stalks were still standing. The field led, by a gradual ascent, to the ridge occupied by the enemy. Strangely enough, there was no force at the river to dispute our passage.

There was no firing until we had advanced a considerable distance into the cornfield. Then the rebels opened suddenly with a volley that wellnigh made "each particular hair to stand on end." The bullets whistled around us and pattered viciously upon the cornstalks. The enemy being on high ground, the volley passed mostly over our heads. But the bullets came as close as we cared to have them, and quite close enough to appease, in some measure, our yearning desire for a fight. Our unquenchable zeal ought to have carried us right into Murfreesboro that night, but it didn't. In fact everybody was glad enough when the order to retire reached us. We did not know much about war yet, but it seemed to us that our advance was a mistake.

The boys got out of that cornfield in double-quick time, dashed again through the *chevaux de frise* of briers and brambles, in utter darkness, and plunged into the river. There was no panic, no disorder. They simply wanted to get away from there and they did so, promptly. During the retreat, part of the Sixty-fifth lapped over in rear of the Thirteenth Michigan. The latter thought we were rebels advancing upon them and turned upon us with their muskets, but fortunately did no damage. The enemy continued a desultory fire until the brigade had recrossed the river.

We did not escape without casualties. The Sixty-fourth and Sixty-fifth had each three or four men wounded. Two were killed in the Thirteenth Michigan and one in the Fifty-first Indiana. It was hardly less than a miracle that the loss was not tenfold greater. Among the wounded was "Sam" Snider, a lad of sixteen, belonging to Company D, Sixty-fifth, and a universal favorite in the regiment. A bullet, flying transversely across his face, struck his nose and made a bad wreck of that organ. The doctors succeeded in patching it up in good shape, and with their assistance nature repaired the damage so that in a short time he returned to duty, with a nose that was good enough for all practical purposes, if it was not quite as ornamental as before.

It may be remarked here that twenty-five years after the war "Sam" was a member of Congress from Minnesota. At the same time the Sixty-fourth was also represented in Congress, Wilbur F. Sanders, the first adjutant of that regiment, being a United States Senator from Montana.

Through some oversight, Companies B and E of the Sixty-fifth, which had been deployed as skirmishers during this escapade, did not receive the order to recross the river, and remained on the rebel side for two or three hours. They could plainly hear the commotion in the enemy's camp, caused by the wholly unexpected demonstration. Regiments were forming in line, and the voices of the officers giving commands could be distinctly heard. All along the line the rebels were busily engaged in throwing up intrenchments, with a great noise of axes and shovels. Major Whitbeck, who commanded the skirmishers, thinking that they had been forgotten, finally sent a messenger to Colonel Harker, informing him of their position and asking whether they should remain. The colonel was greatly surprised to learn these facts.

"Get on my horse," said he to the messenger, "ride as fast as possible, and tell Major Whitbeck to withdraw instantly, but with extreme caution and silence!" The two companies succeded in recrossing the river without molestation.

It was a strange thing to attempt such a movement, under the circumstances. Unquestionably the order was far less wise and prudent than its revocation. Had we pressed forward we would have encountered, as we afterward learned, a force greatly superior to Wood's division, and with the river between us and the main army the result would most likely have been disastrous. Van Horne, the historian of the Army of the Cumberland, says of our adventure in the cornfield:

> General Rosecrans countermanded his own order and recalled the troops to their former position. Even this movement was critical, as Colonel Harker's brigade had crossed Stone river, and had driven

Breckinridge's advance upon his main line, and Hascall's brigade and Bradley's battery were in the river, advancing in rear. However, Colonel Harker's adroitness and the veil of darkness secured their withdrawal with only slight loss.

Marching back a few hundred yards from the river we bivouacked for the night in the edge of a cotton field. At last the boys had something to talk about. There were many tales of hair-breadth escapes. Rebel bullets passed within half an inch of the head of every man in the brigade!

As soon as the brigade recrossed the river the Sixty-fourth was ordered on picket, the line stretching along the margin of the stream. The men threw up little barricades of timber, stones and earth. These proved of great service the next day as a protection from the enemy's pickets, with whom there was constant skirmishing. During that day the Sixty-fourth suffered a loss of one man killed—Wesley Hetherington, the first death in the regiment from a hostile bullet—and five or six wounded.

We expected to advance or fight, and probably both, on the 30th, but we did neither. The exercises of the previous day had been of such a character that we had made up our minds that after tramping over four states looking for trouble, we were at last going to be accommodated—and we were, but not that day.

We were called into line at four o'clock and directed to be in readiness to advance at daylight, but that was all. The only movement we made was a very hasty change of position, several hundred yards to the rear, to get out of the way of the shells that a rebel battery on the ridge across the river kept throwing at us. They seemed to have more hardware than they wanted and insisted on sharing it with us. But we were well supplied and their motives were not appreciated. So we just "climbed" for the rear to get out of range. This was about the middle of the forenoon. We could see their cannon glistening in the sunlight, less than a mile distant. There would be a puff of smoke and then *whizz! boom!* and everybody would be dodging to get out of the way of the pieces. Captain Bradley brought his battery to the front and replied with a lively fire, which soon silenced the enemy's guns. One of Bradley's carriages was struck by a solid shot and badly splintered. The Sixth battery men stood bravely to their work. It was clear that they could be depended upon.

The firing was kept up all day at intervals, not only in our front but at other points on the line. Our pickets, posted along the river bank, were almost constantly exchanging compliments with the rebel outposts.

During the afternoon several pigs wandered within the lines of the Sixty-fifth. They were surrounded and bayoneted without mercy. Our meat rations were running short, and the presence of the enemy did not prevent the boys from looking out for their stomachs. Colonel Cassil viewed the slaughter with complacency. He didn't make any fuss about it, and partook of a sparerib with evident enjoyment.

Just at dusk we drew rations. The Sixty-fifth was ordered to report forthwith for picket duty, to relieve the Sixty-fourth. As we moved to the river bank the batteries on both sides opened with a tremendous fire. The roar was terrific, but it was mostly noise, only three or four men in our brigade being wounded by fragments of shell. Captain Bradley had all of his six guns going. He paid strict attention to the rebel battery on the ridge, which had suddenly become very active. We took our positions for the night along the bank, behind the little breastworks which had been thrown up by the Sixty-fourth. The night was comparatively quiet, but we had no sleep save an occasional "cat-nap" when on the reserve.

The remainder of the brigade bivouacked in line of battle, as did both armies, the hostile lines being but six hundred yards apart. It was generally known, even among the soldiers, that the mighty grapple of Rosecrans and Bragg would take place on the morrow. By a singular coincidence, each commander had determined to take the offensive at dawn of the 31st, and both had decided upon the same plan of battle—that is, each was to assail the other's right flank. Rosecrans directed the left wing, under Crittenden, to cross Stone river, attack Breckinridge, commanding the Confederate right, drive him from his position covering Murfreesboro, sweep through the town, enfilade Bragg's main line with artillery, and obtain possession of the roads in the Confederate rear. Meanwhile the right, McCook, and the center, Thomas, were to engage the enemy vigorously in their front and prevent the sending of reinforcements to Breckinridge. All this looked very feasible, on paper, but circumstances which we could not control interfered very materially with the carrying out of the well arranged program. Bragg's plan was to mass, during the night, a heavy column and at daylight hurl it upon the Union right, sweep the line and seize the Nashville turnpike, Rosecrans's avenue of retreat in case of disaster.

Long before daylight, officers and orderly sergeants moved quietly along the line and aroused the soldiers. There was no sound of drum or bugle, as the men seized their muskets and took their places in the ranks. For an hour they stood waiting and watching for the dawn. Each man had forty rounds of ammunition in his cartridge box and forty more in his pockets, a haversack well filled with rations, and a canteen of water. Nearly all had blankets, but thousands of these were flung away during the day. The confronting lines were about three miles in length. Stone river, by a sharp bend, cut the Confederate line, so that the main body of the rebel army was on the same side as our own. At the extreme Union left the river flowed between us and the enemy under Breckinridge.

In accordance with the orders of General Rosecrans, Van Cleve's division crossed Stone river at the lower ford and moved in battle array to assail the Confederate right. Our division (Wood's) was to cross at the upper ford, connect with Van Cleve's right, and join in the attack. Wood's leading brigade (Hascall's) was already in the stream and ours (Harker's) was at the brink prepared to follow. No opposition had been encountered, and thus far all was working well. As the sun rose we could plainly see the glistening guns of a rebel battery posted on high ground half a mile from the river, but up to this time they had given no sound.

Now the storm burst with the greatest fury upon the Union right, under McCook. In furtherance of his plan, Bragg had massed at that point two-fifths of his army, and a sudden and most impetuous assault threw McCook's flank into immediate confusion. His position was faulty and

Murfreesboro: *Negley's Union division strikes across Stone River*

the consequences well nigh proved fatal. Many of the troops were not in line but were at breakfast, while the horses of some of the batteries were not even harnessed. Johnson's division, the extreme right, was swept in disorder from the field, after a brief resistance, losing nearly all of its artillery. Davis's division, next in line, was also disrupted and streamed to the rear, a mass of broken battalions. Next was the division of "Phil" Sheridan, and that officer and his men, breasting the tide with superb heroism, checked the onward rush of the enemy and gave priceless moments for General Rosecrans to make the new dispositions demanded by the unexpected onslaught of the Confederates. It is not my province to write a history of the battle, but only of our part in it. I have said thus much to recall the alarming aspect of affairs at the time a staff officer dashed up on a mad gallop and delivered an order suspending our movement across the river, and recalling the division of Van Cleve.

"Attention—Battalion!" and away we went at double-quick toward the cedar thicket upon the right, whence came the unceasing roar of battle. Immediate succor was needed, and Harker's brigade—soon followed by others—was ordered to the point where the stress was greatest. Just as we started from the river bank the rebel battery, of which mention has been made, opened upon us with shell. One of these missiles struck Company B, of the Sixty-fifth, and burst, killing Joseph Bull—the first man of the Sixty-fifth to fall in battle—and wounding several others. Our rapid movement soon carried us out of range.

On and on we went, at the greatest possible speed. Every man was in his place, his nerves wrought up to the highest tension, and none thought of weariness. We passed through a large space of open ground, which presented a scene of the wildest excitement and chaos that can be conceived. Demoralized stragglers from the right wing were seeking safety at the rear, while officers, mounted and on foot, shouting and cursing, were endeavoring to stay the tide of panic; teamsters, in a delirium of fright, lashed their mules into a furious gallop, as they sought to reach the pike with ammunition, supply and baggage wagons; bodies of troops were hurrying forward to meet the advancing and exultant foe; generals and staff officers gathered here and there giving their orders; while shouts and yells and the braying of mules filled the air with a hideous din. It was a scene never to be forgotten.

Through this mass of frenzied men and animals we threaded our way, still on the double-quick. We saw many wounded making their way to the rear, unaided, or borne upon stretchers, or in ambulances. This was indeed war; the crucial test was before us. Every man clutched his musket with a tighter grip and nerved himself to face the storm, already so near that we could feel its fiery breath. There was no sign of flinching, and yet I may safely say that we hardly felt that raging desire to plunge into the blazing vortex of death, which had so often found expression on our weary marches and around the camp-fires, during the previous year. But the truly brave man is he who realizes the danger and willingly faces it at the call of duty.

Still on, and a shell from a rebel battery bursts above us and the fragments hurtle around us. The droning buzz of spent bullets is heard. We hastily form in line of battle, connecting with the right of a brigade of

Van Cleve's division. "Forward!" and the line moves steadily on. Two hundred yards in advance of us are Union troops fiercely engaged, whom we are ordered to support. The need is not immediate and we are directed to lie down. For a long time, as it seems to us—probably about twenty minutes—we remain prone upon the earth awaiting the issue. A staff officer dashes up to Colonel Harker and points toward the right. The rebels have overlapped the Union line and disaster is imminent.

Instantly each regiment receives the command: "Battalion—rise up!" We face to the right and dash off upon the run. Farther and farther we go until a line of rebels is descried advancing toward us. We halt, face to the front, and move forward in battle array to meet the foe. The Seventy-third Indiana, Sixty-fourth and Sixty-fifth Ohio are in the first line, supported by the Fifty-first Indiana and Thirteenth Michigan. The Sixth Ohio battery is upon the right of the Sixty-fifth. Two companies from each regiment in front are deployed as skirmishers. Five minutes, and they engage those of the enemy.

Now we are at the edge of the storm. Hissing bullets strike in our ranks and one and then another is stricken down, dead or wounded, Lieutenant Pealer, of Company A, Sixty-fifth, being one of the first to fall, grievously wounded in the thigh. We cannot pause to give them aid; our duty is—yonder. More thickly come the bullets, and soon a dozen, twenty, are stretched upon the ground. We glance sorrowfully at the sufferers, nor can we repress a shudder as a comrade falls at our side, but we move steadily forward. The skirmishers are withdrawn; the hostile lines are separated by a distance of but two hundred yards.

At last we are face to face with the foe. "Commence firing!" and "Fire at will!" are the orders in quick succession. The enemy delivers a volley and at once the fighting becomes fierce. Officers and men are killed or wounded by scores. In the Sixty-fourth Captain Sweet, of Company K, falls in immediate death. In the Sixty-fifth Captain Christofel, of Company I, receives a fatal wound; Adjutant Massey is thrice hit and mortally hurt; Lieutenant Vankirk, of Company G, is struck squarely in the forehead and falls dead; Lieutenant-Colonel Cassil is disabled by his horse, which is shot, falling upon him; Major Whitbeck, upon whom devolves the command of the regiment, is pierced through the shoulder but pluckily refuses to quit the field. The courage and steadiness of the men are above praise. The ground about them is thickly strewn with the dead and dying, but with ceaseless vigor hands fly to cartridge boxes, bullets are rammed home, and muskets blaze defiance to the enemy.

A short distance to our right the Sixth battery is hotly engaged with the rebel artillery, posted at the left of the hostile line. Four guns, embracing the right and center sections, commanded respectively by Lieutenant Oliver H. P. Ayres and First Sergeant George W. Smetts, face directly to the front. The left section, Lieutenant Baldwin, which had been ordered to swing over and go into position a hundred yards to the right and rear, is in a furious duel with two or three Confederate guns which occupy an advanced position on the extreme flank. Baldwin's rapid and well-directed fire silences the guns of the enemy and the section moves quickly up to the line of the battery, taking post at the right of a small building which intervenes between these two pieces and the four others of the battery. Captain Bradley, cool and collected, directs with judgment and deliberation the fire of his guns. Officers and men stand gallantly to their work, serving their pieces with tireless energy. Men and horses are struck, but not for an instant does the firing slacken.

At length the brigade of Van Cleve's division upon our left, gives way before a charge of the enemy and falls back. By its recession our brigade, which is the extreme right of the line, is seriously compromised, both its flanks being now exposed. Following hard after the retreating troops of Van Cleve, the rebels are swiftly advancing. In a few minutes we will be enveloped. To remain would be fatal and we are ordered to retire. We do so, rapidly, for two hundred yards, but rally behind the partial cover of a cedar fence, and again send our deadly greeting to the enemy.

Before the break in the infantry line, the Fifty-first Indiana had shifted to the right to support the Sixth battery. "Stick to them," shouts Colonel Streight, "the Fifty-first will see you through!" But when the infantry falls back it would be folly for the battery to "stick" longer. An order from Colonel Harker directs its retirement. The rebels are advancing with loud yells and the need of haste is urgent. Every instant of delay increases the imminence of the peril. Quickly the sections of Ayres and Smetts are limbered up and go whirling back nearly to the line of the fence behind which the infantry has rallied. Here the four pieces are unlimbered and again blaze defiance at the foe. Baldwin's section, separated from the others as before mentioned, does not, in the confusion, receive the order to fall back, and so intent are the men upon their work that they are ignorant of the movement to the rear. The section receives a galling fire of both infantry and artillery. Two horses of Sergeant Stewart Miller's piece are killed by a cannon ball, and driver William Corey has an arm torn off. The guns are in the greatest jeopardy, for the exultant rebels are charging toward them. Just in time, the dead and wounded horses are cut loose and the section dashes to the rear. As it reaches a depression in the ground the Confederates deliver a volley from their muskets. The bullets whiz over the heads of Baldwin's men, but strike with deadly effect the two sections which had first retired. Sergeant George W. Howard and Private Samuel M. Scott fall in death, and a number of others are wounded. Horses go down on every hand.

After a brief but fierce struggle at the fence we are again flanked upon the left and our decimated line is torn by a biting enfilading fire. There is no alternative and again we fall back, with the advancing rebels at our heels. We come upon the Twenty-seventh and Fifty-first Illinois regiments, of Sheridan's division, lying in line. They have been sent to our aid. As soon as we have passed over them they rise, deliver a volley, and charge with fixed bayonets. Before that charge the Confederates recoil, turn about and scamper back to their own lines. Our fighting for the day is ended.

The infantry having yielded its position, the battery can no longer hold its place, and "Limber to the rear!" is again the order. It is executed with desperate haste. Two of the guns—one each in the sections of Ayres and Smetts—have lost eleven of their twelve horses. The four other guns of the battery dash away, but the rebels are close at hand, there is no chance to attach the prolongs, and the two pieces are abandoned. But they have been rendered harmless, for they have been spiked by Corporal David H. Evans. With exultant shouts the rebels take possession of the two guns. Not long do they hold their prize. The Thirteenth Michigan is lying among the rocks, a short distance to the rear. Colonel Shoemaker orders the Thirteenth to charge. Almost in a moment it snatches the guns from their captors, the prolongs are attached, and they are dragged back amidst a tempest of cheers. The battery takes up a new position near the pike. The rebels run out a battery which opens from a distance of four hundred yards. Colonel Harker directs Captain Bradley to "smash that battery." The men spring to their pieces and a few well-aimed shells send the rebel guns galloping to the rear.

We re-formed our broken lines; but how much shorter they were than in the morning! There were many vacant places in the ranks. In the Sixty-fifth but five officers remained unhurt out of sixteen who went into the battle. For the time, the regiment was organized into a battalion of four companies. The enemy made no further demonstration in our front. We stacked arms, and details were sent to bring in as many of our wounded as could be found. Those who were not wholly disabled had made their way to the hospitals. The greater part of our loss was incurred at our first position, and when we fell back we were reluctantly compelled to leave behind those who were so severely wounded as to be helpless. They fell into the hands of the rebels, and after the latter had been driven back they were between the lines. Every one who could be reached was brought back, but many lay upon the ground, without surgical aid, through all the long and bitterly cold night that followed. They and many hundreds of other wounded suffered unspeakable agonies.

That night at a council of General Rosecrans with his subordinate commanders, a few timorous ones advised a retreat to Nashville.

"Gentlemen," said Rosecrans, "we fight or die right here!"

Before dawn he had readjusted his lines, which were so rudely broken the day before by the blows of his impetuous adversary; confidence was restored, and he was fully prepared to meet the enemy, should the latter again assail him. During the battle of Wednesday, Rosecrans gave abundant evidence of his high personal courage. He rode along the lines in the thickest of the fight, cheering and encouraging his hard-pressed soldiers. While galloping across a field, with his chief of staff by his side, the latter, Colonel Garesche, was instantly killed, a cannon ball taking off his head.

During the night we returned to our proper place in Crittenden's left wing. The ground was covered with a heavy white frost, which creaked under our feet as we marched across the battlefield, among the stiffened, lifeless forms of the dead. We went into position just west of the Nashville railroad, and rested till an hour before daybreak, when we were aroused to stand at arms. Sleep was scarcely possible. Chilled and benumbed by the keen, frosty air we were compelled to move about to keep the blood flowing in our veins. Soon after dawn we made a little coffee and ate a hasty breakfast, ready to instantly grasp our arms in case of need.

Bragg evidently thought that Rosecrans ought to know that he was whipped, and retreat. About eight o'clock a heavy rebel force advanced in our front, probably to find out whether there was any fight left in the Union army. The long line was in plain view, at a distance of three-quarters of a mile, moving forward in battle array. The Sixth Ohio and two or three other batteries at once opened a tremendous fire. General Rosecrans rode up and dashed here and there, shouting, "Pour it into them, boys! Pour it into them!" The rebels were soon satisfied that our pugnacity was not all gone and they gave it up, the whole line retiring in haste out of range.

Throughout the remainder of the day the armies, weary and sore from the buffetings of the previous day, lay comparatively inactive. Neither was disposed to resume the offensive, though each made every preparation to receive an attack. There was constant firing between the pickets; and sharpshooters, on both sides, with their long-range rifles, made themselves particularly obnoxious.

At noon the Sixth battery was stationed in an advanced position, facing what was known as the "round woods," where it remained during the night, with guns shotted. Captain Baldwin says: "It fell to the writer to be on duty from midnight until three o'clock in the morning. The night was cloudy and dark. About two o'clock cries were heard near our immediate front, asking for help and calling for a cup of water. Corporal Kimberk was directed to take a canteen of water and try to reach the wounded soldier. He had not proceeded more than twenty-five yards when *bang!* went a gun and the whizzing bullet struck a gun-tire within two feet of the writer. Corporal Kimberk returned and said if that fellow, whether friend or foe, needed any help, some one else might go, for he believed it was a plot on the part of the rebel pickets to make a widow up north, and he was not going to be the man to risk himself on that kind of a game. To stand picket with a battery was something new to us. But here we were, without a solitary infantryman between our lines and the enemy. Consequently we had to exercise extraordinary vigilance. If an attack had taken place there was nothing to meet it but the guns of the battery. Fortunately, the night passed without any movement by the enemy."

Friday morning, January 2nd, half of the Sixty-fifth was ordered on picket. As we relieved those who had been on duty during the night, six or eight pieces of artillery on the other side opened upon us a furious fire. At the outposts were V-shaped piles of rails, which had been laid by our predecessors for a shelter from musketry. Two or three of these were struck by shells and knocked into kindling wood. Several of our men were wounded, but none were killed.

As soon as the rebel guns opened, the Sixth Ohio battery, which had moved to a knoll just in rear of the main line of our brigade, responded with the greatest spirit. For an hour the firing was terrific. We, upon the outposts, flattened ourselves out as thin as possible upon the ground, while the screaming missiles passed both ways directly over our heads. For the time the deafening roar almost deprived us of our senses. The Eighth Indiana battery, which had been firing from the right of the Sixth Ohio, suffered so severely from the rebel "hardware" that it limbered up and galloped to the rear. The Sixth Ohio held its ground bravely. Every man stood to the guns, the steady, rapid fire of which was very effective.

At this time the Chicago Board of Trade battery was ordered up from the rear to engage the enemy. By a strange mistake, its commander, believing the Sixth Ohio to be a rebel battery, halted at a distance of three or four hundred yards, and opened upon it with grape. Before the firing could be stopped the blunderers had killed a number of horses and wounded several men of the Sixth, including Lieutenant Ayres. Captain Bradley was naturally thrown into a paroxysm of excitement and indignation. He thought he could hold his own with any of the rebel gunners, but to be sandwiched between two batteries, firing upon him from front and rear, made things a little too warm for comfort. Lieutenant Baldwin was ordered to proceed to the Chicago battery and stop its firing. Springing upon his horse, he had passed over about half the distance when the Chicago gunners let fly again. By this discharge his horse was killed, but Baldwin, who was uninjured, took the double-quick on foot, reached the battery, and by the use of very vigorous English brought the Chicago people to their senses. The Sixth battery stayed there, and its fire completely silenced the rebel guns. The Sixty-fourth Ohio, which was supporting the Sixth, also suffered from the ill-judged fire of the Chicago artillerists.

In the afternoon, part of the Sixty-fifth—under the command of Captain Brown, of Company H, and Captain Matthias, of Company K—was personally directed by Colonel Harker to advance from the outposts, charge the rebel pickets and drive them out of a thick grove, from which their fire was exceedingly annoying. We swept over the ground and occupied the grove, the rebels taking to their heels upon our approach. We suffered from their fire, one man of Company H being killed and six or eight in that and other companies wounded. We advanced as far as the spot that had been occupied by the rebel battery with which the Sixth Ohio was so severely engaged in the forenoon. Two exploded caissons and more than a dozen dead horses attested the efficacy of Captain Bradley's fire.

The same afternoon there was more hard fighting on the extreme left. It was not a general engagement. General Rosecrans had returned to his original plan of moving against the Confederate right, and to that end threw a strong force across Stone river. Bragg ordered Breckinridge to dislodge it, and the latter, with his division, attacked savagely. Major Mendenhall, General Crittenden's chief of artillery, hastily drew together ten batteries—fifty-eight guns in all—and posted them on high ground upon the west bank of the river. These guns completely enfiladed the lines of Breckinridge, and their fire, tremendous in volume, was most destructive. The rebels were driven back in confusion, with a loss of seventeen hundred men. The Sixth Ohio was conspicuous in this artillery firing for the rapid manner in which its guns were served. The ardor of its officers and men was illustrated by an incident. General Rosecrans rode up and asked:

"What battery is this?"

"The Sixth Ohio, sir!" said Captain Bradley, saluting.

"Well, be a little more deliberate and take good aim. Don't fire so d——d fast!"

It was determined to hold the position on the east bank of the river and Crittenden's entire corps was ordered to that side. We crossed in the evening, advanced to a position upon high ground, and threw up intrenchments of rails, logs, stones and earth. By this time our rations were completely exhausted. For three days we had lived upon what we had in our haversacks when we went into the battle on Wednesday morning. Many of the men had, in one way or another, lost their haversacks during the fighting, and those who had clung to their supplies divided their scanty store with those who had none. While working upon the intrenchments that night, we received the welcome intelligence that a supply train had arrived from Nashville, and we were directed to send details across the river for hardtack, bacon and coffee. The detachments returned about midnight. The conditions were such that no fires could be permitted, and we appeased our ravenous appetites with crackers and raw bacon. We were thankful to be able to do even that.

Saturday, January 3rd, was cold, rainy and wretchedly disagreeable, as we were entirely without shelter. The armies did little to disturb each other, although a continual fire was kept up along the picket lines. As a matter of fact, Bragg, finding that Rosecrans had no intention of retreating, had concluded to do so himself, and all day Saturday was immersed in the work of preparation for the exodus of his army, sending off by railroad his sick and wounded, and surplus stores and munitions. He kept up a brave show at the front, and his retreat was not suspected, until it was disclosed by the dawn of Sunday.

During Saturday night the river rose rapidly, in consequence of copious rains. Not knowing that the rebels were then getting away as fast as they could, General Rosecrans feared that the safety of his army would be jeopardized, should the river become unfordable, with Crittenden's corps thus separated from the main body. So, at midnight we were ordered to recross, which we did, in the storm and darkness, by fording, the water in places reaching to our hips. We marched a short distance from the river, stacked arms, and were permitted to rest till daylight.

The news that the rebels admitted themselves beaten and had gone to look for another place to fight, spread with lightning rapidity through the Union army. All that Sunday morning the woods were vocal with shouts and cheers. As appropriate to the day, somebody in the Sixty-fourth started to sing: "Praise God from Whom All Blessings Flow!" The whole regiment caught up the music, and never were the stately strains of "Old Hundred" sung with greater effect. The doxology ran through the entire brigade and spread to others. I know not when or where it stopped.

Soon after breakfast we marched to a spot near the scene of our engagement on Wednesday, and large details, with picks and shovels, were sent from each regiment to bury its dead. It was done in this way in order that the bodies, which had lain for four days, might be identified. It was a mournful duty to gather up the mangled remains of loved comrades and messmates, with whom we had marched so many weary miles, and whose companionship we had enjoyed around so many camp-fires. Those were not unmanly tears that moistened the eyes of the men engaged in this sad task. For the dead of each regiment a long trench, seven feet wide was dug, and the bodies, each tenderly wrapped in a blanket, were laid in side by side and covered from sight. At the head of each was placed a bit of board—a piece of a cracker or ammunition box—with the name and regiment of the soldier marked upon it. No shaft of polished marble was ever reared with more genuine affection than that which found expression in those rude boards above the remains of our heroic and cherished dead.

We found the body of Captain Christofel in the posture in which he had died—sitting upon the ground, with his back against a tree. He appeared so natural that it was difficult, for a moment, to believe that he was dead. A musket ball had passed through his leg, evidently severing an artery. He had tied his suspenders around the limb, in an effort to stanch the flow of blood. It was without avail.

Among the dead of Company B, Sixty-fifth, was Morris Johnston. An examination of his body showed that he had been shot through the shoulder, leg and head, and had three bayonet wounds in the abdomen. He was one of the bravest of the brave, but excitable, and his hatred of the rebels was most bitter. Beyond question, he received the bayonet thrusts while lying wounded, when the enemy passed the spot, closely following us as we fell back. Johnston's comrades, knowing his disposition, believe that after he was disabled by the wounds in leg and shoulder, and could not retreat with the fragment of his company, he continued to fire upon the rebels as they came on with mad yells, determined to sell his life dearly, and that he was then shot in the head and bayoneted. The circumstances indicate that such was the case.

Of the wounded of both regiments, more than a quarter died of their wounds. The battle of Stone River cost the Sherman Brigade the lives of one hundred and twenty men, out of eight hundred and fifty engaged. Among them were many of the bravest and best non-commissioned officers and privates.

STONEWALL JACKSON
MARCHES NORTH

THE SOUTH TOOK HEART from Lee's victories in defense of Richmond. Southern armies would carry the fight to the Union, menace Washington, force the North to seek an end to hostilities. Stonewall Jackson could see it plain:

"McClellan's army was manifestly thoroughly beaten, incapable of moving until it had been reorganized and reinforced. There was danger that the fruits of victory would be lost, as they had been lost after Bull Run. The Confederate army should at once leave the malarious district round Richmond and, moving northward, carry the horrors of invasion across the border."*

In July, Lee sent Jackson north to threaten Washington and, if possible, to draw into battle General Pope's Army of Virginia, entrusted with the defense of the capital. Lee was sure President Lincoln would order McClellan's army, still at Harrison's Landing, to join Pope. Thus, with two Union armies tied up protecting Washington, the threat to Richmond would be definitely removed. Jackson marched north to Gordonsville and fought a battle with part of Pope's forces at Cedar Run. He won a narrow victory, then waited for Lee's army to join him. By the middle of August General Lee had moved into position with Jackson. Lee decided to attack Pope without delay, for McClellan was coming north to join Pope on the Rappahannock River. Pope's "whole force was now concentrated on the road which runs from Sulphur Springs through Warrenton and Gainesville to Washington and Alexandria."† Lee would divide his army into two wings. "Jackson, marching northward was to cross the Bull Run Mountains at Thoroughfare Gap, ten miles as the crow flies from the enemy's right, and strike the railway which formed Pope's line of supply. The Federal commander, who would meanwhile be held in play by Longstreet, would be compelled to fall back in a northeasterly direction to save his communications, and thus be drawn away from McClellan. Longstreet would then follow Jackson, and it was hoped that the Federals, disconcerted by these movements, might be attacked in detail or forced to fight at a disadvantage. The risk, however, was very great.

* G. F. R. Henderson, *Stonewall Jackson*, p. 397.
† *Ibid.*, p. 431.

"An army of 55,000 men was about to march into a region occupied by 100,000, who might easily be reinforced to 150,000; and it was to march in two wings, separated from each other by two days' march. If Pope were to receive early warning of Jackson's march, he might hurl his whole force on one or the other. Moreover, defeat, with both Pope and McClellan between the Confederates and Richmond, spelt ruin and nothing less. But as Lee said after the war, referring to the criticism evoked by maneuvers, in this as in other of his campaigns, which were daring even to rashness, 'Such criticism is obvious, but the disparity of force between the contending forces rendered the risks unavoidable.' In the present case the only alternative was an immediate retreat; and retreat, so long as the enemy was not fully concentrated, and there was a chance of dealing with him in detail, was a measure which neither Lee nor Jackson was ever willing to advise.

"On the evening of the 24th Jackson began his preparations for the most famous of his marches."*

Second Manassas†

BY G. F. R. HENDERSON

LONG BEFORE DAWN THE DIVISIONS WERE AFOOT. The men were hungry, and their rest had been short; but they were old acquaintances of the morning star, and the march while the east was still grey had become a matter of routine. But as their guides led northward, and the sound of the guns, opening along the Rappahannock, grew fainter and fainter, a certain excitement began to pervade the column. Something mysterious was in the air. What their movement portended not the shrewdest of the soldiers could divine; but they recalled their marches in the Valley and their inevitable results, and they knew instinctively that a surprise on a still larger scale was in contemplation. The thought was enough. Asking no questions, and full of enthusiasm, they followed with quick step the leader in whom their confidence had become so absolute. The flood had subsided on the Upper Rappahannock, and the divisions forded it at Hinson's Mill, unmolested and apparently unobserved. Without halting it pressed on, Boswell with a small escort of cavalry leading the way. The march led first by Amissville, thence north to Orleans, beyond Hedgeman's River, and thence to Salem, a village on the Manassas Gap Railroad. Where the roads diverged from the shortest line the troops took to the fields. Guides were stationed by the advanced-guard at each gap and gate

* *Ibid.*, p. 433.
† Condensed from *Stonewall Jackson.*

which marked the route. Every precaution was taken to conceal the movement. The roads in the direction of the enemy were watched by cavalry, and so far as possible the column was directed through woods and valleys. The men, although they knew nothing of their destination, whether Winchester, or Harper's Ferry, or even Washington itself, strode on mile after mile, through field and ford, in the fierce heat of the August noon, without question or complaint. "Old Jack" had asked them to do their best, and that was enough to command their most strenuous efforts.

Near the end of the day Jackson rode to the head of the leading brigade, and complimented the officers on the fine condition of the troops and the regularity of the march. They had made more than twenty miles, and were still moving briskly, well closed up, and without stragglers. Then, standing by the wayside, he watched his army pass. The sun was setting, and the rays struck full on his familiar face, brown with exposure, and his dusty uniform. Ewell's division led the way, and when the men saw their general, they prepared to salute him with their usual greeting. But as they began to cheer he raised his hand to stop them, and the word passed down the column, "Don't shout, boys, the Yankees will hear us"; and the soldiers contented themselves with swinging their caps in mute acclamation. When the next division passed a deeper flush spread over Jackson's face. Here were the men he had so often led to triumph, the men he had trained himself, the men of the Valley, of the First Manassas, of Kernstown, and M'Dowell. The Stonewall regiments were before him, and he was unable to restrain them; devotion such as theirs was not to be silenced at such a moment, and the wild battle-yell of his own brigade set his pulses tingling. For once a breach of discipline was condoned. "It is of no use," said Jackson, turning to his staff, "you see I can't stop them"; and then, with a sudden access of intense pride in his gallant veterans, he added, half to himself, "Who could fail to win battles with such men as these?"

It was midnight before the column halted near Salem village, and the men, wearied outright with their march of six-and-twenty miles, threw themselves on the ground by the piles of muskets, without even troubling to unroll their blankets. So far the movement had been entirely successful. Not a Federal had been seen, and none appeared during the warm midsummer night. Yet the soldiers were permitted scant time for rest. Once more they were aroused while the stars were bright; and, half awake, snatching what food they could, they stumbled forward through the darkness. As the cool breath of the morning rose about them, the dark forests of the Bull Run Mountains became gradually visible in the faint light of the eastern sky, and the men at last discovered whither their general was leading them. With the knowledge, which spread quickly through the ranks, that they were making for the communications of the boaster Pope, the regiments stepped out with renewed energy. "There was no need for speech, no breath to spare if there had been—only the shuffling tramp of marching feet, the rumbling of wheels, the creak and clank of harness and accoutrements, with an occasional order, uttered under the breath, and always the same: 'Close up, men! Close up!'"

Through Thoroughfare Gap, a narrow gorge in the Bull Run range, with high cliffs, covered with creepers and crowned with pines on either hand, the column wound steadily upwards; and, gaining the higher level, the troops looked down on the open country to the eastward. Over a vast area of alternate field and forest, bounded by distant uplands, the shadows of the clouds were slowly sailing. Issuing from the mouth of the pass, and trending a little to the south-east, ran the broad high-road, passing through two tiny hamlets, Haymarket and Gainesville, and climbing by gentle gradients to a great bare plateau, familiar to the soldiers of Bull Run under the name of Manassas Plains. At Gainesville this road was crossed by another, which, lost in dense woods, appeared once more on the open heights to the far north-east, where the white buildings of Centreville glistened in the sunshine. The second road was the Warrenton and Alexandria highway, the direct line of communication between Pope's army and Washington, and it is not difficult to divine the anxiety with which it was scrutinised by Jackson. If his march had been detected, a far superior force might already be moving to intercept him. At any moment the news might come in that the Federal army was rapidly approaching; and even were that not the case, it seemed hardly possible that the Confederate column, betrayed by the dust, could escape the observation of passing patrols or orderlies. But not a solitary scout was visible; no movement was reported from the direction of Warrenton; and the troops pressed on, further and further round the Federal rear, further and further from Lee and Longstreet. The cooked rations which they carried had been consumed or thrown away; there was no time for the slaughter and distribution of the cattle; but the men took tribute from the fields and orchards, and green corn and green apples were all the morning meal that many of them enjoyed. At Gainesville the column was joined by Stuart, who had maintained a fierce artillery fight at Waterloo Bridge the previous day; and then, slipping quietly away under cover of the darkness, had marched at two in the morning to cover Jackson's flank. The sun was high in the heavens, and still the enemy made no sign. Munford's horsemen, forming the advanced-guard, had long since reached the Alexandria turnpike, sweeping up all before them, and neither patrols nor orderlies had escaped to carry the news to Warrenton.

So the point of danger was safely passed, and thirteen miles in rear of Pope's headquarters, right across the communications he had told his troops to disregard, the long column swung swiftly forward in the noon-day heat. Not a sound, save the muffled roll of many wheels, broke the stillness of the tranquil valley; only the great dust cloud, rolling always eastward up the slopes of the Manassas plateau, betrayed the presence of war.

Beyond Gainesville Jackson took the road which led to Bristoe Station, some seven miles south of Manassas Junction. Neither the success which had hitherto accompanied his movement, nor the excitement incident on his situation, had overbalanced his judgment. From Gainesville the Junction might have been reached in little more than an hour's march; and prudence would have recommended a swift dash at the supply depot, swift destruction, and swift escape. But it was always possible that Pope might have been alarmed, and the railroad from Warrenton Junction supplied him with the means of throwing a strong force of infantry rapidly to his rear. In order to obstruct such a movement Jackson had detemined to seize Bristoe Station. Here, breaking down the railway bridge over Broad Run, and establishing his main body in an almost impregnable position behind the stream, he could proceed at his leisure with the destruction of the stores at Manassas Junction. The advantages promised by this manœuvre more than compensated for the increased length of the march.

The sun had not yet set when the advanced-guard arrived within striking distance of Bristoe Station. Munford's squadrons, still leading the way, dashed upon the village. Ewell followed in hot haste, and a large portion of the guard, consisting of two companies, one of cavalry and one of infantry, was immediately captured. A train returning empty from Warrenton Junction to Alexandria darted through the station under a heavy fire. The line was then torn up, and two trains which followed in the same direction as the first were thrown down a high embankment. A fourth, scenting danger ahead, moved back before it reached the break in the road. The column had now closed up, and it was already dark. The escape of the two trains were most unfortunate. It would soon be known, both at Alexandria and Warrenton, that Manassas Junction was in danger. The troops had marched nearly five-and-twenty-miles, but if the object of the expedition was to be accomplished, further exertions were absolutely necessary. Trimble, energetic as ever, volunteered with two regiments, the 21st Georgia and 21st North Carolina, to move on Manassas Junction. Stuart was placed in command, and without a moment's delay the detachment moved northward through the woods. The night was hot and moonless. The infantry moved in order of battle, the skirmishers in advance; and pushing slowly forward over a broken country, it was nearly midnight before they reached the Junction. Half a mile from the depot their advance was greeted by a salvo of shells. The Federal garrison, warned by the fugitives from Bristoe Station, were on the alert; but so harmless was their fire that Trimble's men swept on without a check. The two regiments, one on either side of the railroad, halted within a hundred yards of the Federal guns. The countersign was passed down the ranks, and the bugles sounded the charge. The Northern gunners, without waiting for the onset, fled through the darkness, and two batteries, each with its full complement of guns and wagons, became the prize of the Confederate infantry. Stuart, coming up on the flank, rode down the fugitives. Over 300 prisoners were taken, and the remainder of the garrison streamed northward through the deserted camps. The results of this attack more than compensated for the exertions the troops had undergone. Only 15 Confederates had been wounded, and the supplies on which Pope's army, whether it was intended to move against Longstreet or merely to hold the line of the Rappahannock, depended both for food and ammunition were in Jackson's hands.

The next morning Hill's and Taliaferro's divisions joined Trimble. Ewell remained at Bristoe; cavalry patrols were sent out in every direction, and Jackson, riding to Manassas, saw before him the reward of his splendid march. Streets of warehouses, stored to overflowing, had sprung up round the Junction. A line of freight cars, two miles in length, stood upon the railway. Thousands of barrels, containing flour, pork, and biscuit, covered the neighbouring fields. Brand-new ambulances were packed in regular rows. Field-ovens, with the fires still smouldering and all the para-phernalia of a large bakery, attracted the wondering gaze of the Confed-erate soldiery; while great pyramids of shot and shell, piled with the symmetry of an arsenal, testified to the profusion with which the enemy's artillery was supplied.

It was a strange commentary on war. Washington was but a long day's march to the north; Warrenton, Pope's headquarters, but twelve miles distant to the south-west; and along the Rappahannock, between Jackson and Lee, stood the tents of a host which outnumbered the whole Con-federate army. No thought of danger had entered the minds of those who selected Manassas Junction as the depot of the Federal forces. Pope had been content to leave a small guard as a protection against raiding cavalry. Halleck, concerned only with massing the whole army on the Rappahan-nock, had used every effort to fill the storehouses. It was impossible to carry away even a tithe of the stores, and when an issue of rations had been made, the bakery set working, and the liquor placed under guard, the regiments were let loose on the magazines. Such an opportunity occurs but seldom in the soldier's service, and the hungry Confederates were not the men to let it pass. "Weak and haggard from their diet of green corn and apples, one can well imagine," says Gordon, "with what surprise their eyes opened upon the contents of the sutlers' stores, containing an amount and variety of property such as they had never conceived. Then came a storming charge of men rushing in a tumultuous mob over each other's heads, under each other's feet, anywhere, everywhere, to satisfy a craving stronger than a yearning for fame. There were no laggards in the charge, and there was abundant evidence of the fruits of victory. Men ragged and famished clutched tenaciously at whatever came in their way, whether of clothing or food, of luxury or necessity. Here a long yellow-haired, barefooted son of the South claimed as prizes a toothbrush, a box of candles, a barrel of coffee; while another, whose butternut homespun hung round him in tatters, crammed himself with lobster salad, sardines, potted game and sweetmeats, and washed them down with Rhenish wine. Nor was the outer man neglected. From piles of new clothing the Southerners arrayed themselves in the blue uniforms of the Federals. The naked were clad, the barefooted were shod, and the sick provided with luxuries to which they had long been strangers."

It was no time, however, to indulge in reflections on the irony of fortune. All through the afternoon, while the sharp-set Confederates were sweeping away the profits which the Northern sutlers had wrung from Northern soldiers, Stuart's vigilant patrols sent in report on report of the Federal movements. From Warrenton heavy columns were hurry-ing over the great highroad to Gainesville, and from Warrenton Junction a large force of all arms was marching direct on Bristoe. There was news, too, from Lee. Despite the distance to be covered, and the proximity of the enemy, a trooper of the "Black Horse," a regiment of young planters which now formed Jackson's escort, disguised as a countryman, made his way back from headquarters, and Jackson learned that Longstreet, who had started the previous evening, was following his own track by Orleans, Salem, and Thoroughfare Gap. It was evident, then, that the whole Federal army was in motion northwards, and that Longstreet had crossed

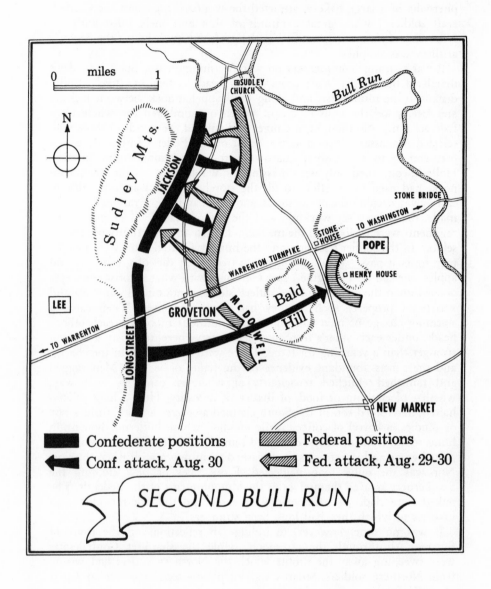

SECOND BULL RUN

miles
0 — 1

N

Bull Run

SUDLEY CHURCH

Sudley Mts.

JACKSON

STONE BRIDGE

STONE HOUSE

TO WASHINGTON

WARRENTON TURNPIKE

POPE

HENRY HOUSE

Bald Hill

LEE

GROVETON

McDOWELL

TO WARRENTON

LONGSTREET

NEW MARKET

Confederate positions

Federal positions

Conf. attack, Aug. 30

Fed. attack, Aug. 29-30

the Rappahannock. But Longstreet had many miles to march and Thoroughfare Gap to pass before he could lend assistance; and the movement of the enemy on Gainesville threatened to intervene between the widely separated wings of the Confederate army.

It was no difficult matter for Jackson to decide on the course to be adopted. There was but one thing to do, to retreat at once; and only one line of escape still open, the roads leading north and north-west from Manassas Junction. To remain at Manassas and await Lee's arrival would have been to sacrifice his command; 20,000 men, even with the protection of intrenchments, could hardly hope to hold the whole Federal army at bay for two days; and it was always possible that Pope, blocking Thoroughfare Gap with a portion of his force, might delay Lee for even longer than two days. Nor did it recommend itself to Jackson as sound strategy to move south, attack the Federal column approaching Bristoe, and driving it from his path to escape past the rear of the column moving to Gainesville. The exact position of the Federal troops was far from clear. Large forces might be encountered near the Rappahannock, and part of McClellan's army was known to be marching westward from Aquia Creek. Moreover, such a movement would have accentuated the separation of the Confederate wings, and a local success over a portion of the hostile army would have been but a poor substitute for the decisive victory which Lee hoped to win when his whole force was once more concentrated.

About three in the afternoon the thunder of artillery was heard from the direction of Bristoe. Ewell had sent a brigade along the railroad to support some cavalry on reconnaissance, and to destroy a bridge over Kettle Run. Hardly had the latter task been accomplished when a strong column of Federal infantry emerged from the forrest and deployed for action. Hooker's division of 5,500 men, belonging to McClellan's army, had joined Pope on the same day that Jackson had crossed the Rappahannock, and had been dispatched northwards from Warrenton Junction as soon as the news came in that Manassas Junction had been captured. Hooker had been instructed to ascertain the strength of the enemy at Manassas, for Pope was still under the impression that the attack on his rear was nothing more than a repetition of the raid on Catlett's Station. Striking the Confederate outposts at Kettle Run, he deployed his troops in three lines and pushed briskly forward. The batteries on both sides opened, and after a hot skirmish of an hour's duration Ewell, who had orders not to risk an engagement with superior forces, found that his flanks were threatened. In accordance with his instructions he directed his three brigades to retire in succession across Broad Run. This difficult manœuvre was accomplished with trifling loss, and Hooker, ascertaining that Jackson's whole corps, estimated at 30,000 men, was near at hand, advanced no further than the stream. Ewell fell back slowly to the Junction; and shortly after midnight the three Confederate divisions had disappeared into the darkness. The torch had already been set to the captured stores; warehouses, trains, camps, and hospitals were burning fiercely, and the dark figures of Stuart's troopers, still urging on the work, passed to and fro amid the flames. But the effect of their destruction on the Federal operations was for the time being overwhelming. And of this destruction Pope himself was a witness. The fight with Ewell had just ceased, and the troops were going into bivouac, when the Commander-in-Chief, anxious to ascertain with his own eyes the extent of the danger to which he was exposed, reached Bristoe Station. There, while the explosion of the piles of shells resembled the noise of a great battle, from the ridge above Broad Run he saw the sky to the north-east lurid with the blaze of a vast conflagration; and there he learned for the first time that it was no mere raid of cavalry, but Stonewall Jackson, with his whole army corps, who stood between himself and Washington.

The capture of Manassas, to use Pope's own words, rendered his position at Warrenton no longer tenable, and early on the 27th, the army, instead of concentrating on Warrenton, was ordered to move to Gainesville (from Gainesville it was easy to block Thoroughfare Gap); Buford's cavalry brigade was thrown out towards White Plains to observe Longstreet, and Hooker was dispatched to clear up the situation at Manassas. This move, which was completed before nightfall, could hardly have been improved upon. The whole Federal army was now established on the direct line of communication between Jackson and Lee, and although Jackson might still escape, the Confederates had as yet gained no advantage beyond the destruction of Pope's supplies. It seemed impossible that the two wings could combine east of the Bull Run Mountains. But on the evening of the 27th, after the conclusion of the engagement at Bristoe Station, Pope lost his head. The view he now took of the situation was absolutely erroneous. Ewell's retreat before Hooker he interpreted as an easy victory, which fully compensated for the loss of his magazines. He imagined that Jackson had been surprised, and that no other course was open to him than to take refuge in the intrenchments of Manassas Junction and await Lee's arrival. Orders were at once issued for a manœuvre which should ensure the defeat of the presumptuous foe. The Federal army corps, marching in three columns, were called up to Manassas, a movement which would leave Thoroughfare Gap unguarded save by Buford's cavalry. Some were to move at midnight, others "at the very earliest blush of dawn." "We shall bag the whole crowd, if they are prompt and expeditious," said Pope, with a sad lapse from the poetical phraseology he had just employed.

And so, on the morning of the 28th, a Federal army once more set out with the expectation of surrounding Jackson, to find once more that the task was beyond their powers.

The march was slow. Pope made no movement from Bristoe Station until Hooker had been reinforced by Kearney and Reno; McDowell, before he turned east from Gainesville, was delayed by Sigel's trains, which crossed his line of March, and it was not till noon that Hooker's advanced-guard halted amid the still smouldering ruins on the Manassas plateau. The march had been undisturbed. The redoubts were untenanted. The woods to the north were silent. A few grey-coated vedettes watched the operations from far-distant ridges; a few stragglers, overcome perhaps by their Gargantuan meal of the previous evening, were picked up in the copses, but Jackson's divisions had vanished from the earth.

The explanation was simple. Jackson was moving north by three roads; and before morning broke A. P. Hill was near Centreville, Ewell had

crossed Bull Run by Blackburn's Ford, and Taliaferro was north of
Bald Hill, with a brigade at Groveton, while Stuart's squadrons formed
a screen to front and flank. Then, as the Federals slowly converged on
Manassas, Hill and Ewell, marching unobserved along the north bank of
Bull Run, crossed the Stone Bridge; Taliaferro joined them, and before
Pope had found that his enemy had left the Junction, the Confederates
were in bivouac north of Groveton, hidden in the woods, and recovering
from the fatigue of their long night march.

Jackson's arrangements for deceiving his enemy, for concealing his
line of retreat, and for drawing Pope northward on Centreville, had
been carefully thought out. The march from Manassas was no hasty
movement to the rear. Established on his enemy's flank, he could avoid
the full shock of his force should Lee be delayed, or he could strike
effectively himself; and it was to retain the power of striking that he had
not moved further northward, and secured his front by camping beyond
Catharpen Run. It was essential that he should be prepared for offensive action. The object with which he had marched upon Manassas had
only been half accomplished. Pope had been compelled to abandon the
strong line of the Rappahannock, but he had not yet been defeated; and
if he were not defeated, he would combine with McClellan, and advance
in a few days in overwhelming force. Lee looked for a battle with Pope
before he could be reinformed, and to achieve this end it was necessary that the Federal commander should be prevented from retreating
further; that Jackson should hold him by the throat until Lee should
come up to administer the *coup de grâce*.

It was with this purpose in his mind that Jackson had taken post
near Groveton, and he was now awaiting the information that should
tell him the time had come to strike. But, as already related, the march
of the Federals on Manassas was slow and·toilsome.

During the afternoon, however, the cavalry captured a Federal courier,
carrying McDowell's orders for the movement of the left and centre,
which had been placed under his command, to Manassas Junction, and
this important document was immediately forwarded to Jackson. Says
General Taliaferro, "The captured dispatch roused Jackson like an electric shock. He was essentially a man of action. He rarely, if ever,
hesitated. He never asked advice. He called no council to discuss the
situation, disclosed by this communication, although his ranking officers
were almost at his side. He asked no conference of opinion. He made
no suggestion, but simply, without a word, except to repeat the language
of the message, turned to me and said: 'Move your division and attack
the enemy'; and to Ewell, 'Support the attack.' The slumbering soldiers
sprang from the earth at the first murmur. They were sleeping almost
in ranks; and by the time the horses of their officers were saddled, the
long lines of infantry were moving to the anticipated battle-field.

"The two divisions, after marching some distance to the north of the
turnpike, were halted and rested, and the prospect of an engagement on
that afternoon seemed to disappear with the lengthening shadows. The
enemy did not come. The Warrenton turnpike, along which it was
supposed he would march, was in view, but it was as free from Federal

soldiery as it had been two days before, when Jackson's men had streamed along its highway."

Jackson, however, was better informed than his subordinate. Troops were still moving through Gainesville, and, instead of turning off to Manassas, were marching up the turnpike on which so many eyes were turned from the neighbouring woods. King's division, while on the march to Manassas, had been instructed to countermarch and make for Centreville, by Groveton and the Stone Bridge. Ricketts, who had been ordered by McDowell to hold Thoroughfare Gap, was already engaged with Longstreet's advanced-guard, and of this Jackson was aware; for Stuart, in position at Haymarket, three miles north of Gainesville, had been skirmishing all day with the enemy's cavalry, and had been in full view of the conflict at the Gap.

Jackson, however, knew not that one division was all that was before him. The Federal movements had covered so wide an extent of country, and had been so well concealed by the forests, that it was hardly possible for Stuart's patrols, enterprising as they were, to obtain accurate information. Unaccustomed to such disjointed marches as were now in progress across his front, Jackson believed that King's column was the flank-guard of McDowell's army corps.

Within the wood due north of the Dogan House, through which ran an unfinished railroad, Ewell's and Taliaferro's divisions, awaiting the propitious moment for attack, were drawn up in order of battle. Eight brigades, and three small batteries, which had been brought across country with great difficulty, were present, and the remainder of the artillery was not far distant. Taliaferro, on the right, had two brigades (A. G. Taliaferro's and the Stonewall) in first line; Starke was in second line, and Bradley Johnson near Groveton village. Ewell, on the left, had placed Lawton and Trimble in front, while Early and Forno formed a general reserve. This force numbered in all about 8,000 men, and even the skirmishers, thrown out well to the front, were concealed by the undulations of the ground.

The Federal division commanded by General King, although unprovided with cavalry and quite unsupported, was no unworthy enemy. It was composed of four brigades of infantry, led by excellent officers, and accompanied by four batteries. The total strength was 10,000 men. The absence of horsemen, however, placed the Northerners at a disadvantage from the outset.

The leading brigade was within a mile of Groveton, a hamlet of a few houses at the foot of a long descent, and the advanced-guard, deployed as skirmishers, was searching the woods in front. On the road in rear, with the batteries between the columns, came the three remaining brigades—Gibbon's, Doubleday's, and Patrick's—in the order named.

The wood in which the Confederates were drawn up was near a mile from the highway, on a commanding ridge, overlooking a broad expanse of open ground, which fell gently in successive undulations to the road. The Federals were marching in absolute unconsciousness that the enemy, whom the last reports had placed at Manassas, far away to the right, was close at hand. No flank-guards had been thrown out. General King was at Gainesville, sick, and a regimental band had just struck up a merry quickstep. On the open fields to the left, bathed in sunshine, there was not a sign of life. The whitewashed cottages, surrounded by green orchards, which stood upon the slopes, were lonely and untenanted, and on the edge of the distant wood, still and drooping in the heat, was neither stir nor motion. The troops trudged· steadily forward through the dust; regiment after regiment disappeared in the deep copse which stands west of Groveton, and far to the rear the road was still crowded with men and guns. Jackson's time had come.

Two Confederate batteries, trotting forward from the wood, deployed upon the ridge. The range was soon found, and the effect was instantaneous. But the confusion in the Northern ranks was soon checked; the troops found cover inside the bank which lined the road, and two batteries, one with the advanced-guard and one from the centre of the column, wheeling into the fields to the left, came quickly into action. About the same moment Bradley Johnson became engaged with the skirmishers near Groveton.

The Confederate infantry, still hidden by the rolling ground, was forming for attack, when a Federal brigade, led by General Gibbon, rapidly deploying on the slopes, moved forward against the guns. It was Stuart's horse-artillery, so the Northerners believed, which had fired on the column, and a bold attack would soon drive back the cavalry. But as Gibbon's regiments came forward the Southern skirmishers, lying in front of the batteries, sprang to their feet and opened with rapid volleys; and then the grey line of battle, rising suddenly into view, bore down upon the astonished foe. Taliaferro, on the right, seized a small farmhouse near Gainesville, and occupied the orchard; the Stonewall Brigade advanced upon his left, and Lawton and Trimble prolonged the front towards the Douglass House. But the Western farmers of Gibbon's brigade were made of stubborn stuff. The Wisconsin regiments held their ground with unflinching courage. Both flanks were protected by artillery, and strong reinforcements were coming up. The advanced-guard was gradually falling back from Groveton; the rear brigades were hurrying forward up the road. The two Confederate batteries, overpowered by superior metal, had been compelled to shift position; only a section of Stuart's horse-artillery under Captain Pelham had come to their assistance, and the battle was confined to a frontal attack at the closest range. In many places the lines approached within a hundred yards, the men standing in the open and blazing fiercely in each other's faces. Here and there, as fresh regiments came up on either side, the grey or the blue gave way for a few short paces; but the gaps were quickly filled, and the wave once more surged forward over the piles of dead. Men fell like leaves in autumn. Ewell was struck down, and Taliaferro, and many of their field officers, and still the Federals held their ground. Night was settling on the field, and although the gallant Pelham, the boy soldier, brought a gun into action within seventy paces of Gibbon's line, yet the front of fire, flashing redly through the gloom, neither receded nor advanced. A flank attack on either side would have turned the scale, but the fight was destined to end as it had begun. The Federal commander, ignorant of the enemy's strength, and reaching the field when the fight was hottest, was reluctant to engage his last reserves. Jackson had ordered

Early and Forno, moving through the wood west of the Douglass House, to turn the enemy's right; but within the thickets ran the deep cuttings and high embankments of the unfinished railroad; and the regiments, bewildered in the darkness, were unable to advance. Meanwhile the fight to the front had gradually died away. The Federals, outflanked upon the left, and far outnumbered, had slowly retreated to the road. The Confederates had been too roughly handled to pursue.

Strategically, however, the engagement was decisive. Jackson had brought on the fight with the view of drawing the whole Federal army on himself, and he was completely successful.

But Pope, full of the idea that Jackson had been stopped in attempting to retreat through Thoroughfare Gap, altogether misunderstood the situation. He was badly informed. He did not know even the position of his own troops. His divisions, scattered over a wide extent of country, harrassed by Stuart's cavalry, and ignorant of the topography, had lost all touch with the Commander-in-Chief. Important dispatches had been captured. Messages and orders were slow in arriving, if they arrived at all. Even the generals were at a loss to find either the Commander-in-Chief or the right road. McDowell had ridden from Gainesville to Manassas in order to consult with Pope, but Pope had gone to Centreville. McDowell thereupon set out to rejoin his troops, but lost his way in the forest and went back to Manassas. He was not aware that after a long skirmish at Thoroughfare Gap, Longstreet had opened the pass by sending his brigades over the mountains on either hand, threatening both flanks of the Federals, and compelling them to retire. He was not aware that King's division, so far from intercepting Jackson's retreat, had abandoned the field of Groveton at 1 A.M., and finding its position untenable in face of superior numbers, had fallen back on Manassas; or that Ricketts, who had by this time reached Gainesville, had in consequence continued his retreat in the same direction.

Seldom have the baneful effects of dispersion been more strikingly illustrated, and the difficulty, under such circumstances, of keeping the troops in the hand of the Commander-in-Chief.

Jackson's army corps bivouacked in the position they had held when the fierce musketry of Groveton died away. It was not till long after daybreak on the 29th that his cavalry patrols discovered that King's troops had disappeared, and that Longstreet's advanced-guard was already through Thoroughfare Gap. Nor was it till the sun was high that Lee learned the events of the previous evening, and these threw only a faint light on the general situation.

Longstreet had indeed cleared the pass, and the Federals who guarded it had retreated; but the main body of the Confederate army had still twelve miles to march before it could reach Jackson, and Jackson was confronted by superior numbers. On the plateau of Bull Run, little more than two miles from the field of Groveton, were encamped over 20,000 Federals, with the same number at Manassas. At Centreville, a seven miles' march, were 18,000; and at Bristoe Station, about the same distance, 11,000.

It was thus possible for Pope to hurl a superior force against Jackson before Lee could intervene; and although it would have been sounder strategy, on the part of the Federal commander, to have concentrated towards Centreville, and have there awaited reinforcements, now fast coming up, he had some reasons for believing that he might still, unaided, deal with the enemy in detail. The high virtue of patience was not his.

So on the morning of the 29th Jackson had to do with an enemy who had resolved to overwhelm him by weight of numbers. Nor could he expect immediate help. The Federal cavalry still stood between Stuart and Thoroughfare Gap, and not only was Jackson unaware that Longstreet had broken through, but he was unaware whether he *could* break through. In any case, it would be several hours before he could receive support, and for that space of time his three divisions, worn with long marching and the fierce fight of the previous evening, would have to hold their own unaided. The outlook, to all appearance, was anything but bright. But on the opposite hills, where the Federals were now forming in line of battle, the Valley soldiers had already given proof of their stubborn qualities on the defensive. The sight of their baptismal battle-field and the memories of Bull Run must have gone far to nerve the hearts of the Stonewall regiments, and in preparing once more to justify their proud title the troops were aided by their leader's quick eye for a position. While it was still dark the divisions which had been engaged at Groveton took ground to their left, and passing north of the hamlet, deployed on the right of A. P. Hill. The long, flat-topped ridge, covered with scattered copses and rough undergrowth, which stands north of the Warrenton-Centreville road, commands the approaches from the south and east, and some five hundred yards below the crest ran the unfinished railroad.

Behind the deep cuttings and high embankments the Confederate fighting-line was strongly placed. The left, slightly thrown back, rested on a rocky spur near Bull Run, commanding Sudley Springs Ford and the road to Aldie Gap. The front extended for a mile and three-quarters south-west. Early, with two brigades and a battery, occupied a wooded knoll where the unfinished railroad crosses the highroad, protecting the right rear, and stretching a hand to Longstreet.

The flanks were secured by Stuart. A portion of the cavalry was placed at Haymarket to communicate as soon as possible with Longstreet. A regiment was pushed out towards Manassas, and on the left bank of Bull Run Fitzhugh Lee's brigade watched the approaches from Centreville and the north. Jackson's strength, deducting the losses of the previous day, and the numerous stragglers left behind during his forced marches, can hardly have exceeded 18,000 muskets, supported by 40 guns, all that there was room for, and some 2,500 cavalry. These numbers, however, were ample for the defence of the position which had been selected. Excluding the detached force on the extreme right, the line occupied was three thousand yards in length, and to every yard of this line there were more than five muskets, so that half the force could be retained in third line or reserve. The position was thus strongly held and strong by nature. The embankments formed stout parapets, the cuttings deep ditches.

Before the right and the right centre the green pastures, shorn for thirteen hundred yards of all obstacles save a few solitary cottages, sloped almost imperceptibly to the brook which is called Young's Branch. The left centre and left, however, were shut in by a belt of timber, from four hundred to six hundred yards in width, which we may call the Groveton wood. This belt closed in upon, and at one point crossed, the railroad, and, as regards the field of fire, it was the weakest point. In another respect, however, it was the strongest, for the defenders were screened by the trees from the enemy's artillery. The rocky hill on the left, facing north-east, was a point of vantage, for an open corn-field lay between it and Bull Run. Within the position, behind the copses and undulations, there was ample cover for all troops not employed on the fighting-line; and from the ridge in rear the general could view the field from commanding ground.

Shortly after 5 A.M., while the Confederates were still taking up their positions, the Federal columns were seen moving down the heights near the Henry House. Jackson had ridden round his lines, and ordering Early to throw forward two regiments east of the turnpike, had then moved to the great battery forming in rear of his right centre. His orders had already been issued. The troops were merely to hold their ground, no general counterstroke was intended, and the divisional commanders were to confine themselves to repulsing the attack. The time for a strong offensive return had not yet come.

The enemy advanced slowly in imposing masses. Shortly after seven o'clock, hidden to some extent by the woods, four divisions of infantry deployed in several lines at the foot of the Henry Hill, and their skirmishers became engaged with the Confederate pickets. . . .

Through the day four Union divisions, Schurz', Steinwehr's, Hooker's, and Reno's, had been hurled in succession against Jackson's front. Their losses had been enormous. Grover's brigade had lost 461 out of 2,000, of which one regiment, 283 strong, accounted for 6 officers and 106 men; three regiments of Reno's lost 530; and it is probable that more than 4,000 men had fallen in the wood which lay in front of Hill's brigades.

The fighting, however, had not been without effect on the Confederates. The charges to which they had been exposed, impetuous as they were, were doubtless less trying than a sustained attack, pressed on by continuous waves of fresh troops, and allowing the defence no breathing space. Such steady pressure, always increasing in strength, saps the *morale* more rapidly than a series of fierce assaults, delivered at wide intervals of time. But such pressure implies on the part of the assailant an accumulation of superior force, and this accumulation the enemy's generals had not attempted to provide. In none of the four attacks which had shivered against Hill's front had the strength of the assailants been greater than that of his own division; and to the tremendous weight of such a stroke as had won the battles of Gaines' Mill or Cedar Run, to the closely combined advance of overwhelming numbers, Jackson's men had not yet been subjected.

The battle, nevertheless, had been fiercely contested, and the strain of constant vigilance and close-range fighting had told on the Light Division. The Federal skirmishers, boldly advancing as Pender's men fell back, had once more filled the wood, and their venomous fire allowed the defenders no leisure for repose. Ammunition had already given out; many of the men had but two or three cartridges remaining, and the volunteers who ran the gauntlet to procure fresh supplies were many of them shot down. Moreover, nine hours' fighting, much of it at close range, had piled the corpses thick upon the railroad, and the ranks of Hill's brigades were terribly attenuated. The second line had already been brought up to fill the gaps, and every brigade had been heavily engaged.

It was about four o'clock, and for a short space the pressure on the Confederate lines relaxed. The continuous roar of the artillery dwindled to a fitful cannonade; and along the edge of the wood, drooping under the heat, where the foliage was white with the dust of battle, the skirmishers let their rifles cool. But the Valley soldiers knew that their respite would be short. The Federal masses were still marching and countermarching on the opposite hills; from the forest beyond long columns streamed steadily to the front, and near the Warrenton turnpike fresh batteries were coming into action.

While Pope was hurling division after division against the Confederate left. Lee, with Longstreet at his side, observed the conflict from Stuart's Hill, the wooded eminence which stands south-west of Groveton. On this wing, though a mile distant from Jackson's battle, both Federals and Confederates were in force. At least one half of Pope's army had gradually assembled on this flank. Here were Reynolds and McDowell, and on the Manassas road stood two divisions under Porter.

Within the woods on Stuart's Hill, with the cavalry on his flank, Longstreet had deployed his whole force, with the exception of Anderson, who had not yet passed Thoroughfare Gap. But although both Pope and Lee were anxious to engage, neither could bring their subordinates to the point. Pope had sent vague instructions to Porter and McDowell, and when at length he had substituted a definite order it was not only late in arriving, but the generals found that it was based on an absolutely incorrect view of the situation. The Federal commander had no knowledge that Longstreet, with 25,000 men, was already in position beyond his left. So close lay the Confederates that under the impression that Stuart's Hill was still untenanted, he desired Porter to move across it and envelop Jackson's right. Porter, suspecting that the main body of the Southern army was before him, declined to risk his 10,000 men until he had reported the true state of affairs. A peremptory reply to attack at once was received at 6:30, but it was then too late to intervene.

Nor had Lee been more successful in developing a counterstroke. Longstreet, with a complacency it is difficult to understand, has related how he opposed the wishes of the Commander-in-Chief. Three times Lee urged him forward. The first time he rode to the front to reconnoitre, and found that the position, in his own words, was not inviting. Again Lee insisted that the enemy's left might be turned. While the question was under discussion, a heavy force (Porter and McDowell) was reported advancing from Manassas Junction. No attack followed, however, and Lee repeated his instructions. Longstreet was still unwilling. A large portion of the Federal force on the Manassas road now marched northward to join Pope, and Lee, for the last time, bade Longstreet attack towards Groveton. "I suggested," says the latter, "that the day being far spent, it might be as well to advance before night on a forced reconnaissance, get our troops into the most favourable positions, and have all things ready for battle the next morning. To this General Lee reluctantly gave consent, and orders were given for an advance to be pursued under cover of night, until the main position could be carefully examined. It so happened that an order to advance was issued on the other side at the same time, so that the encounter was something of a surprise on both sides." Hood, with his two Texan brigades, led the Confederates, and King's division, now commanded by Hatch, met him on the slopes of Stuart's Hill. Although the Federals, since 1 A.M. the same morning, had marched to Manassas and back again, the fight was spirited. Hood, however, was strongly supported, and the Texans pushed forward a mile and a half in front of the position they had held since noon. Longstreet had now full leisure to make his reconnaissance. The ground to which the enemy had retreated was very strong. He believed it strongly manned, and an hour after midnight Hood's brigades were ordered to withdraw.

The firing, even of the skirmishers, had long since died away on the opposite flank. The battle was over, and the Valley army had been once more victorious. But when Jackson's staff gathered round him in the bivouac, "their triumph," says Dabney, "bore a solemn hue." Their great task had been accomplished, and Pope's army, harassed, starving, and bewildered, had been brought to bay. But their energies were worn down. The incessant marching, by day and night, the suspense of the past week, the fierce strife of the day that had just closed, pressed heavily on the whole force. Many of the bravest were gone. Trimble, that stout soldier, was severely wounded, Field and Forno had fallen, and in Gregg's brigade alone 40 officers were dead or wounded. Doctor McGuire, fresh from the ghastly spectacle of the silent battle-field, said, "General, this day has been won by nothing but stark and stern fighting." "No," replied Jackson, very quietly, "it has been won by nothing but the blessing and protection of Providence." And in this attitude of acknowledgment general and soldiers were as one. When the pickets had been posted, and night had fallen on the forest, officers and men, gathered together round their chaplains, made such preparations for the morrow's battle as did the host of King Harry on the eve of Agincourt.

During the night of August 30 the long line of camp-fires on the heights above Bull Run, and the frequent skirmishes along the picket line, told General Lee that his enemy had no intention of falling back behind the stream. And when morning broke the Federal troops were observed upon every ridge.

The Confederate leader, eager as he had been to force the battle to an issue on the previous afternoon, had now abandoned all idea of attack. The respite which the enemy had gained might have altogether changed the situation. It was possible that the Federals had been largely reinforced. Pope and McClellan had been given time, and the hours of the night might have been utilised to bring up the remainder of the Army of the Potomac. Lee resolved, therefore, to await events. The Federal position was strong; their masses were well concentrated; there was ample space, on the ridges beyond Young's Branch, for the deployment of their numerous artillery, and it would be difficult to outflank them. Moreover, a contingent of fresh troops from Richmond, the divisions of D. H. Hill,

McLaws, and Walker, together with Hampton's brigade of cavalry, and part of the reserve artillery, 20,350 men in all, had crossed the Rappahannock. Until this force should join him he determined to postpone further manœuvres, and to rest his army. But he was not without hope that Pope might assume the initiative and move down from the heights on which his columns were already forming. Aware of the sanguine and impatient temper of his adversary, confident in the *morale* of his troops, and in the strength of his position, he foresaw that an opportunity might offer for an overwhelming counterstroke.

Meanwhile, the Confederate divisions, still hidden in the woods, lay quietly on their arms. Few changes were made in the dispositions of the previous day. Jackson, despite his losses, had made no demand for reinforcements; and the only direct support afforded him was a battery of eighteen guns, drawn from the battalion of Colonel S. D. Lee, and established on the high ground west of the Douglass House, at right angles to his line of battle. These guns, pointing north-east, overlooked the wide tract of undulating meadow which lay in front of the Stonewall and Lawton's divisions, and they commanded a field of fire over a mile long. The left of the battery was not far distant from the guns on Jackson's right, and the whole of the open space was thus exposed to the cross-fire of a formidable artillery. It was noticed that notwithstanding the heavy losses they had experienced Jackson's troops were never more light-hearted than on the morning of August 30. Cartridge-boxes had been replenished, rations had been issued, and for several hours the men had been called on neither to march nor fight. As they lay in the woods, and the pickets, firing on the enemy's patrols, kept up a constant skirmish to the front, the laugh and jest ran down the ranks. . . . Pope was in an excellent humour, conversing affably with his staff, and viewing with pride the martial aspect of his massed divisions. Nearly his whole force was concentrated on the hills around him, and Porter, who had been called up from the Manassas road, was already marching northwards through the woods. The retreat of Hood's brigades the preceding night, after their reconnaissance, had induced him to believe that Jackson had been defeated. . . .

At ten o'clock on the morning of August 30, and for many months afterwards, despite his statement that he had fought "the combined forces of the enemy" on the previous day, he was still under the impression, so skilfully were the Confederate troops concealed, that Longstreet had not yet joined Jackson, and that the latter was gradually falling back on Thoroughfare Gap. His patrols had reported that the enemy's cavalry had been withdrawn from the left bank of Bull Run. A small reconnaissance in force, sent to test Jackson's strength, had ascertained that the extreme left was not so far forward as it had been yesterday; while two of the Federal generals, reconnoitring beyond the turnpike, observed only a few skirmishers. On these negative reports Pope based his decision to seize the ridge which was held by Jackson. Yet the woods along the unfinished railroad had not been examined, and the information from other sources was of a different colour and more positive. Buford's cavalry had reported on the evening of the 29th that a large force had passed through Thoroughfare Gap. Porter declared that the enemy was in great strength on the Manassas road. Reynolds, who had been in close contact with Longstreet since the previous afternoon, reported that Stuart's Hill was strongly occupied. Ricketts, moreover, who had fought Longstreet for many hours at Thoroughfare Gap, was actually present on the field. But Pope, who had made up his mind that the enemy ought to retreat, and that therefore he must retreat, refused credence to any report whatever which ran counter to these preconceived ideas. Without making the slightest attempts to verify, by personal observation, the conclusions at which his subordinates had arrived, at midday, to the dismay of his best officers, his army being now in position, he issued orders for his troops to be "immediately thrown forward in pursuit of the enemy, and to press him vigorously."

Porter and Reynolds formed the left of the Federal army. These generals, alive to the necessity of examining the woods, deployed a strong skirmish line before them as they formed for action. Further evidence of Pope's hallucination was at once forthcoming. The moment Reynolds moved forward against Stuart's Hill he found his front overlapped by long lines of infantry, and, riding back, he informed Pope that in so doing he had had to run the gauntlet of skirmishers who threatened his rear. Porter, too, pushing his reconnaissance across the meadows west of Groveton, drew the fire of several batteries. But at this juncture, unfortunately for the Federals, a Union prisoner, recaptured from Jackson, declared that he had "heard the rebel officers say that their army was retiring to unite with Longstreet." So positively did the indications before him contradict this statement, that Porter, on sending the man to Pope, wrote: "In duty bound I send him, but I regard him as either a fool or designedly released to give a wrong impression. No faith should be put in what he says." If Jackson employed this man to delude his enemy, the ruse was eminently successful. Porter received the reply: "General Pope believes that soldier, and directs you to attack"; Reynolds was dismissed with a message that cavalry would be sent to verify his report; and McDowell was ordered to put in the divisions of Hatch and Ricketts on Porter's right.

During the whole morning the attention of the Confederates had been directed to the Groveton wood. Beyond the timber rose the hill northeast, and on this hill three or four Federal batteries had come into action at an early hour, firing at intervals across the meadows. The Confederate guns, save when the enemy's skirmishers approached too close, hardly deigned to reply, reserving their ammunition for warmer work. That such work was to come was hardly doubtful. Troops had been constantly in motion near the hostile batteries, and the thickets below were evidently full of men. Shortly after noon the enemy's skirmishers became aggressive, swarming over the meadows, and into the wood which had seen such heavy slaughter in the fight of yesterday. As Jackson's pickets, extended over a wide front, gave slowly back, his guns opened in earnest, and shell and shrapnel flew fast over the open space. The strong force of skirmishers betrayed the presence of a line of battle not far in rear, and ignoring the fire of the artillery, the Confederate batteries concentrated on the covert behind which they knew the enemy's masses were forming for attack. But, except the pickets, not a single man of either the Stonewall or Lawton's division was permitted to expose himself. A few companies held the railroad, the remainder were carefully concealed. The storm was not long in breaking. Jackson had just ridden along his lines, examining with his own eyes the stir in the Groveton wood, when, in rear of the skirmishers, advancing over the highroad, appeared the serried ranks of the line of battle; 20,000 bayonets, on a front which extended from Groveton to near Bull Run, swept forward against his front; 40,000 formed in dense masses on the slopes in rear, stood in readiness to support them; and numerous batteries, coming into action on every rising ground, covered the advance with a heavy fire.

Pope, standing on a knoll near the Stone House, saw victory within his grasp. The Confederate guns had been pointed out to his troops as the objective of the attack. Unsupported, as he believed, save by the scattered groups of skirmishers who were already retreating to the railroad, and assailed in front and flank, these batteries, he expected, would soon be flying to the rear, and the Federal army, in possession of the high ground, would then sweep down in heavy columns towards Thoroughfare Gap. Suddenly his hopes fell. Porter's masses, stretching far to right and left, had already passed the Dogan House; Hatch was entering the Groveton wood; Ricketts was moving forward along Bull Run, and the way seemed clear before them; when loud and clear above the roar of the artillery rang out the Confederate bugles, and along the whole length of the ridge beyond the railroad long lines of infantry, streaming forward from the woods, ran down the embankment. "The effect," said an officer who witnessed this unexpected apparition, "was not unlike flushing a covey of quails."

Instead of the small rear-guard which Pope had thought to crush by sheer force of overwhelming numbers, the whole of the Stonewall division, with Lawton on the left, stood across Porter's path.

Reynolds, south of the turnpike, and confronting Longstreet, was immediately ordered to fall back and support the attack, and two small brigades, Warren's and Alexander's, were left alone on the Federal left. Pope had committed his last and his worst blunder. Sigel with two divisions was in rear of Porter, and for Sigel's assistance Porter had already asked. But Pope, still under the delusion that Longstreet was not yet up, preferred rather to weaken his left than grant the request of a subordinate.

Under such a leader the courage of the troops, however vehement, was of no avail, and in Porter's attack the soldiers displayed a courage to which the Confederates paid a willing tribute. Morell's division, with the two brigades abreast, arrayed in three lines, advanced across the meadows. Hatch's division, in still deeper formation, pushed through the wood on Morell's right. Nearer Bull Run were two brigades of Ricketts; and to Morell's left rear the division of regulars moved forward under Sykes.

Morell's attack was directed against Jackson's right. In the centre of the Federal line a mounted officer, whose gallant bearing lived long in the memories of the Stonewall division, rode out in front of the column, and, drawing his sabre, led the advance over the rolling grassland. The Confederate batteries, with a terrible cross-fire, swept the Northern ranks from end to end. The volleys of the infantry, lying behind their parapet, struck them full in face. But the horse and his rider lived through it all.

Second Bull Run: *Pope mounts attack on Jackson's left wing*

The men followed close, charging swiftly up the slope, and then the leader, putting his horse straight at the embankment, stood for a moment on the top. The daring feat was seen by the whole Confederate line, and a yell went up from the men along the railroad, "Don't kill him! don't kill him!" But while the cry went up horse and rider fell in one limp mass across the earthwork, and the gallant Northerner was dragged under shelter by his generous foes. Three times, as the lines in rear merged with the first, the Federal officers brought their men forward to the assault, and three times were they hurled back, leaving hundreds of their number dead and wounded on the blood-soaked turf. One regiment of the Stonewall division, posted in a copse beyond the railroad, was driven in; but others, when cartridges failed them, had recourse to the stones which lay along the railway-bed; and with these strange weapons, backed up by the bayonet, more than one desperate effort was repulsed.

For over thirty minutes the battle raged along the front at the closest range. Opposite a deep cutting the colours of a Federal regiment, for nearly half an hour, rose and fell, as bearer after bearer was shot down, within ten yards of the muzzles of the Confederate rifles, and after the fight a hundred dead Northerners were found where the flag had been so gallantly upheld.

Hill, meanwhile, was heavily engaged with Hatch. Every brigade, with the exception of Gregg's, had been thrown into the fighting-line; and so hardly were they pressed, that Jackson, turning to his signallers, demanded reinforcements from his colleague. Longstreet, in response to the call, ordered two more batteries to join Colonel Stephen Lee; and Morell's division, penned in that deadly cockpit between Stuart's Hill and the Groveton wood, shattered by musketry in front and by artillery at short range in flank, fell back across the meadows. Hatch soon followed suit, and Jackson's artillery, which during the fight at close quarters had turned its fire on the supports, launched a storm of shell on the defeated Federals. Some batteries were ordered to change position so as to rake their lines; and the Stonewall division, reinforced by a brigade of Hill's, was sent forward to the counter-attack. At every step the losses of the Federals increased, and the shattered divisions, passing through two regiments of regulars, which had been sent forward to support them, sought shelter in the woods. Then Porter and Hatch, under cover of their artillery, withdrew their infantry. Ricketts had fallen back before his troops arrived within decisive range. Under the impression that he was about to pursue a retreating enemy, he had found on advancing, instead of a thin screen of skirmishers, a line of battle, strongly established, and backed by batteries to which he was unable to reply. Against such odds attack would only have increased the slaughter.

It was after four o'clock. Three hours of daylight yet remained, time enough still to secure a victory. But the Federal army was in no condition to renew the attack. Worn with long marches, deprived of their supplies, and oppressed by the consciousness that they were ill-led, both officers and men had lost all confidence. Every single division on the field had been engaged, and every single division had been beaten back.

As Porter reeled back from Jackson's front, Lee had seen his opportunity. The whole army was ordered to advance to the attack. Longstreet, prepared since dawn for the counterstroke, had moved before the message reached him, and the exulting yells of his soldiers were now resounding through the forest.

The Federal gunners, striving valiantly to cover the retreat of their shattered infantry, met the advance of the Southerners with a rapid fire. Pope and McDowell exerted themselves to throw a strong force on to the heights above Bull Run; and the two brigades upon the left, Warren's and Alexander's, already overlapped, made a gallant effort to gain time for the occupation of the new position.

But the counterstroke of Lee was not to be withstood by a few regiments of infantry. The field of Bull Run had seen many examples of the attack as executed by indifferent tacticians. At the first battle isolated brigades had advanced at wide intervals of time. At the second battle the Federals had assaulted by successive divisions. Out of 50,000 infantry, no more than 20,000 had been simultaneously engaged, and when a partial success had been achieved there were no supports at hand to complete the victory. When the Confederates came forward it was in other fashion. Lee's order for the advance embraced his whole army. Every regiment, every battery, and every squadron was employed. No reserves save the artillery were retained upon the ridge, but wave after wave of bayonets followed closely on the fighting-line.

The field was still covered with Porter's and Hatch's disordered masses when Lee's strong array advanced, and the sight was magnificent. As far as the eye could reach the long grey lines of infantry, with the crimson of the colours gleaming like blood in the evening sun, swept with ordered ranks across the Groveton valley. Batteries galloped furiously to the front; far away to the right fluttered the guidons of Stuart's squadrons, and over all the massed artillery maintained a tremendous fire. The men drew fresh vigour from this powerful combination.

The Federal advanced line, behind which the troops which had been engaged in the last attack were slowly rallying, extended from the Groveton wood to a low hill, south of the turnpike and east of the village. This hill was quickly carried by Hood's brigade of Evan's division. The two regiments which defended it, rapidly outflanked, and assailed by overwhelming numbers, were routed with the loss of nearly half their muster. Jackson's attack through the Groveton wood was equally successful, but on the ridge in rear were posted the regulars under Sykes; and, further east, on Buck Hill, had assembled the remnants of four divisions.

Outflanked by the capture of the hill upon their left, and fiercely assailed in front, Sykes's well-disciplined regiments, formed in lines of columns and covered by a rear-guard of skirmishers, retired steadily under the tremendous fire, preserving their formation, and falling back slowly across Young's Branch. Then Jackson, reforming his troops along the Sudley road, and swinging round to the left, moved swiftly against Buck Hill. Here, in addition to the infantry, were posted three Union batteries, and the artillery made a desperate endeavour to stay the counterstroke.

But nothing could withstand the vehement charge of the Valley soldiers. "They came on," says the correspondent of a Northern journal, "like demons emerging from the earth." The crests of the ridges blazed with musketry, and Hill's infantry, advancing in the very teeth of the canister, captured six guns at the bayonet's point. Once more Jackson reformed his lines; and, as twilight came down upon the battle-field, from position after position, in the direction of the Stone Bridge, the divisions of Stevens, Ricketts, Kearney, and Hooker, were gradually pushed back.

On the Henry Hill, the key of the Federal position, a fierce conflict was meanwhile raging. . . .

The dark masses on the Henry Hill, increased every moment by troops ascending from the valley, held fast, with no hope indeed of victory, but with a stern determination to maintain their ground. Had the hill been lost, nothing could have saved Pope's army. The crest commanded the crossings of Bull Run. The Stone Bridge, the main point of passage, was not more than a mile northward, within the range of artillery, and Jackson was already in possession of the Matthew Hill, not fourteen hundred yards from the road by which the troops must pass in their retreat.

The night, however, put an end to the battle. Even the Valley soldiers were constrained to halt. It was impossible in the obscurity to distinguish friend from foe. The Confederate lines presented a broken front, here pushed forward, and here drawn back; divisions, brigades, and regiments had intermingled; and the thick woods, intervening at frequent intervals, rendered combination impracticable. During the darkness, which was accompanied by heavy rain, the Federals quietly withdrew, leaving thousands of wounded on the field, and morning found them in position on the heights of Centreville, four miles beyond Bull Run.

The position of Centreville was strong. The intrenchments constructed by the Confederates during the winter of 1861 were still standing. Halleck had forwarded supplies; there was ammunition in abundance, and 20,000 infantry under Franklin and Sumner—for the latter also had come up from Washington—more than compensated for the casualties of the battle. But formidable earthworks, against generals who dare manœuvre, are often a mere trap for the unwary.

Before daylight Stuart and his troopers were in the saddle; and, picking up many stragglers as they marched, came within range of the guns at Centreville. Lee, accompanied by Jackson, having reconnoitred the position, determined to move once more upon the Federal rear. Longstreet remained on the battle-field to engage the attention of the enemy and cover the removal of the wounded; while Jackson, crossing not by the Stone Bridge, but by Sudley Ford, was entrusted with the work of forcing Pope from his strong position.

The weather was inclement, the roads were quagmires, and the men were in no condition to make forced marches. Yet before nightfall Jackson had pushed ten miles through the mud, halting near Pleasant Valley, on the Little River turnpike, five miles north-west of Centreville. During the afternoon Longstreet, throwing a brigade across Bull Run to keep the enemy on the *qui vive,* followed the same route. Of these movements Pope received no warning, and Jackson's proclivity for flank manœuvres had evidently made no impression on him, for, in blissful unconsciousness that his line of retreat was already threatened, he ordered all wagons to be unloaded at Centreville, and to return to Fairfax Station for forage and rations.

But on the morning of September 1, although his whole army, including Banks, was closely concentrated behind strong intrenchments, Pope had conceived a suspicion that he would find it difficult to fulfill his promise to Halleck that "he would hold on." The previous night Stuart had been active towards his right and rear, capturing his reconnoitring parties, and shelling his trains. Before noon suspicion became certainty. Either stragglers or the country people reported that Jackson was moving down the Little River turnpike, and Centreville was at once evacuated, the troops marching to a new position round Fairfax Court House.

Jackson, meanwhile, covered by the cavalry, was advancing to Chantilly —a fine old mansion which the Federals had gutted—with the intention of seizing a position whence he could command the road. The day was sombre, and a tempest was gathering in the mountains. Late in the afternoon, Stuart's patrols near Ox Hill were driven in by hostile infantry, the thick woods preventing the scouts from ascertaining the strength or dispositions of the Federal force. Jackson at once ordered two brigades of Hill's to feel the enemy. The remainder of the Light Division took ground to the right, followed by Lawton; Starke's division held the turnpike, and Stuart was sent towards Fairfax Court House to ascertain whether the Federal main body was retreating or advancing.

Reno, who had been ordered to protect Pope's flank, came briskly forward, and Hill's advanced-guard was soon brought to a standstill. Three fresh brigades were rapidly deployed; as the enemy pressed the attack a fourth was sent in, and the Northerners fell back with the loss of a general and many men. Lawton's first line became engaged at the same time, and Reno, now reinforced by Kearney, made a vigorous effort to hold the Confederates in check. Hays' brigade of Lawton's division, commanded by an inexperienced officer, was caught while "clubbed" during a change of formation, and driven back in disorder; and Trimble's brigade, now reduced to a handful, became involved in the confusion. But a vigorous charge of the second line restored the battle. The Federals were beginning to give way. General Kearney, riding through the murky twilight into the Confederate lines, was shot by a skirmisher. The hostile lines were within short range, and the advent of a reserve on either side would have probably ended the engagement. But the rain was now falling in torrents; heavy peals of thunder, crashing through the forest, drowned the discharges of the two guns which Jackson had brought up through the woods, and the red flash of musketry paled before the vivid lightning. Much of the ammunition was rendered useless, the men were unable to discharge their pieces, and the fierce wind lashed the rain in the faces of the Confederates. The night grew darker and the tempest fiercer; and as if by mutual consent the opposing lines drew gradually apart.

Pope's trains and his whole army reached Fairfax Court House without further disaster. But the persistent attacks of his indefatigable foe had broken down his resolution. He had intended, he told Halleck, when Jackson's march down the Little River turnpike was first announced, to attack the Confederates the next day, or "certainly the day after." The action at Chantilly, however, induced a more prudent mood; and, on the morning of the 2nd, he reported that "there was an intense idea among the troops that they must get behind the intrenchments [of Alexandria];

that there was an undoubted purpose, on the part of the enemy, to keep on slowly turning his position so as to come in on the right, and that the forces under his command were unable to prevent him doing so in the open field. Halleck must decide what was to be done." The reply was prompt, Pope was to bring his forces, "as best he could," under the shelter of the heavy guns.

Whatever might be the truth as regards the troops, there could be no question but that the general was demoralised; and, preceded by thousands of stragglers, the army fell back without further delay to the Potomac. It was not followed except by Stuart. "It was found," says Lee, in his official dispatch, "that the enemy had conducted his retreat so rapidly that the attempt to interfere with him was abandoned. The proximity of the fortifications around Alexandria and Washington rendered further pursuit useless."

THE ARMY OF THE
POTOMAC

THE UPSHOT OF THE SECOND MANASSAS BATTLE was the resignation of
General Pope and the appointment of General McClellan to command the
Army of the Potomac. Because Little Mac was popular with the Federal
troops, news that he had taken command boosted their spirits. As he
rode out from Washington to meet them retreating from Manassas, "down
mile after mile of Virginia roads the stumbling columns came alive, and
threw caps and knapsacks into the air, and yelled until they could yell
no more."*

By September, McClellan had reorganized the army and was ready to
march. No one in Washington knew quite where Lee's army was at this
time, but rumor had it the Confederates planned to invade Maryland.
McClellan set out to stop him.

After the Confederate victory at Second Manassas, Lee and his generals
agreed that the time had come to invade the North; the question was,
how far north could they dare to go? It was their nature to be aggressive,
but until now, as Henderson says, they "had played the role of the de-
fender to perfection. No attempt had been made to hold the frontier.
Mobility and not earthworks was the weapon on which they had relied
. . . the Federal generals had consistently refused to run their heads
against earthworks. Their overwhelming numbers would enable them to
turn any position, however formidable; and the only chance of success
lay in keeping these numbers apart and in preventing them from combining. . . .

"The idea that a small army, opposed to one vastly superior, cannot
afford to attack because the attack is costly, and that it must trust for
success to favorable ground, had been effectually dispelled. Lee and
Jackson had taught the Southerners that the secret of success lies not in
strong positions, but in concentration, by means of skillful strategy, of
superior numbers on the field of battle. Their tactics had been essentially
offensive, and it is noteworthy that their victories had not been dearly
purchased.

"But if they had shown that the best defense lies in a vigorous offensive,
their offensive had not yet been applied at the decisive point.

* Bruce Catton, *This Hallowed Ground*, p. 160.

"Such were the ideas entertained by Lee and accepted by the President (Davis), and on the morning of September 2, as soon as it was found that the Federals had sought shelter under the forts of Alexandria, Jackson was instructed to cross the Potomac, and form the advance guard of invasion.

"Lee himself . . . (had) . . . no certain expectation of great results. In advocating invasion he confessed to the President that his troops were hardly fit for service beyond the frontier. . . . The army 'lacks much of the material of war, is feeble in transportation, the animals being much reduced, and the men are poorly provided with clothes and in thousands of instances are destitute of shoes . . . what concerns me most is the fear of getting out of ammunition. . . .'

"As a record of military activity the campaign of the spring and summer of 1862 has few parallels. Jackson's division, since the evacuation of Winchester at the end of February, that is, in six months, had taken part in no less than eight battles and innumerable minor engagements; it had marched nearly a thousand miles, and it had long ago discarded tents. . . .

"It was not only that battle and sickness had thinned the ranks, but that those whose health had been proof against continued hardships, and whose strength and spirit was still equal to further efforts, were so badly shod that a few long marches over indifferent roads were certain to be more productive of casualties than a pitched battle. The want of boots had already been severely felt.

"The captures made in the Valley, in the Peninsula, and in the second Manassas campaign proved of inestimable value. Old muskets were exchanged for new, smooth-bore cannon for rifled guns, tattered blankets for good overcoats. 'Mr. Commissary Banks,' his successor Pope, and McClellan himself, had furnished their enemies with the material of war, with tents, medicines, ambulances, and ammunition wagons. Even the vehicles at Confederate Headquarters bore on their tilts the initials, U.S.A. Many of Lee's soldiers were partially clothed in Federal uniforms, and the bad quality of the boots supplied by the Northern contractors was a very general subject of complaint in the Southern ranks."*

The consequence of these troubles was a marching army of Confederates of only about 40,000. However, a factor on Lee's side which he appreciated keenly was McClellan's belief that the Confederates always outnumbered him. And, as Catton says: "He was not taking as many men into Maryland as he had had on the peninsula. In the middle of September the Army of the Potomac numbered just over eighty-seven thousand, and by no means were all of these combat soldiers; nearly one fifth of the army, at this stage of the war, was occupied on various noncombatant assignments and could not be put on the firing line in battle. McClellan, of course, knew this—he always was acutely aware of his own army's weaknesses—and he could not, for the very life of him, see that the other army was much worse off than his own. The shadowy, unreal host which outnumbered him from the beginning was still opposite him. Luck might have given him the greatest opening any Union general ever had, but when he set about exploiting it he would be very, very careful.

* G. F. R. Henderson, *Stonewall Jackson*, pp. 491–96.

"His first moves were simple and direct.

"He sent one corps to break through the mountains at Crampton's Gap, five or six miles to the south of the main pass near Boonesboro; if it moved fast, this corps ought to be able to rescue the Harper's Ferry garrison before Jackson swallowed it. With the rest of the army McClellan moved straight for Boonesboro Gap, planning to get to the far side of the mountain and destroy the separate pieces of Lee's army before they could reunite.

"The start was made promptly enough, and in each of the passes the Confederates were so greatly outnumbered that they had no chance to fight more than a delaying action. They hung on stoutly, however, aided considerably by the Pinkerton delusion as to numbers; D. H. Hill had five or six thousand soldiers to defend Boonesboro Gap, and the Federal command thought that he had thirty thousand, which meant that the attack could not be driven home until most of the army had come up. In the end, Hill hung on all through September 14, retreating only after night had come. Crampton's Gap was lost sooner, but McClellan's corps commander there, General William B. Franklin, did not think it safe to march boldly for Harper's Ferry until the next morning. When morning came it took time to get his troops moving, and before he could accomplish anything Harper's Ferry had been surrendered and the Confederacy had picked up ten thousand Yankee prisoners, vast quantities of small arms and military stores, and a useful supply of artillery. Jackson rode through the town after the surrender, a remarkably uninspiring-looking man in dusty uniform with an old forage cap pulled down over his eyes—he could no more look like a dashing soldier than could U. S. Grant. One of the surrendered Union soldiers studied him, remarked that he didn't look like much, and then added bitterly: 'But if we had him we wouldn't be in the fix we're in.'

"September 15 saw McClellan through the South Mountain gaps, and Lee was trying desperately to pull his army together before the Yankees could destroy it piecemeal. Lee thought at first that he would have to get everybody back into Virginia as quickly as possible, but when he learned about the capture of Harper's Ferry he changed his mind. He would reassemble at Sharpsburg, a little country town a dozen miles south of Hagerstown, near the Potomac, behind the meandering valley of Antietam Creek; if McClellan wanted to fight they would fight there, and afterward it might be possible to go on with the invasion of the North. In any case, the fight would enable the Confederacy to get the military loot south from Harper's Ferry.

So what there was of Lee's army was ordered to take its place on the rolling hills west of Antietam Creek, and there the advance guard of the Army of the Potomac found it on the evening of September 15."*

* *This Hallowed Ground,* pp. 164–65.

Antietam*

BY MAJOR R. R. DAWES

In THE REORGANIZATION OF THE ARMY which took place at Upton's Hill, our brigade was designated as 4th brigade, 1st division, 1st army corps, Army of the Potomac.

Our camp on the quiet Sabbath morning of September 14th, 1862, was in the valley of the Monocacy, near Frederick, Maryland. There are few fairer landscapes in our country than this valley affords from its eastern range of hills. The morning was bright, warm, and clear. The bells of the city of Frederick were all ringing. It was a rejoicing at the advent of the host for her deliverance, the Army of the Potomac. The spires of the city were glistening in the morning sunlight. To the southwest could be distinctly heard the muttering of cannon. This was General Stonewall Jackson attacking the garrison at Harper's Ferry. From right to left along the valley below us, were stretched the swarming camps of the blue coats, and every soldier felt his courage rise at the sight.

At 8 o'clock A.M., our brigade marched forward on the National turnpike, the sixth Wisconsin in advance. At 11 A.M. we reached the summit of the Katoctin mountain. Fences and trees showed marks of a skirmish of the evening before. From the summit of this mountain a splendid view was spread before us, in the valley of Middleton. Over beyond the valley, eight miles away, from along the slopes of the South Mountain, we could see arising the smoke of battle. We hurried along down the road toward the scene of action, every gun of which we could see and hear. Our march through the little village of Middleton was almost a counterpart of our reception at Frederick City. The people were more excited as the cannon boomed loud and near, and bloodstained soldiers were coming in from the field of battle. We marched on beyond Middleton about a mile and a half and then turned into a field to make our coffee. The fires were not kindled, when an order came to fall in and move forward. It was announced that General Hooker had said "that the crest of that mountain must be carried to-night." The brigade countermarched and advanced again on the National road for half a mile. We then turned to the left into a field and formed in two lines of battle. We had in the ranks of our regiment four hundred men. Simmon's Ohio battery, planted in this field, was firing shell at the rebels on the summit of South Mountain. Before us was a valley, beyond which by a steep and stony slope, rose the South Mountain range. From our position to the summit of South Mountain was perhaps two miles. Two miles away on our right, long lines and heavy columns of dark blue infantry could be seen pressing up

* From *Service with the Sixth Wisconsin Volunteers.*

the green slopes of the mountain, their bayonets flashing like silver in the rays of the setting sun, and their banners waving in beautiful relief against the background of green.

Turner's gap through which the National turnpike passes over the mountain, was directly in our front. To attack this pass was the special duty for which we had been selected. To our left along the wooded slopes, there was a crash of musketry, and the roll of cannon, and a white cloud of battle smoke rose above the trees. From Turner's gap in our front, and along the right on the summit of the mountain, the artillery of the enemy was firing, and we could see the shells bursting over and among our advancing troops. For nearly an hour we laid upon the grassy knoll, passive spectators of the scene. The sun was sinking behind the mountain, when our order came to move forward. The two regiments in front (7th Wisconsin and 19th Indiana) moved in line of battle. Our regiment and the 2nd Wisconsin followed at supporting distance, formed in double columns. Thus we went down into the valley and began to climb the slope of the mountain, which was smooth at first and covered with orchards and cornfields. The regiment was halted in an orchard and two companies were sent forward as skirmishers. Our skirmishers immediately encountered skirmishers of the enemy and drove them slowly up the mountain, fighting for every inch of the ground.

For half a mile of advance, our skirmishers played a deadly game of "Bo-peep," hiding behind logs, fences, rocks and bushes. The enemy now turned upon us the fire of their batteries, planted in the pass near the mountain top, but their shot flew over.

General Gibbon mounted upon his horse and riding upon high ground where he could see his whole line, shouted orders in a voice loud and clear as a bell and distinctly heard throughout the brigade. It was always "Forward! Forward!" Just at dusk we came to a rough, stony field, skirted on its upper edge by timber. Our skirmishers had encounted the enemy in force and were behind a fence. The seventh Wisconsin in front of us, climbed the fence and moved steadily forward across the field and we followed them, our regiment being formed in double column. Suddenly the seventh Wisconsin halted and opened fire, and we could see a rapid spitting of musketry flashes from the woods above and in front of us, and wounded men from the seventh began to hobble by us. The sharpest fire came from a stone wall, running along in a ravine toward the left of the seventh. Captain John B. Callis was in command of that regiment. He ordered a change of front, throwing his right forward to face the wall; but there burst from the woods, skirting the right of the field, a flame of musketry which sent a shower of bullets into the backs of the men of the right wing of the seventh Wisconsin. Many men were shot by the enfilading fire to which they could make no reply. Captain Hollon Richardson came running toward us shouting: "Come forward, sixth!" Sharp and clear rang out on the night, the voice of Bragg: "Deploy column! By the right and left flanks, double quick, march!" The living machine responded to this impulsive force with instant action, and the column was deployed into line of battle. The right wing of our regiment came into open field, but the left wing was behind the seventh. "Major!" ordered Bragg, "take command of the right wing and fire on the woods!"

I instantly ordered: "Attention, right wing, ready, right oblique, aim, fire, load at will, load!" The roll of this wing volley had hardly ceased to reverberate, when Bragg said: "Have your men lie down on the ground, I am going over you." "Right wing, lie down! Look out, the left wing is going over you!" was the command. Bragg had brought the left wing behind the right wing and he ordered them forward over the men of the right wing as they laid upon the ground. The left wing fired a volley into the woods, and the right wing advanced in the same manner over them and fired a volley into the woods. Once more Bragg gave a volley by the left wing. There were four volleys by wing given, at the word of command. In a long experience in musketry fighting, this was the single instance I saw of other than a fire by file in battle. The characteristic of Colonel Bragg in battle, was a remarkably quick conception and instant action. The conduct of the men was worthy of their commander. In the deployment of the column under fire, they hurried over the rough and stony field with the utmost zeal, and while many men were struck by the bullets of the enemy, there was neither hesitation nor confusion. After the four volleys by wing and a welcome cheer by the seventh Wisconsin, there was positive enthusiasm. Our whole line was slowly advanced up the mountain, the men shouting and firing. The rebels behind the stone wall and in the timber would shout: "O, you d——d Yanks, we gave you h——ll again at Bull Run!" Our men would shout back: "Never mind Johnny, its no McDowell after you now. 'Little Mac' and 'Johnny Gibbon' are after you now." The rebels fell back from the woods, but stuck to the stone wall. The hostile lines had approached each other closely and the fire was deadly. It was dark and our only aim was by the flashes of the enemy's guns. Many of our men were falling, and we could not long endure it. Colonel Bragg took the left wing, directing me to keep up the fire with the right wing, and crept up into the woods on our right, advancing a considerable distance up the mountain. He gained higher ground than that of the enemy in our front, and from this position opened fire.

Colonel Bragg directed me to join him with the right wing. Owing to the thick brush and the darkness of the night, it was a difficult matter to scramble up the stony side of the mountain. To add to our difficulties, the rebels opened fire upon us; but our gallant left wing fired hotly in return and the junction was completed. Our cartridges were getting short and our guns were dirty with bad powder. Gradually by direction of Colonel Bragg we ceased firing and lay still on the ground. A man in company "A" exclaimed: "Captain Noyes, I am out of cartridges!" It is likely that the enemy in the woods above us heard him, for they immediately opened upon us a heavy fire. We returned the fire, and for a short time the contest was very sharp. This was the last of the battle. We were nearly out of ammunition and our guns so dirty that we could hardly use them. We lay among thick bushes on the steep rough slope of a mountain in almost total darkness.

We did not dare to let the men sleep. Colonel Bragg sent to General Gibbon for ammunition. General Gibbon replied that it was impossible for him to furnish it, but that he hoped that we would soon be relieved by other troops.

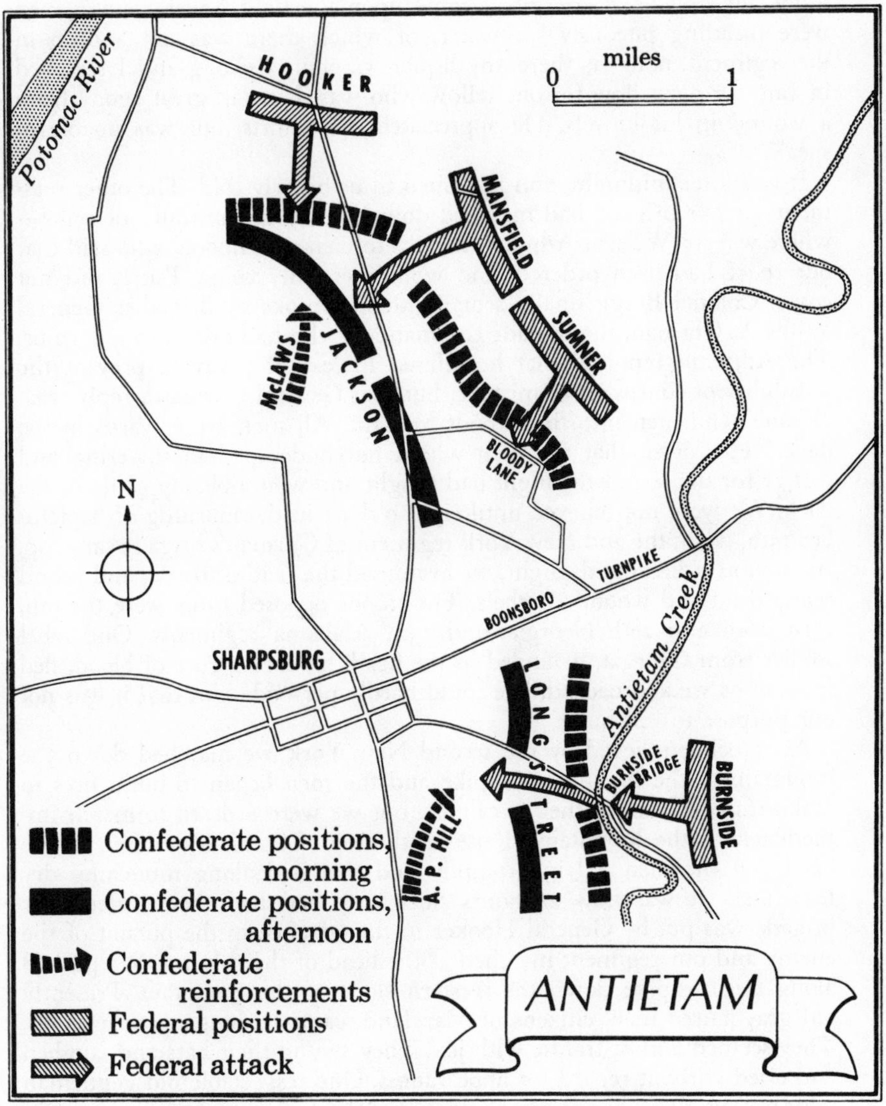

ANTIETAM
Potomac River
HOOKER
miles
0
1
MANSFIELD
SUMNER
JACKSON
McLAWS
BLOODY LANE
N
TURNPIKE
BOONSBORO
SHARPSBURG
Antietam Creek
LONGSTREET
BURNSIDE BRIDGE
BURNSIDE
A. P. HILL
Confederate positions, morning
Confederate positions, afternoon
Confederate reinforcements
Federal positions
Federal attack

The night was chilly, and in the woods intensely dark. Our wounded were scattered over a great distance up and down the mountain, and were suffering untold agonies. Owing to the difficulties of the ground and the night, no stretcher bearers had come upon the field. Several dying men were pleading piteously for water, of which there was not a drop in the regiment, nor was there any liquor. Captain Kellogg and I searched in vain for a swallow for one fellow who was dying in great agony from a wound in his bowels. He appreciated our efforts, but was unable to speak.

It was after midnight, and it seemed to us bitterly cold. The other regiments of our brigade had marched down the mountain, but our relief—where was it? We sent Adjutant Brooks to General Gibbon, who said that our relief had been ordered, and would certainly come. But it did not come. Colonel Bragg finally sent Adjutant Brooks to Brigadier General Willis A. Gorman, the brigade commander, who had orders to relieve us. The Adjutant reported that he offered to lead the way to prevent the possibility of confusion or mistake, but that General Gorman's reply was: "I can't send men into that woods to-night. All men are cowards in the dark." He forgot that the men whom he condemned to shivering and misery for the rest of the night had fought and won a bloody battle in the dark. We were not relieved until eight o'clock in the morning of September 15th, when the 2nd New York regiment of Gorman's brigade came up. As soon as it became daylight, we examined the field of battle, and found many dead and wounded rebels. The troops opposed to us were the 6th, 23rd, 26th and 28th Georgia, and 13th Alabama regiments. One rebel soldier from Georgia, wounded in the head, his face a gore of blood, fled from us as we approached. We could hardly persuade him that it was not our purpose to kill him.

After being relieved by the second New York we marched down the mountain to the National turnpike and the men began to build fires to make coffee and cook their breakfast, but we were ordered to march immediately to the Mountain House on the top of South Mountain. It was hard, but the men fell in promptly and marched along munching dry hard tack. It was now 24 hours since they had had their coffee. Our brigade was put by General Hooker in the advance in the pursuit of the enemy and our regiment marched at the head of the column. We pushed along the turnpike down the western slope of the mountain. Presently old gray-haired men, citizens of Maryland, came rushing up to meet us. They seemed almost frantic with joy. They swung their hats and laughed and cried without regard for appearances. One respectable old gentleman who trotted along beside my horse said; "We have watched for you, Sir, and we have prayed for you and now thank God you have come."

As we approached the village of Boonesboro, it seemed deserted, but when our column entered the streets, doors and windows flew open and the people thronged out to greet us. Flags that had been hidden in the darkest corner were now unfurled. These people informed us that the rebel infantry had passed through the town in haste and in much disorder. Colonels were in some cases, they said, carrying regimental banners. They said that General Lee was present when the retreat commenced. We turned to the left in Boonesboro toward Antietam creek. Our cavalry in front were picking up hundreds of prisoners, stragglers and wounded men from the retreating army. We pushed on five or six miles, passing through the village of Keedysville. When we were on the hill west of that place, the rebels opened fire on us from batteries planted in front of the village of Sharpsburg. We turned off the turnpike into a field and marched into a ravine, where we had protection. Still fragments of bursting shell fell thick in the fields around us. Our batteries came galloping along the turnpike and wheeling rapidly into position along a ridge they returned the fire of the rebel artillery. Unmindful of this clatter, our men rallied for the fences and building fires made their much needed coffee with little regard for the fragments of shell flying around.

After drinking coffee I went up to the ridge where our batteries were firing upon the enemy. I could see on the hills beyond the creek (Antietam) a rebel line of battle stretching over the fields. General Joseph Hooker was there at this time with his field-glass and I heard him say that from appearances the force of the enemy was at least forty thousand. It was now three o'clock in the afternoon. We marched up the Antietam more out of range of the rebel batteries and bivouacked for the night. Our greatly exhausted men were soon sound asleep. At several times during the 16th of September the cannonading was heavy and from our position, we had a good view of the combat. About four o'clock in the afternoon, General Hooker's army corps began to cross Antietam Creek. The division of Pennsylvania Reserves crossed on the bridge above Keedysville, while General Doubleday's division, to which we belonged, forded the creek at a shallow place below. The troops advanced slowly toward the Sharpsburg and Hagerstown Turnpike. We passed over open fields and through orchards and gardens, and the men filled their pockets and empty haversacks with apples. About dusk, sharp musketry and cannonading began in our front. It was nine o'clock at night when our brigade reached the position assigned it. The men lay down upon the ground, formed in close column, muskets loaded and lines parallel with the turnpike. Once or twice during the night, heavy volleys of musketry crashed in the dark woods on our left. There was a drizzling rain, and with the certain prospect of deadly conflict on the morrow, the night was dismal. Nothing can be more solemn than a period of silent waiting for the summons to battle, known to be impending.

About daylight, General Doubleday came galloping along the line, and he ordered that our brigade be moved at once out of its position. He said we were in open range of the rebel batteries. The men were in a heavy slumber. After much shaking and kicking and hurrying, they were aroused, and stood up in their places in the lines. Too much noise was probably made, which appears to have aroused the enemy. The column hurriedly changed direction, according to orders, and commenced moving away from the perilous slope which faced the hostile batteries.

We had marched ten rods, when *whiz-z-z! bang!* burst a shell over our heads; then another; then a percussion shell struck and exploded in the very center of the moving mass of men. It killed two men and wounded eleven. It tore off Captain David K. Noyes's foot, and cut off both arms of a man in his company. This dreadful scene occurred within a few feet of where I was riding, and before my eyes. The column pushed on without a halt, and in another moment had the shelter of a barn. Thus opened the first firing of the great battle of Antietam, in the early morning of September 17th, 1862. The regiment continued moving forward into a strip of woods, where the column was deployed into line of battle. The artillery fire had now increased to the roar of an hundred cannon. Solid shot and shell whistled through the trees above us, cutting off limbs which fell about us. In front of the woods was an open field; beyond this was a house, surrounded by peach and apple trees, a garden, and out-houses. The rebel skirmishers were in this cover, and they directed upon us a vigorous fire. But company "I" deployed as skirmishers, under command of Captain John A. Kellogg, dashed across the field at a full run and drove them out, and the line of the regiment pushed on over the green open field, the air above our heads filled with the screaming missiles of the contending batteries. The right of the regiment was now on the Sharpsburg and Hagerstown Turnpike. The left wing was obstructed in its advance by the picket fence around the garden before mentioned. As the right wing passed on, I ordered the men of the left wing to take hold all together and pull down the fence. They were unable to do so. I had, therefore, to pass the left wing by the flank through a gate with the utmost haste, and form again in the garden. Here Captain Edwin A. Brown, of company "E," was instantly killed. There is in my mind as I write, the spectacle of a young officer, with uplifted sword, shouting in a loud imperative voice the order I had given him, "Company 'E,' on the right by file into line!" A bullet passes into his open mouth, and the voice is forever silent. I urged the left wing forward with all possible speed. The men scrambled over briars and flower-beds in the garden. Beyond the garden, we entered a peach orchard. I hurried forward to a rail fence skirting the front edge of the orchard, where we overtook the right wing. Before us was a strip of open-field, beyond which on the left-hand side of the turnpike, was rising ground, covered by a large corn-field, the stalks standing thick and high. The rebel skirmishers ran into the corn as we appeared at the fence. Owing to our headlong advance, we were far ahead of the general lines of battle. They were in open fields, and we had the cover of the houses and orchard. Colonel Bragg, however, with his usual battle ardor, ordered the regiment forward. We climbed the fence, moved across the open space, and pushed on into the corn-field. The three right companies of the regiment were crowded into an open field on the right-hand side of the turnpike. Thus we pushed up the hill to the middle of the corn-field.

At this juncture, the companies of the right wing received a deadly fire from the woods on their right. To save them, Colonel Bragg, with a quickness and coolness equal to the emergency, caused them to change front and form behind the turnpike fence, from whence they returned the fire of the enemy. Meanwhile, I halted the left wing, and ordered them to lie down on the ground. The bullets began to clip through the corn, and spin through the soft furrows—thick, almost, as hail. Shells burst around us, the fragments tearing up the ground, and canister whistled through the corn above us. Lieutenant Bode of company "F," was instantly killed, and Lieutenant John Ticknor was badly wounded. Sergeant Major Howard J. Huntington now came running to me through the corn.

He said: "Major, Colonel Bragg wants to see you, quick, at the turnpike." I ran to the fence in time to hear Bragg say: "Major, I am shot," before he fell upon the ground. I saw a tear in the side of his overcoat which he had on. I feared that he was shot through the body. I called two men from the ranks, who bundled him quickly into a shelter tent, and hurried away with him. Colonel Bragg was shot in the first fire from the woods and his nerve, in standing up under the shock until he had effected the maneuver so necessary for the safety of his men, was wonderful. I felt a great sense of responsibility, when thrown thus suddenly in command of the regiment in the face of a terrible battle. I stood near the fence in the corn-field, over-looking the companies on the turnpike which were firing on the enemy in the woods, and where I could see the left wing also. I noticed a group of mounted rebel officers, whom I took to be a general and staff. I took a rest over the turnpike fence, and fired six shots at the group, the men handing me loaded muskets. They suddenly scattered.

Our lines on the left now came sweeping forward through the corn and the open fields beyond. I ordered my men up to join in the advance, and commanded: "Forward—guide left—march!" We swung away from the turnpike, and I sent the sergeant-major to Captain Kellogg, command-ing the companies on the turnpike, with this order: "If it is practicable, move forward the right companies, aligning with the left wing." Captain Kellogg said: "Please give Major Dawes my compliments, and say it is impracticable; the fire is murderous."

As we were getting separated, I directed Sergeant Huntington to tell Captain Kellogg that he could get cover in the corn, and to join us, if possible. Huntington was struck by a bullet, but delivered the order. Kellogg ordered his men up, but so many were shot that he ordered them down again at once. While this took place on the turnpike, our companies were marching forward through the thick corn, on the right of a long line of battle. Closely following was a second line. At the front edge of the corn-field was a low Virginia rail fence. Before the corn were open fields, beyond which was a strip of woods surrounding a little church, the Dunkard church. As we appeared at the edge of the corn, a long line of men in butternut and gray rose up from the ground. Simultaneously, the hostile battle lines opened a tremendous fire upon each other. Men, I can not say fell; they were knocked out of the ranks by dozens. But we jumped over the fence, and pushed on, loading, firing, and shouting as we advanced. There was, on the part of the men, great hysterical excitement, eagerness to go forward, and a reckless disregard of life, of every thing but victory. Captain Kellogg brought his companies up abreast of us on the turnpike.

The Fourteenth Brooklyn Regiment, red-legged Zouaves, came into our line, closing the awful gaps. Now is the pinch. Men and officers of New York and Wisconsin are fused into a common mass, in the frantic strug-gle to shoot fast. Every body tears cartridges, loads, passes guns, or shoots. Men are falling in their places or running back into the corn. The soldier who is shooting is furious in his energy. The soldier who is shot looks around for help with an imploring agony of death on his face. After a few rods of advance, the line stopped and, by common impulse, fell back to the edge of the corn and lay down on the ground behind the

Antietam: *The action at Burnside's Bridge* (THE BETTMANN ARCHIVE)

low rail fence. Another line of our men came up through the corn. We all joined together, jumped over the fence, and again pushed out into the open field. There is a rattling fusillade and loud cheers. "Forward" is the word. The men are loading and firing with demoniacal fury and shouting and laughing hysterically, and the whole field before us is covered with rebels fleeing for life, into the woods. Great numbers of them are shot while climbing over the high post and rail fences along the turnpike. We push on over the open fields half way to the little church. The powder is bad, and the guns have become very dirty. It takes hard pounding to get the bullets down, and our firing is becoming slow. A long and steady line of rebel gray, unbroken by the fugitives who fly before us, comes sweeping down through the woods around the church. They raise the yell and fire. It is like a scythe running through our line. "Now, save, who can." It is a race for life that each man runs for the corn-field. A sharp cut, as of a switch, stings the calf of my leg as I run. Back to the corn, and back through the corn, the headlong flight continues. At the bottom of the hill, I took the blue color of the state of Wisconsin, and waving it, called a rally of Wisconsin men. Two hundred men gathered around the flag of the Badger state. Across the turnpike just in front of the haystacks, two guns of Battery "B," 4th U. S. artillery were in action. The pursuing rebels were upon them. General John Gibbon, our brigade commander, who in regular service was captain of this battery, grimed and black with powder smoke in himself sighting these guns of his old battery, comes running to me, "Here, major, move your men over, we must save these guns." I commanded, "Right face, forward march," and started ahead with the colors in my hand into the open field, the men following. As I entered the field, a report as of a thunderclap in my ear fairly stunned me. This was Gibbon's last shot at the advancing rebels. The cannon was double charged with canister. The rails of the fence flew high in the air. A line of union blue charged swiftly forward from our right across the field in front of the battery, and into the corn-field. They drove back the rebels who were firing upon us. It was our own gallant nineteenth Indiana, and here fell dead their leader, Lieutenant Colonel A. F. Bachman; but the youngest captain in their line, William W. Dudley, stepped forward and led on the charge. I gathered my men on the turnpike, reorganized them, and reported to General Doubleday, who was himself there. He ordered me to move back to the next woods in the rear, to remain and await instruction. Bullets, shot, and shell, fired by the enemy in the corn-field, were still flying thickly around us, striking the trees in this woods, and cutting off the limbs. I placed my men under the best shelter I could find, and here we figured up, as nearly as we could, our dreadful losses in the battle. Three hundred and fourteen officers and men had marched with us into battle. There had been killed and wounded, one hundred and fifty-two. Company "C" under Captain Hooe, thirty-five men, was not in the fight in front of the corn-field. That company was on skirmish duty farther to our right. In this service they lost two men. Of two hundred and eighty men who were at the corn-field and turnpike, one hundred and fifty were killed or wounded. This was the most dreadful slaughter to which our regiment was subjected in the war. We were joined in the woods by Captain Ely, who reported to me, as the senior officer present, with the colors and eighteen men of the second Wisconsin. They represented what remained for duty of that gallant regiment.

The roar of musketry to the front about the corn-field and the Dunkard church had again become heavy. Stragglers and wounded streamed in troops toward the rear. This tide growing momentarily stronger, General Gibbons directed me to form a line of the whole brigade, perhaps five hundred men present, to drive back, at the point of the bayonet, all men who were fit for duty at the front. But, soon, the troops engaged about the Dunkard church fell back, and the whole line was formed in rear of batteries, planted on the ridge near Poffenberger's house. We were on the ground from which, at the early dawn, our regiment had moved forward to begin the battle.

At the very farthest point of advance on the turnpike, Captain Werner Von Bachelle, commanding Company F, was shot dead. Captain Bachelle was an ex-officer of the French army. Bachelle had a fine Newfoundland dog, which had been trained to perform military salutes and many other remarkable things. In camp, on the march, and in the line of battle, this dog was his constant companion. The dog was by his side when he fell. Our line of men left the body when they retreated, but the dog stayed with his dead master, and was found on the morning of the 19th of September lying dead upon his body.

It was about noon when we got to our position in rear of the batteries, and we were greatly astonished and rejoiced to meet here our gallant Lieut. Colonel, Edward S. Bragg, who had come back to join us on the field of battle. He was severely wounded and unfit for duty, but he was there, and we had believed him to be dead.

Captain John A. Kellogg showed great ability as a commander of men in battle. He rallied several hundred stragglers of every regiment engaged and organized them as a regiment; posting his line behind a stone wall on the right hand side of the turnpike near the Poffenberger house. He did this while I was deploying the brigade to stop stragglers, as ordered by General Gibbon. General Doubleday, our division commander, seeing his line and not knowing how to account for it, galloped up shouting, "What regiment is this?" "A regiment of stragglers, Sir," said Kellogg. "Have you any orders?" "Stick to the stone wall." Captains P. W. Plummer and Rollin P. Converse, Lieutenants Charles P. Hyatt, Lyman B. Upham and Howard V. Pruyn were always in the lead. But the same is true of all of our line officers who were there. Whoever stood in front of the corn-field at Antietam needs no praise. Captain Converse was shot through both thighs, as we were about to advance in pursuit of the running rebels. He convulsively threw his sword into the soft ground and said, "Hyatt, I can't run after them, I am shot, take command," and he hobbled off, refusing help.

The excitement of the men at the point of the battle when the rebels began to run before us, is illustrated by curious incidents. Private Thomas Barcus of company "I," like Captain Converse, was shot in such a manner as to disable the flexor tendons of his legs. Finding he could not run, he shouted, "Here is where you get your stiff legs!" Corporal Sherman of company "D," after shooting several times at a rebel color, saw it fall. At that moment a bullet went through his arm. He was boasting in a loud voice that he had "fetched it," and seemed greatly surprised to find his own arm paralyzed.

During the remainder of the day we were in position in support of the heavy line of batteries. About 4 P.M., while the musketry of General Burnside's battle upon the left was crashing, the enemy suddenly opened upon us a heavy fire of artillery. Our cannon, I believe about forty in number, replied with great vigor, and for half an hour a Titanic combat raged. We lay as closely as possible to the ground. I was upon the same oil-cloth with Captain John A. Kellogg, when a large fragment of shell passed into the ground between us, cutting a great hole in the oil-cloth, and covering us with dirt. It was a mystery how this could be and neither of us be struck.

The piles of dead on the Sharpsburg and Hagerstown Turnpike were frightful. The "angle of death" at Spottsylvania, and the Cold Harbor "slaughter pen," and the Fredericksburgh Stone Wall, where Sumner charged, were all mentally compared by me, when I saw them, with this turnpike at Antietam. My feeling was that the Antietam Turnpike surpassed all in manifest evidence of slaughter. When we marched along the turnpike on the morning of September 19th the scene was indescribably horrible. Great numbers of dead, swollen and black under the hot sun, lay, upon the field. My horse, as I rode through the narrow lane made by piling the bodies along beside the turnpike fences, trembled in every limb with fright and was wet with perspiration. Friend and foe were indiscriminately mingled.

In climbing the two post and rail fences that lined the turnpike, great numbers of men were killed. They climbed these fences as the shortest cut to the woods through fear of retreating before the fire over the open fields. In climbing, they made themselves an easy mark. Our own troops climbed these fences under the same circumstances on their several retreats from the woods around the Dunkard Church.

In front of the haystacks where Battery B, 4th U. S. Artillery, had been planted was seen a horse, apparently in the act of rising from the ground. Its head was held proudly aloft, and its fore legs set firmly forward. Nothing could be more vigorous or lifelike than the pose of this animal. But like all surrounding it on that horrid Aceldama, the horse was dead.

WE WILL HAVE TO
FIGHT HERE

THE BATTLE OF ANTIETAM ENDED with the Federals in possession of the field, and the Confederates in retreat, so despite the extremely heavy bluecoat casualties it was, technically at least, a northern victory. Abraham Lincoln certainly considered Antietam a victory; he used it to justify the issuance of his greatest document, the Emancipation Proclamation, which in effect ended slavery in America. But Little Mac was not one to accept success gladly. Lincoln and Halleck pressed him to pursue Lee and force a decisive battle, but October passed with no significant movement, other than the embarrassment of another cavalry raid by Jeb Stuart around the Union army. At last, on November 7, McClellan was relieved and General Ambrose Everett Burnside replaced him as commander of the Army of the Potomac.

With Richmond as his objective, Burnside moved southeast to the Rappahannock opposite Fredericksburg, where he hoped to cross the river before Lee could arrive on the opposite bank.

Confederate General James Longstreet says: "About the 18th or 19th of November, we received information through our scouts that Sumner, with his grand division of more than thirty thousand men, was moving toward Fredericksburg. Evidently he intended to surprise us and cross the Rappahannock before we could offer resistance. On receipt of the information, two of my divisions were ordered down to meet him. We made a forced march and arrived on the hills around Fredericksburg about three o'clock on the afternoon of the 21st. Sumner had already arrived, and his army was encamped on Stafford Heights, overlooking the town from the Federal side.

"About the 26th or 27th it became evident that Fredericksburg would be the scene of a battle, and we advised the people who were still in the town to prepare to leave, as they would soon be in danger if they remained. The evacuation of the place by the distressed women and helpless men was a painful sight. Many were almost destitute and had nowhere to go, but, yielding to the cruel necessities of war, they collected their portable effects and turned their backs on the town. Many were forced to seek shelter in the woods and brave the icy November nights to escape the approaching assault from the Federal army.

"Very soon after I reached Fredericksburg the remainder of my corps

297

arrived from Culpeper Court House, and as soon as it was known that all the Army of the Potomac was in motion for the prospective scene of battle Jackson was drawn down from the Blue Ridge. In a very short time the Army of Northern Virginia was face to face with the Army of the Potomac.

"At a point just above the town, a range of hills begins, extending from the river edge out a short distance and bearing around the valley somewhat in the form of a crescent. On the opposite side are the noted Stafford Heights, then occupied by the Federals. At the foot of these hills flows the Rappahannock River. On the Confederate side nestled Fredericksburg, and around it stretched the fertile bottoms from which fine crops had been gathered and upon which the Federal troops were to mass and give battle to the Confederates. On the Confederate side nearest the river was Taylor's Hill, and south of it the now famous Marye's Hill; next, Telegraph Hill, the highest of the elevations on the Confederate side (later known as Lee's Hill, because during the battle General Lee was there most of the time), where I had my headquarters in the field; next was a declination through which Deep Run Creek passed on its way to the Rappahannock River; and next was the gentle elevation at Hamilton's Crossing, not dignified with a name, upon which Stonewall Jackson massed thirty thousand men.

"The hills occupied by the Confederate forces, although over-crowned by the heights of Stafford, were so distant as to be outside the range of effective fire by the Federal guns, and, with the lower receding grounds between them, formed a defensive series that may be likened to natural bastions. Taylor's Hill, on our left, was unassailable; Marye's Hill was more advanced toward the town, was of a gradual ascent and of less height than the others, and we considered it the point most assailable, and guarded it accordingly.

"This was the situation of the 65,000 Confederates massed around Fredericksburg, and they had twenty-odd days in which to prepare for the approaching battle.

"On the morning of the 11th of December, 1862, an hour or so before daylight, the slumbering Confederates were awakened by a solitary cannon thundering on the heights of Marye's Hill. Again it boomed, and instantly the aroused Confederates recognized the signal of the Washington Artillery and knew that the Federal troops were preparing to cross the Rappahannock to give us the expected battle. The Federals came down to the river's edge and began the construction of their bridges, when Barksdale opened fire with such effect that they were forced to retire. Again and again they made an effort to cross, but each time they were met and repulsed by the well-directed bullets of the Mississippians. This contest lasted until 1 o'clock, when the Federals, with angry desperation, turned their whole available force of artillery on the little city, and sent down from the heights a perfect storm of shot and shell, crushing the houses with a cyclone of fiery metal. From our position on the heights we saw the batteries hurling an avalanche upon the town whose only offense was that near its edge in a snug retreat nestled three thousand Confederate hornets that were stinging the Army of the Potomac into a frenzy. It was terrific, the pandemonium which that little squad of Confederates had provoked.

The town caught fire in several places, shells crashed and burst, and solid shot rained like hail. In the midst of the successive crashes could be heard the shouts and yells of those engaged in the struggle, while the smoke rose from the burning city and the flames leaped about, making a scene which can never be effaced from the memory of those who saw it. But, in the midst of all this fury, the little brigade of Mississippians clung to their work. At last, when I had everything in readiness, I sent a peremptory order to Barksdale to withdraw, which he did, fighting as he retired before the Federals, who had by that time succeeded in landing a number of their troops. The Federals then constructed their pontoons without molestation, and during the night and the following day the grand division of Sumner passed over into Fredericksburg.

"About a mile and a half below the town, where the Deep Run empties into the Rappahannock, General Franklin had been allowed without serious opposition to throw two pontoon-bridges on the 11th, and his grand division passed over and massed on the level bottoms opposite Hamilton's Crossing, thus placing himself in front of Stonewall Jackson's corps. The 11th and 12th were thus spent by the Federals in crossing the river and preparing for battle."*

Fredericksburg †

BY THE SURVIVORS OF THE
118TH PENNSYLVANIA VOLUNTEERS

THERE HAD BEEN FREQUENT PRELIMINARY ORDERS to be in readiness to move immediately, to move at a ˙moment's notice, to move at once, to move without delay. It was the usual phraseology then so familiar and aroused but little comment, as a soldier was about as ready to move at one time as another. They were accompanied by directions to carry five days' cooked rations, and the orders, following each other so closely, kept that supply continually on hand.

The thunder of heavy cannonading about four o'clock on the morning of the 11th of December, followed promptly by the "general," dissipated the flippant treatment with which the preliminary directions had been received, and, amid some bustle and confusion, the regiment was without delay in line, awaiting the order to march.

The sun, great and round, rose ominously red. Camp-fixtures were to remain standing and the troops to be equipped in light-marching order only. The soldiers had not yet conceived that much was intended beyond

* "Battle of Fredericksburg," *Battles and Leaders,* III, 70, 72, 73, 75.
† From *The History of the 118th Pennsylvania Volunteers.*

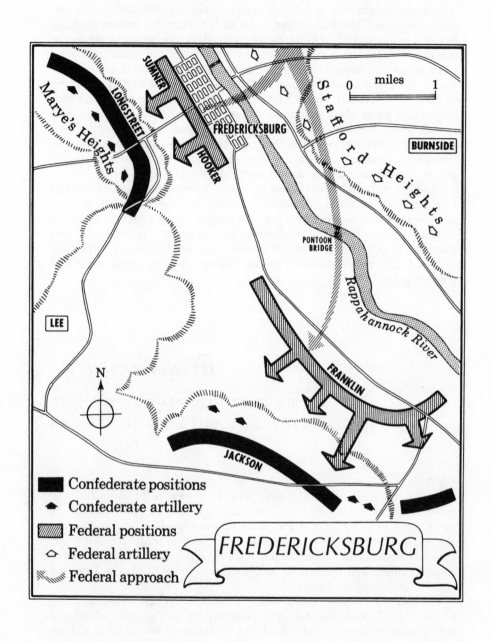

Marye's Heights

SUMNER

LONGSTREET

HOOKER

FREDERICKSBURG

Stafford Heights

0 miles 1

BURNSIDE

LEE

PONTOON BRIDGE

Rappahannock River

N

FRANKLIN

JACKSON

■ Confederate positions
◂ Confederate artillery
▨ Federal positions
⬠ Federal artillery
〰 Federal approach

FREDERICKSBURG

a reconnoissance in heavy force. This, though, was one of those hopeful conceptions to drive off the notion that there would be a fight.

The company cooks were metamorphosed; that is, these professional gentlemen had been promoted to the ranks, exchanged their ladles for muskets and cartridge-boxes, and were given an opportunity to pepper the enemies of their country instead of the bean soup. One of them, whose rotund form and unctuous face made his usual occupation unmistakable, hearing the boom of the heavy guns, asked what the noise was.

He was answered: "The rebel artillery."

"You fellers needn't think you can fool me. I've heard that noise too often in Philadelphia; they're unloading boards somewhere."

Afterward, when the man of pots and pans heard the screech of the shells and saw them falling in the river near the engineers who were laying the pontoons, he went lumbering to the rear as though he had forgotten something, and his oleaginous form faded in the distance.

At seven o'clock the column was in motion, not in the familiar direction towards Hartwood Church, but by the shortest and most practicable route to Falmouth and the Rappahannock. Evidences were everywhere abroad of preparation for desperate and bloody work. Ambulance trains were parked in every direction; every safe and readily accessible location was occupied by hospital tents. Stretchers in unlimited supply were being hurried to the front for immediate use. Fresh, clean straw, neatly bundled had been distributed where the wounded were to be brought for treatment. The thunder of the guns continued in uninterrupted roar.

The march was soon accomplished. The whole of the Centre Grand Division was massed on "Stafford Heights," the prominent bluffs on the left bank of the river, commanding a full view of the city of Fredericksburg, the stream and the lowlands and hills upon the other side. Line upon line, should to shoulder, this closely packed body of men awaited, in quiet resoluteness, the order that should send them forward to measure strength and courage with their adversaries. It was a martial sight.

The stream, inconsiderable in width, is navigable for steamboats. The water-front of the city extended about a mile, with streets at right-angles, lined with substantial brick and stone buildings reaching back from the water about half that distance. The city lay on a plain away below the heights which overlooked it. At the distance of half a mile arose a formidable hill, of easy, gentle slope, then modestly known by its owner's name as Marye's Heights. It was to become famous as the scene of most desperate and valorous assaults. Marye's Heights were lined with earthwork, planned and constructed by skilled engineers, defended by soldiers tried in battle, mounted with guns handled by the best artillerists. They appeared almost impregnable. The enemy's cannon answered in active response to the Union guns. All this was in full view, and as the column passed over the bluffs and down to the bridges, all those "thinking bayonets" could not but conclude that a direct assault would be hopeless.

Whilst the infantry massed about the heights suffered but little annoyance from the enemy's artillery, the engineers and pontooniers were at a difficult and perilous task. Every house on the river-bank had its riflemen, and small earthworks had been constructed for others whom the houses could not shelter. Each attempt to lay the boats was met with terrific and fatal volleys; the loss was appalling. In sheer desperation, the afternoon well spent, the engineers, resting from their labor, had sought such shelter as could be found at the foot of the bluffs and on the edge of the river. The pontoon boats, dismounted from their wagons, lay useless on the shore. Suddenly bodies of men, pelted as relentlessly as were the engineers, rushed to the shore. With commendable precision, regardless of their terrible loss, they took the places allotted them in the boats and pushed them into the stream. They were rapidly pulled across, the galling fire continuing until a landing effected upon the other side in a measure silenced it. The laying of the bridges soon followed, but it was late in the afternoon before they were fitted for a passage.

It did not fall to the lot of our division to cross that night, and about five o'clock it retired a mile or so for a bivouac near a spot designated as "White House"; but whence it derived its name is inconceivable, as no settlement was thereabouts and nothing observable but a solitary white-washed shanty.

Mr. Henry K. Jewell, a well-known citizen of Philadelphia and an acquaintance of many of the officers of the regiment, opportunely appeared during the afternoon. He was connected in some civic capacity with the Commissary Department. The soldier rarely knows much that is reliable, except what is occurring immediately around him. He gathers his information afterwards when the newspapers reach the front. Mr. Jewell said the cause of the delay in attacking Fredericksburg was the non-arrival of the pontoons, and also told of General Sumner's demand, through General Patrick, on General Lee, to surrender the city, and its refusal. The story of both circumstances subsequently appeared fully in the newspapers, and is now historically recorded. The delay in forwarding the pontoons has been the frequent subject of severe comment and harsh criticism, and it has fallen mostly upon General Halleck, on whom it was alleged the responsibility rested.

Jewell was a thoughtful fellow. He had loaded himself with canteens, all he could carry, filled to the brim with an excellent quality of ardent spirits. He freely and cheerfully distributed this among his friends who had the conveniences at hand to carry it. It was carefully husbanded, and proved a priceless *jewel* in the next day's engagement, when it was judiciously dispensed to many a wounded sufferer.

At eight o'clock on the morning of the 12th the regiment returned to the same spot it had held on the day before. All day long the big guns on the bluffs and the field-batteries tore away persistently at the enemy's works on Marye's Heights. The roar was continuous, but apparently little damage followed the cannonading; certainly none to the entrenchments, though it probably caused some loss among the soldiery. Smoke in great volumes hung over everything, lifting occasionally, when there was a lull in the firing, to permit a cursory observation.

All day long Sumner's Right Grand Division was pouring over the pontoons amid a storm of the enemy's shells. The enemy seemed to have a pretty fair knowledge of where the bridges were, and were tolerably successful in securing the range. So close, indeed, did the shells from the Confederate batteries fall to the pontoons that the crossing soldiers were frequently splashed with the water that flew up from the places where they struck the river. It was cooling, but not refreshing.

From the Phillips House, a most pretentious mansion, which was General Burnside's head-quarters, staff-officers, at frightful pace, were continually coming and going. Night settled before things were in complete readiness, and the regiment rested where it was, awaiting the breaking of the portentous morn.

Saturday, the 13th, dawned in an almost impenetrable fog, so dense that it, with the smoke of the battle, made objects close at hand scarcely distinguishable. It was of such density that there was a fear that in a close engagement friends might be mistaken for foes. To avoid such a contingency the very unusual precaution of a word of recognition was adopted, and the watchword "Scott" was given to be used in such an emergency.

Between nine and ten o'clock the fog lifted a little, and unfolded a scene thrilling in its inspiration and awful in its terror. The streets of the city were literally packed with soldiers. Glistening rifle-barrels, sombre blue, surged in undistinguishable columns, pressing for the open country to seek some relief from the deadly plunge of cannon-shots dealing mercilessly their miseries of wounds and death. But the same batteries on Marye's Heights were again encountered, more frowning and formidable than ever, and wicked in their renewed determination to punish the temerity that dared assault these formidable entrenchments. With such gunnery, fog and smoke settled again and the scene was lost to view from Stafford Heights, the continuing noise alone indicating the progress of the battle.

Amid all these stirring scenes four officers of the regiment indulged in a game of euchre. Intent upon their amusement, they were lost to the terrors around them, and apparently heedless of the greater dangers they were soon to face when it should be their turn to be active participants in the pending combat. As the game progressed and the interest increased it was suddenly interrupted by orders that started the command on its way to where the battle was the hottest. The game was resumed from time to time at the frequent halts that occur in the movements of large bodies of troops across narrow bridgeways, and it was not completed until the near approach to the action stiffened every nerve to its highest tension.

Then the custody of the *deck* became a subject for consideration. Every one of the quartet tried to convince every other one that the best possible thing for him to do was to carry it. Unanimously, and finally, it was concluded that, as they were fighting for the existence of a republic, it would not be seemly, should they fall, to have it transpire that they had been taking care of kings and queens. Royalty and knavery were, consequently, allowed to float down towards the sea on the waters of the Rappahannock.

In these peaceful days, and to those unacquainted with army life during an active campaign, this amusement in the face of danger might seem stolid and reckless indifference. Not so. It passed away the wretched time of waiting, every minute of which would otherwise seem an hour, and quieted the nerves which would be thrilling with excitement if the mind had nothing to dwell upon but the possibilities of the pending battle.

About one o'clock the regiment was called to attention and, with the

division, began the movement to the bridges. It was tedious, halting and
hesitating. The bridges were crowded and the streets jammed from the
slow deployments under the withering fire which met the fresh victims
fed to the slaughter, as the troops in advance reached the open country. It
was but a short distance to the bluffs and then the battle in all its fury
was spread out to view. Upon the slope of Marye's Heights were long
lines of blue formed with regularity, moving with precision, disappearing
as speedily as they were seen before the furious cannonade and the deadly
musketry. Thought was rife and expression free with the selfish hope that
some effective service might be done by those already in to save others
from the terrible ordeal, revealed in ghastly horror everywhere, into the
very jaws of which the regiment was about to plunge. The futility of open
assaults was manifest. The disasters which had been plainly seen to follow
each other so rapidly were woefully dispiriting. But all such hopes were
vain.

About two o'clock the regiment entered the town. It had been reported
that $65,000 worth of tobacco, in boxes, had been thrown overboard from
the wharf near the pontoons. Some of the men belonging to the regiments
already in the town were diving for and bringing up the tobacco, which
they sold to their comrades by the box or in job-lots to suit the pocket. A
cool transaction in December and under the enemy's fire. Sergeant Con-
ner, of G, invested $25 in these speculative "job lots," and, placing them
in his knapsack, essayed to carry his purchase until a fitting opportunity
was afforded to realize. But his venture proved unsuccessful, as he
abandoned his knapsack when the regiment assaulted the heights beyond
the lines.

The view from the other side of the river gave but a faint conception
of what was within the town. On every hand were ruin and pillage. The
city had been rudely sacked; household furniture lined the streets. Books
and battered pictures, bureaus, lounges, feather-beds, clocks and every
conceivable article of goods, chattels and apparel had been savagely torn
from the houses and lay about in wanton confusion in all directions. Fires
were made for both warmth and cooking with fragments of broken furniture. Pianos, their harmonious strings displaced, were utilized as horse-
troughs, and, amid all the dangers, animals quietly ate from them. There
was a momentary, irresistible desire to seek some shelter from the havoc
of the guns in the deserted houses. It was manfully conquered and the
men heroically held to their places.

The march was continued under all the dreadful shelling along what
was apparently the main thoroughfare, which ran at a right angle to the
river, to a street that crossed it parallel with the stream, and on towards
the farther edge of the city. Turning into this street there was a halt for
some time in line of battle, closed well up to the sidewalk. Upon the side
of the street nearest the enemy some protection was afforded from the
shower of death-dealing missiles that had poured down so relentlessly
from the moment of entering the town; but bricks, window-shutters and
shingles, struck by the shells and solid shot, flew around unceasingly.
Opposite the centre, in the rear, was a house that had been most roughly
handled. It was evidently the residence of some person of culture and
refinement. Several solid shots had passed through the upper rooms and

a shell, bursting in the library, had made bricks, mortar and books a heap of rubbish. A tastefully bound copy of "Ivanhoe" which had escaped the wreck tempted the literary tastes of an officer, and he picked it up, intending that it should help to while away an hour of loneliness in some quieter time. Light as was the load, he soon became weary of it and his book was abandoned.

The dashing charge over the level plain, the determined advance against breastworks lined with threatening bayonets, the splendid resistance to columns of assault, are tests of courage and endurance of frequent occurrence. It is seldom, however, that the mettle of men is tested in column in the crowded streets, where there can be no resistance, into which, from unseen positions, the artillery strikes its rapid, telling blows, and will not and can not be silenced. Courageous men, well fitted to meet in a conflict, the purpose of which is seen, an adversary behind his own entrenchments, at his own guns, may well quake when submitting unresistingly to continuous punishment in mass, where their manhood is lost and their power sacrificed in apparently hopeless confusion. So, when the soldiers of the Right and Centre Grand Divisions passed through such a bitter experience of war in the streets of Fredericksburg, and then valiantly assailed the formidable heights beyond, they proved that the Union soldiery possessed a tenacity and courage equal to any standard vaunted in Anglo-Saxon song or story.

There is scarcely any situation which, however serious, cannot sustain the ludicrous. Never do colored servants, except in rare individual instances, follow when soldiers are exposed to such dangers as the regiment had passed through, and which still surrounded it where it had last halted, near the outskirts. A romping, rollicking little darkey, who had been christened Scipio Africanus, because his qualities were the very opposite of those of that distinguished Roman general, was standing upon a door which had fallen from its hinges and lay upon the pavement, and was grinning and chippering, exposing his pearl-white teeth till they resembled, embedded in his ebony jaws, chalk upon a blackboard. He was in full view of the entire command, who were hugely enjoying his guffaws, wondering whether such unusual hilarity, in such a trying situation, was not assumed. Suddenly a solid shot whizzed wickedly over head, struck the front of a brick house upon the opposite side of the street, glanced, flew up into the air and, returning, struck violently the other end of the door upon which the boy was standing. Up, away up, bounded the darkey, unhurt, but scared apparently beyond the recollection that aught was left of him.

It was a ridiculous sight. Shouts and laughter from the whole line greeted him as he landed some ten or fifteen feet from where he started. He waited for no comments, but, with his face changed almost to a deadly pallor, evidently with no conception that he was yet moving of his own volition, disappeared somewhere to safer quarters, not even catching the quaint remark which followed him as he flew away: "What's de matter wid you, honey? You's been foolin' wid a torpedo, ha?"

The same shot upset a wooden step and platform in front of a house and exposed three small boxes of tobacco that had been hidden underneath. There was a rush by the men to secure the plunder.

During the halt Colonel Gwyn exercised the regiment for some time in the manual of arms, at the conclusion of which it was ordered to load.

The crucial moment was fast approaching. The brigade moved off, passing its brigade commander, who was intently observing the temper and bearing of his soldiers, back into the main highway from which it had been withdrawn for a little rest and less exposure. The head the column must have been seen; the rapidity of the firing increased; the roar was deafening; shot and shell screeched in maddening sounds; they fell thicker and faster, dropping with wonderful accuracy right into the midst of the column. Every gun seemed trained upon this very street; and so they were, for it was afterwards learned that batteries, specially planted for the purpose, raked every highway leading from the river. Soldiers, some malingerers, some skulkers, often demoralized, stood behind houses at the corners watching the column. Some had been in and had withdrawn discomfited and dejected; others were of the class who generally manage to elude danger. Sullen and silent, their conduct was no incentive and their presence no encouragement to those not of the sterner sort, who had not yet felt the hot blast of the musketry. Two brass guns in action at the end of the street were pounding away vigorously and effectively at the enemy, the gunners holding heroically to their places in spite of the severe punishment they were receiving.

The Confederate shells performed some curious and fanciful gyrations. One in particular fell obliquely, striking in the centre of the hard, solid roadway, then ricocheted, struck a house, flew up the wall, tore off a window-shutter, then crossed over to the other side, striking the house opposite, down again into the street, passed back to the other side over the heads of Company H, and finally fell upon the steps of the house it had first struck and lay there without exploding. This was fortunately the case with much of their ammunition, which appeared to be remarkably faulty.

It is not to be supposed that the column moved upon the highway with the steadiness of a parade occasion. There was hesitancy and some unsteadiness, but no dropping out, no skulking, no concealment.

Avoiding the middle of the street, where it was soon observed the fire was the most direct, and closing to the pavement, the men held their places with reasonable accuracy and moved under the trying circumstances with commendable precision.

As the regiment debouched from the town, upon the edge of the closely built thoroughfare, was a sign, in large black letters; "Van Haugen's Variety Store." It had scarcely come into view when a shell burst and tore it to fragments. The pieces of the shell and sign fell into the ranks of Company K. Their loss was not so serious as that of the 1st Michigan, in the rear, where, at about the same time, another shell burst, killing or maiming some sixteen of its soldiers, whose startled shrieks could be heard above the din and roar of the battle. The column now plunged into and waded through the mill-race. This was done as quickly as possible, for the Confederates had trained a battery on this spot. In the mill-race were noticed very many solid shot and unexploded shells, which had evidently rolled back into the water after striking the side of the embankment. Private John Mensing was carrying his piece at "arms port": a shell struck and shivered it to fragments, but beyond a severe cut on his right hand he was not injured. Another tore off the right arm of Private John Fisher just below the elbow and knocked down four sergeants in one company. They were more or less bruised and hurt, but none of them seriously.

The right of the brigade had now reached an open level space on the left of the road, some four hundred yards in width, as well as observation could estimate it. At its farther edge the ground rose abruptly, as if the earth had been cut away. This perpendicular rise or cut was the extreme base of the slope that approached and terminated in the gun-capped Marye's Heights. The artillery played with unintermitting vigor.

The usual rotations brought the regiment on the right of the brigade, on the 13th. It had about covered its front from where the right first struck the open plain, where by the "forward into line" the left was extended into the plain. It was intended that the right should rest on the road. There was some confusion attending the formation, but a line was ultimately established pressed close up to the edge of the abrupt rise, over which and beyond to the top of the hill everything was in full view. Beyond the summit was another elevation, and just below it a stone fence, lined with rebel infantry, whence the musketry rolled unceasingly.

A board fence, with some of the boards displaced, others torn from the top, stood between the abrupt rise and the stone fence, nearer to the latter. It had evidently greatly retarded the previous advances and what was left of it was yet in the road to impede others.

Humphrey's division had just charged up the hill, and, although they had failed to carry the heights, hundreds of men lay prone upon the ground in fair alignment, apparently too spirited to withdraw entirely from their futile effort. It seems scarcely credible, but a closer inspection showed all these men, apparently hundreds in number, to be killed or too seriously wounded to move.

The regiment still hugged the ground closely where it had first established its line. Instinctively, in taking up a movement indicated by an advance by another portion of the line, for the terrible roar drowned the voice of command, it began its desperate work of assault. Under the appalling musketry and amid great disorder, the advance was maintained with reasonable regularity to a brick-yard, with its kiln standing, through which tore shot and shell, and from which bricks flew in every direction. The little shelter afforded by the kiln had enticed the wounded within its reach to crawl to it for cover, and their mangled, bleeding forms lay strewn everywhere, closely packed together. Sweeping by this, right into the very mouth of the cannon, upward and onward the advance continued to the board fence. The fence was about five feet high, of three boards, with intervals between them. Opposite the centre and right, the boards had been torn off down to the one nearest the ground. The fatality that had followed the delay in their removal was marked by the bodies of the dead lying there, one upon another. To the left, the boards still remained; the men heroically seized and tore them all away, some climbing over. Thinned out, exhausted, with energies taxed to their limit, in the face of such fearful odds, instinctively the line halted.

Major Herring here received a ball in his right arm. He was sitting on his horse at the time. As the ball struck him, some one said, "This is

Fredericksburg: *Sumner's division assaults Confederate positions*

awful!" "This is what we came here for," quietly replied the major, as he dismounted. Subsequently, another ball passed through his left arm, and buckshot through his coat. At nightfall, his wounds needing surgical attention, he was forced to go to the hospital for treatment. He made several efforts to reach the front again, but his strength failed him. It was feared amputation would be necessary, but he insisted upon conservative surgery, and it saved him his arm. The absence of his strong directing mind at such a critical time was a serious misfortune.

From the place of the halt to the stone fence, behind which belched the deadly musketry, was between two and three hundred feet. At that distance, halted with little or no cover, such punishment was unbearable.

There was still about two hours of daylight. Some two hundred yards to the left, but no greater distance from the stone fence, there was decidedly better cover, and to this undulation, broad enough to include the entire regimental front, the command was moved within a few moments from the time it had halted. Colonel Barnes, commanding the brigade, rode the full length of the line before it started, calling to the men to fall in. Although in full view of the Confederates, and the target for their shots, he escaped injury.

It seems remarkable that men could live at all that close to the enemy's lines, but there the regiment remained all that night, all of Sunday's daylight and well into the night, suffering but few casualties, and those happening principally when necessity forced exposure, or temerity prompted rashness. But safety was only found in hugging the ground as tight as a human body could be made to hold on to the earth. Darkness was a relief from the stiff and uncomfortable postures, but during those ten or twenty hours of that winter's daylight, there was no safety except with bodies prone and flattened to their fullest length. A raise of the head, or a single turn not unfrequently proved fatal.

Just as the day was closing a regiment advanced immediately to the rear of where the command lay. It had been ordered to charge the works, and had got thus far on its mission, but had no one to conduct it farther. All its officers had disappeared; its men, hopeless as was their task were even yet anxious to fulfil it. Colonel Gwyn, informed of its situation, and understanding its anxiety to still go forward, valiantly stepped to its front and centre, and gallantly tendered his services to lead it on. Colonel Barnes, comprehending the fruitless purpose of the undertaking, forbade it, and ordered the regiment to retire to some convenient shelter and await the further direction of its brigade commander. This it was not disposed to do, but mingled with the others on the front line, and remained with them until they were withdrawn.

The combat ceased with the night. Its lengthening shadows were gratefully hailed as a relief from the terrors of a day of suffering and death.

In getting to the front, one of Company H's men had been severely wounded, but had managed to crawl up to his company. After nightfall some of his comrades got a stretcher and carried him into the town. Leaving him at one of the improvised hospitals, the men started in search of quarters, intending, for one night at least, to sleep with a roof over their heads. A corner store, with a dwelling above, seemed a suitable place. But doors and windows were fastened. An entrance, by the aid of a couple of bayonets, was soon effected. A newspaper was produced and lighted, dropping pieces of half-burned paper as the party passed through the store into the back room, searching for a candle. One was found in a candle-stick, lighted, and a reconnoissance in force was made, to discover what the enemy had left. Returning to the store, the party found, right in the track of the burned paper, an unexploded shell. The precious thing was picked up very carefully, and put tenderly away in a closet. An iron teakettle was found in the house, a well in the yard, and clapboards on the building. These helping, a steaming pot of coffee was made and drunk. Then, alternately mounting guard, the party indulged in a luxuri-ous sleep, with bare boards for feathers, and starting betimes, reached the front again before daylight.

Sunday morning broke bright and clear. Just as the day dawned the men at the front, who had been sleeping as best they could, rose and walked up and down briskly to warm their chilled blood. The whole line seemed to be in motion. Suddenly, without the least warning, the Con-federates poured in upon them a heavy volley. Every man promptly dropped to the ground. In one place they were crowded together too closely for comfort. Beyond, a man who, with the cape of his overcoat over his head, was apparently asleep, there was room for two or three.

"Wake him up, and tell him to move along," some one cried. The soldier next to him gave him a shake, and said:

"I can't, he's too fast asleep."

"You must."

The soldier pulled the overcoat cape back, intending to give him a vigorous shake. As he uncovered the head, the colorless side-face, and a triangular hole in the neck told the tale. He was sleeping his last sleep. He must have been struck by a shell the day before, and fallen just where he lay, and some comrade's hand had thrown the cape over his head to hide the ghastly wound.

If there was remembrance of the Christian Sabbath there was no recog-nition of its religious observances. The city was a charnel-house, its churches and its dwellings hospitals, and its streets rumbling with vehicles and crowded with stretcher-bearers carrying the wounded sufferers.

The cannonading ceased. The cannon, that for three days had thundered so incessantly, had opportunity to cool, and the gunners rested from their unceasing toil. The quiet—there was no noise save from the occasional discharge of a musket—was in striking contrast to the continuous roar that had preceded it.

Fortunately the rigors of winter weather had not yet arrived. Save from the constrained position of their bodies, and the want of water, the men of the regiments in the front line suffered no discomfort and but little loss. There was still sufficient in the haversacks for nourishment, but all looked longingly for the night to come. There was scarcely any firing from the Union side, save where some one more daring than his fellows would rise in his place, discharge his piece, and quickly seek cover again. They frequently suffered for their exposure.

Sergeant Geo. W. Stotsenberg, of Company K, turned the cartridges out of his box into his cap, loaded, knelt upon one knee, waited, and, when-ever a head appeared above the stone wall, blazed away at it, and reloaded.

He kept his position for more than two hours, and though the bullets sang about his ears and ploughed little furrows in the ground before him, he was not even touched.

Captain Crocker could not long brook this forced restraint. He had suffered greatly from his close confinement. Angered beyond endurance at the foe who kept him thus confined, he threw a taunting menace in their teeth. About noon, saying naught to any one, he rose suddenly from his place, seized the colors, advanced with them a few paces to the front, and jammed the staff well into the ground, shaking his fist angrily and firing a round of epithets in no polite or cultured strain. His greetings were responded to in language equally cultured, accompanied by a volley of balls. His temerity lost him nothing except the emptying of his canteen, which was struck. Lieutenant Kelley, who was close beside him, observed the contents escaping to the ground, and before Crocker was aware of what he was losing, rose to his knees, placed the hole to his lips, and drained whatever remained to the dregs. Kelley got a "ball," if Crocker did not.

Captain Bankson was not to be outdone by this daring feat of Crocker's, and he followed with one of like temerity. He left his place, proceeded to where the colors had been planted, seized them, waved them several times defiantly at the enemy, and then returned. A similar salute of musketry greeted him, but he, too, escaped unharmed.

It has been observed that the human voice was sometimes so drowned by the din of battle that the utterance of commands was useless. Successful obedience only followed close observance and apt attention. Any inattention or failure to comprehend what was likely to be done frequently separated the best of soldiers from their commands. A misunderstanding resulting from this condition of things happened in the regiment at its halt just beyond the board fence. The attention of some was momentarily distracted, more particularly by the casualties that there befell some of the best men. In what appeared but an instant, the regiment had moved by the left flank to a position three hundred yards away, where it remained during the rest of the engagement. Those who had not observed the movement were left where they were. The first conclusion was that the regiment had withdrawn entirely. There was considerable confusion, and the soldiers of one command intermingled with others. Nor was it possible to distinguish organizations, as the men were flattened tight to the earth, with their faces downward. They might recognize any one standing up, especially because few were in such position, but for one who stood to recognize those who were lying, was an impossibility. This impossibility of recognition was a further difficulty in the way of removing the conviction that there had been a formal withdrawal.

In the full assurance that their belief was well founded, those who had been left retired for a better cover to the rear of the brick-kiln. There, rumors from the town that the regiment had been seen in the city confirmed their belief, and they remained awaiting a favorable opportunity to rejoin it. To attempt it just then was an invitation for a volley, and a great personal risk, which, as the regiment was believed not to be engaged, the occasion did not seem to demand.

As the detachment lay behind the kiln, an officer was noticed approaching them, oblivious to all the dangers around him, shot at by volleys, aimed at singly, coolly stopping to examine the faces of the dead he passed, moving with deliberation and ease. He finally safely reached the cover of the kiln wall. It was Lieutenant William Wilson, of Company A. He reported that as the regiment left the city he had become separated from it, and had ever since been employed in a hopeless search for it. He was told of the misfortune which had happened to the detachment, the conviction that the regiment had been withdrawn, and the apparent confirmation by the stories that had come from the town, and he was advised to remain where he was. This did not, however, satisfy him. He said he had met a number of the men, but had not yet seen the field-officers and colors, and as he had pretty faithfully hunted the city, he was determined to prosecute his search further at the front.

In a few moments he left and was again exposed to the same startling dangers. Volleys upon volleys greeted him, but alone, bold and erect, a most inviting target, bent upon his purpose, he continued his errand and disappeared from view still unhurt. It was an exhibition of splendid heroism. By mere accident he reached the position which the regiment occupied, but was unaware of it until he was recognized and hailed by his name.

As has been noticed, when the brick-kiln was passed on the advance, wounded, more than could be covered, were in indiscriminate confusion about it, and since then the number had sensibly increased. If there were any on hand to administer relief the force was wholly inadequate to the occasion. Strangely, large numbers of blocks of ribbon were scattered around. How they came there was inconceivable, nor was there any disposition to inquire. Their usefulness was soon apparent. Generous hands quickly unwound the blocks, and tenderly, it may be awkwardly, applied the ribbon to wounds gaping, exposed and yet untreated, and bandaged hurts, possibly nearing fatality from want of care. But whether life was saved or not, it was a comfort and consolation for kindly hands to minister to those pressing needs.

During the time the detachment was at the brick-kiln another advance appeared, moving up the hillside. One regiment, with its commandant gallantly riding in its front, maintained a most excellent alignment. It preserved its shapely formation until just in rear of the brick-yard, when the commanding officer fell seriously wounded. Three of his soldiers bore him away and his command then seemingly disappeared entirely.

With this advance appeared a battery of twelve-pound Napoleons. It had scarce unlimbered before every horse and rider fell. The men left without firing a shot. The officers remained a moment gesticulating violently, apparently endeavoring to enforce the return of their men, and then they too disappeared and the deserted guns alone remained. No guns could be served at such a point and no gunners could live in such exposure. It seemed madness to have ordered a battery in action there.

The detachment at the brick-kiln gradually drew off to the city and collecting about the outskirts moved after dark to the river-bank, where it bivouacked for the night. After daylight communication with the front was again wholly cut off and it was impossible for them to rejoin their fellows; nor was it necessary, as the fight had subsided to an indifferent sort of a skirmish, with no prospect of an assault by the enemy. The bivouac was consequently maintained until the command was retired from the front line.

Shortly before ten o'clock on Sunday night the regiment was relieved from its perilous and trying post at the extreme front and withdrawn to the bivouac on the river-bank, where the missing detachment was. Here it remained during Monday. A little after noon General Burnside and his staff rode down to the bridge and passed over. There was always a kindly feeling for Burnside, but now his presence stirred no enthusiasm; his appearance aroused no demonstration. It may have been a coincidence that, as he rode by, he drew his hat further down over his face. Unuttered thoughts were rife that somebody had seriously blundered. But sadly and silently the men viewed their commander, with the deepest consideration for the anxiety and solicitude which at that moment must have almost overwhelmed him.

At dusk the brigade started for the front again. It took a position on the highway at the farther end of the city, as it was subsequently learned, to cover, with other troops, the withdrawal of the entire army to the other side of the river. Absolute quiet was cautioned and conversation forbidden. That silence might be maintained strictly, the rattling of the tin-cups was prevented by removing them from the belts. It was a weird night. The wind blew a gale, fortunately directly from the enemy, and, with the extreme quiet prevailing in our lines, voice and noise were distinctly audible in theirs. Window-shutters banged and rattled, and shots rang out frequently on the picket-line. An attack was momentarily expected and every one was ready to resist the anticipated assault.

In the rear of the centre of the regiment was J. H. Roy's drug store. Within all was impenetrable darkness, but there came from it continually the sound of breaking glass. All the dangers could not deter the pilfering soldier. Groping about for something desirable, a whole shelf of bottles would fall at once, creating a tremendous rattle, penetrating in the extreme quiet, scattering their contents in every direction. Repeated orders were given to arrest these purloiners, but the seizure of one would speedily be followed by the approach of another in the darkness readily eluding the guard. His presence would soon be known by another smashing of glassware. An officer, annoyed beyond restraint, rushed in himself and seized a marauder with a bottle in his hand. Violently shaking himself loose and escaping, the man left a bottle in the officer's hand which, on bringing to the street, he discovered to be labelled "Ayer's Cherry Pectoral." This he put in his pocket, but, soon forgetting it, resumed his place on the cellar-door, where he had been previously resting, and shivered the bottle to fragments. The contents, of a sticky consistency, soaked his clothing.

About four o'clock in the morning there was a sudden call to attention and a rapid movement to the lower end of the town. The officer who brought the order to retire indicated the wrong direction. Pretty much everything had been withdrawn and all movements required alacrity, but, reaching the river at the point where the officer conveying the order directed, the bridge, which had been there was found to have been removed. The brigade was the last to cross; daylight was close at hand and the mistake threatened disaster. The column was counter-marched with amazing rapidity and headed for the centre bridge. It, too, was in course of removal, but the engineers hurriedly replaced the planks and, in the midst of a drenching rain, which then began to fall, the column crossed to the other side. Day was just breaking when the movement was completed.

Fredericksburg was fought and lost. The Army of the Potomac, battered about and abused, had become indifferent to results. A victory, where the enemy was pursued, routed or brought to terms, had never been theirs to achieve. After a battle it therefore accepted a withdrawal or advance with equal complacency, maintaining the consciousness that it had done all men could do to accomplish a designated purpose. But always before it had administered punishment commensurate with what it had received. There was a conviction, at least with the troops thrown against the works on Marye's Heights, that such was not the result at Fredericksburg. It was too apparent, even to the obtuse observer, that the heavy sufferers on that fatal hillside were the soldiers who assaulted, and not the soldiers who defended. It was too plain that for the multitude of dead and wounded who covered its slope no corresponding number of disabled soldiery lay behind the powerful entrenchments.

There is no need of any comments, only such as suggest themselves to any soldier. Burnside is dead. We all admired his frank and manly character. His assumption of all blame for the defeat is worthy of him. But it will not atone for the slaughter of so many brave men.

After this battle there remained in the army little confidence in his capacity for this command. He has since been reported as saying: "No one will ever know how near I came to achieving a great success," and to this we will add, *"No one ever will."*

The loss of the Federal army was 1,180 killed, 9,028 wounded, and 2,145 missing, and on the part of the Confederates it was 5,309 killed, wounded and missing.

HOOKER MAKES
HIS MOVE

BURNSIDE'S TROOPS HAD TAKEN A SEVERE BEATING at Fredericksburg, but Burnside stubbornly refused to admit it. He ordered a new attack on Lee's position. Aghast, his generals finally convinced him of his folly. The Army of the Potomac retreated across the Rappahannock, having suffered more than 12,000 casualties—more than twice the Confederate loss.

The weather continued to be unusually mild, and the Virginia roads were dry and acceptable for marching. Burnside, hoping to redeem himself, decided to risk a sudden change to bad weather and ordered the army to make another crossing of the Rappahannock. The troops moved out of camp on January 20, and as they began their march, the skies clouded over and then rain begin to fall. The army bogged down in the mud and cold, but Burnside insisted that the troops push on to the river.

Once there, the exhausted men could look across the river and see the Confederates leaning on their rifles, waiting for them to attempt the crossing. The attack was doomed before it could begin; this time, Burnside wisely ordered a return to camp. Winter had set in with a vengeance, and almost as many troops were lost through exhaustion, exposure, and sickness as if they had fought. This second debacle brought Burnside's relief, and the command was given to General "Fighting Joe" Hooker.

By the time spring arrived, Hooker had injected new life in the troops and they were ready to do battle again. Reinforcements swelled the army to 134,000, more than double the size of Lee's army across the river. "The position of the Confederates on the other side of the Rappahannock had not changed since the battle of Fredericksburg. As then, they occupied at the end of April the line of fortified heights extending from Skenker's Creek to the point where they touched the river above Falmouth. On this side, however, they had extended their lines by covering, with fortifications occupied with troops, the only two feasible crossings between Falmouth and the point where the Rapidan empties into the Rappahannock: Banks and United States fords. And these two fords were passable only in the summer. Everywhere else the steep and wooded banks of the two rivers presented a barrier which could not be passed. It was a stretch of twenty to twenty-five miles to defend. The rebel army did not number more than sixty thousand in front of Hooker, when, on April 27, the latter began his movement on Chancellorsville.

"Chancellorsville is not a village, or even a hamlet. It is a solitary house in the midst of a cultivated clearing, surrounded on all sides by woods, which have given that region the name of *Wilderness*. A veritable solitude, impenetrable for the deploying or quick manœuvring of an army. So that it was not there that Hooker had planned to give battle. But it was a well chosen point for concentrating his forces, three or four miles southeast of United States Ford. From that point he could strike the enemy, taken in reverse, or, at least, force him to come out of his position, as weak from the rear as it was strong from the front. If the Confederate army fell back on Richmond, it presented its flank to our attack, and, if he were stopped or delayed by some obstacle and pursued at the same time by a force strong enough to vigorously press his rearguard, his retreat might be changed to a rout. If, on the contrary, he marched towards Chancellorsville to meet us, he was forced to accept battle in the open field, in unforeseen conditions, exposed to attack by a pursuing army as much as on the Richmond road. Attacked at the same time both in front and rear, Lee ran the chance of being cut in pieces, and would be very fortunate if he saved the remnant of his forces.

"Such was Hooker's well concerted plan, the secret of which was confided to no one, not even to his most intimate friends amongst the officers.

"The point on which everything depended for success was to be able to assemble the army at Chancellorsville before the enemy could oppose him at that point. This part of the plan was as admirably executed as it had been ably conceived, and it can be truly said that up to that point General Hooker showed himself to be an able tactician.

"In the first place, he detached all his cavalry, under the orders of General Stoneman, to cut the enemy's lines of communication with Richmond. The undertaking was not very dangerous, for Stoneman took with him more than ten thousand horse, who could meet with no serious resistance. Under his instructions, after crossing the Rappahannock, he was to divide his force into two columns: one, under command of General Averill, was to threaten the force the enemy might have at Culpeper and Gordonsville, while the other, led by Stoneman himself, would attempt to accomplish the main object of the expedition. Both columns were to come together at a given point, to attack the enemy in case he retreated directly towards Richmond, and to harass him if he took the road to Gordonsville.

"At the same time that the cavalry started, the Eleventh and Twelfth Corps (Howard and Slocum) marched for Kelly's Ford, above the mouth of the Rapidan and twenty-seven miles distant from Fredericksburg. There, on the 28th, they were met by Meade's corps (the Fifth), which was to join them. The passage of the Rappahannock was made that night without opposition. On the 29th, that of the Rapidan was effected happily, in two columns, and, the movement continuing with a promptness of good augury, the three corps arrived at Chancellorsville on the afternoon of the 30th. Their advance opened United States Ford, behind which the Second Corps (Couch) was waiting, in order to throw across a pontoon bridge and join the other corps, which was done before night. Hooker himself arrived at the appointed rendezvous, to finish up the work he had so brilliantly commenced.

"While these important movements were being accomplished on one side, the attention of the enemy was concentrated in the opposite direction, towards what seemed to him to be a prelude to an attack in force. In fact, on the 29th, at daybreak, while our right, having already crossed the Rappahannock, was advancing towards the Rapidan, a bridge of boats was established by force at the same point where, on the 13th of December preceding, Franklin had passed the river, and the Sixth Corps (Sedgwick) after having driven back the enemy's sharpshooters, advanced into the plain below Fredericksburg. A little further down, the First Corps (Reynolds) did the same thing, and, finally, the Third Corps (Sickles) took position in reserve, ready to cross over in its turn if necessary. This was the force designed to hold the enemy in his intrenchments by the menace of an immediate attack, or to pursue him, if, discovering the danger which threatened him, he should abandon his position.

"During that day the demonstration succeeded to our best wishes. The enemy appeared only to prepare his defence on the side where it was not intended to attack him.

"The next day, the 30th, the Confedreates not stirring, Hooker called the Third Corps to Chancellorsville. We started immediately, making a forced march in order to arrive in time for the decisive attack. That night we made our fires at a short distance from the bridge across which the Second Corps had marched in the morning.

"So there, on the 30th, at night, the Confederates, still motionless in their positions in rear of Fredericksburg, prepared for an attack on their right, indicated by the movements of the two corps of Sedgwick and Reynolds, while in rear of their left four other corps were already united, and about to be joined by a fifth. On one side, Sedgwick, with forty thousand men, including Gibbon's division of the Second Corps, which, having its camp in full view of the enemy, had not yet moved; on the other, Hooker, with about seventy thousand men in a position which seemed an assurance, in advance, of a victory. 'Now,' said he, in an order of the day to the army, 'the enemy must flee shamefully or come out of his defences to accept a battle on our ground, where he is doomed to certain destruction!' And every one repeated, 'He is in our power!' Nobody doubted that, before two days, all our past reverses would be effaced by the annihilation of Lee's army.*

* From Regis de Trobriand, *Four Years with the Potomac Army.*

Chancellorsville*

BY COLONEL REGIS deTROBRIAND

WHAT HOOKER CALLED "OUR GROUND" to give battle on was about half-way from Chancellorsville to Fredericksburg, outside of that region covered with almost impenetrable woods, where we were at that time. On that side the country was open and favorable for the manœuvring of an army. It was then important to get there at the earliest possible moment. Two broad roads led to it, coming together near a church called Tabernacle, while a third road, running near the river, led to Banks Ford. By these three roads, Hooker renewed his movement in advance, on Friday morning, May 1. Slocum, with the Twelfth Corps, held the right by the plank road; Sykes, with a division of the Fifth Corps, supported by Hancock's division of the Second Corps, advanced in the centre, along the principal road, called the Macadamized road (although it was not); and Meade led the column composed of Humphreys' and Griffin's divisions along the road near the river. The three other corps, the Second, the Third, and the Eleventh, were to follow the movement, so as to come into line of battle outside of the forest, at two o'clock in the afternoon.

But before Hooker had left Chancellorsville Lee had started to meet him. Informed, the evening before, of the true state of affairs, he had collected his forces in all haste, and, leaving behind him only Early's division reënforced by one brigade, he had hurried forward all the rest at midnight, in the direction of Chancellorsville. Between ten and eleven o'clock in the morning, his advance guard encountered our cavalry skirmishers, and forced them back. But behind them Sykes had already deployed his division. He charged the enemy resolutely, drove them back in his turn, and established himself in the position which had been assigned to him by his instructions.

Everything went well with us. On the right, Slocum had encountered no opposition; on the left, Meade had arrived in full view of Banks Ford, without the least obstacle. He had only to form promptly in order of battle. The corps in the rear would have had time to get into line while the enemy made his disposition on his side, on the ground where General Hooker had "devoted him to certain destruction."

Well, as if Heaven wished to take up that arrogant defiance to adverse fortune, it was at this time and at this very place that General Hooker virtually lost the battle of Chancellorsville by an error as unexpected as inexplicable.

Instead of supporting Sykes' division strongly, and pushing his forces

* *Ibid.*

forward, he hurriedly sent the order to the three columns to return to the positions they had occupied the night before. Amongst the general who were in position to judge for themselves, I know not one who considered the measure otherwise than deplorable. Couch, before withdrawing Hancock's division, sent to pray the general-in-chief to countermand the order; Warren, who commanded the corps of topographical engineers, and who was in the advance, hurried himself to headquarters with the same errand. Nothing availed. The decision was maintained. The columns fell back uneasy, astonished above all that the first order given by Hooker as general in command in front of the enemy was to retreat without fighting. That did not at all resemble Hooker commanding a division.

The position which we voluntarily abandoned to the enemy was excellent; the position which we took in place of it was detestable. In the first, we could deploy and fight, well connected together on a crest of ground running in the direction of our lines; in the second, we were as if penned up in the midst of natural obstacles, on low and flat ground, which neutralized any advantage in numbers by the difficulty of movement. In the first, we barred to the enemy the only three routes by which he could penetrate into the Wildnerness; in the second position, we gave up to him the plank road, and it will soon be seen what use he made of it against us. Finally, in the first case we preserved all the material and moral advantage of the offensive; in the second, we subjected ourselves to all the disadvantage of a defensive accepted without necessity, as it was without preparation.

The enemy took possession immediately of the position which we so benevolently abandoned to him. He planted his guns there, and followed our retreating troops closely. The afternoon was passed on his side in feeling of our lines at several points by direct demonstrations; on our side, by protecting ourselves by abatis, by regulating the position of the different corps, and awaiting events.

Towards four o'clock, the Third Corps, which had remained in reserve between Chancellorsville and the river, received orders to advance. In the woods, on the right and left we passed a great number of troops, massed without apparent order and filling all the small clearings. Soon we came out on the Fredericksburg road, in front of which stretched our line of battle. Berry's division, which had preceded ours, deployed in the open ground around the farm. As we turned to the right, to take position further on, the skirmishing fire told us that the enemy extended along our front, on the other side of some great woods, which concealed his movements from us. He had his batteries already in position on that side, for the shells and balls reached the troops while they were deploying. One struck a colonel of the Excelsior Brigade. We saw him fall from his horse, without letting go his bridle rein, although he was dead. His men hastened to him and carried off his body.

To discover the enemy's movements, five or six daring men had climbed to the top of the highest trees, from which they had a view over the surrounding woods. The position was very dangerous, for they might become targets for the rebel sharpshooters. In order to guard against it as much as possible, they kept up a continual shaking of the trees in which they were; they could be seen thus balancing in the air more than a hundred feet above the ground, braving the double danger of the enemy's bullets and a fall—death in either event.

Firing ceased a little after dark. The moon rose calm and smiling, and nothing troubled the tranquillity of the night.

The next morning, May 2, an order was sent to the First Corp, to join us. Sedgwick then remained alone below Fredericksburg with the Sixth Corps and Gibbon's division of the Second; twenty-six to twenty-seven thousand men in all.

At Chancellorsville our line was disposed in the following order: On the left, the Fifth Corps and Hancock's division extended from the vicinity of the river to the turnpike, facing towards Fredericksburg; in the centre, the Twelfth Corps, forming an obtuse angle with the left, and covering the road in front and parallel to which it stretched; then, in the same direction, Birney's division of the Third Corps; finally, the Eleventh Corps on the right. Two divisions of the Third Corps (Berry and Whipple) and one division of the Second Corps (French) were held in reserve.

In the morning, the enemy contenting himself with attacking Hancock's pickets, without approaching his line, Hooker began to be troubled about what was passing in our front, beyond the curtain of woods, which limited our view in that direction. He sent forward the troops of the Twelfth Corps, who, being received by a deadly fire, could not force their way, and were compelled to fall back, leaving the general commanding in the same uncertainty as before. But almost immediately, through an opening in the woods before the Twelfth Corps, there appeared a column of rebels marching rapidly from the left to the right, and which consequently presented its flank to our whole line of battle.

This movement threatened our right, which appeared to be unprepared for it. As it was the opposite side from that by which the enemy had advanced from Fredericksburg, less disposition was made against an attack there than elsewhere. The whole Eleventh Corps prolonged the general line parallel to the road. But a small brigade thrown back barred this road with two guns, resting on nothing, leaving our extreme right completely in the air.

General Hooker had visited that part of the line in good season, without prescribing any change. Only, when the movement of the enemy revealed to him the possibility of an attack from that direction, he sent some additional instructions to General Howard, which had no other effect than to cause an advance of the pickets. There was no change made in the disposition of the troops. The fact is that General Hooker did not believe in the danger of such an attack, and that he preferred to regard the movement as a retreat of the army of Lee on Gordonsville. Otherwise he would not have telegraphed a few hours later to General Sedgwick: "Take Fredericksburg and everything you find there, and pursue the enemy vigorously. *We know that he is in full retreat,* endeavoring to save his trains. Two of Sickles' division are upon him."

General Slocum was far from sharing that confidence. Towards noon I met him visiting our front to see how we were placed, and examining attentively the position of the Eleventh Corps.

"Let me recommend you to fortify yourself as well as possible," he said to me. "The enemy is massing a considerable force on our right. In two or three hours he will fall on Howard, and you will have him upon you in strong force. You had better protect yourself as well as possible, at least by an abatis on your front."

I was about to follow his advice when the division received orders to advance. We moved forward out of the woods, and crossed the open ground which extended in our front. It was an effort to cut in two the column of the enemy, which continued to defile before us, and to sweep away what must be his rearguard.

Our advance was delayed in the woods. We had to build or rebuild some bridges over some brooks. We had to cut our way painfully through the thick underbrush, a network of branches and briars. But these detentions afforded the Second Division time to support us. Finally, by main force, our first regiments reached the crossroads on which the rear of the enemy's column was marching. A brisk fire was opened immediately; our men charged upon the enemy surprised at seeing an attack made upon them from a thicket which they thought absolutely impenetrable. They fell into confusion. Some fled, others surrendered; the Twenty-seventh Georgia resisted stoutly; but it was soon surrounded and compelled to lay down its arms. More than five hundred prisoners remained in our hands, and were immediately sent to the rear.

We had in this way, continually on the run, reached some abandoned furnaces. Birney had just formed the division in a square across the road by which the enemy had disappeared, and he waited the arrival of the Second Division, reënforced by two brigades, one from the Eleventh and one from the Twelfth Corps. The men took breath, laid off their knapsacks, and reloaded their pieces. The officers laughed and conversed together, relating the different episodes of the combat.

Suddenly the noise of a distant firing came through the air. Our ranks became silent, as if by magic. Each one listened, and turned his head towards Chancellorsville. There is no more doubt; there is where the fight will be made. The musketry fire increases and rolls uninterruptedly. Soon the roar of cannon breaks out like a clap of thunder, at first by a volley of batteries, then by shots hurried, furious, as in combat à *outrance*.

In a moment the aids passed at a gallop along the front of our regiments. The command rang out, from one end of the division to the other, *Forward!* Double quick! March! And we were soon swiftly returning on the run by the road over which we had just come. Hurry up! Jackson has crushed our right; the Eleventh Corps is in an utter rout. Hurry up! Quick! or we will be cut off!

Harassed and out of breath, yet in good order, we finally reached the edge of the open ground that we had first crossed on leaving our lines. Our artillery was still there, but turned against the same woods we had occupied a few hours before. Firing had ceased. Jackson's troops filled the intrenchments which the Eleventh Corps had raised, and the rebel flag floated behind the abatis which, in the morning, had protected the front of our division. Evening had come. We silently formed in line of battle near the artillery, and awaited the fate which the night had in store for us.

We then heard a detailed account of what had happened in our absence. General Lee, having found our lines too strong to be carried on our left or centre, had agreed to Stonewall Jackson's proposition to lead an attack on our extreme right. The movement was not without risk, for, in order to do it, it was necessary to march on one single road, at a short distance from our front, a long column of twenty-five thousand men, and to divide in two parts an army which, altogether, was yet inferior in number to ours. But the position taken since the evening by General Hooker was so absolutely defensive, the difficulty of moving so as to get out of it so manifest, that the general commanding the enemy thought that a few demonstrations would suffice to keep him on the defensive. Jackson commenced his movement early in the morning, and although the head of his column had been noticed between nine and ten o'clock, he continued to march with impunity along our front the greater part of the day. When, at last, in the afternoon, our division was sent to cut him in two, we were only able to reach his rearguard, which merely hastened his march.

Jackson, having gone beyond the point where our lines extended, turned to the right, by a road which led into the turnpike, near an inn known as Old Wilderness Tavern, and massed his forces there for one of those terrible attacks which have rendered his name celebrated in this war. This movement was made known to General Devens, who commanded the last division in that direction, and to General Howard, his corps commander, by two soldiers sent out to reconnoitre. Several times a brisk fire was opened upon the line of pickets of the Eleventh Corps, showing the presence of the enemy's skirmishers. Yet, notwithstanding all that, no new measure was taken, and the small brigade across the road remained alone, with two regiments in reserve, to meet an attack against our right, already turned.

About five o'clock, the picket firing was suddenly renewed, then redoubled, and came nearer. Soon the men appeared falling-back hurriedly on both sides of the road. A moment more, and the enemy, emerging from the woods in deep masses, with the rebel yell, threw himself upon the few regiments which were opposing him. The latter endeavored to resist, but they were quickly swept away and beaten down. The remainder of the division, taken in flank, melted away, was broken, and rolled upon the next division, which it carried with it; while along the road, in the midst of the fleeing multitude, the wagons, the ambulances, horses and mules, which had been imprudently left in that part of the field, were precipitated pell-mell. In vain, a few superior officers endeavored to stop the flight. In order to meet the attack it was necessary to change front to the rear, and, during this movement, their ranks were broken and carried along with the torrent. It was not an engagement, it was a rout, in the midst of which a few regiments, keeping their order, endeavored to hold together. Two brigade commanders, Schimmelpfennig of Schultz's division, and Bushbeck of Steinwehr's division, succeeded in effecting their change of front, and fought until, overwhelmed and carried away by numbers, they were compelled to fall back on the Twelfth Corps. All the rest went on in the greatest confusion towards Chancellorsville and the road to the Rappahannock.

In the midst of the rout and tumult, Hooker hurried up. Very fortunately, he found at hand, back of the road on which the enemy was sweeping everything before him, Berry's division, the one which he had so long commanded. "Forward!" he cried, "with the bayonet!" The division, supported by Hay's brigade of the Second Corps, advanced, with a firm and steady step, cleaving the multitude of disbanded men as the bow of a vessel cleaves the waves of the sea. It struck the advance of the Confederates obliquely, and stopped it with the aid of the Twelfth Corps artillery.

Jackson's attack, arrested on the left and in front, was thrown towards the right, that is to say, into the woods between the road and the intrenchments abandoned by the Eleventh Corps. It was drawing near the position that Birney had occupied in the morning, and thus a new, terrible, and imminent danger presented itself to us. In the open ground, and in front of the woods, and two or three hundred yards from the intrenchment, the division had left its artillery without protection, while advancing towards the furnaces. The guns were there on low ground, in full view, under the guard of the cannoneers only. Multitudes of flying men had taken this direction, to escape more quickly, and wagons, ambulances, and pieces of artillery rolled at a gallop across the field, in the hope of finding, further on, an opportunity to get back into our lines. The moment was most critical. Who should save the guns from almost certain capture?

At this instant, General Pleasonton, who had accompanied us in our forward movement, returned with two regiments of cavalry, which he had found it impossible to use to advantage in the midst of the thickets. While marching, one of his aids, who had gone on in advance, came back in haste to announce that the Eleventh Corps was fleeing in disorder, and that cavalry was necessary to stop it. Pleasonton put his columns at a gallop, and, on arriving, recognized at a glance the imminence of the peril. Then, consulting only his inspiration in the responsibility he was about to take, he assumed the direct command of the artillery at that point.

To put it in position, he must have at least ten or twelve minutes, minutes more than precious in such a case. He called Major Keenan of the Eighth Pennsylvania, and said to him: "Major, charge into the woods with your regiment and hold the rebels in check until I can get these pieces into position. It must be done at all hazards."

"General, I will do it," simply replied Major Keenan.

It was nearly certain death. He knew it; but the honor of the duty assigned, and the importance of the service to be done, lighted up his features with a noble smile. He had but four or five hundred men. Riding at their head, he charged furiously at the enemy, advancing victoriously, and fell lifeless on the line whose advance he seemed to still bar with his dead body. This intrepid charge caused the attack to hesitate for a short time, and Pleasonton gained the ten minutes which he required.

All he had to do more was to clear the ground of stragglers and vehicles, and to put in position, near the two batteries of the division, the one he had brought with him, and a few pieces of the Eleventh Corps, which had retired in that direction. When the remains of the Eighth Pennsylvania cavalry had fallen back to the right and left, Pleasonton had twenty-two guns in line, loaded with double charges of canister, and ready to open fire. In the rear, the Seventeenth Pennsylvania, half concealed by a roll of the ground, awaited the moment to charge in its turn, in case of necessity.

Soon the wood was full of rebels. A moment later, their flags appeared

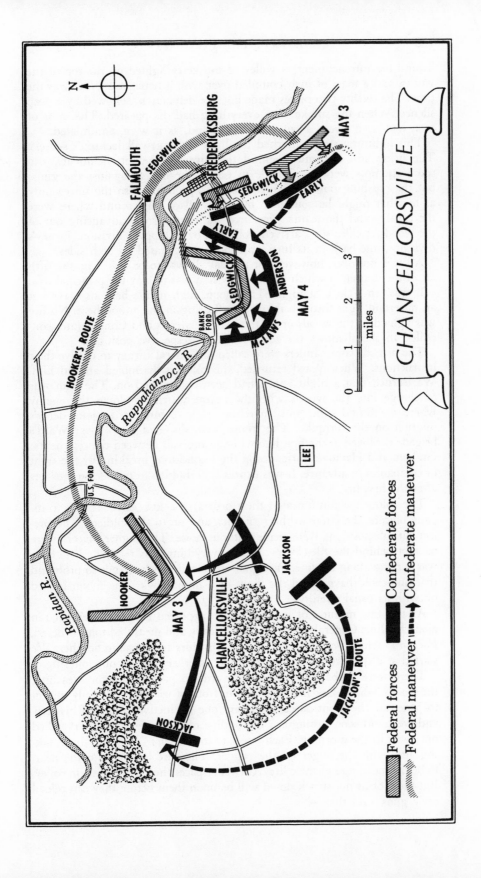

CHANCELLORSVILLE

Federal forces
Federal maneuver

Confederate forces
Confederate maneuver

miles

0   1   2   3

N

FALMOUTH
SEDGWICK
FREDERICKSBURG
SEDGWICK
EARLY
MAY 3

EARLY
SEDGWICK
ANDERSON
MAY 4
McLAWS
BANKS FORD

HOOKER'S ROUTE
Rappahannock R.

Rapidan R.
U.S. FORD
HOOKER
MAY 3

LEE

WILDERNESS
CHANCELLORSVILLE
JACKSON
JACKSON
JACKSON'S ROUTE

behind the intrenchment; a volley of musketry lighted up the top of the works, and a mass of men bounded over with a fierce yell. Now was the time. The twenty-two pieces made but one detonation, followed by a deep silence. When the smoke rose, everything had disappeared. The mass of men had been swept away at a stroke, and, as it were, annihilated.

This lightning stroke marked the limit of Stonewall Jackson's success. The firing still continued behind the cover of the intrenchments, and some attempts were even made to renew the charge against the guns; but the crushing power of their fire, and, probably, also the uncertainty as to what might be concealed by the swell of the ground where were the cavalry and the teams, prevented the enemy from advancing out of the woods. Sickles soon arrived, followed by Whipple's division. Birney's division came back in its turn, and the contest ceased on both sides.

All was not over, however, for the day. It was to be closed by the fifth act of the drama, in which Birney's division was to play the principal role.

It was ten o'clock at night. The moon, high in the heavens, gave but an uncertain light through the vapors floating in the atmosphere. No fire was lighted in the woods or on the plain. Federals and Confederates concealed in the shadows the secret of their respective positions.

The brigade commanders were called to General Birney to receive their instructions. When Ward returned, the colonels assembled around him. We learned that a night attack had been determined on. The plan was to charge into the woods with the bayonet, striking down the enemy where we found him, and, marching right before us, to join Berry's division on the turnpike. The troops were disposed as follows: Ward's brigade deployed in the first line without intervals between the regiments; Graham and Hayman's brigades in the second line, breaking by the right of companies in advance. It was expressly forbidden to reload the muskets after the first fire.

The colonels communicated their orders in a low voice to their company officers, the latter to the sergeants, and on to the soldiers. The preliminary dispositions were made without noise. The higher officers were on foot behind the file-closers. When everything was ready and nothing was stirring along the line, the signal was awaited in a silence so profound that one could have heard the flight of a night-hawk. The moon looked on with its usual serenity.

After a few minutes of waiting which appeared long a movement ran along the line. General Ward had, in a steady and measured tone, ordered, *Forward!* which was repeated in low murmurs from one to another. We started at a quick step, gun on shoulder, neither hurried nor loitering.

There were perhaps two hundred yards to pass over before reaching the woods, whose dark line appeared in front of us. All eyes vainly sought to penetrate the silent obscurity. Every one instinctively hurried his step, and we could soon distinguish the outline of the intrenchments sketched out by us in the morning. Each one said to himself: "They are there, taking aim, with the finger on the trigger. They are letting us come near, to be the more sure of their fire. At twenty paces they will fire their volley. But those of us not struck down will be upon them before they can reload their guns, and then—"

The nearer we approached, the lower dropped the point of the bayonets of the front rank.

At a distance of twenty steps there was no sign of movement. Well, it was said, the contest will be at bayonets' point; so much the better.

In such moments one has an excessive delicacy of hearing. A cracking of branches and a footstep on the dead leaves were heard on our right. It was the Ninety-ninth Pennsylvania, which was advancing into the woods without encountering any one. In an instant, we were there in our turn. The enemy—I do not know why, even now—had neglected to occupy the border of the woods. He was farther back, in a line of intrenchments more complete and on higher ground. Perhaps, also, we surprised him in the midst of some movement preparatory for the next day's battle. However that might have been, profiting by the fortunate accident, without seeking the cause, we continued to advance through the thicket, but not in as good order.

We had moved forward about fifty yards, and my regiment was crossing a rough and muddy ravine, when a voice cried out, "Halt! who goes there?" Nearly at the same time one shot, then ten, twenty, a hundred; the word *Forward!* was heard on all sides; a loud hurrah responded, and the bloody contest commenced.

The ground on which we found ourselves was not only very wooded, but also very rough. There were unequal little hillocks and small winding ravines, at the bottom of which crept or stagnated the water from springs or from rainfall. The trees grew very irregularly, scattered, here high, there brushy, and covered with thorns. The line of the brigade was broken in an instant: the regiments obliqued to the right or the left, led astray by the slope of the ground. The companies were mingled together while crossing the obstacles; the left of the Ninety-ninth Pennsylvania was thrown over into my right. The Third Maine, on the other hand, was separated from my left. My regiment itself was divided into two parts. We ran to one side to reëstablish order, and on the other the companies dashed forward on the run. Some carried the intrenchments before them without firing a shot; others recoiled before a deadly fire. The defence was as confused as the attack. Terrible at some points, at others it was a mere nothing. But, instead of ceasing, the fire redoubled on our side. In spite of orders, the men reloaded their pieces, some while marching, others posted behind trees.

The second line, entering in its turn into the woods, carried away by the noise of the firing, began to fire also. A hundred voices were immediately raised above the noise of the tumult: "Stop firing there below! You are firing on us!" A few men fell, struck from the rear. Then all dashed forward, pell-mell, as they were able. The enemy, broken already at several points, did not await the shock. They disappeared, running, leaving not a man in the intrenchments.

The confusion was extreme. I had around me about a hundred men of the Thirty-eighth, mingled with others of different regiments. They were brave men. They marched with mine, without thinking of profiting by the opportunity to slip away. For the rest, I did not trouble myself about the companies out of my sight. I knew they were well commanded, and all inflamed with honorable rivalry between those of the right, belonging to the old Thirty-eighth, and those of the left, belonging to the old Fifty-fifth. I had but one thing to fear, which was that the desire of each to surpass the others might carry them too far.

However, the repeated hurrahs showed clearly that the Third Maine had advanced farther than we had. We hurried forward to rejoin them, the more eagerly inasmuch as four of my companies would be with it. The ranks being reformed as well as possible, we again took up our march, crossing obliquely a second hollow. We had scarcely commenced to ascend the opposite slope, when, at a distance of fifty yards, the crest burst into a flame like a volcano, and sent us a hail of bullets. Happily for us, the enemy, deceived by the darkness, had fired too soon. The avalanche of lead passed, whistling, over our heads. Hardly a man was hit. We fell back towards the left, to turn the position, following the curve of the ravine, and there we found a fire by file from the same quarter where the Third Maine must have passed. Where was the enemy? Where were our men? We could not tell anything about it. In this obscure labyrinth of ravines and hillocks, of dwarfed thickets and giant trees, we had lost our direction.

How could we find it again? We were fired on from all sides; from the front, from the right, from the left, and even from the rear, where the fragments of the second line, scattered like ours, marched at hazard, and fired in the same manner. The moon was hidden; we could not see ten steps. Around me, men fell or disappeared. The part of the wood where we were had become the focus to which all the firing converged. The bullets struck the trees all around us; shells crossed their sparks from all directions, and filled the air with the noise and flash of their bursting. The groans of the wounded, the orders of the officers, the oaths of the soldiers, the whistling of the balls, the roaring of the conical projectiles, the crackling of the branches, the rolling of the fusillade, the thunder of the artillery—everything united in a concert infernal.

I was there joined by Colonel Pierson, of the First New York. He belonged to the second line, and had hardly twenty men with him. He endeavored to lead forward those who were giving way. Half a dozen of the latter had taken refuge behind an epaulement, where they were cowering. We tried to make them march; but it was of no use, and I had no time to lose.

With a handful of men, who still followed me, I turned my steps towards a point where the firing seemed to have ceased. All at once, I felt the ground moving under my feet, and cries issuing from it. It was a square hole, from which the dirt had been taken out, without doubt, for the intrenchments. Five or six poltroons had lain down there flat on the ground, literally packed like sardines in a box. We passed over them, and continued our advance.

In the midst of a clearing, there was growing a great tree. Around its trunk five men were crowded, thinking they were protected from the fire. There were two on one side, and three on the other. The precaution was of little use, where the balls came from all quarters.

A few steps further on I met an officer, going in the opposite direction. He was alone, and appeared to be looking for his company.

"Have you seen any men of the Thirty-eighth?" I asked him.

"I do not know; I saw some troops in that direction; but they belonged to the Twelfth Corps, and we were fired upon. A nice mess!" grumbled he. "The devil himself would not know where he was."

Nevertheless, the information was useful to me. It served to set me right. Knowing the position occupied by General Slocum, I turned immediately to the left. I walked as fast as possible, putting aside the small branches with the point of my sabre. I thought I recognized a path which must lead to the turnpike. I immediately took it, hoping to find my lost companies there.

Passing around a thick bush, a man ran against me. He wore a light blue jacket (color of the uniform of the old Fifty-fifth), trimmed with black on the sleeves. The man recognized me immediately.

"Don't go that way, colonel," said he to me. "The rebels are in force a few steps away. They hold the line of the road by which we advanced out of the woods this morning, and are picking up all who pass. They have taken a good many prisoners from us, and I came near being gobbled up myself. A wounded man warned me in time, and told me that General Ward had been taken, with two or three officers of his staff."

While listening to him I had turned about to retrace my steps. I saw that I was alone with my informant. The last men who had followed me had taken a different direction.

It appeared quite improbable to me that General Ward had been taken prisoner at the extreme left of his brigade, in the very direction where, as he well knew, the greater part of the force of the enemy was. But, if the report were true, the command devolved upon me, and, without believing it, I resolved to find out about it. The melee had finished, evidently to our advantage. The two lines of rifle-pits taken from the enemy were vacant. To the continual fusillade had succeeded the occasional shot, and the shells burst only at intervals. Soldiers were going back and forth looking for their regiments, or helping the wounded. The dead were lying alongside of the living.

On returning towards the edge of the woods, I recognized my lieutenant-colonel walking behind me.

"Colonel Allason," I said to him, immediately, "where are our men?"

"All around, colonel; at least, I suppose so. The companies of the right have just gone out of the woods, where the Fourth Maine occupies a part of the intrenchments taken from the enemy. Two or three other regiments have the same orders that we have, to reform near the guns. But five companies are lacking, of whom I have no news since the commencement of the action. Were you with them?"

"No," I told him. "They took the lead from the beginning, and must have reached the main road where Berry's division is."

On the open ground we found, in fact, one half of the regiment, around which rallied, from time to time, the men strayed away during the contest. General Ward was near there, inquiet about two officers of his staff who were missing. We did not know whether they were dead or prisoners. The latter supposition was the true one. This was, without doubt, what had given rise to the report I had heard.

By inquiring of every one, and sending out in search of them, I finally found out what had become of my missing companies.

Three of them, belonging to the old Fifty-fifth, finding the ground easier than elsewhere, had advanced under the command of Captains Williams and Demasure and Lieutenant Suraud. But they had not advanced faster than the company of the Thirty-eighth, commanded by Captain Brady. They charged the intrenchments together, overcame the force they found there, and, after a moment's halt, saw a short distance away the flashing of the fire from a battery of artillery. The idea of carrying the battery came to them immediately, and, with one accord, they took that direction. We must believe that, in the tumult, the cannoneers did not hear them approach, or that, if they were seen, the direction from which they came caused the gunners to hesitate. However that may be, they advanced right up to the mouths of the guns.

One of the first to leap into the battery was a great German, nearly six feet high, named Johann. He wore in the front of his cap a red lozenge, the distinguishing mark of the First Division, Third Corps.

"Hello! who are you?" cried one of the cannoneers.

"Thirty-eighth New York," cried Johann, brandishing his bayonet.

"Hold on! don't fire!" cried a score of voices at once. "This is the Twelfth Corps, General Slocum."

And my men, completely mystified, recognized General Slocum himself, in the midst of the artillerymen, revolver in hand, ready to be slain at his pieces rather than not defend them at all risks. The general complimented the officers on the vigor with which they had led the charge, and the four companies were put in line to defend the artillery they had so nearly attacked.

The last company to hear from was one belonging to the old Thirty-eighth, commanded by Captain Althouse. The captain, without troubling himself about what was going on elsewhere, or turning to right or left, had marched straight ahead, with well closed ranks. He fortunately crossed the two intrenched lines, and continued his march without stopping. Reaching a piece of woods thicker than the rest, he saw himself surrounded and summoned to surrender. All resistance was useless. He had advanced directly into what appeared to be the enemy's lines. The captain, with chagrin, was about to surrender his sabre when a joyous voice called out, in a shout of laughter, "Well, that is a good joke! This is the First Division."

The Company was in the midst of a brigade of Berry's division. It was the only one, to my knowledge, which arrived at its destination.

At that time we were still ignorant of the most important event of that nocturnal combat. We had taken two rows of rifle-pits from some of the enemy's regiments, but at a very heavy cost to us. But what gave the engagement the importance of a victory gained for us was the fact that Stonewall Jackson, the most to be dreaded of our adversaries after Lee, had fallen, mortally wounded, a few steps from us in the same woods, a witness of a melee as bloody as it was confused.

Encouraged by the day's success, full of confidence in the fortunes of the morrow, Jackson had made his disposition to throw himself on our rear, and cut off our line of retreat to United States Ford. After having himself overlooked some changes in the disposition of his troops, he had advanced out of his lines, with a few officers of his staff, in order to see himself the exact position we occupied. In this way he reached the turnpike, where he had before him Berry's division, where the attack commenced against the most advanced of his regiments in the woods. In an instant he recognized that it was something more serious than a skirmisher's alarm. He turned his horse to reënter his lines, and took the most direct road. His troops were under arms, eyes and ears open, as may be imagined. At the noise of horses galloping, they thought it was a charge of cavalry, and fired. Jackson fell, struck by several bullets, one of which broke his arm. Two or three of his officers were killed or wounded. The others made themselves known. A litter was hastily brought. The general was placed thereon, and they hurried to get him into his own lines. They had scarcely started when one of the bearers fell, struck by a ball or by a piece of shell. The general was roughly thrown to the ground. The fall aggravated his wound, and doubled his suffering.

Thus ended the second day of May, 1863.

We had about two hours of repose. Before daybreak the brigade was assembled, and we received an order to form line behind the artillery, in the field which extended between the Chancellorsville house and the woods which we had swept clean of living rebels, while leaving there a large number of our own dead. It was on that side a renewed attack was expected. By leaving Birney's division where it was, along with Whipple's, we would have had an excellent defensive position at that point, for we should have taken the enemy between two fires, both in front and in flank. It was deemed preferable to draw back the whole Third Corps between the house and the woods, perpendicular to the main road. The result was that the enemy, finding the ground free, which we had just quitted, promptly took possession of it, and placed his artillery there, giving him a converging fire, without hindrance, upon the centre of our position. And yet the retreat of our corps was not made without difficulty. Although the day had hardly broken, the brigade which brought up the rear was attacked as soon as it was put in motion. But General Graham, who commanded it, held back forces much superior to his own, and effected a retreat in good order, without breaking.

Then began a desperate battle, the brunt of which the Third Corps had still to bear. The enemy advanced in three lines sustained by strong reserves, between the main road and the ground where his guns replaced those which Pleasonton had so well defended. The movement then was simply the continuation of that which, the evening before, had swept away the Eleventh Corps. The resistance was terrible as the attack was desperate. The musketry and artillery fire mowed down the Confederate ranks; but the more they fell the more came on, and they continued to advance, crying: "Remember Jackson!"

During this time Ward's brigade was receiving blows without being able to return them. The bullets ricocheted in our ranks, shells burst around us, and the balls which passed over the first line found a mark in the second. As we were without cover, we had caused the men to lie down, to avoid useless losses; the officers alone remaining standing. In spite of this precaution, the number of wounded increased more and more, when we received an order to throw ourselves rapidly on the other side of the road, where a violent fire had broken out, and extended into the thicket.

In order not to return to the first phase of the day's action, I will say that, up to this time, the troops of the Third Corps had to sustain alone the furious attack of which we have just spoken. They defended the ground foot by foot, until they had fired their last cartridge, and were compelled to fall back to the rest of the army, saving their artillery, but abandoning that part of the plateau of Chancellorsville to the enemy.

During the fight, General Hooker had been wounded on the threshold of the Chancellorsville house. He was standing under a verandah, watching the approach of the Confederates, when he was violently knocked down by one of the columns sustaining the roof, which had been struck by a cannon ball. The shock was so great that he remained unconscious during the most of the battle, and did not appear to have recovered his faculties during the rest of the day—which, I think, explains many things, and especially why the Third Corps received neither support nor reënforcements at the time when it had the most urgent need of them.

Let us return now to the woods where our brigade had just disappeared.

Generally, on reading the description of a battle, one witnesses, as it were, from the upper air, as formerly the Olympian divinities witnessed the heroic combats of the Greeks and Trojans. We see the movement of the right, the left, and the centre of each army; we see the reënforcements arrive, the reserves put in action, and in that view of the whole, well pictured, the details are of little account. But to a colonel who is in the action matters are presented under an entirely different aspect. Of the general field he sees nothing; of the details very little. Unless good fortune gives him an exceptional position, his visual horizon does not extend beyond his brigade, and is often bounded by the line of his regiment. Where he receives the order to go, there he goes; forward, backward, to the right, to the left. His sphere of action is limited to take his regiment in on a charge; to hold it steady on a retreat; in every event to execute rapidly and correctly the changes of position which he is directed to make. Aside from that, the battle may be won or lost; he knows nothing about it. He will learn that later. What happens elsewhere is none of his business.

As an example, here is a copy of my pencil notes, May 3, during the battle of Chancellorsville, from the time when I left off my story:

"Being able to penetrate the thicket only on foot, I turned my horse over to Couillou (a sapper), with orders to bring him to me by a detour, to a clearing towards which we were going. Arriving there, neither man nor horse was to be seen. The fire continued with extreme violence. It must be Berry's division which stops the enemy's movements on this side. They are firing through the thickets, without being able to charge. Our men hold firm. No hurrahs, but a deafening noise of musketry. What the devil has become of Couillou?

"The firing came nearer and stronger at the centre. Clearly the enemy was driving us back at that point.

"We are now on the left centre, near the Twelfth Corps. We have hurried forward with our utmost ability. It seems that the time is critical. We formed our line twenty or thirty paces from the first, which, after all, had not given way. In this direction, the rebels are giving voice to their sharp yell, and our men reply by distinct hurrahs, as if there were not enough noise without that! As we had a great number of wounded, we were made to fall back to the edge of a road, where the men can at least lie down in the ditch. The bullets do us much less injury; the shells continue to trouble us. A great column of black smoke towards our left, then sheets of flame; the Chancellorsville house is burning. At the rate they are going on in our front, they will soon use up all their ammunition, and it will be our turn to take their place. The wounded are continually passing through our lines. One of them, half naked, is as black as a Negro. He runs shrieking towards the ambulances. It is an artilleryman, wounded by the explosion of a caisson. Couch passes by at a light trot, a little switch in his hand, as usual. Sickles goes by in his turn at a walk, with a smiling air, smoking a cigar. 'Everything is going well,' said he, in a loud voice, intended to be heard. Then, in a lower tone, giving me his hand, he whispered in my ear a congratulation and a promise. It would appear that I won a star in the fight by moonlight, the night before.

"We returned to the right, always on the double quick. The enemy's artillery rains projectiles upon us. Our lot for to-day is to receive blows from all sides, without being able to return them. A lieutenant of the Third Maine is cut in two by a shell bursting in his body; legs thrown to one side, the trunk to the other. One of our batteries has silenced the one which troubled us so much. General Berry has just been killed near us. An excellent man and a brave soldier. An hour of respite. It is as hot as summer; my cloak oppresses me, and I have no horse! Nothing in my stomach for twenty-four hours, but a cup of black coffee and a big swallow of whiskey, which a staff officer gave me a short time ago.

"Fifth change of position to the rear. Interval employed in covering ourselves with light intrenchments. This time, we are in the front line. The two other brigades of the division return at last to join us. General Mott is wounded. Colonel MacKnight, of the One Hundred and Fifth Pennsylvania, is killed; also Colonel Shylock, of the Fifth Michigan. In General Birney's staff, two officers are wounded, Clarke and Walker. The latter, division inspector, belongs to my regiment. He is said to be maimed for life.

"Two batteries have just come into position on our line. At half after four, the firing recommences, and stops at five o'clock.

"We learn that the First Corps arrived last night, coming from Fredericksburg, and that the Sixth carried the heights above the city this morning."

One can judge by this extract how much a colonel sees and knows about a battle in which he has all the time manœuvred his regiment. Here, now, is what occurred:

Every effort of the enemy was against the Third Corps. When that corps, out of ammunition, began to fall back to the rear, from the right to the other side of the road, Stuart, who succeeded Jackson, extended his attack on his left, hoping to take us in reverse, and reach our line of retreat towards the Rappahannock. There he struck French's division of the Second Corps, which not only held its ground, but even compelled its assailants to fall back. It was to sustain him that Ward's brigade had been ordered into the woods.

In this part of the field, our right was facing to the west, while our centre looked south, and our left east.

In the meanwhile, Lee, having learned of the success of Stuart on our right, and seeing us all engaged in that direction, attacked our left centre vigorously, so that for a moment it was in danger of being broken. Upon which our brigade was hurried over to reënforce the Twelfth Corps.

The danger past, Stuart returned to the charge, reënforced by new troops, and now forced French to retire. This was the reason for our precipitate return near the clearing where we had first taken position.

But our comrades of the Third Corps were not yet out of the difficulty, notwithstanding their having fallen back and changed front. The enemy, who had just effected a junction of his two wings on the plateau of Chancellorsville, and who had not been able to force, at the angle to our left, the intrenched line of our advanced posts admirably defended by Colonel Nelson A. Miles, now commenced again the attack against Sickles with renewed vigor. Our men, short of ammunition, had no other resource than the bayonet. They availed themselves of it brilliantly and with great success. The New Jersey brigade, amongst others, commanded by General Mott, broke the first line of the Confederates, and, advancing, took flags and trophies from their second line.

General Hooker, recovering from his unconsciousness, although still feeling the effects of the accident, had resumed the command of the army, left for some hours to General Couch. He gave the order to retire to a stronger line of defence which he had had traced out the night before by the engineer officers. There the other two brigades of the division came to join us.

Thus ended the third day of May, 1863.

Our new position rested, at one end, on the Rappahannock, the other on the Rapidan. On the left it faced southeast, on the right southwest, making a very open angle, at whose apex, opposite the enemy's centre, was formed a great trilateral work. This was the point occupied by the Third Corps. As the army made no further movement until it repassed the river, we can leave it behind its breastworks and join the corps at Fredericksburg.

On the afternoon of the 2d, Hooker, seeing his right broken in, and the Third Corps compromised by Jackson's attack, had thought immediately of making a diversion from the other side, which would turn Lee. He sent an order to General Sedgwick to cross the Rappahannock as quickly as possible, and march out on the Chancellorsville road, attacking and destroying what ever force might bar his way. Sedgwick received the despatch about midnight, having already crossed the river by virtue of a preceding order directing him to take the Bowling Green road and "any other." He immediately changed his dispositions, and marched on Fredericksburg without loss of time. His instructions were: "You will leave your train behind you, except the mules carrying ammunition, and will march so as to be in the neighborhood of the general in command at daylight. You will probably strike the rear of the forces commanded by General Lee, and, between you and the major-general commanding, the latter hopes to make a finish of his adversary."

The silence as to the fortified heights seemed to imply that the general-in-chief supposed that they had been stripped of troops since the morning; without that, the contest to be entered on at that posiion should have entered explicitly into the calcaulation in reference to the time allowed to Sedgwick to reach the neighborhood of Chancellorsville. Now, not a company had been withdrawn by the enemy from that strong position, which was still defended by Early's division, reënforced by a brigade.

The Sixth Corps was surrounded by a cordon of rebel pickets, whose firing gave warning of the march as soon as it began. Early, forewarned, prepared for an attack. Immediately, on entering Fredericksburg, Sedgwick sent four regiments to try the heights; they were received with a deadly fire, and were compelled to retire. The preparations for a final assault occupied the last hours of the night. It would appear that they were not moved with the promptness which circumstances demanded, for it was not till eleven o'clock in the morning that the two columns of attack charged the intrenchments. Colonel Spear of the Sixty-first Pennsylvania, who led the right, was killed. Colonel Johns of the Seventh Massachusetts, commanding the left, was severely wounded; but, in spite of the vigor of the defence, Marye's Heights were carried by main force. At the same time Howe's division carried the enemy's position on the left, and the whole line was ours, with a part of the artillery and a large number of prisoners.

Without loss of time, the troops reformed, and the Sixth Corps advanced on the Chancellorsville road, leaving Gibbon's division of the Second Corps at Fredericksburg, as the order of General Hooker had directed. Those of the enemy who had retired in that direction were driven back without stopping to Salem Heights, in front of Banks Ford. There Brooks' division, which had the advance, met with a determined resistance. It was then about four o'clock in the afternoon (Sunday, May 3). We note the hour, for at this moment the army under the immediate command of Hooker was already inclosed behind the second intrenched line, and the battle there was virtually finished, entirely to the advantage of Lee.

Leaving in front of us what troops were necessary to hold us in our lines, in the cramped position which we occupied, hardly able to move, Lee sent MacLaws' division, strengthened by Mahone's brigade, against Sedgwick. These forces reached Salem in time to reënforce Wilcox's brigade, which, abandoning the guard of Banks Ford, had hurried on to bar the road against the Sixth Corps. The enemy was, at first, driven back from the heights he occupied, but, when his reënforcements reached him, he retook them, notwithstanding an obstinate resistance, forcing Brooks and Newton to fall back. Sedgwick's advance was arrested, when night came to put an end to the engagement.

Behold us now, on Monday, May 4. What has become of the plan so ably conceived, so happily executed in the beginning? That plan which would leave to Lee's army only the alternative of a shameful flight or certain destruction? Hooker lost the benefit of everything he had done up to that time when, on the 1st of May, he had abruptly stopped a series of fine offensive manœuvres, to take up a purely defensive attitude on his first meeting the enemy. From that moment he no longer attacked. He simply stood on the defensive, and he defended himself badly.

On the 2d his right was swept away. That the Eleventh Corps, compos-

Chancellorsville: *Hooker's men under heavy Confederate pressure*

ing the right, had fought poorly or not at all; that some regiments had fled, leaving their arms stacked, or throwing them away so as to run faster, is a fact that must unfortunately be acknowledged. But would all this have happened if the Eleventh Corps had been prepared to receive the attack from the side on which it was absolutely defenceless? We must judge matters coolly. The facts prove that the attack had not been foreseen either by General Howard or by General Hooker. The latter visits and examines that part of the line in the morning, and when General Howard asks him if the dispositions made are satisfactory he replies in the affirmative, in the presence of General Devens, commanding the division placed on the extreme right. Only, on his return to head-quarters, he sent a note to the commanders of the Eleventh and Twelfth Corps to direct them to "examine the ground and decide what positions they must take in the eventuality of an attack on the flank, in order to be prepared to receive the enemy from whatever direction he might present himself." That done, as if to clear his conscience, and without assuring himself that any modification was made of the defective dispositions of the Eleventh Corps, he stripped his lines himself by sending Sickles with two divisions to run after the tail of the enemy's column, when it had nearly all passed by. To support it, he detached a brigade from Slocum's command, another from that of Howard; then he ordered General Pleasonton to follow with his cavalry, and do the enemy, "who was march-ing in the direction of Gordonsville," all the injury he could. We know the result of it.

The following night is devoted partly to firing on ourselves. It might have been more profitably employed.

On the 3d the enemy continued to force back our right, and to press us strongly on our centre. He found before him only the Third and Twelfth Corps, each supported by a division of the Second. No combina-tions, no manœuvres. Each one defends himself as best he can, and in the position he is occupying, some by firing, others by the bayonet. And, all this time, one half the army remains inactive in the rear. The First, the Fifth, and the Eleventh (which must have been eager to make amends for the evening before) move only to fall back when the whole line retires to a position more crowded, and still more on the defensive.

Thus we find the army paralyzed at the very time when the capture of Fredericksburg Heights by Sedgwick, and his approach to the rear of Lee, should have been the signal to us for a redoubling of efforts, the decisive moment to throw the First Corps on the flank of Stuart, with the Fifth and the Eleventh Corps strike the centre of Lee, weakened by the loss of the troops he had been compelled to send against the Sixth Corps, and crush these forces between the two mills of iron and fire. Everything could yet have been saved; but all was lost. Hooker was no longer Hooker. The blow of the miserable piece of wood which had stretched him senseless across the sill of the Chancellorsville house had left him com-pletely shattered, and as though there was a cloud over his faculties.

When General Warren, arriving from Salem, where he had assisted in the fight, came to report to Hooker, and asked him if there were any instructions to send to Sedgwick, Hooker replied, "None."

However, the Sixth Corps could not be left there in danger of being cut in pieces without a knowledge of the state of affairs. Warren took upon himself to write to Sedgwick: "We have drawn our lines in somewhat, and repulsed the last assault easily. General Hooker wishes that the Confederates would attack him to-morrow, if they so desire. He does not wish you to attack them as yet in force, unless he attacks at the same time. He says that you are too far from him for him to direct your movements. Look well to the safety of your corps, and keep your communications open with General Benham at Banks Ford, and with Fredericksburg. You may retire on either point, if you think it better to cross the river. Banks Ford would bring you within supporting distance of the rest of the army, and would be preferable to a retreat on Fredericksburg."

But when Sedgwick received that despatch (on the 4th) he had no longer any choice. Early advanced from the direction of Fredericksburg, reënforced by the troops which Lee, left free by Hooker's inaction, had sent to envelop the Sixth Corps. Threatened from two sides at once, Sedgwick was compelled to fight in a disadvantageous position. Howe's division, attacked from the direction of the river, defends itself vigorously, facing to the rear. After giving way a moment on the left, it gains the advantage, and ends by decidedly repelling the enemy, while, from the direction of the road, Brooks holds his position without much difficulty.

And, during that whole afternoon, we heard the cannon roaring without stirring ourselves, or even making any pretence of moving. Did Hooker, with six army corps, expect that Sedgwick, with seventeen or eighteen thousand men, was coming to deliver him from the false position in which he had placed himself? Or, rather, did he have any other idea than that of recrossing the Rappahannock without further fighting?

As soon as night came on, Sedgwick took advantage of it to draw back his three divisions on Banks Ford, and the morning's sun found the Sixth Corps safe and sound on the left bank of the river. Perhaps Lee, freed from all embarrassment in that direction, would have tried a general attack on us, with his whole force, if a rain in torrents, which came on in the afternoon, had not forcibly delayed his preparations until the following day. But Hooker did not wait for the attack which he had desired the evening before. In the night of the 5th the whole army recrossed the river, without hindrance, and, for the second time in five months, returned beaten to its encampment.

The victory cost the enemy only thirteen thousand men; defeat cost us seventeen thousand. The Third Corps and the Sixth, together, bore half the loss. The other half was shared principally between the Second, the Eleventh, and the Twelfth. As to the First and Fifth, they lost enough only to mention it.

Except the small force commanded by General Pleasonton, the cavalry had poorly performed its mission. Stoneman had scattered his column in every direction, without any appreciable result, except a lively alarm in the neighborhood of Richmond. Averill had not led his troops further than the Rapidan.

So that we were completely beaten—beaten on account of the general-in-chief, who, after having prepared for his army the best opportunity for being victorious which it had ever had, threw to the winds all his advantage. For one moment he had held the enemy in his hand; he had only, so to speak, to stretch it forth, to crush him; and he had not only allowed the enemy to escape, but had delivered himself up to him, by falling backward in such a manner as to paralyze his own movements. By one fault after another, and one error after another, he lost the opportunity to repossess himself of fortune's favors, and condemned one-half of his army to a fatal inaction, even to the humiliating extremity of escaping by night from a position yet formidable, before forces decidedly inferior to his own.

LEE INVADES PENNSYLVANIA

STONEWALL JACKSON'S ARM WAS AMPUTATED and his health seemed to improve, until, still suffering exhaustion from shock and exposure, he contracted pneumonia. This disease, a greater killer those days than now, had its way with Jackson. On May 10, the South lost its most famous general; General Lee said, "I have lost my right arm."

At Chancellorsville, the Federals had once again taken a licking at the hands of Lee and Jackson. Although General Hooker had had a decided advantage over Lee when the fighting began, he did not see in time, as Federal generals before him had not seen, the vulnerability of Lee's army, especially when Jackson took off on his end run to hit the Federal right flank. Nor had Sedgwick moved quickly enough to put pressure on Lee's rear. Sedgwick's troops had captured the heights above Fredericksburg, but because of poor communications with Hooker he had fought Lee not knowing the rest of the Union troops had already drawn back on the Rappahannock to insure their escape route. Sedgwick made no headway, for Lee could now deal solely with Sedgwick's attack. Both Hooker and Sedgwick retreated across the river.

Lee's Army of Northern Virginia had shown itself to be a superb fighting force and Lee was seriously considering a new invasion of the North. He had the backing of most of the Confederate leaders, who clung to the belief that a victory on Union soil would bring recognition from England and France and the accompanying prestige and power resulting therefrom. Such a victory also would encourage the antiwar party in the North in their efforts to persuade the rest of the Union that continuation of the war was futile. And surely any invasion that threatened Washington would bring the Army of the Potomac rushing north, thus moving the war out of Virginia.

A minority opinion existed in the South (as evidenced by General Longstreet) that part of Lee's army should be detached and sent west to help defend Vicksburg and the Mississippi valley. Lee resisted such a move and his record of success was sufficient for him to withstand opposition and keep his army intact.

Lee divided his 70,000 men into three corps. First Corps remained with Lieutenant General James Longstreet. Second Corps was given to Richard Ewell, and Third Corps went to A. P. Hill, both of whom were appointed Lieutenant Generals.

Early in June, General Ewell's corps swung northwest into the Shenandoah Valley, then marched north into Maryland, heading for Pennsylvania. Longstreet and Hill followed soon after. Once in Pennsylvania, Ewell sent off two attack columns, one of which captured York and Wrightsville, while the other threatened Harrisburg.

General Hooker had received news that Lee was heading north, but he proposed to Washington that the Army of the Potomac strike for Richmond, pointing out that any such move should bring Lee rushing back to Virginia. But Stanton, who was dissatisfied with Hooker, ordered him to turn around and march north, keeping his men between Lee and the capital.

Getting rid of Hooker presented a problem to Stanton and Lincoln. They had decided to replace him but feared that an outright removal would cause political repercussions. Stanton set out to frustrate and irritate Hooker to a point where, in a rage, he would offer his resignation. At the end of June, Hooker did just that, and the offer was promptly accepted. General George Meade, who had commanded the V Corps in the Army of the Potomac, took over the command on June 28.

As the Army of the Potomac continued its march north toward Harrisburg, it advanced on a front, according to Catton, "35 to 40 miles from tip to tip." Progress was slow while Union cavalry under General John Buford searched for Lee's army. At Gettysburg on June 30, Buford finally made contact with Confederate patrols. That night he occupied a position on Seminary Ridge northwest of the town and, believing that Lee's army was near, sent out scouts to locate it.

For once the Federals were better informed than the Confederates. Since June 25, Stuart had been riding in a long cast around the Army of the Potomac (from east to west), expecting to meet forward elements of Lee's army in southern Pennsylvania. By cutting to the east of the Army of the Potomac he could take a short cut and molest the Federals' supply routes. But Stuart kept running into Federal troops. This slowed his progress, thus depriving Lee of news of Meade's activities. When Lee finally discovered the Federals hot on his heels he ordered Ewell, Longstreet, and Hill to converge at Gettysburg. Divisions from both Hill to the west and Ewell in the north began arriving in Gettysburg on July 1.

At daybreak Buford's cavalry pickets saw Confederate troops marching directly toward their positions on Seminary Ridge. Buford placed his troops, now dismounted, in battle formation. He hoped to delay the Confederates long enough for the main body of Federal troops approaching from the south to reach Gettysburg.

As more and more Confederate troops appeared over the western ridge Buford sent couriers to hurry the Federal divisions. The first to arrive was General Reynolds' I Corps. They went into position with Buford on Seminary Ridge.

In the early stages of the battle the Federals successfully stood off the forward elements of Hill's corps, but when the main body arrived the Federals were outnumbered. "The battle lines grew and grew until they formed a great semicircle west and north of the town. . . . Another Yankee corps, the XI, came up and went through the town on the double, colliding head on with Confederates who were marching south. . . . These

Confederates cut around both flanks of the XI Corps' line, crumpled them, punched holes in the line, and late in the afternoon drove the survivors back through the village in rout; then the line west of town caved in, and by evening the Federals who were left (they had had upwards of 10,000 casualties) were reassembling on the high ground south and east of Gettysburg, grimly determined to hold on until the rest of the army came up, but not at all certain that they could do it."*

Federal troops were marching hard and fast. One of the approaching columns was part of the V Corps, and one of its regiments, the 20th Maine, would have a vital role to play the next day.

"Off to the west there were disturbances of the atmosphere, as though someone were beating a rug, far over the horizon. Late in the afternoon they went into bivouac near Hanover, then right out of bivouac again, for a lathered horseman arrived with bad news that soon spread through the entire corps. The report said that the First Corps and the Eleventh Corps had run into Lee at a place called Gettysburg, fourteen or fifteen miles to the west, and had been hurt badly. General Reynolds, the First Corps commander, had been killed; the two corps had been driven back through the town of Gettysburg and now were dug in on some hills this side of the town, waiting for the rest of the army to arrive.

"This meant that the march of the Fifth Corps would continue into the night. The bugles sounded 'Forward!' and they were pushing westward again. In midevening, the moon came up, illuminating the countryside with a clear blue light, and suddenly a phantom was riding ahead of them. 'At a turn of the road a staff officer, with an air of authority, told each colonel as he came up that McClellan was in command again, and riding ahead of us on the road,' Colonel Chamberlain reported. And Private Theodore Gerrish of the 20th Maine wrote, 'Men waved their hats and cheered until they were hoarse and wild with excitement.' No one knew how the false rumor got started, but for a time that evening they marched believing that their beloved McClellan was once again leading them into battle. The men were intensely keyed up. Later there would be a rumor that the spirit of George Washington was accompanying them, riding on a white horse.

"It was a night that Gerrish always remembered. He wrote, 'The people rushed from their homes and stood by the roadside to welcome us, men, women, and children all gazing on the strange spectacle. Bands played, the soldiers and the people cheered, banners waved, and white handkerchiefs fluttered from doors and windows, as the blue, dusty column surged on.'

"But as the evening wore on, excitement gave way to weariness. The cheering died away. Many of the men began to stagger, half asleep on their feet. They had now marched over twenty-five miles. Some time after midnight a halt was called and they got two or three hours' sleep, lying in the dust and the dew beside the road.

"Around four-thirty the sun came up red, indicating another hot day. They arose, dazed and stiff, and continued the march. Arriving on some level, open ground, the two divisions of the Fifth Corps then present

* Bruce Catton, *This Hallowed Ground*, p. 251.

formed as though for a grand review, with colors unfurled, lines dressed, pieces at the right shoulder. Detail cleared away fences in front, and they advanced in formation—great blocks of dusty blue, with the flags and the shimmer of steel over them in the morning light. There was a remarkable stillness in the ranks, broken only by low-voiced commands and the swishing of legs through growing grain, hay, and low bushes. Coming to the crest of a knoll, they saw a group of rough, wooded hills ahead, with the brown scars of earthworks on them . . . wagon and artillery parks . . . rows of stacked muskets where troops were resting . . . other evidences that they were in the rear of a battle line.

"East of the hills, the Fifth Corps division maneuvered into a line facing generally north, and there was a lot of waiting and standing around. Officers got out in front of their regiments and read an order from General Meade. A number of phrases filtered through to tired brains . . . 'enemy are on our soil . . . whole country now looks anxiously to this army to deliver it . . . homes, firesides and domestic altars are involved.' It sounded pretty serious. And then came a grim and remarkable sentence that made them realize just how serious it was. 'Corps and other commanders are authorized to order the instant death of any soldier who fails in his duty at this hour.'

"Later in the forenoon the corps moved, crossed a creek, and went into a reserve position in a field just off the Baltimore Pike near an orchard. The town and the scene of yesterday's fighting were not visible, being hidden by the hills and some woods on high ground west of them. They could see a lot of activity. Ambulances coming up. Staff officers riding furiously on mysterious errands. Wagons distributing ammunition. But aside from the occasional boom of a cannon, it seemed mighty peaceful for a battlefield.

"The men stretched out and got some much needed rest. It felt good to have the earth pressing against the back instead of the feet. They dozed off. From off behind the hills and the woods, someone began popping corn. First one kernel went pop. Then others softly—pop, pop, pop, pop, p-p-p-popopopopopopop—the sound of musketry, muffled by heat, distance and intervening terrain. The sound started in the northwest, then ran around to the west and finally died away. A few eyes opened, then closed. It was just skirmish firing. The men of the 20th Maine dozed and slept. The scent of trampled and crushed grass rose around them. Summer breathed hot on their upturned faces. It was quiet at Gettysburg."*

---

* From John J. Pullen, *The Twentieth Maine*, pp. 95, 96, 97.

Gettysburg: Second Day*

BY JOHN J. PULLEN

WHILE THE TIRED SOLDIERS of the 20th Maine slept behind Powers Hill, the stage was being set for their entrance, and various actors were moving about in the wings.

Chief of these was Major General George Gordon Meade, former Fifth Corps commander, now commanding general of the Army of the Potomac. Meade was not a spectacular leader but he was a safe one, and a man of character—not given to throwing soldiers' lives away needlessly. This seems to have been a virtue that had impressed the men of the 20th Maine. Private Theodore Gerrish described Meade thus: "He had not the dashing appearance of many other generals, but when we saw that tall, bowed form, enveloped in a great brown overcoat, riding to the front, we always felt safe." Gerrish also remembered that Meade appeared to be continually bent over by the great burdens placed upon his shoulders; as the General rode along "he always seemed to be looking upon the ground, at a point about twenty yards in advance of him."

This overborne appearance, combined with sharp eyes, a deeply lined face, and a large Roman nose, usually gave Meade the look of a tired eagle, but on this morning of July 2, somewhere between eight and nine o'clock, as he came out of the little house in the rear of Cemetery Ridge serving as his headquarters, he was wearing a cheerful face, relatively speaking. Captain George Meade, his son and aide, said that "to one who was familiar with the general's manner and tones of voice in different moods he seemed in excellent spirits, as if well pleased with affairs as far as they had proceeded."

And well he might be pleased. In falling back from their defeat west and north of the town on the previous day, the First Corps and the Eleventh Corps had occupied and held excellent ground. Arriving on the field shortly after midnight, General Meade had found them dug in and reinforced on hills south of Gettysburg. Now the rest of the army, with the exception of one corps, had arrived and had occupied more of the high ground.

The line, as planned by Meade that morning, looked like a big fishhook. The hook itself, with point to the east, lay on a group of rather steep hills just south of the village. The long shank of the hook ran south along a ridge known as Cemetery Ridge. The eye of the shank was supposed to rest upon a rough, rocky hill called Little Round Top. Opposite Cemetery Ridge, on Seminary Ridge about a mile to the west, and curv-

* From Pullen, *op. cit.*

ing through the town of Gettysburg, lay the Confederate line. It was longer than the Union line; troops had to be moved farther in any maneuvers along it. With higher ground, with shorter interior lines, Meade had the advantage.

But things started to go wrong for him, and there were hints of trouble early in the day. The southernmost corps in line was the Third Corps, commanded by Major General Daniel E. Sickles. Sickles was a brave officer, affectionately regarded by his men, but he was a "political general," and the West Pointers were inclined to look upon him with a certain amount of suspicion. General Meade told his son, Captain Meade, to go down and see what Sickles was doing. Captain Meade rode down the Taneytown Road and came upon the temporary headquarters of the Third Corps in a patch of woods west of the road. He was told that General Sickles had been up all night and was now in his tent resting; that the Third Corps was not in position; and that General Sickles didn't know exactly where he was supposed to go.

Captain Meade thereupon galloped hastily back to army headquarters and told his father of this seeming indecision on the part of General Sickles. In Meade's mind the picture was clear; the shank of the fishhook was to run straight south; half that shank was the Second Corps; and below it, resting its left upon Little Round Top, the Third Corps. Sharply and decisively, he told Captain Meade to gallop back to Sickles again and tell him that his instructions were to go into position on the left of the Second Corps. His right was to connect with the Second Corps and he was to prolong the line of that corps, occupying the "position that General Geary had held the night before."

Back down the Taneytown Road rode Captain Meade once more. At General Sickles' headquarters, he found the tents struck, staff officers hustling about, and a movement of some sort under way. General Sickles, a thick-set man with a large head, full round face and heavy moustache, was sitting on his horse. There are good days and bad days, depending on your name, and for the name Dan Sickles July 2, 1863, wasn't going to be a good day. It was starting wrong already. The commanding general of the army had assigned his corps to an area that he, Sickles, considered completely indefensible. Cemetery Ridge was no ridge at all here. It sank away into low ground, with high ground a few hundred yards in front, where Sickles believed the enemy could plant artillery and make his own position untenable.

And now here was this young whippersnapper of an aide telling him something about getting into a position held by General Geary on the night before, and implying that he ought to be quick about it. However, it is politic to be civil to a general's aide, particularly if the aide is the general's son, and Sickles told young Meade that his troops were then moving and would be in position shortly. But he also muttered that General Geary had no battle position the night before; his troops were merely massed in that vicinity. Captain Meade rode back to army headquarters, where it was assumed that Sickles now knew where he was supposed to place his men, and was acting accordingly.

Around eleven o'clock, General Sickles appeared briefly at Meade's headquarters. He was fussing about his position. Meade went over it again with him, explaining that Sickles' corps was to prolong the line of the Second Corps down toward Little Round Top. Reference was apparently made again to the position as that held by General Geary the night before and Sickles said Geary hadn't had any position, and so on and so on. Sickles wanted to know if he couldn't use his own judgment in posting his corps and Meade said, "Certainly, within the limits of the general instructions I have given you; any ground within those limits you choose to occupy, I leave to you."

Sickles then got General Hunt, the army chief of artillery, to accompany him back to his area to have a look at the ground. A Confederate attack would be—Sickles thought—disastrous if he remained where he was. What did Hunt think about that ridge of high ground out in front? Wouldn't that be a better position for Sickles' artillery? Shouldn't Sickles move his corps out there? Hunt advised him to wait for orders before making any such move. Later Hunt went back to army headquarters and reported that the advanced position Sickles was contemplating had some good points and some bad ones—and that if he were the commanding general he wouldn't put troops out there until he had gone and looked it over for himself. About this time there was a disturbance over to the right, and this seems to have given Meade and Hunt something else to think about.

At about the same time—farther to the south, out to the west and southwest of the Round Tops—another loose end was coming unraveled. Here General John Buford was patrolling with two brigades of cavalry. Buford and his men had brought the Confederates to their first halt on the day before and had stood them off until the Union infantry corps arrived. They had continued to fight beside the infantrymen all day, taking heavy losses. Now they were out of rations and forage. Many of the horses had thrown their shoes and were unfit for service.

Buford had sent word of all this to his superior, General Alfred Pleasonton, the cavalry chief. Pleasonton, and General Dan Butterfield, now army chief of staff, had apparently given Meade the impression that other cavalry was immediately available to replace Buford. Pleasonton now reported that Buford wanted to go to the rear and refit, since the rest of the army was nearly all up. All right, said Meade, let Buford go as a guard with the army trains back to Westminster and refit there. Meade assumed that Pleasonton would substitute other cavalry for Buford's, so that this watchful and protective screen in front of the army's left would be maintained. This Pleasonton failed to do. And Butterfield—fine composer of bugle calls, great designer of badges and banners, but right at this moment somewhat lacking in the qualities of a desirable chief of staff—failed to see that Pleasonton had slipped up.

So Buford moved back and no one went out in his place. From this area, out beyond the Round Tops, the Union left was now open to surprise and to a sudden, smashing attack of troops in mass.

The blow was on the way. It had been under consideration for several hours, and it was the first move over which Robert E. Lee exercised personal direction. The fight of the day before had been one that had boiled up from a chance encounter when advanced elements of the two armies had run into one another near Gettysburg. But now General Lee was taking charge. And if one would believe Longstreet's account, Lee was like a man who saw a fateful struggle ahead of him, and who knew that he could postpone it, perhaps to a more favorable time and place, but who found further waiting intolerable. Arriving at Gettysburg at five o'clock on the afternoon of July 1, Longstreet had found his chief on Seminary Ridge, watching the Union forces taking positions on the opposite height of land after their initial defeat. Lee had pointed out the Union positions. Longstreet had raised his glasses and studied the landscape for five or ten minutes, intently, for there were questions of life and death in every patch of woods, every ridge or hollow of the ground, and if men were going to get killed out there, they had better get killed advantageously. It seemed to Longstreet that the big decision hinged on a couple of round-topped hills that stuck up starkly on the south end of what appeared to be the Union line.

Longstreet lowered his glasses and proposed a plan: Move way around those hills. Get behind the Union left. Get between Meade's army and Washington, in a strong defensive position. Then Meade would attack, and on ground of Lee's expert choosing the Union army could be badly beaten. Or if Meade did not attack immediately, they could pick another strong position nearer Washington and move to it at night. Then Meade —and Washington too—would be frantic. The Union army would be forced to attack, into some trap of the terrain that Lee could set.

But Robert E. Lee, ordinarily as composed as steel and stone, had been gripped in a fixity of purpose that, for the good gray general, seemed almost like a passion. Lee had struck the air with his clenched fist and declared, "The enemy is there, and I am going to attack him there."

Once again Longstreet had urged his scheme, pointing out that the move around the Union left would give Lee control of the roads to Washington and Baltimore. But Lee had vehemently declared, "No; they are there in position, and I am going to whip them or they are going to whip me."

And again on the following morning—July 2—Longstreet had proposed that the army move all the way around the Round Tops to Meade's left and rear. But the great commander still would not listen.

Lee's plan was to attack frontally with part of his army, while Longstreet's Corps made a concealed movement to the right, falling upon the Union left flank and driving it in. Once in position on Meade's flank, Longstreet was to attack in a northeasterly direction, guiding his left on the Emmitsburg Road.

After a long delay—Longstreet waiting for one of his brigades, Law's, to come up—the flanking move finally got under way around eleven o'clock in the forenoon. Longstreet was lacking Pickett's Division, but with the two big divisions of Hood and McLaw's he still had a massive force. The corps started moving south, keeping behind Seminary Ridge and other high ground in order to avoid observation from Union signal units on Little Round Top. Longstreet was in a bad mood, deeply resenting the fact that his recommendations had been disregarded. He was further exacerbated when it began to appear that the route reconnaissance, performed by one of Lee's engineer officers, had been done badly, resulting in many halts and countermarches. And Longstreet had another grumble. Stuart, who with his cavalry was supposed to be the eyes and ears of the army, was off galloping around somewhere miles away from Gettysburg. The little cavalry that remained with the army was elsewhere on the field. Here where Longstreet was making his move, not so much as one trooper was available to precede him. In the absence of cavalry, Longstreet ordered General Hood, one of his division commanders, to send out picked scouts in advance, so that the infantry would not be walking into the area entirely blind.

With many troublesome delays, Longstreet's column moved south. It got to be one and two and three o'clock, and they still had not arrived at the attack position.

Back at the little house behind Cemetery Ridge, Meade's headquarters, a conference was called, to assemble shortly after three. The battle of Gettysburg was a great one for conferences and consultations on the Union side, and the corps commanders were arriving to talk things over. But the conference didn't last long. Major General Gouverneur K. Warren, Meade's chief of engineers, came in with a report to the effect that General Sickles had advanced his corps and was way out of position. Warren made this startling disclosure to General Meade.

It was now somewhere around three-thirty. Longstreet's sweating infantrymen were coming into position on a low ridge slanting across the Emmitsburg Road. Ahead of them on their right, they saw the Round Tops. Ahead, and much closer on their left, a peach orchard, and here there was a surprise—Yankee guns and infantry in the orchard, also extending up the Emmitsburg Road. From the peach orchard, the Union line seemed to angle back toward the Round Tops. It was Sickles' Corps, thrust out in a salient, with one arm facing generally west, the other southwest. If Sickles' move had seemed questionable to Meade's staff officers, it now seemed devilishly inconvenient for the Confederate commanders. Their orders were to attack up the Emmitsburg Road. But here was a strong force of bluecoats to overcome before they could even start.

The situation began to look more favorable, however, when reports came back from the scouts that Hood had sent out. The reports said that the Round Tops were unoccupied, and this whole area seemed to be lightly, if at all, defended. The scouts had climbed Big Round Top and, looking down, had seen Union wagon trains parked just east of the hills.

General Hood now urged Longstreet to alter the course of the attack so as to move around Big Round Top and come in on the Union left and rear. This was, substantially, what Longstreet had wanted Lee to do with the whole army. But Longstreet was now sullen—and stubborn. Lee's orders were to attack up the Emmitsburg Road. Well, then, they would attack up the Emmitsburg Road.

With McLaws' Division preparing to advance on the peach orchard, Hood took his division far to the right in order to envelop the southward-facing arm of Sickles' salient and be in position to strike at the undefended Round Tops.

At headquarters, Army of the Potomac, the conference of corps commanders had broken up with explosive suddenness. First had come Warren's report of Sickles' new and highly original position. Then from far
over on the left, cannonading and a few rattles of musketry had been
heard. And now to the conference came General Sickles, having previously been detained. Meade told him not to get off his horse. He told
General George Sykes, the Fifth Corps commander, to go get his corps
and move it over there to the left. General Sykes, a little man with a big
nose and a fine suit of whiskers, flew off to rouse up the Fifth Corps, still
resting in rear of Powers Hill. Meade then told General Sickles to get
back to his corps and he would follow him and see just what the situation
was. Even though prepared by Warren's report, Meade was shocked,
when he arrived, to see how far forward Sickles had actually posted the
Third Corps—entirely disconnected from the rest of the army and far
out beyond the possibility of support from existing positions.

General Sickles was deeply sorry. He said that he would withdraw his
troops. Meade replied, "Yes, you may as well, at once. The enemy will
not let you withdraw without taking advantage of your position, but
you have to come back, and you may as well do it at once as at any
other time."

General Sickles turned to give the necessary orders; just then Longstreet's cannoneers pulled their lanyards and the sky smashed over the
Emmitsburg Road. It was now too late to withdraw. Meade told Sickles
to hold on and do the best he could and that some way or other he would
be supported. A projectile shrieked past. Meade's mount reared, plunged
and went crazy. Meade was carried from the scene on a runaway horse—
the final touch of frustration. It was now around four o'clock.

Meanwhile, General Gouverneur K. Warren had arrived on the summit of Little Round Top to play his big part, on his Big Day in history.
A slight, dark, intense officer who bore a faint resemblance to Edgar
Allan Poe, Warren had come to this elevated point to see what was going
on out there beyond the Round Tops to the west. The hill was unoccupied
except for a few signalmen. Since he was a military engineer, Warren
presumably had recognized the importance of Little Round Top long
before this. But he had not realized that it was completely undefended,
and this discovery was highly disturbing. He also saw that off to the west
there was a long line of woods, which made an excellent concealment for
the enemy. Acting on a sudden inspiration, Warren sent word down to
a battery emplaced on a smaller hill below (Devil's Den) where Sickles
line ended, and asked the artillerymen to fire a shot into the woods. The
projectile, flying among the trees, caused the Confederate infantrymen
to look upward, and the corresponding gleam of reflected sunlight on
shifting rifle barrels and bayonets revealed their position to Warren. It
also gave him a nasty shock. For here was a long line of battle that would
far outflank the Union left when it advanced. With a thrill of mortal
danger, Warren saw what would happen. The right of Longstreet's attack
would sweep over Little Round Top. With this point in their possession,
the Confederates would have the key to the battlefield. Starting here they
could enfilade and roll up the Union line in a wholesale disaster. Troops
here would be in command of the vital Taneytown Road. And if Meade's

troops were routed, Lee would be between them and Washington, a most embarrassing possibility, in the light of Meade's orders from that city.

There was only one thing to do: get some soldiers up here as soon as the Lord would let him. Warren sent an aide flying off to find Meade and request at least a division. He sent another down to Sickles asking for a brigade. Sickles had to say no. He had enough fighting to do right where he was. By now the attack had begun and Longstreet was starting to smash in his salient with an overwhelming violence that was to cost Sickles his corps and his right leg. (The Third Corps was practically destroyed. The leg, shattered by a shell, had to be amputated. General Sickles sent it to the Army Medical Museum, where the bones can be seen today. Sickles used to visit the museum and stand for minutes at a time, looking at his bones and thinking—no doubt—about the day that was not his day at Gettysburg.)

So there was no help to be expected from Sickles. But help was at hand from another source—the Fifth Corps which General Sykes had started forward at Meade's order. The reconnaissance officers and advance elements of the Fifth Corps were now appearing, passing north of Little Round Top, and going out to the support of Sickles.

The leading brigade was Vincent's, and right near the front was the 20th Regiment Infantry, Maine Volunteers.

Summoned to support the unhooked and unhinged salient of General Sickles, the 1st Division of the Fifth Corps had marched rapidly toward the firing. The 20th Maine, near the head of the column in Vincent's Brigade, reached the edge of a wheatfield, where the brigade halted momentarily to await instructions.

The woods ahead, beyond the field and out toward the Emmitsburg Road, was roaring and smoking; tiny flashes of lightning winked over the treetops, changing instantly to lazily drifting puffballs; the ground shook, and underneath was the sound of musketry, the shrill piping of far-off yells and the almost human screams of horses being struck in the short-range artillery duel.

But Colonel Chamberlain and his Maine soldiers didn't have long to look, or listen. Warren's call for help was being directed to Colonel Vincent, their brigade commander. A staff officer came dashing up to Vincent, and the focus of attention suddenly shifted to the left and rear. There was a great deal of shouting and pointing at Little Round Top— an ugly, rock-strewn hill with woods all over it except on the western face. Vincent turned his horse and made for the hill with an urgent squeak of saddle leather, leaving word for the brigade to follow. His standard-bearer galloped after him. Chamberlain and the others saw the two horsemen try to ride up the northwest face of Little Round Top, but it was too rough; they couldn't make it. They then skirted the northern foot of the hill and disappeared in the woods behind the crest. The triangular flag with its red Maltese cross flashed once or twice between the trees. Near it, a shellburst blossomed with a growling roar. The Confederates, too, had their eye on Little Round Top. The artillery fire intensified as the brigade, following Vincent, scrambled up the lower gradient of the hill. In this movement, the 20th Maine now came last.

Three Chamberlain brothers were riding abreast: Colonel Joshua; Tom, now a lieutenant acting as adjutant; and another brother, John Chamberlain, who had arrived at Gettysburg with the Christian Commission and who had chosen to go along with the 20th Maine to help the chaplain and the ambulance men. A large, unseen object swished past their faces. Said the Colonel, "Boys, I don't like this. Another such shot might make it hard for mother. Tom, go to the rear of the regiment, and see that it is well closed up! John, pass up ahead and look out a place for our wounded."

The regiment scrambled up the northern face of the hill under a heavy artillery fire from the Confederates. Shells were bursting among the trees and on the rocks and there were miserable slashing and humming sounds in the air—fragments of iron and splintered stone flying, sliced-off branches tumbling down. Mounted officers got off their horses, sending the animals to sheltered positions in the rear. The Maine men turned south behind the summit, getting some protection from the crest, and on the southern slope of the hill they found Colonel Strong Vincent putting the brigade into line of battle.

Within the fifteen minutes or so available, Vincent was doing one of the war's best jobs of reconnaissance, selection and occupation of position. His regiments were following him in this order:

> 44th New York
> 16th Regiment
> 83rd Pennsylvania
> 20th Maine

Vincent had chosen a line of defense that would start on the west slope of Little Round Top and continue around the hill in a quarter circle—not on the crest, but well below it. As the regiments arrived, he put them into line carefully, even taking time to defer to a whim voiced by Colonel James C. Rice, commander of the 44th New York. The 44th and the 83rd Pennsylvania were known as Butterfield's Twins, and going into line in the order in which they were arriving, the two regiments would be separated by the 16th Michigan. Colonel Rice had a seizure of superstition or sentiment, and he said to Vincent, "Colonel, the 83rd and 44th have always fought side by side in every battle, and I wish they may do the same today."

He was accommodated. The 16th marched past the 44th and took position first, on the west slope. The Twins, following, went into line side by side, curving around the hill. Coming up last in the column, the 20th Maine extended the formation to the east, and Vincent told Chamberlain, "This is the left of the Union line. You understand. You are to hold this ground at all costs!"

Chamberlain ordered his regiment in "on the right by file into line." This was a slow maneuver, made even more awkward by the rough ground, rocks and trees, but it anchored the right of the 20th firmly to the left of the 83rd, and each man was ready to commence firing as soon as he came into position. They now saw that they were on the brink of a smooth, shallow valley, lightly forested and strewn with rocks. Across this valley to the south, facing them: Big Round Top, gigantic, covered with forest and huge boulders, apparently impassable. On their right, the rest of the brigade.

On the left, nothing!

Chamberlain was looking off in that direction, studiously. To his men it afterward seemed that the Colonel had the ability to see through forests and hills and to know what was coming. This apparently magical gift of great infantry officers was something that Chamberlain had caught on to; it was merely a matter of studying the terrain closely, imagining all kinds of horrible things that might happen, and planning counter-measures in advance.

Knowing that he had no support on the left, Chamberlain sent Company B, commanded by Captain Walter G. Morrill, out in that direction to guard his exposed flank and act as the necessities of the battle would require. Chamberlain didn't know quite what these necessities would be, but he knew Morrill and he was the sort of fellow who would do something and probably do it right.

Holding the left of the entire four-or-five mile Union line, the 20th Maine had stepped, all unawares, into the spotlight of history. Off to the west, Sickles' salient was caving in. Up from the south was coming the powerful right hook of Longstreet's attack. If this point failed, the Confederates would be smashing into the rear of a Union line that was already wildly confused by a massive frontal attack. Robert E. Lee and the Confederacy were never so close to victory.

So here on this hidden corner of the battlefield, one of the world's decisive small-unit military actions was about to begin. And upon this spot were converging many chains of cause and effect- starting from previous events that had seemed, in their time, unimportant.

When Hood's Division swung across the Emmitsburg Road and prepared to attack, its right brigade, Law's Alabamians, had already marched twenty-eight miles since 3 A.M. In the 15th Alabama, canteens were empty and the men were thirsty. A detail of twenty-two men collected all the canteens and started for a well a hundred yards or so to the rear to fill them and return. But before they could get back the advance started. As the Alabama brigade approached Big Round Top, the men saw near the western foot of the hill what appeared to be a small regiment in an advanced position. These Yankees were beyond good shooting range, but puffs of smoke appeared from among them and Alabama soldiers began to fall in alarming numbers. Later they were to learn that this regiment was the 2nd U. S. Sharpshooters. Including a company of Maine marksmen, as well as sharpshooters from other states, this was a group of men who could each put ten consecutive shots into a target at six hundred feet with an average distance from the center of less than five inches. Against this deadly fire, one of Law's regiments almost broke, but they rallied and the brigade swept on, a long line of veterans in sun-bleached gray, bayonets shining, color staffs slanting forward, the flags of the Confederacy flickering above them. When they got to where they could start giving it back to the Yankees, the sharpshooters suddenly withdrew; part of them went back to a little hill on the left (Devil's Den) and the other part ran up Big Round Top and disappeared among the trees and boulders.

From this position the sharpshooters began sniping again at the right flank of the Confederate advance. On this wing in command of the 15th Alabama, with the 47th Alabama also acting under his direction, was Colonel William C. Oates, a mustachioed and bewhiskered officer who was both courageous and perceptive. Not wanting to go on and leave the hornet's nest of sharpshooters in his rear, Oates ordered the advance to extend to the right, up over Big Round Top, to clear his flank. It was a brutal climb. (It's an exhausting climb today on the smooth path the Park Service has built.) For infantrymen who had already marched twenty-eight miles, who had to climb over boulders and through brush, who were laden with arms and ammunition, and who had to fight dead-shot Yankees on the way, it was an ordeal. Several fainted in the heat. But the sharpshooters finally disappeared, and the right of the 15th Alabama reached the top, where Colonel Oates told them to stop and rest.

Here they hoped the water-carriers would catch up with them. But the canteen party was destined never to arrive; it had walked into a concealed party of sharpshooters and had been captured to a man. The men of the 15th Alabama always thought that the loss of this water detail had a lot to do with losing the battle of Gettysburg.

During the break, Colonel Oates found a place on the summit from which he could peer through the heavy July foliage and get some idea of where he was, and what was going on. He was amazed at the prospect. He could see Gettysburg in the distance. He could see the battle smoke drifting up from Devil's Den and hear the racket of the fighting that was starting around Little Round Top. He realized that he was on the highest point in the neighborhood. It was like sitting high in a box seat, over-looking the flank of the Union line.

Oates also realized that he held what could be the key of the battlefield. Drag up some artillery, cut down a few trees to clear a field of fire, and he could command not only Little Round Top, but the whole Union line all the way up Cemetery Ridge. Oates was entranced with the idea of a position here on Big Round Top. He thought . . . "within half an hour I could convert it into a Gibraltar that I could hold against ten times the number of men that I had." A staff officer from Law, now act-ing division commander, came up and Oates urged a halt for the purpose of occupying Big Round Top; that, clearly, was the thing to do. The staff officer admitted that Oates was probably right, but their orders were to find and turn the left of the Union line, and the left of the Union line was not up here, it was down there on Little Round Top. And there was no time to go back and find someone with authority to change those orders. (The absence of general officers on this critical right end of the Confederate line was a deficiency that Oates was to deplore to his dying day.) But orders were orders, and so Oates told his weary men to get up and start down the slope of the hill toward Little Round Top.

As they were descending, Oates saw, only a few hundred yards away, the Federal trains, including an extensive park of ordnance wagons. If he could work his way a little farther east, he would be completely in the rear of Meade's army. By the time he reached the bottom of the hill,

Oates had moved his troops by the right flank and had them in a column of fours. Rapidly, the column headed eastward through the thinly wooded valley between the Round Tops. As soon as he got past the Union flank, Oates would bring his command to a "front" and go crashing into the Yankee rear in an attack that ought to start the Union left falling like a row of tenpins.

Back on Little Round Top, the men of the 20th Maine had been waiting. These minutes of inactivity would be almost intolerable, but blind instinct would be getting their bodies ready—blood beating harder and faster through the arteries; lungs seeming to dilate deep down, reaching for more oxygen; stomach and intestines shrinking and stopping all movement; and tension rising to the point where it could shake a man like the passage of a powerful electric current. When it came, any kind of action would be a relief—and the reaction would be explosive.

The Maine men had watched Morrill's Company B disappear into the trees on their left front, walking warily, rifles held high. Now they turned their attention to the right front, where the shallow valley opened out toward Devil's Den. There was a great commotion in that direction. Minié balls began to whistle through the branches overhead, twigs and leaves falling around them. An order ran along the line: *Come to the ready . . . take good aim. . . .* They heard volleys crash out from the rest of Vincent's Brigade on their right, followed by the frantic rattling of ramrods and the "thugging" of leaden cones being driven home in rifle barrels. They heard something else that raised the hair on the backs of their necks. It was a shrill, undulating yell—sharp and chilling as a winter wind, full of hate, exultation, and "Let's go get 'em!" It was the rebel yell, and they were coming on with a rush.

The order-in-line of the forces about to confront each other was as follows:

LAW'S BRIGADE (Plus 4th and 5th Texas)

CONFEDERATE RIGHT
15th Ala., 47th Ala., 4th Ala., 5th Tex., 4th Tex., 48th Ala., 44th Ala.

VINCENT'S BRIGADE

UNION LEFT
20th Maine, 83rd Pennsylvania, 44th New York, 16th Michigan

Neither was an actual straight line. The Union regiments were in a quarter circle around part of the hill. Of the Confederate regiments, the 15th Alabama and the 47th Alabama were behind the others, retarded by their climb over Big Round Top. The two Texas regiments didn't belong with Law's Brigade, but had got into the middle of it in a shuffle during the advance. The 44th Alabama did not come all the way to Little Round Top, but turned off and attacked Devil's Den.

The first troops the 20th Maine caught sight of were those of the 4th Alabama—fierce, lean men who were charging up the hill on their right, then drawing back as the fire of the rest of the Union brigade came out at them, then extending farther up the valley. They soon reached the right front of the 20th Maine and the regiment opened fire. Confined in the rocky valley, the noise became a continuously re-echoing roar, punctuated with the spanging of soft lead on stones and the yowling of ricochets. The attacking force gradually covered the entire front of the 20th Maine, and the smoke of the firing grew thick, hanging in the sultry air.

But this fighting had no more than started when Lieutenant James H. Nichols, commanding Company K, ran up to tell Colonel Chamberlain that something very strange was going on *behind* the attacking Confederate line. Mounting a rock, Chamberlain saw a solid gray mass advancing along the valley toward his left, partially screened by the smoke and the fighting already in progress on his front.

This was Oates and his flanking column. By itself, it was a large force, outnumbering the 20th Maine almost two to one, and the sight gave Chamberlain a real jolt. What did the book say to do, in a situation like this?

The order-in-line of the 20th Maine companies (less Company B, detached as skirmishers and now presumably cut off by the Confederate flanking column) was as represented here:

Colors

Left G C H A F D K I E

In the face of the impending flank attack, the obvious countermove was to change front with the whole regiment, in order to face to the left and thus guard the flank of the brigade against the heavy assault that would presently be coming in from that direction. But Chamberlain quickly saw that this wouldn't work. The 20th Maine was on a spur of high ground extending out from Little Round Top. In changing front, in order to keep his right in contact with the 83rd Pennsylvania, Chamberlain would have to swing the whole regiment back. This would relinquish part of the high ground to the enemy. Also, much of the 20th Maine was already participating in the fire-fight that had involved the rest of the brigade.

Rejecting the obvious maneuver, Chamberlain called his company commanders and gave them instructions that were completely fantastic, considering the fact that the regiment was already under fire. Chamberlain decided to move the left wing (left half) of the regiment to the left and rear, facing it at right angles with the original line. Meanwhile the right wing would extend itself by taking intervals to the left and forming a single rank, so that the regiment would stand thus:

F   D   K   I   E

A

H

C

G

As the left wing moved, the right wing was instructed to stay in contact with it, the men taking side steps to the left, meanwhile keeping up their fire to the front, without regard to the effect or whether or not the fire was needed. This would tend to conceal the movement.

The plan was executed in a way that never thereafter ceased to be a source of wonder to the officers of the 20th Maine. With bullets smashing into it, and the roar of gunfire making commands inaudible, the regiment writhed and twisted into the new formation like a single, living organism responding to a sense of imminent danger. Or—it was almost as though every man had been party to a quiet conference, where everything had been diagrammed and perfectly understood. On the right wing, men were firing, shouting, dodging from rock to rock and tree to tree, and gradually forming a single rank that covered the entire original front of the regiment. Chamberlain remembered that while this was going on there seemed to be no slackening of fire on that front.

Meanwhile the men of the bent-back wing were forming a solid line facing to the left, taking what concealment they could find behind rocks and undergrowth. Their presence came as a grievous surprise to the 15th Alabama.

When the Alabamians came to a front and charged up on what had been a few moments before an unguarded flank, the Maine men rose above the rocks and a volley flashed out that lighted all the fires of hell in that hot, shadowed backyard of the battle. At close range, it was a deadly blast, followed by hoarse screams, the sound of bodies falling in the bushes, the clatter of rifles dropped on the rocks by stricken men. Broken by the fire, the Alabama charge stopped momentarily. But these were hard men and they came on again, this time right up into the Maine line. Squads of them bayoneted their way through and had to be disposed of in horrid hand-to-hand grappling. The Maine men hadn't fixed bayonets; they clubbed their muskets and chopped with them like axes.

No one could ever describe this part of the fight coherently, or tell just how long it lasted. From here on everything was a medley of monstrous noises and a blur . . . muzzle-flashes blazing . . . gray forms appearing through the smoke . . . faces looming up with red, open, yelling mouths ringed with the black of cartridge biting . . . strangled animal sounds . . . and the queer-sounding resonances of skulls struck by musket butts. Chamberlain remembered that "the edge of conflict swayed to and fro, with wild whirlpools and eddies. At times I saw around me more of the enemy than of my own men; gaps opening, swallowing, closing again with sharp convulsive energy; squads of stalwart men who had cut their way through us, disappearing as if translated. All around, strange, mingled roar. . . ."

Somehow, the line held, in one form or another, although the fighting was raging up and down in such a way that often no definite line could be seen. Nearly everyone but the hospital attendants of the 20th Maine were in ranks, and all were fighting like madmen. One young fellow was cut down with a ghastly wound across the forehead, and Chamberlain, thinking that he might be saved with prompt attention, sent him to the rear. Soon he saw him in the fight again with a bloody bandage around his head.

George Washington Buck, a boy who had been unjustly reduced to private at Stoneman's Switch, made sergeant again. Chamberlain came across Private Buck lying on his back, tearing his shirt away from his chest. What he saw convinced him—and the Colonel—that there wasn't much time left. Chamberlain bent over him and told him that he was promoting him to sergeant on the spot. Sergeant Buck was carried to the rear and died shortly afterward.

There were other transformations in the flame of battle. Two mutineers from the 2nd Maine, who were being held with the regiment as prisoners awaiting court-martial, chose this moment to return to duty. Picking up rifles, the two 2nd Mainers waded into the fray and laid about them so lustily that Chamberlain resolved to get the charges against them dropped if he survived.

And the Colonel saw something else he was always to remember—a grouping that could have been a model for the sort of heroic statuary that came out of the war to adorn village squares. "I saw through a sudden rift in the thick smoke our colors standing alone. I first thought some optical illusion imposed upon me. But as forms emerged through the drifting smoke, the truth came to view. The cross-fire had cut keenly; the center had been almost shot away; only two of the color guard had been left, and they fighting to fill the whole space; and in the center, wreathed in battle smoke, stood the color-sergeant, Andrew Tozier. His color staff planted in the ground at his side, the upper part clasped in his elbow, so holding the flag upright, with musket and cartridges seized from the fallen comrade at his side he was defending his sacred trust in the manner of the songs of chivalry."

The fight was seen through many eyes, but all seem to have seen it through the same red, smoky haze. Private Gerrish described the action where Company H was fighting, out on the bent-back wing. "If a rock promised shelter, down went a man behind it, and a rifle barrel gleamed and flamed above it. Every tree was also utilized, but a great majority of the troops were not thus provided for. As the moments passed the conflict thickened; the cartridge boxes were pulled around in front and left open; the cartridges were torn out and crowded into the smoking muzzles of the guns with a terrible rapidity. The steel rammers clashed and clanged in barrels heated with burning powder."

Gerrish saw the first sergeant, Charles W. Steele, stagger up to the company commander with a big hole in his chest. "I am going, Captain," the sergeant reported. In reply, Captain Joseph F. Land shouted, "My God, Sergeant!" and sprang to catch him, but too late, and Steele was dead by the time his body struck the ground. Another sergeant, Isaac N. Lathrop—a giant of a man—went crashing down with a mortal wound. Gerrish recalled that "of twenty-eight of that company, fifteen were either killed or wounded, and in other companies the slaughter had been equally as great. Not only on the crest of the hill, among the blue coats, was blood running in little rivulets and forming crimson pools, but in the gray ranks of the assailants there had also been a fearful destruction."

The 20th Maine had sixty rounds per man, and in the relatively short time of an hour or an hour and a half, they fired nearly every round. This meant that over twenty thousand bullets went out, and many more than that came back, slashing across the valley, flattening on rocks and flying in tearing ricochets.

Trees on the slope were gashed and peppered with white scars up to a height of six feet. One three- or four-inch tree in front of the left of Company F was gnawed completely off about two feet off the ground, the ragged edges of the cut showing that it had been made by bullets and not by a shell.

Everywhere, men going down . . .

Colonel Oates of the 15th Alabama saw a bullet strike Captain J. Henry Ellison in the head. "He fell upon his left shoulder, turned upon his back, raised his arms, clenched his fists, gave one shudder, his arms fell, and he was dead."

And then more of his officers falling . . . "Captain Brainard, one of the bravest and best officers in the regiment, in leading his company forward, fell, exclaiming, 'O, God! that I could see my mother' and instantly expired. Lieutenant John A. Oates, my dear brother, succeeded to the command of the company, but was pierced through by a number of bullets, and fell mortally wounded. Lieutenant Cody fell mortally wounded, Captain Bethune and several other officers were seriously wounded, while the carnage in the ranks was appalling."

And later, "My dead and wounded were then nearly as great in number as those still on duty. They literally covered the ground. The blood stood in puddles in some places on the rocks. . . ."

There were charges and countercharges up and down the slope. Colonel Oates believed that he drove the Federals from their position five times, and each time they rallied and drove back, twice coming to the point of hand-to-hand combat. He remembered that once "a Maine man reached to grasp the staff of the colors when Ensign Archibald stepped back and Sergeant Pat O'Connor stove his bayonet through the head of the Yankee, who fell dead."

Then came a lull when the Confederates drew back temporarily, and the Maine soldiers could have agreed with Oates that the scene had taken on a decidedly reddish tinge. The 20th had lost almost a third of its strength. They saw their dead and wounded out in front of them, mingled with those of the enemy. During the countercharges they had been scattered all the way down the slope to the very feet of the enemy, now rallying for another attempt.

Across the valley, a Confederate soldier saw Colonel Chamberlain standing by himself, in the open, behind the center of the 20th Maine's line. It was evident from Chamberlain's uniform and his actions that he was an important officer, well worth a careful shot. The soldier found himself a place between two big rocks, rested his rifle over one of them and looked at Chamberlain over the sights, taking steady aim. When he started to pull the trigger, a queer feeling came over him and he stopped. Ashamed of himself, he once again lined up his sights, but for some reason that he couldn't explain, he was unable to pull the trigger. Years later, he wrote to Chamberlain saying he was glad that he hadn't fired and he hoped that Chamberlain was too.

Over on the right of the 20th Maine, the rest of Vincent's Brigade had been holding its own. The right wing had almost broken once but was rallied by Colonel Vincent himself, and the 140th New York had arrived in time to hurl back the Confederate attack at this point. But Vincent had fallen with a bullet in his left groin, saying as they carried him back, "This is the fourth or fifth time they have shot at me, and they have hit me at last." On this western part of Little Round Top, Hazlett's Battery had also arrived, and the men of the 20th Maine could hear Hazlett's guns pounding, with heavy musketry also telling of desperate fighting. There was no hope of assistance from that quarter. The left of the 20th Maine had now been bent so far back that bullets from the attacking Confederates were falling into the rest of the brigade from the rear. The acting adjutant of the 83rd Pennsylvania came dodging and scrambling over to Chamberlain, wanting to know if his left had been turned.

Chamberlain sent word to Captain O. S. Woodward, commander of the 83rd, that the enemy was pushing his left back almost double upon his right and asked for a company. Woodward replied that he couldn't spare a company, but if the 20th Maine would pull its right companies to the left, he would move over and fill up the gap.

This move was made and brought some relief, but the 20th Maine had been bent back so far that it was in the rear of the army, in rear of the brigade, and in rear of itself. Let it give way in another Confederate charge, and Lee might be rolling up the Army of the Potomac like a rug.

And that was not the worst. There were hoarse cries of "Ammunition!" up and down the line, and soldiers were scrambling around looking for cartridges in the boxes of the dead and wounded. Chamberlain saw men fire their last rounds and then look back at him as if to say, "What now?"

The Colonel's alert brain ticked off the alternatives. The Confederates were gathering for another assault, but the 20th Maine couldn't withdraw; its orders were to hold the ground at all costs. He knew that they could not withstand another charge. And they couldn't continue the fire-fight for the reason that they had run out of ammunition. (Later Chamberlain figured that this was a good thing, for if they had continued, the enemy with superior numbers would have finished them off on a musket-to-musket basis.) Chamberlain decided that there was only one thing to do: fix bayonets and charge down into the Alabamians, hoping that surprise and shock action would drive them.

But here, too, there was a serious difficulty. With the left of the 20th Maine bent back so far, a charge might disperse the regiment or cause it to split in two at the angle. The left wing therefore had to begin the charge and swing around abreast of the right before the whole line could move forward. Colonel Chamberlain limped along the line, giving the necessary instructions. (His right instep had been cut by a flying shell fragment or rock splinter, and his left thigh had been badly bruised when a Minié ball bent his steel scabbard against it.)

As Chamberlain was returning to the center. Lieutenant Holman S. Melcher of Company F came up to him and asked permission to go out and get some of his wounded who lay between the 20th and the enemy line. To Melcher's surprise, the Colonel said, "Yes, sir. Take your place with your company. I am about to order a right wheel forward of the whole regiment."

Chamberlain stepped to the colors and his voice rang out. "Bayonet!" There was a moment of hesitation along the line, an intaking of breath like that of a man about to plunge into a cold, dark river. But along with it there was a rattling of bayonet shanks on steel. Intent on his wounded, Lieutenant Melcher sprang out in front of the line with his sword flashing, and this seems to have been the spark. The colors rose in front. A few men got up. Then a few more. They began to shout. The left wing, which was fighting off an attack at the time, suddenly charged, drove off its opponents and kept on until it had swung around abreast of the right wing. Then the regiment plunged down the slope in a great right wheel, Captain A. W. Clark's Company E holding the pivot against the 83rd Pennsylvania. To an officer of the 83rd, the 20th Maine looked as though it were moving "like a great gate upon a post."

The Confederate troops at the bottom of the slope were taken completely off guard. There were, perhaps, physical as well as psychological reasons to explain the apparent miracle that followed. The Confederates had been weakened by their strenuous approach march, thirst, and their efforts during the fighting. There was no time to fire a decisive volley and the Maine bayonets were shining in their faces almost before they knew what had happened. For a moment they fought in a daze. Then, before this roaring, downward-lunging assault, they gave backward and the affair took on the qualities of a dream. With one hand an Alabama officer fired a big revolver in Colonel Chamberlain's face, missed, and promptly handed over his sword with the other hand. Men were running, tripping, falling. The Confederate line broke up in confusion.

Farther on, the Alabamians made a stand with squads of the formidable 4th and 5th Texas, and it might have gone badly with the 20th Maine had there not been a fortuitous intervention. Even as the 20th Maine had been saving the army's left flank, so now it was itself about to be aided by one of its own fragments. This was Captain Morrill's Company B. After moving out as a skirmish party, Company B had not been heard from. Supposedly it had been cut off or captured by the sudden advance of the Alabamians. But the men of Company B had been very much alive all the while, hidden behind a stone wall. Now, having been joined by some of the sharpshooters that Oates had driven over Big Round Top, they rose up and fired a volley into the Confederate rear, at the same time making a loud demonstration.

The exhausted and staggered Alabamians were being pressed back by the charging Maine regiment in front—back so far that they were also receiving fire from the rest of the Yankee brigade on their left. And now, suddenly, bullets were coming from their right and rear. Morrill and his men had unleashed one of the most fearsome weapons of war—surprise, which explodes in the brain and destroys the power to reason. Oates saw a dreadful thing: men being shot in the face, while others beside them were being shot in the back, and still others were being struck by bullets coming simultaneously from two or three different directions. The growing panic that set in is traceable in the reports coming to Oates from his company commanders. In one of these reports Morrill's little band was magnified into two regiments. Another report had it that there was a line of dismounted Union cavalrymen in the Confederate rear, although there is no record of cavalrymen in the Little Round Top fight, either mounted or dismounted. Oates believed that he was completely surrounded, and his regiment would have to cut its way out. "I . . . had the officers and men advised the best I could that when the signal was given that we would not try to retreat in order, but every one should run in the direction from whence we came. . . . When the signal was given we ran like a herd of wild cattle, right through the line of dismounted cavalrymen. . . . As we ran, a man named Keils, of Company H, from Henry County, who was to my right and rear, had his throat cut by a bullet, and he ran past me breathing at his throat and the blood spattering."

In spite of their numbers, their courage, and their almost superhuman exertions, the Confederate troops had suffered a baffling defeat.

Part of the reason had been superb handling of a regiment by a college professor who had been in the army less than a year. And part had been —well, everything going against them, events combining in a way that might not happen again in a thousand years.

To find any parallel, it would almost be necessary to go back to Second Kings, 7, wherein the four leprous men had said to one another, "Why sit we here until we die?" and had then risen up and advanced into the camp of the Syrians, the Lord at the proper moment causing the Syrians to hear "a noise of chariots, and a noise of horses, even the noise of a great host," so that they all fled for their lives.

After sweeping the front of the brigade clear and rounding up an estimated four hundred prisoners, the 20th Maine returned to its original position on Little Round Top, and it was a triumphant but a sobering walk. The slaughter had been sudden, prodigious—and sickening, now that there was time to look at the results. As Oates had noted, the ground was literally covered with bodies. Some moaning and moving and bleeding. Others silent, lying in the ridiculous, rag-doll postures of the dead. They were scattered everywhere, among rocks, behind trees. The 20th Maine had suffered 130 casualties, including forty killed or mortally wounded. Mingled with these were around 150 dead and wounded Confederates.

In his official report Colonel Chamberlain stated, "We went into the fight with 386, all told—358 guns. Every pioneer and musician who could carry a musket went into the ranks. Even the sick and footsore, who could not keep up in the march, came up as soon as they could find their regiments, and took their places in line of battle, while it was battle, indeed."

Now that there was time to stop and think about what had happened, it was enough to give a man the shakes.

The thing that was most frightening about it was how the weight of a momentous battle could have come to rest so disproportionately upon just a few ordinary men—farmers, fishermen and woodsmen. Seldom if ever before had one small regiment been in such a fantastic spot.

And seldom had a regiment fought so fantastically. The maneuver whereby the double line of battle had stretched itself out into a single line, extending and bending back under fire with the noise making ordinary commands impossible, was something out of a dream.

The charge, the swinging and straightening of the left wing back into line, the plunge down the slope had succeeded simply because it had been so improbable.

And if the Maine men had been in any mood to reflect, they might have mused upon the workings of a Providence that had brought them past Antietam, Fredericksburg and Chancellorsville to arrive at this spot with the unfit weeded out, but with the lean fighting muscle of the regiment largely unimpaired.

It was immediately clear to a lot of people that one of the most important actions of the war had just been fought. Corporal William T. Livermore recorded the day's events in his diary. "The Regiment we fought and captured was the 15th Alabama. They fought like demons and said they never were whipped before and never wanted to meet the 20th Maine again. . . . Ours was an important position, and had we been driven from it, the tide of battle would have been turned against us and what the result would have been we cannot tell."

But the man who had seen the Confederacy's lost opportunity more clearly than anyone else was Colonel Oates. Roll call that night revealed that less than half of his once-great regiment remained. In later years he would reflect, "There never were harder fighters than the Twentieth Maine men and their gallant Colonel. His skill and persistency and the great bravery of his men saved Little Round Top and the Army of the Potomac from defeat. Great events sometimes turn on comparatively small affairs."

And later, for this day's work, would come the Congressional Medal of Honor for Joshua Chamberlain.

It was, as Maine men would say, *"a caution!"* But right now, with nostrils filled with the sulphurous, sickish-sweet smell of burned gunpowder, heads dazed, and ears ringing, they weren't saying or thinking much of anything.

The smoke settled and the shadows deepened in the little valley. Westward, trees turned black against a sultry purple sunset. To the west and north, the roar of battle died away in a slow, rumbling diminuendo. Darkness came, and in barns and other buildings where the wounded had been taken, the surgeons were working desperately by candlelight.

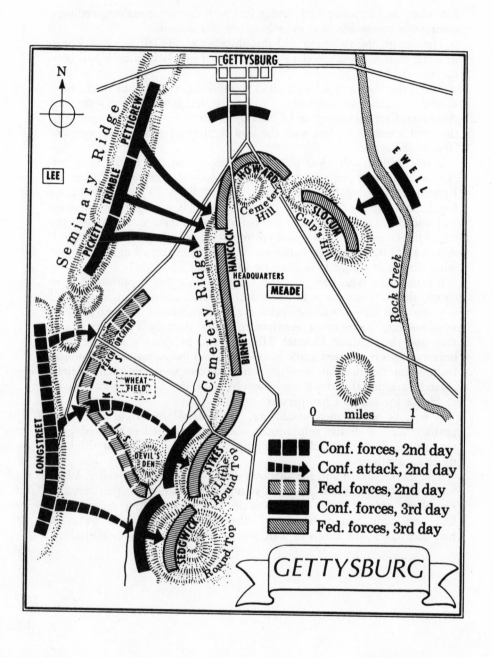

GETTYSBURG

Conf. forces, 2nd day
Conf. attack, 2nd day
Fed. forces, 2nd day
Conf. forces, 3rd day
Fed. forces, 3rd day

0 miles 1

THE LULL BEFORE
THE STORM

THE DAY BEGAN WITH A FIGHT between Confederate troops who controlled the lower half of Culp's Hill on the Federal right flank. Fierce fighting surged back and forth as the Confederates tried to reach the top of the hill from which they could threaten the whole Union right flank and rear. By 10:30 A.M. they had worn themselves out in frontal charges, and an ominous quiet settled over the battlefield.

Robert E. Lee had failed to turn either Federal flank. Now he was considering an assault on the Federal center at Cemetery Ridge. General Longstreet felt the attack would be a disaster and he said so, emphatically, without effect. Lee ordered Longstreet to send the Confederate divisions into battle.

Not until 2 P.M. was the silence of the battlefield broken. Then: "rebel artillery, from all points, in a circle radiating around our own, began a terrific and concentrated fire on Cemetery Hill. A flock of pigeons, which not ten minutes previously had darkened the sky above, were scarcely thicker than the flock of horrible missiles that now, instead of sailing harmlessly above, descended on our position. The storm broke upon us so suddenly that soldiers and officers—who leaped, as it began, from their tents and from lazy siesta on the grass—were stricken in their rising with mortal wounds, and died, some with cigars between their teeth, some with pieces of food in their fingers, and one at least—a pale young German from Pennsylvania—with a miniature of his sister in his hands, which seemed more fit to grasp an artist's pencil than a musket. Horses fell, shrieking awful cries. The boards of fences flew in splinters through the air. The earth, torn up in clouds, blinded the eyes of hurrying men."*

And: "holes like graves were gouged in the earth by exploding shells. The flowers in bloom upon the graves at the Cemetery were shot away. Tombs and monuments were knocked to pieces, and ordinary gravestones shattered in rows."†

The men on Cemetery Ridge had expected a fight this day, but they were not prepared for the onslaught to come.

* From a reporter for the New York *World*, as reported in *The Rebellion Record*, Vol. VII.
† From Warren L. Goss, *Recollections of a Private*.

Gettysburg: Third Day*

BY COLONEL FRANK HASKELL

At four o'clock on the morning of the third, I was awakened by General Gibbon's pulling me by the foot and saying: "Come, don't you hear that?" I sprang up to my feet. Where was I? A moment and my dead senses and memory were alive again, and the sound of brisk firing of musketry to the front and right of the Second Corps, and over at the extreme right of our line, where we heard it last in the night, brought all back to my memory. We surely were on the field of battle, and there were palpable evidences to my reason that to-day was to be another blood. Oh! for a moment the thought of it was sickening to every sense and feeling! But the motion of my horse as I galloped over the crest a few minutes later, and the serene splendor of the morning now breaking through rifted clouds and spreading over the landscape, soon assured me. Come day of battle! Up Rebel hosts, and thunder with your arms! We are all ready to do and to die for the Republic!

I found a sharp skirmish going on in front of the right of the Second Corps, between our outposts and those of the enemy, but save this—and none of the enemy but his outposts were in sight—all was quiet in that part of the field. On the extreme right of the line the sound of musketry was quite heavy; and this I learned was brought on by the attack of the Second Division, Twelfth Corps, General Geary, upon the enemy in order to drive him out of our works which he had sneaked into yesterday, as I have mentioned The attack was made at the earliest moment in the morning when it was light enough to discern objects to fire at.

The enemy could not use the works, but was confronting Geary in woods, and had the cover of many rocks and trees, so the fight was an irregular one, now breaking out and swelling to a vigorous fight, now subsiding to a few scattering shots; and so it continued by turns until the morning was well advanced, when the enemy was finally wholly repulsed and driven from the pits, and the right of our line was again re-established in the place it first occupied.

The heaviest losses the Twelfth Corps sustained in all the battle occurred during this attack, and they were here quite severe. I heard General Meade express dissatisfaction at General Geary for making this attack, as a thing not ordered and not necessary, as the works of ours were of no intrinsic importance, and had not been captured from us by a fight, and Geary's position was just as good as they, where he was during the night. And I heard General Meade say that he sent an order to have the

* From *The Battle of Gettysburg*.

fight stopped; but I believe the order was not communicated to Geary until after the repulse of the enemy.

Late in the forenoon the enemy again tried to carry our right by storm. We heard that old Rebel Ewell had sworn an oath that he would break our right. He had Stonewall Jackson's Corps and possibly imagined himself another Stonewall, but he certainly *hankered* after the right of our line—and so up through the woods, and over the rocks, and up the steeps he sent his storming parties—our men could see them now in the day time. But all the Rebel's efforts were fruitless, save in one thing, slaughter in his own men.

These assaults were made with great spirit and determination, but as the enemy would come up, our men lying behind their secure defenses would just singe them with the blaze of their muskets, and riddle them, as a hail-storm the tender blades of corn. The Rebel oath was not kept, any more than his former one to support the Constitution of the United States. The Rebel loss was very heavy indeed, here, ours but trifling.

I regret that I cannot give more of the details of this fighting upon the right—it was so determined upon the part of the enemy, both last night and this morning—so successful to us. About all that I actually saw of it during its progress, was the smoke, and I heard the discharges. My information is derived from officers who were personally in it. Some of our heavier artillery assisted our infantry in this by firing, with the piece elevated, far from the rear, over the heads of our men, at a distance from the enemy of two miles, I suppose. Of course they could have done no great damage. It was nearly eleven o'clock that the battle in this part of the field subsided, not to be again renewed. All the morning we felt no apprehension for this part of the line, for we knew its strength, and that our troops engaged, the Twelfth Corps and the First Division, Wadsworth's, of the First, could be trusted.

For the sake of telling one thing at a time, I have anticipated events somewhat, in writing of this fight upon the right. I shall now go back to the starting point, four o'clock this morning, and, as other events occurred during the day, second to none in the battle in importance, which I think I saw as much of as any man living, I will tell you something of them, and what I saw, and how the time moved on.

The outpost skirmish that I have mentioned soon subsided. I suppose it was the natural escape of the wrath which the men had during the night hoarded up against each other, and which, as soon as they could see in the morning, they could no longer contain, but must let it off through their musket barrels, at their adversaries. At the commencement of the war such firing would have awaked the whole army and roused it to its feet and to arms; not so now. The men upon the crest lay snoring in their blankets, even though some of the enemy's bullets dropped among them, as if bullets were harmless as the drops of dew around them. As the sun arose to-day, the clouds became broken, and we had once more glimpses of sky, and fits of sunshine—a rarity, to cheer us.

From the crest, save to the right of the Second Corps, no enemy, not even his outposts could be discovered, along all the position where he so thronged upon the Third Corps yesterday. All was silent there—the wounded horses were limping about the field; the ravages of the conflict were still fearfully visible—the scattered arms and the ground thickly dotted with the dead—but no hostile foe. The men were roused early, in order that the morning meal might be out of the way in time for whatever should occur. Then ensued the hum of an army, not in ranks, chatting in low tones, and running about and jostling among each other, rolling and packing their blankets and tents.

They looked like an army of rag-gatherers, while shaking these very useful articles of the soldier's outfit, for you must know that rain and mud in conjunction have not had the effect to make them clean, and the wear and tear of service have not left them entirely whole. But one could not have told by the appearance of the men, that they were in battle yesterday, and were likely to be again to-day. They packed their knapsacks, boiled their coffee and munched their hard bread, just as usual—just like old soldiers who know what campaigning is; and their talk is far more concerning their present employment—some joke or drollery—than concerning what they saw or did yesterday.

As early as practicable the lines all along the left are revised and reformed, this having been rendered necessary by yesterday's battle, and also by what is anticipated to-day.

It is the opinion of many of our Generals that the Rebel will not give us battle to-day—that he had enough yesterday—that he will be heading towards the Potomac at the earliest practicable moment, if he has not already done so; but the better, and controlling judgment is, that he will make another grand effort to pierce or turn our lines—that he will either mass and attack the left again, as yesterday, or direct his operations against the left of our center, the position of the Second Corps, and try to sever our line. I infer that General Meade was of the opinion that the attack to-day would be upon the left—this from the disposition he ordered, I know that General Hancock anticipated the attack upon the center.

The dispositions to-day upon the left are as follows:

The Second and Third Divisions of the Second Corps are in the position of yesterday; then on the left come Doubleday's—the Third Division and Col. Stannard's brigade of the First Corps; then Colwell's [Caldwell's]— the First Division of the Second Corps; then the Third Corps, temporarily under the command of Hancock, since Sickles' wound. The Third Corps is upon the same ground in part, and on the identical line where it first formed yesterday morning, and where, had it stayed instead of moving out to the front, we should have many more men to-day, and should not have been upon the brink of disaster yesterday. On the left of the Third Corps is the Fifth Corps, with a short front and deep line; then comes the Sixth Corps, all but one brigade, which is sent over to the Twelfth. The Sixth, a splendid Corps, almost intact in the fight of yesterday, is the extreme left of our line, which terminates to the south of Round Top, and runs along its western base in the woods, and thence to the Cemetery. This Corps is burning to pay off the old scores made on the 4th of May, there back of Fredericksburg.

Note well the position of the Second and Third Divisions of the Second Corps—it will become important. There are nearly six thousand men and officers in these two Divisions here upon the field—the losses were quite heavy yesterday, some regiments are detached to other parts of the field

—so all told there are less than six thousand men now in the two Divisions, who occupy a line of about a thousand yards. The most of the way along this line upon the crest was a stone fence, constructed of small, rough stones, a good deal of the way badly pulled down, but the men had improved it and patched it with rails from the neighboring fences, and with earth, so as to render it in many places a very passable breastwork against musketry and flying fragments of shells.

These works are so low as to compel the men to kneel or lie down generally to obtain cover. Near the right of the Second Division, and just by the little group of trees that I have mentioned there, this stone fence made a right angle, and extended thence to the front, about twenty or thirty yards, where with another less than a right angle it followed along the crest again.

The lines were conformed to these breastworks and to the nature of the ground upon the crest, so as to occupy the most favorable places, to be covered, and still be able to deliver effective fire upon the enemy should he come there. In some places a second line was so posted as to be able to deliver its fire over the heads of the first line behind the works; but such formation was not practicable all of the way. But all the force of these two divisions was in line, in position, without reserves, and in such a manner that every man of them could have fired his piece at the same instant. The division flags, that of the Second Division, being a white trefoil upon a square blue field, and of the Third Division, a blue trefoil upon a white rectangular field, waved behind the divisions at the points where the Generals of Division were supposed to be; the brigade flags, similar to these but with a triangular field, were behind the brigades; and the national flags of the regiments were in the lines of their regiments. To the left of the Second Division, and advanced something over a hundred yards, were posted a part of Stannard's Brigade, two regiments or more, behind a small bush-crowned crest that ran in a direction oblique to the general line. These were well covered by the crest, and wholly concealed by the bushes, so that an advancing enemy would be close upon them before they could be seen. Other troops of Doubleday's Division were strongly posted in rear of these in the general line.

I could not help wishing all the morning that this line of the two divisions of the Second Corps was stronger; it was, so far as numbers constitute strength, the weakest part of our whole line of battle. What if, I thought, the enemy should make an assault here to-day, with two or three heavy lines—a great overwhelming mass; would he not sweep through that thin six thousand?

But I was not General Meade, who alone had power to send other troops there; and he was satisfied with that part of the line as it was. He was early on horseback this morning, and rode along the whole line, looking to it himself and with glass in hand sweeping the woods and fields in the direction of the enemy, to see if aught of him could be discovered. His manner was calm and serious, but earnest. There was no arrogance of hope, or timidity of fear discernible in his face; but you would have supposed he would do his duty conscientiously and well and would be willing to abide the result. You would have seen this in his face. He was well pleased with the left of the line to-day, it was so strong with good troops. He had no apprehension for the right where the fight now was going on, on account of the admirable position of our forces there. He was not of the opinion that the enemy would attack the center, our artillery had such sweep there, and this was not the favorite point of attack with the Rebel. Besides, should he attack the center, the General thought he could reinforce it in good season. I heard General Meade speak of these matters to Hancock and some others, at about nine o'clock in the morning, while they were up by the line, near the Second Corps.

No further changes of importance except those mentioned were made in the disposition of the troops this morning, except to replace some of the batteries that were disabled yesterday by others from the artillery reserve, and to brace up the lines well with guns wherever there were eligible places, from the same source. The line is all in good order again, and we are ready for general battle.

Save the operations upon the right, the enemy, so far as we could see, was very quiet all the morning. Occasionally the outposts would fire a little, and then cease. Movements would be discovered which would indicate the attempt on the part of the enemy to post a battery. Our Parrotts would send a few shells to the spot, then silence would follow.

At one of these times a painful accident happened to us, this morning. First Lieutenant Henry Ropes, 20th Massachusetts, in General Gibbon's Division, a most estimable gentleman and officer, intelligent, educated, refined, one of the noble souls that came to the country's defense, while lying at his post with his regiment, in front of one of the Batteries, which fired over the Infantry, was instantly killed by a badly made shell, which, or some portion of it, fell but a few yards in front of the muzzle of the gun. The same accident killed or wounded several others. The loss of Ropes would have pained us at any time, and in any manner; in this manner his death was doubly painful.

Between ten and eleven o'clock, over in a peach orchard in front of the position of Sickles yesterday, some little show of the enemy's infantry was discovered; a few shells scattered the gray-backs; they again appeared, and it becoming apparent that they were only posting a skirmish line, no further molestation was offered them. A little after this some of the enemy's flags could be discerned over near the same quarter, above the top and behind a small crest of a ridge. There seemed to be two or three of them—possibly they were guidons—and they moved too fast to be carried on foot. Possibly, we thought, the enemy is posting some batteries there. We knew in about two hours from this time better about the matter.

Eleven o'clock came. The noise of battle has ceased upon the right; not a sound of a gun or musket can be heard on all the field; the sky is bright, with only the white fleecy clouds floating over from the West. The July sun streams down its fire upon the bright iron of the muskets in stacks upon the crest, and the dazzling brass of the Napoleons. The army lolls and longs for the shade, of which some get a hand's breadth, from a shelter tent stuck upon a ramrod. The silence and sultriness of a July noon are supreme. Now it so happened that just about this time of day a very original interesting thought occurred to General Gibbon and several of his staff; that it would be a very good thing and a very good time, to have something to eat. When I announce to you that I had not tasted a mouthful of food since yesterday noon, and that all I had had to drink since that time, but the most miserable muddy warm water, was a little drink of whiskey that Major Biddle, General Meade's aide-de-camp, gave me last evening, and a cup of strong coffee that I gulped down as I was first mounting this morning, and further, that, save the four or five hours in the night, there was scarcely a moment since that time but that I was in the saddle, you may have some notion of the reason of my assent to this extraordinary proposition. Nor will I mention the doubt I had as to the feasibility of the execution of this very novel proposal, except to say that I knew this morning that our larder was low; not to put too fine a point upon it, that we had nothing but some potatoes and sugar and coffee in the world. And I may as well say here, that of such, in scant proportion, would have been our repast, had it not been for the riding of miles by two persons, one an officer, to procure supplies; and they only succeeded in getting some few chickens, some butter, and one huge loaf of bread, which last was bought of a soldier, because he had grown faint in carrying it, and was afterwards rescued with much difficulty and after a long race from a four-footed hog, which had got hold of and had actually eaten a part of it. "There is a divinity," etc.

Suffice it, this very ingenious and unheard of contemplated proceeding, first announced by the General, was accepted and at once undertaken by his staff. Of the absolute quality of what we had to eat, I could not pretend to judge, but I think an unprejudiced person would have said of the bread that it was good; so of the potatoes before they were boiled. Of the chickens he would have questioned their age, but they were large and in good *running* order. The toast was good, and the butter. There were those who, when coffee was given them, called for tea, and vice versa, and were so ungracious as to suggest that the water that was used in both might have come from near a barn. Of course it did not. We all came down to the little peach orchard where we had stayed last night, and, wonderful to see and tell, ever mindful of our needs, had it all ready, had our faithful John. There was an enormous pan of stewed chickens, and the potatoes, and toast, all hot, and the bread and the butter, and tea and coffee. There was satisfaction derived from just naming them all over. We called John an angel, and he snickered and said he "knowed" we'd come.

General Hancock is of course invited to partake, and without delay we commence operations. Stools are not very numerous, two in all, and these the two Generals have by common consent. Our table was the top of a mess chest. By this the Generals sat. The rest of us sat upon the ground, cross-legged, like the picture of a smoking Turk, and held our plates upon our laps. How delicious was the stewed chicken. I had a cucumber pickle in my saddle bags, the last of a lunch left there two or three days ago, which George brought, and I had half of it. We were just well at it when General Meade rode down to us from the line, accompanied by one of his staff, and by General Gibbon's invitation, they dismounted and joined us. For the General commanding the Army of the Potomac, George, by an effort worthy of the person and the occasion, finds an empty cracker box for a seat. The staff officer must sit upon the ground with the rest of us. Soon Generals Newton and Pleasonton, each with an aide, arrive. By an almost superhuman effort a roll of blankets is found, which upon a pinch, is long enough to seat these Generals both, and room is made for them. The aides sit with us. And fortunate to relate, there was enough cooked for us all, and from General Meade to the youngest second lieutenant we all had a most hearty and well relished dinner. Of the "past" we were "secure."

The Generals ate, and after, lighted cigars, and under the flickering shade of a very small tree, discoursed of the incidents of yesterday's battle and of the probabilities of today. General Newton humorously spoke of General Gibbon as "this young North Carolinian," and how he was becoming arrogant and above his position, because he commanded a corps. General Gibbon retorted by saying that General Newton had not been long enough in such a command, only since yesterday, to enable him to judge of such things. General Meade still thought the enemy would attack his left again to-day towards evening; but he was ready for them. General Hancock thought that the attack would be upon the position of the Second Corps. It was mentioned that General Hancock would again assume command of the Second Corps from that time, so that General Gibbon would again return to the Second Division.

General Meade spoke of the Provost Guards, that they were good men, and that it would be better to-day to have them in the works than to stop stragglers and skulkers, as these latter would be good for but little even in the works; and so he gave the order that all the Provost Guards should at once temporarily rejoin their regiments. Then General Gibbon called up Captain Farrell, First Minnesota, who commanded the provost guard of his division, and directed him for that day to join the regiment. "Very well, sir," said the Captain, as he touched his hat and turned away. He was a quiet, excellent gentleman and thorough soldier. I knew him well and esteemed him. I never saw him again. He was killed in two or three hours from that time, and over half of his splendid company were either killed or wounded.

And so the time passed on, each General now and then dispatching some order or message by an officer or orderly, until about half-past twelve, when all the Generals, one by one, first General Meade, rode off their several ways, and General Gibbon and his staff alone remained.

We dozed in the heat, and lolled upon the ground, with half-open eyes. Our horses were hitched to the trees munching some oats. A great lull rests upon all the field. Time was heavy, and for want of something better to do, I yawned, and looked at my watch. It was five minutes before one o'clock. I returned my watch to my pocket, and thought possibly that I might go to sleep, and stretched myself upon the ground accordingly. *Ex uno disce omnes.* My attitude and purpose were those of the General and the rest of the staff.

What sound was that? There was no mistaking it. The distinct sharp sound of one of the enemy's guns, square over to the front, caused us to open our eyes and turn them in that direction, when we saw directly above the crest the smoke of the bursting shell, and heard its noise. In an instant, before a word was spoken, as if that was the signal gun for general work, loud, startling, booming, the report of gun after gun in rapid succession smote our ears and their shells plunged down and exploded all around us.

We sprang to our feet. In briefest time the whole Rebel line to the West was pouring out its thunder and its iron upon our devoted crest. The wildest confusion for a few moments obtained sway among us. The shells came bursting all about. The servants ran terror-stricken for dear life and disappeared. The horses, hitched to the trees or held by the slack hands of the orderlies, neighed out in fright and broke away and plunged riderless through the fields. The General at the first had snatched his sword, and started on foot for the front. I called for my horse; nobody responded. I found him tied to a tree, nearby, eating oats, with an air of the greatest composure, which under the circumstances, even then struck me as exceedingly ridiculous. He alone, of all beasts or men near, was cool. I am not sure but that I learned a lesson then from a horse. Anxious alone for his oats, while I put on the bridle and adjusted the halter, he delayed me by keeping his head down, so I had time to see one of the horses of our mess wagon struck and torn by a shell. The pair plunge— the driver has lost the reins—horses, driver and wagon go into a heap by a tree. Two mules close at hand, packed with boxes of ammunition, are knocked all to pieces by a shell. General Gibbon's groom has just mounted his horse and is starting to take the General's horse to him, when the flying iron meets him and tears open his breast. He drops dead and the horses gallop away. No more than a minute since the first shot was fired, and I am mounted and riding after the General.

The mighty din that now rises to heaven and shakes the earth is not all of it the voice of the rebellion; for our guns, the guardian lions of the crest, quick to awake when danger comes, have opened their fiery jaws and begun to roar—the great hoarse roar of battle. I overtake the General half way up to the line. Before we reach the crest his horse is brought by an orderly. Leaving our horses just behind a sharp declivity of the ridge, on foot we go up among the batteries. How the long streams of fire spout from the guns, how the rifled shells hiss, how the smoke deepens and rolls. But where is the infantry? Has it vanished in smoke? Is this a nightmare or a juggler's devilish trick? All too real. The men of the infantry have seized their arms, and behind their works, behind every rock, in every ditch, wherever there is any shelter, they hug the ground, silent, quiet, unterrified, little harmed. The enemy's guns now in action are in position at their front of the woods along the second ridge that I have before mentioned and towards their right, behind a small crest in the open field, where we saw the flags this morning. Their line is some two miles long, concave on the side towards us, and their range is from one thousand to eighteen hundred yards. A hundred and twenty-five rebel guns, we estimate, are now active, firing twenty-four pound, twenty, twelve and ten-pound projectiles, solid shot and shells, spherical, conical, spiral.

The enemy's fire is chiefly concentrated upon the position of the Second Corps. From the Cemetery to Round Top, with over a hundred guns, and to all parts of the enemy's line, our batteries reply, of twenty and ten-pound Parrotts, ten-pound rifled ordnance, and twelve-pound Napoleons, using projectiles as various in shape and name as those of the enemy. Captain [John G.] Hazard commanding the artillery brigade of the Second Corps was vigilant among the batteries of his command, and they were all doing well. All was going on satisfactorily. We had nothing to do, therefore, but to be observers of the grand spectacle of battle. Captain Wessels, Judge Advocate of the Division, now joined us, and we sat down behind the crest, close to the left of Cushing's Battery, to bide our time, to see, to be ready to act when the time should come, which might be at any moment.

Who can describe such a conflict as is raging around us? To say that it was like a summer storm, with the crash of thunder, the glare of lightning, the shrieking of the wind, and the clatter of hailstones, would be weak. The thunder and lightning of these two hundred and fifty guns and their shells, whose smoke darkens the sky, are incessant, all pervading, in the air above our heads, on the ground at our feet, remote, near, deafening, ear-piercing, astounding; and these hailstones are massy iron, charged with exploding fire. And there is little of human interest in a storm; it is an absorbing element of this. You may see flame and smoke, and hurrying men, and human passion at a great conflagration; but they are all earthly and nothing more. These guns are great infuriate demons, not of the earth, whose mouths blaze with smoky tongues of living fire, and whose murky breath, sulphur-laden, rolls around them and along the ground, the smoke of Hades. These grimy men, rushing, shouting, their souls in frenzy, plying the dusky globes and the igniting spark, are in their league, and but their willing ministers. We thought that at the second Bull Run, at the Antietam and at Fredericksburg on the 11th of December, we had heard heavy cannonading; they were but holiday salutes compared with this. Besides the great ceaseless roar of the guns, which was but the background of the others, a million various minor sounds engaged the ear. The projectiles shriek long and sharp. They hiss, they scream, they growl, they sputter; all sounds of life and rage; and each has its different note, and all are discordant. Was ever such a chorus of sound before? We note the effect of the enemies' fire among the batteries and along the crest. We see the solid shot strike axle, or pole, or wheel, and the tough iron and heart of oak snap and fly like straws. The great oaks there by Woodruff's guns heave down their massy branches with a crash, as if the lightning smote them. The shells swoop down among the battery horses standing there apart. A half a dozen horses start, they tumble, their legs stiffen, their vitals and blood smear the ground. And these shot and shells have no respect for men either. We see the poor fellows hobbling back from the crest, or unable to do so, pale and weak, lying on the ground with the mangled stump of an arm or leg, dripping their life-blood away; or with a cheek torn open or a shoulder mashed. And many, alas! hear not the roar as they stretch upon the ground with upturned faces and open eyes, though a shell should burst at their very ears. Their ears and their bodies this instant are only mud. We saw them but a moment since there among the flame, with brawny arms and muscles of iron, wielding the rammer and pushing home the cannon's plethoric load.

Strange freaks these round shot play! We saw a man coming up from the rear with his full knapsack on, and some canteens of water held by the straps in his hands. He was walking slowly and with apparent unconcern, though the iron hailed around him. A shot struck the knapsack, and it and its contents flew thirty yards in every direction, the knapsack disappearing like an egg thrown spitefully against a rock. The soldier stopped and turned about in puzzled surprise, put up one hand to his back to assure himself that the knapsack was not there, and then walked slowly on again unharmed, with not even his coat torn. Near us was a man crouching behind a small disintegrated stone, which was about the size of a common water bucket. He was bent up, with his face to the ground, in the attitude of a Pagan worshipper before his idol. It looked so absurd to see him thus, that I went and said to him, "Do not lie there like a toad. Why not go to your regiment and be a man?" He turned up his face with a stupid, terrified look upon me, and then without a word turned his nose again to the ground. An orderly that was with me at the time told me a few moments later, that a shot struck the stone, smashing it in a thousand fragments, but did not touch the man, though his head was not six inches from the stone.

All the projectiles that came near us were not so harmless. Not ten yards away from us a shell burst among some small bushes, where sat three or four orderlies holding horses. Two of the men and one horse were killed. Only a few yards off a shell exploded over an open limber box in Cushing's battery, and at the same instant, another shell over a neighboring box. In both the boxes the ammunition blew up with an explosion that shook the ground, throwing fire and splinters and shells far into the air and all around, and destroying several men. We watched the shells bursting in the air, as they came hissing in all directions. Their flash was a bright gleam of lightning radiating from a point, giving place in the thousandth part of a second to a small, white puffy cloud, like a fleece of the lightest, whitest wool. These clouds were very numerous. We could not often see the shell before it burst; but sometimes, as we faced toward the enemy, and looked above our heads, the approach would be heralded by a prolonged hiss, which always seemed to me to be a line of something tangible, terminating in a black globe, distinct to the eye, as the sound had been to the ear. The shell would seem to stop, and hang suspended in the air an instant, and then vanish in fire and smoke and noise.

We saw the missiles tear and plow the ground. All in rear of the crest for a thousand yards, as well as among the batteries, was the field of their blind fury. Ambulances, passing down the Taneytown road, with wounded men, were struck. The hospitals near this road were riddled. The house which was General Meade's headquarters was shot through several times, and a great many horses of officers and orderlies were lying dead around it. Riderless horses, galloping madly through the fields, were brought up, or down rather, by these invisible horse-tamers, and they would not run any more. Mules with ammunition, pigs wallowing about, cows in the pastures, whatever was animate or inanimate, in all this broad range, were no exception to their blind havoc. The percussion shells would strike, and thunder, and scatter the earth and their whistling fragments; the Whitworth bolts would pound and ricochet, and bowl far away sputtering, with the sound of a mass of hot iron plunged in water; and the great solid shot would smite the unresisting ground with a sounding "thud," as the strong boxer crashes his iron fist into the jaws of his unguarded adversary. Such were some of the sights and sounds of this great iron

battle of missiles. Our artillerymen upon the crest budged not an inch, nor
intermitted, but, though caisson and limber were smashed, and guns
dismantled, and men and horses killed, there amidst smoke and sweat,
they gave back, without grudge, or loss of time in the sending, in kind
whatever the enemy sent, globe, and cone, and bolt, hollow or solid, an
iron greeting to the rebellion, the compliments of the wrathful Republic.

An hour has droned its flight since the war began. There is no sign of
weariness or abatement on either side. So long it seemed, that the din and
crashing around began to appear the normal condition of nature there,
and fighting man's element. The General proposed to go among the men
and over to the front of the batteries, so at about two o'clock he and I
started. We went along the lines of the infantry as they lay there flat upon
the earth, a little to the front of the batteries. They were suffering little,
and were quiet and cool. How glad we were that the enmy were no better
gunners, and that they cut the shell fuses too long. To the question asked
the men, "What do you think of this?" the replies would be "O, this is
bully," "We are getting to like it," "O, we don't mind this." And so they
lay under the heaviest cannonade that ever shook the continent, and among
them a thousand times more jokes than heads were cracked.

We went down in front of the line some two hundred yards, and as
the smoke had a tendency to settle upon a higher plain than where we
were, we could see near the ground distinctly all over the fields, as well
back to the crest where were our own guns as to the opposite ridge where
were those of the enemy. No infantry was in sight, save the skirmishers,
and they stood silent and motionless—a row of gray posts through the
field on one side confronted by another of blue. Under the grateful shade
of some elm trees, where we could see much of the field, we made seats
of the ground and sat down. Here all the more repulsive features of the
fight were unseen, by reason of the smoke. Man had arranged the scenes,
and for a time had taken part in the great drama; but at last, as the plot
thickened, conscious of his littleness and inadequacy to the mighty part,
he had stepped aside and given place to more powerful actors. So it
seemed; for we could see no men about the batteries. On either crest we
could see the great flaky streams of fire, and they seemed numberless, of
the opposing guns, and their white banks of swift, convolving smoke;
but the sound of the discharges was drowned in the universal ocean of
sound. Over all the valley the smoke, a sulphury arch, stretched its lurid
span; and through it always, shrieking on their unseen courses, thickly
flew a myriad iron deaths. With our grim horizon on all sides round
toothed thick with battery flame, under that dissonant canopy of warring
shells, we sat and heard in silence. What other expression had we that was
not mean, for such an awful universe of battle?

A shell struck our breastwork of rails up in sight of us, and a moment
afterwards we saw the men bearing some of their wounded companions
away from the same spot; and directly two men came from there down
toward where we were and sought to get shelter in an excavation near
by, where many dead horses, killed in yesterday's fight, had been thrown.
General Gibbon said to these men, more in a tone of kindly expostulation
than of command: "My men, do not leave your ranks to try to get shelter
here. All these matters are in the hands of God, and nothing that you

can do will make you safer in one place than in another." The men went quietly back to the line at once. The General then said to me: "I am not a member of any church, but I have always had a strong religious feeling; and so in all these battles I have always believed that I was in the hands of God, and that I should be unharmed or not, according to his will. For this reason, I think it is, I am always ready to go where duty calls, no matter how great the danger."

Half-past two o'clock, an hour and a half since the commencement, and still the cannonade did not in the least abate; but soon thereafter some signs of weariness and a little slacking of fire began to be apparent upon both sides. First we saw Brown's battery retire from the line, too feeble for further battle. Its position was a little to the front of the line. Its commander was wounded, and many of its men were so, or worse; some of its guns had been disabled, many of its horses killed; its ammunition was nearly expended. Other batteries in similar case had been withdrawn before to be replaced by fresh ones, and some were withdrawn afterwards. Soon after the battery named had gone, the General and I started to return, passing towards the left of the division, and crossing the ground where the guns had stood. The stricken horses were numerous, and the dead and wounded men lay about, and as we passed these latter, their low, piteous call for water would invariably come to us, if they had yet any voice left. I found canteens of water near—no difficult matter where a battle has been—and held them to livid lips, and even in the faintness of death the eagerness to drink told of their terrible torture of thirst. But we must pass on. Our infantry was still unshaken, and in all the cannonade suffered very little. The batteries had been handled much more severely. I am unable to give any figures. A great number of horses had been killed, in some batteries more than half of all. Guns had been dismounted. A great many caissons, limbers and carriages had been destroyed, and usually from ten to twenty-five men to each battery had been struck, at least along our part of the crest. Altogether the fire of the enemy had injured us much, both in the modes that I have stated, and also by exhausting our ammunition and fouling our guns, so as to render our batteries unfit for further immediate use. The scenes that met our eyes on all hands among the batteries were fearful. All things must end, and the great cannonade was no exception to the general law of earth. In the number of guns active at one time, and in the duration and rapidity of their fire, this artillery engagement, up to this time, must stand alone and preeminent in this war. It has not been often, or many times, surpassed in the battles of the world. Two hundred and fifty guns, at least, rapidly fired for two mortal hours. Cipher out the number of tons of gunpowder and iron that made these two hours hideous.

Of the injury of our fire upon the enemy, except the facts that ours was the superior position, if not better served and constructed artillery, and that the enemy's artillery hereafter during the battle was almost silent, we know little. Of course, during the fight we often saw the enemy's caissons explode, and the trees rent by our shot crashing about his ears, but we can from these alone infer but little of general results. At three o'clock almost precisely the last shot hummed, and bounded and fell, and the cannonade was over. The purpose of General Lee in all this fire

Gettysburg: *High tide of the Confederacy, July 3, 1863*

of his guns—we know it now, we did not at the time so well—was to disable our artillery and break up our infantry upon the position of the Second Corps, so as to render them less an impediment to the sweep of his own brigades and divisions over our crest and through our lines. He probably supposed our infantry was massed behind the crest and the batteries; and hence his fire was so high, and his fuses to the shells were cut so long, too long. The Rebel General failed in some of his plans in this behalf, as many generals have failed before and will again. The artillery fight over, men began to breathe more freely, and to ask, What next, I wonder? The battery men were among their guns, some leaning to rest and wipe the sweat from their sooty faces, some were handling ammunition boxes and replenishing those that were empty. Some batteries from the artillery reserve were moving up to take the places of the disabled ones; the smoke was clearing from the crests. There was a pause between the acts, with the curtain down, soon to rise upon the great final act, and catastrophe of Gettysburg. We have passed by the left of the Second Division, coming from the First; when we crossed the crest the enemy was not in sight, and all was still—we walked slowly along in the rear of the troops, by the ridge cut off now from a view of the enemy in his position, and were returning to the spot where we had left our horses. General Gibbon had just said that he inclined to the belief that the enemy was falling back, and that the cannonade was only one of his noisy modes of covering the movement. I said that I thought that fifteen minutes would show that, by all his bowling, the Rebel did not mean retreat. We were near our horses when we noticed Brigadier General Hunt, Chief of Artillery of the Army, near Woodruff's Battery, swiftly moving about on horseback, and apparently in a rapid manner giving some orders about the guns. Thought we, What could this mean? In a moment afterwards we met Captain Wessels and the orderlies who had our horses; they were on foot leading the horses. Captain Wessels was pale, and he said, excited: "General, they say the enemy's infantry is advancing." We sprang into our saddles, a score of bounds brought us upon the all-seeing crest. To say that men grew pale and held their breath at what we and they there saw, would not be true. Might not six thousand men be brave and without shade of fear, and yet, before a hostile eighteen thousand, armed, and not five minutes' march away, turn ashy white?

None on that crest now needs be told that *the enemy is advancing*. Every eye could see his legions, an overwhelming resistless tide of an ocean of armed men sweeping upon us! Regiment after regiment and brigade after brigade move from the woods and rapidly take their places in the lines forming the assault. Pickett's proud division, with some additional troops, hold their right; Pettigrew's (Worth's) their left. The first line at short interval is followed by a second, and that a third succeeds; and columns between support the lines. More than half a mile their front extends; more than a thousand yards the dull gray masses deploy, man touching man, rank pressing rank, and line supporting line. The red flags wave, their horsemen gallop up and down; the arms of eighteen thousand men, barrel and bayonet, gleam in the sun, a sloping forest of flashing steel. Right on they move, as with one soul, in perfect order, without impediment of ditch, or wall or stream, over ridge and slope, through orchard and meadow, and cornfield, magnificent, grim, irresistible.

All was orderly and still upon our crest; no noise and no confusion. The men had little need of commands, for the survivors of a dozen battles knew well enough what this array in front portended, and, already in their places, they would be prepared to act when the right time should come. The click of the locks as each man raised the hammer to feel with his fingers that the cap was on the nipple; the sharp jar as a musket touched a stone upon the wall when thrust in aiming over it, and the clicking of the iron axles as the guns were rolled up by hand a little further to the front, were quite all the sounds that could be heard. Cap-boxes were slid around to the front of the body; cartridge boxes opened, officers opened their pistol-holsters. Such preparations, little more was needed. The trefoil flags, colors of the brigades and divisions moved to their places in rear; but along the lines in front the grand old ensign that first waved in battle at Saratoga in 1777, and which these people coming would rob of half its stars, stood up, and the west wind kissed it as the sergeants sloped its lance towards the enemy. I believe that not one above whom it then waved but blessed his God that he was loyal to it, and whose heart did not swell with pride towards it, as the emblem of the Republic before that treason's flaunting rag in front.

General Gibbon rode down the lines, cool and calm, and in an unimpassioned voice he said to the men, "Do not hurry, men, and fire too fast, let them come up close before you fire, and then aim low and steadily." The coolness of their General was reflected in the faces of his men. Five minutes has elapsed since first the enemy have emerged from the woods—no great space of time surely, if measured by the usual standard by which men estimate duration—but it was long enough for us to note and weigh some of the elements of mighty moment that surrounded us; the disparity of numbers between the assailants and the assailed; that few as were our numbers we could not be supported or reinforced until support would not be needed or would be too late; that upon the ability of the two trefoil divisions to hold the crest and repel the assault depended not only their own safety or destruction, but also the honor of the Army of the Potomac and defeat or victory at Gettysburg. Should these advancing men pierce our line and become the entering wedge, driven home, that would sever our army asunder, what hope would there be afterwards, and where the blood-earned fruits of yesterday? It was long enough for the Rebel storm to drift across more than half the space that had at first separated us. None, or all, of these considerations either depressed or elevated us. They might have done the former, had we been timid; the latter had we been confident and vain. But, we were there waiting, and ready to do our duty—that done, results could not dishonor us.

Our skirmishers open a spattering fire along the front, and, fighting, retire upon the main line—the first drops, the heralds of the storm, sounding on our windows. Then the thunders of our guns, first Arnold's then Cushing's and Woodruff's and the rest, shake and reverberate again through the air, and their sounding shells smite the enemy. The General said I had better go and tell General Meade of this advance. To gallop to

General Meade's headquarters, to learn there that he had changed them to another part of the field, to dispatch to him by the Signal Corps in General Gibbon's name the message, "The enemy is advancing his infantry in force upon my front," and to be again upon the crest, were but the work of a minute. All our available guns are now active, and from the fire of shells, as the range grows shorter and shorter, they change to shrapnel, and from shrapnel to canister; but in spite of shells, and shrapnel and canister, without wavering or halt, the hardy lines of the enemy continue to move on. The Rebel guns make no reply to ours, and no charging shout rings out to-day, as is the Rebel wont; but the courage of these silent men amid our shots seems not to need the stimulus of other noise. The enemy's right flank sweeps near Stannard's bushy crest, and his concealed Vermonters rake it with a well-delivered fire of musketry. The gray lines do not halt or reply, but withdrawing a little from that extreme, they still move on.

And so across all that broad open ground they have come, nearer and nearer, nearly half the way, with our guns bellowing in their faces, until now a hundred yards, no more, divide our ready left from their advancing right. The eager men there are impatient to begin. Let them. First, Harrow's breastworks flame; then Hall's; then Webb's. As if our bullets were the fire coals that touched off their muskets, the enemy in front halts, and his countless level barrels blaze back upon us. The Second Division is struggling in battle. The rattling storm soon spreads to the right, and the blue trefoils are vying with the white. All along each hostile front, a thousand yards, with narrowest space between, the volleys blaze and roll; as thick the sound as when a summer hail-storm pelts the city roofs; as thick the fire as when the incessant lightning fringes a summer cloud. When the Rebel infantry had opened fire our batteries soon became silent, and this without their fault, for they were foul by long previous use. They were the targets of the concentrated Rebel bullets, and some of them had expended all their canister. But they were not silent before Rorty was killed, Woodruff had fallen mortally wounded, and Cushing, firing almost his last canister, had dropped dead among his guns shot through the head by a bullet. The conflict is left to the infantry alone.

Unable to find my general when I had returned to the crest after transmitting his message to General Meade, and while riding in the search having witnessed the development of the fight, from the first fire upon the left by the main lines until all of the two divisions were furiously engaged, I gave up hunting as useless—I was convinced General Gibbon could not be on the field; I left him mounted; I could easily have found him now had he so remained—but now, save myself, there was not a mounted officer near the engaged lines—and was riding towards the right of the Second Division, with purpose to stop there, as the most eligible position to watch the further progress of the battle, there to be ready to take part according to my own notions whenever and wherever occasion was presented. The conflict was tremendous, but I had seen no wavering in all our line.

Wondering how long the Rebel ranks, deep though they were, could stand our sheltered volleys, I had come near my destination, when—great heaven! were my senses mad? The larger portion of Webb's brigade—my

God, it was true—there by the group of trees and the angles of the wall, was breaking from the cover of their works, and, without orders or reason, with no hand lifted to check them, was falling back, a fear-stricken flock of confusion! The fate of Gettysburg hung upon a spider's single thread! A great magnificent passion came on me at the instant, not one that overpowers and confounds, but one that blanches the face and sublimes every sense and faculty. My sword, that had always hung idle by my side, the sign of rank only in every battle, I drew, bright and gleaming, the symbol of command. Was that not a fit occasion, and these fugitives the men on whom to try the temper of the Solingen steel? All rules and properties were forgotten; all considerations of person, and danger and safety despised; for, as I met the tide of these rabbits, the damned red flags of the rebellion began to thicken and flaunt along the wall they had just deserted, and one was already wavering over one of the guns of the dead Cushing. I ordered these men to "halt," and "face about" and "fire," and they heard my voice and gathered my meaning, and obeyed my commands. On some unpatriotic backs of those not quick of comprehension, the flat of my sabre fell not lightly, and at its touch their love of country returned, and, with a look at me as if I were the destroying angel, as I might have become theirs, they again faced the enemy. General Webb soon came to my assistance. He was on foot, but he was active, and did all that one could do to repair the breach, or to avert its calamity. The men that had fallen back, facing the enemy, soon regained confidence in themselves, and became steady.

This portion of the wall was lost to us, and the enemy had gained the cover of the reverse side, where he now stormed with fire. But Webb's men, with their bodies in part protected by the abruptness of the crest, now sent back in the enemies' faces as fierce a storm. Some scores of venturesome Rebels, that in their first push at the wall had dared to cross at the further angle, and those that had desecrated Cushing's guns were promptly shot down, and speedy death met him who should raise his body to cross it again. At this point little could be seen of the enemy, by reason of his cover and the smoke, except the flash of his muskets and his waving flags. These red flags were accumulating at the wall every moment, and they maddened us as the same color does the bull. Webb's men are falling fast, and he is among them to direct and to encourage; but, however well they may now do, with that walled enemy in front, with more than a dozen flags to Webb's three, it soon becomes apparent that in not many minutes they will be overpowered, or that there will be none alive for the enemy to overpower. Webb has but three regiments, all small, the 69th, 71st and 72d Pennsylvania—the 106th Pennsylvania, except two companies, is not here to-day—and he must have speedy assistance, or this crest will be lost.

Oh, where is Gibbon? where is Hancock?—some general—anybody with the power and the will to support that wasting, melting line? No general came, and no succor! I thought of Hays upon the right, but from the smoke and war along his front, it was evident that he had enough upon his hands, if he stayed the in-rolling tide of the Rebels there. Double-day upon the left was too far off and too slow, and on another occasion I had begged him to send his idle regiments to support another line battling with thrice its numbers, and this "Old Sumter Hero" had declined. As a last resort I resolved to see if Hall and Harrow could not send some of their commands to reinforce Webb. I galloped to the left in the execution of my purpose, and as I attained the rear of Hall's line, from the nature of the ground and the position of the enemy it was easy to discover the reason and the manner of this gathering of Rebel flags in front of Webb. The enemy, emboldened by his success in gaining our line by the group of trees and the angle of the wall, was concentrating all his right against and was further pressing that point. There was the stress of his assault; there would he drive his fiery wedge to split our line.

In front of Harrow's and Hall's Brigades he had been able to advance no nearer than when he first halted to deliver fire, and these commands had not yielded an inch. To effect the concentration before Webb, the enemy would march the regiment on his extreme right of each of his lines by the left flank to the rear of the troops, still halted and facing to the front, and so continuing to draw in his right, when they were all massed in the position desired, he would again face them to the front, and advance to the storming. This was the way he made the wall before Webb's line blaze red with his battle flags, and such was the purpose there of his thick-crowding battalions.

Not a moment must be lost. Colonel Hall I found just in rear of his line, sword in hand, cool, vigilant, noting all that passed and directing the battle of his brigade. The fire was constantly diminishing now in his front, in the manner and by the movement of the enemy that I have mentioned, drifting to the right. "How is it going?" Colonel Hall asked me, as I rode up. "Well, but Webb is hotly pressed and must have support, or he will be overpowered. Can you assist him?" "Yes." "You cannot be too quick." "I will move my brigade at once." "Good." He gave the order, and in briefest time I saw five friendly colors hurrying to the aid of the imperilled three; and each color represented true, battle-tried men, that had not turned back from Rebel fire that day nor yesterday, though their ranks were sadly thinned. To Webb's brigade, pressed back as it had been from the wall, the distance was not great from Hall's right. The regiments marched by the right flank. Colonel Hall superintended the movement in person. Colonel Devereux coolly commanded the 19th Massachusetts. His major, Rice, had already been wounded and carried off. Lieutenant Colonel Macy, of the 20th Massachusetts, had just had his left hand shot off, and so Captain Abbott gallantly led over this fine regiment. The 42d New York followed their excellent Colonel Mallon. Lieutenant Colonel Steele, 7th Michigan, had just been killed, and his regiment, and the handful of the 59th New York, followed their colors. The movement, as it did, attracting the enemy's fire, and executed in haste, as it must be, was difficult; but in reasonable time, and in order that is serviceable, if not regular, Hall's men are fighting gallantly side by side with Webb's before the all important point. I did not stop to see all this movement of Hall's, but from him I went at once further to the left, to the 1st brigade. General Harrow I did not see, but his fighting men would answer my purpose as well. The 19th Maine, the 15th Massachusetts, the 32d New York and the shattered old thunderbolt, the 1st Minnesota—

poor Farrell was dying then upon the ground where he had fallen—all men that I could find I took over to the right at the *double quick*.

As we were moving to, and near the other brigade of the division, from my position on horseback I could see that the enemy's right, under Hall's fire, was beginning to stagger and to break. "See," I said to the men, "See the *chivalry!* See the gray-backs run!" The men saw, and as they swept to their places by the side of Hall and opened fire, they roared, and this in a manner that said more plainly than words—for the deaf could have seen it in their faces, and the blind could have heard it in their voices—*the crest is safe!*

The whole Division concentrated, and changes of position, and new phases, as well on our part as on that of the enemy, having as indicated occurred, for the purpose of showing the exact present posture of affairs, some further description is necessary. Before the 2d Division the enemy is massed, the main bulk of his force covered by the ground that slopes to his rear, with his front at the stone wall. Between his front and us extends the very apex of the crest. All there are left of the White Trefoil Division—yesterday morning there were three thousand eight hundred, this morning there were less than three thousand—at this moment there are somewhat over two thousand; twelve regiments in three brigades are below or behind the crest, in such a position that by the exposure of the head and upper part of the body above the crest they can deliver their fire in the enemy's faces along the top of the wall. By reason of the disorganization incidental in Webb's brigade to his men's having broken and fallen back, as mentioned, in the two other brigades to their rapid and difficult change of position under fire, and in all the division in part to severe and continuous battle, formation of companies and regiments in regular ranks is lost; but commands, companies, regiments and brigades are blended and intermixed—an irregular extended mass—men enough, if in order, to form a line of four or five ranks along the whole front of the division. The twelve flags of the regiments wave defiantly at intervals along the front; at the stone wall, at unequal distances from ours of forty, fifty or sixty yards, stream nearly double this number of the battle flags of the enemy. These changes accomplished on either side, and the concentration complete, although no cessation or abatement in the general din of conflict since the commencement had at any time been appreciable, now it was as if a new battle, deadlier, stormier than before, had sprung from the body of the old—a young Phoenix of combat, whose eyes stream lightning, shaking his arrowy wings over the yet glowing ashes of his progenitor.

The jostling, swaying lines on either side boil, and roar, and dash their flamy spray, two hostile billows of a fiery ocean. Thick flashes stream from the wall, thick volleys answer from the crest. No threats or expostulation now, only example and encouragement. All depths of passion are stirred, and all combatives fire, down to their deep foundations. Individuality is drowned in a sea of clamor, and timid men, breathing the breath of the multitude, are brave. The frequent dead and wounded lie where they stagger and fall—there is no humanity for them now, and none can be spared to care for them. The men do not cheer or shout; they growl, and over that uneasy sea, heard with the roar of musketry, sweeps the muttered thunder of a storm of growls. Webb, Hall, Devereux, Mallon, Abbott among the men where all are heroes, are doing deeds of note. Now the loyal wave rolls up as if it would overleap its barrier, the crest. Pistols flash with the muskets. My "Forward to the wall" is answered by the Rebel counter-command "Steady, men!" and the wave swings back. Again it surges, and again it sinks. These men of Pennsylvania, on the soil of their own homesteads, the first and only to flee the wall, must be the first to storm it.

"Major ———, *lead* your men over the crest, they will follow." "By the tactics I understand my place is in rear of the men." "Your pardon, sir; I see *your* place is in rear of the men. I thought you were fit to lead." "Captain Sapler, come on with your men." "Let me first stop this fire in the rear, or we shall be hit by our own men." "Never mind the fire in the rear; let us take care of this in front first." "Sergeant, forward with your color. Let the Rebels see it close to their eyes once before they die." The color sergeant of the 72d Pennsylvania, grasping the stump of the severed lance in both his hands, waved the flag above his head and rushed towards the wall. "Will you see your color storm the wall alone?" One man only starts to follow. Almost half way to the wall, down go color bearer and color to the ground—the gallant sergeant is dead. The line springs—the crest of the solid ground with a great roar heaves forward its maddened load, men, arms, smoke, fire, a fighting mass. It rolls to the wall—flash meets flash, the wall is crossed—a moment ensues of thrusts, yells, blows, shots, and the undistinguishable conflict, followed by a shout universal that makes the welkin ring again, and the last and bloodiest fight of the great battle of Gettysburg is ended and won.

General Meade rode up, accompanied alone by his son, who is his aide-de-camp, an escort, if select, not large for a commander of such an army. The principal horseman was no bedizened hero of some holiday review, but he was a plain man, dressed in a serviceable summer suit of dark blue cloth, without badge or ornament, save the shoulder-straps of his grade, and a light, straight sword of a General or general staff officer. He wore heavy, high-top boots and buff gauntlets, and his soft black felt hat was slouched down over his eyes. His face was very white, not pale, and the lines were marked and earnest and full of care.

As he arrived near me, coming up the hill, he asked, in a sharp, eager voice: "How is it going here?" "I believe, General, the enemy's attack is repulsed," I answered. Still approaching, and a new light began to come in his face, of gratified surprise, with a touch of incredulity, of which his voice was also the medium, he further asked: *"What! Is the assault already repulsed?"* his voice quicker and more eager than before. "It is, sir," I replied. By this time he was on the crest, and when his eye had for an instant swept over the field, taking in just a glance of the whole— the masses of prisoners, the numerous captured flags which the men were derisively flaunting about, the fugitives of the routed enemy, disappearing with the speed of terror in the woods—partly at what I had told him, partly at what he saw, he said, impressively, and his face lighted: "Thank God." And then his right hand moved as if it would have caught off his hat and waved it; but this gesture he suppressed, and instead he waved his hand, and said "Hurrah!" The son, with more youth in his blood and less rank upon his shoulders, snatched off his cap, and roared out his three "hurrahs" right heartily.

The General then surveyed the field, some minutes, in silence. He at length asked who was in command—he had heard that Hancock and Gibbon were wounded—and I told him that General Caldwell was the senior officer of the Corps and General Harrow of the Division. He asked where they were, but before I had time to answer that I did not know, he resumed: "No matter; I will give my orders to you and you will see them executed." He then gave direction that the troops should be re-formed as soon as practicable, and kept in their places, as the enemy might be mad enough to attack again. He also gave directions concerning the posting of some reinforcements which he said would soon be there, adding: "If the enemy does attack, charge him in the flank and sweep him from the field; do you understand?" The General then, a gratified man, galloped in the direction of his headquarters.

When the prisoners were cleared away and order was again established upon our crest, where the conflict had impaired it, until between five and six o'clock, I remained upon the field, directing some troops to their position, in conformity to the orders of General Meade. The enemy appeared no 'more in front of the Second Corps; but while I was engaged as I have mentioned, farther to our left some considerable force of the enemy moved out and made show of attack. Our artillery, now in good order again, in due time opened fire, and the shell scattered the "Butternuts," as clubs do the gray snow-birds of winter, before they came within range of our infantry. This, save unimportant outpost firing, was the last of the battle.

CHICKAMAUGA

On July 4, Lee began his retreat to the Potomac. The river was high from heavy rains. The last Confederate did not cross until July 13, but Meade's pursuit was too slow to cause trouble. Lee had left a third of his army on the field of Gettysburg, but Meade's own casualties of 25,000 helped reinforce his natural caution. Both armies had been through hell.

To the people in the North, however, the news of Lee's repulse and the fall of Vicksburg, both received on the Fourth of July, were cause for jubilant celebration. Then on July 9, Port Hudson fell, and "the Father of Waters flowed unvexed to the sea." The noose was drawing ever tighter around the Confederacy, but there were still plenty of trouble spots for the Union. General Grant describes one which concerned him greatly in the summer of 1863:

"After the fall of Vicksburg I urged strongly upon the Government the propriety of a movement against Mobile. General Rosecrans had been at Murfreesboro, Tennessee, with a large and well-equipped army from early in the year 1863, with Bragg confronting him with a force quite equal to his own at first, considering that it was on the defensive. But after the investment of Vicksburg, Bragg's army was largely depleted to strengthen Johnston, in Mississippi, who was being reënforced to raise the siege. I frequently wrote to General Halleck suggesting that Rosecrans should move against Bragg. By so doing he would either detain the latter's troops where they were, or lay Chattanooga open to capture. General Halleck strongly approved the suggestion, and finally wrote me that he had repeatedly ordered Rosecrans to advance, but that the latter had constantly failed to comply with the order, and at last, after having held a council of war, replied, in effect, that it was a military maxim 'not to fight two decisive battles at the same time.' If true, the maxim was not applicable in this case. It would be bad to be defeated in two decisive battles fought the same day, but it would not be bad to win them. I, however, was fighting no battle, and the siege of Vicksburg had drawn from Rosecrans's front so many of the enemy that his chances of victory were much greater than they would be if he waited until the siege was over, when these troops could be returned. Rosecrans was ordered to move against the army that was detaching troops to raise the siege. Finally, on the 24th of June, he did move, but ten days afterward Vicksburg surrendered, and the troops sent from Bragg were free to return. . . .

388

"Soon it was discovered in Washington that Rosecrans was in trouble and required assistance. As fast as transports could be provided all the troops except a portion of the Seventeenth Corps were forwarded under Sherman, whose services up to this time demonstrated his superior fitness for a separate command. I also moved McPherson, with most of the troops still about Vicksburg, eastward, to compel the enemy to keep back a force to meet him. Meanwhile Rosecrans had very skillfully manœuvred Bragg south of the Tennessee River, and through and beyond Chattanooga. If he had stopped and intrenched, and made himself strong there, all would have been right, and the mistake of not moving earlier partially compensated. But he pushed on, with his forces very much scattered."

Rosecrans thought Bragg was retreating. He sent three Union corps under Thomas, McCook and Crittenden fanning out south of Chattanooga. Because of mountainous terrain and the lack of lateral roads, the three corps became widely extended, forty miles separating the right and left wings. If Bragg could catch a single corps by itself he could easily destroy it.

Bragg, meanwhile, was twenty-five miles south of Chattanooga. Not only was he no longer retreating, he was trying to get his generals to mount an attack, and he was receiving substantial reinforcements. By the time Bragg was ready to move on September 18, Rosecrans had sensed the danger and ordered his three corps to come together. McCook and Thomas wheeled north to form a defensive line south of Chattanooga and west of Chickamauga Creek.

Bragg's plan of attack was to smash into the Federal left, drive between Rosecrans and Chattanooga, and roll the Union forces into the mountains, where they could be cut up piecemeal. First Bragg would cross the Chickamauga, march north along its banks, then wheel eastward, where he would assault the Union positions which were facing south. According to Catton, if Bragg could cut "the north-south road that ran from Lafayette to Chattanooga Rosecrans' army would be done for.

"That was what Bragg planned, and he probably would have got it if he had been able to start the fighting twenty-four hours earlier. On September 18 the Federal left rested at Lee and Gordon's Mills, where the Lafayette road crossed the Chickamauga, and nobody but Crittenden was there to hold it. The country off to the northeast, downstream, across which Bragg proposed to attack, was empty except for cavalry, Thomas and McCook were still coming in from the distant right, and Confederate infantry could have marched straight to the Lafayette road, deep in the Federal rear. But on September 18, while this balky Confederate army was moving down its side of the river, driving Yankee cavalry away from the crossings and getting itself properly organized, Thomas' four divisions were making a prodigious hike. They left their camp in the afternoon and they kept on marching all night, setting fences on fire to light the way, infantry stumbling with fatigue but plowing on regardless; and by the morning of September 19, when Bragg's army at last opened its offensive, Thomas had most of his people in line east of the Lafayette road several miles north of Crittenden, drawn up squarely in the path of the Confederate divisions that were coming west from the river.

"So the Yankee army was not where Bragg thought it was. It was

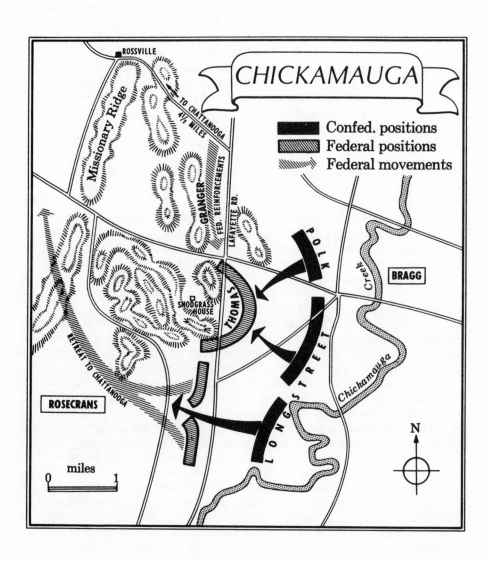

still highly vulnerable, to be sure; if the left ever gave way the whole army would be lost, and Bragg's army had shown at Stone's River that when it struck a blow it struck with bone-crushing power. But Bragg's army could no longer win by maneuver. It would have to fight for everything it got, and although at last it got a good deal it did not get what it needed most. The battle of Chickamauga went by nobody's plan, once the first shots were fired. A Federal brigadier summed it up perfectly when he wrote that it was 'a mad, irregular battle, very much resembling guerrilla warfare on a vast scale, in which one army was bushwhacking the other, and wherein all the science and the art of war went for nothing.' The Confederate Senator G. A Henry of Tennessee called the turn before the battle began when he told President Davis that the Army of Tennessee needed better leadership and warned him: 'As sure as you are born, that army is better than its commanders.' Both armies were.

"It began a little west of the Chickamauga on that morning of September 19, when Bedford Forrest's cavalry—advancing dismounted, as competent foot-soldiers as any infantry—collided with one of Thomas' brigades near Reed's bridge. Confederate infantry moved up to help, and before long both armies were heavily engaged. Rosecrans brought McCook's weary corps in on Thomas' right and pulled Crittenden back from Lee and Gordon's, and all day long his army fought desperately to keep the Confederates away from the Lafayette road, with Thomas' corps drawn up in a long shallow crescent and taking most of the pressure. The country was full of trees and underbrush, with little clearings here and there; nobody could see much of his enemy's position, it was almost impossible to move artillery along the narrow country lanes, both armies were sodden with weariness, drinking water was hard to find, casualties were extremely heavy, and by nightfall all anyone could be sure of was that there had been a terrible fight and that it would be worse tomorrow.

"That night there was a full moon, lighting the smoky fields and woods where lay so many thousands of dead and wounded men. In each army, generals who went to headquarters to report and compare notes felt a pervading air of depression and uncertainty; it was the hard fighting men, John B. Hood and Phil Sheridan, who were most struck by it. Rosecrans got a dozen of his chief lieutenants into a cramped log cabin owned by a lady who comes down in history simply as 'the Widow Glenn'; there was a cot for the commanding general to rest on, and a camp chair for General Thomas, but everyone else sat on the floor or lounged against the wall. A fire flickered in the fireplace, and some aide lit a candle, with an inverted bayonet for a candle-holder. The generals were subdued, and the innumerable small noises of the surrounding camp could be heard in the little room; for some reason, when men spoke they spoke in low tones or even in whispers. Thomas was practically torpid for want of sleep. He kept dozing in his chair, rousing himself now and then to say, 'I would strengthen the left,' and then drowsing again.

"His advice was sound. The Federal army held a long, irregular line facing eastward, in front of the Lafayette road. The Confederates had tried all day to crush the northern end of that line—the left, held by Thomas—so that they could get in between Rosecrans and Chattanooga, and they were certain to renew the pressure in the morning. Rosecrans had some thought of shifting his troops into a position from which he could make a counterattack, but he felt that the men were too exhausted to be disturbed. The most he could do was to tell McCook and Crittenden to contract their lines in the morning so that they could send additional help over to Thomas in case he needed it.

"A few miles away, on the Confederate side of this most dismal of battlefields, in a country so tangled that a general could get lost making a simple trip to his superior officer's headquarters, Bragg was revising his command arrangements. It was natural that he should do this, in view of the way some of his generals had performed, although it was a risky thing to do in the middle of a big battle; one suspects that he was trying to find a way to make full use of the talents of General Longstreet, who reached the scene that evening, ready for action even though only five of his brigades were on hand. At any rate, Bragg divided his army into two wings, giving the right wing to Polk and the left to Longstreet. Polk was to make an all-out assault on Thomas at daybreak, and Longstreet was to apply pressure at the other end of the Federal line, making a full-scale attack of his own as soon as Polk's offensive showed progress.

"As usual, there was a hitch. Polk's attack did not get under way until somewhere around nine o'clock in the morning, for reasons now indecipherable: Bragg blamed Polk, Polk blamed D. H. Hill, Hill proclaimed his utter innocence, and probably the real trouble was simply that the chain of command was distressingly loose and that the units of this unhappy army moved with a time-lag much like the one that was habitual in the Army of the Potomac. At any rate, the attack on Thomas was badly delayed, and the delay may have saved the life of the Union army because when at last Polk's troops attacked they struck with enormous force and if they had come in before Rosecrans could send reinforcements from his right Thomas' corps would probably have been overpowered.

"The attack flamed all along his front, overlapping his left as he had feared, and men from McCook's and Crittenden's corps were sent to the left, where Thomas already had more than half of the Union army under his command. Thomas touched the edge of final disaster, once, when John Breckinridge broke past his flank with his division and put two brigades squarely on the vital Lafayette road; these brigades swung around, astride that fateful sandy highway, and came charging south straight into the Union rear, and for a time part of Thomas' line was under attack from two sides at once. By a prodigious effort, the Federals broke these brigades and drove them away, mangling them so badly that they had to be taken out of action altogether; but after they were gone another Confederate corps came in in their place, and the fight had to be made all over again, and Thomas notified Rosecrans that he had to have more help.

"The unexpected result of this pressure on the Union left was that the Union right collapsed. In the hot confusion of battle, army headquarters at last lost track of the shifting and counter-marching that had been ordered, and Rosecrans finally pulled the division of Major General Thomas J. Wood out of Crittenden's line and sent it off to the left. This left a big gap in the line, and before anyone could fill it Longstreet made his own attack, striking with five divisions at the precise spot that had just been vacated, handling his men with the cold professional competence that prevailed in Lee's army. A third of Rosecrans' army was crumpled and driven off to the west, Sheridan's entire division and most of Jeff Davis', with elements from other commands, going all the way beyond the lower end of Missionary Ridge and shambling in disorganized rout toward the crossroads of Rossville, five miles north of battlefield. With them went Rosecrans himself and two of his corps commanders, McCook and Crittenden. Since the last word the unhappy Rosecrans had from Thomas indicated that the left was in dire straits, Rosecrans seems to have assumed now that the entire army had been broken up, and he himself went all the way to Chattanooga in the belief that the commander of a beaten army ought to return to his base and make arrangements for a last-ditch stand.

"That left Thomas to pick up the pieces and save the army, and Thomas did all any soldier could have done. He contracted his original lines and formed a long extension on Snodgrass Hill to the west, getting his men into a huge horseshoe-shaped formation, determined to hold on until dusk and make the final withdrawal an orderly one. He was powerfully helped by two circumstances: Polk's wing had been so roughly handled in the morning's fighting that it was unable to renew the assault until late in the day, and a Federal reserve corps under Major General Gordon Granger, three brigades that had been stationed east of Rossville, came hurrying down to buttress the lines on Snodgrass Hill."[*]

General Granger's reserve corps had been "distributed over a long stretch of country,[†] its rear at Murfreesboro and its van on the battlefield of Chickamauga. These troops had been posted to cover the rear and left flank of the army (of the Cumberland). During September 19, the first day of the battle, they were engaged in some skirmishing and stood at arms expecting an attack. On the evening of the 19th every indication pointed to a renewal of the battle early the next day. The night was cold for that time of the year. Telltale fires were prohibited. The men slept on their arms. All was quiet save in the field hospitals in the rear. A bright moon lighted up the fields and woods. Along the greater part of a front of eight miles the ground was strewn with the intermingled dead of friend and foe. The morning of Sunday, the 20th, opened with a cloudless sky, but a fog had come up from the warm water of the Chickamauga and hung over the battle-field until 9 o'clock. A silence of desertion was in the front. This quiet continued till nearly 10 o'clock; then, as the peaceful tones of the church-bells, rolling over the land from the east, reached the meridian of Chickamauga, they were made dissonant by the murderous roar of the artillery of Bishop Polk, who was opening the battle on Thomas's front. Granger, who had been ordered at all hazards to hold fast where he was, listened and grew impatient. Shortly before 10 o'clock, calling my attention to a great column of dust moving from our front toward the point from which came the sound of battle, he said, 'They are concentrating over there. That is where we ought to be.' The corps flag marked his headquarters in an open field near the Ringgold

---

[*] Bruce Catton, *Never Call Retreat*, pp. 245, 246, 247, 248, 249.

[†] The following narrative of Granger's reinforcement of Thomas is by J. S. Fullerton, from Vol. III of *Battles and Leaders*, pp. 665 to 667.

road. He walked up and down in front of his flag, nervously pulling his beard. Once stopping, he said, 'Why the —— does Rosecrans keep me here? There is nothing in front of us now. There is the battle'—pointing in the direction of Thomas. Every moment the sounds of battle grew louder, while the many columns of dust rolling together here mingled with the smoke that hung over the scene.

"At 11 o'clock, with Granger, I climbed a high hayrick near by. We sat there for ten minutes listening and watching. Then Granger jumped up, thrust his glass into its case, and exclaimed with an oath:

" 'I am going to Thomas, orders or no orders!'

" 'And if you go,' I replied, 'it may bring disaster to the army and you to a court-martial.'

" 'There's nothing in our front now but ragtag, bobtail cavalry,' he replied. 'Don't you see Bragg is piling his whole army on Thomas? I am going to his assistance.'

"We quickly climbed down the rick, and, going to Steedman, Granger ordered him to move his command 'over there,' pointing toward the place from which came the sounds of battle. Colonel Daniel McCook was directed to hold fast at McAfee Church, where his brigade covered the Ringgold road. Before half-past 11 o'clock Steedman's command was in motion. Granger, with his staff and escort, rode in advance. Steedman, after accompanying them a short distance, rode back to the head of his column.

"Thomas was nearly four miles away. The day had not grown very warm, yet the troops marched rapidly over the narrow road, which was covered ankle-deep with dust that rose in suffocating clouds. Completely enveloped in it, the moving column swept along like a desert sandstorm. Two miles from the point of starting, and three-quarters of a mile to the left of the road, the enemy's skirmishers and a section of artillery opened fire on us from an open wood. This force had worked round Thomas's left, and was then partly in his rear. Granger halted to feel them. Soon becoming convinced that it was only a large party of observation, he again started his column and pushed rapidly forward. I was then sent to bring up Colonel McCook's brigade, and put it in position to watch the movements of the enemy, to keep open the Lafayette road, and to cover the open fields between that point and the position held by Thomas. This brigade remained there the rest of the day. Our skirmishers had not gone far when they came upon Thomas's field-hospital, at Cloud's house, then swarming with the enemy. They came from the same body of Forrest's cavalry that had fired on us from the wood. They were quickly driven out, and our men were warmly welcomed with cheers from dying and wounded men.

"A little farther on we were met by a staff-officer sent by General Thomas to discover whether we were friends or enemies; he did not know whence friends could be coming, and the enemy appeared to be approaching from all directions. All of this shattered Army of the Cumberland left on the field was with Thomas; but not more than one-fourth of the men of the army who went into battle at the opening were there. Thomas's loss in killed and wounded during the two days had been dreadful. As his men dropped out his line was contracted to half its length. Now its flanks were bent back, conforming to ridges shaped like a horse-shoe.

"On the part of Thomas and his men there was no thought but that of fighting. He was a soldier who had never retreated, who had never been defeated. He stood immovable, the 'Rock of Chickamauga.' Never had soldiers greater love for a commander. He imbued them with his spirit, and their confidence in him was sublime.

"To the right of Thomas's line was a gorge, then a high ridge, nearly at right angles thereto, running east and west. Confederates under Kershaw (McLaws's division of Hood's corps) were passing through the gorge, together with Bushrod Johnson's division, which Longstreet was strengthening with Hindman's division; divisions were forming on this ridge for an assault; to their left the guns of a battery were being unlimbered for an enfilading fire. There was not a man to send against the force on the ridge, none to oppose this impending assault. The enemy saw the approaching colors of the Reserve Corps and hesitated.

"At 1 o'clock Granger shook hands with Thomas. Something was said about forming to fight to the right and rear.

"'Those men must be driven back,' said Granger, pointing to the gorge and ridge. 'Can you do it?' asked Thomas.

"'Yes. My men are fresh, and they are just the fellows for that work. They are raw troops, and they don't know any better than to charge up there.'

"Granger quickly sent Aleshire's battery of 3-inch rifle guns which he brought up to Thomas's left to assist in repelling another assault about to be made on the Kelly farm front. Whitaker's and Mitchell's brigades under Steedman were wheeled into position and projected against the enemy in the gorge and on the ridge. With ringing cheers they advanced in two lines by double-quick—over open fields, through weeds waist-high, through a little valley, then up the ridge. The enemy opened on them first with artillery, then with a murderous musketry fire. When well up the ridge the men, almost exhausted, were halted for breath. They lay on the ground two or three minutes, then came the command, 'Forward!' Brave, bluff old Steedman, with a regimental flag in his hand, led the way. On went the lines, firing as they ran and bravely receiving a deadly and continuous fire from the enemy on the summit. The Confederates began to break and in another minute were flying down the southern slope of the ridge. In twenty minutes from the beginning of the charge the ridge had been carried.

"Granger's hat had been torn by a fragment of shell; Steedman had been wounded; Whitaker had been wounded, and four of his five staff-officers killed or mortally wounded. Of Steedman's two brigades, numbering 3,500, twenty per cent had been killed and wounded in that twenty minutes; and the end was not yet.

"The enemy massed a force to retake the ridge. They came before our men had rested; twice they assaulted and were driven back. During one assault, as the first line came within range of our muskets, it halted, apparently hesitating, when we saw a colonel seize a flag, wave it over his head, and rush forward. The whole line instantly caught his enthusiasm, and with a wild cheer followed, only to be hurled back again. Our men ran down the ridge in pursuit. In the midst of a group of Confederate dead and wounded they found the brave colonel dead, the flag he carried spread over him where he fell.

"Soon after 5 o'clock Thomas rode to the left of his line, leaving Granger the ranking officer at the center. The ammunition of both Thomas's and Granger's commands was now about exhausted. When Granger had come up he had given ammunition to Brannan and Wood, and that had exhausted his supply. The cartridge-boxes of both our own and the enemy's dead within reach had been emptied by our men. When it was not yet 6 o'clock, and Thomas was still on the left of his line, Brannan rushed up to Granger, saying, 'The enemy are forming for another assault; we have not another round of ammunition—what shall we do?' 'Fix bayonets and go for them,' was the reply. Along the whole line ran the order, 'Fix bayonets.' On came the enemy—our men were lying down. 'Forward,' was sounded. In one instant they were on their feet. Forward they went to meet the charge. The enemy fled. So impetuous was this counter-charge that one regiment, with empty muskets and empty cartridge-boxes, broke through the enemy's line, which, closing in their rear, carried them off as in the undertow."

Late that evening Thomas collected his battered forces and retreated into Chattanooga. As Catton says, Bragg "had fought to the limit of his army's capacity for two days in an attempt to drive Rosecrans away from Chattanooga, and he had at last driven him straight into it. He had won a victory he could not use."[*]

Bragg now occupied Missionary Ridge overlooking Chattanooga, as well as Lookout Mountain to the west. The Federals had Chattanooga but they were in trouble. As Grant wrote, "Halleck . . . directed all the forces that could be spared from my department to be sent to Rosecrans, suggesting that a good commander like Sherman or McPherson should go with the troops; also that I should go in person to Nashville to superintend the movement. Long before this dispatch was received Sherman was already on his way, and McPherson also was moving east with most of the garrison of Vicksburg.

"All supplies for Rosecrans had to be brought from Nashville. The railroad between this base and the army was in possession of the Government up to Bridgeport, the point at which the road crosses to the south side of the Tennessee River; but Bragg, holding Lookout and Raccoon mountains west of Chattanooga, commanded the railroad, the river, and the shortest and best wagon roads both south and north of the Tennessee, between Chattanooga and Bridgeport. The distance between these two places is but twenty-six miles by rail; but owing to this position of Bragg all supplies for Rosecrans had to be hauled by a circuitous route, north of the river, and over a mountainous country, increasing the distance to over sixty miles. This country afforded but little food for his animals, nearly ten thousand of which had already starved, and none was left to draw a single piece of artillery or even the ambulances to convey the sick. The men had been on half rations of hard bread for a considerable time, with but few other supplies, except beef driven from Nashville across the country. The region along the road became so exhausted of food for the cattle

---

* Bruce Catton, *Never Call Retreat*, p. 250.

that by the time they reached Chattanooga they were much in the condition of the few animals left alive there, 'on the lift.' Indeed, the beef was
so poor that the soldiers were in the habit of saying, with a faint facetious-
ness, that they were living on half rations of hard bread and 'beef dried
on the hoof.' Nothing could be transported but food, and the troops were
without sufficient shoes or other clothing suitable for the advancing season. What they had was well worn. The fuel within the Federal lines
was exahusted, even to the stumps of trees. There were no teams to draw
it from the opposite bank, where it was abundant. The only means for
supplying fuel, for some time before my arrival, had been to cut trees
from the north bank of the river, at a considerable distance up the stream,
form rafts of it, and float it down with the current, effecting a landing
on the south side, within our lines, by the use of paddles or poles. It would
then be carried on the shoulders of the men to their camps. If a retreat
had occurred at this time it is not probable that any of the army would
have reached the railroad as an organized body, if followed by the enemy.

"On the morning of the 20th of October I started by train with my staff,
and proceeded as far as Nashville. . . . On the morning of the 21st we took
the train for the front, reaching Stevenson, Alabama, after dark. Rosecrans was there on his way north.* He came into my car, and we held a
brief interview in which he described very clearly the situation at Chattanooga, and made some excellent suggestions as to what should be done.
My only wonder was that he had not carried them out. We then proceeded to Bridgeport, where we stopped for the night. From here we
took horses and made our way by Jasper and over Waldron's Ridge to
Chattanooga. There had been much rain and the roads were almost impassable from mud knee-deep in places, and from washouts on the moun-
tain-sides. The roads were strewn with the debris of broken wagons and
the carcasses of thousands of starved mules and horses. I went directly to
Thomas's headquarters, and remained there a few days until I could
establish my own.

"During the evening most of the general officers called in to pay their
respects and to talk about the condition of affairs. They pointed out on the
maps the line marked with a red or blue pencil which Rosecrans had
contemplated falling back upon. If any of them had approved the move,
they did not say so to me. I found General W. F. Smith occupying the
position of chief engineer of the Army of the Cumberland. I had known
Smith as a cadet at West Point, but had no recollection of having met him
after my graduation, in 1843, up to this time. He explained the situation
of the two armies and the topography of the country so plainly that I
could see it without an inspection. I found that he had established a saw-
mill on the banks of the river, by utilizing an old engine found in the
neighborhood; and by rafting logs from the north side of the river above
had got out the lumber and completed pontoons and roadway plank for a
second bridge, one flying-bridge being there already. He was also rapidly
getting out the materials for constructing the boats for a third bridge. In
addition to this he had far under way a steamer for plying between Chat-

* Rosecrans had been relieved, and General Thomas was now in command at
Chattanooga.

tanooga and Bridgeport whenever he might get possession of the river. This boat consisted of a scow made of the plank sawed out at the mill, housed in, with a stern-wheel attached which was propelled by a second engine taken from some shop or factory.

"I telegraphed to Washington this night, notifying Halleck of my arrival, and asking to have Sherman assigned to the command of the Army of the Tennessee, headquarters in the field. The request was at once complied with.

"The next day, the 24th, I started out to make a personal inspection, taking Thomas and Smith with me, besides most of the members of my personal staff. We crossed to the north side of the river, and, moving to the north of detached spurs of hills, reached the Tennessee, at Brown's Ferry, some three miles below Lookout Mountain, unobserved by the enemy. Here we left our horses back from the river and approached the water on foot. There was a picket station of the enemy, on the opposite side, of about twenty men, in full view, and we were within easy range. They did not fire upon us nor seem to be disturbed by our presence. They must have seen that we were all commissioned officers. But, I suppose, they looked upon the garrison of Chattanooga as prisoners of war, feeding or starving themselves, and thought it would be inhuman to kill any of them except in self-defense. That night I issued orders for opening the route to Bridgeport—a 'cracker line,' as the soldiers appropriately termed it. They had been so long on short rations that my first thought was the establishment of a line over which food might reach them."*

$\mathcal{L}$ifting the Siege of $\mathcal{C}$hattanooga †

BY GENERAL U. S. GRANT

CHATTANOOGA IS ON THE SOUTH BANK OF THE TENNESSEE, where that river runs nearly due west. It is at the northern end of a valley five or six miles in width through which runs Chattanooga Creek. To the east of the valley is Missionary Ridge, rising from five to eight hundred feet above the creek, and terminating somewhat abruptly a half-mile or more before reaching the Tennessee. On the west of the valley is Lookout Mountain, 2,200 feet above tide-water. Just below the town, the Tennessee makes a turn to the south and runs to the base of Lookout Mountain, leaving no level ground between the mountain and river. The Memphis and Charles-

* U. S. Grant, "Chattanooga," *Battles and Leaders,* Vol. III.
† *Ibid.*

ton railroad passes this point, where the mountain stands nearly perpendicular. East of Missionary Ridge flows the South Chickamauga River; west of Lookout Mountain is Lookout Creek; and west of that, the Raccoon Mountain. Lookout Mountain at its northern end rises almost perpendicularly for some distance, then breaks off in a gentle slope of cultivated fields to near the summit, where it ends in a palisade thirty or more feet in height. The intrenched line of the enemy commenced on the north end of Missionary Ridge and extended along the crest for some distance south, thence across Chattanooga Valley to Lookout Mountain. Lookout Mountain was also fortified and held by the enemy, who also kept troops in Lookout Valley and on Raccoon Mountain, with pickets extending down the river so as to command the road on the north bank and render it useless to us. In addition to this there was an intrenched line in Chattanooga Valley extending from the river east of the town to Lookout Mountain, to make the investment complete.

Thus the enemy, with a vastly superior force, was strongly fortified to the east, south, and west, and commanded the river below. Practically the Army of the Cumberland was besieged. The enemy, with his cavalry north of the river, had stopped the passing of a train loaded with ammunition and medical supplies. The Union army was short of both, not having ammunition enough for a day's fighting.

Long before my coming into this new field, General Halleck had ordered parts of the Eleventh and Twelfth corps, commanded respectively by Generals Howard and Slocum, Hooker in command of the whole, from the Army of the Potomac, to reënforce Rosecrans. It would have been folly to have sent them to Chattanooga to help eat up the few rations left there. They were consequently left on the railroad, where supplies could be brought them. Before my arrival Thomas ordered their concentration at Bridgeport.

General W. F. Smith had been so instrumental in preparing for the move which I was now about to make, and so clear in his judgment about the manner of making it, that I deemed it but just to him that he should have command of the troops detailed to execute the design, although he was then acting as a staff-officer, and was not in command of troops.

On the 24th of October, after my return to Chattanooga, the following details were made: General Hooker, who was now at Bridgeport, was ordered to cross to the south side of the Tennessee and march up by Whiteside's and Wauhatchie to Brown's Ferry. General Palmer, with a division of the Fourteenth Corps, Army of the Cumberland, was ordered to move down the river on the north side, by a back road, until opposite Whiteside's, then cross and hold the road in Hooker's rear after he had passed. Four thousand men were at the same time detailed to act under General Smith directly from Chattanooga. Eighteen hundred of them, under General Hazen, were to take sixty pontoon-boats and, under cover of night, float by the pickets of the enemy at the north base of Lookout, down to Brown's Ferry, then land on the south side and capture or drive away the pickets at that point. Smith was to march with the remainder of the detail, also under cover of night, by the north bank of the river, to Brown's Ferry, taking with him all the material for laying the bridge, as soon as the crossing was secured.

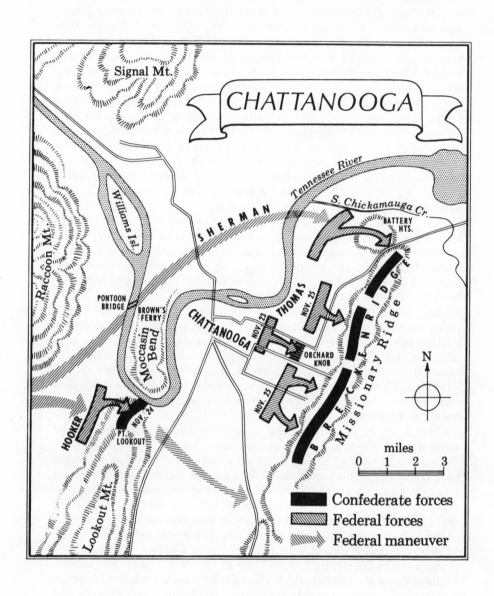

CHATTANOOGA

Signal Mt.

Tennessee River

Williams Isl.

Raccoon Mt.

SHERMAN

S. Chickamauga Cr.

BATTERY HTS.

PONTOON BRIDGE

BROWN'S FERRY

Moccasin Bend

CHATTANOOGA

NOV. 23

THOMAS

NOV. 25

ORCHARD KNOB

NOV. 25

BRECKENRIDGE

Missionary Ridge

N

HOOKER

PT. LOOKOUT

NOV. 24

Lookout Mt.

miles
0 1 2 3

◼ Confederate forces
▨ Federal forces
〰 Federal maneuver

On the 26th Hooker crossed the river at Bridgeport and commenced his eastward march. At three o'clock on the morning of the 27th Hazen moved into the stream with his sixty pontoons and eighteen hundred brave and well-equipped men. Smith started enough in advance to be near the river when Hazen should arrive. There are a number of detached spurs of hills north of the river at Chattanooga, back of which is a good road parallel to the stream, sheltered from view from the top of Lookout. It was over this road Smith marched. At five o'clock Hazen landed at Brown's Ferry, surprised the picket-guard and captured most of it. By seven o'clock the whole of Smith's force was ferried over and in possession of a height commanding the ferry. This was speedily fortified while a detail was laying the pontoon-bridge. By ten o'clock the bridge was laid, and our extreme right, now in Lookout Valley, was fortified and connected with the rest of the army. The two bridges over the Tennessee River—a flying one at Chattanooga and the new one at Brown's Ferry—with the road north of the river, covered from both the fire and the view of the enemy, made the connection complete. Hooker found but slight obstacles in his way, and on the afternoon of the 28th emerged into Lookout Valley at Wauhatchie. Howard marched on to Brown's Ferry, while Geary, who commanded a division in the Twelfth Corps, stopped three miles south. The pickets of the enemy on the river below were cut off and soon came in and surrendered.

The river was now open to us from Lookout Valley to Bridgeport. Between Brown's Ferry and Kelley's Ferry the Tennessee runs through a narrow gorge in the mountains, which contracts the stream so much as to increase the current beyond the capacity of an ordinary steamer to stem. To get up these rapids, steamers must be cordelled, that is, pulled up by ropes from the shore. But there is no difficulty in navigating the stream from Bridgeport to Kelley's Ferry. The latter point is only eight miles from Chattanooga, and connected with it by a good wagon road, which runs through a low pass in the Raccoon Mountain on the south side of the river to Brown's Ferry, thence on the north side to the river opposite Chattanooga. There were several steamers at Bridgeport, and abundance of forage, clothing, and provisions.

On the way to Chattanooga I had telegraphed back to Nashville for a good supply of vegetables and small rations, which the troops had been so long deprived of. Hooker had brought with him from the east a full supply of land transportation. His animals had not been subjected to hard work on bad roads without forage, but were in good condition. In five days from my arrival at Chattanooga the way was open to Bridgeport, and, with the aid of steamers and Hooker's teams, in a week the troops were receiving full rations. It is hard for any one not an eye-witness to realize the relief this brought. The men were soon reclothed and well fed; an abundance of ammunition was brought up, and a cheerfulness prevailed not before enjoyed in many weeks. Neither officers nor men looked upon themselves any longer as doomed. The weak and languid appearance of the troops, so visible before, disappeared at once.

The enemy was surprised by the movement which secured to us a line of supplies. He appreciated its importance, and hastened to try to recover the line from us. His strength on Lookout Mountain was not equal to

Hooker's command in the valley below. From Missionary Ridge he had to march twice the distance we had from Chattanooga, in order to reach Lookout Valley. But on the night of the 28th–29th [of October] an attack was made on Geary, at Wauhatchie, by Longstreet's corps. When the battle commenced, Hooker ordered Howard up from Brown's Ferry. He had three miles to march to reach Geary. On his way he was fired upon by rebel troops from a foot-hill to the left of the road, and from which the road was commanded. Howard turned to the left, and charged up the hill, and captured it before the enemy had time to intrench, taking many prisoners. Leaving sufficient men to hold this height, he pushed on to reënforce Geary. Before he got up, Geary had been engaged for about three hours against a vastly superior force. The night was so dark that the men could not distinguish one another except by the light of the flashes of their muskets. In the darkness and uproar Hooker's teamsters became frightened, and deserted their teams. The mules also became frightened, and, breaking loose from their fastenings, stampeded directly toward the enemy. The latter no doubt took this for a charge, and stampeded in turn. By four o'clock in the morning the battle had entirely ceased, and our "cracker line" was never afterward disturbed.

In securing possession of Lookout Valley, Smith lost one man killed and four or five wounded. The enemy lost most of his pickets at the ferry by capture. In the night engagement of the 28th–29th Hooker lost 416 killed and wounded. I never knew the loss of the enemy, but our troops buried over 150 of his dead, and captured more than 100.

Having got the Army of the Cumberland in a comfortable position, I now began to look after the remainder of my new command. Burnside was in about as desperate a condition as the Army of the Cumberland had been, only he was not yet besieged. He was a hundred miles from the nearest possible base, Big South Fork of the Cumberland River, and much farther from any railroad we had possession of. The roads back were over mountains, and all supplies along the line had long since been exhausted. His animals, too, had been starved, and their carcasses lined the road from Cumberland Gap, and far back toward Lexington, Kentucky. East Tennessee still furnished supplies of beef, bread, and forage, but it did not supply ammunition, clothing, medical supplies, or small rations, such as coffee, sugar, salt, and rice.

Stopping to organize his new command, Sherman had started from Memphis for Corinth on the 11th of October. His instructions required him to repair the road in his rear in order to bring up supplies. The distance was about 330 miles through a hostile country. His entire command could not have maintained the road if it had been completed. The bridges had all been destroyed by the enemy and much other damage done; a hostile community lived along the road; guerrilla bands infested the country, and more or less of the cavalry of the enemy was still in the west. Often Sherman's work was destroyed as soon as completed, though he was only a short distance away.

The Memphis and Charleston road strikes the Tennessee River at Eastport, Mississippi. Knowing the difficulty Sherman would have to supply himself from Memphis, I had previously ordered supplies sent from St. Louis on small steamers, to be convoyed by the navy, to meet him at Eastport. These he got. I now ordered him to discontinue his work of repairing roads, and to move on with his whole force to Stevenson, Alabama, without delay. This order was borne to Sherman by a messenger who paddled down the Tennessee in a canoe, and floated over Muscle Shoals; it was delivered at Iuka on the 27th. In this Sherman was notified that the rebels were moving a force toward Cleveland, east Tennessee, and might be going to Nashville, in which event his troops were in the best position to beat them there. Sherman, with his characteristic promptness, abandoned the work he was engaged upon and pushed on at once. On the 1st of November he crossed the Tennessee at Eastport, and that day was in Florence, Alabama, with the head of column, while his troops were still crossing at Eastport, with Blair bringing up the rear.

Sherman's force made an additional army, with cavalry, artillery, and trains, all to be supplied by the single-track road from Nashville. All indications pointed also to the probable necessity of supplying Burnside's command, in east Tennessee, 25,000 more, by the same road. A single track could not do this. I therefore gave an order to Sherman to halt General G. M. Dodge's command of eight thousand men at Athens, and subsequently directed the latter to arrange his troops along the railroad from Decatur, north toward Nashville, and to rebuild that road. The road from Nashville to Decatur passes over a broken country, cut up with innumerable streams, many of them of considerable width, and with valleys far below the road-bed. All the bridges over these had been destroyed and the rails taken up and twisted by the enemy. All the locomotives and cars not carried off had been destroyed as effectually as they knew how to destroy them. All bridges and culverts had been destroyed between Nashville and Decatur, and thence to Stevenson, where the Memphis and Charleston and the Nashville and Chattanooga roads unite. The rebuilding of this road would give us two roads as far as Stevenson over which to supply the army. From Bridgeport, a short distance farther east, the river supplements the road.

General Dodge, besides being a most capable soldier, was an experienced railroad builder. He had no tools to work with except those of the pioneers—axes, picks, and spades. With these he was able to intrench his men and protect them against surprises by small parties of the enemy. As he had no base of supplies until the road could be completed back to Nashville, the first matter to consider, after protecting his men, was the getting in of food and forage from the surrounding country. He had his men and teams bring in all the grain they could find, or all they needed, and all the cattle for beef, and such other food as could be found. Millers were detailed from the ranks to run the mills along the line of the army; when these were not near enough to the troops for protection, they were taken down and moved up to the line of the road. Blacksmith shops, with all the iron and steel found in them, were moved up in like manner. Blacksmiths were detailed and set to work making the tools necessary in railroad and bridge building. Axemen were put to work getting out timber for bridges, and cutting fuel for the locomotives when the road should be completed; car-builders were set to work repairing the locomotives and cars. Thus every branch of railroad-building, making tools to work with, and supplying the workingmen with food, was all going on at once, and without the aid of a mechanic or laborer except what the command itself furnished. But rails and cars the men could not make without material, and there was not enough rolling stock to keep the road we already had worked to its full capacity. There were no rails except those in use. To supply these deficiencies I ordered eight of the ten engineers General McPherson had at Vicksburg to be sent to Nashville, and all the cars he had, except ten. I also ordered the troops in west Tennessee to points on the river and on the Memphis and Charleston road, and ordered the cars, locomotives, and rails from all the railroads, except the Memphis and Charleston, to Nashville. The military manager of railroads, also, was directed to furnish more rolling stock, and, as far as he could, bridge material. General Dodge had the work assigned him finished within forty days after receiving his orders. The number of bridges to rebuild was 182, many of them over deep and wide chasms. The length of road repaired was 182 miles.

My orders for the battle were all prepared in advance of Sherman's arrival, except the dates, which could not be fixed while troops to be engaged were so far away. The possession of Lookout Mountain was of no special advantage to us now. Hooker was instructed to send Howard's corps to the north side of the Tennessee, thence up behind the hills on the north side, and to go into camp opposite Chattanooga; with the remainder of the command Hooker was, at a time to be afterward appointed, to ascend the western slope between the upper and lower palisades, and so get into Chattanooga Valley.

The plan of battle was for Sherman to attack the enemy's right flank, form a line across it, extend our left over South Chickamauga River, so as to threaten or hold the railroad in Bragg's rear, and thus force him either to weaken his lines elsewhere or lose his connection with his base at Chickamauga Station. Hooker was to perform like service on our right. His problem was to get from Lookout Valley to Chattanooga Valley in the most expeditious way possible; cross the latter valley rapidly to Rossville, south of Bragg's line on Missionary Ridge, form line there across the ridge, facing north, with his right flank extended to Chickamauga Valley east of the ridge, thus threatening the enemy's rear on that flank and compelling him to reënforce this also. Thomas, with the Army of the Cumberland, occupied the center, and was to assault while the enemy was engaged with most of his forces on his two flanks.

To carry out this plan, Sherman was to cross the Tennessee at Brown's Ferry and move east of Chattanooga to a point opposite the north end of Missionary Ridge, and to place his command back of the foot-hills out of sight of the enemy on the ridge. There are two streams called Chickamauga emptying into the Tennessee River east of Chattanooga: North Chickamauga, taking its rise in Tennessee, flowing south and emptying into the river some seven or eight miles east; while the South Chickamauga, which takes its rise in Georgia, flows northward, and empties into the Tennessee some three or four miles above the town. There were now 116 pontoons in the North Chickamauga River, their presence there being unknown to the enemy.

At night a division was to be marched up to that point, and at two o'clock in the morning moved down with the current, thirty men in each boat. A few were to land east of the mouth of the South Chickamauga, capture the pickets there, and then lay a bridge connecting the two banks of the river. The rest were to land on the south side of the Tennessee, where Missionary Ridge would strike it if prolonged, and a sufficient number of men to man the boats were to push to the north side to ferry over the main body of Sherman's command, while those left on the south side intrenched themselves. Thomas was to move out from his lines facing the ridge, leaving enough of Palmer's corps to guard against an attack down the valley. Lookout Valley being of no present value to us, and being untenable by the enemy if we should secure Missionary Ridge, Hooker's orders were changed. His revised orders brought him to Chattanooga by the established route north of the Tennessee. He was then to move out to the right to Rossville.

The next day after Sherman's arrival I took him, with Generals Thomas and Smith and other officers, to the north side of the river and showed them the ground over which Sherman had to march, and pointed out generally what he was expected to do. As soon as the inspection was over, Sherman started for Bridgeport to hasten matters, rowing a boat himself, I believe, from Kelley's Ferry. Sherman had left Bridgeport the night of the 14th, reached Chattanooga the evening of the 15th, made the above-described inspection the morning of the 16th, and started back the same evening to hurry up his command, fully appreciating the importance of time.

His march was conducted with as much expedition as the roads and season would admit of. By the 20th he was himself at Brown's Ferry with head of column, but many of his troops were far behind, and one division, Ewing's, was at Trenton, sent that way to create the impression that Lookout was to be taken from the south. Sherman received his orders at the ferry, and was asked if he could not be ready for the assault the following morning. It was impossible to get Sherman's troops up for the next day. I then asked him if they could not be got up to make the assault on the morning of the 22d, and ordered Thomas to move on that date. But the elements were against us. It rained all the 20th and 21st. The river rose so rapidly that it was difficult to keep the pontoons in place.

Meantime Sherman continued his crossing, without intermission, as fast as his troops could get up. The crossing had to be effected in full view of the enemy on the top of Lookout Mountain. Once over, the troops soon disappeared behind the detached hills on the north side, and would not come to view again, either to watchmen on Lookout Mountain or Missionary Ridge, until they emerged between the hills to strike the bank of the river. But when Sherman's advance reached a point opposite the town of Chattanooga, Howard, who, it will be remembered, had been concealed behind the hills on the north side, took up his line of march to join the troops on the south side. His crossing was in full view both from Missionary Ridge and the top of Lookout, and the enemy, of course, supposed these troops to be Sherman's. This enabled Sherman to get to his assigned position without discovery.

During the night of the 21st the rest of the pontoon-boats, completed, one hundred and sixteen in all, were carried up to and placed in North

Chickamauga. The material for the roadway over these was deposited out of view of the enemy within a few hundred yards of the bank of the Tennessee where the north end of the bridge was to rest.

Lookout Mountain[*]

BY GENERAL J. S. FULLERTON

G ENERAL GRANT'S PLAN, IN BRIEF, now was to turn Bragg's right. He selected his old army—the Army of the Tennessee, under Sherman—to open the battle, to make the grand attack, and to carry Missionary Ridge as far as Tunnel Hill. The Army of the Cumberland was simply to get into position and coöperate.

No battle-field in our war, probably none in history, where large armies were engaged, was so spectacular or so well fitted for a display of soldierly courage and daring as the amphitheater of Chattanooga. Late on the night of November 22d a sentinel who had deserted from the enemy was brought to General Sheridan, and informed him that Bragg's baggage was being reduced and that he was about to fall back. On account of these indications and reports, General Grant decided not to wait longer for General Sherman's troops to come up, but to find out whether Bragg was in fact withdrawing, and, if so, to attack him at once. Therefore, at eleven o'clock on the morning of the 23d, he directed General Thomas to "drive in the enemy's pickets," and feel his lines for the purpose of finding out whether he still held in force. Thus Grant was about to change his plans. He was compelled to depart from his original purpose, and was obliged to call on troops of the Army of the Cumberland to make the first offensive movement.

General Thomas ordered General Granger, commanding the Fourth Corps, to throw one division forward in the direction of Orchard Knob, with a second division in support, to discover if the enemy still remained near his old camp.

Orchard Knob is a rough, steep hill, one hundred feet high, covered with a growth of small timber, rising abruptly from the Chattanooga Valley, and lying about half-way between our outer pits and the breastworks of logs and stones. At its western base, and extending for a mile beyond, both north and south of the hill, were other rifle-pits, hid in part by a heavy belt of timber that extended about a quarter of a mile from the foot of the hill into the plain. Between this belt of timber and our lines were open fields, in which there was not a tree, fence, or other obstruction,

[*] From "The Army of the Cumberland at Chattanooga," *Battles and Leaders,* Vol. III.

save the bed of the East Tennessee Railroad. On the plain were hundreds of little mounds, thrown up by our own and the enemy's pickets, giving it the appearance of an overgrown prairie-dog village.

At noon General Grant, Assistant Secretary of War Dana, General Thomas, Generals Hooker, Granger, Howard, and other distinguished officers stood on the parapet of Fort Wood facing Orchard Knob, waiting to see this initial movement—the overture to the battle of Chattanooga. At half-part twelve, Wood's division, supported by Sheridan, marched out on the plain in front of the fort. It was an inspiriting sight. Flags were flying; the quick, earnest steps of thousands beat equal time. The sharp commands of hundreds of company officers, the sound of the drums, the ringing notes of the bugle, companies wheeling and countermarching and regiments getting into line, the bright sun lighting up ten thousand polished bayonets till they glistened and flashed like a flying shower of electric sparks—all looked like preparations for a peaceful pageant, rather than for the bloody work of death.

Groups of officers on Missionary Ridge looked down through their glasses, and the enemy's pickets, but a few hundred yards away, came out of their pits and stood idly looking on, unconcernedly viewing what they supposed to be preparations for a grand review. But at half-past one o'clock the advance was sounded. Instantly Wood's division, moving with the steadiness of a machine, started forward. Not a straggler or laggard was on the field, and, what was probably hardly ever before seen, drummers were marching with their companies, beating the charge. Now the enemy realized, for the first time, that it was not a review. His pickets fell back to their reserves. The reserves were quickly driven back to the main line. Firing opened from the enemy's advanced rifle-pits, followed by a tremendous roll of musketry and roar of artillery. Men were seen on the ground, dotting the field over which the line of battle had passed. Ambulances came hurrying back with the first of the wounded. Columns of puffy smoke arose from the Orchard Knob woods. A cheer, faint to those on the parapet of Fort Wood, indicated that the boys in blue were carrying the breastworks on the Knob! A sharp, short struggle, and the hill was ours.

About four o'clock in the afternoon of November 23d, when it became certain that Osterhaus, cut off by the breaking of the pontoon-bridge at Brown's Ferry, would be attached to Hooker's command, General Thomas directed Hooker to make a demonstration against Lookout Mountain the next morning, and, if the demonstration showed it could be carried, to proceed to take it. Later in the day, orders to the same effect came to General Hooker from General Grant. The success at Orchard Knob, and the breaking of the bridge, caused this radical change to be made in Grant's plans. Yet he still held to the chief feature, which was to turn Bragg's right.

The morning of November 24th opened with a cold, drizzling rain. Thick clouds of mist were settling on Lookout Mountain. At daybreak Geary's division, and Whitaker's brigade of Cruft's division, marched up to Wauhatchie, the nearest point at which Lookout Creek, swelled by recent rains, could be forded, and at eight o'clock they crossed. The heavy clouds of mist reaching down the mountain-side hid the movement from

Lookout Mountain: *The battle above the clouds*

the enemy, who was expecting and was well prepared to resist a crossing at the Chattanooga road below. As soon as this movement was discovered, the enemy withdrew his troops from the summit of the mountain, changed front, and formed a new line to meet our advance, his left resting at the palisade, and his right at the heavy works in the valley, where the road crossed the creek. Having crossed at Wauhatchie, Whitaker's brigade, being in the advance, drove back the enemy's pickets, and quickly ascended the mountain till it reached the foot of the palisade. Here, firmly attaching its right, the brigade faced left in front, with its left joined to Geary's division. Geary now moved along the side of the mountain, and through the valley, thus covering the crossing of the rest of Hooker's command. In the meantime Grose's brigade was engaging the enemy at the lower road crossing, and Woods' brigade of Osterhaus's division was building a bridge rather more than half a mile farther up the creek. Geary, moving down the valley, reached this point at eleven o'clock, just after the bridge was finished, and as Osterhaus's division and Grose's brigade were crossing. Hooker's command, now united in the enemy's field, was ready to advance and sweep around the mountain. His line, hanging at the base of the palisades like a great pendulum, reached down the side of the mountain to the valley, where the force that had just crossed the creek was attached as its weight. Now, as, at the command of Hooker, it swung forward in its upward movement, the artillery of the Army of the Cumberland, on Moccasin Point, opened fire, throwing a stream of shot and shell into the enemy's rifle-pits at the foot of the mountain, and into the works thickly planted on the "White House" plateau. At the same time the guns planted by Hooker on the west side of the creek opened on the works which covered the enemy's right. Then followed a gallant assault by Osterhaus and Grose. After fighting for nearly two hours, step by step up the steep mountain-side, over and through deep gullies and ravines, over great rocks and fallen trees, the earth-works on the plateau were assaulted and carried, and the enemy was driven out and forced to fall back. He did so slowly and reluctantly, taking advantage of the rough ground to continue the fight. It was now two o'clock. A halt all along the line was ordered by General Hooker, as the clouds had grown so thick that further advance was impracticable, and as his ammunition was almost exhausted and more could not well be brought up the mountain. But all the enemy's works had been taken. Hooker had carried the mountain on the east side, had opened communication with Chattanooga, and he commanded the enemy's line of defensive works in Chattanooga Valley.

At two o'clock Hooker reported to General Thomas and informed him that he was out of ammunition. Thomas at once sent Carlin's brigade from the valley, each soldier taking with him all the small ammunition he could carry. At five o'clock Carlin was on the mountain, and Hooker's skirmishers were quickly supplied with the means of carrying on their work.

In the morning it had not been known in Chattanooga, in Sherman's army, or in Bragg's camp, that a battle was to be fought. Indeed, it was not definitely known even to General Grant; for Hooker was only ordered to make a demonstration, and, if this showed a good chance for success, then to make an attack. Soon after breakfast, Sherman's men at the other end of the line, intent on the north end of Missionary Ridge, and Thomas's men in the center, fretting to be let loose from their intrench-ments, were startled by the sound of artillery and musketry firing in Lookout Valley. Surprise possessed the thousands who turned their anxious eyes toward the mountain. The hours slowly wore away; the roar of battle increased, as it came rolling around the point of the mountain, and the anxiety grew. A battle was being fought just before and above them. They could hear, but could not see how it was going. Finally, the wind, tossing about the clouds and mist, made a rift that for a few minutes opened a view of White House plateau. The enemy was seen to be in flight, and Hooker's men were in pursuit! Then went up a mighty cheer from the thirty thousand in the valley that was heard above the battle by their comrades on the mountain.

As the sun went down, the clouds rolled away, and the night came on clear and cool. A grand sight was old Lookout that night. Not two miles apart were the parallel camp-fires of the two armies, extending from the summit of the mountain to its base, looking like streams of burning lava, while in between, the flashes from the skirmishers' muskets glowed like giant fire-flies.

The next morning there was silence in Hooker's front. Before daylight eight adventurous, active volunteers from the 8th Kentucky Infantry scaled the palisades and ran up the Stars and Stripes. The enemy had stolen away in the night.

Although General Grant had twice changed his original plan, first in the movement from the center, then in the reconnoissance and resulting attack on Lookout Mountain, he still adhered to his purpose of turning Bragg's right, and made no change in the instructions given to General Sherman, except as to the time of attack. Every necessary preparation for crossing Sherman's troops had been made secretly, under direction of General W. F. Smith; 116 pontoons had been placed in North Chicka-mauga Creek, and in ravines near its mouth, and many wagon-loads of "balks" (stringers) and chess (flooring) had been hid near by. Sherman had his troops well massed on the north side of the river. After dark, November 23d, Colonel James Barnett, the gallant and skillful Chief of Artillery, of the Army of the Cumberland under Rosecrans, to whom was assigned the duty of covering Sherman's crossing, and protecting the pon-toon bridge, planted the guns of six six-gun batteries on the low foot-hills, and a battery of siege guns on the higher ground on the north side of the river. At midnight General Giles A. Smith's brigade entered the pontoons, floated out of North Chickamauga Creek, and was rowed to the south bank of the river. Landing quietly, he surprised and captured the enemy's pickets, and secured a firm foothold. The pontoons were sent across the river, and with these and the small steamboat brought up from Chat-tanooga General Morgan L. Smith's and General John E. Smith's divi-sions were ferried over the river. As soon as these troops had been landed, work was commenced on the pontoon-bridge, which was skillfully laid under the supervision of General W. F. Smith. The bridge was 1,350 feet in length, and was completed by eleven o'clock in the morning, when General Ewing's division and Sherman's artillery crossed. At one o'clock, just as Hooker was rounding the front of Lookout Mountain, the roar of

Missionary Ridge: *Thomas's Union troops charging uphill*

his battle stirring the blood of the veterans of the Army of the Tennessee, General Sherman gave the command, "Forward!" At three thirty General Sherman took the hill which was supposed to be the north end of the ridge, and soon afterward took another hill a little in advance, both separated by a deep depression from the heavily fortified Tunnel Hill, on which Bragg's right flank rested and which was Sherman's objective point.

None of the men of the Army of the Cumberland, who for nine weeks were buried in the trenches at Chattanooga, can ever forget the glorious night of the 24th of November. As the sun went down, the clouds rolled up the mountain, and the mist was blown out of the valley. Night came on clear, with the stars lighting up the heavens. But there followed a sight to cheer their hearts and thrill their souls. Away off to their right, and reaching skyward, Lookout Mountain was ablaze with the fires of Hooker's men, while off to their left, and reaching far above the valley, the north end of Missionary Ridge was aflame with the lights of Sherman's army. The great iron crescent that had, with threatening aspect, so long hung over them, was disappearing. The only thought that dampened their enthusiasm was that the enemy was being destroyed on the flanks, while they were tied down in the center, without a part in the victories. But late that night General Grant, thinking that General Sherman had carried Tunnel Hill, and acting in that belief, gave orders for the next day's battle. General Sherman was directed to attack the enemy at early dawn, Thomas to co-operate with him, and Hooker, to be ready to advance into Chattanooga Valley, to hold the road that zigzagged from the valley to the summit. Early the next morning, when General Grant learned that the ridge had not been carried as far as Tunnel Hill, and that Lookout Mountain had been evacuated by the enemy, he suspended his orders, except those to Sherman, and directed Hooker to come down from the mountain, to carry the pass at Rossville, and then operate on Bragg's left and rear. Bragg's army was now concentrated on Missionary Ridge, and in the valley at the east foot. Cheatham's and Stevenson's divisions had been withdrawn from Lookout Mountain on the night of the 24th, and, marching all night, were seen at dawn the next morning moving along the summit of Missionary Ridge, on the way to reënforce Bragg's right. For several hours after daylight the flowing of this steady stream of troops continued.

Early in the morning of the 25th General Grant and General Thomas established their headquarters on Orchard Knob, a point from which the best view of the movements of the whole army could be had. At sunrise General Sherman commenced his attack, but after repeated assaults and severe fighting, it appearing to be impossible for General Sherman to take the enemy's works, operations ceased early in the afternoon.

Meanwhile Hooker was detained three hours at Chattanooga Creek, while a bridge that the retreating enemy had burned was being rebuilt. As soon as he had taken Rossville, he moved against the south end of Missionary Ridge. The ridge was quickly carried, and, sweeping northward, Hooker soon came upon Stewart's division, posted on the summit, and behind the earth-works which the Army of the Cumberland had thrown up the day after Chickamauga. Cruft's division assaulted and carried the works, thus having the good fortune of retaking the works they themselves had constructed. It was by this time nearly sundown. Hooker reached the south end of the ridge too late in the day to relieve the pressure on Sherman, who was at the north end six miles off. Bragg's right had not been turned. Success had not followed Sherman's movement. The battle as planned had not been won.

Late on this memorable afternoon there was an accident—an accident like the charge at Balaklava; though, unlike this theme for poetry, it called for greater daring, and was attended by complete success, and yielded most important results, for it led to the complete shattering of the enemy's army, and drove him from the field. On Orchard Knob, and opposite the center of Missionary Ridge, were four divisions of the Army of the Cumberland. On the left was Baird's division; then Wood's and Sheridan's divisions occupying the lines which, two days before, they had taken in their magnificent advance; on the right was R. W. Johnson's division—all under the personal command of Thomas. It was past three o'clock. General Sherman had ceased operations. General Hooker's advance had not yet been felt. The day was dying, and Bragg still held the ridge. If any movement to dislodge him was to be made that day it must be made at once. At half-past three o'clock an attack was ordered by General Grant. He had changed his plan of battle. At once orders were issued that at the firing, in rapid succession, of six guns on Orchard Knob, Thomas's whole line should instantaneously move forward, Sheridan's and Wood's divisions in the center, Sheridan to be supported on the right by Johnson, and Wood on the left by Baird. This demonstration was to be made to relieve the pressure on Sherman. The only order given was to move forward and take the rifle-pits at the foot of the ridge. In Sheridan's division the order was, "As soon as the signal is given, the whole line will advance, and you will take what is before you."

Between Orchard Knob and Missionary Ridge was a valley, partly covered with a small growth of timber. It was wooded in front of the right of Baird's and of the whole of Wood's division. In front of Sheridan's and Johnson's it had been almost entirely cleared. At the foot of the ridge were heavy rifle-pits, which could be seen from Orchard Knob, and extending in front of them, for four and five hundred yards, the ground was covered with felled trees. There was a good plain for both direct and enfilading fire from the rifle-pits, and the approaches were commanded by the enemy's artillery. At this point the ridge is five or six hundred feet high. Its side, scored with gullies and showing but little timber, had a rough and bare appearance. Half-way up was another line of rifle-pits, and the summit was furrowed with additional lines and dotted over with epaulements, in which were placed fifty pieces of artillery. Directly in front of Orchard Knob, and on the summit of the ridge, in a small house was Bragg's headquarters.

At twenty minutes before four the signal guns were fired. Suddenly twenty thousand men rushed forward, moving in line of battle by brigades, with a double line of skirmishers in front, and closely followed by the reserves in mass. The big siege-guns in the Chattanooga forts roared above the light artillery and musketry in the valley. The enemy's rifle-pits were ablaze, and the whole ridge in our front had broken out like another Aetna. Not many minutes afterward our men were seen working through the felled trees and other obstructions. Though exposed to such a terrific fire, they neither fell back nor halted. By a bold and desperate push they broke through the works in several places and opened flank and reverse fires. The enemy was thrown into confusion, and took precipitate flight up the ridge. Many prisoners and a large number of small-arms were captured. The order of the commanding general had now been fully and most successfully carried out. But it did not go far enough to satisfy these brave men, who thought the time had come to finish the battle of Chickamauga. There was a halt of but a few minutes, to take breath and to re-form lines; then, with a sudden impulse, and without orders, all started up the ridge. Officers, catching their spirit, first followed, then led. There was no thought of supports or of protecting flanks, though the enemy's line could be seen, stretching on either side.

As soon as this movement was seen from Orchard Knob, Grant quickly turned to Thomas, who stood by his side, and I heard him say angrily: "Thomas, who ordered those men up the ridge?" Thomas replied, in his usual slow, quiet manner: "I don't know; I did not." Then, addressing General Gordon Granger, he said, "Did you order them up, Granger?" "No," said Granger; "they started up without orders. When those fellows get started all hell can't stop them." General Grant said something to the effect that somebody would suffer if it did not turn out well, and then, turning, stoically watched the ridge. He gave no further orders.

As soon as Granger had replied to Thomas, he turned to me, his chief-of-staff, and said: "Ride at once to Wood, and then to Sheridan, and ask them if they ordered their men up the ridge, and tell them, if they can take it, to push ahead." As I was mounting, Granger added: "It is hot over there, and you may not get through. I shall send Captain Avery to Sheridan, and other officers after both of you." As fast as my horse could carry me, I rode first to General Wood, and delivered the message. "I didn't order them up," said Wood; "they started up on their own account, and they are going up, too! Tell Granger, if we are supported, we will take and hold the ridge!" As soon as I reached General Wood, Captain Avery got to General Sheridan, and delivered his message. "I didn't order them up," said Sheridan; "but we are going to take the ridge!" He then asked Avery for his flask and waved it at a group of Confederate officers, standing just in front of Bragg's headquarters, with the salutation, "Here's at you!" At once two guns—the "Lady Breckinridge" and the "Lady Buckner"—in front of Bragg's headquarters were fired at Sheridan and the group of officers about him. One shell struck so near as to throw dirt over Sheridan and Avery. "Ah!" said the general, "that is ungenerous; I shall take those guns for that!" Before Sheridan received the message taken by Captain Avery, he had sent a staff-officer to Granger, to inquire whether "the order given to take the rifle-pits meant the rifle-pits at the base, or those on the top of the ridge." Granger told this officer that "the order given was to take those at the base." Conceiving this to be an order to fall back, the officer, on his way to Sheridan, gave it to General Wagner, commanding the Second Brigade of the division, which was then nearly half-way up the ridge. Wagner ordered his brigade back to the rifle-pits at the base, but it only remained there till Sheridan, seeing the mistake, ordered it forward. It again advanced under a terrific fire.

The men, fighting and climbing up the steep hill, sought the roads, ravines, and less rugged parts. The ground was so broken that it was impossible to keep a regular line of battle. At times their movements were in shape like the flight of migratory birds—sometimes in line, sometimes in mass, mostly in V-shaped groups, with the points toward the enemy. At these points regimental flags were flying, sometimes drooping as the bearers were shot, but never reaching the ground, for other brave hands were there to seize them. Sixty flags were advancing up the hill. Bragg was hurrying large bodies of men from his right to the center. They could be seen hastening along the ridge. Cheatham's division was being withdrawn from Sherman's front. Bragg and Hardee were at the center, urging their men to stand firm and drive back the advancing enemy, now so near the summit—indeed, so near that the guns, which could not be sufficiently depressed to reach them, became useless. Artillerymen were lighting the fuses of shells, and bowling them by hundreds down the hill. The critical moment arrived when the summit was just within reach. At six different points, and almost simultaneously, Sheridan's and Wood's divisions broke over the crest—Sheridan's first, near Bragg's headquarters; and in a few minutes Sheridan was beside the guns that had been fired at him, and claiming them as captures of his division. Baird's division took the works on Wood's left almost immediately afterward; and then Johnson came up on Sheridan's right. The enemy's guns were turned upon those who still remained in the works, and soon all were in flight down the eastern slope. Baird got on the ridge just in time to change front and oppose a large body of the enemy moving down from Bragg's right to attack our left. After a sharp engagement, that lasted till dark, he drove the enemy back beyond a high point on the north, which he at once occupied.

The sun had not yet gone down, Missionary Ridge was ours, and Bragg's army was broken and in flight! Dead and wounded comrades lay thickly strewn on the ground: but thicker yet were the dead and wounded men in gray. Then followed the wildest confusion, as the victors gave vent to their joy. Some madly shouted; some wept from very excess of joy; some grotesquely danced out their delight—even our wounded forgot their pain, to join in the general hurrah. But Sheridan did not long stop to receive praise and congratulations. With two brigades he started down the Mission Mills road, and found, strongly posted on a second hill, the enemy's rear. They made a stout resistance, but by a sudden flank movement he drove them from the heights and captured two guns and many prisoners. The day was succeeded by a clear moonlight night. At seven o'clock General Granger sent word to General Thomas that by a bold dash at Chickamauga Crossing he might cut off a large number of the enemy now supposed to be leaving Sherman's front, and that he proposed to move in that direction. It was midnight before guides could be found, and then General Sheridan again put his tired and well-worn men in motion. He reached the creek just as the rear-guard of the enemy was crossing, and pressed it so closely that it burned the pontoon-bridge before all its troops were over. Here Sheridan captured several hundred prisoners, a large number of quartermasters' wagons, together with caissons, artillery, ammunition, and many small-arms.

In this battle Sheridan's and Wood's divisions—the two center assaulting divisions—took 31 pieces of artillery, several thousand small-arms, and 3,800 prisoners. In that one hour of assault they lost 2,337 men in killed and wounded—over 20 per cent of their whole force! On the northern end of the ridge General Sherman lost in his two days' fighting 1,697 in killed and wounded. Of these, 1,268 were in his own three divisions. During the night the last of Bragg's army was withdrawn from Missionary Ridge, and Chattanooga from that time remained in undisputed possession of the Union forces.

THE BLOCKADE-RUNNERS

AFTER ADMIRAL FARRAGUT TOOK NEW ORLEANS he wanted to move immediately against the forts in Mobile Bay, either to occupy the city of Mobile or seal off the harbor from use by blockade-runners. President Lincoln had other plans; he ordered Farragut to proceed up the Mississippi River to attack Vicksburg. There, in 1862, Farragut's fleet took a hammering from shore batteries. He returned to the Gulf, but it was then too late to risk an attack solely with his wooden ships. The forts defending the entrance to the Bay had been strengthened, and it was rumored that the Confederates were building rams. Farragut would need ironclads to get past the forts, but he wouldn't receive any until 1864. In the meantime, he blockaded the Gulf coast.

"To guard the ordinary entrances to these ports was comparatively a simple task. There was, however, a greater difficulty to be met; for the outer coast-line is only the exterior edge of a series of islands between which and the mainland there is an elaborate network of navigable sounds and passages, having numerous inlets communicating with the sea. These inlets were frequently changing under the influence of the great storms; new channels would be opened and old ones filled up. As soon as we closed a port, by stationing vessels at the main entrance thereto, the blockade-runners would slip in at some of the numerous remote inlets, reaching their destination by the inside passages; so that blockade-running flourished until we were able to procure as many blockaders as there were channels and inlets to be guarded. The extreme diversity of the services required of these blockading vessels made it difficult to obtain ships that could meet the varying necessities. They must be heavy enough to contend with the enemy's rams, or they would be driven away from the principal ports. They must be light enough to chase and capture the swift blockade-runners. They must be deep enough in the water to ride out in safety the violent winter gales, and they must be of such light draft as to be able to go near enough to the shallow inlets to blockade them efficiently.

"The blockading fleets of all the important harbors were composed of several very heavy ships, with a few vessels of the lighter class; the rest of the fleet represented some of the other classes needed. But it was impossible to do this along the entire coast, and it sometimes happened that the Confederate ironclads perversely attacked the lighter vessels, as in the case of the rams at Charleston selecting for their victims the *Mercedita* and the *Keystone State,* instead of the heavier ships; while, on the other hand, the swift blockade-runners disclosed themselves most frequently to the ponderous and slow-moving ships that were least able to catch them. . . ."*

The struggle to make the blockade work was naturally countered by Confederate evasive measures. "Four categories of ships engaged in blockade-running: those owned by the Confederate government; those owned by the state governments; those owned by private individuals or groups of speculators; and foreign ships. Of these the third and fourth categories were the most important, though government-owned blockade-runners gave a good account of themselves. It has been estimated that altogether some 600 ships were engaged, at one time or another, in the lucrative and exciting business of blockade-running, but this estimate is palpably too low; that there were, altogether, some 8,000 violations of the blockade; and that blockade-runners brought in altogether over 600,000 small arms, 550,000 pair of shoes, and large quantities of meat, coffee, saltpeter, lead, and other items. At the same time substantial quantities of supplies were brought in from Mexico, across the Rio Grande, and there was at all times a lively trade with the North: General Sherman said that Cincinnati furnished more goods to the Confederacy than Charleston!

"All this would indicate that the blockade was but loosely enforced, and it cannot be denied that it was pretty ineffective in 1861 and even in 1862. Thereafter, however—what with the fall of New Orleans and of Fort Royal and the sealing up of other harbors—it became increasingly effective, and the South felt the pinch seriously. It is estimated that the chances of capture were one in ten in 1861, but one in three by 1864, and with the capture of Wilmington in January 1865 blockade-running practically ceased."†

But in 1863, when blockade-runners were most successful, Horace Wait says, "the arrivals and departures were equal to one steamer a day, taking all of the Confederate ports together. Prior to this no such attempts had ever been made to violate a blockade. The industrial necessities of the principal maritime nations stimulated them to unusual efforts, in return for which they looked forward to a rich harvest. The British especially had abundant capital, the finest and swiftest ships ever built, manned by the most energetic seamen. They felt confident that they could monopolize the Southern cotton and the markets of the Confederacy; but when it was found that neither swift steamers, skilled officers, nor desperate efforts could give security to their best investments of capital, and that the perils to their beautiful vessels and precious cargoes increased as fast as their efforts to surmount them, ultimately becoming even greater in proportion than the enormous gains of the traffic when successful, they were at last driven off from our coast entirely, and kept at bay, though armed and supported by the greatest of foreign powers. They finally gave up the business, admitting that the blockade was a success. A Confederate officer

* From Horace Wait, *The Blockade of the Confederacy.*
† Henry Steele Commager, *The Blue and the Gray,* pp. 846–47.

stated that when Fort Fisher fell their last port was gone, and blockade-running was at an end.

"This signal defeat of that extraordinary development of our Civil War has been spoken of as one of the great moral lessons of our struggle. After the war British officers frankly stated to our naval officers that they considered the blockade and its enforcement the great fact of the war. This was the first time in the history of naval warfare that a steam navy had been kept at sea for so long a period. The Confederates menaced the blockading fleets with nine ironclads which would have been a match for any ironclads in the French or English navy afloat at that time; therefore it becomes manifest that a fleet which could hold in check ironclads, as well as shut out blockade-runners that were the swiftest steamers built at that time, must have combined speed and power to an extent never before displayed in naval warfare. . . ."*

Meanwhile, in August, 1864, Admiral Farragut got his ironclad monitors. Several months before, the Confederate ram *Tennessee* had been observed in the Bay. She was considered "the strongest and most powerful iron-clad ever put afloat. She looked like a great turtle; her sloping sides were covered with iron plates six inches in thickness, thoroughly riveted together, and she had a formidable iron beak projecting under the water. Her armament consisted of six heavy Brooke rifles, each sending a solid shot weighing from 95 to 110 pounds—a small affair compared with the heavy guns of the present time, but irresistible then against everything but the turrets of the monitors. In addition to these means of resistance, the narrow channel to within a few hundred yards of the shore had been lined with torpedoes. These were under the water, anchored to the bottom. Some of them were beer-kegs filled with powder, from the sides of which projected numerous little tubes containing fulminate, which it was expected would be exploded by contact with the passing vessels, but the greater part were tin cones fitted with caps.

"Except for what Farragut had already accomplished on the Mississippi, it would have been considered a foolhardy experiment for wooden vessels to attempt to pass so close to one of the strongest forts on the coast."†

Farragut planned his attack for August 5. Lieutenant Kinney described the situation in Mobile Bay. The Bay "gradually widens from the city to the gulf, a distance of thirty miles. The entrance is protected by a long narrow arm of sand, with Fort Morgan on the extreme western point. Across the channel from Fort Morgan, and perhaps three miles distant, is Dauphine Island, a narrow strip of sand with Fort Gaines at its eastern end. Further to the west is little Fort Powell, commanding a narrow channel through which light-draught vessels could enter the bay. Between Dauphine Island and Fort Morgan, and in front of the main entrance to the bay, is Sand Island, a barren spot, under the lee of which three of our monitors were lying. The army signal officers were sent on board the fleet, not with any intention of having their services used in passing the forts, but in order to establish communication afterward between the fleet and the army, for the purpose of cooperating in the cap-

* Wait, *op. cit.*
† From John C. Kinney, "Farragut at Mobile Bay," *Battles and Leaders*, IV, 382.

ture of the forts. The primary objects of Admiral Farragut in entering the bay were to close Mobile to the outside world, to capture or destroy the *Tennessee,* and to cut off all possible means of escape from the garrisons of the forts. . . . There was no immediate expectation of capturing the city of Mobile, which was safe by reason of a solid row of piles and torpedoes across the river, three miles below the city. Moreover, the larger vessels of the fleet could not approach within a dozen miles of the city, on account of shallow water."*

Farragut at Mobile Bay†

BY LIEUTENANT JOHN C. KINNEY

AT SUNSET THE LAST ORDERS HAD BEEN ISSUED, every commander knew his duty, and unusual quiet prevailed in the fleet. The sea was smooth, a gentle breeze relieved the midsummer heat, and the night came on serenely and peacefully, and far more quietly than to a yachting fleet at Newport. For the first hour after the candles were lighted below, the stillness was almost oppressive. The officers of the *Hartford* gathered around the ward-room table, writing letters to loved ones far away, or giving instructions in case of death. As brave and thoughtful men, they recognized the dangers that they did not fear, and made provision for the possibilities of the morrow. But this occupied little time, and then, business over, there followed an hour of unrestrained jollity. Many an old story was retold and ancient conundrum repeated. Old officers forgot, for the moment, their customary dignity, and it was evident that all were exhilarated and stimulated by the knowledge of the coming struggle. There was no other "stimulation," for the strict naval rules prevented. Finally, after a half-hour's smoke under the forecastle, all hands turned in. The scene on the flag-ship was representative of the night before the battle throughout the fleet.

It was the admiral's desire and intention to get under way by daylight, to take advantage of the inflowing tide; but a dense fog came on after midnight and delayed the work of forming line.

It was a weird sight as the big ships "balanced to partners," the dim outlines slowly emerging like phantoms in the fog. The vessels were lashed together in pairs, fastened side by side by huge cables. All the vessels had been stripped for the fight, the top-hamper being left at Pensacola, and the starboard boats being either left behind or towed on the port side. The admiral's steam-launch, the *Loyall,* named after his son, steamed alongside the flag-ship on the port side.

* Kinney, *op. cit.,* p. 385.
† *Ibid.,* pp. 385–400.

It was a quarter of six o'clock before the fleet was in motion. Meantime a light breeze had scattered the fog and left a clear, sunny August day. The line moved slowly, and it was an hour after starting before the opening gun was fired. This was a 15-inch shell from the *Tecumseh,* and it exploded over Fort Morgan. Half an hour afterward the fleet came within range and the firing from the starboard vessels became general, the fort and the Confederate fleet replying. The fleet took position across the entrance to the bay and raked the advance vessels fore and aft, doing great damage, to which it was for a time impossible to make effective reply. Gradually the fleet came into close quarters with Fort Morgan, and the firing on both sides became terrific. The wooden vessels moved more rapidly than the monitors, and as the *Brooklyn* came opposite the fort, and approached the torpedo line, she came nearly alongside the rear monitor. To have kept on would have been to take the lead, with the ram *Tennessee* approaching and with the unknown danger of the torpedoes underneath. At this critical moment the *Brooklyn* halted and began backing and signaling with the army signals. The *Hartford* was immediately behind and the following vessels were in close proximity, and the sudden stopping of the *Brooklyn* threatened to bring the whole fleet into collision, while the strong inflowing tide was likely to carry some of the vessels to the shore under the guns of the fort.

On the previous night the admiral had issued orders that the army signal officers were not to be allowed on deck during the fight, but were to go into the cockpit, on the lower deck, and assist the surgeons. The reason assigned was that these officers would not be needed during the passage of the forts, but would be wanted afterward to open communication with the army, and that therefore it would be a misfortune to have any of them disabled. The two army signal officers on the *Hartford* disrelished this order exceedingly, and, after consulting together, decided that in the confusion of the occasion their presence on deck would probably not be noticed, and that they would evade the command if possible. In this they were successful until shortly before passing Sand Island and coming within range of Fort Morgan. Then the executive officer, Lieutenant-Commander Lewis A. Kimberly, who never allowed anything to escape his attention, came to them very quietly and politely, and told them the admiral's order must be obeyed. We were satisfied from his manner that the surgeons had need of us, and, without endeavoring to argue the matter, made our way to the stifling hold, where Surgeon Lansdale and Assistant-Surgeon Commons, with their helpers, were sitting, with their paraphernalia spread out ready for use.

Nearly every man had his watch in his hand awaiting the first shot. To us, ignorant of everything going on above, every minute seemed an hour, and there was a feeling of great relief when the boom of the *Tecumseh*'s first gun was heard. Presently one or two of our forward guns opened, and we could hear the distant sound of the guns of the fort in reply. Soon the cannon-balls began to crash through the deck above us, and then the thunder of our whole broadside of nine Dahlgren guns kept the vessel in a quiver. But as yet no wounded were sent down, and we knew we were still at comparatively long range. In the intense excitement of the occasion it seemed that hours had passed, but it was just twenty minutes from the time we went below, when an officer shouted down the hatchway: "Send up an army signal officer immediately; the *Brooklyn* is signaling." In a moment the writer was on deck, where he found the situation as already described. Running on to the forecastle, he hastily took the *Brooklyn's* message, which imparted the unnecessary information, "The monitors are right ahead; we cannot go on without passing them." The reply was sent at once from the admiral, "Order the monitors ahead and go on." But still the *Brooklyn* halted, while, to add to the horror of the situation, the monitor *Tecumseh,* a few hundred yards in the advance, suddenly careened to one side and almost instantly sank to the bottom, carrying with her Captain Tunis A. M. Craven and the greater part of his crew, numbering in all 114 officers and men. The pilot, John Collins, and a few men who were in the turret jumped into the water and were rescued by a boat from the *Metacomet,* which, under charge of Acting Ensign Henry C. Nields, rowed up under the guns of the fort and through a deadly storm of shot and shell and picked them up. Meantime the *Brooklyn* failed to go ahead, and the whole fleet became a stationary point-blank target for the guns of Fort Morgan and of the rebel vessels. It was during these few perilous moments that the most fatal work of the day was done to the fleet.

Owing to the *Hartford's* position, only her few bow guns could be used, while a deadly rain of shot and shell was falling on her, and her men were being cut down by scores, unable to make reply. The sight on deck was sickening beyond the power of words to portray. Shot after shot came through the side, mowing down the men, deluging the decks with blood, and scattering mangled fragments of humanity so thickly that it was difficult to stand on the deck, so slippery was it. The old expression of the "scuppers running blood," "the slippery deck," etc., give but the faintest idea of the spectacle on the *Hartford.* The bodies of the dead were placed in a long row on the port side, while the wounded were sent below until the surgeons' quarters would hold no more. A solid shot coming through the bow struck a gunner on the neck, completely severing head from body. One poor fellow (afterward an object of interest at the great Sanitary Commission Fair in New York) lost both legs by a cannon-ball; as he fell he threw up both arms, just in time to have them also carried away by another shot. At one gun, all the crew on one side were swept down by a shot which came crashing through the bulwarks. A shell burst between the two forward guns in charge of Lieutenant Tyson, killing and wounding fifteen men. The mast upon which the writer was perched was twice struck, once slightly, and again just below the foretop by a heavy shell, from a rifle on the Confederate gun-boat *Selma.* Fortunately the shell came tumbling end over end, and buried itself in the mast, butt-end first, leaving the percussion-cap protruding. Had it come point first, or had it struck at any other part of the mast than in the reënforced portion where the heel of the topmast laps the top of the lower mast, this contribution to the literature of the war would probably have been lost to the world, as the distance to the deck was about a hundred feet. As it was, the sudden jar would have dislodged any one from the crosstrees had not the shell been visible from the time it left the *Selma,* thus giving time to prepare for it by an extra grip around the top of the mast. Looking out over the water, it was easy to trace the course of every shot, both from the guns of the *Hartford* and from the Confederate fleet. Another signal message from the *Brooklyn* told of the sinking of the *Tecumseh,* a fact known already, and another order to "go on" was given and was not obeyed.

Soon after the fight began, Admiral Farragut, finding that the low-hanging smoke from the guns interfered with his view from the deck, went up the rigging of the mainmast as far as the futtock-shrouds, immediately below the maintop. The pilot, Martin Freeman, was in the top directly overhead, and the fleet-captain was on the deck below. Seeing the admiral in this exposed position, where, if wounded, he would be killed by falling to the deck, Fleet-Captain Drayton ordered Knowles, the signal-quartermaster, to fasten a rope around him so that he would be prevented from falling.

Finding that the *Brooklyn* failed to obey his orders, the admiral hurriedly inquired of the pilot if there was sufficient depth of water for the *Hartford* to pass to the left of the *Brooklyn*. Receiving an affirmative reply, he said: "I will take the lead," and immediately ordered the *Hartford* ahead at full speed. As he passed the *Brooklyn* a voice warned him of the torpedoes, to which he returned the contemptuous answer, "Damn the torpedoes." This is the current story, and may have some basis of truth. But as a matter of fact, there was never a moment when the din of the battle would not have drowned any attempt at a conversation between the two ships, and while it is quite probable that the admiral made the remark it is doubtful if he shouted it to the *Brooklyn*.

Then was witnessed the remarkable sight of the *Hartford* and her consort, the *Metacomet,* passing over the dreaded torpedo ground and rushing ahead far in advance of the rest of the fleet, the extrication of which from the confusion caused by the *Brooklyn*'s halt required many minutes of valuable time. The *Hartford* was now moving over what is called the "middle ground," with shallow water on either side, so that it was impossible to move except as the channel permitted. Taking advantage of the situation, the Confederate gun-boat *Selma* kept directly in front of the flag-ship and raked her fore and aft, doing more damage in reality than all the rest of the enemy's fleet. The other gun-boats, the *Gaines* and the *Morgan,* were in shallow water on our starboard bow, but they received more damage from the *Hartford*'s broadsides than they were able to inflict. Meanwhile the ram *Tennessee,* which up to this time had contented herself with simply firing at the approaching fleet, started for the *Hartford,* apparently with the intention of striking her amidships. She came on perhaps for half a mile, never approaching nearer than a hundred yards, and then suddenly turned and made for the fleet, which, still in front of the fort, was gradually getting straightened out and following the *Hartford*. This change of course on the part of the ram has always been a mystery. The captain of the ram, in papers published since the war, denies that any such move was made, but it was witnessed by the entire fleet, and is mentioned by both Admiral Farragut and Fleet-Captain Drayton in their official reports.

The *Hartford* had now run a mile inside the bay, and was suffering chiefly from the raking fire of the *Selma,* which was unquestionably managed more skillfully than any other Confederate vessel. Captain (now Admiral) Jouett, commanding the *Hartford*'s escort, the *Metacomet,* repeatedly asked permission of the admiral to cut loose and take care of the *Selma,* and finally, at five minutes past eight, consent was given. In an instant the cables binding the two vessels were cut, and the *Metacomet,* the fastest vessel in the fleet, bounded ahead. The *Selma* was no match for her, and, recognizing her danger, endeavored to retreat up the bay. But she was speedily overhauled, and when a shot had wounded her captain and killed her first lieutenant she surrendered. Before this the *Gaines* had been crippled by the splendid marksmanship of the *Hartford*'s gunners, and had run aground under the guns of the fort, where she was shortly afterward set on fire, the crew escaping to the shore. The gunboat *Morgan,* after grounding for a few moments on the shoals to the east of Navy Cove, retreated to the shallow water near the fort, whence she escaped the following night to Mobile. The *Hartford,* having reached the deep water of the bay, about three miles north of Dauphine Island, came to anchor.

Let us now return to the other vessels of the fleet, which we left massed in front of Fort Morgan by the remarkable action of the *Brooklyn* in stopping and refusing to move ahead. When the ram *Tennessee* turned away from the *Hartford,* as narrated, she made for the fleet, and in their crowded and confused condition it seemed to be a matter of no difficulty to pick out whatever victims the Confederate commander (Admiral Franklin Buchanan) might desire, as he had done in 1861 when commanding the *Merrimac* in Hampton Roads. Before he could reach them the line had become straightened, and the leading vessels had passed the fort. Admiral Jenkins, who commanded the *Richmond* during the fight, writing of this part of the fight, for the use of the present writer, says:

During the delay under the guns of Fort Morgan and the water-battery by the backing of the *Brooklyn,* the vessels astern had remained apparently stationary, so that the nearest one to the *Richmond* was about half a mile off, and some of them paid very dearly, for the men of the water-battery, who had been driven away from their guns and up the sand hills by the fire of the *Richmond* and *Chickasaw,* had time to return and attack them. When the *Hartford* "cut adrift" from the *Brooklyn* and *Richmond*—the only safe thing possible to do —the *Tennessee* and the three gun-boats pursued her. That is, the *Tennessee,* after getting above the lines of torpedoes, turned into the main ship-channel and followed the *Hartford,* while the gun-boats were in shallow water to the northward, where our heavy vessels could not go after them. When the *Tennessee* was within probably half a mile of the *Hartford,* she suddenly turned her head toward the *Brooklyn* and *Richmond* (both close together). As she approached, every one on board the *Richmond* supposed that she would ram the *Brooklyn;* that, we thought, would be our opportunity, for if she struck the *Brooklyn* the concussion would throw her port side across our path, and being so near to us, she would not have time to "straighten up," and we would strike her fairly and squarely, and most likely sink her.

The guns were loaded with solid shot and heaviest powder charge; the forecastle gun's crew were ordered to get their small-arms and fire into her gun-ports; and as previously determined, if we came in collision at any time, the orders were to throw gun charges of powder in bags from the fore and main yard-arms down her smoke-stack (or at least try to do so). To our great surprise, she sheered off from the *Brooklyn,* and at about one hundred yards put two shot or shells through and through the *Brooklyn's* sides (as reported), doing much damage.

Approaching, passing, and getting away from the *Richmond,* the ram received from us three full broadsides of 9-inch solid shot, each broadside being eleven guns. They were well aimed and all struck, but when she was examined next day, no other indications were seen than scratches. The musketry fire into the two ports prevented the leveling of her guns, and therefore two of her shot or shell passed harmlessly over the *Richmond,* except the cutting of a ratline in the port main-shroud, just under the feet of the pilot, while the other whistled unpleasantly close to Lieutenant Terry's head. The *Tennessee* passed toward the *Lackawanna,* the next vessel astern, and avoided her—wishing either to ram Captain Strong's vessel (the *Monongahela*), or cross his bow and attack McCann's vessel (the *Kennebec,* Strong's consort). Strong was ready for her, and, anticipating her object, made at her, but the blow (by the quick manœuvring of the *Tennessee*) was a glancing one, doing very little damage to either Strong's or McCann's vessel. Thence the *Tennessee,* after firing two broadsides into the *Oneida,* proceeded toward the fort, and for a time entirely disappeared from our sight. During this time the three gun-boats were proceeding, apparently, up the bay, to escape. The *Hartford* was closely watched with our glasses, and soon after the *Tennessee* had left Strong, the *Metacomet* (Jouett) was seen to cast off; and divining the purpose, the *Port Royal* (Gherardi) was ordered to cast off from the *Richmond* and go in chase of the enemy, pointing in the direction of the three gun-boats of the enemy. George Brown (in the *Itasca*) cast off from the *Ossipee* and (I believe) McCann did also, and steered for the enemy. By this time Jouett had come up with the *Selma,* and the fight commenced. A very few minutes after Gherardi had left the side of the *Richmond,* and the other small vessels had left their consorts, a thick mist, with light rain (just enough to wet the deck), passed over the *Richmond,* obscuring from sight every object outside the vessel; indeed, for a few minutes the bowsprit of the *Richmond* could not be seen from the poop-deck. This mist and rain, in a cloudless sunshiny day, were slowly wafted over the waters toward the fort and pilot town, enabling John W. Bennett, commanding one of the enemy's gun-boats, and George W. Harrison, commanding the other, to shape their courses for safety, in shoal water, and finally under Fort Morgan. Gherardi in the *Port Royal* (as soon as he could see) saw only the *Selma* and *Metacomet,* and continued his course for them.

Whatever damage was done by the *Tennessee* to the fleet in passing the fort was by the occasional discharge of her guns. She failed to strike a single one of the Union vessels, but was herself run into by the *Mononga-hela,* Captain Strong, at full speed. The captain says in his report:

> After passing the forts I saw the rebel ram *Tennessee* head on for our line. I then sheered out of the line to run into her, at the same time ordering full speed as fast as possible. I struck her fair, and swinging around poured in a broadside of solid 11-inch shot, which apparently had little if any effect upon her.

This modest statement is characteristic of the gallant writer, now dead, as are so many others of the conspicuous actors in that day's work. The *Monongahela* was no match for the *Tennessee,* but she had been strengthened by an artificial iron prow, and being one of the fastest—or rather, *least slow*—of the fleet, was expected to act as a ram if opportunity offered. Captain Strong waited for no orders, but seeing the huge ram coming for the fleet left his place in the line and attacked her, as narrated. It was at this time that the *Monongahela*'s first lieutenant, Roderick Prentiss, a brave and gifted young officer, received his death wound, both legs being shattered.

At last all the fleet passed the fort, and while the ram ran under its guns the vessels made their way to the *Hartford* and dropped their anchors, except the *Metacomet, Port Royal, Kennebec,* and *Itasca.* After the forts were passed, the three last named had cut loose from their escorts and gone to aid the *Metacomet* in her struggle with the *Selma* and *Morgan.*

The thunder of heavy artillery now ceased. The crews of the various vessels had begun to efface the marks of the terrible contest by washing the decks and clearing up the splinters. The cooks were preparing breakfast, the surgeons were busily engaged in making amputations and binding arteries, and under canvas, on the port side of each vessel, lay the ghastly line of dead waiting the sailor's burial. As if by mutual understanding, officers who were relieved from immediate duty gathered in the ward-rooms to ascertain who of their mates were missing, and the reaction from such a season of tense nerves and excitement was just setting in when the hurried call to quarters came and the word passed around, "The ram is coming."

The *Tennessee,* after remaining near Fort Morgan while the fleet had made its way four miles above to its anchorage—certainly as much as half an hour—had suddenly decided to settle at once the question of the control of the bay. Single-handed she came on to meet the whole fleet, consisting now of ten wooden vessels and the three monitors. At that time the *Tennessee* was believed to be the strongest vessel afloat, and the safety with which she carried her crew during the battle proved that she was virtually invulnerable. Fortunately for the Union fleet she was weakly handled, and at the end fell a victim to a stupendous blunder in her construction—the failure to protect her rudder-chains. The spectacle afforded the Confederate soldiers, who crowded the ramparts of the two forts—

the fleet now being out of range—was such as has very rarely been furnished in the history of the world. To the looker-on it seemed as if the fleet was at the mercy of the ram, for the monitors, which were expected to be the chief defense, were so destitute of speed and so difficult to manœuvre that it seemed an easy task for the *Tennessee* to avoid them and sink the wooden vessels in detail. Because of the slowness of the monitors, Admiral Farragut selected the fastest of the wooden vessels to begin the attack. While the navy signals for a general attack of the enemy were being prepared, the *Monongahela* (Captain Strong) and the *Lackawanna* (Captain Marchand) were ordered by the more rapid signal system of the army to "run down the ram," the order being immediately repeated to the monitors.

The *Monongahela,* with her prow already somewhat weakened by the previous attempt to ram, at once took the lead, as she had not yet come to anchor. The ram from the first headed for the *Hartford,* and paid no attention to her assailants, except with her guns. The *Monongahela,* going at full speed, struck the *Tennessee* amidships—a blow that would have sunk almost any vessel of the Union navy, but which inflicted not the slightest damage on the solid iron hull of the ram. (After the surrender it was almost impossible to tell where the attacking vessel had struck.) Her own iron prow and cutwater were carried away, and she was otherwise badly damaged about the stern by the collision. The *Lackawanna* was close behind and delivered a similar blow with her wooden bow, simply causing the ram to lurch slightly to one side. As the vessels separated the *Lackawanna* swung alongside the ram, which sent two shots through her and kept on her course for the *Hartford,* which was now the next vessel in the attack. The two flag-ships approached each other, bow to bow, iron against oak. It was impossible for the *Hartford,* with her lack of speed, to circle around and strike the ram on the side; her only safety was in keeping pointed directly for the bow of her assailant. The other vessels of the fleet were unable to do anything for the defense of the admiral except to train their guns on the ram, on which as yet they had not the slightest effect.

It was a thrilling moment for the fleet, for it was evident that if the ram could strike the *Hartford* the latter must sink. But for the two vessels to strike fairly, bows on, would probably have involved the destruction of both, for the ram must have penetrated so far into the wooden ship that as the *Hartford* filled and sank she would have carried the ram under water. Whether for this reason or for some other, as the two vessels came together the *Tennessee* slightly changed her course, the port bow of the *Hartford* met the port bow of the ram, and the ships grated against each other as they passed. The *Hartford* poured her whole port broadside against the ram, but the solid shot merely dented the side and bounded into the air. The ram tried to return the salute, but owing to defective primers only one gun was discharged. This sent a shell through the berth-deck, killing five men and wounding eight. The muzzle of the gun was so close to the *Hartford* that the powder blackened her side.

The admiral stood on the quarter-deck when the vessels came together, and as he saw the result he jumped on to the port-quarter rail, holding to the mizzen-rigging, a position from which he might have jumped to

Capture of the Confederate ram Tennessee

the deck of the ram as she passed. Seeing him in this position, and fearing for his safety, Flag-Lieutenant Watson slipped a rope around him and secured it to the rigging, so that during the fight the admiral was twice "lashed to the rigging," each time by devoted officers who knew better than to consult him before acting. Fleet-Captain Drayton had hurried to the bow of the *Hartford* as the collision was seen to be inevitable, and expressed keen satisfaction when the ram avoided a direct blow.

The *Tennessee* now became the target for the whole fleet, all the vessels of which were making toward her, pounding her with shot, and trying to run her down. As the *Hartford* turned to make for her again, we ran in front of the *Lackawanna,* which had already turned and was moving under full headway with the same object. She struck us on our starboard side, amidships, crushing halfway through, knocking two portholes into one, upsetting one of the Dahlgren guns, and creating general consternation. For a time it was thought that we must sink, and the cry rang out over the deck: "Save the admiral! Save the admiral!" The port boats were ordered lowered, and in their haste some of the sailors cut the "falls," and two of the cutters dropped into the water wrong side up, and floated astern. But the admiral sprang into the starboard mizzen-rigging, looked over the side of the ship, and, finding there were still a few inches to spare above the water's edge, instantly ordered the ship ahead again at full speed, after the ram. The unfortunate *Lackawanna,* which had struck the ram a second blow, was making for her once more, and, singularly enough, again came up on our starboard side, and another collision seemed imminent. And now the admiral became a trifle excited. He had no idea of whipping the rebels to be himself sunk by a friend, nor did he realize at the moment that the *Hartford* was as much to blame as the *Lackawanna.* Turning to the writer he inquired. "Can you say 'For God's sake' by signal?" "Yes, sir," was the reply. "Then say to the *Lackawanna,* 'For God's sake get out of our way and anchor!' " In my haste to send the message, I brought the end of my signal flag-staff down with considerable violence upon the head of the admiral, who was standing nearer than I thought, causing him to wince perceptibly. It was a hasty message, for the fault was equally divided, each ship being too eager to reach the enemy, and it turned out all right, by a fortunate accident, that Captain Marchand never received it. The army signal officer on the *Lackawanna,* Lieutenant Myron Adams (now pastor of Plymouth Congregational Church in Rochester, N. Y.), had taken his station in the foretop, and just as he received the first five words—"For God's sake get out"—the wind flirted the large United States flag at the mast-head around him, so that he was unable to read the conclusion of the message.

The remainder of the story is soon told. As the *Tennessee* left the *Hartford* she became the target of the entire fleet, and at last the concentration of solid shot from so many guns began to tell. The flag-staff was shot away, the smoke-stack was riddled with holes, and finally disappeared. The monitor *Chickasaw,* Lieutenant-Commander Perkins, succeeded in coming up astern and began pounding away with 11-inch solid shot, and one shot from a 15-inch gun of the *Manhattan* crushed into the side sufficiently to prove that a few more such shots would have made the casemate untenable. Finally, one of the *Chickasaw*'s shots cut the rudder-chain of the ram and she would no longer mind her helm. At this time, as Admiral Farragut says in his report, "she was sore beset. The *Chickasaw* was pounding away at her stern, the *Ossipee* was approaching her at full speed, and the *Monongahela, Lackawanna,* and this ship were bearing down upon her, determined upon her destruction." From the time the *Hartford* struck her she did not fire a gun. Finally the Confederate admiral, Buchanan, was severely wounded by an iron splinter or a piece of a shell, and just as the *Ossipee* was about to strike her the *Tennessee* displayed a white flag, hoisted on an improvised staff through the grating over her deck. The *Ossipee* (Captain Le Roy) reversed her engine, but was so near that a harmless collision was inevitable. Suddenly the terrific cannonading ceased, and from every ship rang out cheer after cheer, as the weary men realized that at last the ram was conquered and the day won. The *Chickasaw* took the *Tennessee* in tow and brought her to anchor near the *Hartford*. The impression prevailed at first that the *Tennessee* had been seriously injured by the ramming she had received and was sinking, and orders were signaled to send boats to assist her crew, but it was soon discovered that this was unnecessary.

Fort Powell, was evacuated about 10 P.M. that night, the officers and men escaping to the mainland. The *Chickasaw* also tackled Fort Gaines on the 6th, and speedily convinced the commanding officer that it would be folly to attempt to withstand a siege. The result was a surrender to the army and navy the next morning.

Fort Morgan was at once invested, and surrendered on the 23d of August.

ON TO ATLANTA

THE CAMPAIGNS WAGED BY THE UNION GENERALS in the West had been strikingly more successful than those in the East. Abraham Lincoln, a midwesterner himself, asked U. S. Grant to come East and run the whole war. He made Grant a Lieutenant General, the first officer in the U. S. Army to hold so high a rank since George Washington. This meant that Grant was commander-in-chief of all Union forces. Since Grant chose not to operate from a desk in Washington, Halleck was appointed chief of staff. Grant would take to the field and lead the Army of the Potomac against Lee.

But first Grant wanted to see General Sherman, his successor in the West, to confer on broad, basic strategy. In Cincinnati, the two generals agreed on the essentials necessary to defeat the Confederacy. As Lloyd Lewis says,, Sherman marveled "that Grant should decide to 'go East, a stranger almost among strange troops; . . . a more daring thing was never done by man on earth.' But at any rate he and his friend had the war in their own hands. Each believing that 'in war a town is a military weakness,' they did not need to reassure each other that from now on there would be no more scattering of troops to hold citadels. Grant, with the simplicity of genius, said that there were but two objectives: one, Lee's army in Virginia, the other (army), mobilized at Dalton, thirty miles south of Chattanooga, under J. E. Johnston, now restored to command. The Confederacy would have its best leaders against them. Every effort must now be bent toward endless, relentless fighting, summer, winter, all the time—the kind of warfare both Grant and Sherman had preached, 'blows, thick and fast.' It would be hideous carnage, but the most merciful in the end if it could halt these years of wastage."* Or as General Sherman said after the war, "He was to go for Lee and I was to go for Joe Johnston." Sherman's first job was to reorganize the western armies, and he set about doing it.

By May 6, he had 98,000 troops and 254 cannon ready to move against the Confederates at Dalton, Georgia. There would be no frontal assault on the Confederate positions in the mountains before Dalton; instead, General McPherson's corps was sent around Johnston's rear to cut his

---

* *Sherman: Fighting Prophet,* p. 345.

supply lines at the railroad center of Resaca. Sherman's attack, according to Lewis, made the best use of his generals—"slow, unconquerable Thomas in the center as a bulwark against counterattack; McPherson and Schofield, younger, more aggressive men, on the flanks with smaller, fleeter armies marching in swiftly traveled arcs, feinting, swerving, feinting again, then suddenly striking like hammers into Johnston's ribs. If McPherson should seize the railroad in Johnston's rear, the latter would be driven into the less hilly country to the east, where Sherman felt certain he would destroy half the Confederate army and capture its cannon."*

McPherson failed to take Resaca before Johnston supplied reinforcements. Sherman then sent both Thomas and Schofield around Johnston's flank, which forced Johnston to pull his army out of Dalton. Wherever possible, Sherman resorted to artful flanking movements and Johnston continued to retreat rather than contest Sherman. Johnston's failure to cope with end runs may be better understood when one considers that he had only 65,000 troops, while Sherman had 110,000. The extra men gave Sherman greater mobility.

At Kennesaw Mountain Sherman varied his tactics. Again the Confederates were strongly entrenched, and they had weakened their center in order to strengthen their flanks. Sherman tried to break through the center but met with little success. Then, to avoid stalling his drive, Sherman resumed his flanking tactics—and once more Johnston was forced to retreat.

By the middle of July Sherman's armies had crossed the Chattahoochee River a few miles from Atlanta. The Georgia city was second only to Richmond in industrial importance. Its capture would deprive the Confederacy of sorely needed arms and munitions and an important rail center.

Because Johnston had failed to mount a major counterattack to stop Sherman's drive, President Davis was under pressure to install a more aggressive general. On July 17 General John Bell Hood was given command of the Confederate troops in Atlanta.

A fiery Texan, Hood wasted little time. On July 20 he struck the Union armies first at Peachtree creek north of the city, and on July 22 he attacked a Union flanking force east of Atlanta. Here he almost succeeded in destroying McPherson's corps. But the attacks were not coordinated and both were repelled. Hood then turned to preparing Atlanta for siege. But he reckoned without Sherman, who had already sent a strong force to outflank the city, this time to the west.

* *Ibid.*, p. 357.

The Fall of Atlanta*

BY CAPTAIN W. F. HINMAN

THE SOUTHERN PEOPLE WANTED A GENERAL who would fight rather than run. Such a one they found in Hood. He was a brave man, but rash and not properly equipped to handle a large army and conduct a great campaign. He had served two years in Lee's Virginia army, and was wounded at Gettysburg. Going west with Longstreet, in command of a division, he lost a leg at Chickamauga. In the spring of 1864 he was assigned to the command of a corps in the army of Johnston at Dalton. General Schofield and General McPherson were classmates of Hood at West Point. General Sherman inquired of them as to his characteristics and at once made up his mind that the change "meant fight." He immediately issued orders to his corps, division, brigade and regimental commanders to hold themselves and their commands at all times in readiness for instant action. Events soon proved that these cautionary words were timely and judicious.

On the 19th the Sixty-fourth Ohio and Twenty-seventh Illinois, under the command of Colonel Robert C. Brown, were ordered to make a reconnoisance along the Decatur road, if possible as far as Peachtree creek. About three miles out, the column reached the creek and found the enemy's pickets in strong rifle-pits on the opposite bank, and the bridge burned. The situation was reported back to headquarters, and in a short time Colonel Brown's command was relieved by Stanley's division.

Hood did not wait long before showing his purpose to fight. He made the 20th of July an exciting day for us and many others of Sherman's army. On that day was fought the battle of Peachtree creek. The stress of the fighting fell upon the Twentieth corps, but we got enough of it to make it decidedly interesting. During the early part of the day we did a good deal of wild maneuvering, evidently in search of a place where we would be expected to do something. At length we seemed to have found it, and our brigade was formed in mass for a charge upon the Confederate works, which were on high ground some four hundred yards distant, the intervening space being open, with no cover. With a vivid recollection of our experience at Kennesaw, we did not relish the prospect before us, and no regrets were expressed when, after a more careful survey of the ground, the plan was changed and the order to assault was revoked.

At this time Hooker's Twentieth corps became heavily engaged at some distance to our right. Sherman's line was much attenuated and broken, McPherson and Schofield being six or eight miles to the left. It was

* From *The Story of the Sherman Brigade.*

Hood's evident purpose to burst through the Union center and disrupt the line. The roar of musketry and artillery upon our right indicated fierce fighting. Our division was advanced to support Hooker's left and foil any attempt to turn his flank. The first and second brigades were in the advance; ours, in reserve. The former halted and began to throw up intrenchments. They had not half finished their work, when a large mass of the enemy, in three successive lines, emerged from the woods and charged them, with blood-curdling yells. The Union soldiers withheld their fire until the rebels were within fifty yards and then delivered a volley so destructive that the assailants recoiled and fled in disorder.

At the left of the Second brigade was a deep ravine which was not occupied by our troops. It was soon discovered that a column of the enemy was moving through this ravine for the apparent purpose of gaining our rear. Our brigade was instantly dispatched to check this movement. We formed line of battle to the left of the road and parallel to it, and advanced. Reaching the crest of a low ridge our skirmishers came upon those of the enemy, not more than thirty yards distant. In their rear we could see a heavy line advancing upon us. Our position was not advantageous for defence, and our single brigade was evidently greatly inferior in strength to the force we must encounter. We were instantly ordered to "about face" and move back to the road, which was upon high ground and a good place to fight. We made our change of base at double-quick, and the rebels, supposing us to be in full retreat, followed swiftly, with loud cheers. Our officers were cautioned not to permit their men to keep on running after regaining the road, but to halt them there, face about and confront the enemy.

There was little need for the caution; our soldiers were too well schooled in war. There seemed to be scarcely a man in the ranks who did not comprehend, as well as those who wore shoulder straps, the situation of affairs and the need of the moment. At the road the men turned by a common impulse, and, partly covered by a fence, faced the foe. The rebel skirmishers were almost at our heels and the main body was not more than two hundred yards away. Our men poured into them a staggering volley and immediately began to "load and fire at will," each man working with the energy of desperation. Never did soldiers stand more bravely to their work. There was scarcely a laggard or a skulker. The rebels halted and delivered a volley, but they were upon much lower ground than ourselves and most of their shots passed harmlessly over our heads.

In the meantime two or three batteries had been brought up, on the other side of Peachtree creek, and so posted as to completely enfilade the rebel line. The guns opened with canister, and scarcly a dozen shots had been fired, when the Confederates broke and fled in dismay to the cover of the ravine, from which they had debouched before forming for the charge. They seemed to be satisfied for that day, as they did not reappear to renew the attack. Our loss was singularly small, the killed and wounded in our brigade numbering less than thirty, while that of the rebels in our front, judging from the dead and severely wounded left upon the field, was more than ten times that number.

As we did not move immediately, details were sent out to care for the rebel wounded. Sixty or more were brought in and received the attention of our surgeons. I have never forgotten a mere boy, belonging to a Georgia regiment, whom we brought in and laid upon a blanket under a tree. He was helpless, a bullet having crushed his thigh. We gave him food and water, and did what else we could to mitigate his suffering. The tears gathered in his eyes as he said:

"They told us that you-all would kill us if you took us prisoners. I didn't think you'd be so kind to me!"

To the right Hooker repelled every assault. He lost near two thousand men, but inflicted upon the enemy a loss twice his own.

During the night of the 21st, the rebels retired within the defences of Atlanta. The forts and earthworks of all kinds were exceedingly strong. Thousands of Negroes had been employed for weeks in their construction. On the 22nd we advanced until we were within half a mile of the fortifications and could go no farther. We were fired upon by a rebel battery with fatal effect. "Pony" Seavolt, a young musician of Company C, Sixty-fifth, was instantly killed by a solid shot. Several were wounded by fragments of shell. On this day occurred, upon the left, the most severe distinct engagement of the entire campaign, in which the much-lamented General McPherson was killed.

That day Captain Alfred A. Reed, of the Sixty-fourth, had an exceedingly close call. A cannon shot knocked into flinders a barricade of rails behind which he was lying. A large splinter struck him upon the head, tearing away a portion of the scalp and laying bare the skull. The doctors patched him up in pretty fair shape, but for a good while he was literally a "sore-head."

From this point dates the "siege of Atlanta," which continued five weeks. General Sherman disposed his army in a semi-circular line extending about half way around the town, and as near to the Confederate fortifications as possible. Orders were promulgated to build works that would be impregnable to assault. For a week the men toiled day and night, strengthening their position and protecting it by all the devices known to military art. For a time the rebels caused us constant annoyance by shelling our lines with the greatest industry. Every day men engaged upon the intrenchments were killed or wounded, but the work went right on. Forts were built and heavy siege guns were brought up and mounted in them. Within a few days after his arrival, Sherman began to throw shells into Atlanta and kept it up at frequent intervals during the siege. Many of the citizens dug caves in the earth, where they slept to escape the unwelcome visitors.

Day and night the Union army lay in the trenches, with muskets constantly loaded and at hand, ready for use. About once a week each regiments was permitted to go to the rear for a day and a night, to rest and "clean up." Here and there was a man who lived in utter disregard of cleanliness. A person directly from home might have thought this of all of us, judging from our appearance, but nine-tenths of the soldiers kept their bodies and their clothing in the best condition possible under the circumstances. In more than one case an incorrigible was taken to a stream by his comrades, who stripped him by main force and scrubbed him from head to foot. If he got mad about it, they only scrubbed the harder.

The enemy made frequent bluffs with both musketry and artillery, and at all times we were called to stand at the works, often for hours together. We changed our location several times as the line was now and then readjusted. Every possible chance was improved to gain an advantage of position. Tents were pitched close to the works, and during the quiet hours the men lay in their little shelters, sleeping, reading, writing or playing with the "pasteboards." The latter was the most popular method of whiling away the time. If a few shots were heard every man seized his musket and in ten seconds was in his place at the intrenchments. Whenever the rebel artillery opened there was a scramble for the shelter of the works. At the more exposed points many of the soldiers dug "gopher holes" into which they dodged like prairie dogs to avoid the missiles. A very strong line of outposts was maintained and picket duty was frequent and arduous. All the posts were protected by works impervious to bullets. In many cases the changing of pickets, once in twenty-four hours, had to be done at night, as the exposure by day was certain to provoke the enemy's fire.

The men of the Sixth battery constructed a furnace for heating shot, the material therefor being supplied by an old brick chimney. One afternoon in the early part of August, they put a lot of twelve-pound solid shot into the furnace, brought them to a red heat, and in the evening threw them over into Atlanta. A large fire was soon seen, which, according to statements of rebel pickets the next morning, was caused by the shot. It is scarcely necessary to say that the battery boys did not undertake the experiment of heating shells.

At this time some changes were made in the composition of our brigade and the number of its regiments was reduced from nine to seven. The term of the Twenty-second and Twenty-seventh Illinois, which were non-veteran regiments, expired, and they went to the rear to be mustered out of service. Colonel Opdycke was wanted to command the First brigade of the division, and he took the One Hundred and Twenty-fifth Ohio with him. In its place we received the Fifteenth Missouri, Colonel Joseph Conrad. This was a St. Louis regiment, composed almost entirely of Germans. The men talked "Dutch" among themselves and the officers gave their commands in that language. But it was a most excellent regiment. One of its distinctive features was its splended corps of trained buglers. After the death of McPherson, General Howard was taken to command the Army of the Tennessee, and General David S. Stanley succeeded to the command of the Fourth corps.

Two or three times we engaged in making those riotous demonstrations against the rebels, the purpose of which was to amuse them and divert their attention from some movement that was being executed at another point on our line. One of these, in the early part of August, was particularly protracted and noisy. The Army of the Tennessee was to undertake some important operation, and the men upon the outposts along the front of the Fourth corps were ordered to fire incessantly, yell, and in every way raise all the racket possible, to lead the Johnnies to believe we were going to assault. In the ordinary conditions of life deception is not classed among the Christian virtues, but "everything is fair in love and war," and it "went" in the army. In order to make the affair more impressive, an extra regiment from each brigade was sent to the outpost to swell the volume of noise. We happened to be on picket that day, and the boys had great sport. The rebel pickets were so near us that voices could be easily heard.

When the hour fixed for the demonstration arrived, the officers shouted with all the lung power at their command: "Forward! Double-quick! March!" and the buglers almost blew their heads off in sounding the advance. Then the fusillade began. From their well-intrenched posts the men fired a withering volley, shouting and yelling like savages. Then they kept loading and firing, each on his own account, with furious energy. The rebels returned the fire with equal vigor, and for two hours the woods fairly blazed with burning powder. It was hard on the trees and bushes, which were the only sufferers. When it was "all over" they looked as if they had been swept by a mowing machine. In front of one post—the garrison of which had been reinforced for the occasion and numbered twelve or fifteen men—was an oak tree, six or eight inches in diameter. The men concentrated their fire upon that tree and within an hour the bullets cut it down. Its fall was greeted with prodigious yells. During those two hours the men fired from eighty to a hundred rounds each. When the riot ceased, we were relieved and went to the rear to refill our empty cartridge boxes. We do not know whether we scared anybody or not, but if we didn't it certainly was not our fault, for we tried hard and made noise enough. After the order was given to cease firing this colloquy occurred:

"I say, Yank!"

"Hello, Johnny!"

"Think ye'r' raisin' Cain, don't ye?"

"Oh, that's all right, Johnny; jest havin' a little fun with ye! We've got more bullets 'n we know what ter do with 'n' we thought you rebs 'd like ter have a few of 'em. Ye better gather 'em up, ye may need 'em!"

"Oh, come off! We'un's got 'nough ter make you-all mighty sick! Hood's a fighter, he is! But say, when ye goin' ter take Atlanta."

"We'll git thar, Eli, one o' these fine mornin's! Goin' after some more catridges now; watch out when we come back. Good bye, Johnny!"

"Good bye, Yank!"

The weather during August was extremely hot. The men literally sweltered in the trenches and under their "pup" tents. At night myriads of mosquitoes swarmed about the picket posts and gave us as much annoyance as did the rebels. Mails were as regular as could be expected, usually three or four each week. Most of the time we had full rations of the three essentials, hardtack, bacon and coffee, but the daily bill of fare became painfully monotonous. There was no possible chance to do any foraging, and the soldiers would have given a week's pay for a supply of vegetables.

At long intervals fresh beef was issued, cattle being driven on the hoof all the way from Chattanooga. They didn't find much to eat on the way, and by the time they reached the army they were little more than a structural framework of bones. The boys used to say as they picked their bones—that is, the beef bones—that the commissary people killed each night the animals which were so nearly played out that they could not endure another day's march, and this seemed to be very near the truth.

The hind quarters furnished about all the meat that was edible, and even that is not saying much. But the fact that the animals were not all hind quarters caused a great deal of friction in the matter of distribution. Each company always insisted that it was its turn to have steak, and there were many heated arguments between the commissary-sergeants and the orderlies. "Jim" Mills, the purveyor of the Sixty-fifth, was not a profane man; it is a wonder that he did not become so while issuing fresh beef during the Atlanta campaign. Three-quarters of the men only got skinny ribs and lean soup-shanks, and they did swearing enough to go around.

All the commissary sergeants had this cross to bear, for human nature was much alike in all regiments and there was everywhere the same disturbance over the apportionment of fresh beef. It will be appropriate to narrate here a beef incident that occurred in the Sixty-fourth, although its chronological place would be a year earlier. One day, while we were in camp at Hillsboro, Tennessee, Commissary-sergeant William H. Farber had one of his periodical struggles with a beef carcass. He carefully superintended the carving and brought all the energies of his intellect to bear upon the matter of its equitable division. He arranged the pieces in ten piles, referring to a memorandum, which he kept to see which companies were due for steak, and which must this time be content with neck, shank or rib. When he had finished his task he surveyed the heaps with calm satisfaction and then yelled:

"Orderlies, fer yer fresh beef!"

The orderlies were promptly on hand and kicking began at once, with even greater violence than usual, for the "critter" had been a lean one and the spread was not tempting. Two or three of the orderlies, who found steak in their portions, were estopped from joining in the insurrection, but all the others jumped on Farber, vehemently declaring in chorus, that they had neck and shank *all* the time, and nothing else. Conscious of his rectitude, Farber assured them that he had endeavored to divide the beef with perfect fairness. He showed them his record of previous issues, but they pronounced it a fraud. Their memories were short, and none of them could remember ever having had any of the choice cuts. They charged him with always providing a good supply of porterhouse or sirloin for his own mess—the non-commissioned staff. At length Farber got hot under the collar and declared his ultimatum, that each of them could take his assigned portion or go without.

Several of the orderlies, knowing that they would catch "Hail Columbia" from the men, refused to do so. They went at once to their respective company commanders and entered formal complaint against the commissary-sergeant, and this was promptly carried up to Colonel McIlvaine. The latter, in his brusque, excited way, determined to settle the matter once for all. Summoning the company commanders he bore down upon Farber with fire in his eye. In words that scorched, he told Farber, who stood quaking in his shoes, of the complaints that had come to his ears, and of his purpose to go to the bottom of the difficulty, then and there. The officers all stood around those piles of meat and held an inquest over the remains, McIlvaine acting as coroner. The colonel examined Farber's list showing the number of men in each company, and, with a critical eye, scanned the various portions. Farber half expected to be sentenced to have his head shaved and be drummed out of camp to the tune of the "Rogue's March," but he began to breathe freely when Colonel McIlvaine said, addressing the officers:

"If there is one of you who thinks he can make a fairer division than that, I will have the meat thrown into a pile and he can try it."

To this there was no response, and after a pause the colonel added, with a good deal of asperity;

"Go to your quarters, and any officer or man who grumbles hereafter about the division of beef will be at once put under arrest. This thing has got to stop right here!"

And that was the end of the great beef riot in the Sixty-fourth.

When the army left Chattanooga it had with it a herd of three or four thousand cattle, convoyed by an entire brigade of soldiers. One night, near Resaca, a furious thunder-storm stampeded the cattle and several hundred of them galloped directly into the enemy's lines.

Occasionally we received small portions of desiccated vegetables—the result of a scheme evolved by some genius to supply the soldiers with vegetable food. The stuff came in slabs about a foot square and an inch thick. It was composed of a mixture containing pretty nearly everything known to the vegetable kingdom. By hydraulic or some other pressure all the juices were squeezed out, leaving only the fiber, and this would "keep" for an indefinite period. The boys made great sport of it at first, but they found it good and wholesome. It was used in the form of soup, of which a cubic inch would make a quart. Of course its scientific name, "desiccated" was speedily changed to "desecrated" or "consecrated," and the boys never called it anything else. The great Sanitary Commission—a noble organization extending thoughout the entire north—undertook to send supplies of fresh vegetables, such as potatoes and onions, to the soldiers in the field. Most of them were, however, side-tracked at points in the rear, and only a small portion ever reached us. The tear-starting onion, drastic and malodorous, was always warmly welcomed. It was eaten raw, with the keenest relish. Three or four times onions were passed around, at the rate of about a bushel to a regiment. The onion is well known to the medical profession as an anti-scorbutic, and was often used in the hospitals as a remedy for scurvy, or as a preventive. The soldiers would gladly have devoured thousands of bushels if they could have had them.

Many will remember one beautiful Sunday evening toward the end of August, when the sound of strife was hushed and quiet reigned along the lines. One of our bands took position just behind the works and played "The Star-spangled Banner," eliciting loud cheers from the soldiers. A Confederate band responded with "The Bonnie Blue Flag," and it was the turn of the rebels to cheer. For an hour the bands played alternately— "Hail Columbia" and "Dixie"; "Red, White and Blue" and "My Maryland"; "Rally Round the Flag" and "The Palmetto Tree"; "John Brown's Body" and "Ole Virginny"; followed by sentimental selections, such as "Annie Laurie," "Bowld Soger Boy," "The Girl I Left Behind Me," "Old Kentucky Home," "Suwanee River," and "Home, Sweet Home." No shot vexed the ear. The softening strains of music cast their spell over Union and Confederate. For the time the fierce passions of war were hushed, tender thoughts of home and loved ones filled every heart, and a spirit of gentleness and peace brooded over the hostile armies.

Captain Thomas E. Tillotson, of the Sixty-fourth—his comrades usually addressed him by his middle name, Eugene—was at this time serving on the staff of General John Newton commanding the division, his position being that of acting assistant inspector general. While the army was lying in the trenches before Atlanta, Tillotson had an experience that was enough to bleach the hair of the average man. One of his functions was to have supervision of the picket line. Whenever the troops halted in a new position, it was his duty to post the pickets. One day General Newton, who was sometimes a little querulous, asked the captain how many men he had on the picket line covering the front of the division.

"I cannot say exactly, sir," answered Tillotson, saluting, "but we have the usual force out there."

"You don't know!" exclaimed the general, fiercely. "A fine inspector you are, not to know how many men you have on post. It's your business to know, and I want you to find out, and be quick about it, too!"

Now everyone who remembers Tillotson as a soldier, knows that he never flinched in the face of danger, and that he was conspicuously faithful and conscientious in the performance of duty. So marked were his courage and efficiency that at the close of the war he was brevetted major, for "gallant and meritorious services."

Stung by the sharp and ungracious words of his chief, his face flushed as he touched his hat and replied: "All right, General, I'll find out at once and let you know." Then he put spurs to his horse and dashed away.

Tillotson decided that the way to obtain the desired information was to go and see. He determined not to go on foot, either, although that would have been far less dangerous. So he picked his way on horseback through the opening in the abatis and brush in front of the breastworks, and rode out so near to the picket line that he could see the piles of fresh earth which indicated the location of the picket posts; for all the videttes were protected by small intrenchments. So close were the hostile lines that the change of pickets could only be made at night. He began at the left and counted the dirt piles, multiplying the total by three, that being the number of men on each post. They were stationed in this way so that if one or two should be killed or wounded, the post would not be left unguarded.

Soon after the captain started on his perilous ride, he was discovered by the sharp eyes of the rebel pickets, who promptly opened fire upon him. The firing rapidly increased until it seemed that an attack upon the Union line was about to be made. The bullets flew thickly above and around him, but Tillotson heeded them not until his task was fully accomplished. Then he galloped back within the works as fast as his horse could carry him. That he was not struck by the flying missiles was to him as strange as it was gratifying.

Meanwhile, the rebel fusillade had been attended with the usual result. The entire division was formed in line of battle at the works, to await the onslaught of the foe. But our pickets did not come in, as they would have done had the enemy advanced, and the scare soon wore itself out. After Tillotson disappeared the firing ceased.

Captain Tillotson rode directly to the spot where he had left General

Newton, whom he supposed to be impatiently awaiting the report for which he had made such a peppery demand. But the general had returned to his headquarters as soon as he discovered that the noise on the picket line did not mean business. Tillotson found him and reported the exact number of men on the line of outposts. The general had evidently forgotten the errand upon which he had sent him, for as he looked at man and horse, both dripping with perspiration, he asked:

"How do you know?"

"I counted them sir!" said Tillotson.

"Was that you out there in front drawing the fire of the rebels, which alarmed the army and caused that rush to the works?"

"Yes, General, it was!"

"Well, sir," replied Newton, "all I have to say is that you were a fool!" prefacing the last word with the usual sheolic adjective.

"Yes, General Newton, I believe I was!" said Tillotson, dumbfounded to find that his dangerous ride had been worse than useless.

During all these weeks General Sherman had been seeking a solution of the perplexing problem—how to take Atlanta. To carry its formidable defences by assault was out of the question; no weak spot could be found which offered promise of success. Nothing could be gained by lying idly where we were. It only remained to try the effect of another great turning movement, and this Sherman decided to do, by throwing the body of his army upon the railroads to the southward of Atlanta. Orders were issued on the 24th of August to march that night. The Twentieth corps was directed to take post at the Chattahoochee River, to protect the railroad bridge. The movement began soon after nightfall. At the usual hour all the buglers blew the customary calls, "retreat" and "tattoo," and fires were replenished. All this was to inform the enemy that there was nothing going on out of the ordinary within the Union lines. The movement was by the right, to the west and south of the town, by a wide detour, to avoid detection as long as possible. Beginning at the extreme left of the long line, one regiment and brigade after another broke off, silently left the trenches, and marched swiftly to the right, in rear of the intrenchments.

At dark we struck tents and put ourselves in order for traveling. We were directed to be ready to march at ten o'clock, but it was much later when we got off. Hour after hour the troops from the left streamed past in continuous procession. Soon after midnight our brigade moved out into the darkness. Silence was enjoined upon all. The wheels of the artillery were muffled to deaden their noise. For two hours our journey was exceedingly wearisome. We halted and marched alternately, five minutes at a time, and by two o'clock we had made but a couple of miles. By that time they got the kinks out of the long column and we marched very rapidly until daylight. We halted in rear of the Seventeenth corps, and, after an hour for breakfast, began, from sheer force of habit, to throw up intrenchments. Before the work was fairly under way we were ordered to fall in, and off we went, making but a few brief halts until four o'clock in the afternoon. when we pitched tents on the bank of Utoy creek. After two hours of hard labor, building breastworks, we ate our suppers and threw ourselves upon the ground to sleep. The men had not closed their eyes since morning of the previous day. Many were prostrated by heat and exertion and all were greatly exhausted.

The peering eyes and listening ears of the Confederate pickets around Atlanta did not until dawn discover the evacuation. When morning broke they missed the familiar crack of muskets. Venturing to reconnoiter, they found the Union works deserted. Sherman's army had disappeared as completely as if it had been swallowed by an earthquake. The rebels at once jumped to the conclusion that Sherman had given it up as a bad job. General Hood gleefully telegraphed to Richmond and other points in the south that the siege was raised and the Yankees were in full retreat. The south was thrown into a paroxysm of rejoicing. Congratulations poured in upon General Hood, while his soldiers indulged in frantic demonstrations of delight. But this did not last long. Before twenty-four hours had passed, Hood knew that Sherman was flanking again, and bestirred himself to meet the menace to his rear.

In the afternoon of the 27th we resumed the march, advancing about six miles. We traveled slowly and it was nearly dark when we halted for the night. The Sixty-fifth was ordered to occupy a hill a short distance in front of the line, and there we worked till midnight, fortifying our position. Since leaving Atlanta we had passed through a country abounding in forage of all kinds, and supplied ourselves plenteously with green corn and vegetables, and an occasional pig or chicken.

During the ensuing three days we hitched along slowly, a few miles at a time, building half a dozen lines of breastworks and skirmishing with rebel cavalry that hovered around us. We reached the Montgomery railroad and followed it some distance toward Atlanta. The track had been totally destroyed by troops in advance of us, all the ties having been burned and the rails bent and twisted. We learned that a picnic train had passed toward Atlanta half an hour before the troops reached the road. However, the left of the line captured the train—seven cars with their load of fried chicken, etc., as well as the fair damsels who expected a good time in celebrating the raising of the siege of Atlanta. The ladies were allowed to make their way homeward on foot.

During the night of the 30th, being on picket, we observed and reported the southward movement of a large body of Confederate troops, by a road half a mile in our front. This was the force sent by Hood, under Hardee, to Jonesboro, where it was soundly whipped by the Fourteenth corps. On the 31st we were kept constantly dodging about from one point to another. We built that day four different lines of intrenchments, and didn't fire a shot from either of them. At night we came to a pause within a mile of the railroad to Macon. Wood's division had already reached this road, and a long stretch of smoke told that it was engaged in the work of destruction. Every man in Sherman's army knew that the success of the movement was already assured, and the night was vocal with shouts and cheers.

On the morning of September 1st we took an early start and marched to the Macon railroad. Our division stacked arms and the men were told to "go in." They went, with a glad alacrity that cannot be described. We had suffered a good many times from the cutting of our cracker-line, and this was the first time our boys had found an opportunity to administer to the rebels a dose of their own medicine. It was a novel experience, and officers and men sprang to the work with the greatest zeal and vigor, not forgetting to give vent to their satisfaction in loud and repeated yells. A long row of men ranged themselves, as close together as they could stand, at one side of the track. Seizing the rails and ties they just tipped over the track, bottom side up. The ties were then disengaged, laid in piles, and the torch was applied. Across these piles the rails were laid. The flames were stimulated by brush and dry logs that were heaped upon them. When the rails were at a red heat in the middle, for a distance of three or four feet, they were bent around trees and stumps, twisted and distorted into all imaginable shapes, and left to cool. Railroad iron worn out or destroyed in the south could not be replaced, and we knew that it would be many a day before *that* road would be used again, for the job was well and thoroughly done.

About the middle of the afternoon we rested from our labors, having finished the task assigned us. After an interview with our haversacks, we fell in and marched to a point near Jonesboro, where severe fighting was in progress. The Fourteenth corps captured an entire brigade and ten pieces of artillery. The Fourth was scheduled to get in the rear and cut off the retreat of the enemy. We tried hard to reach the right spot on time, but the distance was too great, and the rebels got away. We captured a large field hospital, in which were several hundred Confederate wounded. We do not claim any glory for that achievement, but it lay directly in our path, and we took possession. One of the most unpleasant sights I ever looked upon was a heap of eight or ten legs and arms that had been amputated.

During the night of September 1st we were startled by heavy and continuous explosions in the direction of Atlanta. At times it sounded like the roar of artillery, as though a battle were in progress. Later the sky was illumined by the glare of a conflagration. We did not *know* what caused the disturbance but we guessed, and correctly, that Hood was evacuating Atlanta. Early in the morning of the 2nd, a reconnoitering force from the Twentieth corps, at the crossing of the Chattahoochee, entered Atlanta unopposed, and soon afterward the city was formally surrendered by the mayor to General Slocum. Before noon of that day a courier reached General Sherman with a message from Slocum informing him of the event, and it was immediately published to the army. *Such* yelling! "Atlanta is ours, and fairly won," was the dispatch sent by Sherman to Washington. It electrified the people of the north, being everywhere greeted with the liveliest rejoicing and patriotic enthusiasm.

About ten o'clock on the 2nd, the Fourth corps started in pursuit of the rebel force which had retreated after the battle of the previous day. Passing through Jonesboro, we continued southward to Lovejoy's station, where, in the afternoon, we found the enemy occupying a strong position and hard at work throwing up intrenchments. Bradley's brigade was in the advance and it was ordered to storm the rebel works, which were upon the crest of a ridge, the intervening space being an open field, without cover of any kind. It had an ugly look, and pulses quickened and hearts throbbed as we lay in momentary expectation of the word to go forward. After a careful inspection of the position and a consultation of the generals, it was decided that an assault would be extra-hazardous, inevitably entailing great loss of life, and the enterprise was abandoned. The brigade was ready to go at command, but there was not a man in it who did not experience a sense of relief when word was passed along the line that the order to charge had been countermanded.

The Sixty-fourth had a very warm encounter with the enemy's skirmishers at Lovejoy's. Sergeant Andrew Towsley, of Company G, a most excellent soldier, was killed, and a number were wounded.

Here ended the Atlanta campaign, which, for continuous marching, fighting and intrenching, tenacity of purpose on the part of the commanding general, and the courage and endurance of the officers and soldiers composing his army, has no parallel in the record of the war except in the contemporaneous campaign of General Grant against Lee. The losses of the Sixty-fourth, from Rocky Face ridge to Lovejoy's, were: officers, three killed, six wounded; enlisted men, twenty-five killed, one hundred wounded, three captured—total, one hundred and thirty-seven. The Sixty-fifth lost: officers, two killed (besides General Harker), four wounded; enlisted men, nine killed, fifty-five wounded, two missing—total, seventy-two. The loss of the Sixth battery was: killed or mortally wounded, one officer, four enlisted men; wounded, seven. Harker's brigade entered the campaign in May with about twenty-six hundred men. Its losses in killed and wounded were ten hundred and forty-one—40 per cent.

At Lovejoy's we bade good-bye to our "esteemed contemporary," the Third Kentucky. Its time having expired, it was ordered to the rear to be mustered out. For eighteen months this excellent regiment had been a member of our brigade family, and we had formed many warm attachments among its members. Hearty cheers were exchanged as the brave, warm-hearted Kentuckians turned their steps homeward. Just before it started, it was visited by many officers and men of the Sixty-fourth and Sixty-fifth, who mingled with their comrades, congratulated them that their long and faithful service was ended, and gave them friendly farewells. We always liked the Third Kentucky. It was composed of excellent material and its record was without a stain. Whenever we were in a tight place, if that regiment was at hand we knew it could be depended upon to stay by to the last extremity. In one of its companies the last of five brothers was killed at Kennesaw.

After lying two days at Lovejoy's, we marched leisurely back to Atlanta, the prize of the four months' campaign. We pitched our camp a mile and a half east of the town, near the battle ground of July 22nd, where General McPherson was killed. It was understood that we would remain there a considerable time, for a season of rest after the arduous service since leaving Chattanooga in May. It is likely that this program would have been carried out had not General Hood perversely spoiled our calculations. As it was we stayed at Atlanta just sixteen days.

MAKING GEORGIA HOWL

ON SEPTEMBER 2, SHERMAN'S FOOTSORE RIFLEMEN marched into Atlanta. Hood retreated southeast to Lovejoy's Station. For a month "Uncle Billy" Sherman rested his troops. They had marched steadily for almost four months. Now, three-year enlistments were up for many of them. Sherman waited for new recruits to fill up the ranks, and calmly calculated his next move.

Because of Atlanta's industrial importance to the South, he considered leaving an occupation force, but this would immobilize 30,000 troops. Next he considered reducing the manpower of the city by shifting a quarter of it elsewhere—many citizens were highly skilled in the making of arms and munitions—but this proposal provoked howls of protest. Eventually Sherman decided to put the torch to the foundries and munition factories and evacuate the city. After that, he would lead his army on through Georgia, cutting a swath through the heart of the South which, so far, had been untouched by the war. His troops would have to live off the country, because supply lines to depots in the North could not be maintained.

Meanwhile Hood decided to shift his army to the southwest, outflank Sherman, and then drive north for Tennessee; on the way he would attack and destroy Sherman's already overextended supply lines. Sherman had been concerned with just such a move. He had telegraphed General Grant to explain how he would deal with this threat: "It will be a physical impossibility to protect the roads, now that Hood, Forrest and Wheeler, and the whole batch of devils are turned loose without home or habitation. . . . I propose we break up the railroad from Chattanooga, and strike out with wagons to Milledgeville, Millen and Savannah. Until we can repopulate Georgia, it is useless to occupy it, but the utter destruction of its roads, houses and people will cripple their military resources. By attempting to hold the roads we will lose 1,000 men monthly, and will gain no result. I can make the march, and make Georgia howl."

The telegram had hardly been sent before Hood headed north. Sherman wired Grant again: "I would infinitely prefer to make a wreck of the road and of the country from Chattanooga to Atlanta . . . and, with my effective army, move through Georgia, smashing things to the sea. Hood may turn into Tennessee and Kentucky, but I believe he will be forced to follow me. Instead of being on the defensive, I would be on the offensive; instead of guessing at what he means to do, he would have to guess at my plans. The difference in war is full 25 per cent. I can make Savannah, Charleston or the mouth of the Chattahoochee."

Grant replied: "If you were to cut loose, I do not believe you would meet Hood's army, but would be bushwacked by all the old men, little boys, and such railroad guards as are still left at home. . . . If there is any way of getting at Hood's army, I would prefer that, but I must trust to your own judgment. I find I shall not be able to send a force from here to act with you at Savannah. Your movements, therefore, will be independent of mine, at least until the fall of Richmond takes place."

Sherman sent George Thomas back to Nashville to organize an army to deal with Hood and released two corps from Atlanta to follow Thomas north. Thomas would keep his troops concentrated at Nashville and Chattanooga so that Hood's cavalry could not cut them up.

Of Sherman's decision, B. H. Liddell Hart says, "It was a supreme act of moral courage. To leave the enemy in his rear, to divide his army, to cut himself adrift from railroad and telegraph, from supplies and reinforcements, and launch not a mere raiding force of cavalry but a great army into the heart of a hostile country—pinning his faith and his fortune on a principle which he had deduced by reasoning contrary to orthodoxy. And with nothing to fortify his spirit beyond that reasoning, for his venture was to be made under the cloud of the dubious permission of his military superior, the anxious fears of his President, and the positive objections of their advisors. If it requires great moral courage under such gloomy conditions to launch an army to an attack from a secure base, how much greater the effort and strength of will required to launch an army 'into the blue.' "[*]

The March to the Sea[†]

BY MAJOR GEORGE W. NICHOLS

BEFORE FAIRLY ENTERING UPON A RECITAL of the incidents attending the great march seaward, it is important to glance at the organization of the army, and to gain at least a general idea of its main features.

The grand army under the supreme command of General Sherman is divided into two armies, called the Right and Left Wings, each of which has a separate army commander—General Howard, of the right wing, and General Slocum, of the left.

---

[*] B. H. Liddell Hart, *Sherman*, p. 330.
[†] Condensed from *Story of the Great March*.

The right wing of the army is called the Army of Tennessee, and is commanded by General Howard. It is composed of two corps, the 15th and the 17th.

The left wing of the army is called the Army of Georgia, and is commanded by General Slocum. It also contains two corps, the 14th and the 20th.

The order of march is issued by the army commanders the preceding night, from them to the corps commanders, and then passed along until every soldier, teamster, and camp-follower knows that an early start is to be made. "The second division will be on the Milledgeville road promptly at five o'clock" reads an order, by way of instance.

At three o'clock the watch-fires are burning dimly, and, but for the occasional neighing of horses, all is so silent that it is difficult to imagine that twenty thousand men are within a radius of a few miles. The ripple of the brook can be distinctly heard as it breaks over the pebbles, or winds petulantly about the gnarled roots. The wind sweeping gently through the tall pines overhead only serves to lull to deeper repose the slumbering soldier, who in his tent is dreaming of his far-off Northern home.

But in an instant all is changed. From some commanding elevation the clear-toned bugle sounds out the *reveille,* and another and another responds, until the startled echoes double and treble the clarion calls. Intermingled with this comes the beating of drums, often rattling and jarring on unwilling ears. In a few moments the peaceful quiet is replaced by noise and tumult, arising from hill and dale, from field and forest. Camp-fires, hitherto extinct or smouldering in dull gray ashes, awaken to new life and brilliancy, and send forth their sparks high into the morning air. Although no gleam of sunrise blushes in the east, the harmless flames on every side light up the scene, so that there is no disorder or confusion.

The aesthetic aspects of this sudden change do not, however, occupy much of the soldier's time. He is more practically engaged in getting his breakfast ready. The potatoes are frying nicely in the well-larded pan; the chicken is roasting delicately on the red-hot coals, and grateful fumes from steaming coffee-pots delight the nostrils. The animals are not less busy. An ample supply of corn and huge piles of fodder are greedily devoured by these faithful friends of the boys in blue, and any neglect is quickly made known by the pawing of neighing horses and the fearful braying of the mules. Amid all this the busy clatter of tongues and tools— a Babel of sound, forming a contrast to the quiet of the previous hour as marked as that between peace and war.

Then the animals are hitched into the traces, and the droves of cattle relieved from the night's confinement in the corral. Knapsacks are strapped, men seize their trusty weapons, and as again the bugles sound the note of command, the soldiers fall into line and file out upon the road.

A day's march varies according to the country to be traversed or the opposition encountered. If the map indicates a stream crossing the path, probably the strong party of mounted infantry or of cavalry which has been sent forward the day before has found the bridges burned, and then the pontoons are pushed on to the front. If a battle is anticipated, the trains are shifted to the rear of the centre. Under any circumstances, the divisions having the lead move unencumbered by wagons, and in close fighting trim. The ambulances following in the rear of the division are in such close proximity as to be available if needed. In the rear of each regiment follow the pack-mules, laden with every kind of camp baggage, including blankets, pots, pans, kettles, and all the kitchen-ware needed for cooking. Here will be found the led horses, and with them the Negro servants, who form an important feature of the *menage*.

Having placed the column upon the road, let us now follow that long line of muskets gleaming in the rays of the morning sunlight, and ride, heedless of the crack of the rifles, to the head of the column. The advance are driving a squad of Rebel cavalry before them so fast that the march is not in the least impeded. The flankers spread out, on a line parallel to the leading troops, for several hundred yards, more or less, as the occasion may require. They search through the swamps and forests, ready for any concealed foe, and anxiously looking out for any line of works which may have been thrown up by the enemy to check our progress. Here the General of the division, if a fighting man, is most likely to be found; his experienced eye noting that there is no serious opposition, he orders up a brigade or another regiment, who, in soldier's phraseology, send the Rebel rascals "kiting," and the column moves on. A large plantation appears by the road-side. If the "bummers" have been ahead, the chances are that it has been visited, in which event the interior is apt to show evidences of confusion; but the barns are full of corn and fodder, and parties are at once detailed to secure and convey the prize to the road-side. As the wagons pass along they are not allowed to halt, but the grain or fodder is stuffed into the front and rear of the vehicles as they pass, the unhandy operation affording much amusement to the soldiers, and not unfrequently giving them a poor excuse for swearing as well as laughing.

When the treasure-trove of grain, and poultry, and vegetables has been secured, one man is detailed to guard it until the proper wagon comes along. Numbers of these details will be met, who, with proper authority, have started off early in the morning, and have struck out miles away from the flank of the column. They sit upon some cross-road, surrounded with their spoils—chickens, turkeys, geese, ducks, pigs, hogs, sheep, calves, nicely-dressed hams, buckets full of honey, and pots of fresh white lard.

A Roman consul returning with victorious eagles could not wear a more triumphant air than this solitary guard. The soldiers see it, and gibe him as they pass:

"Say, you thar! where did you steal them pigs?"

"Steal!" is the indignant response; "steal!—perhaps you would like to have one of '*them*' pigs yourself."

An officer who is riding along gazes upon the appetizing show. He has recently joined, never has been on one of Sherman's raids, and does not know that a soldier will not sell his chickens for any price.

"Ah! a nice pair of ducks you have there, soldier; what will you take for them?"

Firmly, but respectfully, the forager makes answer, touching his cap the while, "They are not in the market. We *never* sell our stuff, sir—couldn't think of it."

Marching through Georgia

The officer rides away through a battery of wide grins from the by-standers, and never again offers to buy the spoils of a forager.

As rumors of the approach of our army reached the frightened inhabitants, frantic efforts were made to canceal not only their valuable personal effects, plate, jewelry, and other rich goods, but also articles of food, such as hams, sugar, flour, etc. A large part of these supplies were carried to the neighboring swamps; but the favorite method of concealment was the burial of the treasures in the pathways and gardens adjoining the dwelling-houses. Sometimes, also, the grave-yards were selected as the best place of security from the "vandal hands of the invaders." Unfortunately for these people, the Negroes betrayed them, and in the early part of the march the soldiers learned the secret. It is possible that supplies thus hidden may have escaped the search of our men; but, if so, it was not for want of diligent exploration. With untiring zeal the soldiers hunted for concealed treasures. Wherever the army halted, almost every inch of ground in the vicinity of the dwellings was poked by ramrods, pierced with sabres, or upturned with spades. The universal digging was good for the garden land, but its results were distressing to the Rebel owners of exhumed property, who saw it rapidly and irretrievably "confiscated." It was comical to see a group of these red-bearded, barefooted, ragged veterans punching the unoffending earth in an apparently idiotic, but certainly most energetic way. If they "struck a vein" a spade was instantly put in requisition, and the coveted wealth was speedily unearthed. A woman standing upon the porch of a house, apparently watching their proceedings, instantly became an object of suspicion, and she was watched until some movement betrayed a place of concealment. The fresh earth recently thrown up, a bed of flowers just set out, the slightest indication of a change in appearance or position, all attracted the gaze of these military agriculturists. It was all fair spoil of war, and the search made one of the excitements of the march.

There is a halt in the column. The officer in charge of the pioneer corps, which follows the advance guard, has discovered an ugly place in the road, which must be "corduroyed" at once, before the wagons can pass. The pioneers quickly tear down the fence near by and bridge over the treacherous place, perhaps at the rate of a quarter of a mile in fifteen minutes. If rails are not near, pine saplings and split logs supply their place. Meanwhile the bugles have sounded, and the column has halted. The soldiers, during the temporary halt, drop out of line on the road-side, lying upon their backs, supported by their still unstrapped knapsacks. If the halt is a long one, the different regiments march by file right, one behind the other, into the fields, stacking their muskets, and taking their rest at ease, released from their knapsack.

These short halts are of great benefit to the soldier. He gains a breathing-spell, has a chance to wipe the perspiration from his brow and the dust out of his eyes, or pulls off his shoes and stockings to cool his swollen, heated feet, though old campaigners do not feel the need of this. He munches his bit of hard bread, or pulls out a book from his pocket, or oftener a pipe, to indulge in that greatest of luxuries to the soldier, a soothing, refreshing smoke. Here may be seen one group at a brook-side, bathing their heads and drinking; and another, crowded round an old song-book, are making very fair music. One venturesome fellow has kindled a fire, and is brewing a cup of coffee. All are happy and jolly; but when the bugle sounds "fall in," "attention," and "forward," in an instant every temporary occupation is dropped, and they are on the road again.

This massing of brigades and wagons during a halt is a proper and most admirable arrangement. It keeps the column well closed up; and if a brigade or division has by some means been delayed, it has the opportunity to overtake the others. The 20th Corps manage this thing to perfection.

A great many of the mounted officers ride through the fields, on either side of the line of march, so as not to interfere with the troops. General Sherman always takes to the fields, dashing through thickets or plunging into the swamps, and, when forced to take the road, never breaks into a regiment or brigade, but waits until it passes, and then falls in. He says that they, and not he, have the right to the road.

Sometimes a little creek crosses the path, and at once a foot-bridge is made upon one side of the way for those who wish to keep dry-shod; many, however, with a shout of derision, will dash through the water at a run, and then they all shout the more when some unsteady comrade misses his footing and tumbles in at full length. The unlucky wight, however, takes the fun at his expense in the best of humor. Indeed, as a general rule, soldiers are good-humored and kind-hearted to the last degree. I have seen a soldier stand at a spring of water for ten minutes, giving thirsty comers cool draughts, although it would delay him so that he would have to run a quarter of a mile or more to overtake his company. The troops, by the way, kept their ranks admirably during this Georgia campaign. Occasionally, however, they would rush for a drink of water, or for a beehive which they would despoil of its sweets with a total disregard of the swarm of bees buzzing about their ears, but which, strange to say, rarely stung.

But the sun has long since passed the zenith, the droves of cattle which have been driven through the swamps and fields are lowing and wandering in search of a corral, the soldiers are beginning to lag a little, the teamsters are obliged to apply the whip oftener, ten or fifteen miles have been traversed, and the designated halting-place for the night is near. The column must now be got into camp.

Officers ride on in advance to select the ground for each brigade, giving the preference to slopes in the vicinity of wood and water. Soon the troops file out into the woods and fields, the leading division pitching tents first, those in the rear marching on yet farther, ready to take their turn in the advance the next day.

As soon as the arms are stacked, the boys attack the fences and rail-piles, and with incredible swiftness their little shelter-tents spring up all over the ground. The fires are kindled with equal celerity, and the luxurious repast prepared, while "good digestion waits on appetite, and health on both." After this is heard the music of dancing or singing, the pleasant buzz of conversation, and the measured sound of reading. The wagons are meanwhile parked and the animals fed. If there has been a fight during the day, the incidents of success or failure are recounted; the poor fellow who lies wounded in "the anguish-laden ambulance" is not forgotten, and the brave comrade who fell in the strife is remembered with words of loving praise.

By-and-by the tattoo rings out on the night air. Its familiar sound is understood. "Go to rest, go to rest," it says, plainly as organs of human speech.

Shortly after follows the peremptory command of "Taps." "Out lights, out lights, out lights!" The soldier gradually disappears from the camp-fire. Rolled snugly in his blanket, the soldier dreams again of home, or revisits in imagination the battle-fields he has trod. The animals, with dull instinct, lie down to rest, and with dim gropings of consciousness ruminate over "fresh fields and pastures new." The fires, neglected by the sleeping men, go out, gradually flickering and smouldering, as if unwilling to die.

MILLEDGEVILLE, NOVEMBER 24TH

We are in full possession of the capital of the State of Georgia, and without firing a gun in its conquest. A few days ago, the Legislature, which had been in session, hearing of our approach, hastily decamped without any adjournment. The legislative panic spread among the citizens to such an extent as to depopulate the place, except a few old gentlemen and ladies and the Negroes.

General Slocum, with the 20th Corps, first entered the city, arriving by way of Madison, having accomplished his work of destroying the rail-roads and valuable bridges at that place. The fright of the legislators, as described by witnesses, must have been comical in the extreme. They little imagined the movement of our left wing, hearing first of the advance of Kilpatrick on the extreme right toward Macon, and supposing that to be another raid. What their opinion was when Howard's army appeared at M'Donough it would be difficult to say; and their astonishment must have approached insanity when the other two columns were heard from —one directed toward Augusta, and the other swiftly marching straight upon their devoted city.

It seemed as if they were surrounded upon all sides except toward the east, and that their doom was sealed. With the certain punishment for their crimes looming up before them, they sought every possible means of escape. Private effects, household furniture, books, pictures, were conveyed to the depot, and loaded into the cars until they were filled and heaped, and the flying people could not find standing-room.

Any and every price was obtained for a vehicle. A thousand dollars was cheap for a common buggy, and men rushed about the streets in an agony of fear lest they should "fall victims to the ferocity of the Yankees."

Several days of perfect quiet passed after this exodus, when, on a bright sunshiny morning, a regiment entered the city, with a band playing national airs, which music had long been hushed in the capital of Georgia.

But few of the troops were marched through the city. Two or three regiments were detailed, under the orders of the engineers, to destroy certain property designated by the General Commanding. The magazines, arsenals, depot buildings, factories of various kinds, with store-houses containing large amounts of government property, and about seventeen hundred bales of cotton, were burned. Private houses were respected every where, even those of noted Rebels, and I heard of no instance of pillage or insult to the inhabitants. One or two of the latter, known as having been in the Rebel army, were made prisoners of war, but the surgeons at the hospitals, the principal of the Insane Asylum, and others, expressed their gratitude that such perfect order was maintained throughout the city.

General Sherman is at the executive mansion, its former occupant having, with extremely bad grace, fled from his distinguished visitor, taking with him the entire furniture of the building. As General Sherman travels with a *menage* (a roll of blankets and a haversack full of "hard-tack"), which is as complete for a life in the open air as in a palace, this discourtesy of Governor Brown was not a serious inconvenience.

Just before his entrance into Milledgeville, General Sherman camped on one of the plantations of Howell Cobb. It was a coincidence that a Macon paper, containing Cobb's address to the Georgians as General Commanding, was received the same day. This plantation was the property of Cobb's wife, who was a Lamar. I do not know that Cobb ever claimed any great reputation as a man of piety or singular virtues, but I could not help contrasting the call upon his fellow-citizens to "rise and defend their liberties, homes, etc., from the step of the invader, to burn and destroy every thing in his front, and assail him on all sides," and all that, with his own conduct here, and the wretched condition of his Negroes and their quarters.

We found his granaries well filled with corn and wheat, part of which was distributed and eaten by our animals and men. A large supply of sirup made from sorghum (which we have found at nearly every plantation on our march) was stored in an out-house. This was also disposed of to the soldiers and the poor decrepit Negroes which this humane, liberty-loving major general left to die in this place a few days ago. Becoming alarmed, Cobb sent for and removed all the able-bodied mules, horses, cows, and slaves. He left here some fifty old men—cripples—and women and children, with nothing scarcely covering their nakedness, with little or no food, and without means of procuring it. We found them cowering over the fireplaces of their miserable huts, where the wind whirled through the crevices between the logs, frightened at the approach of the Yankees, who, they had been told, would kill them. A more forlorn, neglected set of human beings I never saw.

General Sherman distributed to the Negroes with his own hands the provisions left here, and assured them that we were their friends, and they need not be afraid that we were foes. An old man answered him: "I spose dat you'se true; but, massa, you'se 'll go way to-morrow, and anudder white man'll come." He had never known any thing but persecutions and injury from the white man, and had been kept in such ignorance of us that he did not dare to put faith in any white man.

General Sherman invites all able-bodied Negroes (others could not make the march) to join the column, and he takes especial pleasure on some occasions, when they join the procession, in telling them they are free; that Massa Lincoln has given them their liberty, and that they can go where they please; that if they earn their freedom they should have it, but that Massa Lincoln had given it to them any how. They seem to understand that the proclamation of freedom had made them free; and I have met but few instances where they did not say they expected the Yankees were coming down some time or other, and very generally they are possessed with the idea that we are fighting for them, and that their freedom is the object of the war.

General Sherman's opening move in the present campaign has been successful in the highest degree. First marching his army in three columns, with a column of cavalry on his extreme right, upon eccentric lines, he diverted the attention of the enemy, so that the Rebels concentrated their forces at extreme points, Macon and Augusta, leaving unimpeded the progress of the central columns.

The roads each column was to follow were carefully designated, the number of miles each day to be traveled, and the points of rendezvous were given at a certain date. All of these conditions were fulfilled to the letter. Slocum, with the 20th Corps, arrived at Milledgeville on the 22d instant, preceding Davis, with the 14th Corps, one day. On the same day Kilpatrick struck the Macon and Western road, destroying the bridge at Walnut Creek. The day following, Howard, with the 15th and 17th Corps, arrived at Gordon, and began the destruction of the Georgia Central Railroad.

It was near here that the most serious fight of the campaign has occurred up to this date. General Walcott, in command of a detachment of cavalry and a brigade of infantry, was thrown forward to Griswoldville, toward Macon, for demonstrative purposes merely. The enemy, about five thousand strong, advanced upon our troops, who had thrown up temporary breastworks, with a section of battery in position. The cavalry fell slowly back on either flank of the brigade, protecting them from attack in flank and rear. The Rebels were chiefly composed of militia, although a portion of Hardee's old corps was present, having been brought up from Savannah.

With the ignorance of danger common to new troops, the Rebels rushed upon our veterans with the greatest fury. They were received with grape-shot and musketry at point-blank range, our soldiers firing coolly, while shouting derisively to the quivering columns to come on, as if they thought the whole thing a nice joke. The Rebels resumed the attack, but with the same fatal results, and were soon in full flight, leaving more than three hundred dead on the field. Our loss was some forty killed and wounded, while their killed, wounded, and prisoners are estimated to exceed two thousand five hundred. A pretty severe lesson they have received.

NEAR TENNILLE STATION, ON THE GEORGIA CENTRAL RAILROAD, NOVEMBER 27TH

Since writing the above the army has moved forward all along the line. The Rebels seem to have understood, but too late, that it was not Sherman's intention to make a serious attack upon Macon. They have, however, succeeded in getting Wheeler across the Oconee at a point below the railroad bridge. We first became aware of their presence in our front by the destruction of several small bridges across Buffalo Creek, on the two roads leading to Sandersville, over which were advancing the 20th and 14th Corps.

We were delayed but a few hours. The passage was also contested by the Rebel cavalry under Wheeler, and they fought our front all the way, and into the streets of Sandersville. The 20th Corps had the advance, deploying a regiment as skirmishers, and forming the remainder of a brigade in line of battle on either side of the road. The movement was executed in the handsomest manner, and was so effectual as not to impede the march of the column in the slightest degree, although the roll of musketry was unceasing. Our loss was not serious—about twenty killed and wounded.

As the 20th Corps entered the town they were met by the 14th, whose head of column arrived at the same moment. While these two corps had found the obstructions above mentioned, the army under General Howard was attempting to throw a pontoon across the Oconee at the Georgia Central Railroad bridge. Here they met a force under the command of General Wayne, which was composed of a portion of Wheeler's cavalry, militia, and a band of convicts who had been liberated from the penitentiary upon the condition that they would join the army.

The most of these desperadoes have been taken prisoners, dressed in their state prison clothing. General Sherman has turned them loose, believing that Governor Brown had not got the full benefits of his liberality. The Rebels did not make a remarkably stern defense of the bridge, for Howard was able to cross his army yesterday, and began breaking railroad again to-day. In fact, all the army, except one corps, is engaged in this same work. Wayne, with his army, was hardly able to reach this point, where he met General Hardee, who had managed to get around here from Macon. Our troops struck the railroad at this station a few hours after the frightened band escaped.

We had been told that the country was very poor east of the Oconee, but our experience has been a delightful gastronomic contradiction of the statement. The cattle trains are getting so large that we find difficulty in driving them along. Thanksgiving-day was very generally observed in the army, the troops scorning chickens in the plenitude of turkeys with which they had supplied themselves.

Vegetables of all kinds, and in unlimited quantities, were at hand, and the soldiers gave thanks as soldiers may, and were merry as only soldiers can be. In truth, so far as the gratification of the stomach goes, the troops are pursuing a continuous thanksgiving.

In addition to fowls, vegetables, and meats, many obtain a delicious sirup made from sorghum, which is cultivated on all the plantations, and stored away in large troughs and hogsheads. The mills here and there furnish fresh supplies of flour and meal, and we hear little or nothing of "hardtack"—that terror to weak mastication. Over the sections of country lately traversed I find very little cultivation of cotton. The commands of Davis appear to have been obeyed; and our large droves of cattle are turned nightly into the immense fields of ungathered corn to eat their fill, while the granaries are crowded to overflowing with both oats and corn.

We have also reached the sand regions, so that the fall of rain has no terrors; the roads are excellent, and would become firmer from a liberal wetting. The rise of the rivers will not trouble us much, for each army corps has its pontoon, and the launching of its boats is a matter of an hour.

TENNILLE STATION, NOVEMBER 28TH

The destruction of railroads in this campaign has been most thorough. The work of demolition on such long lines of road necessarily requires time, but the process is performed as expeditiously as possible, in order to prevent any serious delay of the movement of the army. The method of destruction is simple, but very effective. Two ingenious instruments have been made for this purpose. One of them is a clasp, which locks under the rail. It has a ring in the top, into which is inserted a long lever, and the rail is thus ripped from the sleepers. The sleepers are then piled in a heap and set on fire, the rails roasting in the flames until they bend by their own weight. When sufficiently heated, each rail is taken off by wrenches fitting closely over the ends, and by turning in opposite directions, it is so twisted that even a rolling-machine could not bring it back into shape. In this manner we have destroyed thirty miles of rails which lay in the city of Atlanta, and all on the Augusta and Atlanta Road from the last-named place to Madison, besides the entire track of the Central Georgia line, from a point a few miles east of Macon to the station where I am now writing.

NEAR JOHNSTON, SOUTH SIDE OF THE GEORGIA RAILROAD, NOVEMBER 29TH

All day long the army has been moving through magnificent pine-woods—the savannas of the South, as they are termed. I have never seen, and I can not conceive a more picturesque sight than the army winding along through these grand old woods. The pines, destitute of branches, rise to a height of eighty or ninety feet, their tops being crowned with tufts of pure green. They are widely apart, so that frequently two trains of wagons and troops in double column are marching abreast. In the distance may be seen a troop of horsemen—some General and his staff—turning about here and there, their gray uniforms and red and white flags contrasting harmoniously with the bright yellow grass underneath and the deep evergreen.

The most pathetic scenes occur upon our line of march daily and hourly. Thousands of Negro women join the column, some carrying household goods, and many of them carrying children in their arms, while older boys and girls plod by their side. All these women and children are ordered back, heartrending though it may be to refuse them liberty. One begs that she may go to see her husband and children at Savannah. Long years ago she was forced from them and sold. Another has heard that her boy was in Macon, and she is "done gone with grief goin' on four years."

But the majority accept the advent of the Yankees as the fulfillment of the millennial prophecies. The "day of jubilee," the hope and prayer of a lifetime, has come. They can not be made to understand that they must remain behind, and they are satisfied only when General Sherman tells them, as he does every day, that we shall come back for them some time, and that they must be patient until the proper hour of deliverance arrives.

The other day a woman with a child in her arms was working her way along among the teams and crowds of cattle and horsemen. An officer called to her kindly: "Where are you going, aunty?"

She looked up into his face with a hopeful, beseeching look, and replied:

"I'se gwine whar you'se gwine, massa."

NOVEMBER 30TH

With the exception of the 15th Corps, our army is across the Ogeechee without fighting a battle. This river is a line of great strength to the Rebels, who might have made its passage a costly effort for us, but they have been outwitted and outmanœuvred. I am more than ever convinced that, if General Sherman intends to take his army to the sea-board, it is his policy to avoid any contest which will delay him in the establishment of a new base of operations and supplies; if he is able to establish this new base, and at the same time destroy all the lines of communication from the Rebel armies with the great cities, so that they will be as much isolated as if those strong-holds were in our hands, he will have accomplished the greatest strategic victory in the war, and all the more welcome because bloodless. Macon, Augusta, Savannah, or Charleston are of no strategic value to us, except that they are filled with munitions of war, and that the two latter might be useful to us as a base of supplies, with the additional moral advantage which would result from their capture. All these places, however, are vitally important to the enemy, as the source of a large part of their supplies of ammunition and commissary stores.

We have heard to-day from Kilpatrick and from Millen. Kilpatrick has made a splendid march, fighting Wheeler all the way to Waynesboro, destroying the railroad bridge across Brier Creek, between Augusta and Millen. It is with real grief that we hear he was unable to accomplish the release of our prisoners in the prison-pen at Millen. It appears that for some time past the Rebels have been removing our soldiers from Millen; the officers have been sent to Columbia, South Carolina, and the privates farther south, somewhere on the Gulf Railroad.

We have had very little difficulty in crossing the Ogeechee. The 20th Corps moved down the railroad, destroying it as far as the bridge. The 17th Corps covered the river at that point, where a light bridge was only partially destroyed. It was easily repaired, so that the infantry and cavalry could pass over it, while the wagons and artillery used the pontoons. The Ogeechee is about sixty yards in width at this point. It is approached on the northern or western side through swamps, which would be impassable but for the sandy soil, which packs solidly when the water covers the roads, although in places there are treacherous quicksands which we are obliged to corduroy.

This evening I walked down to the river, where a striking and novel spectacle was visible. The fires of pitch pine were flaring up into the mist and darkness; figures of men and horses loomed out of the dense shadows in gigantic proportions; torch-lights were blinking and flashing away off in the forests; and the still air echoed and re-echoed with the cries of teamsters and the wild shouts of the soldiers. A long line of the troops marched across the foot-bridge, each soldier bearing a torch, and, as the column marched, the vivid light was reflected in quivering lines in the swift-running stream.

Soon the fog, which here settles like a blanket over the swamps and forests of the river-bottoms, shut down upon the scene; and so dense and dark was it that torches were of but little use, and our men were directed here and there by the voice.

"Jim, are you there?" shouted one.

"Yes, I *am* here," was the impatient answer.

"Well, then, go straight ahead."

"Straight ahead! where in thunder is 'straight ahead?' "

And so the troops shuffled upon and over each other, and finally blundered into their quarters for the night.

As we journey on from day to day, it is curious to observe the attentions bestowed by our soldiers upon camp pets. With a care which almost deserves the name of tenderness, the men gather helpless, dumb animals around them; sometimes an innocent kid whose mother has been served up as an extra ration, and again a raccoon, a little donkey, a dog, or a cat. One regiment has adopted a fine Newfoundland dog, which soon became so attached to its new home that it never strayed, but became a part of the body, recognizing the face of every man in it. These pets are watched, fed, protected, and carried along with a faithfulness and affection which constantly suggest the most interesting psychological queries.

The favorite pet of the camp, however, is the hero of the barn-yard. There is not a regiment nor a company, not a teamster nor a Negro at head-quarters, nor an orderly, but has a "rooster" of one kind or another. When the column is moving, these haughty game-cocks are seen mounted upon the breech of a cannon, tied to the pack-saddle of a mule, among pots and pans, or carried lovingly in the arms of a mounted orderly; crowing with all his might from the interior of a wagon, or making the woods re-echo with his triumphant notes as he rides perched upon the knapsack of a soldier. These cocks represent every known breed, Polish and Spanish, Dorkings, Shanghais and Bantams—high-blooded specimens travelling with those of their species who may not boast of noble lineage. They must all fight, however, or be killed and eaten. Hardly has the army gone into camp before these feathery combats begin. The cocks use only the spurs with which Nature furnishes them; for the soldiers have not yet reached the refinement of applying artificial gaffs, and so but little harm is done. The game-cocks which have come out of repeated conflicts victorious are honored with such names as "Bill Sherman," "Johnny Lo-

gan," etc.; while the defeated and bepecked victim is saluted with derisive
appellations, such as "Jeff. Davis," "Beauregard," or "Bob Lee."

Cock-fighting is not, perhaps, one of the most refined or elevating of
pastimes, but it furnishes food for a certain kind of fun in camp; and as
it is not carried to the point of cruelty, the soldiers can not be blamed
for liking it.

MILLEN, DECEMBER 3D

Pivoted upon Millen, the army has swung slowly round from its eastern
course, and is now moving in six columns upon parallel roads southward.
Until yesterday it was impossible for the Rebels to decide whether or not
it was General Sherman's intention to march upon Augusta. Kilpatrick
had destroyed the bridge above Waynesboro, and, after falling back, had
again advanced, supported by the 14th Army Corps, under General Davis.
South of this column, moving eastward through Birdsville, was the 20th
Corps, commanded by General Slocum. Yet farther south, the 17th Corps,
General Blair in command, followed the railroad, destroying the track
as it advanced. West and south of the Ogeechee, the 15th Corps, General
Osterhaus in immediate command, but under the eye of General Howard,
has moved in two columns.

Until now, Davis and Kilpatrick have been a cover and shield to the
real movement of the army. At no time has it been possible for Hardee
to interpose any serious obstacle to the advance of our main body, for our
left wing has always been a strong arm thrust out in advance, ready to
encounter any force which might attempt to bar the way.

The Rebel councils of war appear to have been completely deceived,
for we hear it reported that Bragg and Longstreet are at Augusta, with
ten thousand men made up of militia, two or three South Carolina regiments, and a portion of Hampton's Legion, sent there for remount. It is
possible, now that the curtain has been withdrawn, and as it may appear
that we are marching straight for Savannah, that these generals, with
their ten thousand men, may attempt to harass our rear, but they can
accomplish nothing more than the loss of a few lives. They can not check
our progress.

The work so admirably performed by our left wing, so far as it obliged
the Rebels in our front constantly to retreat, by threatening their rear,
now becomes the office of the 15th Corps, which is divided, and will
operate on the right and left banks of the river. These two columns are
marching, one day in advance of the main body, down the peninsula
formed by the Savannah and Ogeechee rivers, with a detachment thrown
over to the south side of the latter stream.

These flank movements are of the greatest necessity and value. They
have taken place in the following order: first, the right wing, with Kilpatrick's cavalry, moved upon Macon, in the early part of the campaign;
next, after disappearing from that flank, to the great amazement of the
Rebels, the same troops marched across our rear and suddenly appeared
upon our left flank, supported by Davis, and demonstrating savagely upon
Augusta; and now Howard is performing the same office on our right.
This style of manœuvring has not been practiced on account of any appre-

hension that we can not run over and demolish any Rebel force in Georgia, for all the troops of the enemy in the state could not stand for a moment against this army on any battle-field; but because General Sherman neither wishes to sacrifice life needlessly nor be detained. A very small force of infantry or cavalry in position at a river-crossing could delay a marching column half a day, or longer: our flanking column prevents this. Besides, our soldiers have tired of chickens, sweet potatoes, sorghum, etc., and have been promised oysters at the sea-side—oysters roasted, oysters fried, oysters stewed, oysters on the half shell, oysters in abundance, without money and without price. In short, the soldiers themselves don't wish to be delayed!

The railroad, which has received our immediate attention within the last week, is altogether the best I have seen in the state, though the rail itself is not so heavy as the T rail on the Augusta and Atlanta road. The rail on the Georgia Central is partially laid with the U, and partly with light T rail, but it is all fastened to parallel string-pieces, which are again fixed to the ties. The station-houses are generally built of brick, in the most substantial manner, and are placed at distances of fifteen or twenty miles apart. They have been destroyed by our army all the way along from Macon. The extensive depot at Millen was a wooden structure of exceedingly graceful proportions. It was ignited in three places simultaneously, and its destruction was a brilliant spectacle; the building burning slowly, although there was sufficient wind to lift the vast volume of smoke and exhibit the exquisite architecture traced in lines of fire. This scene was so striking that even the rank and file observed and made comments upon it among themselves—a circumstance which may be counted as unusual, for the taste for conflagrations has been so cultivated of late in the army that any small affair of that kind attracts very little attention.

We daily traverse immense corn-fields, each of which covers from one hundred to one thousand acres. These fields were once devoted to the cultivation of cotton, and it is surprising to see how the planters have carried out the wishes or orders of the Rebel Government; for cotton has given way to corn. A large amount of cotton has been destroyed by our army in this campaign, but it must have been a small portion even of the limited crop raised, as our destruction has chiefly been upon the line of the railroads. As nearly as I can learn, two thirds of this cotton has been sent over the Georgia Central Railroad to Augusta by way of Millen; thence a limited amount has been transported to Wilmington for transAtlantic shipment; the remainder is at Columbia, South Carolina, at Columbus, Georgia, and at Montgomery, Alabama. I think it will be found, however, when the facts are known, that no large amounts of cotton are stored in any one place. The policy of scattering the crop is probably the wisest the Rebels could have adopted.

It is well ascertained that the country west of the Savannah River is expected to furnish supplies for the Rebel armies in the West; for although corn and beef are sent from this district to Lee's army, he draws the bulk of his supplies from the states east of the Savannah, and there is no region so prolific as that about Columbia. I note this fact because I wish to correct the impression, so general at the North, that the Eastern

armies are fed from the Southwest. One thing is certain, that neither the
West nor the East will draw any supplies from the counties in this state
traversed by our army for a long time to come. Our work has been the
next thing to annihilation.

OGEECHEE CHURCH, DECEMBER 6TH

For two days past the army has been concentrated at this point, which
is the narrowest part of the peninsula. General Howard is still on the
west side of the Ogeechee, but he is within supporting distance, and has
ample means of crossing the river, should it be necessary, which is not at
all probable.

Kilpatrick has again done noble work. On Sunday last, while marching
toward Alexander for the purpose of more thoroughly completing the
destruction of the railroad bridge crossing Brier Creek, he found Wheeler
near Waynesboro and fought him several times, punishing him severely
in each instance, driving his infantry and cavalry before him through
Waynesboro and beyond the bridge, which was completely destroyed.
Kilpatrick, having performed this feat, rejoined the main body of our
army, then marching southward.

One important object of this eccentric movement of Kilpatrick is to
impress the Rebel leaders with the conviction that we intend to march
upon Augusta. To divide and and scatter their force is our main purpose.
Let them keep a large army in Augusta until we reach the sea, and then
they can go where they please!

DECEMBER 8TH

The army has been advancing slowly and surely, but as cautiously as
if a strong army were in our front. The relative position of the troops has
not materially changed during the past few days, except that we are all
farther south. From fifteen to twenty miles distant lies Savannah, a city
which is probably in some perturbation at the certainty of our approach.
If the Rebels intend fighting in defense of the city, the battle will be an
assault of fortifications; for as yet we have only skirmished with parties
of cavalry.

DECEMBER 10TH

The army has advanced some six miles to-day, and has met everywhere
a strong line of works, which appear to be held by a large force, with
heavy guns in position. Their line, although extended, is more easily
defended because of a succession of impassable swamps which stretch
across the peninsula. All the openings between these morasses and the
roads which lead through them are strongly fortified, and the approaches
have been contested vigorously, but with little loss to us. General Sherman seems to avoid the sacrifices of life, and I doubt his making any
serious attack until he has communicated with the fleet.

We have now connected our lines, so that the corps are within supporting distance of each other. The soldiers are meanwhile in most cheerful spirits, displaying the unconcern which is the most characteristic feature of our troops.

The necessity of an open communication with the fleet is becoming apparent, for the army is rapidly consuming its supplies, and replenishment is vitally important. Away in the distance, across the rice-fields, as far as the banks of the Ogeechee, our signal-officers are stationed, scanning the seaward horizon in search of indications of the presence of the fleet, but thus far unsuccessfully. On the other side of the river, within cannon range, stand the frowning parapets of Fort McAllister, its ponderous guns and rebel garrison guarding the only avenue open to our approach.

This evening a movement of the greatest importance has begun. Hazen's division of the 15th Corps is marching to the other side of the river. Fort McAllister must be taken. To-morrow's sun will see the veterans whom Sherman led upon the heights of Missionary Ridge within striking distance of its walls.

FORT McALLISTER, DECEMBER 13TH

Fort McAllister is ours. I saw the heroic assault from the point of observation selected by General Sherman at the adjacent rice-mill.

During the greater part of to-day the General gazed anxiously toward the sea, watching for the appearance of the fleet. About the middle of the afternoon he descried a light column of smoke creeping lazily along over the flat marshes, and soon the spars of a steamer were visible, and then the flag of our Union floated out.

The sun was now fast going down behind a grove of water-oaks, and as his last rays gilded the earth, all eyes once more turned toward the Rebel fort. Suddenly white puffs of smoke shot out from the thick woods surrounding the line of works. Hazen was closing in, ready for the final rush of his column directly upon the fort. A warning answer came from the enemy in the roar of heavy artillery—and so the battle opened.

General Sherman walked nervously to and fro, turning quickly now and then from viewing the scene of conflict to observe the sun sinking slowly behind the tree-tops. No longer willing to bear the suspense, he said:

"Signal General Hazen that he must carry the fort by assault, to-night if possible."

The little flag waved and fluttered in the evening air, and the answer came:

"I am ready, and will assault at once!"

The words had hardly passed when from out the encircling woods there came a long line of blue coats and bright bayonets, and the dear old flag was there, waving proudly in the breeze. Then the fort seemed alive with flame; quick, thick jets of fire shooting out from all its sides, while the white smoke first covered the place and then rolled away over the glacis. The line of blue moved steadily on; too slowly, as it seemed to us, for we exclaimed, "Why don't they dash forward?" but their measured step was unfaltering. Now the flag goes down, but the line does not halt. A moment longer, and the banner gleams again in the front. Then the enemy's fire redoubled in rapidity and violence. The line of blue entered the enshrouding folds of smoke. The flag was at last dimly seen, and then it went out of sight altogether.

"They have been repulsed!" said one of the group of officers who watched the fight.

The firing ceased. The wind lifted the smoke. Crowds of men were visible on the parapets, fiercely fighting—but our flag was planted there. There were a few scattering musket-shots, and then the sounds of battle ceased. Then the bomb-proofs and parapets were alive with crowding swarms of our men, who fired their pieces in the air as a *feu de joie*. Victory! The fort was won.

This evening we have enjoyed unrestricted opportunities of examining Fort McAllister. It is a large inclosure, with wide parapets, a deep ditch, and thickly-planted palisades, which latter are broken in several places where our men passed through. The dead and wounded are lying where they fell. Groups of soldiers are gathered here and there, laughing and talking of the proud deed that had been done. One said:

"If they had had embrasures for these guns," pointing to them, "we should have got hurt."

SAVANNAH, DECEMBER 20TH

The fall of Fort McAllister has been quickly followed by the evacuation of this great commercial city, which we gain without a battle.

Two events combined to insure this important result: first, the capture of Fort McAllister by direct assault, a feat which seems to have impressed the Rebels in a manner which can only be appreciated by talking with the deserters who constantly come into our lines in squads, and who assert that the soldiers in Savannah did not hesitate openly to declare that it was a useless sacrifice of life to defend the city. This terror was shared by the citizens in a magnified degree; and now we know for a certainty that the mayor and alderman, with a large body of citizens, waited upon General Hardee and insisted upon the surrender of the city.

The second reason was a flank movement, which was in process of operation. In two days more we should have had a division operating with Foster upon Savannah by way of Broad River, which would have rendered escape impossible. Practically, all avenues to the city were closed up by our army, which stretched from the Savannah to the Ogeechee rivers, and by Foster's troops, which covered the Savannah and Charleston Railroad.

The path by which Hardee finally escaped led through swamps which were previously considered impracticable. The Rebel general obtained knowledge of our movement through his spies, who swarmed in our camp.

It was fortunate that our troops followed so quickly after the evacuation of the city by the enemy, for a mob had gathered in the streets, and were breaking into the stores and houses. They were with difficulty dispersed by the bayonets of our soldiers, and then, once more, order and confidence prevailed throughout the conquered city.

We have won a magnificent prize—the city of Savannah, more than two hundred guns, magazines filled with ammunition, thirty-five thousand bales of cotton, three steam-boats, several locomotives, and one hundred and fifty cars, and stores of all kinds. We had not been in occupation forty-eight hours before the transport steamer *Canonicus,* with General Foster on board, lay alongside a pier, and our new line of supplies was formed.

ON THE ROAD TO RICHMOND

WHEN SHERMAN MOVED SOUTH from Chattanooga, Grant had been in Washington only six weeks. But in that time, he had worked hard. According to Catton, "Grant reorganized his cavalry, bringing tough little Phil Sheridan in from the West to turn the cavalry corps into a fighting organization. As April wore away, the effect of all this began to be felt, and the army displayed a quiet new confidence. Lee might be just over the Rapidan, but there was a different feeling in the air; maybe this spring it would be different.

"Maybe it would; what a general could do would be done. But in the last analysis everything would depend on the men in the ranks, and both in the East and in the West the enlisted man was called on that winter to give his conclusive vote of confidence in the conduct of the war. He gave his vote in the most direct way imaginable—by re-enlisting voluntarily for another hitch.

"Union armies in the Civil War did not sign for the duration. They enlisted by regiments, and the top term was three years. This meant—since the hard core of the United States Army was made up of the volunteers who had enlisted in 1861—that as the climactic year of 1864 began the army was on the verge of falling apart. Of 956 volunteer infantry regiments, as 1863 drew to a close 455 were about to go out of existence because their time would very soon be up. Of 158 volunteer batteries, 81 would presently cease to exist.

"There was no way on earth by which these veterans could be made to remain in the army if they did not choose to stay. If they took their discharges and went home—as they were legally and morally entitled to do—the war effort would simply collapse. New recruits were coming in but because Congress in its wisdom had devised the worst possible system for keeping the army up to strength, the war could not be won without the veterans. Enlistments there were, in plenty; and yet—leaving out of consideration the fact that raw recruits could not hope to stand up to the battle-trained old-timers led by Lee and Johnston—they were not doing the army very much good. Heavy cash bounties were offered to men who would enlist; when cities, states, and Federal government offers were added up, a man might get as much as a thousand dollars just for joining the army. This meant that vast numbers of men were enlisting for the

469

money they would get and then were deserting as quickly as possible—which was usually pretty quickly, since the Civil War authorities never really solved the problem of checking desertion—and going off to some other town to enlist all over again under a different name, collecting another bounty, and then deserting again to try the same game in still a third place. The 'bounty man' was notorious as a shirker, and the veterans detested him. Grant once estimated that not 12 per cent of the bounty men ever did any useful service at the front.

"There was a draft act, to be sure, but it contained a flagrant loophole. A man who was drafted could avoid service (unless and until his number was drawn again) by paying a three-hundred-dollar commutation fee; better yet, he could permanently escape military service by hiring a substitute to go to war for him. Clever entrepreneurs eager to make a quick dollar set themselves up in business as substitute brokers, and any drafted man who could afford the price—which often ran up to a thousand dollars or more—could get a broker to find a substitute for him. The substitutes who were thus provided were, if possible, even more worthless as a class than the bounty men. Cripples, diseased men, outright half-wits, epileptics, fugitives from workhouse and poor farm—all were brought forward by the substitute brokers and presented to the harassed recruiting agents as potential cannon fodder. The brokers made such immense profits that they could usually afford any bribery that might be necessary to get their infirm candidates past the medical examination, and the great bulk of the men they sent into the army were of no use whatever.

"Any regiment that contained any substantial percentage of bounty men or substitutes felt itself weakened rather than strengthened by its reinforcements. The 5th New Hampshire—originally one of the stoutest combat units in the Army of the Potomac—got so many of these people that it leaked a steady stream of deserters over to the Confederacy; so many, indeed, that at one time the Rebels opposite this regiment sent over a message asking when they might expect to get the regimental colors, and put up a sign reading: 'Headquarters, 5th New Hampshire Volunteers. Recruits wanted.' It is recorded that a Federal company commander finding some of his bounty men actually under fire, sharply ordered the men to take cover: 'You cost twelve hundred dollars apiece and I'm damned if I am going to have you throw your lives away—you're too expensive!'

"The war could not be won, in other words, unless a substantial percentage of the veterans would consent to re-enlist, and the most searching test the Union cause ever got came early in 1864, when the government—hat in hand, so to speak—went to the veteran regiments and pleaded with the men to join up for another hitch. It offered certain inducements—a four-hundred-dollar bounty (plus whatever sum a man's own city or county might be offering), a thirty-day furlough, the right to call oneself a 'veteran volunteer,' and a neat chevron that could be worn on the sleeve.

"Astoundingly, 136,000 three-year veterans re-enlisted. They were men who had seen the worst of it—men who had eaten bad food, slept in the mud and the rain, made killing marches, and stood up to Rebel fire in battles like Antietam and Stone's River, Chickamauga and Gettysburg—and they had long since lost the fine flush of innocent enthusiasm that had brought them into the army in the first place. They appear to have signed up for a variety of reasons. The furlough was attractive, and an Illinois soldier confessed that the four-hundred-dollar bounty 'seemed to be about the right amount for spending money while on furlough.' Pride in the regiment was also important; to be able to denominate one's regiment veteran volunteers, instead of plain volunteers, meant a good deal. In many cases the men had just got used to soldiering. . . .

"Whatever their reason, the men did re-enlist, and in numbers adequate to carry on the war. It was noteworthy that re-enlistments were hardest to get in the Army of the Potomac; when Meade added up the results at the end of March he found that he had twenty-six thousand re-enlistments, which meant that at least half of the men whose time was expiring had refused to stay with the army. Nevertheless, even this figure was encouraging. It was insurance; the army would not dissolve just when Grant was starting to use it."*

U. S. Grant believed the war would be won only if General Lee's army could be defeated.† He would seek battle with Lee wherever possible. He had the guns, the manpower, the supplies—and unlike his predecessors he meant to apply pressure continuously, ruthlessly, and with full knowledge of his own power.

And so, on May 4, the Army of the Potomac moved out of camp, across the Rapidan, and into the Wilderness, to try again what four previous attempts had failed to do—crush Lee's army and capture Richmond.

From the Wilderness
to Cold Harbor ‡

BY PRIVATE FRANK WILKESON

THE ENLISTED MEN OF THE BATTERY I SERVED WITH ate breakfast and struck their camp at Brandy Station before sunrise. It was a beautiful morning, cool and pleasant. The sun arose above an oak forest that stood to the east of us, and its rays caused thousands of distant rifle barrels and steel bayonets to glisten as fire points. In all directions troops were falling into line. The air resounded with the strains of martial music. Standards

* From Bruce Catton, *This Hallowed Ground*, pp. 317, 318, 319.

† Grant had dispatched 35,000 troops under Butler to the James River, to bring pressure on Richmond from the east. Butler accomplished nothing more than a standoff with Beauregard who was entrenched on a line between the James and Appomattox rivers.

‡ Condensed from *Recollections of a Private Soldier in the Army of the Potomac*.

were unfurled and floated lazily in the light wind. Regiments fell into line on the plain before us. We could see officers sitting on their horses before them, as though making brief speeches to their soldiers, and then the banners would wave, and the lines face to the right into column of fours and march off; and then the sound of·exultant cheering would float to us. Short trains of white-capped and dust-raising wagons rolled across the plain. The heavy-artillery regiment of Germans serving as infantry, which had been encamped to our left during the winter, fell into line. We light-artillery men laughed to see the burdens these sturdy men had on their backs. Jellet, the gunner of the piece I served on, joined me as I stood leaning against a cool gun. He smiled, and said, significantly: "They will throw away those loads before they camp to-night." A word of command rang out in front of their regiment. They faced to the right and marched toward Ely's Ford of the Rapidan, and toward the Wilderness that lay beyond. "Boots and saddles!" was cheerily blown. The light-artillery men stood to their guns. The horses were harnessed and hitched in, the drivers mounted, and we moved off to take position in the column directly behind the heavily laden Germans. We were in high spirits; indeed we were frisky, and walked along gayly. The men talked of the coming battle, and they sang songs about the soul of John Brown, alleged to be marching on, songs indicative of a desire to hang Jeff. Davis to a sour apple-tree.

We marched toward Ely's Ford pretty steadily for a couple of hours. As we drew near it, we saw that the troops were beginning to jam around its approaches. They were being massed quicker than they could cross. We halted at a short distance from the ford and impatiently waited for our turn to cross. I noticed that the Germans in our front were sitting on their knapsacks engaged in mopping their faces with red handkerchiefs.

A staff officer rode out of the apparently confused mass of men jammed around the ford, and galloped toward us. As he passed the German soldiers, they slowly arose and, resuming their back-breaking burdens, marched off. The staff officer rode to us, and told our captain to follow the Germans closely.

We crossed the Rapidan on a pontoon bridge, and filled our canteens and drank deeply as we crossed. Then we marched over a narrow strip of valley land; then came a long, steep hill that led up to the comparatively level table-land of the Wilderness. This was the hill that caused the Germans to part with their personal property. Spare knapsacks, bursting with richness, were cast aside near its base. Near the top of the hill we found many well-filled haversacks, and we picked up every one of them and hung them on the limbers and caissons and guns. The mine was rich, and we worked it thoroughly. Now we began to come on stragglers—men who had overloaded themselves, or who were soft and unfit to march in their gross condition.

We felt it a duty to tenderly inquire into the condition of the health of these exhausted men, and did so pleasantly; but they, the ill-conditioned persons, resented our expressions of love and pity as though they had been insulting remarks.

On the upland we marched briskly. I saw no inhabitants in this region. They had fled before our advance, abandoning their homes. The soil was poor and thin, and the fields were covered with last year's dead grass, and this grass was burning as we passed by. We marched steadily until the old Chancellorsville House was in sight. Many of the trees standing around us were bullet-scarred. We stood idly in the road for some time, then went on for a few hundred yards, and parked in a field by the road, with the Germans in camp ahead of us.

During the day we had occasionally heard the faint report of distant rifles or the heavy, muffled report of a gun, and we suspected that our cavalry was feeling of Lee's men, who were intrenched near Mine Run, but whose pickets were all over the adjacent country. All of the enlisted men hoped that they would get through the Wilderness—a rugged, broken area of upland that extends from the Rapidan River close to Spotsylvania —without fighting. The timber is dense and scrubby, and the whole region is cut up by a labyrinth of roads which lead to clearings of charcoal pits and there end. Deep ravines, thickly clad with brush and trees, furrow the forest. The Confederates knew the region thoroughly. We knew nothing, excepting that the Army of the Potomac, under Hooker, had once encountered a direful disaster on the outskirts of this desolate region.

In the evening, after supper, I walked with a comrade to the spot where General Pleasanton had massed his guns and saved the army under Hooker from destruction, by checking the impetuous onslaught of Stonewall Jackson's Virginian infantry, fresh from the pleasures of the chase of the routed Eleventh Corps. We walked to and fro over the old battle-field, looking at bullet-scarred and canister-riven trees. The men who had fallen in that fierce fight had apparently been buried where they fell, and buried hastily. Many polished skulls lay on the ground. Leg bones, arm bones, and ribs could be found without trouble. Toes of shoes, and bits of faded, weather-worn uniforms, and occasionally a grinning, bony, fleshless face peered through the low mound that had been hastily thrown over these brave warriors. As we wandered to and fro over the battle-ground, looking at the gleaming skulls and whitish bones, and examining the exposed clothing of the dead to see if they had been Union or Confederate soldiers, many infantrymen joined us. It grew dark, and we built a fire at which to light our pipes close to where we thought Jackson's men had formed for the charge, as the graves were thickest there, and then we talked of the battle of the preceding year. One veteran told the story of the burning of some of the Union soldiers who were wounded during Hooker's fight around the Wilderness, as they lay helpless in the woods.

"This region," indicating the woods beyond us with a wave of his arm, "is an awful place to fight in. The utmost extent of vision is about one hundred yards. Artillery cannot be used effectively. The wounded are liable to be burned to death. I am willing to take my chances of getting killed, but I dread to have a leg broken and then to be burned slowly; and these woods will surely be burned if we fight here. I hope we will get through this chaparral without fighting," and he took off his cap and meditatively rubbed the dust off of the red clover leaf which indicated the division and corps he belonged to. As we sat silently smoking and listening to the story, an infantry soldier who had, unobserved by us, been prying into the shallow grave he sat on with his bayonet, suddenly rolled a skull on the ground before us, and said in a deep, low voice:

"That is what you are all coming to, and some of you will start toward it to-morrow." It was growing late, and this uncanny remark broke up the group, most of the men going to their regimental camps. A few of us still sat by the dying embers and smoked. As we talked we heard picket-firing, not brisk, but at short intervals the faint report of a rifle quickly answered. And we reasoned correctly that a Confederate skirmish line was in the woods, and that battle would be offered in the timber. The intelligent enlisted men of the Second Corps with whom I talked that night listened attentively to the firing, now rising, now sinking into silence, to again break out in another place. All of them said that Lee was going to face Grant in the Wilderness, and they based their opinion on the presence of a Confederate skirmish line in the woods. And all of them agreed that the advantages of position were with Lee, and that his knowledge of the region would enable him to face our greatly superior army in point of numbers, with a fair prospect of success.

It was past midnight when I crept under the caisson of my gun and pillowed my head on my knapsack. The distant rifle-shots on the picket-line grew fainter and fainter, then were lost in the nearer noises of the camps, and I slept.

The next morning I was awakened by a bugle call to find the battery I belonged to almost ready to march. I hurriedly toasted a bit of pork and ate it, and quickly chewed down a couple of hard tack, and drank deeply from my canteen, and was ready to march when the battery moved. We struck into the road, passed the Chancellorsville House, turned to the right, and marched up a broad turnpike toward the Wilderness forest. After marching on this road for a short distance we turned to the left on an old dirt road, which led obliquely into the woods. The picket firing had increased in volume since the previous evening, and there was no longer any doubt that we were to fight in the Wilderness. The firing was a pretty brisk rattle, and steadily increasing in volume. About ten o'clock in the morning the soft spring air resounded with a fierce yell, the sound of which was instantly drowned by a roar of musketry, and we knew that the battle of the Wilderness had opened. The battery rolled heavily up the road into the woods for a short distance, when we were met by a staff officer, who ordered us out, saying:

"The battle has opened in dense timber. Artillery cannot be used. Go into park in the field just outside of the woods."

We turned the guns and marched back and went into park. Battery after battery joined us, some coming out of the woods and others up the road from the Chancellorsville House, until some hundred guns or more were parked in the field. We were then the reserve artillery.

Ambulances and wagons loaded with medical supplies galloped on the field, and a hospital was established behind our guns. Soon men, singly and in pairs or in groups of four or five, came limping slowly or walking briskly, with arms across their breasts and their hands clutched into their blouses, out of the woods. Some carried their rifles. Others had thrown them away. All of them were bloody. They slowly filtered through the immense artillery park and asked, with bloodless lips, to be directed to a hospital. Powder smoke hung high above the trees in thin clouds. The noise in the woods was terrific. The musketry was a steady roll, and high above it sounded the inspiring charging cheers and yells of the now thoroughly excited combatants.

By noon I was quite wild with curiosity, and, confident that the artillery would remain in park, I decided to go to the battle-line and see what was going on. I neglected to ask my captain for permission to leave the battery, because I feared he would not grant my request, and I did not want to disobey orders by going after he had refused me. I walked out of camp and up the road. The wounded men were becoming more and more numerous. I saw men, faint from loss of blood, sitting in the shade cast by trees. Other men were lying down. All were pale, and their faces expressed great suffering. As I walked I saw a dead man lying under a tree which stood by the roadside. He had been shot through the chest and had struggled to the rear; then, becoming exhausted or choked with blood, he had lain down on a carpet of leaves and died. His pockets were turned inside out. A little farther on I met a sentinel standing by the roadside.

He eyed me inquiringly, and answered my question as to what he was doing there, saying: "Sending stragglers back to the front." Then he added, in an explanatory tone: "No enlisted man can go past me to the rear unless he can show blood."

I explained to the sentinel that I was a light-artillery man, and that I wanted to see the fight.

"Can I go past you?" I inquired.

"Yes," he replied, "you can go up. But you had better not go," he added. "You have no distinctive mark or badge on your dress to indicate the arm you belong to. If you go up, you may not be allowed to return, and then," he added, as he shrugged his shoulders indifferently, "you may get killed. But suit yourself."

So I went on. There was very heavy firing to the left of the road in a chaparral of brush and scrubby pines and oaks. There the musketry was a steady roar, and the cheers and yells of the fighters incessant. I left the road and walked through the woods toward the battle-ground, and met many wounded men who were coming out. They were bound for the rear and the hospitals. Then I came on a body of troops lying in reserve —a second line of battle, I suppose. I heard the hum of bullets as they passed over the low trees. Then I noticed that small limbs of trees were falling in a feeble shower in advance of me. It was as though an army of squirrels were at work cutting off nut and pine cone-laden branches preparatory to laying in their winter's store of food. Then, partially obscured by a cloud of powder smoke, I saw a straggling line of men clad in blue. They were not standing as if on parade, but they were taking advantage of the cover afforded by trees, and they were firing rapidly. Their line officers were standing behind them or in line with them. The smoke drifted to and fro, and there were many rifts in it. I saw scores of wounded men. I saw many dead soldiers lying on the ground, and I saw men constantly falling on the battle-line. I could not see the Confederates, and, as I had gone to the front expressly to see a battle, I pushed on, picking my way from protective tree to protective tree, until I was about forty yards from the battle-line. The uproar was deafening; the bullets flew through the air thickly. Now our line would move forward a few yards, now fall back. I stood behind a large oak tree, and peeped around its trunk. I heard bullets "spat" into this tree, and I suddenly realized that I was in danger. My heart thumped wildly for a minute; then my throat and mouth felt dry and queer. A dead sergeant lay at my feet, with a hole in his forehead just above his left eye. Out of this wound bits of brain oozed, and slid on a bloody trail into his eye, and thence over his cheek to the ground. I leaned over the body to feel of it. It was still warm. He could not have been dead for over five minutes. As I stooped over the dead man, bullets swept past me, and I became angry at the danger I had foolishly gotten into. I unbuckled the dead man's cartridge belt, and strapped it around me, and then I picked up his rifle. I remember standing behind the large oak tree, and dropping the ramrod into the rifle to see if it was loaded. It was not. So I loaded it, and before I fairly understood what had taken place, I was in the rear rank of the battle-line, which had surged back on the crest of a battle billow, bareheaded, and greatly excited, and blazing away at an indistinct, smoke-and-tree-obscured line of men clad in gray and slouch-hatted. As I cooled off in the heat of the battle fire, I found that I was on the Fifth Corps' line, instead of on the Second Corps' line, where I wanted to be. I spoke to the men on either side of me, and they stared at me, a stranger, and briefly said that the regiment, the distinctive number of which I have long since forgotten, was near the left of the Fifth Corps, and that they had been fighting pretty steadily since about ten o'clock in the morning, but with poor success, as the Confederates had driven them back a little. The fire was rather hot, and the men were falling pretty fast. Still it was not anywhere near as bloody as I had expected a battle to be. As a grand, inspiring spectacle, it was highly unsatisfactory, owing to the powder smoke obscuring the vision. At times we could not see the Confederate line, but that made no difference; we kept on firing just as though they were in full view. We gained ground at times, and then dead Confederates lay on the ground as thickly as dead Union soldiers did behind us. Then we would fall back, fighting stubbornly, but steadily giving ground, until the dead were all clad in blue.

Between two and three o'clock the fire in our front slackened. We did not advance. Indeed I saw no general officer on the battle-line to take advantage of any opportunity that the battle's tide might expose to a man of military talent. I had seen some general officers near the reserves, but none on the front line. I noticed the lack of artillery and saw that the nature of the ground forbade its use. Our line was fed with fresh troops and greatly strengthened. Boxes of cartridges were carried to us, and we helped ourselves. We were standing behind trees or lying on the ground, and occasionally shooting at the Confederate line, or where their line should have been. Some of the old soldiers muttered about things in general, and rebel dodges in particular, and darkly hinted that the sudden slackening of the fire in our front boded no good to us. Soon a storm of yells, followed instantly by a roar of musketry, rolled to us from the left, and not distant. Almost instantly it was followed by a cheer and a volley of musketry. We sprang to our feet and were in line, but there was nothing in strength ahead of us. To the left the noise increased in volume. The musketry was thunderous. Soon affrighted men rushed through the woods to our rear, not in ones and twos, but in dozens and scores, and as they swept past us they cried loudly:

"We are flanked! Hill's corps has got around our left."

Officers gave commands which I did not understand, but I did as my comrades did, and we were speedily placed at right angles to our original position, which was held by a heavy skirmish line. Many of the men who were running from the battle-field dropped into our line and remained with us until nightfall. I saw men from a dozen different regiments standing in our line. We were dreadfully nervous, and felt around blindly for a few minutes, not knowing what to do. Then we were reassured by seeing a staff officer explaining something to the commander of the regiment, a young major. This officer passed the word along the line that the Second Corps had come up just in time to close up a gap between the two corps, through which the Confederate general, Hill, had endeavored to thrust a heavy column of infantry. Speedily we got back into our original position. In a few minutes we saw a thin line of gray figures, not much heavier than a strong skirmish line, advancing rapidly toward us. They yelled loudly and continuously. We began firing rapidly, and so did they. They came quite close to us, say within seventy-five yards, and covered themselves as well as they could. We could see them fairly well, and shot many of them, and they killed and wounded many Union soldiers. Soon we drove them to cover, and they were comparatively quiet. The noise to the left, where Hancock's corps was fighting, almost drowned the racket we were making. The Confederate charge against the portion of the Fifth Corps where I was fighting was not delivered with vim. It impressed me as a sham. Their line, as I said, was thin, and it lacked momentum. I spoke to my fellows about it, and they all agreed that it was not earnest fighting, but a sham to cover the real attack on our left. There the battle raged with inconceivable fury for about two hours. Then the fight died down, and excepting for picket-firing, the lines were silent.

The wounded soldiers lay scattered among the trees. They moaned piteously. The unwounded troops, exhausted with battle, helped their stricken comrades to the rear. The wounded were haunted with the dread of fire. They conjured the scenes of the previous year, when some wounded men were burned to death, and their hearts well-nigh ceased to beat when they thought they detected the smell of burning wood in the air. The bare prospect of fire running through the woods where they lay helpless, unnerved the most courageous of men, and made them call aloud for help. I saw many wounded soldiers in the Wilderness who hung on to their rifles, and whose intention was clearly stamped on their pallid faces. I saw one man, both of whose legs were broken, lying on the ground with his cocked rifle by his side and his ramrod in his hand, and his eyes set on the front. I knew he meant to kill himself in case of fire—knew it as surely as though I could read his thoughts. The dead men lay where they fell. Their haversacks and cartridges had been taken from their bodies. The battle-field ghouls had rifled their pockets. I saw no dead man that night whose pockets had not been turned inside out.

Soon after dark the story of the fight on our left had been gathered by the newsmongers, and we learned that the Second Corps had saved itself from rout and the army from defeat by the most dogged fighting, and that they had required the aid of Getty's division of the Sixth Corps to enable them to hold their own. That news was sufficient to start me. So I went down the line, walking through the woods, stumbling over the dead and being cursed by the living, until I came to the Second Corps. There I found a regiment, the Fortieth New York, if I correctly recall the number, some of whose soldiers I knew. They told me the story of the fight. It was really told by the windrows of dead men, and the loud and continuous shrieks and groans of the wounded. I was still bareheaded, and I fitted myself with a hat from a collection of hats lying near some dead men. And I took a pair of blankets from the shoulders of a dead man and slept in them that night.

Early the next morning, long before sunrise, I had my breakfast, and having seen sufficient of the fighting done by infantry, and strongly impressed with the truth that a light-artillery man had better stay close to his guns, I bade my acquaintances good-by, and walked off, intent on getting to my gun and comparative comfort and safety. But I hung on to my rifle and belt. They were to be trophies of the battle, and I meant to excite the envy of my comrades by displaying them. Stepping into the road I walked along briskly, and saw many other unwounded men rearward bound. A sentinel, with rifle at the carry, halted me, and demanded to see blood. I could show none. I assured him that I belonged to the light artillery, and that I had gone to the front the previous day just to see the battle.

He said: "You have a rifle; you have a belt and a cartridge box. Your mouth is powder-blackened. You have been fighting as an infantryman, and you shall so continue to fight. You go back, or I will arrest you, and then you will be sent back.

I longed to kill him—longed to show the Army of the Potomac one dead provost guard; but I was afraid to shoot him, for fear that his comrades might see me do it. So I turned and hastened back to the front. I determined to fight that day, and go home to the battery the succeeding night.

Away off to the right, toward the Rapidan, the battle rose with the sun. In our front, the Second Corps, there was little movement discernible. But so dense was the cover that we could see but little at a distance of two hundred yards. I saw that the soldiers had thrown up a slight intrenchment during the previous night. About five o'clock we were ordered to advance, and pushed ahead, fighting as we went, and forced Hill's men back, killing many, wounding more, and taking scores of prisoners. We crossed a road, which a wounded Confederate told me was the Brock road. I saw many dead Confederates during this advance. They were poorly clad. Their blankets were in rolls, hanging diagonally from the left shoulder to the right side, where the ends were tied with a string or a strap. Their canvas haversacks contained plenty of corn-meal and some bacon. I saw no coffee, no sugar, no hard bread in any of the Confederate haversacks I looked into. But there was tobacco in plugs on almost all the dead Confederates. Their arms were not as good as ours. They were poorly shod. The direful poverty of the Confederacy was plainly indicated by its dead soldiers. But they fought.

The Confederates seemed to be fighting more stubbornly, fighting as though their battle-line was being fed with more troops. They hung on to the ground they occupied tenaciously, and resolutely refused to fall back further. Then came a swish of bullets and a fierce exultant yell, as of thousands of infuriated tigers. Our men fell by scores. Great gaps were struck in our lines. There was a lull for an instant, and then Longstreet's men sprang to the charge. It was swiftly and bravely made, and was within an ace of being successful. There was great confusion in our line. The men wavered badly. They fired wildly. They hesitated. I feared the line would break; feared that we were whipped. The line was fed with troops from the reserve. The regimental officers held their men as well as they could. We could hear them close behind us, or in line with us, saying: "Steady, men, steady, steady, steady!" as one speaks to frightened and excited horses. The Confederate fire resembled the fury of hell in intensity, and was deadly accurate. Their bullets swished by in swarms. It seems to me that I could have caught a pot full of them if I had had a strong iron vessel rigged on a pole as a butterfly net. Again our line became wavy and badly confused, and it was rapidly being shot into a skirmish-like order of formation. Speedily a portion of the Ninth Corps came to our assistance, and they came none too soon. They steadied the line and we regained heart. During this critical time, when the fate of the Second Corps was trembling in the balance, many officers rushed to and fro behind us, but I saw no major-generals among them; but then I had sufficient to do to look ahead and fall back without falling down, and they may have been on the battle-line, only I did not see them. The Confederates got a couple of batteries into action, and they added to the deafening din. The shot and shell from these guns cut great limbs off of the trees, and these occasionally fell near the battle-line, and several men were knocked down by them. Our line strengthened, we, in our turn, pushed ahead, and Longstreet's men gave ground slowly before us, fighting savagely for every foot. The wounded lay together. I saw, in the heat of this fight, wounded men of the opposing forces aiding each other to reach the protective shelter of trees and logs, and, as we advanced, I saw a Confederate and a Union soldier drinking in turn out of a Union canteen, as they lay behind a tree.

There was another lull, and then the charging line of gray again rushed to the assault with inconceivable fury. We fired and fired and fired, and fell back fighting stubbornly. We tore cartridges until our teeth ached. But we could not check the Confederate advance, and they forced us back and back and back until we were behind the slight intrenchments along the Brock road. A better charge, or a more determined, I never saw. We fought savagely at the earthworks. At some points the timber used in the earthworks was fired, and our men had to stand back out of the line of flame and shoot through it at the Confederates, who were fighting in front of the works. And the woods, through which we had fallen back, were set on fire, and many wounded soldiers were burned to death. We beat off the Confederates, and they, with the exception of the picket line, disappeared. Our line was straightened, reserves were brought up, and some of the battle-torn troops were relieved. We had half an hour's rest, during which time many of us ate and smoked, and drank out of our canteens; and we talked, though not so hopefully as in the early morning.

Men missed old comrades, and with only seeming indifference figuratively reckoned they had "turned up their toes." Firing had almost ceased. It was as the cessation of the wind before the approach of a cyclone. A tempest of fire and balls and yells broke out on the right. We were out of it. The real battle raged furiously in the woods to the right, while a heavy line of Confederate skirmishers, who lurked skilfully behind trees and who fired briskly and accurately, made things decidedly unpleasant for us, and effectually prevented any men being drawn from our portion of the line to strengthen the right. How we fretted while this unseen combat raged! We judged that our men were being worsted as the battle-sounds passed steadily to our rear. Then the fugitives, the men quick to take alarm and speedy of foot when faced to the rear, began to pass diagonally through the woods behind us. While we stood quivering with nervous excitement, and gazing anxiously into each other's eyes we heard a solid roll of musketry, as though a division had fired together, cheers followed, and then the battle-sound rapidly advanced toward the Confederate line. Then all was quiet, and the fighting on the left of our line was over. Soon word was passed along the line that the charging Confederates had broken through the left of the Ninth Corps, and would have cut the army in twain if General Carroll had not caught them on the flank and driven them back with the Third Brigade of the Second Division of the Second Corps.

The enlisted men supposed the day's fighting was over. And so did our generals. But the Confederates marched swiftly on many parallel roads, and were massed for an attack on our right, the Sixth Corps. They were skilfully launched and ably led, and they struck with terrific violence against Shaler's and Seymour's brigades, which were routed, with a loss of 4,000 prisoners. The Confederates came within an ace of routing the Sixth Corps; but the commanders restored and steadied the lines, and the Confederate charge was first checked and then bloodily repulsed.

The day's offensive fighting on the part of the Confederates, as we, the enlisted men, summed it up, had consisted of two general assaults delivered all along our line, as though to feel of us and discover where we were the weakest, and to promptly take advantage of the knowledge gained, to attack in force and with surprising vim and stanchness first one flank and then the other. Both of the assaults were dangerously near being successful.

The sun sank, and the gloom among the trees thickened and thickened until darkness reigned in the forest where thousands of dead and wounded men lay. The air still smelled of powder-smoke. Many soldiers cleaned out their rifles. We ate, and then large details helped carry their wounded comrades to the road, where we loaded them into ambulances and wagons. I determined to join my battery. I threw away my rifle and belt, and as the first wagons loaded with wounded men moved to the rear, I walked by the side of the column and passed the guards, if there were any stationed on that road, without being challenged. When I was well to the rear, I for the first and last time became a "coffee boiler." I cooked and ate a hearty supper, and then rolled myself in the dead soldier's blankets, which I had hung on to, and slept soundly until morning, when I found the battery I belonged to without much trouble, and was promptly punished for being absent without leave.

That evening the troops began to pour out of the woods in columns. The infantry soldiers marched soberly past the artillery. There were no exultant songs in those columns. The men seemed aged. They were very tired and very hungry. They seemed to be greatly depressed.

There was a gap in the column, and my battery moved on to the road, and other batteries followed us. We marched rapidly and without halting, until we reached a point where another road, which led in the direction of the right of our battle-line, joined the road we were on. Here we met a heavy column of troops marching to the rear, as we were. The enlisted men were grave, and rather low in spirits, and decidedly rough in temper.

"Here we go," said a Yankee private; "here we go, marching for the Rapidan, and the protection afforded by that river. Now, when we get to the Chancellorsville House, if we turn to the left, we are whipped—at least so say Grant and Meade. And if we turn toward the river, the bounty-jumpers will break and run, and there will be a panic."

"Suppose we turn to the right, what then?" I asked.

"That will mean fighting, and fighting on the line the Confederates have selected and intrenched. But it will indicate the purpose of Grant to fight," he replied.

Grant's military standing with the enlisted men this day hung on the direction we turned at the Chancellorsville House. If to the left, he was to be rated with Meade and Hooker and Burnside and Pope—the generals who preceded him. At the Chancellorsville House we turned to the right. Instantly all of us heard a sigh of relief. Our spirits rose. We marched free. The men began to sing. The enlisted men understood the flanking movement. That night we were happy.

May 8, 1864. The bloody battle of the Wilderness was a thing of the past. That dense chaparral in which the unburied dead Union and Confederate soldiers lay scattered thickly was being left behind us as we marched. In the morning the guns of the Fifth Corps notified the Union troops that the Confederates had been found. The Fifth Corps had been in the advance in the flank movement to the left out of the Wilderness, and Longstreet's corps had marched parallel with it, and had taken position behind the river Ny, which was more properly a creek. We were not in this fight, but correctly judged that it was not severe, as at no time did the battle's roar rise to the volume which indicates a fierce engagement. On May 9th the army was clear of the Wilderness. We took position around Spotsylvania Court House. Wherever we went there were heavy earthworks, behind which the veteran Confederate infantry lurked. The day was spent in getting into position and in bloody wrangling between the opposing pickets and in sharpshooting. At intervals would be a crash of musketry and a cheer; then the artillery would open and fire briskly for a few minutes. But there was no real fighting. That night we heard that General Sedgwick, commanding the Sixth Corps, had been killed by a sharpshooter or by a stray ball from the Confederate picket line.

May 10th, and the fighting began. The din of the battle was continuous, and as much of the artillery had been drawn to the battle-line the noise

Spottsylvania: *The bloody struggle at the Salient*

was far louder than it had been in the Wilderness. The troops fought all day. A solid roll of musketry, mingled with the thunderous reports of cannon quickly served, caused the air to quiver. After fighting all day, we spent a large portion of the night in fruitless endeavors to flank the Confederate position. Spent it in following staff officers, to find that we were again in front of earthworks, which were lined with keen-eyed, resolute infantry soldiers. In Spotsylvania we fought by day, we marched by night, and our losses were exceedingly large.

One day the battery I served with was parked for rest near a road down which wounded men were streaming in a straggling column. These men, tired, weakened by loss of blood, and discouraged, tumbled exhausted into the angles of worm fences, and spread their blankets from rail to rail to make a shade. There they rested and patiently waited for their turn at the surgeons' tables. They were a ghastly array. The sight of these poor, stricken men as they helped one another, as they bound one another's wounds, as they painfully hobbled to and fro for water, was a most pathetic one. They lined the roadside for half a mile, a double hedgerow of suffering and death, as men were dying in the fence corners every few minutes. Down the road we heard the stirring music of a martial band. Soon the head of a column of troops came in sight. Officers were riding at the head of the soldiers on horses that pranced. The men were neatly clad, and their brass shoulder-plates shone brightly in the sun.

"The heavy-artillery men from the fortifications around Washington," one of my comrades murmured.

These fresh soldiers were marching beautifully. They were singing loudly and tunefully. They were apparently pleased with the prospect of fighting in defence of their country. For some reason the infantry of the line—the volunteer infantry—did not admire heavy-artillery men. They liked light-artillery men, and were encouraged by the presence of the guns on the battle-line. There was something inspiring in the work of the gunners and in the noisy reports of the cannon; and, then, cannon were deadly, and if well served and accurately aimed, they could and did pulverize charging columns. But heavy-artillery men were soldiers of a different breed. There was a widespread belief among us that these men had enlisted in that arm because they expected to fight behind earthworks, or to safely garrison the forts which surrounded Washington. We did not like these troops. The head of the heavy-artillery column, the men armed as infantry, was thrust among the wounded who lined the roadside. These bloody wrecks of soldiers derided the new-comers. Men would tauntingly point to a shattered arm, or a wounded leg, or to bloody wounds on their faces, or to dead men lying in fence corners, and derisively shout: "That is what you will catch up yonder in the woods!" and they would solemnly indicate the portion of the forest they meant by extending arms from which blood trickled in drops. I saw one group of these wounded men repeatedly cover and uncover with a blanket a dead man whose face was horribly distorted, and show the courage-sapping spectacle to the marching troops, and faintly chuckle and cause their pale cheeks to bulge with derisive tongue-thrusts, as they saw the heavy-artillery men's faces blanch. Still others would inquire in mock solicitous tones as to the locality of their cannon, and then tenderly inquire of some soldier whose bearing or dress caught their attention: "Why, dearest, why did you leave your earthwork behind you?" And they would hobble along and solemnly assure the man that he had made a serious mistake, and that he should have brought the earthwork along, as he would need it in yonder woods, pointing with outstretched bloody arms to the forest, where the battle's roar resounded. Others assumed attitudes of mock admiration and gazed impudently and contemptuously at the full regiments as they marched by. Long before the heavy-artillery men had passed through the bloody gauntlet their songs were hushed.

The movable fight dragged along until May 12th. We fought here. We charged there. We accomplished nothing. But early on the morning of May 12th the Second Corps carried by assault the Confederate works held by Johnston's division of Ewell's corps, capturing about three thousand five hundred prisoners and thirty guns. Our troops caught the battle-exhausted Confederates asleep in their blankets. The Confederate line was broken. Their army was cut in twain. But it amounted to nothing. If the advantage had been intelligently followed up, it might have had decisive results. As it was, many thousands of enlisted men were killed and wounded in a furious fight which lasted all day, and the next morning we found that the Confederates had fortified a line in rear of the captured works, and our losses of thousands of brave men resulted in nothing but the capture of twenty guns (ten of these guns which were captured by the Second Corps were wrested from them by Ewell's men in the fights that ensued).

That night a wounded Second Corps soldier came into our battery, and joined me at the fire. He asked for food. I had plenty, and as the man's right arm was stiff from a wound, I told him I would cook a supper for him if he would wait. He greedily accepted the invitation. Soon I had a mess of pork and hardtack frying and coffee boiling, and as I had that day found a haversack—truth is that its owner, a heavy-artilleryman, was asleep when I found it—which contained a can of condensed milk and half a loaf of light bread, the wounded soldier and I had a feast. After supper we smoked and talked.

"The Wilderness," said my wounded guest, "was a private's battle. The men fought as best they could, and fought stanchly. The generals could not see the ground, and if they were on the front line, they could not have seen their troops. The enlisted men did not expect much generalship to be shown. All they expected was to have the battle-torn portions of the line fed with fresh troops. There was no chance for a display of military talent on our side, only for the enlisted men to fight, and fight, and fight; and that they did cheerfully and bravely. Here the Confederates are strongly intrenched, and it was the duty of our generals to know the strength of the works (we all knew the dogged fighting capacity of their defenders) before they launched the army against them." My guest was tired, and first exacting a promise from me that I would give him his breakfast, he lay on his back behind a tree, and after I had bathed his wounded arm he slept.

We marched to and fro. The infantry were almost constantly engaged in feeling of the Confederate lines to find a weak place, and finding all points stanchly defended. The artillery was pleasantly employed in burying good iron in Confederate earthworks. The list of our killed and wounded and missing grew steadily and rapidly, longer and longer, as their cartridge-boxes grew lighter and lighter. One day a brisk fight was going on in front of us. We were ordered to the top of a hill and told to fire over our infantry into the edge of the woods, where the Confederates lay. The battery swung into action. Below us, in the open, was a pasture field. In it were two batteries and a line of infantry. The former were noisily engaged; the latter were not doing much of any thing. The Confederates were behind an earthwork that stood, shadowed by trees, in the edge of the forest, and it was evident that they meant to stay there. Our infantry charged, and at some points they entered the edge of the woods, out of which they speedily came, followed by a disorderly and heavy line of Confederate skirmishers. The batteries in the open were skilfully handled and admirably served, but it was a matter of a very short time for them. As soon as our infantry got out of range in a ravine, the Confederate skirmishers dropped prone on the ground, disappeared behind trees, sank into holes, squatted behind bushes, and turned their attention to the Union batteries, which were within rifle range of the skirmishers, and the guns were almost instantly driven from the field, leaving many horses, and men clad in blue, lying on the ground. Then the Confederate skirmishers ran back to their earthworks and clambered over. The battery I served with was firing three-inch percussion bolts at the Confederate line and doing no harm. One of my comrades spoke to me across the gun, saying: "Grant and Meade are over there," nodding his head to indicate the direction in which I was to look. I turned my head and saw Grant and Meade sitting on the ground under a large tree. Both of them were watching the fight which was going on in the pasture field. Occasionally they turned their glasses to the distant wood, above which small clouds of white smoke marked the bursting shells and the extent of the battle. Across the woods that lay behind the pasture, and behind the bare ridge that formed the horizon, and well within the Confederate lines, a dense column of dust arose, its head slowly moving to our left. I saw Meade call Grant's attention to this dust column, which was raised either by a column of Confederate infantry or by a wagon train. We ceased firing, and sat on the ground around the guns watching our general, and the preparations that were being made for another charge. Grant had a cigar in his mouth. His face was immovable and expressionless. His eyes lacked lustre. He sat quietly and watched the scene as though he was an uninterested spectator. Meade was nervous, and his hand constantly sought his face, which it stroked. Staff officers rode furiously up and down the hill carrying orders and information. The infantry below us in the ravine formed for another charge. Then they started on the run for the Confederate earthworks, cheering loudly the while. We sprang to our guns and began firing rapidly over their heads at the edge of the woods. It was a fine display of accurate artillery practice, but, as the Confederates lay behind thick earthworks, and were veterans not to be shaken by shelling the outside of a dirt bank behind which they lay secure, the fire resulted in emptying our limber chests, and in the remarkable discovery that three-inch percussion shells could not be relied upon to perform the work of a steam shovel. Our infantry advanced swiftly, but not with the vim they had displayed a week previous; and when they got within close rifle range of the works, they were struck by a storm of rifle-balls and canister that smashed the front line to flinders. They broke for cover, leaving the ground thickly strewed with dead and dying men. The second line of battle did not attempt to make an assault, but returned to the ravine. Grant's face never changed its expression. He sat impassive and smoked steadily, and watched the short-lived battle and decided defeat without displaying emotion. Meade betrayed great anxiety. The fight over, the generals arose and walked back to their horses, mounted and rode briskly away, followed by their staff. No troops cheered them. None evinced the slightest enthusiasm.

Toward evening of the eighth day's fighting a furious attack was made on our right by Ewell's corps. This attack was repulsed, and then the battle died down to picket-firing and sharpshooting. Now and then a battery would fire a few shot into a Confederate earthwork, just to let its defenders know that we still lived. We were strongly intrenched, and it was evident to the enlisted men that the battles fought around Spotsylvania belonged to the past. We estimated our losses up to this time at from forty-five thousand to fifty thousand men, or about two fifths of the men whom Grant took across the Rapidan. I slept from 6 P.M. of the eighth day's fighting until 2 P.M. of the ninth day's fighting. I made up the losses of sleep incurred during the eight days and nights of almost continuous fighting and marching. This sleep was so profound that I barely heard the guns as they occasionally roared over my head. I was easy in my mind, as I knew that some hollow-eyed comrade would awaken me if I was needed at the guns or if we moved.

On the morning of May 28, 1864, the Second Corps crossed the Pamunkey River. Close by the bridge on which we crossed, and to the right of it, under a tree, stood Generals Grant, Meade, and Hancock, and a little back of them was a group of staff officers. Grant looked tired. He was sallow. He held a dead cigar firmly between his teeth. His face was as expressionless as a pine board. He gazed steadily at the enlisted men as they marched by, as though trying to read their thoughts, and they gazed intently at him. He had the power to send us to our deaths, and we were curious to see him. Grant stood silently looking at his troops and listening to Hancock, who was talking and gesticulating earnestly. Meade stood by Grant's side and thoughtfully stroked his own face.

During the afternoon we heard considerable firing in front of us, and toward evening we marched over ground where dead cavalrymen were plentifully sprinkled. The blue and the gray lay side by side, and their arms by them. With the Confederates lay muzzle-loading carbines, the ramrods of which worked upward on a swivel hinge fastened near the muzzle of the weapon. It was an awkward arm and far inferior to the Spencer carbine with which our cavalry was armed. There were ancient and ferocious-looking horse-pistols, such as used to grace the Bowery stage, lying by the dead Confederates. The poverty of the South was plainly shown by the clothing and equipment of her dead. These dead men were hardly stiff when we saw them. All of their pockets had been turned inside out. That night, while searching for fresh, clean water, I found several dead cavalrymen in the woods, where they had probably crawled after being wounded. I struck a match so as to see one of these men plainly, and was greatly shocked to see large black beetles eating the corpse. I looked at no more dead men that night.

The next day the sound of battle arose again. At distant points it would break out furiously and then die down. In our immediate front heavy skirmishing was going on, and wounded men began to drift to the rear in search of hospitals. They said that there was a stream of water, swamps, and a line of earthworks, behind which lay the Confederate infantry, in our front, and that we could not get to the works. At no time did the fire rise to a battle's volume; it was simply heavy and continuous skirmishing, in which our men fought at great disadvantage, and were severely handled. Finding that these works were too strong to be taken by assault, Grant moved the army to the left. On June 1st we heard heavy fighting to our left, and that night we learned that a portion of the Sixth Corps, aided by ten thousand of Butler's men from Bermuda Hundred, had forced the Chickahominy River at a loss of three thousand men, and that they held the ground they had taken. The news-gatherers said that the Confederates were strongly intrenched, and evidently had no intention of fighting in the open. We knew that a bloody battle was close at hand, and instead of being elated the enlisted men were depressed in spirits. That night the old soldiers told the story of the campaign under McClellan in 1862. They had fought over some of the ground we were then camped on. Some of the men were sad, some indifferent; some so tired of the strain on their nerves that they wished they were dead and their troubles over. The infantry knew that they were to be called upon to assault perfect earthworks, and though they had resolved to do their best, there was no eagerness for the fray, and the impression among the intelligent soldiers was that the task cut out for them was more than men could accomplish.

On June 2d the Second Corps moved from the right to the left. We saw many wounded men that day. We crossed a swamp or marched around a swamp, and the battery I belonged to parked in a ravine. There were some old houses on our line of march, but not a chicken or a sheep or a cow to be seen. The land was wretchedly poor. The night of June 2d was spent in getting into battle-line. There was considerable confusion as the infantry marched in the darkness. In our front we could see tongues of flames dart forth from Confederate rifles as their pickets fired in the direction of the noise they heard, and their bullets sang high above our heads. My battery went into position just back of a crest of a hill. Behind us was an alder swamp, where good drinking water gushed forth from many springs. Before we slept we talked with some of the Seventh New York Heavy Artillery, and found that they were sad of heart. They knew that they were to go into the fight early in the morning, and they dreaded the work. The whole army seemed to be greatly depressed the night before the battle of Cold Harbor.

Before daybreak of June 3d the light-artillery men were aroused. We ate our scanty breakfast and took our positions around the guns. All of us were loath to go into action. In front of us we could hear the murmurs of infantry, but it was not sufficiently light to see them. We stood leaning against the cool guns, or resting easily on the ponderous wheels, and gazed intently into the darkness in the direction of the Confederate earthworks. How slowly dawn came! Indistinctly we saw moving figures. Some on foot rearward bound, cowards hunting for safety; others on horseback riding to and fro near where we supposed the battle-lines to be; then orderlies and servants came in from out the darkness leading horses, and we knew that the regimental and brigade commanders were going into action on foot. The darkness faded slowly, one by one the stars went out, and then the Confederate pickets opened fire briskly; then we could see the Confederate earthworks, about six hundred yards ahead of us—could just see them and no more. They were apparently deserted, not a man was to be seen behind them; but it was still faint gray light. One of our gunners looked over his piece and said that he could see the sights, but that they blurred. We filled our sponge buckets with water and waited, the Confederate pickets firing briskly at us the while, but doing no damage. Suddenly the Confederate works were manned. We could see a line of slouch hats above the parapet. Smoke in great puffs burst forth from their line, and shell began to howl by us. Their gunners were getting the range. We sprung in and out from the three-inch guns and replied angrily. To our left, to our right, other batteries opened; and along the Confederate line cannon sent forth their balls searching for the range. Then their guns were silent. It was daylight. We, the light-artillery men, were heated with battle. The strain on our nerves was over. In our front were two lines of blue-coated infantry. One well in advance of the other, and both lying down. We were firing over them. The Confederate pickets sprang out of their rifle pits and ran back to their main line of works. Then they turned and warmed the battery with long-range rifle practice, knocking a man over here, killing another there, breaking the leg of a horse yonder, and generally behaving in an exasperating manner. The Confederate infantry was always much more effective than their artillery, and the battery that got under the fire of their cool infantry always suffered severely. The air began to grow hazy with powder smoke. We saw that the line of slouch-hatted heads had disappeared from the Confederate earthworks, leaving heads exposed only at long intervals. Out of the powder smoke came an officer from the battle-lines of infantry. He told us to stop firing, as the soldiers were about to charge. He disappeared to carry the message to other batteries. Our cannon became silent. The smoke drifted off of the field. I noticed that the sun was not yet up. Suddenly the foremost line of our troops, which were lying on the ground in front of us, sprang to their feet and dashed at the Confederate earthworks at a run. Instantly those works were manned. Cannon belched forth a torrent of canister, the works glowed brightly with musketry, a storm of lead and iron struck the blue line, cutting gaps in it. Still they pushed on, and on, and on. But, how many of them fell! They drew near the earthworks, firing as they went, and then, with a cheer, the first line of the Red Division of the Second Corps (Barlow's) swept over it. And there in our front lay, sat, and stood the second line, the supports; why did not they go forward and make good the victory? They did not. Intensely excited, I watched the portion of the Confederate line which our men had captured. I was faintly conscious of terrific firing to our right and of heavy and continuous cheering on that portion of our line which was held by the Fifth and Sixth Corps. For once the several corps had delivered a simultaneous assault, and I knew that it was to be now or never. The powder smoke curled lowly in thin clouds above the captured works. Then the firing became more and more thunderous. The tops of many battle-flags could be seen indistinctly, and then there was a heavy and fierce yell, and the thrilling battle-cry of the Confederate infantry floated to us. "Can our men withstand the charge?" I asked myself. Quickly I was answered. They came into sight clambering over the parapet of the captured works. All organization was lost. They fled wildly for the protection of their second line and the Union guns, and they were shot by scores as they ran. The Confederate infantry appeared behind their works and nimbly climbed over, as though intent on following up their success, and their fire was as the fury of hell. We manned the guns and drove them to cover by bursting shell. How they yelled! How they swung their hats! And how quickly their pickets ran forward to their rifle pits and sank out of sight! The swift, brave assault had been bravely met and most bloodily repulsed. Twenty minutes had not passed since the infantry had sprung to their feet, and ten thousand of our men lay dead or wounded on the ground. The men of the Seventh New York Heavy Artillery came back without their colonel. The regiment lost heavily in enlisted men and line officers. Men from many commands sought shelter behind the crest of the hill we were behind. They seemed to be dazed and utterly discouraged. They told of the strength of the Confederate earthworks, and asserted that behind the line we could see was another and stronger line, and all the enlisted men insisted that they could not have taken the second line even if their supports had followed them. These battle-dazed visitors drifted off after a while and found their regiments, but some of them drifted to the rear and to coffee pots. We drew the guns back behind the crest of the hill, and lay down in the sand and waited. I noticed that the sun was now about a half an hour high. Soldiers came to the front from the rear, hunting for their regiments, which had been practically annihilated as offensive engines of war. Occasionally a man fell dead, struck by a stray ball from the picket line. By noon the stragglers were mostly gathered up and had rejoined their regiments, and columns of troops began to move to and fro in our rear in the little valley formed by the alder swamp. A column of infantry marching by fours passed to our right. I watched them, listlessly wondering if they were going to get something to eat, as I was hungry. I saw a puff of smoke between the marchers and myself, heard the report of a bursting shell, and twelve men of that column were knocked to the earth. Their officers shouted, "Close up! close up!" The uninjured men hurriedly closed the gap and marched on. The dead and wounded men lay on the ground, with their rifles scattered among them.

Soon some soldiers came out of the woods and carried the wounded men off, but left the dead where they fell. We buried them that night. Then, as the day wore away, and the troops were well in hand again, I saw staff officers ride along the lines, and then I saw the regimental commanders getting their men into line. About four o'clock in the afternoon I heard the charging commands given. With many an oath at the military stupidity which would again send good troops to useless slaughter, I sprang to my feet and watched the doomed infantry. Men, whom I knew well, stood rifle in hand not more than thirty feet from me, and I am happy to state that they continued to so stand. Not a man stirred from his place. The army to a man refused to obey the order, presumably from General Grant, to renew the assault. I heard the order given, and I saw it disobeyed. Many of the enlisted men had been up to and over the Confederate works. They had seen their strength, and they knew that they could not be taken by direct assault, and they refused to make a second attempt. That night we began to intrench.

By daylight we had our earthwork finished and were safe. The Seventh New York Heavy Artillery, armed as infantry, were intrenched about eighty yards in front of us. We were on the crest of a ridge; they were below us. Behind us, for supports, were two Delaware regiments, their combined strength being about one hundred and twenty men. Back of us was the alder swamp, where springs of cool water gushed forth. The men in front of us had to go to these springs for water. They would draw lots to see who should run across the dangerous, bullet-swept ground that intervened between our earthworks and theirs. This settled, the victim would hang fifteen or twenty canteens around him; then, crouching low in the rifle-pits, he would give a great jump, and when he struck the ground he was running at the top of his speed for our earthwork. Every Confederate sharpshooter within range fired at him. Some of these thirsty men were shot dead; but generally they ran into the earthwork with a laugh. After filling their canteens, they would sit by our guns and smoke and talk, nerving themselves for the dangerous return. Adjusting their burden of canteens, they would go around the end of our works on a run and rush back over the bullet-swept course, and again every Confederate sharpshooter who saw them would fire at them. Sometimes these water-carriers would come to us in pairs. One day two Albany men leaped into our battery. After filling their canteens, they sat with us and talked of the beautiful city on the Hudson, and finally started together for their rifle-pits. I watched through an embrasure, and saw one fall. Instantly he began to dig a little hollow with his hands in the sandy soil, and instantly the Confederate sharpshooters went to work at him. The dust flew up on one side of him, and then on the other. The wounded soldier kept scraping his little protective trench in the sand. We called to him. He answered that his leg was broken below the knee by a rifle ball. From the rifle-pits we heard his comrades call to him to take off his burden of canteens, to tie their strings together, and to set them to one side. He did so, and then the thirsty men in the pits drew lots to see who should risk his life for the water. I got keenly interested in this dicing with death, and watched intently. A soldier sprang out of the rifle-pits. Running obliquely, he stooped as he passed the canteens, grasped the strings, turned, and in a flash was safe. Looking through the embrasure, I saw the dust rise in many little puffs around the wounded man, who was still digging his little trench, and, with quickening breath, felt that his minutes were numbered. I noted a conspicuous man, who was marked with a goitre, in the rifle-pits, and recognized him as the comrade of the

Cold Harbor: *A Federal charge into Confederate lines*

stricken soldier. He called to his disabled friend, saying that he was coming for him, and that he must rise when he came near and cling to him when he stopped. The hero left the rifle-pits on the run; the wounded man rose up and stood on one foot; the runner clasped him in his arms; the arms of the wounded man twined around his neck, and he was carried into our battery at full speed, and was hurried to the rear and to a hospital. To the honor of the Confederate sharpshooters, be it said, that when they understood what was being done they ceased to shoot.

One day during this protracted Cold Harbor fight, a battery of Cohorn mortars was placed in position in the ravine behind us. The captain of this battery was a tall, handsome, sweet-voiced man. He spent a large portion of his time in our earthworks, watching the fire of his mortars. He would jump on a gun and look over the works, or he would look out through the embrasures. Boy-like, I talked to him. I would have talked to a field-marshal if I had met one. He told me many things relative to mortar practice, and I, in turn, showed him how to get a fair look at the Confederate lines without exposing himself to the fire of the sharpshooters, most of whom we had "marked down." He playfully accused me of being afraid, and insisted that at six hundred yards a sharpshooter could not hit a man. But I had seen too many men killed in our battery to believe that. So he continued to jump on guns and to poke his head into embrasures. One day I went to the spring after water. While walking back I met four men carrying a body in a blanket. "Who is that?" I asked. "The captain of the mortars," was the reply. Stopping, they uncovered his head for me. I saw where the ball had struck him in the eye, and saw the great hole in the back of his head where it had passed out.

The killed and wounded of the first day's fight lay unburied and uncared for between the lines. The stench of the dead men became unbearable, and finally a flag of truce was sent out. There was a cessation of hostilities to bury the dead and to succor the wounded. I went out to the ground in front of our picket line to talk to the Confederate soldiers, and to trade sugar and coffee for tobacco. Every corpse I saw was as black as coal. It was not possible to remove them. They were buried where they fell. Our wounded—I mean those who had fallen on the first day on the ground that lay between the picket lines—were all dead. I saw no live man lying on this ground. The wounded must have suffered horribly before death relieved them, lying there exposed to the blazing southern sun o' days, and being eaten alive by beetles o' nights.

One evening just before sunset I went to the spring to fill some canteens. Having filled them, I loaded my pipe and smoked in silent enjoyment. Looking up, I saw two Confederate infantry soldiers walking slowly down the ravine. They were tall, round-shouldered men. I clasped my knees and stared at them. They walked toward me, then halted, and dropping their musket-butts to the ground, they clasped their hands over the muzzles of their rifles and stared at me as I stared at them. I could not understand what two fully armed Confederate soldiers could be doing within our lines. After gazing at one another in silence for an instant, one of them smiled (I could almost hear the dirt on his face crack, and was agreeably interested in the performance) and inquired kindly,

"Howdy?" So I said, still seated and sucking my pipe, "Howdy," as that seemed to be the correct form of salutation in Virginia. Then I asked indifferently what they were doing within our lines. They told me that they had been captured and that they were on their way to our rear. That statement struck me as decidedly funny. I did not believe it, and my face expressed my disbelief. They then said that they were lost, that they were afraid to return to the front for fear of being killed, that they were afraid to keep on travelling for fear of running against the Union pickets on the flanks, and that they were out of provisions and were hungry. That last statement appealed strongly to me. I imagined myself prowling between the front and the rear of the Confederate army, with an empty haversack dangling at my side, and nothing to hope for but a Confederate prison, and my heart went out to these men. I opened my haversack and shared my hardtack with them, and then showed them the road which led to our rear.

During the fighting of the fourth day, which was not severe, a headquarters' orderly rode into the battery and delivered an order to our captain. He read it, and then calling me to him, handed me the order to read. With military brevity it commanded him to send Private Frank Wilkeson to army head-quarters at once to report to Adjutant-General Seth Williams. My heart sank. I had been doing a lot of things which I should not have done, and now I was in for it. The captain said: "Wash up and accompany the orderly. Get a horse from the chief of caissons and return promptly."

I ignored the first portion of the order, but secured the horse and rode off, pants in boots, slouch-hatted, flannel-shirted, blouseless, a strap around my waist and supremely dirty. I was tortured with the belief that I was to be punished. A certain sheep, which I had met in a field near Bowling Green, weighed heavily on me. A large bunch of haversacks, which I had found o'nights, dangled before me. I ransacked my memory and dragged forth all my military misdeeds and breaches of discipline and laid them one after the other on my saddle-bow and thoughtfully turned them over and over and looked at them, regretfully at first, then desperately and recklessly. I knew that I ought to be court-martialed and that I deserved to be shot.

I rode into a village of tents, one of which was pointed out to me as General Williams'. Sentinels paced to and fro; nice, clean men they were too. I dismounted, hitched my horse, and walked to Williams' tent. I was halted, sent in my name, and was admitted. I strode in defiant, hat on head, expecting to be abused, and resolved to take a hand in the abuse business myself.

I saw a handsome, kind-faced, middle-aged officer standing before me. He smiled kindly, and inquired, as he extended his hand to me, "Have I the pleasure of addressing Lieutenant Frank Wilkeson?" My hat came off instantly; my heart went out to Seth Williams, and I replied: "No, General; I am Private Frank Wilkeson." He smiled again and looked curiously at me. How I did wish I had washed my face and brushed the dirt off of my clothes. He bade me to be seated, and skilfully set me to talking. He asked me many questions, and I answered as intelligently as I could. Growing confidential, I told him that I had been dreadfully frightened by being summoned to head-quarters, and confessed the matters of the sheep and the haversacks, and my misconception of his duties. He tried to look severely grave, but laughed instead, and said pleasantly: "You are not to be shot. The crimes you have committed hardly deserve that punishment. I have called you to me to say that Secretary of War Stanton has ordered your discharge, and that you are to be appointed a second lieutenant in the Fourth Regiment of United States Artillery. When you want your discharge, claim it from your captain. He has the order to discharge you. When you get it, come to me if you need money to travel on, and I will lend you sufficient to take you to Washington and to buy you some clothing. When you arrive there, report to the Secretary of War, and he will tell you what to do."

Kind Seth Williams! So gracious, and sweet, and sympathetic was he to me, a dirty private, that my eyes filled with tears, and I could not talk, could not thank him. I returned to my battery and resumed work on my gun. I thought that the Army of the Potomac might win the next battle, and end the war. If it did, I preferred to be a private in a volunteer battery which was serving at the front, rather than to be a lieutenant in the United States Artillery, stationed at Camp Barry, near Washington.

One night, of these six Cold Harbor nights, I was on guard in the battery. I walked up and down behind the guns. Voices whispering outside of our work startled me. Then I heard men scrambling up the face of the earthwork. In the indistinct light I made out four. They were carrying something. They stood above me on the parapet, and in reply to my challenge poked fun at me. They said they loved me, and had brought me a present. They threw down to me a dead man, and with a light laugh went off. I called to them to come back—insisted that they should carry their corpse and bury it, but they stood off in the darkness and laughed at me, and insisted that they had made me a present of him. "You can have him; the battery can have him," and disappeared, leaving the dead man with me.

I was young, and therefore soft; and the lack of good food and loss of sleep told hard on me. Indeed, I got utterly used up. So one afternoon of this battle that lasted nearly a week, when but little was going on, I said to my sergeant: "I am exhausted, and want a night's sleep. I will dig a trench back here. If possible, let me sleep to-night, or I will be on the sick-list." He promised to let me sleep unless something urgent happened in the night. I ate my supper, wrapped my blanket around me, and lay down in my trench. The guns roared about me, the bullets whistled over me; but, overcome with exhaustion, I fell into a deep sleep. I was awakened with a strong grip on my shoulders, was lifted up and violently shaken, and the earnest voice of the gunner told me to run to my gun. "They have got an enfilading fire on us," the sergeant cried to me. Dazed, half awake, stupid from the deep sleep and coming sickness, I sat on the brink of my trench and wondered where I was. I heard, "Ho, Frank! Yah! No. 1!" sharply screamed. I heard the shot crash into our horses. Still not awake, I started for my gun. I saw the blaze of the fuses of the shells as they whizzed by. I saw countless fireflies; and, in my exhausted, half-awake condition, I confounded the shells and fireflies together, and thought they were all shells. The shock to me, in my weak, nervous condition, when I saw, as I thought, the air actually stiff with shells, required all my pride to stand up under. It woke me up and left me with a fit of trembling that required ten minutes warm work at the guns to get rid of. The enfilading fire did not amount to much, and I soon returned to my trench and deep sleep.

One day four men carrying a pale infantryman stopped for an instant in my battery. The wounded man suffered intensely from a wound through the foot. My sympathy was excited for the young fellow, and as we at the moment were doing nothing, I asked for half an hour's leave. Getting it, I accompanied him back into the woods to one of the Second Corps' field hospitals. Here, groaning loudly, he awaited his turn, which soon came. We lifted him on the rude table. A surgeon held chloroform to his nostrils, and under its influence he lay as if in death. The boot was removed, then the stocking, and I saw a great ragged hole on the sole of the foot where the ball came out. Then I heard the coatless surgeon who was making the examination cry out, "The cowardly whelp!" So I edged around and looked over the shoulders of an assistant surgeon, and saw that the small wound on the top of the foot, where the ball entered, was blackened with powder! I, too, muttered "The coward" and was really pleased to see the knife and saw put to work and the craven's leg taken off below the knee. He was carried into the shade of a tree, and left there to wake up. I watched the skilful surgeons probe and carve other patients. The little pile of legs and arms grew steadily, while I waited for the object of my misplaced sympathy to recover his senses. With a long breath he opened his eyes. I was with him at once, and looked sharply at him. I will never forget the look of horror that fastened on his face when he found his leg was off. Utter hopelessness and fear that look expressed. I entered into conversation with him; and he, weakened and unnerved by the loss of the leg, and the chloroform, for once told the truth. Lying on his back, he aimed at his great toe, meaning to shoot it off; but being rudely joggled by a comrade at the critical instant, his rifle covered his foot just below the ankle, and an ounce ball went crashing through the bones and sinews. The wound, instead of being a furlough, was a discharge from the army, probably into eternity. Our guns at the front began to howl at the Confederates again, and I was forced to leave the hospital. So I hastened back to my guns. The utter contempt of the surgeons, their change from careful handling to almost brutality, when they discovered the wound was self-inflicted, was bracing to me. I liked it, and rammed home the ammunition in gun No. 1 with vim.

Constantly losing men in our earthwork, shot not in fair fight, but by sharpshooters, we all began to loathe the place. At last, one afternoon the captain ordered us to level the corn-hills between the battery and the road, so that we could withdraw the guns without making a noise. At once understanding that a flank movement was at hand, we joyfully gathered up shovels and spades, and went at the obstructions with a will. No. 3 of No. 1 gun, an Albany man, was at my side. I was bent over shovelling. I straightened myself up. He leaned over to sink his shovel, pitched forward in a heap, dead, and an artilleryman beyond him clasped his stomach and howled a death howl. No. 3 was shot from temple to temple. The ball passed through his head and hit the other man in the stomach, fatally wounding him. They were the last men our battery lost at Cold Harbor.

That evening the horses were brought up, and all the guns but mine, No. 1, were taken off. We sat and watched them disappear in the darkness. Soon heavy columns of infantry could be indistinctly seen marching by the alder swamp in our rear. Then all was quiet, excepting the firing of the pickets. We sat and waited for the expected advance of the Confederates; but they did not come. Towards midnight an officer rode into the earthwork and asked lowly who was in command. The sergeant stepped forward and received his orders. Turning to us he whispered, "Limber to the rear." Silently the horses swung around. The gun was limbered, and, with the caisson in the lead, we pulled out of the earthwork, slowly drove across the cornfield, struck into a dusty road in the forest, and marched for the James River and the bloody disasters that awaited us beyond that beautiful stream.

SIDE-SLIPPING TO THE JAMES

THE TWO-DAY BATTLE IN THE WILDERNESS had cost the Army of the Potomac 17,600 casualties, and General Lee's Army of Northern Virginia still barred the road to Richmond. But Grant, breaking a dismal eastern tradition, gave the order to advance rather than retreat. He marched his troops around Lee's right flank, heading for the crossroads at Spotsylvania. He hoped to get there before Lee, thus placing himself between Lee and Richmond. But the Confederates reached Spotsylvania first—they had the shorter interior line of march—and here, as we saw in Wilkeson's selection, a second furious battle was fought.

Catton says, "The fight that started at Spotsylvania lasted for ten uninterrupted days, and it was even worse than the Wilderness fight had been. It was like the Wilderness . . . in that so much of the ground was heavily wooded and the troops had to fight blindly, nobody from commanding general down to private ever being quite sure just where everybody was and what was going on. As the fight developed, Grant's army kept on edging around to the left, trying vainly to get around the Confederate flank and interpose between the battlefield and the Confederate capital. It never quite made it, but in the ten days the two armies swung completely around three quarters of a circle, and on May 12 they had what may have been the most vicious fight of the whole war—a headlong contest for a horseshoe-shaped arc of Confederate trench guarding the principal road crossing, with hand-to-hand fighting that lasted from dawn to dusk, in a pelting rain, over a stretch of breastworks known forever after as the Bloody Angle."*

The losses continued to be huge. But as General Grant says, "During three long years the armies of the Potomac and Northern Virginia had been confronting each other. . . . They had fought more desperate battles than it probably ever before fell to the lot of two armies to fight, without materially changing the vantage-ground of either. The Southern press and people, with more shrewdness than was displayed in the North, finding that they had failed to capture Washington and march on to New York, as they had boasted they would do, assumed that they only defended their capital and Southern territory. Hence, Antietam, Gettysburg,

* Bruce Catton, *This Hallowed Ground*, pp. 326, 327.

and all the other battles that had been fought were by them set down as failures on our part and victories for them. Their army believed this. It produced a morale which could only be overcome by desperate and continuous hard fighting. The battles of the Wilderness, Spotsylvania, North Anna, and Cold Harbor, bloody and terrible as they were on our side, were even more damaging to the enemy, and so crippled him as to make him wary ever after of taking the offensive. His losses in men were probably not so great, owing to the fact that we were, save in the Wilderness almost invariably the attacking party; and when he did attack, it was in the open field."*

Confederate General Law says, "So far as the Confederates were concerned, it would be idle to deny that they (as well as General Lee himself) were disappointed at the result of their efforts in the Wilderness on the 5th and 6th of May, and that General Grant's constant 'hammering' with his largely superior force had, to a certain extent, a depressing effect upon both officers and men. 'It's no use killing these fellows; a half-dozen take the place of every one we kill,' was a common remark in our army. We knew that our resources of men were exhausted, and that the vastly greater resources of the Federal Government, if brought fully to bear even in this costly kind of warfare, must wear us out in the end."†

The story of the fight for Richmond continues from the Confederate side.

Falling Back to Richmond ‡

BY MAJOR ROBERT STILES

THE 10TH OF MAY, '64, was preeminently a day of battle with the Army of Northern Virginia. I know, of course, that the 12th is commonly regarded as the pivotal day, the great day, and the Bloody Angle as the pivotal place, the great place, of the Spotsylvania fights, and that for an hour or so, along the sides and base of that angle, the musketry fire is said to have been heavier than it ever was at any other place in all the world, or for any other hour in all the tide of time. But for frequency and pertinacity of attack, and repetition and constancy of repulse, I question if the left of General Lee's line on the 10th of May, 1864, has ever been surpassed. I cannot pretend to identify the separate attacks or to distinguish between them, but should think there must have been at least a dozen of them. One marked feature was that, while fresh troops poured

---

* *Battles and Leaders*, IV, 149.
† *Ibid.*, pp. 143–44.
‡ From *Four Years Under Marse Robert*.

to almost every charge, the same muskets in the hands of the same men met the first attack in the morning and the last at night; and so it was that the men who in the early morning were so full of fight and fun that they leaped upon the breastworks and shouted to the retiring Federals to come a little closer the next time, as they did not care to go so far after the clothes and shoes and muskets—were so weary and worn and heavy at night that they could scarcely be roused to meet the charging enemy.

The troops supporting the two Napoleon guns of the Howitzers were, as I remember, the Seventh (or Eighth) Georgia and the First Texas. Toward the close of the day everything seemed to have quieted down, in a sort of implied truce. There was absolutely no fire, either of musketry or cannon. Our weary, hungry infantry stacked arms and were cooking their mean and meagre little rations. Some one rose up, and looking over the works—it was shading down a little toward the dark—cried out: "Hello! What's this? Why, here come our men on a run, from—no, by Heavens! it's the Yankees!" and before any one could realize the situation, or even start toward the stacked muskets, the Federal column broke over the little work, between our troops and their arms, bayonetted or shot two or three who were asleep before they could even awake, and dashed upon the men crouched over their low fires—with cooking utensils instead of weapons in their hands. Of course they ran. What else could they do?

The Howitzers—only the left, or Napoleon section, was there—sprang to their guns, swinging them around to bear inside our lines, double-shotted them with canister and fairly spouted it into the Federals, whose formation had been broken in the rush and the plunge over the works, and who seemed to be somewhat massed and huddled and hesitating, but only a few rods away. Quicker almost than I can tell it, our infantry supports, than whom there were not two better regiments in the army, had rallied and gotten to their arms, and then they opened out into a V-shape, and fairly tore the head of the Federal column to pieces. In an incredibly short time those who were able to do so turned to fly and our infantry were following them over the intrenchments; but it is doubtful whether this would have been the result had it not been for the prompt and gallant action of the artillery.

There was an old Captain Hunter—it seems difficult to determine whether of the Texas or the Georgia regiment—who had the handle of his frying pan in his hand, holding the pan over the hot coals, with his little slice of meat sizzling in it, when the enemy broke over. He had his back to them, and the first thing he knew his men were scampering past him like frightened sheep. He had not been accustomed to that style of movement among them, and he sprang up and tore after them, showering them with hot grease and hotter profanity, but never letting go his frying pan. On the contrary, he slapped right and left with the sooty, burning bottom, distributing his favors impartially on Federal and Confederate alike—several of his own men bearing the black and ugly brand on their cheeks for a long time after and occasionally having to bear also the captain's curses for having made him lose his meat that evening. He actually led the counter-charge, leaping upon the works, wielding and waving his frying pan, at once as sword and banner.

It is an interesting coincidence that on this very day, the 10th of May, '64, at the point christened two days later as "The Bloody Angle," the Second Howitzers rendered a service even more important and distinguished perhaps than the gallant conduct of the First Company just recorded; a service which, in the opinion of prominent officers thoroughly acquainted with the facts and every way competent and qualified to judge, was deemed to have saved General Lee's army from being cut in twain.

There is one other feature or incident of the closing fight of the 10th of May which may be worthy of record, not alone because of its essentially amusing nature, but also because of a very pleasant after-clap or reminder of it later on. There were two men in the First Howitzers, older than most of us, of exceptionally high character and courage, who, because of the deafness of the one and the lack of a certain physical flexibility and adaptation in the other, were not well fitted for regular places in the detachment or service about the gun. For a time one or both of them took the position of driver, but this scarcely seemed fitting, and finally they were both classed as "supernumeraries," but with special duties as our company ambulance corps, having charge, under the surgeon of the battalion, of our company litters and our other simple medical and surgical outfit. For this and other reasons, the elder of these two good and gritty soldiers was always called "Doctor."

When the break occurred these two men, always on the extremest forward verge of our battle line, were overwhelmed with amazment, not so much at the irruption of the enemy, as at what seemed to be the demoralized rout of the Georgians and Texans. They ran in among them asking explanation of their conduct, then appealing to them and exhorting them—the Doctor in most courteous and lofty phrase: "Gentlemen, what does this mean? You certainly are not flying before the enemy! Turn, for God's sake; turn, and drive them out!" Then, with indignant outburst: "Halt! you infernal cowards!" and suiting the action to the word, these choleric cannoneers tore the carrying poles out of their litters, and sprang among and in front of the fugitives, belaboring them right and left, till they turned, and then turned with them, following up the retreating enemy with their wooden spears.

Some weeks later, after we had reached Petersburg, in the nick of time to keep Burnside out of the town, and had taken up what promised to be a permanent position and were just dozing off into our first nap in forty-eight hours, an infantry command passing by, in the darkness, stumbled over the trail handspikes of our guns and broke out in the usual style:

"Oh, of course! Here's that infernal artillery again; always in the way, blocking the roads by day and tripping us up at night. What battery is this, any way?"

Some fellow, not yet clean gone in slumber, grunted out:

"First Company, Richmond Howitzers."

What a change! Instantly there was a perfect chorus of greetings from the warm-hearted Texans.

"Boys, here are the Howitzers! Where's your old deaf man? Trot out your old Doctor. They're the jockeys for us. We are going to stay right here. We won't get a chance to run if these plucky Howitzer boys are with us."

Billy tells me that he remembers, word for word, the last crisp sentence Colonel Stephen D. Lee uttered the morning he complimented the old battery on the field of Frazier's Farm; that he said, "Men, hereafter when I want a battery, I'll know where to get one!" Two years later, at the base of the Bloody Angle, General Ewell seems to have been of the same opinion. He held our centre, which had just been pierced and smashed and his artillery captured. He wanted guns to stay the rout and steady his men, and he sent to the extreme left for Cabell's Battalion. I do not mean that the old battalion, or either of its batteries, was counted among the most brilliant artillery commands of the army, but I do claim that the command did have and did deserve the reputation of "staying where it was put," and of doing its work reliably and well.

The 11th had been a sort of off-day with us, very little business doing; but the 12th made up for it. As I remember, it was yet early on the morning of the 12th that we were sent for. We went at once, and did not stand upon the order of our going, though I think two guns of the Howitzers led the column, followed by two guns of Carlton's battery, the Troupe Artillery. If I remember correctly, our other guns occupied positions on the line from which they could not be withdrawn. As Colonel Cabell and I rode ahead, as before mentioned in another connection, to learn precisely where the guns were to be placed, we passed General Lee on horseback, or he passed us. He had only one or two attendants with him. His face was more serious than I had ever seen it, but showed no trace of excitement or alarm. Numbers of demoralized men were streaming past him and his voice was deep as the growl of a tempest as he said: "Shame on you, men; shame on you! Go back to your regiments; go back to your regiments!"

I remember thinking at the moment that it was the only time I ever knew his faintest wish not to be instantly responded to by his troops; but something I have since read induces me to question whether he did not refer to some special rendezvous, somewhere in the rear, appointed for the remnants of the shattered commands to rally to. Be this as it may, every soldier of experience knows that when a man has reached a certain point of demoralization and until he has settled down again past that point, it is absolutely useless to attempt to rouse him to a sense of duty or of honor. I have seen many a man substantially in the condition of the fellow who, as he executed a flying leap over the musket of the guard threatening to shoot and crying "Halt!"—called back, "Give any man fifty dollars to halt me, but can't halt myself!"

When we came back to our four guns and were leading them to the lines and the positions selected for them, just as we were turning down a little declivity, we passed again within a few feet of General Lee, seated upon his horse on the crest of the hill, this time entirely alone, not even a courier with him. I was much impressed with the calmness and perfect poise of his bearing, though his centre had just been pierced by forty thousand men and the fate of his army trembled in the balance. He was completely exposed to the Federal fire, which was very heavy. A half dozen of our men were wounded in making this short descent. In this connection I have recently heard from a courier—who, with others, had ridden with the General to the point where we saw him—that, observing and remarking upon the peril to which they were subjected, he ordered all his couriers to protect themselves behind an old brick kiln, some one hundred and fifty yards to the left, until their services were required, but refused to go there himself. This habit of exposing himself to fire, as they some-times thought, unnecessarily, was the only point in which his soldiers felt that Lee ever did wrong. The superb stories of the several occasions during this campaign when his men refused to advance until he retired, and, with tears streaming down their faces, led his horse to the rear, are too familiar to justify repetition, especially as I did not happen to be an eye-witness of either of these impressive scenes.

Our guns were put in at the left base of the Salient, and there, in full sight and but a short distance up the side of the angle, stood two or three of the guns from which our men had been driven, or at which they had been captured. The Howitzers had two clumsy iron three-inch rifles, and Captain McCarthy and I offered, with volunteers from that company, to draw these captured guns back into our lines, provided we were allowed to exchange our two iron guns for two of these, which were brass Napoleons. This would have given the battery a uniform armament and prevented the frequent separation of the sections. There was not at the time a Federal soldier in sight, and some of us walked out to or near these guns without being fired upon. It might have been a perilous undertaking, yet I think General Ewell would have given his consent; but the officer to whose command the guns belonged protested, saying he would himself have them drawn off later in the day. If it ever could have been done, the opportunity was brief; later it became impracticable, and the guns were permanently lost.

Barrett, Colonel Cabell's plucky little courier, rode almost into the works with us, and we had left our horses with him, close up, but in a position which we thought afforded some protection. In a few moments some one shouted that Barrett was calling lustily for me. I ran back where I had left him and was distressed to see my good horse, Mickey, stretched on the ground. Barrett said he had just been killed by a piece of shell which struck him in the head. The poor fellow's limbs were still quivering. I could see no wound of any consequence about the head or anywhere else; while I was examining him he shuddered violently, sprang up, snorted a little blood and was again "as good as new." As soon as practicable, how-ever, we sent Barrett and the three horses behind that brick kiln back on the hill, or to some place near by of comparative safety. I was afraid that Mickey, who seemed to have "gotten his hand in," might keep up this trick of getting "killed," as Barrett said, once too often. I may as well say right here that the noble horse got safely through the war, but was cap-tured with his master at Sailor's Creek.

When our guns first entered the works, or rather were stationed on the line just back of the little trench, there seemed to be comparatively few infantrymen about. One thing that pleased us greatly was, that our old Mississippi brigade, Barksdale's, or Humphreys', was supporting us; but it must have been just the end of their brigade line, and a very thin line it was. We saw nothing of the major-general of our division. General Rodes, of Ewell's corps, was the only major-general we saw. He was a man of very striking appearance, of erect, fine figure and martial bearing. He constantly passed and repassed in rear of our guns, riding a black horse that champed his bit and tossed his head proudly, until his neck and shoulders were flecked with white froth, seeming to be conscious that he carried Cæsar. Rodes' eyes were everywhere, and every now and then he would stop to attend to some detail of the arrangement of his line or his troops, and then ride on again, humming to himself and catching the ends of his long, tawny moustache between his lips.

It had rained hard all night and was drizzling all day, and everything was wet, soggy, muddy, and comfortless. General Ewell made his headquarters not far off, and seemed busy and apprehensive, and we gathered from everything we saw and heard, especially from General Lee's taking his position so near, that he and his generals anticipated a renewal of the attack at or about this point. From the time of our first approach, stragglers from various commands had been streaming past. I noticed that most of them had their arms and did not seem to be very badly shattered, and I tried hard to induce some of them to turn in and reinforce our thin infantry line. But they would not hearken to the voice of the charmer, charming never so wisely, and finally I appealed to General Rodes and asked him for a detail of men to throw off a short line at right angles to the works so as to catch and turn in these stragglers. He readily assented, and we soon had a strong, full line, though at first neither Rodes' own men nor our Mississippians seemed to appreciate this style of reinforcement.

One point more, with regard to our experience at the left base of the Salient, and we have done with the "Bloody Angle." Every soldier who was there, if he opens his mouth to speak or takes up his pen to write, seems to feel it solemnly incumbent upon him to expatiate upon the fearful fire of musketry. What I have to say about the matter will doubtless prove surprising and disappointing to many; but first let me quote Colonel Taylor's account of it . . . so frequently referred to:

> The army was thus cut in twain, and the situation was well calculated to test the skill of its commander and the nerve and courage of the men. Dispositions were immediately made to repair the breach, and troops were moved up to the right and left to dispute the further progress of the assaulting column. Then occurred the most remarkable musketry fire of the war—from the sides of the Salient, in the possession of the Federals, and the new line forming the base of the triangle, occupied by the Confederates, poured forth from continuous lines of hissing fire an incessant, terrific hail of deadly missiles. No living man nor thing could stand in the doomed space embraced within those angry lines; even large trees were felled, their trunks cut in twain by the bullets of small arms.

Every intelligent soldier, on either side, is aware of Colonel Taylor's deserved reputation for careful and unprejudiced observation and investigation, and for correct and accurate statement. General Fitz Lee, in his "Life of General Robert E. Lee," at p. 335, fully agrees with Colonel

Taylor, saying: "The musketry fire, with its terrific leaden hail, was beyond comparison the heaviest of the four years of war. In the bitter struggle, trees, large and small, fell, cut down by bullets."

Still, I am bound to say I saw nothing that approached a justification of these vivid and powerful descriptions. Of course the fire was at times heavy, but at no time, *in front of our position,* did it approximate, for example, the intensity of the fire during the great attack at Cold Harbor, a few weeks later. One singular feature of the matter is that we appear to have been at the very place where this fire is said to have occurred, and at the very time; for we were sent for by General Ewell, as I recollect, early on the morning of the 12th, and we remained at the left base of the Salient and within sight of some of the captured guns all that day and until the line was moved back out of the bottom, to the crest of the little ridge above mentioned. The only explanation I can suggest is that the fighting must have been much hotter *further to the right.*

It may be well just here to explain, while we cannot excuse, the existence not alone of the great Salient of Spotsylvania, with its soldier nickname of "Bloody Angle," and its fearful lesson of calamity, but also of other like faulty formations in our Confederate battle lines.

It was noticeable toward the close of the war what skilful, practical engineers the rank and file of the Army of Northern Virginia had become; how quickly and unerringly they detected and how unsparingly they condemned an untenable line—that is, where they were unprejudiced critics, as for instance, where fresh troops were brought in to reinforce or relieve a command already in position. I seem to hear, even now, their slashing, impudent, outspoken comment:

"Boys, what infernal fool do you reckon laid out this line? Why, any one can see we can't hold it. We are certain to be infiladed on this flank, and the Yankees can even take us in reverse over yonder. Let's fall back to that ridge we just passed!"

But where troops had themselves originally taken position, it was a very different matter. This was one point where Johnny was disposed to be unreasonable and insubordinate—not to consider consequences or to obey orders. He did not like to fall back from any position he had himself established by hard fighting, especially if it was in advance of the general line. So well recognized was his attitude in this regard that it had well nigh passed into a proverb:

"No, sir! *We fought for this dirt, and we're going to hold it.* The men on our right and left ought to be here alongside of us, and would be if they had fought as hard as we did!"

Of course, Johnny would not violate or forget the fundamental maxim of geometry and war, that *a line must be continuous;* that his right must be somebody's left and his left somebody's right; but the furthest he would go in recognition of the maxim was the compromise of bending back his flanks, so as to connect with the troops on his right and left who had failed to keep up. So this was done, he did not seem to care how irregular the general line of battle was. One cannot look at a map of any of our great battles without being impressed with the tortuous character of our lines.

I have myself heard a major-general send a message back to Army Headquarters, by a staff officer of General Lee, that he didn't see why his division should be expected to abandon the position they had fought for just to accommodate General ———, whose troops had fallen back where his had driven the enemy. On that very occasion, if my memory serves me, this selfish, stupid obstinacy cost us the lives of hundreds of men.

One word more in connection with the straightening of our lines. Of course we moved after dark, and, as I remember, but a short distance. After we got to our new position I discovered that I had lost my pocket-knife, or some such trivial article of personal outfit, but difficult to replace; so, contrary to Colonel Cabell's advice—he didn't forbid my going—I went back, on foot and in the dark, to look or feel for it. I had no difficulty in finding the spot where we had been lying, and began to grope and feel about for the knife, having at the time an unpleasant consciousness that I was running a very foolish and unjustifiable risk, for the Minies were hissing and singing and spatting all about me.

There was a man near me, also on his hands and knees, looking or feeling for something. While glancing at the shape, dimly outlined, I heard the unmistakable thud of a bullet striking flesh. There was a muffled outcry, and the crouching or kneeling figure lay stretched upon the ground. I went to it and felt it. The man was dead.

In a very brief time I was back in our new position and not thinking of pocket-knives.

After feeling our lines, feinting several times, and making, on the 18th, what might perhaps be termed a genuine attack, Grant, on the evening of the 20th, slid off toward Bowling Green; but although he got a little the start of Lee, yet, when he reached his immediate objective, Lee was in line of battle at Hanover Junction, directly across the line of further progress. It is the belief of many intelligent Confederate officers that if Lee had not been attacked by disabling disease, the movements of the two armies about the North Anna would have had a very different termination. Grant ran great risk in taking his army to the southern bank of the river with Lee on the stream between his two wings; it is fair to add that he seems to have realized his peril and to have withdrawn in good time.

General Lee's indisposition, about this time, was really serious. Some of us will never forget how shocked and alarmed we were at seeing him in an ambulance. General Early says of this matter:

> One of his three corps commanders had been disabled by wounds at the Wilderness, and another was too sick to command his corps, while he himself was suffering from a most annoying and weakening disease. In fact nothing but his own determined will enabled him to keep the field at all; and it was there rendered more manifest than ever that he was the head and front, the very life and soul of his army.

It was about this date that General Lee, as I remember a second time, broached the idea that he might be compelled to retire—an idea which no one else could contemplate with any sort of composure; happily, as soon as the disease was checked his superb physical powers came to his aid, and he soon rallied and regained his customary vigor and spirits.

Perhaps no other position of equal labor and responsibility can be mentioned, nor one which makes such drafts upon human strength and endurance, as the command of a great army in a time of active service. I recall during the Gettysburg campaign being equally impressed with the force of this general proposition, and with the almost incredible physical powers of General Lee. On two occasions, just before and just after we recrossed the Potomac, I was sent upon an errand which required my visiting army, corps, and division headquarters, and, so far as practicable, seeing the respective commanding officers in person. On the first round I did not find General Lee at his quarters, and was told that he had ridden down the road to the lines. When I reached the lines I heard he had passed out in front. Following him up, I found him in the rain with a single piece of horse artillery, feeling the enemy. My second ride was made largely at night, and, as I remember, every officer I desired to see was asleep, except at Army Headquarters, where I found Colonel Taylor in his tent on his knees, with his prayer-book open before him, and General Lee in his tent, wide-awake, poring over a map stretched upon a temporary table of rough plank, with a tallow candle stuck in a bottle for a light. I remember saying to myself, as I delivered my message and withdrew, "Does he never, never sleep?"

Again General Grant slid to the east, and we moved off upon a parallel line. I think it was during this detour—or it may have been an earlier or a later one—that I was sent ahead, upon a road which led through a tract of country which had not been desolated by the encampments or the battles of armies, to select a night's resting place for the battalion. Forests were standing untouched, farm lands were protected by fences, crops were green and untrampled, birds were singing, flowers blooming—Eden everywhere. Even my horse seemed to feel the change from the crowded roads, the deadly lines, the dust, the dirt, the mud, the blood, the horror. We were passing through a quiet wood at a brisk walk, when suddenly he roused himself and quickened his gait, breaking of his own accord into a long trot, his beautiful, sensitive ears playing back and forth in the unmistakable way which, in a fine horse, indicates that he catches sounds interesting and agreeable to him. It was, perhaps, several hundred yards before we swung around out of the forest into the open land where stood a comfortable farm house, and there in a sweet and sunny corner were several chubby little children chatting and singing at their play. Mickey, dear old Mickey, trotted right up to the little people, with low whinnies of recognition and delight, and rubbed his head against them. They did not seem at all afraid, but pulled nice tufts of grass for him, which he ate with evident relish and gratitude.

If I remember correctly, it was the evening of the same day, after Mickey and I had kissed and left the children, and I had found a beautiful camping ground for the battalion—a succession of little swells of land crowned with pine copses and covered with broom-sedge, with a clear, cool stream flowing between the hills; and after the batteries were all up and located in this soldier paradise—guns parked, horses watered and fed and all work done—I say, I think it was after all this, that the bugles of each of the batteries blew such sweet and happy notes as I never heard from any one of them before, and then, while I was lying on the broom-sedge, bathing my soul in this peace, and Mickey was browsing near-by, over across the stream, the Howitzer Glee Club launched out into a song, the first they had sung since we broke camp at Morton's Ford, three weeks before.

As the song ceased and the day was fading into the twilight, I caught, up the road, the low murmur of conversation and the rattle of canteens, and following the sound with my eye, saw two infantrymen, from a command that had followed us and camped further back from the stream, wending their way to water. Just as they came fully within sight and hearing, two of the Howitzer Club struck up "What Are the Wild Waves Saying?"—one of them, in a fine falsetto, taking the sister's part. As the clear, sweet female voice floated out on the still evening air my two infantrymen stood transfixed, one putting his hand upon the other's arm and saying with suppressed excitement, "Stop, man; there's a woman!" They were absolutely silent during the singing of the sister's part, but when the brother took up the song they openly wondered whether she would sing again. "Yes, there she is; listen, listen!"

And so, until the song was done, and they had waited, and it had become evident she would sing no more—and then a deep sigh from both the spell-bound auditors, and one of them, making use of the strongest figure he could command, exclaimed, from the bottom of a full heart, "Well, it beats a furlough hollow!"

We almost began to hope that Grant had gotten enough. Even his apparent, yes, real, success at the Salient did not embolden him to attack again at Spotsylvania. He had retired without any serious fighting at Hanover Junction or North Anna, and after feeling our position about Atlee's, he had once more slipped away from our front. Where was he going? What did he intend to do? Any one of his predecessors would have retired and given it up long ago. Was he about to do so?

The fact is, Grant was waiting for reinforcements. He had been heavily reinforced at Spotsylvania after the 12th of May, but not up to the measure of his desires, or of his needs, either; for he really needed more men—and more, and more. He needed them, he asked for them, and he got them. He had a right to all he wanted. His original contract so provided; it covered all necessary drafts. He wanted especially Baldy Smith and his men from the transports, and they were coming. They were stretching out hands to each other. When they clasped hands, then Grant would attack once more; would make his great final effort. When and where would it be?

When Grant slid away from Lee at Atlee's, we felt satisfied that he was, as usual, making for the south and east, so Hoke was ordered toward Cold Harbor, and Kershaw (now our division general, McLaws never having returned from the West) toward Beulah Church. Colonel Cabell received orders on the evening of the 31st of May, or early on the morning of the 1st of June, to make for the latter point; but he was not upon the same road as Kershaw's division, and our orders said nothing about joining it. They seemed to contemplate our going by the most direct route, and we went—that is, as far as we could. No infantry apparently had received any orders to go with us, certainly none went, and we soon passed beyond the apparent end of our infantry line, at least on the road we were traveling. Very soon we reached a stout infantry picket, which I interviewed, and they said there were no Confederate troops down that road, unless perhaps a few cavalry videttes.

I was on very intimate terms with my colonel, and I went to him and suggested whether there was not danger in our proceeding as we were, a battalion of artillery unaccompanied by infantry, out and beyond the last picket post. The colonel was a strict constructionist, and he shut me up at once by saying: "Stiles, that is the responsibility of the general officer who sent me my orders. I am ordered to Beulah Church and to Beulah Church I am going. This is the nearest road." I looked up at him in some little surprise, but said no more; having fired, I now fell back on my reserves, in pretty fair order, but slightly demoralized.

My reserves were the officers and men of the battalion, all of whom I think were fond of me. If I mistake not, Frazier's battery led the column. I am certain it did a little later. Calloway, its commanding officer, to whom we have already been introduced, was one of the very best of soldiers, as the reader will soon be prepared to admit. He was the first man I fell in with as I fell back, Colonel Cabell and little Barrett, his courier, being ahead of the column. Calloway asked me if I didn't think we were running some risk, entirely unsupported as we seemed to be, and outside our lines. I told him what had occurred, and he smiled grimly.

Then I fell back further to the old battery. The column was pretty closed up that morning; everybody seemed to feel it well to be so. I was strongly attached to the old company and particularly to the captain, who was a magnificent fellow. It was early on a beautiful summer morning, and we were again passing through a tract of undesolated, undesecrated country—greenness, quiet, the song of birds, the scent of flowers, all about us. Captain McCarthy was on foot, walking among his men, his great arms frequently around the necks of two of them at once—a position which displayed his martial, manly figure to great advantage. I dismounted, one of the fellows mounting my horse, and walked and talked and chatted with the men, and particularly with the captain.

He was altogether an uncommon person, marked by great simplicity, sincerity, kindliness, courage, good sense, personal force, and a genius for commanding men. He had been rather a reckless, pugnacious boy, difficult to manage, impatient of control. The war had proved a real blessing to him. It let off the surplus fire and fight. Its deep and powerful undertone was just what was needed to harmonize his nature. His spirit had really been balanced and gentled and sweetened by it. He was not essentially an intellectual man, nor yet a man of broad education, and he had under him some of the most intellectual and cultivated young men I ever met, yet he was easily their leader and commander; in the matter of control and for the business in hand, "from his shoulders and upward, taller than any of the people." And these intellectual and cultivated men freely recognized his supremacy and admired and loved him. He seemed to be somewhat subdued and quiet that morning; even more than ordinarily affectionate and demonstrative, but not cheerful or chatty. Several of us noticed his unusual bearing and speculated as to the cause.

As the morning wore on and we were leaving our infantry further and further behind, my uneasiness returned; and besides, I had been away long enough from the colonel, so I remounted and rode forward to the head of the column. He had been very emphatic in repelling my suggestions, but I thought it my duty to renew them, and I did. He was even more emphatic than before, saying he had been ordered to take that battalion to Beulah Church, and he proposed to do it, and he even added that when he wanted any advise from me he would ask it. I felt a nearer approach to heat than ever before or after, in all my intercourse with my friend and commander, and I assured him I would not obtrude my advice again.

I reined in my horse, waiting for Calloway, and rode with him at the head of his battery. I had scarcely joined him, when Colonels Fairfax and Latrobe, of Longstreet's staff, and Captain Simonton, of Pickett's, dashed by, splendidly mounted, and disappeared in a body of woods but a few hundred yards ahead. Hardly had they done so, when *pop! pop! pop!* went a half dozen carbines and revolvers; and a moment later the three officers galloped back out of the forest, driving before them two or three Federal cavalrymen on foot—Simonton leaning over his horse's head and striking at them with his riding whip. On the instant I took my revenge, riding up to Colonel Cabell, taking off my hat with a profound bow, and asking whether it was still his intention to push right on to Beulah Church? Meanwhile, Minié balls began to drop in on us, evidently fired by sharpshooters from a house a short distance to our left and front. The Colonel turned toward me with a smile, and said, in a tone that took all the sting out of his former words, if any was ever intended to be in them: "Yes, you impudent fellow, it is my intention, but let's see how quickly you can drive those sharpshooters out of that house!"

Scarce sooner said than done. I sprang from my horse. Calloway's guns were in battery on the instant, I, by his permission, taking charge of his first piece as gunner. Making a quick estimate of the distance, I shouted back to No. 6 at how many seconds to cut the fuse, and the shell reached the gun almost as soon as I did. A moment—and the gun was loaded, aimed and fired; a moment more and the house burst into flame. The shell from the other three guns were exploded among the retiring skirmishers, who ran back toward the woods; while from the side of the house nearest to us two women came out, one very stout and walking with difficulty, the other bearing a baby in her arms and two little children following her. Calling to the gunner to take charge of his piece, I broke for these women, three or four of the men running with me. There was a fence between us and them and could not have been less than four and a half feet high, which I cleared, "hair and hough," while the rest stopped to climb it. I took the baby and dragged the youngest child along with me, telling the other to come on, and sent the younger woman back to help the elder. When the reinforcements arrived we re-arranged convoys, I still keeping the baby. By the time we reached the battery more of the guns were in action, shelling the woods, and I became interested in the firing. The number fives as they ran by me with the ammunition would stop a moment to pat the baby, who was quite satisfied, and seemed to enjoy the racket, cooing and trying to pull my short hair and beard. This thing had been going on for several minutes, and I had not been conscious of any appeal to me, until one of the men ran up, and, pulling me sharply around, pointed to the two women, who were standing back down the hill, and as far as possible out of the line of the bullets, which were still annoying us. There was a rousing laugh and cheer as I started back to deliver the little infant artilleryman to his mother. It turned out that the elder of the two women was the mother of the other, and had been bedridden for several years. We were exceedingly sorry to have burned their little house, but some of the boys suggested that if the cure of the mother proved permanent, the balance, after all, might be considered rather in our favor.

I do not recall the events of the next few hours with any distinctness, or in any orderly sequence, nor how we got into connection with our division, Kershaw's; but we did so without serious mishap; so, perhaps, Colonel Cabell may have been more nearly right than I after all. The first definite recollection I have, after what I have just related, is of the breaking of Colonel Lawrence M. Keitt's big South Carolina regiment, which had just come to the army and been entered in Kershaw's old brigade, and probably outnumbered all the balance of that command. General Kershaw had put this and another of his brigades into action not far from where we had burned the house to dislodge the skirmishers. Keitt's men gave ground, and in attempting to rally them their colonel fell mortally wounded. Thereupon the regiment went to pieces in abject rout and threatened to overwhelm the rest of the brigade. I have never seen any body of troops in such a condition of utter demoralization; they actually groveled upon the ground and attempted to burrow under each other in holes and depressions. Major Goggin, the stalwart adjutant-general of the division, was attempting to rally them, and I did what I could to help him. It was of no avail. We actually spurred our horses upon them, and seemed to hear their very bones crack, but it did no good; if compelled to wriggle out of one hole they wriggled into another.

So far as I recollect, however, this affair was of no real significance. Our other troops stood firm, and we lost no ground. I think none of the guns of the battery were engaged. Meanwhile the three divisions of our corps—the First, since Longstreet's wounding, under command of Major-General R. H. Anderson—had settled into alignment in the following order, beginning from the left: Field, Pickett, Kershaw. On the right of Kershaw's was Hoke's division, which had been under Beauregard and had joined the Army of Northern Virginia only the night before. The ground upon which our troops had thus felt and fought their way into line was the historic field of Cold Harbor, and the day was the first of June, 1864.

In the afternoon a furious attack was made on the left of Hoke and right of Kershaw; and Clingman's, the left brigade of Hoke, and Wofford's, the right brigade of Kershaw, gave way and the Federal troops poured into the gap over a marshy piece of ground which had not been properly covered by either of these two brigades. Both Field and Pickett sent aid to Kershaw, and several of the guns of our battalion—I am not sure of which batteries, though I think two belonged to the Howitzers, came into battery on the edge of a peach orchard which sloped down to the break, and poured in a hot infilade fire on the victorious Federals, who, after a manly struggle, were driven back, though we did not quite regain all we had lost, and our lines were left in very bad shape.

While Wofford was bending back the right of his line to connect with Hoke, who, even with the aid sent him, had not quite succeeded in regaining his original position, Kershaw's old brigade, which had more perfectly recovered from its little contretemps, was pressing and driving the enemy, both advancing and extending its line upon higher and better ground, a feat it would never have been able to accomplish but for the aid of one of Calloway's guns, which, under command of Lieutenant Robert Falligant, of Savannah, Ga., held and carried the right flank of the brigade, coming into battery and fighting fiercely whenever the enemy seemed to be holding the brigade in check, and limbering up and moving forward with it, while it was advancing; and this alternate advancing and firing was kept up until a fresh Federal force came in and opened fire on the right flank, and all of Falligant's horses fell at the first volley. The enemy made a gallant rush for the piece, but they did not get it. It was in battery in a moment, belching fire like a volcano, and very hot shot, too. The brigade, whose flank it had held, now sprang to its defense, and after a furious little fight the gun was for the present safe, and every one began to dig and to pile up dirt.

The brigade did not, however, advance one foot after Falligant's horses were shot; but it was already considerably in advance of Wofford's left, with which it was not connected at all, until the entire line was rectified on the night of the 2d—nor was there at any time a Confederate infantry soldier to the right of this piece, nor a spadeful of earth, except the little traverse we threw up to protect the right of the gun. It may just as well be added now that this lone gun held the right of Kershaw's brigade line that evening and night—it was getting dark when the extreme advanced position was reached—and all the next day, and was moved back by hand the night of the 2d of June. I have no hesitation in saying that in all my experience as a soldier I never witnessed more gallant action than this of Lieutenant Falligant and his dauntless cannoneers, nor do I believe that any officer of his rank made a more important contribution than he to the success of the Confederate arms in the great historic battle.

Both sides anticipated battle on the 3d, as it really occurred. General Grant in his memoirs says in express terms, "The 2d of June was spent in getting troops into position for attack on the 3d"; and the "Official Journal" of our corps says, under date of June 3d, "The expected battle begins early." This journal also notes the weakness of "Kershaw's Salient," and that the enemy was aware of it, and was "massing heavily" in front of it. Three brigades were sent to support Kershaw—Anderson's, Gregg's, and Law's. We also set to work to rectify the lines about this point. General E. M. Law, of Alabama, is probably entitled to the credit of this suggestion, which had so important a bearing upon our success. He laid off the new line with his own hand and superintended the construction of it during the night of the 2d. The record of the 3d might have been a very different one if this change had not been made. Under Colonel Cabell's instructions and with the aid of the division pioneer corps, I opened roads through the woods for the more rapid and convenient transmission of artillery ammunition, and put up two or three little bridges across ravines with the same view.

While I was superintending this work, the fire at the time being lively, I heard some one calling in a most lugubrious voice, "Mister, Mister, won't you please come here!" I glanced in the direction of the cry and saw a man standing behind a large tree in a very peculiar attitude, having the muzzle of his musket under his left shoulder and leaning heavily upon it. Supposing he was wounded, I went to him and asked what he wanted. He pointed to the butt of his gun, under which a large, vigorous, venomous copperhead snake was writhing; and the wretched skulker actually had the face to whine to me, "Won't you please, sir, kill that snake!" I knew not what to say to the creature, and fear what I did say was neither a very Christian nor a very soldierly response; but no one who has not seen a thoroughly demoralized man can form the slightest conception of how repulsive a thing such a wretch is.

The headquarters of General Kershaw at Cold Harbor was close up to the lines and just back of the position of some of our guns. It was but a short distance, too, from where the caissons bringing in ammunition turned to the right, on a road I had cut, running along the slope of a declivity at the crest of which our guns were stationed, some of them before and all of them after the lines were rectified. He might have found a safer place, but none nearer the point of peril and the working point of everything. The position, however, was so exposed that he found himself compelled to protect it, which he did by putting up a heavy wall of logs, back of which the earth was cut away and pitched over against the face, which was toward the lines. His quarters were thus cut deep into the hillside, and had besides, above the surface and toward the enemy, this wall of logs faced with earth. Thus he had a place where he and his officers could safely confer and at a very short distance from their commands; but it was after all a ghastly place, and very difficult and dangerous of approach. All the roads or paths leading to it were not only swept by an almost continuous and heavy fire of musketry, but I had to keep a force of axe-men almost constantly at work cutting away trees felled across the ammunition roads by the artillery fire of the enemy. Colonel Charles S. Venable, reputed to be one of the roughest and most daring riders on General Lee's staff—later, professor of mathematics at the University of Virginia, and chairman of the faculty—told me he believed this headquarter position of Kershaw's at Cold Harbor was the worst place he was ever sent to. Colonel Cabell was necessarily a great part of the time at these headquarters, and I also, when not engaged at some special work, or with some of the guns, or on the way from one to another. At Cold Harbor these journeys had to be made on foot, and necessarily consumed a good deal of time, an artillery battalion frequently covering, say, half a mile of the line.

Up to the night of the 2d of June, when it was moved back, every time Falligant's gun fired while I was at headquarters, General Kershaw would repeat his admiration of his courage, and ask me to explain to him again and again the isolated and exposed position of the piece, and then he would express his determination that Falligant's gallantry and services should receive their merited reward. Once, when I happened to be there, a soldier from a South Carolina regiment in Kershaw's old brigade, one of those supporting Falligant's gun, came in, reporting that his part of the line was almost out of ammunition, and asking that some be sent in at once. He may have had a written order, but at all events he represented that the case was urgent; that they could not trust to getting it into the line at some safe point and having it passed along by hand, because it would take too long, and besides all the troops were scantily supplied and it would never get to his regiment; and lastly, because the officer who sent him had ordered him to bring it himself. The man was intelligent, self-possessed, and determined. I well remember, too, how pale and worn and powder-begrimed he looked. He confirmed all I had said as to the position and services of Falligant's gun, and was enthusiastic about him and his detachment.

I told him I was going down there and would help him. Boxes of ammunition were piled up in a corner of the cellar, as it might be called, in which we were sitting, and we knocked the top from one or more, and putting two good, strong oilcloths together, poured into them as many cartridges as either of us could conveniently carry at a pretty good rate of speed. We then tied up the cloths, making a bag of double thickness and having two ends to hold by. Together we could run quite rapidly with it, and in case either of us should be killed or wounded, the other could get along fairly well. We then took the course I had already several times taken in reaching the gun—that is, we went down behind Wofford's left flank, and from that point ran across a field covered with scattering sassafras bushes, to a point on Kershaw's line, a little to the left of our gun. This route afforded the best protection, but after we left Wofford's position the "protection" amounted to nothing. The sharpshooters had two-thirds of a circle of fire around the piece, and they popped merrily at us as we stepped across the field, but they never touched either of us; we got in safe and each of us "counted a *coup*," as the French Canadian trappers used to say.

After shaking hands with the infantry, hearing my plucky comrade complimented on his quick and successful trip, and seeing the men draw their rations of powder and ball, I made my way to the gun, told Bob and his gallant detachment what the General had said about them, looked to their fortification and ammunition, and was just about to take the perilous trip back again when the enemy began to press us in a very determined way. There was heavy timber immediately in front, and their mode of attack was to thicken a skirmish line into a line of battle behind the trees, and then try to rush us at very short range. The infantry ammunition had been replenished just in time, but it must be remembered there was not an infantry soldier to our right. If the woods had been as close upon us in that direction they would undoubtedly have captured the piece, but they did not relish coming out into the open.

I was struck with the splendid fighting spirit of Campbell, the tall, lean, keen-eyed, black-haired gunner of the piece; but he was entirely too reckless, standing erect except when bending over the handspike in sighting the piece, and not much "sighting" is done at such short range. Every time the gun belched its deadly contents into the woods Campbell would throw his Glengarry around his head and yell savagely. I cautioned him again and again, reminding him that the other men of the detachment were fighting, and fighting effectively, on their hands and knees. When his commanding officer or I ordered him to "get down" he would do so for a moment, but spring up again when the gun fired. Suddenly I heard the thud of a Minié striking a man, and Campbell's arms flew up as he fell backward, ejaculating, "O God! I'm done forever!" We lifted the poor fellow around, across the face of the little work, under the mouth of the piece, and Falligant kneeled by him and pressed his finger where the blood was spouting, while I took the gunner's place at the trail. Every time the gun was discharged I noticed how Campbell's face—which was almost directly under the bellowing muzzle—was contorted, but he urged me to keep up the fire, until finally, observing a sort of lull in the fight, I proposed to cease firing and note the effect, and the poor fellow said brokenly, "Well, if you think it's safe, Adjutant!" Then he added, "Tell my mother I died like a soldier"—and he was gone.

During this flurry one of the enemy bounded over the work and landed right in among us; but he ran on toward the rear and brought up in a sitting posture on a pile of earth one of the infantry had thrown out of a hole he had dug to cook in—a sort of safety-kitchen. The man's back was turned toward us, his elbows were on his knees, and his head sunk in his hands. After Campbell's death, as he was still sitting there, thinking he must be wounded, I proposed to one of the men to run out with me and bring him back into the work. We tried it, but he cast off our hands and we had to leave him to his fate. In a few moments he was shot in the head and tumbled in upon the cook in the kitchen—dead.

The 2d of June, 1864, was the heaviest, the hardest-worked and the most straining day of my life. Not only did I have my ordinary duties of a day of battle to perform, but I had, in addition, to open and to keep open roads for getting in ammunition, to bridge two or three ravines, to visit Falligant's gun several times and to keep it supplied with ammunition, which had to be passed along the infantry line by hand for quite a long distance. When night came I believe I was more nearly worn out than on any other occasion during the entire war. Colonel Cabell insisted I should go back to our headquarters camp, which was about midway between the lines and the drivers' camp, and sleep; and, in view of what impended on the morrow, I consented to do so. But first, and just before dark, I took Calloway over all the obscure and confusing part of the road to Falligant's gun, the road by which he was to bring it out later. I omitted to say that General Kershaw highly approved our determination to save that piece, if at all possible. I greatly disliked not going with the party to fetch the gun out, but Calloway and every one concerned insisted that I must not think of attempting it, fearing that I would utterly give way if I did so. So I yielded, and after showing and explaining everything to Calloway, I went back to camp and lay down.

I had scarcely gotten to sleep when I had to get up to pilot an officer who had important orders for General Kershaw, and had been unable to find his headquarters. Once more I stretched out and dozed off. How long I dozed or slept I cannot say, but I was awakened by Calloway bending over me and saying, "Adjutant, I never was so sorry about anything, but in those woods it is now as dark as Erebus! Nobody but yourself can find and keep the road you showed me, and I don't believe even you can do it."

The noble fellow was evidently much mortified and troubled at being compelled to rouse me, but he well knew I had much rather this should be done than that the chance of saving the gun should be abandoned. So I got up and mounted Mickey, and off we started.

It was very dark. Just before reaching the point where the road turned to the right along the slope of the hill, we found the gun horses and drivers, Calloway and I passing and directing them to follow us, and to keep absolutely quiet. I experienced little difficulty in finding the road, having superintended the cutting of it and being very familiar with it, and we passed on over the little bridge, and were just passing out from behind Wofford's left flank and heading for Kenshaw's line, when some one seized my bridle rein and abruptly stopped my horse; at the same time asking who I was and what I intended to do, and what I meant by bringing artillery horses through his lines without his permission.

The manner and tone of this address was irritating, but suspecting who my interlocutor was and knowing something of his temperament, I answered quietly that I was adjutant of Cabell's Battalion of Artillery, and that the commanding officer of one of our batteries was with me; that the gun out there, which had protected this part of the line all day, belonged to his battery; that we proposed to save it, and that we had brought the horses for the purpose of hauling it off. I could see nothing, but by this time my suspicion had become conviction and I felt sure I was talking with General Wofford. He positively forbade the attempt, and did not seem disposed to yield until my cousin, Colonel Edward Stiles, of the Sixteenth Georgia, of his brigade, who knew the General well, joined us and suggested as a compromise that we should make the attempt without taking the horses any further; to which I agreed, upon condition that he would furnish me with, say, twenty men, to get the gun off by hand, and that in the event of their failing I should then make the effort with the horses, as we had General Kershaw's positive orders to save the gun if possible.

We got the men and started up the hill, leaving drivers and horses to await our return. It was now absolutely dark. I remember putting my hand before my face and being unable to see it. Calloway and I rode side by side, inclining to the left, so as to guard against running out into the enemy through the gap in the lines. There was absolute stillness, save the soft tread of our horses' feet in the sandy soil. In a few moments their heads rustled against dry leaves—the leafy screen which the troops had put up to protect themselves from the baking sun. We knew we were at the infantry line and turned to the right and toward the gun. There was a good deal of smoke in the air from the woods afire out in front, and we soon became conscious of an insufferable odor of burning flesh. My horse being a rapid walker, I kept a little ahead of Calloway, and very soon was stopped again, by some one who spoke almost in a stage whisper. It turned out to be the commanding officer of Kershaw's old brigade, and he, too, forbade our attempt and ordered us back; but the direct authority of his major-general satisfied him, and he begged only that we should wait until his men could be thoroughly roused and ready to resist any attack that might be made; adding that the poor fellows were utterly exhausted by the unrelieved strain of the past thiry-six hours. All true; yet it was fearful to contemplate the risk they ran in sleeping. The colonel told us, too, what we already suspected, that the odor which so offended our nostrils was that of human bodies roasting in the forest fires in front. We plainly heard the officers passing along the lines and rousing the men, and we feared the enemy heard it, too; but preferred this risk to that of a sudden rush upon a slumbering brigade just as we were drawing the gun off.

Soon after we started again, my horse snorted and sprang aside. I knew this meant we had reached the dead horses, and told Calloway we were almost upon the gun. He dismounted, handing his bridle rein to me, and I heard him enter the little trench and feel and fumble his way along it for a few steps, and then heard him call, in a low tone, "Falligant, Falligant!" Then I heard the sort of groan or grumble a tired man gives out when he is half roused from a sound sleep, and after that a low hum of conversation. Then Calloway came up out of the trench, and, groping his way to me, said: "Adjutant, do you know every man in that detachment was fast asleep and the enemy is lying down in line of battle between here and that low fire out there!" I said he must be mistaken, that I could toss a cracker into that fire. He insisted he was right and urged me to dismount and go into the trench and stoop till I could see under the smoke. I did so, and there, sure enough, was a continuous line of blue which the flickering of the flames beyond enabled me to see. My heart stopped beating at the sight, but this was no time for indulgence of over-sensibility, physical or emotional.

As quietly and rapidly as possible we got everything ready for fight or retreat. Our twenty men had brought their muskets and Kershaw's brigade was up in the trench and on their knees. The gun was backed out of the little work, limbered up, and the ammunition chest replaced; some of the men took hold of the wheels and some of the tongue, and the piece was soon moving after us, almost noiselessly, along the sassafras field toward Wofford's line. In a few moments we reached the goal, returning our thanks to the General, and to my cousin and the sturdy, gallant men they lent us; the horses were hitched up and we were rolling over the little bridges and up to the new line and the position selected for this now distinguished piece.

I trust I am not small enough to indulge in any vulgar pride in my part of the trying experiences of this day; yet I scarce recall another day for which I so thank God, or which has had a greater influence on my life. Often, when depressed and disposed to question whether there is, or ever was, in me the salt of a real manhood, I have looked back to the first three days of June, 1864, and felt the revival of a saving self-respect and the determination not to do or suffer anything unworthy of this heroic past of which I was a part.

There were two battles at Cold Harbor, one in '62 and one in '64. In '62 the Confederates attacked and drove the Federals from their position; in '64 the Federals attacked, but were repulsed with frightful slaughter. It is undisputed that both McClellan's army and Grant's outnumbered Lee's —Grant's overwhelmingly—and it is asserted that the position occupied by the Federals in '62 and the Confederates in '64 was substantially the same.

We were in line of battle at Cold Harbor of '64 from the 1st to the 12th of June—say twelve days; the battle proper did not last perhaps that many minutes. In some respects, at least, it was one of the notable battles of history—certainly in its brevity measured in time, and its length measured in slaughter—as also in the disproportion of the losses. A fair epitome of it in these respects would be that in a few moments more than thirteen thousand men were killed and wounded on the Federal side and less than thirteen hundred on the Confederate. As to the time consumed in the conflict, the longest duration assigned is sixty minutes and the shortest less than eight. For my own part, I could scarcely say whether it lasted eight or sixty minutes, or eight or sixty hours—to such a degree were all my powers concentrated upon the one point of keeping the guns fully supplied with ammunition.

The effect of the fighting was not at all appreciated on the Confederate side at the time. Why we did not at least suspect it, when the truce was asked and granted to allow the removal of the Federal dead and wounded, I cannot say, although I went myself with the officers on our side, detailed to accompany them, on account of my familiarity with the lines. I presume the ignorance, and even incredulity, of our side as to the overwhelming magnitude of the Federal losses resulted from two causes mainly—our own loss was so trivial, so utterly out of proportion, and the one characteristic feature of the fight on the Federal side was not then generally known or appreciated by us, namely, that Grant had attacked in column, in phalanx, or in mass. The record of the Official Diary of our corps (Southern Historical Society Papers, Vol. VII., p. 503), under date of June 3, 1864, is very peculiar and in part in these words: "Meantime the enemy is heavily massed in front of Kershaw's salient. Anderson's, Law's, and Gregg's brigades are there to support Kershaw. Assault after assault is made, and each time repulsed with severe loss to the enemy. At 8 o'clock A.M., fourteen had been made and repulsed (this, means, I suppose, fourteen lines advanced)."

This is obviously a hurried field note by one officer, corrected later by another, in accordance with the facts known to the writer, that is, to the officer who made the later note, but not generally known at the time to the public. We suppose, however, it will to-day be admitted by all that there was *but one attack* upon Kershaw up to 8 A.M., and that at that hour the order was issued to the Federal troops to renew the attack, but they failed to advance; that this order was repeated in the afternoon, when the troops again refused to obey, and that at least some of Grant's corps generals approved of this refusal of their men to repeat the useless sacrifice.

Here, then, is the secret of the otherwise inexplicable and incredible butchery. A little after daylight on June 3, 1864, along the lines of Kershaw's salient, his infantry discharged their bullets and his artillery fired case-shot and double shotted canister, at very short range, into a mass of men twenty-eight (28) deep, who could neither advance nor retreat, and the most of whom could not even discharge their muskets at us. We do not suppose that the general outline of these facts will be denied to-day, but it may be as well to confirm the essential statements by a brief extract from Swinton's "Army of the Potomac":

> The order was issued through these officers to their subordinate commanders, and from them descended through the wonted channels, but no man stirred and the immobile lines pronounced a verdict, silent, yet emphatic, against further slaughter. The loss on the Union side in this sanguinary action was over thirteen thousand, while on the part of the Confederates it is doubtful whether it reached that many hundreds.

To like effect, as to the amount and the disproportion of the carnage, is the statement of Colonel Taylor, on page 135 of his book, that:

> I well recall having received a report after the assault from General Hoke—whose division reached the army just previous to this battle— to the effect that the ground in his entire front over which the enemy had charged was literally covered with their dead and wounded; and that up to that time he had not had a single man killed.

So much for the amount, the disproportion, and the cause of the slaughter. A word now as to the effect of it upon the Federal leaders and the Northern people. Is it too much to say that even Grant's iron nerve was for the time shattered? Not that he would not have fought again if his men would, but they would not. Is it not true that he so informed President Lincoln; that he asked for another army; that, not getting it, or not getting it at once, he changed his plan of campaign from a fighting to a digging one? Is it reasonable to suppose that when he attacked at the Bloody Angle or at Cold Harbor, he really contemplated the siege of Petersburg and regarded those operations as merely preparatory? Is it not true that, years later, Grant said—looking back over his long career of bloody fights—that Cold Harbor was the only battle he ever fought that he would not fight over again under the same circumstances? Is it not true that when first urged, as President, to remove a certain Democratic officeholder in California, and later, when urged to give a reason for his refusal, he replied that the man had been a standard-bearer in the Army of the Potomac, and that he would—allow something very unpleasant to happen to him—before he would remove the only man in his army who even attempted to obey his order to attack a second time at Cold Harbor? Is it not true that General Meade said the Confederacy came nearer to winning recognition at Cold Harbor than at any other period during the war? Is it not true that, after Grant's telegram, the Federal Cabinet resolved at least upon an armistice, and that Mr. Seward was selected to draft the necessary papers, and Mr. Swinton to prepare the public mind for the change? And finally, even if none of these things be true, exactly as propounded—yet is it not true, that Cold Harbor shocked and depressed the Federal Government and the northern public more than any other single battle of the war?

A few words as to some of the prominent features, physical and otherwise, of fighting in "the lines," as we began regularly to do in this campaign of '64, particularly at Cold Harbor. Something of this is necessary to a proper understanding and appreciation of some of the incidents that occurred there. And first, as to "the works" of which I have so often spoken. What were they? I cannot answer in any other way one-half so well as by the following vivid quotation from my friend Willy Dame's "Reminiscences":

Just here I take occasion to correct a very wrong impression about the field works the Army of Northern Virginia fought behind in this campaign. All the Federal writers who have written about these battles speak about our works as "formidable earthworks," "powerful fortifications," "impregnable lines"; such works as no troops could be expected to take and *any troops* should be expected to hold.

Now about the parts of the line distant from us, I couldn't speak so certainly—though I am sure they were all very much the same—but about the works all along our part of the line I can speak with exactness and certainty. I saw them, I helped with my own hands to make them, I fought behind them, I was often on top of them and both sides of them. I know all about them. I got a good deal of the mud off them on me (not for purposes of personal fortification, however). Our works were a single line of earth about four feet high and three to five feet thick. It had no ditch or obstruction in front. It was nothing more than a little heavier line of "rifle pits." There was no physical difficulty in men walking right over that bank. I did it often myself, saw many others do it, and twice saw a line of Federal troops walk over it, and then saw them walk *back* over it with the greatest ease, at the rate of forty miles an hour; i.e. except those whom we had persuaded to stay with us, and those the angels were carrying to Abraham's bosom at a still swifter rate. Works they could go over like that couldn't have been much obstacle! They couldn't have made better time on a dead level.

Such were our works actually, and still they seemed to "loom large" to the people in front. I wonder what could have given them such an exaggerated idea of the strength of those modest little works! I wonder if it could have been the *men* behind them! There wasn't a great many of these men! It was a very thin gray line along them, back of a thin red line of clay. But these lines stuck together, very hard, and were very hard indeed to separate. The red clay was "sticky" and the men were just as "sticky," and as the two lines "stuck" together so closely, it made the whole very strong indeed. Certainly it seems they gave to those who tried to force them apart an impression of great strength.

Yes, it must have been the *men!* A story in point comes to my aid here. A handsome, well dressed lady sweeps with a great air past two street boys. They are much struck. "My eye, Jim, but ain't that a stunning dress?" Says Jim with a superior air, "Oh, get out, Bill, the dress ain't no great shakes; it's the woman in it that makes it so killing!" That was the way with the Spotsylvania earthworks. The "works wa'n't no great shakes." It was the men in 'em that made them so "killing."

The original intent of such "works" is to afford protection against regular attack by the full line of battle of the opposite side, advancing out of their works to attack yours. This, of course, every one understands. But this is only an occasional and comparatively rare thing. The constant and wearing feature of "the lines" is the sharpshooting, which never ceases as long as there is light enough to see how to shoot; unless the skirmishers or sharpshooters of the two sides proclaim, or in some way begin, a temporary truce, as I have known them to do. I have also known them to give explicit warning of the expiration of such a truce.

Sharpshooting, at best, however, is a fearful thing. The regular sharpshooter often seemed to me little better than a human tiger lying in wait for blood. His rifle is frequently trained and made fast bearing upon a particular spot—for example, where the head of a gunner must of necessity appear when sighting his piece—and the instant that object appears and, as it were, "darkens the hole," crash goes a bullet through his brain.

The consequence of the sharpshooting is the "covered-way," which, when applied to these rough and ready temporary lines, means any sort of protection—trenches, ditches, traverses, piles of earth, here and there, at what have proved to be the danger points, designed and placed so as to protect as far as possible against the sharpshooters. Only in regular and elaborate lines of "siege," such as we had later about Petersburg, is seen the more perfect protection of regularly covered galleries and ways for passing from one part of the line to another inside; just as, outside and on the face toward the enemy, such elaborate and permanent lines of works are protected by ditches, abatis or felled trees, friezes or sharpened stakes, to make the "works" more difficult of approach, of access, and of capture.

One can readily understand, now, the supreme discomfort and even suffering of "the lines." Thousands of men cramped up in a narrow trench, unable to go out, or to get up, or to stretch or to stand, without danger to life and limb; unable to lie down, or to sleep, for lack of room and pressure of peril; night alarms, day attacks, hunger, thirst, supreme weariness, squalor, vermin, filth, disgusting odors everywhere; the weary night succeeded by the yet more weary day; the first glance over the way, at day dawn, bringing the sharpshooter's bullet singing past your ear or smashing through your skull, a man's life often exacted as the price of a cup of water from the spring. But I will not specify or elaborate further; only, upon the canvas thus stretched, let me paint for you two or three life and death pictures of Cold Harbor of '64.

The reader may recall our "Old Doctor," the chief of our ambulance corps, who helped to rally the Texans and Georgians on the 10th of May at Spotsylvania, first exhorting them as "gentlemen," then berating and belaboring them as "cowards." No man who was ever in the Howitzers but will appreciate the grim absurdity of this man's feeling a lack of confidence in his own nerve and courage; but he did feel it. When the war broke out he was in Europe enjoying himself, but returned to his native State, serving first in some, as he considered it, "non-combatant" position, until that became unendurable to him, and then he joined the Howitzers as a private soldier; and that final flurry of the 10th of May was the first real fight he ever got into. Hearing some one say just as it was over that it had been "pretty hot work," he asked with the greatest earnestness whether the speaker really meant what he said, and when assured that he did, he asked two or three others of his comrades, whom he regarded as experienced soldiers, whether they concurred in this view of the matter, and on their expressing emphatic concurrence, he expressed intense satisfaction at having at last a standard in his mind, and a relieving standard at that; saying that he had feared he would disgrace his family by exhibiting a lack of courage; but if this was really "hot work," he felt that he would be able to maintain himself and do his duty. The story is almost too much for belief, but it is the sober truth and vouched for by gentlemen of the highest character.

I think it was the evening after the big fight at Cold Harbor that I was sitting in the works, with one of the Howitzer detachments, when the Doctor announced his intention of going to the spring for water. I reminded him that it was not quite dark and the sharpshooters would be apt to pay their respects to him; but he said he must have some water, and offered to take down and fill as many canteens as he could carry. His captain was present and I said no more. He was soon loaded up and started off, stepping right up out of the trench on the level ground. I could not help urging him to take the "covered way," but he replied, "I can't do it, Adjutant. It is dirty; a gentleman can't walk in it, sir."

Away he went, walking bolt upright and with entire nonchalance, down the hill; to my great relief reaching the spring in safety, where he was pretty well protected. In due time he started back, loaded with the full canteens and having a tin cup full of water in his right hand. I heard the sharp report of a rifle and saw the Doctor start forward or stumble, and sprang up to go to his relief, but he steadied himself and came right on up the hill without further attention from the sharpshooters, and stepped down into the work. As he did so he handed the captain the cup of water, in the quietest manner apologizing for having spilled part of it, adding that he had met with a trivial accident. The upper joint of his thumb had been shot away, yet he had not dropped the cup. Then he turned to me and asked my pardon for his disregard of my warning and his imprudence in getting shot, protesting still, however, that it was very hard indeed for a gentleman to walk in those filthy, abominable covered ways.

The spring was perhaps the point of greatest power and pathos in all the weird drama of "The Lines." About this date, or very soon after, a few of us were sitting in the part of the trenches occupied by the Twenty-first Mississippi, of our old brigade—Barksdale's, now Humphreys'—which was supporting our guns. There had been a number of Yale men in the Twenty-first—the Sims, Smiths, Brandon, Scott, and perhaps others. A good many were "gone," and those of us who were left were talking of them and of good times at Old Yale, when some one said, "Scott, isn't it your turn to go to the spring?" "Yes," said Scott, submissively, "I believe it is. Pass up your canteens," and he loaded up and started out. There was a particularly exposed spot on the way to water, which we had tried in vain to protect more perfectly, and we heard, as usual, two or three rifle shots as Scott passed that point. In due time we heard them again as he returned, and one of the fellows said, "Ha! they are waking up old Scott, again, on the home stretch."

The smile had not died upon our faces when a head appeared above the traverse and a business-like voice called: "Hello, Company I; man of yours dead out here!" We ran around the angle of the work, and there lay poor Scott, prone in the ditch and almost covered with canteens. We picked him up and bore him tenderly into the trench, and, as we laid him down and composed his limbs, manly tears dropped upon his still face. Each man disengaged and took his own canteen from the slumbering water-carrier. We did not "pour the water out unto the Lord," as David did when the "three mightiest brake through the host of the Philistines and drew water out of the well of Bethlehem that was by the gate"— albeit, in a truer sense than David spoke, this water was the very "blood of this man."

It was about six o'clock in the evening of one of the days that followed close upon the great fight that there befell the company the very saddest loss it had yet experienced. An order had come to Captain McCarthy, from General Alexander, commanding the artillery corps, directing that the effect of the fire of several howitzers, which were operating as mortars, from a position immediately back of the Howitzer guns, should be carefully observed and reported to him. The captain, appreciating at once the responsibility and the peril of the work, with characteristic chivalry, determined to divide it between himself and one of the most competent and careful men in the company. He was not the man to shrink, or slur over, or postpone his own part in any duty, and immediately stationed himself where he could thoroughly discharge it. He had taken his stand but a few moments when he fell back among his men, his brain pierced by a sharpshooter's bullet. The detachment sprang to his aid, but too late even to prevent his fall. His broad breast heaved once or twice as they knelt about him, and it was all over. The men broke down utterly and sobbed like children.

We never found his hat. While his boys were still gazing at him through their tears a Mississippi soldier came working his way along the lines, from a point a hundred feet or more to the right, holding in his hand a little piece of brass, and as he approached the group said: "This here thing has just fell at my feet. I reckon it belongs to some of you artillery fellows"; and then, looking at the noble figure stretched upon the ground, he asked in the dry, matter-of-fact soldier style, "Who's that's dead?" When we told him Captain McCarthy, of the Howitzers, he said musingly: "McCarthy, McCarthy; why, that's the name of the folks that took care o' me, when I was wounded so bad last year. Well, here's the cannons from his hat." And so it was; his hat, as we suppose, had gone over the works, and his badge of cross cannon, dislodged from it by the shock, had fallen at the feet of a man who had been nursed back to life by his mother and sisters in his boyhood's home.

My younger brother was a great favorite in the company. As he had been a sailor, and as we had come from New England to Virginia, he was nicknamed "Skipper." He had a beautiful tenor voice and a unique repertoire of songs from almost every clime and country. Whenever "Skipper" deigned to sing, "the Professor," the trainer of the Glee Club, would enforce absolute silence throughout the camp, under penalty of a heavy battery of maledictions.

The day after Captain McCarthy's death, my brother, being in almost the exact position the Captain occupied when killed, was shot in the left temple, and fell just where the captain had fallen. I was not present at the moment, but the boys reported that as they bent over him, thinking him dead, he raised his head and said, "If you fellows will stand back and give me some air, I'll get up!"—which he not only did, but walked out to the hospital camp, refusing a litter. He also refused to take chloroform, and directed the surgeons in exploring the track of the ball, which had crushed up his temple and the under half of the socket of his eye, and lodged somewhere in behind his nose. After they had extracted the ball and a great deal of crushed bone, he declared there was something else in his head which must come out. The surgeons told him it was more crushed bone which would come away of itself after awhile; but he insisted it was something that did not belong there, and that they must take it away immediately. They remonstrated, but he would not be satisfied, and finally they probed further and drew out a piece of his hat brim, cut just the width of the ball and jammed like a wad into his head; after that he was much easier. I omitted to say we never found his hat, either.

He was blind in the left eye from the moment the ball struck him, and became for a time blind in the other eye also. While in utter darkness he sang most of the time, and I remember our dear mother was troubled by a fancy that, like a mockingbird she once had that went blind in a railroad train, he might sing himself to death. But he recovered the sight of his right eye after a time, and the marvel is that the left eye did not shrink away and was not even discolored. The bony formation of the under-socket of the eye grew up and rectified itself almost entirely, and a lock of his curly hair covered the desperate-looking wound in the temple. It was a wonderful recovery.

THE VALLEY AGAIN

NEITHER LEE NOR GRANT was happy to have his army settle in for a siege of Richmond. Grant had hoped to get flanking forces around to Lee's rear to cut the railroads supplying Richmond. And Lee knew that time was an enemy: time would enable the Federals to increase their strength to a point where sheer numbers would overwhelm the Confederates. There were no new troops to be found for Lee, and supplies were getting shorter and shorter. One faint hope still existed, a hope based on an old tactic that had always worked in the past—an attack force marching up the Shenandoah Valley to threaten Washington. Always before, any threat to Washington had relieved the pressure on Richmond.

In July, General Jubal Early started up the Valley with 14,000 troops; they drove north to within sight of the outlying defenses of the capital. Fortunately for the Federals, Grant rushed a corps up to the city in the nick of time. After only a light skirmish, Early retreated to the Valley.

To clear the Valley, once and for all, General Grant sent General Sheridan into the Valley with about 43,000 men.

"Up to the summer of 1864 the Shenandoah Valley had not been to the Union armies a fortunate place either for battle or for strategy. A glance at the map will go far toward explaining this. The Valley has a general direction from south-west to north-east. The Blue Ridge Mountains, forming its eastern barrier, are well defined from the James River above Lynchburg to Harper's Ferry on the Potomac. Many passes (in Virginia called 'gaps') made it easy of access from the Confederate base of operations; and, bordered by a fruitful country filled with supplies, it offered a tempting highway for an army bent on a flanking march on Washington or the invasion of Maryland or Pennsylvania. For the Union armies, while it was an equally practicable highway, it led away from the objective, Richmond, and was exposed to flank attacks through the gaps from vantage-ground and perfect cover.

"It was not long after General Grant completed his first campaign in Virginia, and while he was in front of Petersburg, that his attention was called to this famous seat of side issues between Union and Confederate armies. With quick military instinct he saw that the Valley was not useful to the Government for aggressive operations. He decided that it must be made untenable for either army. In doing this he reasoned that the

526

advantage would with us, who did not want it as a source of supplies, nor as a place of arms, and against the Confederates, who wanted it for both."*

At Winchester on September 19, Sheridan defeated Early and the Union won, for the first time, a clear-cut victory in the Valley. The next month Early surprised Sheridan's troops at Cedar Run and put them to rout. Only the arrival of Sheridan from Winchester could turn the tide.

Sheridan's Ride †

BY MAJOR GEORGE A. FORSYTH

IN THE MORNING, ABOUT DAYLIGHT, word was brought from the picket-line south of Winchester of heavy firing at the front. General Sheridan interviewed the officer who brought the information, and decided that it must be the result of the reconnoissance that General Wright had notified him the night before was to take place this morning. Little apprehension was occasioned by the report. After breakfast, probably nearly or quite nine o'clock, we mounted and rode at a walk through the town of Winchester to Mill Creek, a mile south of the village, where we found our escort awaiting us.

We could occasionally hear the far-away sound of heavy guns, and as we moved out with our escort behind us I thought that the general was becoming anxious. He leaned forward and listened intently, and once he dismounted and placed his ear near the ground, seeming somewhat disconcerted as he rose again and remounted. We had not gone far, probably not more than a mile, when, at the crest of a little hill on the road, we found the pike obstructed by some supply-trains which had started on their way to the army. They were now halted, and seemingly in great confusion. Part of the wagons faced one way, part the other; others were half turned round, in position to swing either way, but were huddled together, completely blocking the road.

Turning to me, the general said, "Ride forward quickly and find out the trouble here, and report promptly." I role rapidly to the head of the train and asked for the quartermaster in charge, and was told he had gone up the road a short distance.

On reaching him, I found him conversing with a quartermaster-sergeant. They informed me that an officer had come from the front and told them to go back at once, as our army had been attacked at daylight, defeated, and was being driven down the valley. The officer, they said, had gone back towards the front after warning them to come no further.

---

* From General Wesley Merritt, "Sheridan in the Shenandoah Valley," *Battles and Leaders*, Vol. IV.

† From *Thrilling Days in Army Life*.

Galloping back, I made my report. "Pick out fifty of the best-mounted men from the escort," was the response. Riding down the column, with the aid of one of the officers of the regiment, this was soon accomplished, and I reported with the selected men. Turning to his chief of staff, Colonel J. W. Forsyth, the general said something regarding certain instructions he had evidently been giving him, and then said to me, "You and Captain O'Keeffe will go with me"; and nodding good-bye to the other gentlemen of our party, with whom he had probably been conferring while I was making up the cavalry detail, he turned his horse's head southward, tightening the reins of his bridle, and with a slight touch of the spur he dashed up the turnpike and was off. A yard in rear, and side by side, Captain O'Keeffe and myself swept after him, while the escort, breaking from a trot to a gallop, came thundering on behind.

The distance from Winchester to Cedar Creek, on the north bank of which the Army of the Shenandoah lay encamped, is a little less than nineteen miles. The general direction was west of south, and the road to it, by way of the valley pike, ran directly through the road-side hamlets of Milltown, Kearnstown, Newtown, and Middletown. Our army was encamped four miles south of Middletown. The Shenandoah Valley turnpike, over which we were now speeding, was formerly a well-built macadamized road, laid in crushed limestone, and until the advent of the war had been kept in excellent condition. Even now, though worn for three years past by the tread of contending armies with all the paraphernalia of war as they swept up and down the valley, it was a fairly good road; but the army supply-trains, ammunition-wagons, and artillery had worn it into deep ruts in places, and everywhere the dust lay thick and heavy on its surface, and powdered the trees and bushes that fringed its sides, so that our galloping column sent a gray cloud swirling behind us. It was a golden sunny day that had succeeded a densely foggy October morning. The turnpike stretched away, a white, dusty line, over hill and through dale, bordered by fenceless fields, and past farm-houses and empty barns and straggling orchards. Now and then it ran through a woody copse, with here and there a tiny stream of water crossing it, or meandering by its side, so clear and limpid that it seemed to invite us to pause and slake our thirst as we sped along our dusty way. On either side we saw, through the Indian-summer haze, the distant hills covered with woods and fairly ablaze with foliage; and over all was the deep blue of a cloudless Southern sky, making it a day on which one's blood ran riot and he was glad of health and life.

Within a mile we met more supply-trains that had turned back, and the general stopped long enough to order the officer in charge to halt, park his trains just where he was, and await further instructions. Then on we dashed again, only to meet, within a few moments, more supply-trains hurrying to the rear. The general did not stop, but signalling the officer in charge to join him, gave him instructions on the gallop to park his train at once, and use his escort to arrest and stop all stragglers coming from the army, and to send back to the front all well men who might drift to him, under guard if necessary.

Scarcely had we parted from him and surmounted the next rise in the road when we came suddenly upon indubitable evidence of battle and retreat. About a mile in advance of us the road was filled and the fields dotted with wagons and men belonging to the various brigade, division, and corps headquarters, and in among them officers' servants with led horses, and here and there a broken ambulance, sutlers' supply-trains, a battery forge or two, horses and mules hastily packed with officers' mess kits, led by their cooks, and now and then a group of soldiers, evidently detailed enlisted men attached to the headquarters trains. In fact, this was the first driftwood of a flood just beyond and soon to come sweeping down the road. Passing this accumulation of debris with a rush by leaving the pike and galloping over the open fields on the side of the road, we pushed rapidly on; but not so quickly but that we caught an echoing cheer from the enlisted men and servants, who recognized the general, and shouted and swung their hats in glee.

Within the next few miles the pike and adjacent fields began to be lined and dotted everywhere with army wagons, sutlers' outfits, head-quarters supply-trains, disabled caissons, and teamsters with led mules, all drifting to the rear; and now and then a wounded officer or enlisted man on horseback or plodding along on foot, with groups of straggling soldiers here and there among the wagon-trains, or in the fields, or some-times sitting or lying down to rest by the side of the road, while others were making coffee in their tin cups by tiny camp-fires. Soon we began to see small bodies of soldiers in the fields with stacked arms, evidently cooking breakfast. As we debouched into the fields and passed around the wagons and through these groups, the general would wave his hat to the men and point to the front, never lessening his speed as he pressed forward. It was enough; one glance at the eager face and familiar black horse and they knew him, and starting to their feet, they swung their caps around their heads and broke into cheers as he passed beyond them; and then, gathering up their belongings and shouldering their arms, they started after him for the front, shouting to their comrades further out in the fields, "Sheridan! Sheridan!" waving their hats, and pointing after him as he dashed onward; and they too comprehended instantly, for they took up the cheer and turned back for the battle-field.

To the best of my recollection, from the time we met the first stragglers who had drifted back from the army, his appearance and his cheery shout of "Turn back, men! turn back! Face the other way!" as he waved his hat towards the front, had but one result: a wild cheer of recognition, an answering wave of the cap. In no case, as I glanced back, did I fail to see the men shoulder their arms and follow us. I think it is no exaggeration to say that as he dashed on to the field of battle, for miles back the turnpike was lined with men pressing forward after him to the front.

So rapid had been our gait that nearly all of the escort, save the commanding officer and a few of his best-mounted men, had been distanced, for they were more heavily weighted, and ordinary troop horses could not live at such a pace. Once we were safe among our own people, their commander had the good sense to see that his services were no longer a necessity, and accordingly drew rein and saved his horses by following on at a slow trot. Once the general halted a moment to speak to an officer he knew and inquire for information. As he did so he turned and asked me to get him a switch; for he usually rode carrying a light riding-whip, and furthermore he had broken one of the rowels of his spurs. Dismounting, I cut one from a near-by way-side bush, hastily trimmed it, and gave it him. "Thanks, Sandy," said he, and as we started again he struck his splendid black charger Rienzi a slight blow across the shoulder with it, and he at once broke into that long swinging gallop, almost a run, which he seemed to maintain so easily and so endlessly—a most distressing gait for those who had to follow far. These two words of thanks were nearly the only ones he addressed to me until we reached the army; but my eyes had sought his face at every opportunity, and my heart beat high with hope from what I saw there. As he galloped on his features gradually grew set, as though carved in stone, and the same dull red glint I had seen in his piercing black eyes when, on other occasions, the battle was going against us, was there now. Occasionally Captain O'Keeffe and myself exchanged a few words, and we waved our hats and shouted to the men on the road and in the fields as we passed them, pointing to the general and seconding as best we could his energetic shout: "Turn back, men! turn back! Face the other way!" Now and then I would glance at the face of my companion, Captain O'Keeffe, whose gray-blue eyes fairly danced with excitement at the prospect of the coming fray; for if ever a man was a born soldier and loved fighting for chivalry's sake, it was that gallant young Irish gentleman, Joe O'Keeffe.

Each moment that we advanced the road became more closely clogged with stragglers and wounded men, and here the general suddenly paused to speak to one of the wounded officers, from whom I judge he got his only correct idea of the attack by the enemy at dawn, the crushing of our left, and the steady outflanking that had forced our army back to where it was at present, for I caught something of what the officer said, and his ideas seemed to be clear and concise. This pause was a piece of rare good fortune for me, for my orderly happened to be by the side of the road with my led horse, and in a trice he changed my saddle, and I rejoined the general ere he was a hundred yards away, with all the elation that a fresh mount after a weary one inspires in the heart of a cavalryman.

Within a comparatively short distance we came suddenly upon a field-hospital in a farm-house close to the road beyond Newton, where the medical director had established part of his corps. Just ahead of us the road was filled with ambulances containing wounded men, who were being carried into the house to be operated upon, while outside of the door along the foot-path lay several dead men, who had been hastily placed there on being taken from the stretchers. The vicinity was dotted with wounded men, sitting or lying down or standing around, waiting to have their wounds dressed, while the surgeons were flitting here and there doing their best and straining every nerve to meet their necessities. Giving the place a wide berth, after the first glance, and galloping around the line of ambulances that filled the pike, we passed through a fringe of woods, up a slight eminence in the road, and in a flash we were in full view of the battle-field. It was a gruesome sight to meet the eyes of a commanding general who, three short days before, had left it a triumphant host lying quietly in camp, resting securely on its victories, and confident in its own strength. And now!

In our immediate front the road and adjacent fields were filled with sections of artillery, caissons, ammunition-trains, ambulances, battery-wagons, squads of mounted men, led horses, wounded soldiers, broken wagons, stragglers, and stretcher-bearers—in fact, all that appertains to and is part of the rear of an army in action. One hasty glance as we galloped forward and we had taken in the situation. About half or three-quarters of a mile this side of Middletown, with its left resting upon the turnpike, was a division of infantry in line of battle at right angles to the road, with its standards flying, and evidently held well in hand. Near the turnpike, and just to its left, one of our batteries was having a savage artillery duel with a Confederate battery, which was in position on a little hill to the left and rear of Middletown as we faced it. To the left of this battery of ours were the led horses of a small brigade of cavalry, which was holding the ground to the left of the pike, and both the infantry and cavalry dismounted skirmishers were in action with those of the enemy. Further to the left, and slightly to the rear, on a bit of rising ground, was another of our batteries in action. Half a mile to the right, and somewhat to the rear of the division of infantry which was in line of battle, could be seen a body of infantry in column slowly retiring and tending towards the pike; and just beyond these troops was another body of infantry, also in column, and also moving in the same general direction. Further to the right, across a small valley, and more than a mile away from these last-mentioned troops, was a still larger force of infantry, on a side-hill, facing towards the enemy, in line of battle, but not in action. I looked in vain for the cavalry divisions, but concluded rightly that they were somewhere on the flanks of the enemy.

Skirting the road, and avoiding as best we might the impedimenta of battle; the general, O'Keefe, and myself spurred forward. Finally, on the open road and just before we reached the troops in line, which was Getty's division of the Sixth Army Corps, I asked permission to go directly down to the skirmish-line to see the actual condition of things. "Do so," replied the general, "and report as soon as possible." Just then we reached the line, and as I glanced back I saw the chief draw rein in the midst of the division, where he was greeted by a storm of cheers and wild cries of "Sheridan! Sheridan!" while standards seemed to spring up out of the very earth to greet him. A few seconds later and I was on the skirmish-line by the side of Colonel Charles R. Lowell, commanding the regular cavalry brigade.

"Is Sheridan here?"

"Yes."

"Thank goodness for that!"

At this moment Mr. Stillson, the war correspondent of one of the New York newspapers (who had risked his life for news more than once, and in fact was doing it now), rode up and made the same inquiry.

"He is here," was my reply.

"Well? What is he going to do about it?"

"He's going to whale blank out of them."

"He can't do it," shaking his head.

"Wait, and you'll see."

"I wish I may," said the plucky correspondent, "but I doubt it," and he turned and rode back to find the general.

Turning again to Colonel Lowell, I eagerly asked for the facts about the battle, well knowing that there was no cooler head or better brain in all the army, nor one to be more absolutely relied upon. As we rode along the skirmish-line, that I might get a better view of the enemy, he gave me the details as he knew them. Then, as we watched the enemy forming his battalions in the distance for another advance, I put the question:

"Can you hold on here forty minutes?"

"Yes."

"Can you make it sixty?"

"It depends; you see what they are doing. I will if I can."

"Hold on as long as possible," said I; and turning, I rode rapidly back to my chief, whom I found dismounted, surrounded by several general officers, and in the midst of those of his staff who had not gone with us to Washington. Dismounting, I saluted. Stepping on one side from the group, he faced me, and said,

"Well?"

"You see where we are?" (A nod.) "Lowell says that our losses, killed, wounded, and missing, are between three and five thousand, and more than twenty guns, to say nothing of transportation. He thinks he can hold on where he is for forty minutes longer, possibly sixty."

I can see him before me now as I write, erect, looking intently in my eyes, his left hand resting, clinched savagely, on the top of the hilt of his sabre, his right nervously stroking his chin, his eyes with that strange red gleam in them, and his attenuated features set as if cast in bronze. He stood mute and absolutely still for more than ten seconds; then, throwing up his head, he said:

"Go to the right and find the other two divisions of the Sixth Corps, and also General Emory's command [the two divisions of the Nineteenth Corps]. Bring them up, and order them to take position on the right of Getty. Lose no time." And as I turned to mount, he called out: "Stay! I'll go with you!" And springing on his horse, we set off together, followed by the staff.

Riding up closely to him, I said, "Pardon me, general, but I think if I had control of a division I could do good work here."

Looking at me squarely in the eyes for a few seconds, he replied: "Do you? Perhaps I'll give you control of more than that."

Not another word was said, and in a few moments we had reached the head of the nearest division we were seeking. It was ordered on the line— I think by the general himself; and as I started for the head of the other division, he ordered me to ride directly over to General Emory's command (two divisions of the Nineteenth Corps), and order it up, to take position in line of battle on the right of the Sixth Corps. I rode over to General Emory's line, which was about a mile away, and found his troops in good condition, though somewhat shattered by the fortunes of the day, facing towards the enemy, and half covered by small ledges of rock that cropped out of the hill-side. On receiving the order, he called my attention to the fact that in case the enemy advanced on the Sixth Corps, he would be nearly on their flank, and thought best that I apprise the commanding general of the fact, as it might induce him to modify the order. Galloping back, I gave his suggestion to the general.

"No, no!" he replied. "Get him over *at once—at once!* Don't lose a moment!"

I fairly tore back, and the troops were promptly put in motion for their new position, which they reached in due time, and were formed in line of battle in accordance with General Sheridan's orders.

After the whole line was thoroughly formed, I rode over to my chief and urged him to ride down it, that all the men might see him, and know without doubt that he had returned and assumed command. At first he demurred, but I was most urgent, as I knew that in some instances both men and officers who had not seen him doubted his arrival. His appearance was greeted by tremendous cheers from one end of the line to the other, many of the officers pressing forward to shake his hand. He spoke to them all, cheerily and confidently, saying: "We are going back to our camps, men, never fear. I'll get a twist on these people yet. We'll raise them out of their boots before the day is over."

At no time did I hear him utter that "terrible oath" so often alluded to in both prose and poetry in connection with this day's work.

As we turned to go back from the end of the line, he halted on the line of the Nineteenth Corps and said to me: "Stay here and help fight this corps. I will send orders to General Emory through you. Give orders in my name, if necessary. Stay right on this line with it."

"Very good, general," was my reply; and the general and staff left me there and galloped towards the pike.

It must have been nearly or quite half-past twelve o'clock by this time, and as soon as the skirmishers were thrown forward the troops were ordered to lie down; an order gladly obeyed, for they had been on their feet since daylight, fighting and without food. They were to have but a short period of rest, however, for in a few moments the low rustling murmur, that presages the advance of a line of battle through dense woods (the Nineteenth Corps was formed just at the outer edge of a belt of heavy timber) began to make itself felt, and in a moment the men were in line again. A pattering fire in front, and our skirmishers came quickly back through the woods, and were absorbed in the line; then there was a momentary lull, followed by a rustling, crunching sound as the enemy's line pressed forward, trampling the bushes under foot, and crowding through bits of underbrush.

In a flash we caught a glimpse of a long gray line stretching away through the woods on either side of us, advancing with waving standards, with here and there a mounted officer in rear of it. At the same instant the dark blue line at the edge of the woods seemed to burst upon their view, for suddenly they halted, and with a piercing yell poured in a heavy volley, that was almost instantly answered from our side, and then volleys seemed fairly to leap from one end to the other of our line, and a steady roar of musketry from both sides made the woods echo again in every direction. Gradually, however, the sounds became less heavy and intense, the volleys slowly died away, and we began to recognize the fact that the enemy's bullets were no longer clipping the twigs above us, and that their fire had about ceased, while a ringing cheer along our front proclaimed that for the first time that day the Confederate army had been repulsed.

During the attack my whole thought, and I believe that of every officer on the line, had been to prevent our troops from giving way. In one or two places the line wavered slightly, but the universal shout of "Steady, men, *steady, steady!*" as the field-officers rode up and down the line, seemed to be all that was needed to inspire the few nervous ones with renewed courage and hold them well up to their work. As for myself, I was more than satisfied, for only years of personal experience in war enable a man to appreciate at its actual value the tremendous gain when a routed army turns, faces, and checks a triumphant enemy in the open field. It is a great thing to do it with the aid of reinforcements; it is a glorious thing to do it without.

For a few moments the men stood leaning on their arms, and some of us mounted officers rode slowly forward, anxiously peering through the trees, but save for a dead man or two there was no sign of the enemy; the Confederates had fallen back. Word was passed back to the line, and the men were ordered to lie down, which they willingly did. I rode slowly up and down the line of the Nineteenth Corps, and after a few moments grew impatient for orders, for as a cavalryman my first thought, after the repulse of the enemy, was a countercharge. The minutes crept slowly by, and nothing came, not even an aide for information. Twenty minutes elapsed, thirty, forty, fifty, and I could wait no longer, but galloped to army headquarters, which I found to the right of the turnpike, about two hundred yards in rear of the Sixth Corps. Dismounting, I went up and saluted the commanding general, who was half lying down, with his head resting on his right hand, his elbow on the ground, and surrounded by most of his staff. Colonel J. W. Forsyth, his chief of staff, as well as Colonels Alexander and Thom of the Engineer Corps, were with him, having reached the field since I had been on the line with the Nineteenth Corps.

"Well, what is it?" said the general.

"It seems to me, general, that we ought to advance; I have come hoping for orders." He half sat up, and the black eyes flashed. I realized that I had laid myself open to censure; but gradually an amused look overshadowed the anxious face, and the chief slowly shook his head.

"Not yet, not yet; go back and wait."

I saluted, mounted, and rode leisurely back, cogitating as I went. I knew that there must be some good reason for the delay, but as yet I was unable to fathom it. Reaching the rear of the centre of the Nineteenth Corps, I found a shady spot, and dismounting, sat down on the ground just back of the line, holding my horse's bridle in my hand, for I had no orderly with me. Very soon I became interested in watching the various phases of the situation as they developed before me, and I soon saw one reason for delay, and that was that we were steadily growing stronger. The tired troops had thrown themselves on the ground at the edge of the woods, and lay on their arms in line of battle, listlessly and sleepily. Every now and then stragglers—sometimes singly, oftener in groups—came up from the rear, and moving along back of the line, dusty, heavy-footed, and tired, found and rejoined their respective companies and regiments, dropping down quietly by the side of their companions as they came to them, with a gibe or a word or two of greeting on either side, and then they, too, like most of the rest, subsided into an appearance of apathetic indifference. Here and there men loaded with canteens were sent to the rear in search of water; and every few yards soldiers lay munching a bit of hardtack, the first food many of them had had during the day, for they were driven from their camps at daylight.

Little was said by officers or men, for the truth was that nearly all were tired, troubled, and somewhat disheartened by the disaster that had so unexpectedly overtaken them; for even in the light of existing events the Confederates had triumphed. They had been routed from their position, their left overwhelmed, crushed, and driven in upon the centre, and the whole army repeatedly outflanked and forced back beyond Middletown, a distance of nearly five miles, where they now were, with the loss of many cannon, most of their wounded, thousands of prisoners, and quantities of transportation—this, too, by a foe whom they believed practically vanquished, and whom they had defeated in pitched battle twice within the last thirty days. This unpalatable fact burned itself into their brain as they lay prone on the ground, with their rifles beside them, trying to snatch a few moments' troubled sleep for their heavy eyes and weary bodies. It must have been a bitter cud to chew.

As the moments continued to pass with no orders from headquarters I grew impatient again, notwithstanding the fact that the delay was increasing our strength by the return of stragglers and the reorganization of scattered regiments, as well as giving a much-needed rest to the whole army. For the foe was also resting, and probably gaining strength in the same manner, so I mounted and passed through our line, and rode out towards the enemy as far as I could with reasonable safety. Owing to the woods and the conformation of the ground, I could not accurately determine anything, so I came back and went again to army headquarters. I reported my actions, and told the general how I had not been able to satisfy myself as to the present location of the enemy's line, but I thought the men were sufficiently rested to advance in good heart. He did not reply immediately, but seemed thoughtful and perplexed.

Finally he shook his head, and said, "Not yet, not yet; go back and wait patiently."

Riding back to my former location, I dismounted and sat down again, much puzzled to know the reason for this inaction, as it was so unlike what I had seen of my chief, who was always so quick to see and prompt to act, especially on the field of battle. I think it must have been nearly an hour when I again passed to the front of our line, gave my horse to one of the skirmishers, and cautiously stole through the woods, till, on surmounting a slight rise, I distinctly heard sounds that indicated the vicinity of the enemy, and by crawling forward I saw his line in the distance, and made out that the Confederates were piling up stones and rails on the prolongation of a line of stone fences, evidently expecting an advance from our side and preparing for it.

I returned at once, and for the third time reported at army headquarters. As I came up I noticed that the general had evidently just received a report of some kind from an officer who was riding off as I made my appearance. Reporting what I had heard and seen, he glanced up brightly and said:

"It's all right now! I have been kept back by a report of troops coming down in our rear by way of the Front Royal pike. It's not so, however." Then, turning to one of his staff officers, he asked for the time of day.

"Twenty minutes to four," was the reply.

"So late!" said the general. "Why, that's later than I thought!" And then, turning again to me, he said: "Tell General Wright to move forward the Sixth Corps and attack at once, keeping his left on the pike; then tell General Emory to advance at the same time, keeping the left of the Nineteenth Corps well closed on the right of the Sixth Corps; if opportunity offers, swing the right division of the Nineteenth Corps to the left, and drive the enemy towards the pike. I will put what is available of General Crook's forces on the left of the pike and General Merritt's cavalry also, and send Custer well out on Emory's right to cover that flank. Do you clearly comprehend?"

"Certainly! The Sixth and Nineteenth Corps attack, with Merritt's cavalry on the left and Custer's on the right, the right division of the Nineteenth to try and outflank the enemy and swing towards the pike."

"Good!" said the general, with a quick nod, and I saluted and sprang to my saddle with a feeling of elation difficult for one not a soldier to adequately comprehend.

I found General Wright just in rear of his corps, lying on the ground. He sat up as I reported, and I saw that his beard was clotted with blood and his neck and chin swollen, and he spoke with something of an effort. He had been shot just under the chin early in the day, but had retained command of the army until General Sheridan's arrival, and then assumed command of his own corps. On receiving General Sheridan's order, he said:

"Do I understand that General Emory's troops connect with my right flank?"

"Certainly!"

"And General Crook's forces will be on the left of the pike?"

"Yes, and General Merritt's cavalry also."

"Very well."

And as I saluted and turned away he was already giving orders to his aides. I rode rapidly to General Emory and repeated the commanding general's instructions, and then returned to my former station in rear of the right centre of the Nineteenth Corps.

In a few moments the news ran down the line that we were to advance. Springing to their feet at the word of command, the tired troops stood to arms and seemed to resolutely shake off the depression that had sat so heavily upon them, and began to pull themselves together for the coming fray. Everywhere along the line of battle men might be seen to stoop and retie their shoes; to pull their trousers at the ankle tightly together and then draw up their heavy woollen stockings over them; to rebuckle and tighten their waist-belts; to unbutton the lids of their cartridge-boxes and pull them forward rather more to the front; to rearrange their haversacks and canteens, and to shift their rolls of blankets in order to give freer scope to the expansion of their shoulders and an easier play to their arms; to set their forage-caps tighter on their heads, pulling the vizor well down over their eyes; and then, almost as if by order, there rang from one end of the line to the other the rattle of ramrods and snapping of gunlocks as each man tested for himself the condition of his rifle, and made sure that his weapon was in good order and to be depended upon in the emergency that was so soon to arise. Then, grounding arms, they stood at ease, half leaning on their rifles, saying little, but quietly awaiting orders and grimly gazing straight towards the front. In front of the battalions, with drawn swords and set lips, stood their line-officers, slightly craning their heads forward and looking into the woods, as if trying to catch a glimpse of the enemy they knew to be somewhere there, but whom as yet they could not see.

I push through the line slightly forward of the nearest brigade, and in a moment the sharp command, "Attention!" rings down the line. "Shoulder arms! Forward! *March!*" And with martial tread and floating flags the line of battle is away. "Guide left!" shout the line-officers. "Guide left —*left!*" and that is the only order I hear as we press forward through the thick trees and underbrush. I lean well forward on my horse's neck, striving to catch if possible a glimpse of the Confederate line; but hark! Here comes the first shot. "Steady! *Steady,* men!" Another, and now a few scattering bullets come singing through the woods. The line does not halt or return the fire, but presses steadily on to the oft-repeated command of "Forward! *forward!*" that never ceases to ring from one end to the other of the advancing line. Soon the woods become less dense, and through the trees I see just beyond us an open field partly covered with small bushes, and several hundred yards away, crowning a slight crest on its further side, a low line of fence-rails and loose stones, which, as we leave the edge of the woods, and come into the open, suddenly vomits flame and smoke along its entire length, and a crashing volley tells us that we have found the enemy. For an instant our line staggers, but the volley has been aimed too high and few men fall. "Steady—steady, men!" shout the officers. *"Aim!"* and almost instinctively the whole line throw forward their pieces. *"Fire!"* and the next instant a savage volley answers that of the Confederates. I can see that it has told, too, for in several places along the opposite crest men spring to their feet as if to fall back, but their officers promptly rally them. "Pour it into them, men!" shout our officers. "Let them have it. It's our turn now!" for brute instinct has triumphed and the savage is uppermost with all of us. For a moment or two the men stand and fire at will, as rapidly as it is possible to reload, and then the Confederate fire seems to slowly slacken; so, with a universal shout of "Forward! *forward!*" we press towards the enemy's line. Before we are much more than half way across the field, however, they seem to have abandoned our front, for I cannot see anything ahead of us, though I stand up in my stirrups and look eagerly forward. But what—what is that? *Crash! crash!* and from a little bush-covered plateau on our right the enemy sends a couple of rattling volleys on our exposed flank that do us great harm, and I realize that *we are the outflanked!*

For an instant the line gives way, but every mounted officer in the vicinity, among whom I recognize General Fessenden, seems to be instantly on the spot trying to rally the troops and hold the line. *"Steady!*

steady! Right wheel!" is the shout, and the men, after the first flush of surprise, behave splendidly, one young color-bearer rushing to the right and waving his flag defiantly in the new direction from which the enemy's fire is now coming. I ask him to let me take it, as I am mounted and it can be seen better, as there is some undergrowth at this particular spot in the field. At first he demurs, but seeing the point, yields. Holding on to my saddle, the color-bearer accompanies me towards a slight hillock. The line catches sight of it, and the left begins to swing slowly round, the men in our immediate vicinity loading and firing as rapidly as they can in the direction from which the enemy is now advancing. The Confederates are giving it to us hot, and we realize that we have lost the continuity of our line on both flanks.

Suddenly peal on peal of musketry broke out on our right, and the copse in front of us was fairly bullet-swept by repeated volleys. The next moment a portion of one of McMillan's brigades, which he had promptly swung round and faced to the right, dashed forward, and together we moved up to the position just held by the enemy, to find that he was in headlong retreat. One hasty look and I saw that we had pierced the enemy's line, and that his extreme left was cut off and scattered. But I could not see any troops nor anything of his line over in the direction of the pike, as there was a dense belt of woods that shut out the view. Nevertheless, the steady roar of artillery and peals of musketry told us that heavy fighting was going on in that part of the field. General McMillan was already re-forming his men to move over and take up the line and our former direction to the left, when General Sheridan, riding his gray charger Breckenridge, and surrounded by his staff, came out of the woods and dashed up. One glance and he had the situation. "This is all right! this is all right!" was his sole comment. Then turning to General McMillan, he directed him to continue the movement and close up to the left and complete our line of battle as it originally was.

He told me, however, to hold the troops until I saw that Custer had driven the enemy's cavalry from our flank. This we could easily see, as the country was open and the ground lower than where we were. Having given these instructions, the general, followed by his staff, galloped rapidly to the left and rear through the woods, evidently making for the pike, where, judging from the continued roar of field-guns and musketry, the Sixth Corps was having savage work.

As soon as we saw General Custer's squadrons charge across the field and engage the enemy's cavalry, General McMillan ordered the advance, and we pushed forward, driving the enemy ahead of us through the wood, and came out to the left and rear of the Confederate line, enabling our left to pour in a fearful fire on their exposed flank. The enemy was gallantly holding his line behind some stone fences, but "flesh that is born of woman" could not stand such work as this, and the cavalry, having got well in on their right flank about this time, gave way in retreat.

Our whole army now pressed rapidly forward, not stopping to re-form, but driving them from each new line of defence; but it was no walk-over even then, for the Confederates fought splendidly—desperately even. They tried to take advantage of every stone fence, house, or piece of woods on which to rally their men and retard our advance. Their batteries were served gallantly and handled brilliantly, and took up position after position; but it was all in vain, for we outnumbered them, both cavalry and infantry, and their men must have comprehended the fact that our cavalry was turning both their flanks. They made their last stand on the hills just this side of Cedar Creek, occupying the reverse side of some of our own earthworks; and when the infantry I was with came up to Belle Plain, which was the house General Sheridan had occupied as headquarters prior to his departure for Washington, it was already getting quite dark. I dismounted here and ran in a moment to see whether Colonel Tolles and Dr. Ohlenschlaeger, two of General Sheridan's staff who had been wounded by guerillas, were still living. They were still alive, but unconscious, and some one (a Confederate, I think), fearing that the house might be shelled during the action, had placed their mattresses on the floor to keep them as far out of harm's way as possible. Hurrying out, I pushed on with the infantry.

For a few moments the Confederates held their position on the hills, but suddenly abandoned it in haste and sought safety in flight, for some of General Custer's cavalry had crossed the creek at the ford below and were getting in their rear, and to remain was to be captured. I soon caught up with some of our cavalry regiments, and we started in full cry after the enemy. It was no use for them to attempt anything but flight from this on, and they abandoned everything and got away from our pursuing squadrons as best they might, hundreds of them leaving the pike and scattering through the hills. On we went, pell-mell, in the dark. Two regiments, the Fifth New York Cavalry and the First Vermont Cavalry, to the best of my recollection, were the only regimental organizations that went beyond Strasburg. The road was literally crammed with abandoned wagons, ambulances, caissons, and artillery.

At a small bridge, where a creek crosses the road some distance south of the town, we were fired upon from the opposite side by what I thought was the last organized force of General Early's army. I now believe it to have been his provost guard with a large body of our prisoners captured by the enemy early in the day. The planks of this bridge were torn up to prevent the enemy from coming back during the night and carrying off any of the captured property. I then started to return to headquarters, counting the captured cannon as I went. It soon occurred to me that as it was so dark I might mistake a caisson for a gun, so I dismounted and placed my hand on each piece. I reached headquarters about half-past eight or possibly nine o'clock. Camp-fires were blazing everywhere. I went up to the chief, who was standing near a bright fire surrounded by a group of officers and saluted, reporting my return.

"Where do you come from?"

"Beyond Strasburg."

"What news have you?"

"The road is lined with transportation of almost every kind, and we have captured forty-four pieces of artillery."

"How do you *know* that we have forty-four pieces?"

"I have placed my hand on each and every gun."

Standing there in the firelight I saw my chief's face light up with a great wave of satisfaction.

BEFORE PETERSBURG

A STALEMATE OCCURRED AT COLD HARBOR and lasted for about two weeks. Grant could not break the Confederate lines by frontal assault, nor could he continue to sideslip around Lee's right flank; such a maneuver would simply take Grant farther away from Richmond. Instead, he marched south, bearing slightly to the east, toward the banks of the James River where he hoped to make a crossing before Lee could get at him.

Grant made "careful preparations for the formidable movement he was about to undertake, for he was fully impressed by its hazardous nature. The army had to be withdrawn so quietly from its position that it would be able to gain a night's march before its absence could be discovered. The fact that the lines were within thirty to forty yards of each other at some points made this an exceedingly delicate task. Roads had to be constructed over the marshes leading to the lower Chickahominy, and bridges thrown over that stream preparatory to crossing. The army was then to move to the James and cross upon pontoon bridges and improvised ferries. This would involve a march of about fifty miles. . . . Lee, holding interior lines, could arrive there by a march of less than half that distance."*

The maneuver was a great success. By June 16 Grant had the army with all its artillery safely across. A great opportunity to capture Petersburg—an important rail center twenty-two miles south of Richmond, by which the Southern capital was supplied—was missed when two corps of Grant's army failed to coordinate their attack on Beauregard's very thin defenses. On June 20 Lee moved the Army of Northern Virginia into the fortifications around Richmond, and Petersburg was secure. The war could have been shortened by the capture of Petersburg, but at long last Grant had won an important tactical advantage over Lee: he had forced the Confederate general into a siege position, thus depriving the Army of Northern Virginia of its awesomely effective mobility.

Frontal assaults on the Confederate fortifications were launched from time to time, but more as probes than attempts to provoke a major battle. Grant dug and strengthened trenches and continued to extend them to the west, hoping to secure a position from which to cut the two railroads

* From Horace Porter, *Campaigning with Grant.*

still open to Richmond. The most famous attempt to break through the Petersburg defenses was by mine explosion. The mine-blast planner, Colonel Pleasants, had little help from the army engineers, but he refused to be discouraged. He says:

"My regiment was only about four hundred strong. At first I employed but a few men at a time, but the number was increased as the work progressed, until at last I had to use the whole regiment—non-commissioned officers and all. The great difficulty I had was to dispose of the material got out of the mine. I found it impossible to get any assistance from anybody; I had to do all the work myself. I had to remove all the earth in old cracker-boxes; I got pieces of hickory and nailed on the boxes in which we received our crackers, and then iron-clad them with hoops of iron taken from old pork and beef barrels. . . . Whenever I made application I could not get anything, although General Burnside was very favorable to it. The most important thing was to ascertain how far I had to mine, because if I fell short of or went beyond the proper place, the explosion would have no practical effect. Therefore I wanted an accurate instrument with which to make the necessary triangulations. I had to make them on the farthest front line, where the enemy's sharp-shooters could reach me. I could not get the instrument I wanted, although there was one at army headquarters, and General Burnside had to send to Washington and get an old-fashioned theodolite, which was given to me. . . . General Burnside told me that General Meade and Major Duane, chief engineer of the Army of the Potomac, said the thing could not be done—that it was all clap-trap and nonsense; that such a length of mine had never been excavated in military operations, and could not be; that I would either get the men smothered, for want of air, or crushed by the falling of the earth; or the enemy would find it out and it would amount to nothing. I could get no boards or lumber supplied to me for my operations. I had to get a pass and send two companies of my own regiment, with wagons, outside of our lines to rebel saw-mills, and get lumber in that way, after having previously got what lumber I could by tearing down an old bridge."*

The mine was finished by July 22; an attack was to be coordinated with the explosion early on the thirtieth. "Immediately after the explosion two brigades were to pass through the opening made in the enemy's works, in two columns, one to turn to the right, and the other to the left. Three other divisions would charge directly for the summit of the hill. After them would advance the 18th Corps, and our success seemed assured. Once established on the hill, Petersburg would be ours on July 30th.

"The hour set for the explosion was half past three in the morning. Everyone was up, the officers watch in hand, eyes fixed on the fated redan. From after three the minutes were counted. . . . It is still too dark, it was said. . . . At four o'clock it was daylight; nothing stirred as yet. At a quarter past four a murmur of impatience ran through the ranks. What has happened? Has there been a counterorder or an accident?

"What had happened was that the fuse, which was ninety feet long, had gone out at a splice about halfway of its length. Two intrepid men volunteered to relight it. Suddenly the earth trembled under our feet. An

* From *Battles and Leaders*, Vol. IV.

Petersburg: *Slaughter at the Crater*

enormous mass sprang into the air. Without form or shape, full of red flames and carried on a bed of lightning flashes, it mounted toward heaven with a detonation of thunder. It spread out like an immense mushroom whose stem seemed to be of fire and its head of smoke.

"Then everything appeared to break up and fall back in a rain of earth mixed with rocks, beams, timbers and mangled human bodies, leaving floating in the air a cloud of white smoke and a cloud of grey dust, which fell slowly toward the earth. The redan had disappeared. In its place had opened a gaping gulf more than 200 feet long and 50 wide and 25 to 30 feet deep.

"All our batteries opened at once on the enemy's entrenchments, and the 1st Brigade advanced to the assault.

"It had nothing in front of it. The Confederate troops occupying the lines in the immediate vicinity of the mine had fled precipitately. The way was completely open to the summit of the hill.

"The column marched to the crater but instead of turning around it, descended into it. Once at the bottom, finding itself sheltered, it stayed there. The general commanding the division had remained within our lines, in a bombproof.

"The 2nd Brigade was soon mixed up with the other. Several regiments descended into the crater, but only one brigade succeeded in making its way through so as to advance beyond. It found itself then engaged in ground cut up by trenches, by covered ways, by sheltered pits dug in the ground. Worse than that, the enemy, recovering from his surprise, had already placed his guns in position and formed his infantry so as to throw a concentrated fire upon the opening made in his works. The brigade, seeing that it was neither supported nor reinforced, was compelled to fall back with loss.

"The 3rd Brigade had not even made a like attempt. Mingling with the first, it had simply increased the confusion.

"Toward seven o'clock a colored brigade received orders to advance in its turn. The Negroes advanced resolutely, passed over the passive mass of white troops, not a company of whom followed them, and charged under a deadly fire of artillery and musketry, which reached them from all sides at once. They even reached the enemy, took from him 250 prisoners, captured a flag and recovered one of ours taken by him. But they were not sustained. They were driven back by a countercharge and returned running in confusion to our lines where, by this time, a large number of the white troops were eager to return with them.

"In a moment it was a general devil-take-the-hindmost, a confused rush in which those who could run fast enough and escape the Rebel fire returned to our lines. Those who endeavored to resist, or were delayed, were taken prisoners.

"Thus passed away the finest opportunity which could have been given us to capture Petersburg."*

There was heavy skirmishing throughout the rest of the summer into the early fall. Grant continued to extend his lines westward, while Lee

* From Regis de Trobriand, *Four Years with the Army of the Potomac.*

countered by sidestepping with him. Eventually the fortifications stretched more than fifty miles.

The winter months went by, spring came, and still the siege held. Then on April 1, Grant struck a major blow. For the first time since the opening of the campaign he managed to turn Lee's right flank. "The next day Grant ordered an assault all along the main lines. General Horatio Wright and his VI Corps found a place where Lee's force had been stretched too thin and broke it—losing two thousand men in the assault, for even when they were woefully undermanned these Petersburg lines were all but invulnerable—punching a wide hole that could not be repaired. On the evening and night of April 2 Lee evacuated Petersburg and Richmond and began his final retreat.

"A great fire burned in Richmond when Union troops marched in. Retreating Confederates had fired various warehouses full of goods they could not take with them, and in the wild confusion of defeat these flames got out of hand; the victorious Unionists, coming at last into the capital city of the Confederacy, spent their first hours there as a fire brigade, putting out flames, checking looting, and bringing order back to the desolate town. Lincoln himself came up the James River in a gun-boat— he had been at City Point, unable to tear himself away from the military nerve center while the climactic battle was being fought—and he walked up the streets of Richmond with a handful of sailors for an escort, dazed crowds looking on in silence; went to the Confederate White House, sat for a time at Jefferson Davis's desk, and saw for himself the final collapse of the nation he had sworn to destroy.

"Most of Grant's army never got into Richmond, and neither did Grant himself. They were on the road, pushing along furiously to head Lee off and drive him into a pocket where he could be forced to surrender."*

Lee Retreats †

BY MAJOR ROBERT STILES

O<small>N SUNDAY, THE 2D OF APRIL</small>, I stood almost all day on our works overhanging the river, listening to the fire about Petersburg, and noting its peculiar character and progression. I made up my mind what it meant, and had time and space out there alone with God and upon His day to commit myself and mine to Him, and to anticipate and prepare for the immediate future. Late in the afternoon I walked back to my quarters, and soon after, George Cary Eggleston, who was then in a command

---

* Bruce Catton, *This Hallowed Ground*, p. 384.
† From *Four Years Under Marse Robert*.

that held a part of the line near us, dropped in. He tells me now that I asked him then what effect he thought it would have upon our cause if our lines should be broken and we compelled to give up Petersburg and Richmond; and that he declined to answer the question because, as he said, the supposed facts were out of the plane of the practical, and would not and could not happen. Now, years afterwards, recalling the peculiar expression and manner with which I propounded this interrogatory, he asks whether I had then received any official information, and I answer in the negative—no, none whatever. Up to the time Eggleston left my camp for his I knew nothing beyond what my tell-tale ears and prescient soul had told me.

Indeed, we went into our meeting that night without any other information; but I had directed the acting-adjutant to remain in his office and to bring at once to me, in the church, any orders that might come to hand. Our service was one of unusual power and interest. I read with the men the "Soldier Psalm," the ninety-first, and exhorted them, in any special pressure that might come upon us in the near future—the "terror by night" or the "destruction . . . at noon-day"—to abide with entire confidence in that "Stronghold," to appropriate that "Strength."

As I uttered these words, I noticed a well-grown, fine-looking country lad named Blount, who was leaning forward, and gazing at me with eager interest, while tears of sympathy and appreciation were brimming his eyes. The door opened and the adjutant appeared. I told him to stand a moment where he was, and as quietly as possible told the men what I was satisfied was the purport of the paper he held in his hand, and why I was so satisfied. And then we prayed for the realization of what David had expressed in that Psalm—for faith, for strength, for protection. After the prayer I called for the paper and read it over, first silently and then aloud, gave brief directions to the men and dismissed them—first calling upon such officers and non-commissioned officers as had special duties to perform in connection with the magazines, etc., to remain a few moments. The men were ordered to rendezvous at a given hour, and to fall in by companies on the parade, and the company officers were ordered to see that they brought with them only what was absolutely necessary, and a brief approximate list was given of the proper campaign outfit. But the poor fellows had been many months in garrison, and it was maddening work within a short and fixed time, to select from their motley accumulations what was really necessary in the changed conditions ahead of us.

The orders were, in general, that the men of the fleet and of the James River defenses should leave the river about midnight of the 2d of April, exploding magazines and ironclads, and join the Army of Northern Virginia in its retreat. Orders such as these were enough to try the mettle even of the best troops, in the highest condition, but for my poor little battalion they were overwhelming, well-nigh stupefying. The marvel is that they held together at all and left the Bluff, as they did, in pretty fair condition. A few months earlier I question whether they would have been equal to it.

I said they left in pretty fair condition, and so they did, except that they had more baggage piled upon their backs than any one brigade, perhaps I might say division, in General Lee's army was bearing at the same moment. I could hardly blame them, and there was no time to correct the folly; besides, I knew it would correct and adjust itself, as it had done pretty well by morning.

The explosions began just as we got across the river. When the magazines at Chaffin's and Drury's Bluffs went off, the solid earth shuddered convulsively; but as the ironclads—one after another—exploded, it seemed as if the very dome of heaven would be shattered down upon us. Earth and air and the black sky glared in the lurid light. Columns and towers and pinnacles of flame shot upward to an amazing height, from which, on all sides, the ignited shells flew on arcs of fire and burst as if bombarding heaven. I distinctly remember feeling that after this I could never more be startled—no, not by the catastrophes of the last great day.

I walked in rear of the battalion to prevent straggling and, as the successive flashes illumined the darkness, the blanched faces and staring eyes turned backward upon me spoke volumes of nervous demoralization. I felt that a hare might shatter the column. No Confederate soldier who was on and of that fearful retreat can fail to recall it as one of the most trying experiences of his life. Trying enough, in the mere fact that the Army of Northern Virginia was flying before its foes, but further trying, incomparably trying, in lack of food and rest and sleep, and because of the audacious pressure of the enemy's cavalry. The combined and continued strain of all this upon soft garrison troops, unenured to labor and hardship and privation and peril, can hardly be conceived and cannot be described. Its two most serious effects were *drowsiness and nervousness*. We crossed and left James River at midnight on Sunday. . . .

The somewhat disorganized condition of the troops and the crowded condition of the roads necessitated frequent halts, and whenever these occurred—especially after night-fall—the men would drop in the road, or on the side of it, and sleep until they were roused, and it was manifestly impossible to rouse them all. My two horses were in almost constant use to transport officers and men who had given out, especially our doctor, whose horse was for some reason unavailable. Besides, I preferred to be on foot, for the very purpose of moving around among the men and rousing them when we resumed the march. With this view I was a good part of the time at the rear of the battalion; but notwithstanding my efforts in this respect, individually and through a detail of men selected and organized for the purpose of waking the sleepers, we lost, I am satisfied, every time we resumed the march after a halt at night—men who were not found or who could not be roused.

The nervousness resulting from this constant strain of starvation, fatigue, and lack of sleep was a dangerous thing, at one time producing very lamentable results, which threatened to be even more serious than they were. One evening an officer, I think of one of our supply departments, passed and repassed us several times, riding a powerful black stallion, all of whose furnishings—girths, reins, etc.,—were very heavy, indicating the unmanageable character of the horse. When he rode ahead the last time, about dark, it seems that he imprudently hitched his horse by tying his very stout tie rein to a heavy fence rail which was part of the road fence. Something frightened the animal and he reared back, pulling the rail out of the fence and dragging it after him full gallop down the road crowded with troops, mowing them down like the scythe of a war chariot. Someone, thinking there was a charge of cavalry, fired his musket and, on the instant, three or four battalions, mine among them, began firing into each other.

I was never more alarmed. Muskets were discharged in my very face, and I fully expected to be shot down; but after the most trying and perilous experience, the commanding officers succeeded in getting control of their men and getting them again into formation. But while we were talking to them, suddenly the panic seized them again, and they rushed in such a wild rout against the heavy road fence that they swept it away, and many of them took to the woods, firing back as they ran. A second time the excitement was quieted and a third time it broke out. By this time, however, I had fully explained to my men that we had just put out fresh flankers on both sides of the road, that we could not have an attack of cavalry without warning from them, and that the safe and soldierly thing to do was to lie down until everything should become calm. I was much pleased that this third time my command did not fire a shot, while the battalions in our front and rear were firing heavily. A field officer and a good many other officers and men were killed and wounded in these alarms, just how many I do not believe was ever ascertained.

When we next halted for any length of time, during daylight, I formed my men and talked to them fully and quietly about these alarms, explaining the folly of their firing, and impressing upon them simply to lie down, keep quiet, and attempt to catch and obey promptly any special orders I might give. I complimented them upon their having resisted the panicky infection the last time it broke out, and felt that, upon the whole, my men had gained rather than lost by the experience.

On Thursday afternoon we had descended into a moist, green little valley, crossed a small stream called Sailor's Creek, and, ascending a gentle, grassy slope beyond it, had halted, and the men were lying down and resting in the edge of a pine wood that crowned the elevation. A desultory fire was going on ahead and bullets began to drop in. I was walking about among the men, seeing that everything was in order and talking cheerfully with them, when I heard a ball strike something hard and saw a little commotion around the battalion colors. Going there, I found that the flag-staff had been splintered, and called out to the men that we were beginning to make a record.

Next moment I heard an outcry—"There, Brookin is killed!"—and saw one of the men writhing on the ground. I went to him. He seemed to be partially paralyzed below the waist, but said he was shot through the neck. I saw no blood anywhere. He had on his roll of blankets and, sure enough, a ball had gone through them and also through his jacket and flannel shirt; but there it was, sticking in the back of his neck, having barely broken the skin. I took it out and said: "Oh, you are not a dead man by a good deal. Here,"—handing the ball to him—"take that home and give it to your sweetheart. It'll fix you all right." Brookin caught at the ball and held it tightly clasped in his hand, smiling faintly, and the men about him laughed.

Just then I heard a shell whizzing over us, coming from across the creek, and we were hurried into line facing in that direction, that is, *to the rear*. I inferred, of course, that we were surrounded, but could not tell how strong the force was upon which we were turning our backs.

I remember, in all the discomfort and wretchedness of the retreat, we had been no little amused by the Naval Battalion, under that old hero, Admiral Tucker. The soldiers called them the "Aye, Ayes," because they responded "aye, aye" to every order, some times repeating the order itself, and adding, "Aye, aye, it is, sir!" As this battalion, which followed immediately after ours, was getting into position, and seaman's and landsman's jargon and movements were getting a good deal mixed in the orders and evolutions—all being harmonized, however, and licked into shape by the "aye, aye"—a young officer of the division staff rode up, saluted Admiral Tucker, and said: "Admiral, I may possibly be of assistance to you in getting your command into line." The Admiral replied: "Young man, I understand how to talk to my people"; and thereupon followed "a grand moral combination" of "right flank" and "left flank," "starboard" and "larboard," "aye, aye" and "aye, aye"—until the battalion gradually settled down into place.

By this time a large Federal force had deployed into line on the other slope beyond the creek, which we had left not long since; two or three lines of battle, and a heavy park of artillery, which rapidly came into battery and opened an accurate and deadly fire, we having no guns with which to reply and thus disturb their aim. My men were lying down and were ordered not to expose themselves. I was walking backward and forward just back of the line, talking to them whenever that was practicable, and keeping my eye upon everything, feeling that such action and exposure on my part were imperatively demanded by the history and condition of the command and my rather peculiar relations to it. A good many had been wounded and several killed when a twenty-pounder Parrott shell struck immediately in my front, on the line, nearly severing a man in twain, and hurling him bodily over my head, his arms hanging down and his hands almost slapping me in the face as they passed.

In that one awful moment I distinctly recognized young Blount, who had gazed into my face so intently Sunday night; and but for that peculiar paralysis which in battle some times passes upon a man's entire being—excepting only his fighting powers—the recognition might have been too much for me.

In a few moments the artillery fire ceased and I had time to glance about me and note results a little more carefully. I had seldom seen a fire more accurate, nor one that had been more deadly, in a single regiment, in so brief a time. The expression of the men's faces indicated clearly enough its effect upon them. They did not appear to be hopelessly demoralized, but they did look blanched and haggard and awe-struck.

The Federal infantry had crossed the creek and were now coming up the slope in two lines of battle. I stepped in front of my line and passed from end to end, impressing upon my men that no one must fire his musket until I so ordered; that when I said *"ready"* they must all rise, kneeling on the right knee; that when I said *"aim"* they must all aim about the knees of the advancing line; that when I said *"fire"* they must all fire together, and that it was all-important they should follow these directions exactly, and obey, implicitly and instantly, any other instructions or orders I might give.

The enemy was coming on and everything was still as the grave. My battalion was formed upon and around a swell of the hill, which threw it farther to the front than any other command in the division, so that, being likely first to meet the enemy and having received no special orders, I was compelled, as to details, to shape my own course. The Federal officers knowing, as I suppose, that we were surrounded and appreciating the fearful havoc their artillery fire had wrought, probably entertained the hope that we would surrender—some of them, as I remember, having their white handkerchiefs in their hands and waving them toward us as if suggesting that course—and yet they never ceased their advance upon our position, nor sent forward a flag of truce, nor even made any demand or call upon us to surrender; nor, so far as I know or believe or have ever heard, were any white flags or indications of surrender exhibited anywhere in our lines. I do not recall any exact parallel to these circumstances.

I dislike to break the flow and force of the narrative by repeated modifying references to recollection and memory; but it is not safe for a man, so many years after the event, to be positive with regard to details, unless there was special reason why they should have been impressed upon him at the time. I will say, then, that my memory records no musket shot on either side up to this time, our skirmishers having retired upon the main line without firing. The enemy showed no disposition to break into the charge, but continued to advance in the same measured and even hesitating manner, and I allowed them to approach very close—I should be afraid to say just how close—before retiring behind my men, who, as before stated, were lying down. I had continued to walk along their front for the very purpose of preventing them from opening fire; but now I stepped through the line and stationing myself about the middle of it, called out my orders deliberately—everything being in full sight of both parties, and the enemy, as I have every reason to believe, hearing every word. *"Ready!"* To my great relief, the men rose, all together, like a piece of mechanism, kneeling on their right knees and their faces set with an expression that meant—everything. *"Aim!"* The musket barrels fell to an almost perfect horizontal line leveled about the knees of the advancing front line. *"Fire!"*

I have never seen such an effect, physical and moral, produced by the utterance of one word. The enemy seemed to have been totally unprepared for it, and, as the sequel showed, my own men scarcely less so. The earth appeared to have swallowed up the first line of the Federal force in our front. There was a rattling supplement to the volley and the second line wavered and broke.

The revulsion was too sudden. On the instant every man in my battalion sprang to his feet, and, without orders, they rushed, bareheaded and with unloaded muskets, down the slope after the retreating Federals. I tried to stop them, but in vain, although I actually got ahead of a good many of them. They simply bore me on with the flood.

The standard-bearer was dashing by me, colors in hand, when I managed to catch his roll of blankets and jerk him violently back, demanding what he meant, advancing the battalion colors without orders.

As I was speaking, the artillery opened fire again and he was hurled to the earth, as I supposed, dead. I stooped to pick up the flag, when his brother, a lieutenant, a fine officer and a splendid-looking fellow, stepped over the body, saying: "Those colors belong to me, Major!" at the same time taking hold of the staff. He was shot through the brain and fell backward. One of the color guard sprang forward, saying: "Give them to me, Major!" But by the time his hand reached the staff he was down. There were at least five men dead and wounded lying close about me, and I did not see why I should continue to make a target of myself. I therefore jammed the color staff down through a thick bush, which supported it in an upright position, and turned my attention to my battalion, which was scattered over the face of the hill firing irregularly at the Federals, who seemed to be reforming to renew the attack. I managed to get my men into some sort of formation and their guns loaded, and then charged the Federal line, driving it back across the creek, and forming my command behind a little ridge, which protected it somewhat.

I ran back up the hill and had a brief conversation with General Curtis Lee—commanding the division, our brigade commander having been killed—explaining to him that I had not ordered the advance and that we would be cut off if we remained long where we were, but that I was satisfied I could bring the battalion back through a ravine, which would protect them largely from the fire of the enemy's artillery, and reform them on the old line, on the right of the naval battalion, which had remained in position. He expressed his doubts as to this, but I told him I believed my battalion would follow me anywhere, and with his permission I would try it. I ran down the hill again and explained to my men that, when I got to the left of the line and shouted to them, they were to get up and follow me, on a run and without special formation, through a ravine that led back to the top of the hill. Just because these simple-hearted fellows knew only enough to trust me, and because the enemy was not so far recovered as to take advantage of our exposure while executing the movement to the rear and reforming, we were back in the original lines in a few moments—that is, all who were left of us.

It was of no avail. By the time we had well settled into our old position we were attacked simultaneously, front and rear, by overwhelming numbers, and quicker than I can tell it the battle degenerated into a butchery and a confused melee of brutal personal conflicts. I saw numbers of men kill each other with bayonets and the butts of muskets, and even bite each others' throats and ears and noses, rolling on the ground like wild beasts. I saw one of my officers and a Federal officer fighting with swords over the battalion colors, which we had brought back with us, each having his left hand upon the staff. I could not get to them, but my man was a very athletic, powerful seaman, and soon I saw the Federal officer fall.

I had cautioned my men against wearing "Yankee overcoats," especially in battle, but had not been able to enforce the order perfectly—and almost at my side I saw a young fellow of one of my companies jam the muzzle of his musket against the back of the head of his most intimate friend, clad in a Yankee overcoat, and blow his brains out. I was wedged in between fighting men, only my right arm free. I tried to strike the musket barrel up, but alas, my sword had broken in the clash and I could not reach it. I well remember the yell of demoniac triumph with which that simple country lad of yesterday clubbed his musket and whirled savagely upon another victim.

I don't think I ever suffered more than during the few moments after I saw that nothing could affect or change the result of the battle. I could not let myself degenerate into a mere fighting brute or devil, because the lives of these poor fellows were, in some sense, in my hand, though there was nothing I could do just then to shield or save them. Suddenly, by one of those inexplicable shiftings which take place on a battle-field, the fighting around me almost entirely ceased, and whereas the moment before the whole environment seemed to be crowded with the enemy, there were now few or none of them on the spot, and as the slaughter and the firing seemed to be pretty well over, I concluded I would try to make my escape, I had always considered it likely I should be killed, but had never anticipated or contemplated capture.

I think it was at this juncture I encountered General Curtis Lee, but it may have been after I was picked up. At all events, selecting the direction which seemed to be most free from Federal soldiers and to offer the best chance of escape, I started first at a walk and then broke into a run; but in a short distance ran into a fresh Federal force, and it seemed the most natural and easy thing in the world to be simply arrested and taken in. My recollection is that General Lee asked to be carried before the Federal general commanding on that part of the line, who, at his request, gave orders putting a stop to the firing, there being no organized Confederate force on the field. Thus ended my active life as a Confederate soldier, my four years' service under Marse Robert, and I was not sorry to end it thus, in red-hot battle, and to be spared the pain, I will not say humiliation, of Appomattox.

I must, however, mention an incident to which I have already briefly referred, to which it would perhaps have been more delicate not to refer at all; but the reader of this chapter can scarcely have failed to perceive that one of the most deeply stirring episodes in my soldier-life was the struggle I made to lift my battalion out of the demoralization in which I found it; to make my men trust and love me, and to rouse and develop in them the true conception of soldierly duty and devotion, courage and endurance.

Looking back upon the teeming recollections of this first and last retreat and this final battle of the Army of Northern Virginia, amid all the overpowering sadness and depression of defeat, I already felt the sustaining consciousness of a real and a worthy success; but it is impossible to express how this consciousness was deepened and heightened when General Ewell sent for me on the field, after we were all captured, and in the presence of half a dozen generals said that he had summoned me to say, in the hearing of these officers, that the conduct of my battalion had been reported to him, and that he desired to congratulate me and them upon the record they had made.

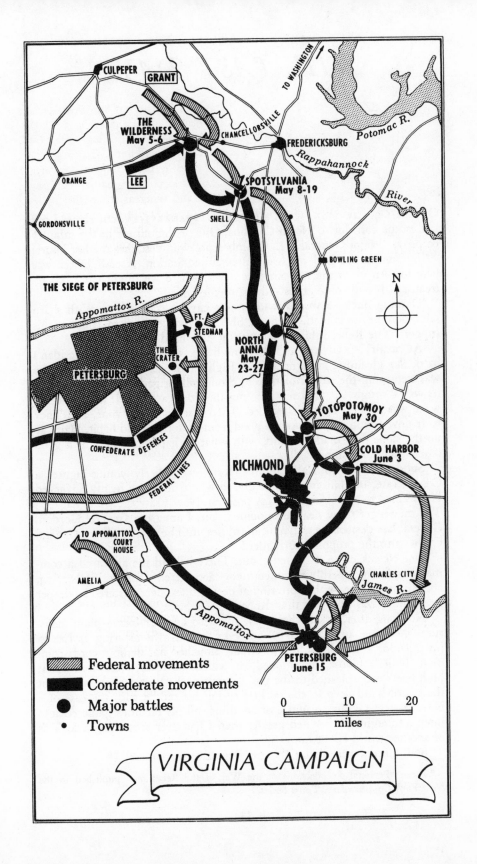

THE SIEGE OF PETERSBURG

Appomattox R.

FT. STEDMAN

THE CRATER

PETERSBURG

CONFEDERATE DEFENSES

FEDERAL LINES

CULPEPER

GRANT

THE WILDERNESS
May 5-6

CHANCELLORSVILLE

TO WASHINGTON

Potomac R.

FREDERICKSBURG

Rappahannock

ORANGE

LEE

SPOTSYLVANIA
May 8-19

River

GORDONSVILLE

SNELL

BOWLING GREEN

N

NORTH
ANNA
May
23-27

TOTOPOTOMOY
May 30

RICHMOND

COLD HARBOR
June 3

TO APPOMATTOX
COURT
HOUSE

CHARLES CITY

James R.

AMELIA

Appomattox

PETERSBURG
June 15

Federal movements

Confederate movements

Major battles

Towns

0   10   20
miles

VIRGINIA CAMPAIGN

THE LAST DAY

ON APRIL 9, SHERIDAN, WITH A CORPS OF INFANTRYMEN, cut across Lee's last escape corridor to North Carolina. One of the officers in the infantry corps was Major General J. L. Chamberlain, who describes the last hours:

"By sunrise we had reached Appomattox Station. A staff officer was here to turn us to the Appomattox River, where we might cut Lee's retreat. . . . It had come at last—the supreme hour.

"Dashing out of a woods road came a cavalry staff officer. With sharp salutation he exclaimed, 'General Sheridan wishes you to come to his support. The Rebel infantry is pressing him hard.'

"At cavalry speed we pushed through the woods, right on Sheridan's battle flag gleaming in an open field. Right before us our cavalry gallantly was stemming the surges of the old Stonewall Brigade, desperate to beat its way through. . . . In a few minutes the tide was turned: the incoming wave was at high flood; it receded. Their last hope was gone. . . . They were now giving way but kept a good front by force of old habit. Halfway up the slope they made a stand, with what perhaps they thought a good omen—behind a stone wall.

"Suddenly rose to sight another form—a soldierly young figure, a Confederate staff officer undoubtedly, to whom someone in my advanced line seemed to be pointing out my position. Now I saw the white flag. . . . The messenger drew near, dismounted. 'Sir, I am from General Gordon. General Lee desires a cessation of hostilities until he can hear from General Grant as to the proposed surrender.'

"One o'clock came. I turned about. There behind me appeared a commanding form, superbly mounted, richly accoutered, of imposing bearing, noble countenance, with expression of deep sadness overmastered by deeper strength. It was no other than Robert E. Lee. . . .

"Not long after, by another road, appeared another form—plain, unassuming, simple and familiar to our eyes, but as awe-inspiring as Lee in his splendor and sadness. It was Grant. Slouched hat without cord; common soldier's blouse, unbuttoned on which, however, were four stars; high boots mudsplashed to the top, trousers tucked inside; no sword, but the sword hand deep in the pocket; sitting his saddle with the ease of a born master; taking no notice of anything, all his faculties gathered into intense thought. He seemed greater than I had ever seen him—a look as of another world about him.

"Staff officers were flying about crying, 'Lee surrenders!' "*

* From "Personal Recollections of the War of the Rebellion," published in the *New York Commandery*, Third Series.

554

The Surrender at
Appomattox Court House*

BY GENERAL HORACE PORTER

ABOUT ONE O'CLOCK the little village of Appomattox Court House, with its half-dozen houses, came in sight, and soon we were entering its single street. It is situated on some rising ground, and beyond the country slopes down into a broad valley. The enemy was seen with his columns and wagon trains covering the low ground. Our cavalry, the Fifth Corps, and part of Ord's command were occupying the high ground to the south and west of the enemy, heading him off completely. Generals Sheridan and Ord, with a group of officers around them, were seen in the road, and as our party came up General Grant said: "How are you, Sheridan?" "First-rate, thank you; how are you?" cried Sheridan, with a voice and look that seemed to indicate that on his part he was having things all his own way. "Is Lee over there?" asked General Grant, pointing up the street, having heard a rumor that Lee was in that vicinity. "Yes, he is in that brick house," answered Sheridan. "Well, then, we'll go over," said Grant.

The general-in-chief now rode on, accompanied by Sheridan, Ord, and some others, and soon Colonel Babcock's orderly was seen sitting on his horse in the street in front of a two-story brick house, better in appearance than the rest of the houses. He said General Lee and Colonel Babcock had gone into this house a short time before, and he was ordered to post himself in the street and keep a lookout for General Grant, so as to let him know where General Lee was.

The house had a comfortable wooden porch with seven steps leading up to it. A hall ran through the middle from front to back, and on each side was a room having two windows, one in front and one in rear. Each room had two doors opening into the hall. The building stood a little distance back from the street, with a yard in front, and to the left was a gate for carriages and a roadway running to a stable in rear. We entered the grounds by this gate and dismounted. In the yard were seen a fine large gray horse, which proved to be General Lee's, and a good-looking mare belonging to Colonel Marshall. An orderly in gray was in charge of them, and had taken off their bridles to let them nibble the grass.

General Grant mounted the steps and entered the house. As he stepped

* From *Battles and Leaders*, Vol. IV.

into the hall Colonel Babcock, who had seen his approach from the window, opened the door of the room on the left, in which he had been sitting with General Lee and Colonel Marshall awaiting General Grant's arrival. The general passed in, while the members of the staff, Generals Sheridan and Ord, and some general officers who had gathered in the front yard, remained outside, feeling that he would probably want his first interview with General Lee to be, in a measure, private. In a few minutes Colonel Babcock came to the front door and, making a motion with his hat toward the sitting-room, said: "The general says, come in." It was then about half-past one of Sunday, the 9th of April. We entered, and found General Grant sitting at a marble-topped table in the center of the room, and Lee sitting beside a small oval table near the front window, in the corner opposite to the door by which we entered, and facing General Grant. Colonel Marshall, his military secretary, was standing at his left. We walked in softly and ranged ourselves quietly about the sides of the room, very much as people enter a sick-chamber when they expect to find the patient dangerously ill. Some found seats on the sofa and the few chairs which constituted the furniture, but most of the party stood.

The contrast between the two commanders was striking, and could not fail to attract marked attention as they sat ten feet apart facing each other. General Grant, then nearly forty-three years of age, was five feet eight inches in height, with shoulders slightly stooped. His hair and full beard were a nut-brown, without a trace of gray in them. He had on a single-breasted blouse, made of dark-blue flannel, unbuttoned in front, and showing a waistcoat underneath. He wore an ordinary pair of top-boots, with his trousers inside, and was without spurs. The boots and portions of his clothes were spattered with mud. He had had on a pair of thread gloves, of a dark-yellow color, which he had taken off on entering the room. His felt "sugarloaf" stiff-brimmed hat was thrown on the table beside him. He had no sword, and a pair of shoulder-straps was all there was about him to designate his rank. In fact, aside from these, his uniform was that of a private soldier.

Lee, on the other hand, was fully six feet in height, and quite erect for one of his age, for he was Grant's senior by sixteen years. His hair and full beard were a silver-gray, and quite thick, except that the hair had become a little thin in front. He wore a new uniform of Confederate gray, buttoned up to the throat, and at his side he carried a long sword of exceedingly fine workmanship, the hilt studded with jewels. It was said to be the sword that had been presented to him by the State of Virginia. His top-boots were comparatively new, and seemed to have on them some ornamental stitching of red silk. Like his uniform, they were singularly clean, and but little travel-stained. On the boots were handsome spurs, with large rowels. A felt hat, which in color matched pretty closely that of his uniform, and a pair of long buckskin gauntlets lay beside him on the table. We asked Colonel Marshall afterward how it was that both he and his chief wore such fine toggery, and looked so much as if they had turned out to go to church, while with us our outward garb scarcely rose to the dignity even of the "shabby-genteel." He enlightened us regarding the contrast, by explaining that when their headquarters wagons had been pressed so closely by our cavalry a few days before, and it was found they would have to destroy all their baggage, except the clothes they carried on their backs, each one, naturally, selected the newest suit he had, and sought to propitiate the god of destruction by a sacrifice of his second-best.

General Grant began the conversation by saying: "I met you once before, General Lee, while we were serving in Mexico, when you came over from General Scott's headquarters to visit Garland's brigade, to which I then belonged. I have always remembered your appearance, and I think I should have recognized you anywhere." "Yes," replied General Lee, "I know I met you on that occasion, and I have often thought of it and tried to recollect how you looked, but I have never been able to recall a single feature." After some further mention of Mexico, General Lee said: "I suppose, General Grant, that the object of our present meeting is fully understood. I asked to see you to ascertain upon what terms you would receive the surrender of my army." General Grant replied: "The terms I propose are those stated substantially in my letter of yesterday—that is, the officers and men surrendered to be paroled and disqualified from taking up arms again until properly exchanged, and all arms, ammunition, and supplies to be delivered up as captured property." Lee nodded an assent, and said: "Those are about the conditions which I expected would be proposed." General Grant then continued: "Yes, I think our correspondence indicated pretty clearly the action that would be taken at our meeting; and I hope it may lead to a general suspension of hostilities and be the means of preventing any further loss of life."

Lee inclined his head as indicating his accord with this wish, and General Grant then went on to talk at some length in a very pleasant vein about the prospects of peace. Lee was evidently anxious to proceed to the formal work of the surrender, and he brought the subject up again by saying:

"I presume, General Grant, we have both carefully considered the proper steps to be taken, and I would suggest that you commit to writing the terms you have proposed, so that they may be formally acted upon."

"Very well," replied General Grant, "I will write them out." And calling for his manifold order-book, he opened it on the table before him and proceeded to write the terms. The leaves had been so prepared that three impressions of the writing were made. He wrote very rapidly, and did not pause until he had finished the sentence ending with "officers appointed by me to receive them." Then he looked toward Lee, and his eyes seemed to be resting on the handsome sword that hung at that officer's side. He said afterward that this set him to thinking that it would be an unnecessary humiliation to require the officers to surrender their swords, and a great hardship to deprive them of their personal baggage and horses, and after a short pause he wrote the sentence: "This will not embrace the side-arms of the officers, nor their private horses or baggage." When he had finished the letter he called Colonel (afterward General) Ely S. Parker, one of the military secretaries on the staff, to his side and looked it over with him and directed him as they went along to interline six or seven words and to strike out the word "their," which had been repeated. When this had been done, he handed the book to General Lee and asked him to read over the letter. It was as follows:

APPOMATTOX CT. H., VA.
April 9, 1865

GENERAL R. E. LEE, Commanding C. S. A.
GENERAL:

In accordance with the substance of my letter to you of the 8th inst., I propose to receive the surrender of the Army of Northern Virginia on the following terms, to wit: Rolls of all the officers and men to be made in duplicate, one copy to be given to an officer to be designated by me, the other to be retained by such officer or officers as you may designate. The officers to give their individual paroles not to take up arms against the Government of the United States until properly [exchanged], and each company or regimental commander to sign a like parole for the men of their commands. The arms, artillery, and public property to be parked, and stacked, and turned over to the officers appointed by me to receive them. This will not embrace the side-arms of the officers, nor their private horses or baggage. This done, each officer and man will be allowed to return to his home, not to be disturbed by the United States authorities so long as they observe their paroles, and the laws in force where they may reside.

Very respectfully,   U. S. GRANT, Lieutenant-General

Lee took it and laid it on the table beside him, while he drew from his pocket a pair of steel-rimmed spectacles and wiped the glasses carefully with his handkerchief. Then he crossed his legs, adjusted the spectacles very slowly and deliberately, took up the draft of the letter, and proceeded to read it attentively. It consisted of two pages. When he reached the top line of the second page, he looked up, and said to General Grant: "After the words 'until properly,' the word 'exchanged' seems to be omitted. You doubtless intended to use that word."

"Why, yes," said Grant; "I thought I had put in the word 'exchanged.' "

"I presumed it had been omitted inadvertently," continued Lee, "and with your permission I will mark where it should be inserted."

"Certainly," Grant replied.

Lee felt in his pocket as if searching for a pencil, but did not seem to be able to find one. Seeing this and happening to be standing close to him, I handed him my pencil. He took it, and laying the paper on the table noted the interlineation. During the rest of the interview he kept twirling this pencil in his fingers and occasionally tapping the top of the table with it. When he handed it back it was carefully treasured by me as a memento of the occasion. When Lee came to the sentence about the officers' side-arms, private horses, and baggage, he showed for the first time during the reading of the letter a slight change of countenance, and was evidently touched by this act of generosity. It was doubtless the condition mentioned to which he particularly alluded when he looked toward General Grant as he finished reading and said with some degree of warmth in his manner: "This will have a very happy effect upon my army."

General Grant then said: "Unless you have some suggestions to make in regard to the form in which I have stated the terms, I will have a copy of the letter made in ink and sign it."

"There is one thing I would like to mention," Lee replied after a short pause. "The cavalrymen and artillerists own their own horses in our army. Its organization in this respect differs from that of the United States." This expression attracted the notice of our officers present, as showing how firmly the conviction was grounded in his mind that we were two distinct countries. He continued: "I would like to understand whether these men will be permitted to retain their horses?"

"You will find that the terms as written do not allow this," General Grant replied; "only the officers are permitted to take their private property."

Lee read over the second page of the letter again, and then said:

"No, I see the terms do not allow it; that is clear." His face showed plainly that he was quite anxious to have this concession made, and Grant said very promptly and without giving Lee time to make a direct request:

"Well, the subject is quite new to me. Of course I did not know that any private soldiers owned their animals, but I think this will be the last battle of the war—I sincerely hope so—and that the surrender of this army will be followed soon by that of all the others, and I take it that most of the men in the ranks are small farmers, and as the country has been so raided by the two armies, it is doubtful whether they will be able to put in a crop to carry themselves and their families through the next winter without the aid of the horses they are now riding, and I will arrange it in this way: I will not change the terms as now written, but I will instruct the officers I shall appoint to receive the paroles to let all the men who claim to own a horse or mule take the animals home with them to work their little farms."

Lee now looked greatly relieved, and though anything but a demonstrative man, he gave every evidence of his appreciation of this concession, and said, "This will have the best possible effect upon the men. It will be very gratifying and will do much toward conciliating our people." He handed the draft of the terms back to General Grant, who called Colonel T. S. Bowers of the staff to him and directed him to make a copy in ink. Bowers was a little nervous, and he turned the matter over to Colonel (afterward General) Parker, whose handwriting presented a better appearance than that of any one else on the staff. Parker sat down to write at the table which stood against the rear side of the room. Wilmer McLean's domestic resources in the way of ink now became the subject of a searching investigation, but it was found that the contents of the conical-shaped stoneware inkstand which he produced appeared to be participating in the general breaking up and had disappeared. Colonel Marshall now came to the rescue, and pulled out of his pocket a small boxwood inkstand, which was put at Parker's service, so that, after all, we had to fall back upon the resources of the enemy in furnishing the stage "properties" for the final scene in the memorable military drama.

Lee in the meantime had directed Colonel Marshall to draw up for his signature a letter of acceptance of the terms of surrender. Colonel Marshall wrote out a draft of such a letter, making it quite formal, beginning with "I have the honor to reply to your communition," etc. General Lee took it, and, after reading it over very carefully, directed that these formal expressions be stricken out and that the letter be otherwise shortened. He afterward went over it again and seemed to change some words, and then told the colonel to make a final copy in ink. When it came to providing the paper, it was found we had the only supply of that important ingredient in the recipe for surrendering an army, so we gave a few pages to the colonel. The letter when completed read as follows:

> HEADQUARTERS, ARMY OF NORTHERN VIRGINIA
> April 9th, 1865
>
> GENERAL:
>
> I received your letter of this date containing the terms of the surrender of the Army of Northern Virginia as proposed by you. As they are substantially the same as those expressed in your letter of the 8th inst., they are accepted. I will proceed to designate the proper officers to carry the stipulations into effect.
>
> R. E. LEE, General
>
> LIEUTENANT-GENERAL U. S. GRANT

While the letters were being copied, General Grant introduced the general officers who had entered, and each member of the staff, to General Lee. The General shook hands with General Seth Williams, who had been his adjutant when Lee was superintendent at West Point, some years before the war, and gave his hand to some of the other officers who had extended theirs, but to most of those who were introduced he merely bowed in a dignified and formal manner. He did not exhibit the slightest change of features during this ceremony until Colonel Parker of our staff was presented to him. Parker was a full-blooded Indian, and the reigning Chief of the Six Nations. When Lee saw his swarthy features he looked at him with evident surprise, and his eyes rested on him for several seconds. What was passing in his mind probably no one ever knew, but the natural surmise was that he at first mistook Parker for a Negro, and was struck with astonishment to find that the commander of the Union armies had one of that race on his personal staff.

Lee did not utter a word while the introductions were going on, except to Seth Williams, with whom he talked quite cordially. Williams at one time referred in rather jocose a manner to a circumstance which occurred during their former service together, as if he wanted to say something in a good-natured way to break up the frigidity of the conversation, but Lee was in no mood for pleasantries, and he did not unbend, or even relax the fixed sternness of his features. His only response to the allusion was a slight inclination of the head. General Lee now took the initiative again in leading the conversation back into business channels. He said:

"I have a thousand or more of your men as prisoners, General Grant, a number of them officers whom we have required to march along with us for several days. I shall be glad to send them into your lines as soon as it can be arranged, for I have no provisions for them. I have, indeed, nothing for my own men. They have been living for the last few days principally upon parched corn, and we are badly in need of both rations and forage. I telegraphed to Lynchburg, directing several train-loads of rations to be sent on by rail from there, and when they arrive I should be glad to have the present wants of my men supplied from them."

At this remark all eyes turned toward Sheridan, for he had captured these trains with his cavalry the night before, near Appomattox Station. General Grant replied: "I should like to have our men sent within our lines as soon as possible. I will take steps at once to have your army supplied with rations, but I am sorry we have no forage for the animals. We have had to depend upon the country for our supply of forage. Of about how many men does your present force consist?"

"Indeed, I am not able to say," Lee answered after a slight pause. "My losses in killed and wounded have been exceedingly heavy, and, besides, there have been many stragglers and some deserters. All my reports and public papers, and, indeed, my own private letters, had to be destroyed on the march, to prevent them from falling into the hands of your people. Many companies are entirely without officers, and I have not seen any returns for several days; so that I have no means of ascertaining our present strength."

General Grant had taken great pains to have a daily estimate made of the enemy's forces from all the data that could be obtained, and, judging it to be about 25,000 at this time, he said: "Suppose I send over 25,000 rations, do you think that will be a sufficient supply?" "I think it will be ample," remarked Lee, and added with considerable earnestness of manner, "and it will be a great relief, I assure you."

General Grant now turned to his chief commissary, Colonel (now General) M. R. Morgan, who was present, and directed him to arrange for issuing the rations. The number of officers and men surrendered was over 28,000. As to General Grant's supplies, he had ordered the army on starting out to carry twelve days' rations. This was the twelfth and last day of the campaign.

Grant's eye now fell upon Lee's sword again, and it seemed to remind him of the absence of his own, and by way of explanation he said to Lee: "I started out from my camp several days ago without my sword, and as I have not seen my headquarters baggage since, I have been riding about without any side-arms. I have generally worn a sword, however, as little as possible, only during the actual operations of a campaign." "I am in the habit of wearing mine most of the time," remarked Lee; "I wear it invariably when I am among my troops, moving about through the army."

General Sheridan now stepped up to General Lee and said that when he discovered some of the Confederate troops in motion during the morning, which seemed to be a violation of the truce, he had sent him (Lee) a couple of notes protesting against this act, and as he had not had time to copy them he would like to have them long enough to make copies. Lee took the notes out of the breast-pocket of his coat and handed them to Sheridan with a few words expressive of regret that the circumstance had occurred, and intimating that it must have been the result of some misunderstanding.

After a little general conversation had been indulged in by those present, the two letters were signed and delivered, and the parties prepared to separate. Lee before parting asked Grant to notify Meade of the surrender, fearing that fighting might break out on that front and lives be uselessly lost. This request was complied with, and two Union officers were sent through the enemy's lines as the shortest route to Meade—some of Lee's officers accompanying them to prevent their being interfered with. At a little before four o'clock General Lee shook hands with General Grant, bowed to the other officers, and with Colonel Marshall left the room. One after another we followed, and passed out to the porch. Lee signaled to his orderly to bring up his horse, and while the animal was being bridled the general stood on the lowest step and gazed sadly in the direction of the valley beyond where his army lay—now an army of prisoners. He smote his hands together a number of times in an absent sort of a way; seemed not to see the group of Union officers in the yard who rose respectfully at his approach, and appeared unconscious of everything about him. All appreciated the sadness that overwhelmed him, and he had the personal sympathy of every one who beheld him at this supreme moment of trial. The approach of his horse seemed to recall him from his reverie, and he at once mounted. General Grant now stepped down from the porch, and, moving toward him, saluted him by raising his hat. He was followed in this act of courtesy by all our officers present; Lee raised his hat respectfully, and rode off to break the sad news to the brave fellows whom he had so long commanded.

General Grant and his staff then mounted and started for the headquarters camp, which, in the meantime, had been pitched near by. The news of the surrender had reached the Union lines, and the firing of salutes began at several points, but the general sent orders at once to have them stopped, and used these words in referring to the occurrence: "The war is over, the rebels are our countrymen again, and the best sign of rejoicing after the victory will be to abstain from all demonstrations in the field."

Mr. McLean* had been charging about in a manner which indicated that the excitement was shaking his system to its nervous center, but his real trials did not begin until the departure of the chief actors in the surrender. Then the relic-hunters charged down upon the manor-house and made various attempts to jump Mr. McLean's claims to his own furniture. Sheridan set a good example, however, by paying the proprietor twenty dollars in gold for the table at which Lee sat, for the purpose of presenting it to Mrs. Custer, and handed it over to her dashing husband, who started off for camp bearing it upon his shoulder. Ord paid forty dollars for the table at which Grant sat, and afterward presented it to Mrs. Grant, who modestly declined it, and insisted that Mrs. Ord should become its possessor. Bargains were at once struck for all the articles in the room, and it is even said that some mementos were carried off for which no coin of the realm was ever exchanged.

Before General Grant had proceeded far toward camp he was reminded that he had not yet announced the important event to the Government. He dismounted by the roadside, sat down on a large stone, and called for pencil and paper. Colonel (afterward General) Badeau handed his order-book to the general, who wrote on one of the leaves the following message, a copy of which was sent to the nearest telegraph station. It was dated 4:30 P.M.:

* Owner of the brick house in which the surrender was signed.

Hon. E. M. STANTON, Secretary of War, Washington:

General Lee surrendered the Army of Northern Virginia this afternoon on terms proposed by myself. The accompanying additional correspondence will show the conditions fully.

U. S. GRANT, Lieut.-General.

Upon reaching camp he seated himself in front of his tent, and we all gathered around him, curious to hear what his first comments would be upon the crowning event of his life. But our expectations were doomed to disappointment, for he appeared to have already dismissed the whole subject from his mind, and turning to General Rufus Ingalls, his first words were: "Ingalls, do you remember that old white mule that so-and-so used to ride when we were in the city of Mexico?" "Why, perfectly," said Ingalls, who was just then in a mood to remember the exact number of hairs in the mule's tail if it would have helped to make matters agreeable. And then the general-in-chief went on to recall the antics played by that animal during an excursion to Popocatepetl. It was not until after supper that he said much about the surrender, when he talked freely of his entire belief that the rest of the rebel commanders would follow Lee's example, and that we would have but little more fighting, even of a partisan nature. He then surprised us by announcing his intention of starting to Washington early the next morning. We were disappointed at this, for we wanted to see something of the opposing army, now that it had become civil enough the first time in its existence to let us get near it, and meet some of the officers who had been acquaintances in former years. The general, however, had no desire to look at the conquered, and but little curiosity in his nature, and he was anxious above all things to begin the reduction of the military establishment and diminish the enormous expense attending it, which at this time amounted to about four millions of dollars a day. When he considered that the railroad was being rapidly put in condition and that he would lose no time by waiting till noon of the next day, he made up his mind to delay his departure.

That evening I made full notes of the occurrences which took place during the surrender, and from these the above account has been written.

There were present at McLean's house, besides Sheridan, Ord, Merritt, Custer, and the officers of Grant's staff, a number of other officers and one or two citizens who entered the room at different times during the interview.

About nine o'clock on the morning of the 10th General Grant with his staff rode out toward the enemy's lines, but it was found upon attempting to pass through that the force of habit is hard to overcome, and that the practice which had so long been inculcated in Lee's army of keeping Grant out of his lines was not to be overturned in a day, and he was politely requested at the picket-lines to wait till a message could be sent to headquarters asking for instructions. As soon as Lee heard that his distinguished opponent was approaching, he was prompt to correct the misunderstanding at the picket-line, and rode out at a gallop to receive him. They met on a knoll that overlooked the lines of the two armies, and saluted respectfully, by each raising his hat. The officers present gave a similar salute, and then grouped themselves around the two chieftains in a semicircle, but withdrew out of ear-shot. General Grant repeated to us that evening the substance of the conversation, which was as follows:

Grant began by expressing a hope that the war would soon be over, and Lee replied by stating that he had for some time been anxious to stop the further effusion of blood, and he trusted that everything would now be done to restore harmony and conciliate the people of the South. He said the emancipation of the Negroes would be no hindrance to the restoring of relations between the two sections of the country, as it would probably not be the desire of the majority of the Southern people to restore slavery then, even if the question were left open to them. He could not tell what the other armies would do or what course Mr. Davis would now take, but he believed it would be best for their other armies to follow his example, as nothing could be gained by further resistance in the field. Finding that he entertained these sentiments, General Grant told him that no one's influence in the South was so great as his, and suggested to him that he should advise the surrender of the remaining armies and thus exert his influence in favor of immediate peace. Lee said he could not take such a course without consulting President Davis first. Grant then proposed to Lee that he should do so, and urge the hastening of a result which was admitted to be inevitable. Lee, however, was averse to stepping beyond his duties as a soldier, and said the authorities would doubtless soon arrive at the same conclusion without his interference.

After the conversation had lasted a little more than half an hour and Lee had requested that such instructions be given to the officers left in charge to carry out the details of the surrender, that there might be no misunderstanding as to the form of paroles, the manner of turning over the property, etc., the conference ended. The two commanders lifted their hats and said good-bye. Lee rode back to his camp to take a final farewell of his army, and Grant returned to McLean's house, where he seated himself on the porch until it was time to take his final departure. During the conference Ingalls, Sheridan, and Williams had asked permission to visit the enemy's lines and renew their acquaintance with some old friends, classmates, and former comrades in arms who were serving in Lee's army. They now returned, bringing with them Cadmus M. Wilcox, who had been General Grant's groomsman when he was married; Longstreet, who had also been at his wedding; Heth, who had been a subaltern with him in Mexico, besides Gordon, Pickett, and a number of others. They all stepped up to pay their respects to General Grant, who received them very cordially and talked with them until it was time to leave. The hour of noon had now arrived, and General Grant, after shaking hands with all present who were not to accompany him, mounted his horse, and started with his staff for Washington without having entered the enemy's lines. Lee set out for Richmond, and it was felt by all that peace had at last dawned upon the land. The charges were now withdrawn from the guns, the camp-fires were left to smolder in their ashes, the flags were tenderly furled—those historic banners, battle-stained, bullet-riddled, many of them but remnants of their former selves, with scarcely enough left of them on which to imprint the names of the battles they had seen—and the Army of the Union and the Army of Northern Virginia turned their backs upon each other for the first time in four long, bloody years.